International Higher Education

An Encyclopedia

Volume 2

◆

Edited by
Philip G. Altbach

GARLAND PUBLISHING, INC.
NEW YORK & LONDON
1991

Library of Congress Cataloging-in-Publication Data

International higher education: an encyclopedia / edited by Philip G. Altbach.
  p. cm. — (Garland reference library of the social sciences; v. 506)
  Includes bibliographical references.
  ISBN 0-8240-4847-4
  1. Education, Higher—Encyclopedias. I. Altbach, Philip G. II. Series: Garland
reference library of social science ; v. 506

LB15.159   1991   90-46952
378'.003—dc20   CIP

10 9 8 7 6 5 4 3 2

Design by Julie Threlkeld

Printed on acid-free, 250-year-life paper
Manufactured in the United States of America

Table of Contents

◆

Volume 1

Topics

Regions and Countries
Africa

Asia

Volume 2

Australia

Europe

AUSTRALIA

Australia

Grant Harman

◆

Australia has well-developed systems of higher education and postsecondary education which closely resemble those of other advanced English-speaking countries, especially Britain, Canada, and New Zealand. Degrees and diplomas awarded by its universities and colleges are widely recognized in other countries and some of its research work, especially in medicine and agriculture, is very well regarded internationally. As in a number of other advanced societies, Australia's higher education and postsecondary education systems are currently undergoing major redirection and reconstruction in order to give governments a greater measure of control and to ensure that higher education institutions more closely serve national economic needs.

From the early 1970s until the end of 1988, postsecondary education in Australia consisted of three major and clearly identified sectors: universities, colleges of advanced education (CAEs), and technical and further education schools.[1] Since January 1, 1989, however, the so-called binary line between universities and CAEs has been abolished and these two sectors have been replaced with a new single, combined sector, the unified national system of higher education.

The main emphasis in this chapter will be on universities and CAEs and on the new unified national system of higher education. For well over a decade government authorities in Australia have referred to university and CAE sectors as constituting the country's higher education system, while the term "tertiary education" has been used to refer to postsecondary education more generally, but especially in universities, CAEs, and technical and further education colleges.

The Three Sectors of Tertiary Education

In 1988 there were nineteen universities, recognized and funded as such by the federal government. They enrolled a total of 194,047 students, of whom 126,141 were studying as internal full-time students. Together they had a total staff of more than 34,000. Except for the Australian National University, located in the nation's capital of Canberra, and established under federal legislation, all universities were state government institutions, responsible to a state minister and parliament. However, except for minor amounts of endowment income and some research grants, all nineteen universities were dependent on the federal government for regular recurrent and capital income. Most students enrolled in universities were studying at the undergraduate level, but in relation to other postsecondary institutions the universities have had a special role in research and postgraduate study. In 1988 about 14 percent of students were studying for higher degrees, about 78 percent for bachelor's degrees, and the remainder for postgraduate diplomas and other awards.

Seen from a distance, the nineteen Australian universities of 1988 all looked very much alike. With the exception of the Australian National University, which was originally established in 1946 as a postgraduate research university, they all pursued similar goals and shared the same dominant values. There was also a high degree of similarity with regard to organizational arrangements and teaching programs. But a closer view would have revealed a number of important differences. The nineteen universities included six old established universities, such as the University of Sydney (founded 1850) and the University of Melbourne (founded 1853), with their traditional academic organization of departments and faculties, and a wide range of professional schools; the immediate post-World War II institutions, created to be strong technological universities, the University of New South Wales (established 1949) and Monash University (established 1958); the "new" capital city suburban universities of the time, modeled largely on the new British universities of the 1960s, such as Macquarie University in Sydney and LaTrobe University in Melbourne (both established 1964); the five regional universities, located outside capital cities, such as the University of New England (established 1954), situated in the country town of Armidale in New South Wales; and the Australian National University, which now comprises seven research schools in the Institute of Advanced Studies (based on the original Australian National University) and the Faculties (based on the Canberra University College, which combined with the original ANU in 1960). Table 1 provides a listing of the nineteen universities, showing the date of establishment for each and 1988 total enrollments.

Apart from these nineteen universities recognized as such by the federal government and funded through the Employment, Education, and Training portfolio, in 1988 there were a small number of additional universities or university-type institutions. These included the Australian Defence Forces Academy (funded through the Defence portfolio and operated academically as a university college linked to the University of New South Wales), the University College of the Northern Territory (funded by the Government of the Northern Territory and academically linked to the University of Queensland), and Bond University, Australia's first private university, established in 1988 by legislation passed by the Queensland Parliament. In addition, two CAEs had been reconstituted as universities by their respective state governments: Curtin University of Technology in Perth, and the University of Technology in

Table 1

Australian Universities 1988

University	Date of Establishment	Total Student Enrollment 1988
University of Sydney	1850	18,236
University of Melbourne	1853	16,733
University of Adelaide	1874	9,177
University of Tasmania	1890	5,376
University of Queensland	1910	18,233
University of Western Australia	1911	10,063
Australian National University	1946	6,651
University of New South Wales	1949	18,706
University of New England	1954	9,427
Monash University	1958	14,768
La Trobe University	1964	13,128
Macquarie University	1964	11,194
University of Newcastle	1965	6,375
Flinders University	1966	6,028
James Cook University of North Queensland	1970	4,244
Griffith University	1971	5,339
Murdoch University	1973	5,196
Deakin University	1975	7,209
University of Wollongong	1975	7,964

Note: This table lists only those institutions recognized by the federal government as universities and funded as such by federal authorities.

Sydney. However, up to the end of 1988, these were not recognized by the federal government as part of the university sector.

In 1988 there were forty-four CAEs that as a group enrolled 215,219 students, of whom 120,275 were studying full time. Together the colleges employed a total of almost 25,000 staff. Although the CAEs were originally developed to offer subdegree courses, by 1988 almost 70 percent of college students were enrolled in bachelor's degree and postgraduate courses. CAEs varied considerably in size, from small institutions with a few hundred students and a limited range of courses to large multischool institutions, such as the Royal Melbourne Institute of Technology, which in 1988 had a total of 11,832 higher education students. However, compared to a decade earlier, the average size of CAEs in 1988 was considerably larger as a result of rapid growth in enrollments and numerous amalgamations. Colleges also tended to be more dispersed geographically, with a significant number located in nonmetropolitan areas. Compared to universities, colleges were less homogeneous, varying from highly specialized "single-purpose" institutions to large broadbased institutions similar in many respects to universities. Like universities, CAEs are funded entirely by the federal government for regular recurrent and capital expenditure, but are subject to a much greater degree of control by state governments. Also, unlike universities, CAEs are subject to external accreditation of courses and awards.

The CAE sector developed from the mid-1960s, following recommendations of the Martin Report,[2] with the aim of diversifying higher education and providing a cheaper alternative to universities, with courses at a lower level and having a more applied and vocational emphasis. The CAE sector grew quickly, responding to strong student demand and with substantial funding provided by the federal government. It absorbed many former nonuniversity institutions including senior technical colleges, teachers colleges, agricultural colleges, and institutions specializing in music, arts, and paramedical studies.[3] Over time, the orientation of most colleges changed, with the introduction of degree studies, the achievement of parity of academic staff salaries with universities, and with the recruitment of academic staff possessing research degrees. By 1988 many of the larger CAEs closely resembled universities, with strong professional faculties and graduate studies, although they were not funded explicitly for research. Clearly the binary line was under strain and challenge.[4]

The technical and further education sector was established in the 1970s, building on a long tradition of technical colleges and mechanics institutes. By 1988 it consisted of a network of 220 major institutions and another thousand annexes and branches, which together enrolled 937,175 students in vocational and technical courses. In addition, another 510,000 students were studying in noncredit adult education courses. In the vocational and technical area, the main emphasis was on courses for basic employment skills, educational preparation, trade and skills, and technician and paraprofessional fields. The main awards were certificates, but since the mid-1980s many TAFE colleges have provided two-year associate diploma courses almost identical to two-year CAE courses. Technical and further education colleges were controlled by separate departments or boards and, while the federal government provided financial assistance, especially for capital works projects, the bulk of funds still came from state (and territory) sources.[5]

Influences on Higher Education

Four main sets of influences have had a major effect on the Australian higher education system. The first set are geographical, and spring from the fact that Australia is still largely a European-based society, inhabiting a large island continent located in the Asian-Pacific region. The population is relatively small (slightly over sixteen million) with large concentrations in a small number of major seaboard cities, but with a very sparse distribution elsewhere. In the pioneering British societies that developed on the Australian continent in the late eighteenth and early nineteenth centuries, higher education developed slowly. Although the first British colony had been established at Sydney Cove in 1788, it was not until 1850 that the first university, the University of Sydney, was established. Even as late as 1939 Australian universities together enrolled just over 14,000 students. Understandably, the early institutions drew largely on British models and experience, although from the start all universities were secular in origin and were established by governments. With strong European cultural ties, Australian higher education institutions continued to be influenced to a major degree by overseas developments and values. Until the 1960s the ties to Britain were close. According to Partridge, pre-1945 Australian universities suffered from considerable isolation from one another, but their ties to Britain were much closer: "Many of the staff were recruited from Universities in the United Kingdom . . . ; most of the native Australian teachers would have done their postgraduate training in a British university; and they usually returned to Britain when their year of sabbatical leave came round. Collectively the universities were dominated by British traditions and practices; they judged themselves by British standards and sought British recognition."[6] While the ties with Britain have since loosened somewhat, Australian institutions are still influenced to a major extent by overseas developments, especially in Britain, North America, and continental Europe.

From the start, however, Australian higher education institutions have had to adapt overseas models to suit the particular characteristics of the local scene. This has resulted in a number of important innovations. One example is the development of external studies or distance education courses, designed to serve a scattered population denied access to regular higher education. First established by the University of Queensland in the 1920s and developed significantly by the University of New England from 1955, external studies has become an important element of the Australian higher education scene. About 12 percent of higher education students are enrolled via external studies, and they pursue their courses using printed materials, audio and video tapes, talk-back radio, teleconferencing, individual telephone and written communications, and visits to the campus for intensive "residential schools."

A second influence stems from the distinctive character of the Australian economy. Australia's export income was first based on two commodities, wool and gold, and even today depends largely on a very limited range of products from farming and mining. Within the broad categories of farm products and mining, there has been considerable diversification; major farm exports now include meat, wheat, sugar, and fruit, while mining produces copper, lead, zinc, and antimony, as well as coal and natural gas. Secondary industry was relatively slow to develop and, with the aid of a strong protection policy, until recently mainly served a local market. The consequences for both industry and higher education have been serious. Industry has tended to be conservative and restricted in nature, largely borrowing ideas from abroad, while higher education has been confined mainly to training for the professions and public sector employment. However, over the past decade deliberate efforts have been made to broaden the nation's export base and to reverse a serious imbalance in external trade. This change in overall economic directions has important implications for the future direction of higher education. If Australia is to be more than a farm and a mine, it will need a broader range of professional expertise and technical skills.

A third influence has come from the distinctive Australian style of federalism. Australia became a nation in 1901, when the six British colonies combined to form the Commonwealth of Australia. The federal constitution specified clear areas of responsibility for the national government; it was assumed that other matters would be the responsibility of state governments. Education was one of the areas it was assumed would remain with state governments, and hence the constitution made no mention of education at all. However, over the years the powers and areas of responsibility of the federal government have enlarged to a major degree.

Despite the lack of a clear-cut specific power relating to education in the constitution, the federal government has become deeply and substantially involved in education at all levels across the nation.[7] Involvement by the federal government in higher education began in a small way prior to World War II. During and immediately after the war it was forced to come to the aid of the severely overstretched and underfinanced universities. In the late 1950s this involvement was regularized as a system of agreed shared financial responsibility, between the Commonwealth and states. In the 1960s the federal government accepted a similar role with respect to CAEs, while in 1974 it took full responsibility for the regular capital and recurrent funding of all higher education institutions. At the same time, at the insistence of the federal government, tuition fees were abolished. As a result of these developments, by the mid-1970s the federal government had become the major source of initiative in the formulation of higher education policy. At times there have been considerable frictions when federal government and state views do not agree.

The expansion of the federal government's powers in higher education have been achieved through the use of two specific constitutional provisions: section 96, which gives the Commonwealth power "to grant financial assistance to any State on such terms and conditions as the Parliament thinks fit," and a 1946 amendment to the constitution (section 51 xxiiiA) through which the Federal Parliament acquired power to make laws "with respect to the provisions of . . . benefits to students" in all states.

A fourth set of influences relate to student demand for courses. The Australian community has always had a somewhat ambivalent view of higher education. There is a strong thread of anti-intellectualism in Australian society, and Australian universities have often been viewed as being somewhat peripheral to the mainstream of cultural and economic life. But in such an egalitarian society higher education provides one of the main avenues for social advancement and employment security. Since World War II, enrollments have increased substantially. University enrollments increased from 25,000 in 1946 to 53,400 in 1960, to 115,600 in 1970, and to almost 200,000 in 1988. CAE enrollments also expanded, from 37,692 in 1970, to 159,466 in 1980, and to over 215,000 in 1988. The rapid growth rate eased off in the late 1970s, largely as a result of a downturn in the economy, but since 1983 growth has again been steady and sustained. Table 2 provides information on university and CAE enrollments from 1984 to 1988. It will be noted that over this period university enrollments increased by 12.7 percent while CAE enrollments increased by 15.7 percent. The current sustained and substantial growth rate can be attributed to a number of factors, including government action in providing additional student places; particular government policies designed to increase access, especially among women and disadvantaged groups; rapidly increasing "retention rates" in secondary schools (nationally retention rates have risen from 40.6 percent in 1983 to 57.6 percent in 1988); and strong demand for graduate employment. Despite the substantial increases provided in student places over recent years, annual surveys have found that up to 20,000 potential students per year have been unable to gain places, even though qualified academically for entry.

Recent Trends, Including the Dawkins Reforms

Since the late 1970s Australian higher education has changed significantly. Reference has been made to the leveling off of growth in enrollments in the late 1970s and to the renewed expansion since about 1983. The drop in the rate of increase in enrollments was largely the result of a marked downturn in the economy, and to a loss of public confidence in higher education, especially as a result of a major problem with graduate unemployment in a number of fields. But it was also in part the result of the policies of the conservative Liberal-National party federal government of the time, led by Malcolm Fraser and in power from 1975 to 1983. The Fraser government attempted to cut public expenditure generally and, under its policy of "New Federalism," attempted to push responsibility for various areas of activity, including aspects of education, back to the state governments. Higher education institutions' budgets were cut, limits were placed on student enrollments in each institution, and an attempt was made to reintroduce tuition fees for second and higher degrees. In addition, to help cut expenditures and deal with a major problem of oversupply of schoolteachers, as part of its "Razor Gang" cuts of April 1981, the Fraser government intimated that thirty CAEs involved exclusively or largely in teacher education had to amalgamate with a larger institution or face loss of federal funding. In the end, after considerable controversy, twenty-six of the specified colleges merged with other institutions.[8]

Early in 1983 a general federal election brought the Hawke Labor government to power. For four years, under Senator Susan

Table 2

University and CAE Enrollments, 1984 to 1988

University	Full-time	Part-time	External	Total
1984	105,480	50,649	15,972	172,101
1985	107,427	51,562	16,487	175,476
1986	110,670	53,211	17,642	181,483
1987	115,774	49,291	15,738	180,803
1988	126,141	51,428	16,478	194,047
CAE				
1984	89,768	67,638	27,289	184,695
1985	96,912	68,516	29,112	194,540
1986	104,575	71,993	31,917	208,485
1987	118,380	64,558	29,993	212,931
1988	120,275	64,337	30,607	215,219

Source: Commonwealth Tertiary Education Comission.

Table 3

Variations in Student Load
Operating Grants and Staff Numbers 1976 to 1985

University	Student Load EFTS	Operating Grants	Academic Staff	General Staff
		(Percentages)		
1976 to 1980	+4.5	+8.6	+6.4	+3.6
1981 to 1985	+9.4	+3.1	+0.1	-0.6
1976 to 1985	+14.4	+11.9	+6.5	+2.9
CAE				
1976 to 1980	+21.7	+19.2	+14.1	+14.8
1981 to 1985	+14.0	+2.9	-1.7	+0.7
1976 to 1985	+38.7	+22.6	+12.2	+15.6

Source: Commonwealth Tertiary Education Commission, *Review of Efficiency and Effectiveness in Higher Education* (Canberra: Australian Government Publishing Service, 1986) p. 37.

Ryan as education minister, the policies of the Fraser government were largely continued, except that deliberate attempts were made to encourage increases in enrollment and the broadening of student access, especially for women and members of minority groups. Enrollments increased substantially, but institutions were forced to become more cost-efficient and additional student load was funded at unsatisfactory marginal rates per student unit. As Table 3 indicates, between 1981 and 1985 the rate of increase in operating grants for higher education institutions was far less than the increase in student load.

In July 1987, following another general federal election in which the Hawke government retained its power, the number of government departments was drastically reduced and John Dawkins became minister in charge of the new "mega" portfolio of Employment, Education, and Training. Dawkins previously held the portfolios of Finance and then Overseas Trade, and was one of a small group of key senior ministers in the cabinet who believed that the Australian economy needed major redirection in order to broaden the export base and correct a dangerously adverse balance of trade. Since late 1987 major changes in the higher education system have been initiated by Dawkins; the results have been more far-reaching and dramatic than most observers expected.

In order to secure greater control over policy direction, Dawkins abolished the Commonwealth Tertiary Education Commission, a statutory agency that had been responsible for advising the minister on forward planning and coordination, and administering grants to institutions and states. A "Green Paper"[9] was prepared and circulated for comment, and this was followed in July 1988 by a "White Paper"[10] that announced major new policy directions. These new directions included abolition of the so-called binary system of separate sectors for universities and CAEs and its replacement by a unified national system; a commitment to extensive amalgamation of institutions and the setting of a minimum limit of two thousand equivalent full-time students units (EFTSU) for institutions in order to gain admission to the unified national system; setting size limits required for institutions to be funded for research (five thousand EFTSU for some research funding, and eight thousand EFTSU for funding of an infrastructure to enable research activities to be carried out over a broad range of fields); a commitment to major expansion in student numbers and the output of graduates; increases in research funding and greater targeting of research funds to areas of national priority; and reform of institutional governance in order to secure greater flexibility, responsiveness, and accountability. Apart from this, under Dawkins a Higher Education Contribution Scheme or "graduate tax" system has been established in order to help finance the planned student expansion, while important concessions were secured in December 1987 on staffing arrangements in industrial negotiations between the federal government, the higher education institutions, and the academic unions. Further still, external studies provisions have been rationalized and eight Distance Education Centers have been designated. These centers will be specifically funded for external studies teaching, and all other institutions will have to offer external studies courses through them.

Implementation of the Dawkins reforms are well under way. All nineteen universities that were federally funded in 1988 have joined the unified national system, along with many CAEs. However, in many cases membership is conditional upon amalgamations being achieved. By 1990 it is likely that the unified national system will consist of thirty to thirty-five institutions, most with the title of university.[11] In New South Wales a state system of six universities and more than fifteen CAEs is to become a system of nine universities. In essence, through a process of forced amalgamations, most CAEs will either be absorbed into existing universities or will become constituent parts of new universities based on a number of former CAEs. A small number of very small CAEs may stay outside the unified national system and be funded at less generous rates on a contract basis for teaching activities only.

Higher Education and Government

The increasing federal government role in higher education has already been noted. Apart from this trend, two major changes have dominated the relationship between higher education institutions and government over the past four decades. The first is that both federal and state governments have experimented with various mechanisms to provide policy advice and coordination, while the second is a belief by higher education institutions that governments have been interfering more and more in their activities.

In order to cope with rapid growth in the higher education system, to facilitate orderly planning, and to achieve some measure of regulation, first the federal government and then the states set up special coordinating agencies for higher education. In 1956 the federal government appointed a committee, presided over by the chairman of the British University Grants Committee, Sir Keith Murray, to inquire into the future of Australian universities. This committee recommended commitment by the federal government to ongoing financial support for university development on a regular basis, and establishment of an Australian University Grants Committee to provide detailed ongoing advice. The recommendations were largely accepted, although the prime minister, R. G. (later Sir Robert) Menzies, decided to establish an Australian Universities Commission as a statutory body rather than a grants committee.[12] With the establishment of the CAE sector, a parallel advisory and coordinating agency for colleges was established, first as an advisory committee and then later as a statutory commission. A statutory body for technical and further education followed in the early 1970s, and in 1977 the three statutory agencies were combined to form the Commonwealth Tertiary Education Commission, which operated for a decade until its closure in 1987. Under John Dawkins, new advisory mechanisms have been established for the portfolio of Employment, Education, and Training, consisting of a National Board of Employment, Education, and Training, with four subsidiary councils with responsibility respectively for higher education, research, schools, and employment and skills formation. Unlike the former coordinating agencies for higher education, the new bodies have a more limited role with full responsibility for program delivery and grant administration lying with the Department of Employment, Education, and Training. While the role that the new advisory bodies are to play is still to be worked out, many experienced observers believe that abolition of the Commonwealth Tertiary Education Commission was an unfortunate step, and one leading to increased government and ministerial control of internal institutional affairs.

The state governments were slower to establish coordinating agencies, but by the late 1970s all six states had established either statutory or advisory bodies, some relating to CAEs alone and others to CAEs and universities, or to all tertiary education. However, recent developments, especially under John Dawkins, have led to review, and most states now have either scaled down the operations of these coordinating agencies or have replaced them with small advisory bodies within the minister's office. In addition, Joint Commonwealth-State Planning Committees have been established to provide a vehicle for negotiation between federal and state authorities.

Overall the federal coordinating mechanisms that operated from 1959 to 1987 worked well, and provided a useful interface between the federal government on the one hand and the state governments and institutions on the other.[13] Similarly, the state agencies performed a useful role, particularly in planning and accreditation of CAE courses and awards. But with a dramatic decrease in the number of institutions, abolition of the binary system, and the ability of federal authorities now to relate directly to each higher education institution, there is no real place for state coordination. Moreover, the current federal government clearly wishes to exercise a greater measure of control and regulation.

Over the past four decades higher education institutions have continued to complain of government encroachment in their affairs and loss of institutional autonomy. Some of these complaints have been unjustified; there is a tendency by some university leaders in particular to appeal to an imaginary past when Australian universities enjoyed almost complete autonomy. But it is true that since World War II in a number of areas governments have come to exercise a more direct influence over internal institutional matters. Some of this increased control sprang from the need to coordinate development and adjudicate on competition between a growing number of separate institutions for funds and new course developments. But, in addition, governments have wished for a more direct influence as the size of higher education has grown, as has its financial costs, and there has developed a strong view that higher education needs to be linked more closely to economic management and labor market needs. Despite occasional claims by a minority of academic staff, however, there has been no real attack on academic freedom: university and CAE staff enjoy similar independence in public comment, teaching, and research as their opposite numbers in the United States or Britain.

Internal Institutional Affairs

Higher education institutions are funded directly by the federal government. Planning is on a rolling triennial basis for recurrent expenditure, with grants being allocated to institutions in a single block sum. Funds for capital projects are allocated on an annual basis. Allocations for recurrent expenditure are based on student load and negotiations on institutional "educational profiles" between institutions and federal authorities. For 1989 total recurrent funds of 2,688 million Australian dollars have been allocated, while 126.7 million has been allocated for major capital works and renovations.

Tuition fees in universities and CAEs were abolished in 1974, as an initiative by the federal Labor government of the time, led by Gough Whitlam. The aim was to increase student access, especially for disadvantaged and lower socioeconomic groups. While access has indeed been broadened since then, the abolition of tuition fees did not change the social composition of the undergraduate population as much as expected,[14] and as in most industrialized countries, the children of upper-income and professional groups participate in higher education more than the children of lower-income groups and those with the least formal education.[15] An unsuccessful attempt was made in the early 1980s by the Fraser government to reintroduce tuition fees for some students, while in 1987 the current Labor government introduced a 250 dollar administration charge on all students. This charge was replaced in 1989 by the Higher Education Contribution Scheme or "graduate tax" system. All enrolled higher education students must contribute to the costs of their courses, either through an "up-front" payment at the beginning of each semester or through a special income tax levy once their income reaches the average income level. For 1989, the annual liability per student has been assessed at 1,800 Australian dollars.

Admission to undergraduate study is generally made on the basis of academic merit as demonstrated by the higher or senior secondary school examinations run by one of the state governments. However, in recent years this has been supplemented by other criteria, including written reports from schools and interviews. For mature-age students entry has become decidedly more flexible, with more emphasis often being given to maturity, motivation, and relevant work experience than to performance on school examinations.

Traditionally, Australian higher education institutions operated on a three-term year, beginning in late February or early March, but in recent years a two-semester system has become the most common pattern.

Universities offer three-year pass degrees in arts, science, and economics, with a fourth year being necessary to qualify for an honors degree. Undergraduate engineering, law, and architecture courses take four years, veterinary science and dentistry five years, and medicine five or six years. At the postgraduate level, research theses for master's degrees and the Ph.D. are usually examined externally. In CAEs the length of courses is similar, except that honors degrees have not been available.

The university academic rank structure is broadly similar to that in British and New Zealand universities. Apart from the short-term junior ranks of tutor and senior tutor, the bottom career appointment is lecturer. Staff may be promoted on merit to the grades of senior lecturer and associate professor (or reader). However, the top grade of professor is generally filled only through open advertisement. About 10 percent of permanent staff are professors, and about another 10 percent are associate professors or readers. The CAE rank structure is similar, except that the term "principal lecturer" is used instead of "associate professor," and "dean" or "head of school" instead of "professor." University salary levels in June 1989 were professor $A63,919; associate professor $A54,192; senior lecturer $A48,086 (maximum); and lecturer $A31,259 (minimum) to $40, 622 (maximum). CAE salaries are almost identical. Salaries for both university and CAE academic staff are nationally determined by the Australian Industrial Relations Commission.

All universities and many CAEs operate under their own acts of parliament. Control is vested in a council, senate, or board of governors consisting of twenty to forty members, drawn from the relevant parliament, the professions, business, and the community, but also including representatives of academic staff, general staff, students, and graduates. Following British provincial tradition, responsibility for academic matters in each institution is delegated to the academic board and committees. In older universities and some CAEs, staff are grouped in departments and faculties, but many newer institutions have adopted a schools structure. The chief executive officer in universities is the vice-chancellor, whereas in CAEs this post usually carries the title of director or principal.

Conclusions

Australia's higher education system, which has been relatively stable for well over two decades, is in the process of major reconstruction and redirection. The so-called binary system, with its separate sectors of universities and CAEs, has been abolished and replaced by a unified national system, which will include a range of institutions, from those with a very heavy emphasis on research and postgraduate study to institutions involved almost exclusively in teaching. Through forced amalgamations the number of institutions is being reduced dramatically and major changes are being made in institutional governance and management and in employment conditions for staff. Student enrollments are planned to continue to be expanded in order to increase the output of graduates. These changes have been initiated by the federal government and its minister for employment, education, and

training, John Dawkins, with the aim of linking higher education more closely to economic reform.

What the long-term implications of these changes will be is by no means clear, but in less than two years the current minister has achieved far more than most observers thought possible. Most institutional leaders have welcomed the planned growth in student enrollments and many of the changes suggested in institutional governance and management. But there is considerable concern about increased government intrusion in institutional decision making, about the future of the more vocationally oriented CAE courses in new amalgamated universities, and about possible tensions in new multilevel "network" universities. In the longer term, what happens as a result of the reforms of Dawkins and the current federal Labor government will depend on efforts to restructure the Australian economy and on public satisfaction with and confidence in the higher education system.

Notes

1. For a further account of these three sectors and their development, see G. S. Harman and C. Selby Smith, eds., *Australian Higher Education: Problems of a Developing System* (Sydney: Angus and Robertson, 1972); Bruce Williams, *Systems of Higher Education: Australia* (New York: Inter-national Council for Educational Develop-ment, 1978); and William Toombs and Grant Harman, eds., *Higher Education and Social Goals in Australia and New Zealand* (University Park: Australian and New Zealand Studies Center, The Pennsylvania State University, 1988).

2. Committee on the Future of Tertiary Education in Australia, *Tertiary Education in Australia: Report to the Australian Universities Commission*, 3 vols. (Melbourne: Government Printer, 1964–65).

3. E. R. Treyvaud and John McLaren, *Equal but Cheaper: The Development of Colleges of Advanced Education* (Carlton, Australia: Melbourne University Press, 1976).

4. Susan Davies, *The Martin Committee and the Binary Policy of Higher Education in Australia* (Surrey Hills, Australia: Ashwood House, 1989).

5. For a discussion of technical and further

education, see Philip C. Candy, ed., *TAFE at the Crossroads: Relationships with Government, Secondary, and Higher Education* (Armidale, Australia: Department of Administrative and Higher Education Studies, University of New England, 1988); and V. Lynn Meek and Ross Harrold, eds., *TAFE and the Reconstruction of Higher Education: A Conference Summary* (Armidale, Australia: Department of Continuing Education, University of New England, 1989).

6. P. H. Partridge, *Society, Schools, and Progress in Australia* (Oxford: Pergamon Press, 1968), 12.

7. Grant Harman and Don Smart, eds., *Federal Intervention in Australian Education* (Melbourne, Australia: Georgian House, 1983).

8. Grant Harman, "The Razor Gang Decisions, the Guidelines to the Commissions, and Commonwealth Education Policy," *Vestes: The Australian Universities Review* 24 (1981): 28–40.

9. *Higher Education: A Policy Discussion Paper* (Canberra: Australian Government Publishing Service, 1987).

10. *Higher Education: A Policy Statement* (Canberra: Australian Government Publishing Service, 1988).

11. *Report of the Task Force on Amalgamations in Higher Education* (Canberra: Australian Government Publishing Service, 1989); and Grant Harman, "The Dawkins Reconstruction of Australian Higher Education," *Higher Education Policy* (forthcoming).

12. A. P. Gallagher, *Co-ordinating Australian University Development: A Study of the Australian Universities Commission, 1959–1970* (St. Lucia, Australia: University of Queensland Press, 1982).

13. Grant Harman, "Australian Experience with Coordinating Agencies for Tertiary Education," *Higher Education* 12 (October 1984): 501–15.

14. D. S. Anderson, R. Boven, P. J. Fensham, and J. P. Powell, *Students in Australian Higher Education: A Study of Their Social Composition Since the Abolition of Fees* (Kensington, Australia: Tertiary Education Research Centre, University of New South Wales, 1978).

15. D. S. Anderson and A. E. Vervoorn, *Access to Privilege: Patterns of Participation in Australian Postsecondary Education* (Canberra: Australian National University, 1983).

EUROPE

Western Europe

Ulrich Teichler

◆

Higher education systems in European countries are based on diverse traditions regarding the relationship between government and institutions of higher education, educational aims and modes, the relationships between research and teaching, the links between higher education and graduate employment, and the organization and management of the institutions. Most experts agree that three different models of higher education shaped higher education systems in Europe and all over the world: the British, which emphasized a sound educational process and training a broad mind; the German, which promoted a close link between research and teaching and supported the freedom of learning; and the French, which was particularly concerned with training the specialist.

This overview cannot hope to offer a complete picture of higher education systems in Western Europe. I have chosen different countries to illustrate the variety of higher education in Europe. I have placed emphasis on the educational rather than on the research function of higher education, and within this framework, on topics in which a substantial exchange of information and "cross-fertilization" in higher education policy were most visible in the 1970s and 1980s: patterns of institutions and course programs, characteristics of curricula, teaching, and examinations, higher education and employment, and the decision-making structures in higher education.

Trends and Policies in Higher Education

After World War II debates on the development of higher education changed dramatically. The higher education systems of the United States and of the Soviet Union became the overt or hidden yardsticks for assessment of the strengths and weaknesses of higher education in the individual Western European or Eastern European countries. In Western Europe, for example, debates about the link between secondary education and higher education, the contribution of higher education to social mobility, the establishment of a nonuniversity sector in the process of higher education expansion, the needs and modes of graduate training, and the management of higher education institutions were strongly influenced by the assumption that the higher education system in the United States was a step ahead of Europe on the way toward the modern higher education system. In Eastern Europe, the socialist countries were influenced by the Soviet emphasis on specialized institutions of higher education, the allocation of a substantial proportion of research outside higher education, quantitative planning based on presumed manpower demand, and positive discrimination regarding traditionally disadvantaged social strata on admission to higher education.

The unprecedented expansion of higher education since World War II and its causes and consequences became the major focus of higher education policies all over Europe. In 1950 5 percent or an even smaller quota of the corresponding age group were enrolled at institutions of higher education. During the 1970s this quota surpassed 20 percent in almost all European countries and approached 30 percent in some cases. Over this period established institutions grew substantially, many new institutions were founded, and many institutions formerly not considered part of higher education were upgraded.[1]

Whereas higher education systems in the Eastern European planned economies were substantially changed in the process of socioeconomic restructuring, Western European countries aimed to stabilize their traditional higher education systems along the economic recovery after World War II. During the 1950s student numbers grew faster in most Eastern than in most Western European countries. Most experts agree that three phases of higher education debates and policies can be observed in most Western European countries from the late 1950s until the late 1970s.[2]

The first phase occurred in most Western European countries during the latter half of the 1950s and the early 1960s. Belief began to spread that a considerable expansion of higher education, and especially an increased number of students, was indispensable for stimulating technical, economic, and social progress. The "sputnik-shock" in the United States and its carryover to Europe, the rising popularity of the economics of education, the OECD's expanding activities in educational fields, the establishment of numerous national planning and counseling bodies—all fell within that period. Governments in many countries gradually turned toward more systematic approaches of quantitative and structural planning. The structural debate focused on types of secondary education and on widening access to higher education not only through expansion of secondary education but also through integration of various types of secondary education or through acceptance of other types of secondary education as appropriate prerequisites for higher education. Substantial attention was paid to the issue as to what extent and under what conditions expansion of higher education could serve both economic growth and reduction of inequality of opportunity.[3]

The second phase of debates and policies can be observed in the late 1960s and early 1970s. Then debates concentrated on the search for a modern structure for higher education systems. Attention was focused on the problem of how the system of higher education could most appropriately absorb the growing number of students who had an increasing variety of educational backgrounds, motives, and aspirations and who would eventually have a wider range of job prospects. In many European countries a second type of institution or course program was established to parallel the traditional university system. Another debate addressed the issue of whether distinct sectors of higher education or other modes of establishing a considerable diversity were preferable and whether such a diversity should be kept in bounds in the framework of comprehensive universities or other integrated models.[4] Student protests in the late 1960s seemed to be the most decisive factor in calling into question traditional views about the function of higher education and in stimulating reforms in decision-making structures, curricular changes, and didactical reforms in higher education. More visible changes in higher education could be observed around 1970 in most Western European countries than during the preceding and subsequent years.

The third phase took place during the 1970s and was frequently characterized in two ways: first, as a shift from optimism or euphoria regarding the needs and the virtues of education expansion toward pessimism or renewed skepticism. This change of mood could be observed most strikingly regarding manpower issues, as the notion of overeducation or overqualification became prevalent. Faith that educational expansion would substantially enhance the opportunities of the hitherto disadvantaged faded. In the wake of this debate and the economic problems subsequent to the oil crisis of 1973, expansion of higher education slowed down in most European countries. Expansion of higher education, however, remained higher in most Western European countries during this period, as observed since the mid-1960s, than in most Eastern European countries. In addition, in Western Europe, those sectors of higher education that seemed to promise their students practical training useful for careers attracted most support.[5]

This third phase was usually characterized by a collapse of faith in societal planning, both in terms of understanding the complexity of higher education and its environment in order to design appropriate innovations and in terms of success in carrying through plans. The rising attention to problems of implementation indicated reduced levels of faith in higher education planning and reform. Many reforms regarding the content, the structures, and the organization of higher education started in the late 1960s or early 1970s came to a complete halt, were realized only in part, or were substantially modified in this context.[6]

Gradually the notion faded that there were definite international trends in higher education systems. Today international discussions continue to deal with common or at least similar needs, problems, and proposals, but countries now focus more on the individual characteristics of their own higher education systems and their contexts.[7]

Similar directions of change in higher education policies became apparent in Eastern European countries as well. Beginning around 1980 in Poland and following a few years later in other planned econo-mies, doubts grew about the feasibility and wisdom of tight manpower planning. More flexible planning approaches and a gradual acceptance of substantial oversupply beyond immediate demands became common. Implementation gaps, the limits of planning, and quality losses caused by bad policies became issues of policy debate and led to a variety of moderate reforms without, however, establishing new overarching general policy concepts.

During the 1980s no single topic dominated higher education debates in Western European countries.[8] But five issues did play a substantial role in many European countries:

1. A need for quality improvement of higher education has been widely emphasized. Proposals made and actions taken in the name of quality improvement, however, have been extraordinarily diverse and varied from country to country: revisions of secondary education and of admission requirements, diversification of higher education institutions and course programs, stimulation of competition between institutions of higher education, the establishment or extension of targeted research promotion programs, a detailed structuring of course requirements and examinations of students, the establishment of graduate course programs, etc.

2. Increased diversity of higher education has been advocated in most Western European countries since the early 1980s. In countries in which the coordinating powers of government regarding higher education curricula were strong, and where in the past a common quality standard had been imposed on universities, diversity for individual institutions, departments, and course programs was now encouraged. Moreover, a wider variation of quality levels with-

in the same institutional type were allowed, though the frame of horizontal and vertical diversity allowed remained much tighter than that in the United States, Japan, and most third world countries.

3. Management in higher education institutions is expected to become more powerful and efficient. Notably, increased power for the head of the institution—rector, president, or vice-chancellor—and for the central administration has been advocated and to some extent implemented in various Western European countries. Associated changes include systems for public demonstration of efficiency, resource allocation informed by evaluation, and the substitution of indirect for direct governmental supervision of higher education.

4. Some substantive issues regarding teaching, learning, and research became the focus of debates. Growing international economic competition, the influential role of new technologies in many areas of research, development, production, and services, and growing ecological problems were frequently named as challenges to which higher education must respond. Targeted support programs, reallocation of resources, and demands for utility of research, teaching, and learning stimulated more optimistic views regarding the employment prospects of the majority of graduates. Concurrently, concern has grown about the future of disciplines not directly favored by the present economic and political climate.

5. Finally, internationalization has been put on the agenda of higher education debates in Europe during the 1980s. An increase has been observed in cross-national research cooperation, organized exchange of students, and new provisions for international mobility of graduates. National governments and international organizations have become strongly involved in supporting further internationalization. The economic and social integration of the European Community was possibly the strongest driving force in this context.

Quantitative Development

Absolute Enrollment Figures

According to UNESCO statistics, the total number of students at institutions of higher education in Europe increased from somewhat more than two million in 1950 to slightly more than four million in 1960 to almost ten million in 1970. One has to take into account, however, that more institutions not previously considered to be part of the higher education system were upgraded during the 1960s than in the preceding and subsequent decades. In 1980 the total student number was 13.8 million; in 1985, 14.8 million.

Enrollment Ratios

In describing the social relevance of student numbers, the ratio of all students to their corresponding age groups or the ratio of all beginner or first-year students to their corresponding age groups are most frequently computed. For example, UNESCO calculates an "enrollment ratio" "by dividing the total enrollment for this level of education, regardless of age, by the population of the group which according to national regulations should be enrolled at this level."[9] The third-level enrollment ratio for all Europe increased from 10.2 percent in 1960 to 17.4 percent in 1970, to 21.8 percent in 1980, and to 23.8 percent in 1985. In the 1980s this ratio for all Europe was less than half of that in North America, substantially lower than in Japan and also a few developing countries, but

Table 1

Proportion of the Age Group Concerned Entering Third-Level Education and Obtaining a Third-Level Qualification in 1986 (percentage)

Country	Entering Higher Education			Obtaining Qualification	
	Level 5	Level 6	Level 5+6	Level 5	Level 6
Austria	4.1	18.4	21.8	3.6	6.8
Belgium	—	—	42.9	15.8	14.9
Denmark	11.7	24.8	36.5	10.3	12.7
Finland	23.5	17.7	41.6	17.0	11.8
France	12.9	20.0	32.9	14.7	15.3
Germany	9.9	17.4	27.3	7.7	12.4
Greece	14.9	18.0	32.8	4.9	10.9
Ireland	—	—	27.6	1.0	10.8
Italy	0.9	24.4	25.3	0.4	7.9
Netherlands	—	16.8	—	16.5	6.8
Norway	—	—	37.6	36.3	16.1
Spain	0	30.4	30.4	0.1	14.7
Sweden	52.8	15.5	67.5	—	—
Switzerland	22.6	12.0	35.3	0.9	6.1
Turkey	2.1	10.1	12.2	1.4	4.4
United Kingdom	15.6	17.5	33.1	12.3	14.2
Yugoslavia	—	—	—	5.8	7.7

Source: Education in OECD Countries 1986–87, pp. 69 and 95.

twice as high as the world total ratio (11.8 percent in 1985). Within Europe, the highest ratio in 1984 or 1985 was reported for Sweden (38.1 percent). It was about 30 percent in Finland, the Netherlands, the German Democratic Republic, France, the Federal Republic of Germany, and Denmark. The majority of Eastern European countries had ratios between 15 and 20 percent. Lower rates were calculated for Portugal (12.6 percent), Romania (11.2 percent), and Albania (7.1 percent).[10] It should be noted, however, that the enrollment ratios thus calculated appear to be highest in countries in which short course programs are rare and prolongation of study is customary.

Table 1 shows the ratio of new entrant students and of those successfully completing higher education course programs in European member states of the OECD. The entering population varies from 67.5 percent in Sweden to 12.2 percent in Turkey. The graduation ratio in the same year ranged from 16.1 percent in Norway to 4.4 percent in Turkey. But one must take into consideration the limits of these statistics. Most of the students named on level 5 (according to the UNESCO definition) in Austria, Finland, Greece, Switzerland, and the United Kingdom were enrolled at institutions or in course programs not considered officially to be part of "higher education" in their home country. Even within the data presented in Table 1, a different range of nonuniversity institutions is taken into account in Norway and in Switzerland in the statistics of new entrant students and graduates, respectively. In Sweden, those students taking short courses not considered to be regular course programs are also included. The distinction of level 5 (nonuniversity third-level education) and level 6 (regular university course programs) became more blurred over the years: in Table 1, Dutch Hoger Beroepsonderwijs and German Fachhochschulen (three- to four-year programs) are included in level 5, whereas students at Spanish Escuelas Universitarias (three-year programs) are part of level 6.

Part-Time Studies

Whereas all Eastern European countries register part-time enrollment separately (the percentage ranged in the mid-

Table 2

Distribution of Students by Groups of Fields of Study (percentage)

Country	Year	Groups of Fields				
		I	II	III	IV	V
Albania	1985	38.47	5.02	4.93	49.26	2.32
Austria	1985	62.52	9.20	12.32	13.53	2.43
Belgium	1985	56.31	8.22	17.33	16.59	1.55
Bulgaria	1985	42.72	7.61	11.09	38.58	—
Cyprus	1985	55.46	7.28	6.67	23.22	7.37
Czechoslovakia	1985	36.73	3.18	7.13	52.64	0.32
Denmark	1984	55.72	6.85	16.24	18.01	3.18
Finland	1985	46.34	12.62	12.77	27.99	0.28
France	1982	56.32	15.58	15.86	9.45	2.79
German Dem. Rep.	1985	32.52	2.75	14.24	37.61	12.88
Germany, Fed. Rep. of	1985	49.83	11.91	14.18	22.86	1.62
Greece	1983	54.69	9.63	12.37	23.31	—
Hungary	1985	59.39	2.24	9.98	27.70	0.69
Iceland	1983	60.88	8.75	21.41	8.96	—
Ireland	1982	49.78	15.67	6.20	24.18	4.17
Italy	1984	51.82	10.10	19.50	16.98	1.60
Luxembourg	1984	54.45	8.66	6.52	30.37	—
Malta	1985	52.72	—	25.71	21.57	—
Netherlands	1984	62.54	3.66	10.49	20.08	3.23
Norway	1984	56.84	8.23	11.47	15.90	7.56
Poland	1985	51.09	4.45	13.52	28.16	2.78
Portugal	1984	58.37	4.76	9.86	23.05	3.96
Romania	1985	16.29	5.10	11.79	66.82	—
Spain	1984	60.61	9.72	10.97	14.43	4.27
Sweden	1984	47.28	7.92	11.77	29.50	3.53
Switzerland	1985	58.09	10.73	9.31	21.87	—
Turkey	1984	61.14	5.46	9.36	24.04	—
United Kingdom	1983	45.39	12.67	15.80	18.47	7.67
USSR	1985	37.91	—	7.30	54.79	—
Yugoslavia	1984	48.29	5.60	8.66	37.55	0.90

I: Humanities and Social Sciences; II: Sciences; III: Medical Fields; IV: Technical Fields; V: Others.

Source: V. Nicolae et al., *Statistics on Higher Education* (Bucharest: CEPES, 1989), p. 36.

1980s from 44 percent in the USSR to 22 percent in Bulgaria), few Western European countries provide corresponding data (the CEPES study reports 60 percent in Switzerland and 42 percent in the United Kingdom).[11] Obviously, a need for the collection of data on part-time enrollment is only felt if specific course programs are provided for part-time students and/or if students have to pay substantial fees and part-time students are entitled to reduction of fees.

Graduate and Other Advanced Studies

Data on enrollment in advanced course programs (UNESCO level 7) are misleading. In the majority of European countries, the first university degree is considered equivalent to an American or English master's degree. Most postdegree professional education is not linked to institutions of higher education. Finally, in many European countries, individual instruction programs rather than graduate school arrangements prevail for doctoral training. About 25 percent of the British students who receive the first university-level degree, about 20 percent of the French students awarded a maîtrise or corresponding degree, and between 10 and 15 percent of graduates in most other European countries proceed to graduate or professional programs.[12]

Female Students

In the mid-1980s more than half of the students enrolled in several East European countries, Iceland, and Portugal were female. According to an overview by CEPES, the mean enrollment of female students in European countries was 46 percent. In the mid-1980s, however, women comprised less than 10 percent of the students in science fields except in Ireland (17 percent) and Italy (11 percent) and less than 20 percent in technical fields in all but for a few Eastern European countries.[13]

Fields of Study

Table 2 shows the distribution of students by fields of study. The proportion of those enrolled in humanities and social sciences was higher than 60 percent in the Netherlands, Austria, Switzerland, Spain, and Iceland; it was less than 40 percent in the majority of Eastern European countries. About 15–25 percent of students in most countries were enrolled in technical fields. But the Eastern European countries averaged 30 percent enrollment. Sweden, with 30 percent, had the highest technical enrollment in Western Europe; the USSR, with 55 percent, and Romania, with 67 percent, had the highest enrollment in Eastern Europe. One has to bear in mind different borderlines between higher education and higher level vocational education; the classification of training for technicians and nurses, for example, vary widely.

Public Expenses for Higher Education

The expansion of student numbers has been associated with rising expenses for higher education. However, the relative costs for higher education are, when viewed in comparative perspective, not very closely linked to enrollment ratios. The proportion of the gross national product spent on higher education in the mid-1980s was highest among Western European countries such as the Netherlands (1.6 percent) and the United Kingdom (1.1 percent). It was about 0.7 to 1.0 percent in most European countries, but only about 0.5 percent in Italy, Spain, Portugal, and Greece.[14] The data are hardly comparable, however, because countries differ notably in the degree to which research is allocated at institutions of higher education, in the extent to which expenses for university hospitals are included, and in the proportion of educational expenses not distributed to educational levels. The OECD calculates the average public expenditure per student as a percentage of per capita gross domestic product. They are higher than 80 percent in the United Kingdom and the Netherlands, more than 50 percent in Portugal, Turkey, and Switzerland, but less than 40 percent in a substantial number of countries—and only 30 percent in France.[15] One should note that students in most European countries do not pay any tuition fees at most institutions of higher education. If tuition fees do have to be paid, the annual amount surpasses average student living costs for two months only in exceptional cases.

Table 3

Foreign Students at Institutions of Higher Education in Europe

Country	Year	Total of Student Enrollment	Foreign Students	Proportion of Foreign Students in the Total Student Enrollment
Albania	1965	12,761	93	0.73
Austria[1]	1985	160,904	15,388	9.56
Belgium	1985	247,499	24,761	10.00
Bulgaria	1985	113,795	7,254	6.37
Czechoslovakia	1985	169,344	4,175	2.47
Denmark	1984	114,559	3,101	2.71
Finland	1985	92,230	979	1.06
France	1985	983,483	131,979	13.41
German Dem. Rep.	1985	432,672	9,231	2.13
Germany, Fed. Rep. of	1985	1,550,211	79,354	5.12
Greece	1982	137,453	6,683	4.86
Hungary	1985	99,344	2,495	2.50
Ireland	1985	55,087	1,774	3.22
Italy	1984	1,181,953	27,548	2.33
Netherlands[2]	1985	317,721	5,705	1.80
Norway	1980	79,117	1,140	1.44
Poland	1985	454,190	2,986	0.66
Portugal	1984	112,851	2,401	2.13
Romania	1985	159,798	10,774	6.74
Spain	1980	681,022	10,997	1.61
Sweden	1980	203,699	13,182	6.47
Switzerland	1985	110,111	17,396	15.80
Turkey	1985	449,414	7,021	1.56
United Kingdom	1985	937,000	63,522	6.78
USSR	1985	5,147,200	66,700	1.30
Yugoslavia	1985	349,013	7,384	2.12

Not included are small European countries.
1. Universities only
2. Full-time students only

Source: V. Nicolae et al., *Statistics on Higher Education* (Bucharest: CEPES, 1989), p. 68.

Foreign Students

Most recently, general statistical overviews on higher education systems also show the proportion of foreign students in the total student enrollment. As Table 3 shows, this proportion was highest in Switzerland (15.8 percent), France (13.4 percent) and Belgium (10.0 percent) in the mid-1980s. The corresponding proportions for the Federal Republic of Germany and the United Kingdom—two countries frequently named as major host countries of foreign students in absolute figures—were 5.1 and 6.8 percent, respectively. The pattern of foreign students clearly varies between European countries. In the mid-1980s African, Asian, and South American students comprised 77 percent of foreign students in France and 73 percent of foreign students in the United Kingdom. In the Federal Republic of Germany 51 percent of foreign students were from these regions. The corresponding proportion was 46 percent for Belgium, 38 percent for Italy, 32 percent for the Netherlands, and only 17 percent for Switzerland. More than 95 percent of European students enrolled abroad study in another European or North American country.[16]

Socioeconomic Background of Students

Finally, overviews on socioeconomic background were a regular part of descriptive profiles of students in the 1960s and part of the 1970s.[17] In the 1980s, however, though many reports about the educational disadvantages of women were published,[18] few reports addressing educational opportunities according to socioeconomic background were issued. In the Federal Republic of Germany students whose fathers had been manual workers comprised about 15 percent of all university students and almost 30 percent of all students at Fachhochschulen as compared to somewhat more than 50 percent among the generation of their parents; these figures hardly changed since the mid-1970s.[19] It might be noteworthy that farmers' children were not a disadvantaged group in every Western European country. For example, 22 percent of new entrant students at institutions of higher education in Ireland in 1986 were from a farming background as compared to 17 percent of the national population under age fifteen in the early 1980s.[20]

Patterns of Institutions and Course Programs
Models Discussed

From the 1960s on, the rapid expansion of higher education led to a search for new institutional patterns and new structures of course programs in Western European countries. Prior to expansion, the research-oriented multidisciplinary universities or university-level institutions that specialized in certain fields were considered to be the major institutions of higher education. A sector of academically less demanding, specialized colleges offering training programs for semiprofessions existed only in a nonsystematic manner. The French *grandes écoles* were the only major exception: they surpassed the universities in reputation regarding their preparatory function for distinct careers.

In the 1960s a consensus seemed to emerge among politicians and experts that the proportion of students enrolled in relatively short, practice-oriented course programs should be increased. Four models were discussed and at least partly implemented: (1) the establishment of (usually two) distinct types of higher education institutions; (2) the introduction of stage models of studies as well as of diplomas and degrees; (3) interinstitutional diversification of what formally had been the same type of institution; (4) intrainstitutional differentiation (comprehensive university models, etc.). No single model is dominant throughout Western Europe, as the following examples show, and there is no trend visible toward a structural convergence.[21]

Some remarks regarding terminology might be appropriate. In most Western European countries those institutions are named universities or considered to be university-type institutions that confer first-level university degrees (no matter whether the institution of higher education itself, the government, or a degree-granting agency actually awards the degree). As a rule, they are also entitled to grant advanced degrees ("licentiatus" in some Scandinavian countries) or doctoral degrees. Four-year degree course programs of most Western European countries (except for some programs in the United Kingdom and in Ireland) are considered equivalent to a master's level education and as a rule entitle the student to proceed to doctoral studies. Only in Ireland, Norway, and the United Kingdom can institutions of higher education not considered to be universities confer—at least in part— degrees identical in names and titles to those conferred at universities. In almost all Western European countries, national legal definitions exist regarding which institutions are considered higher education institutions (in Switzerland, this definition rests within the individual Kanton; in the United Kingdom, no legal definition of higher education exists). The UNESCO and OECD statistics might mention institutions and students on "level 5" that are not considered to belong to higher education by their respective country. Finally, terms such as "postsecondary," "tertiary," or "third-level" higher education are not part of official terminology in most European countries (Ireland is an exception in this respect).

Examples of National Systems

In Italy and Austria universities, university-type course programs clearly dominate.[22] In Italy thirteen years of schooling prior to university education are required. Most course programs require four years of study; some engineering and science programs require five years; and medical programs require six years. Less than 4 percent of students are enrolled in shorter programs. In Austria most university programs require four or five years of study; shorter programs are only provided for a few technical and artistic subjects, and for interpreters. However, Austria has numerous schools for teacher training, social work, health occupations, etc., that are not considered institutions of higher education.

Finland has moved since the mid-1970s toward a relatively homogeneous university system. The Scandinavian tradition (still existing in Denmark and Norway) of two levels of "candidatus"—the lower one involving about three and one-half years of study and the higher one an additional two years—in humanities and sciences was discontinued. All course programs except those for medical fields should comprise 160 to 180 study units requiring about four or five years of study. Most previously shorter programs offered at university-level institutions were incorporated. In the late 1980s moves were visible toward a formal upgrading of higher vocational schools; this upgrading could lead to a new two-type structure.

Since 1977 all Swedish institutions of higher education are formally equal in status in what is now called a comprehensive system of higher education. Two-thirds of the students continue to enroll at universities and one-third in other types of colleges, but structural reforms led to an overlap of types of courses provided at both kinds of institutions. Some colleges now participate in research. Swedish institutions of higher education provide short courses lasting half a year or one year, short semiprofessional programs lasting less than three years, and regular university programs requiring—depending on the field of study—between three and five and one-half years (120–220 points).

University course programs in Spain require at least five years; most engineering and medical fields require six years of study. About 40 percent of diplomas and degrees are granted upon completion of short course programs requiring three years of study. Short programs are mostly provided by "Escuelas Universitarias," formal sections of public universities, or by private institutions that specialize in offering short programs. In the late 1980s, the Spanish government intended to reduce the required duration of university course programs to four years.

In the United Kingdom two major types of higher education have existed since the early 1960s, when Polytechnics, Institutes of Higher Education, and similarly named institutions were formally upgraded. The British pattern, frequently called "binary," is unique, for the two major types of institutions are different in governance and curricular approach, but not in admission prerequisites and duration of course programs. In England and Wales most higher education course programs require thirteen years of prior education and lead toward a bachelor's degree after three years of study. About one-quarter of graduates continue professional studies, take master's courses, or enter a doctoral program. In Scotland, prior schooling is one year shorter, but all university course programs require at least four years of study, and the degree is called a "master's." Some polytechnics and other colleges in England and Wales provide first-degree programs requiring four years, notably those including phases of practical experience ("sandwich" programs). These institutions also offer shorter programs in some subjects leading to a diploma in higher education (Dip HE), and some provide other programs

that are not considered part of higher education, but rather vocational education.

In Belgium two types of institutions of higher education exist with overlapping educational tasks. Course programs at universities require four to five years of study (in a few fields six years). Nonuniversity institutions of higher education provide predominantly short course programs of two or three years' duration. Twelve years of prior schooling is required for all types of higher education program. A general qualification examination has to be passed in order to be entitled for enrollment in university programs. Within the growing nonuniversity sector the proportion of long programs has increased over the years.

In the Federal Republic of Germany two distinct types of institutions and two correspondingly distinct types of course programs dominate. German universities provide course programs that as a rule require four to five years of study and sometimes a final examination period. The second major type of institution, the Fachhochschulen, established since 1971, require twelve years of prior schooling, as compared to thirteen years in the case of universities, and offer course programs usually requiring three years of study, or at most four years, if periods of work experience are included. Exceptions to this general model of two institutional types and corresponding course programs include short programs for some areas of teacher training, fine art courses, and the comprehensive universities. "Gesamthochschulen" offer—in some fields of study—two types of degrees after an initial phase of joint study or in a stage model whereby the degrees in both cases correspond more or less either to the Fachhochschule degree or the university degree, respectively.

Similarly, two different types of course programs and institutions exist in the Netherlands. Universities have required fourteen years of prior schooling ever since two years of preschool education was integrated with the primary schools in the early 1980s. HBO institutions ("hoger beroepsonderwijs"), considered part of higher education since the 1960s but legally upgraded to this sector only in 1986, require thirteen years of prior schooling. Course programs at universities require four years (except for medicine). Those at HBO institutions also require four years, but this includes about one year of work experience. Almost two-thirds of Dutch graduates completed a HBO degree whereby the title "baccalaureus" is conferred. The university degree—the title "doctorandus" is conferred in most fields—is considered equivalent to a master's degree.

Norway has a multitude of levels and institutions. In science and humanities the lower-level university degree of "cand. mag." is awarded after three and one-half to four years of study. A specialized "cand. philog.," "cand. oecon.," etc., can be taken after an additional two years of study. In other fields at universities and equivalent specialized institutions, course programs require four to five years of study. District colleges provide mostly two-year or three-year programs, but also some programs—often combinations of two short programs—leading to a four-year degree. Finally, other small (specialized) colleges for teacher training, social work, technical fields, public administration, etc., provide two-year or three-year programs; admission to some of these programs is possible after less than twelve years of schooling. Altogether, more than 80 percent of Norway's tertiary students graduate after completing course programs requiring less than four years of study.

In France, the *grandes écoles* form the most prestigious sector. They usually require fourteen years of schooling prior to admission. Most applicants choose special preparatory classes (CPGE) for their thirteenth and fourteenth year of schooling. Universities provide course programs at all levels. During the first stage of two years, students might enroll in semispecialized general programs leading to the interim general university diploma (DEUG). Premedical programs or professional programs take two or three years and lead to a Diplome of Scientific and Technical Studies (DEUST). Students transferring to the second "cycle" might be awarded—in humanities and sciences—a "licence" after the third year of study and a "maîtrise" after the fourth year, or—in other fields—a single degree after four or five years of study. The third major type of institutions are Instituts Universitaires de Technologie (IUT), newly created in the 1960s; these are formally components of universities but are administrated separately. They provide mostly two-year programs; though of a lesser duration than universities, their course programs are considered to be very prestigious. In addition, some other two- and three-year course programs are provided by specialized institutions of higher education or in the framework of postsecondary programs at secondary education institutions.

Variety of Patterns Emerged

Thus, clear stage models across all fields corresponding to the sequence of bachelor's and master's which exist only in the United Kingdom and in Ireland were not introduced in any Western European country. Stage models for select fields of study were preserved in France and in some Scandinavian countries, but discontinued in Sweden and Finland. In Belgium, France, and Spain short-cycle professional degrees usually require the same years of study as the first stage of a university degree, but their prestige as compared to a university degree vary substantially between these countries. Two-type models with different entrance and exit levels were introduced in the Federal Republic of Germany and the Netherlands but they are not considered stage models—though transition is possible. There are also variations within Western Europe regarding the allocation of relatively short higher education programs. These might be offered in separate (non-university) institutions, in institutions associated with universities, or within universities themselves; more than one of these models might be found in the same country. In some countries university education clearly dominates; a second sector of institutions or course programs hardly exists or is officially not part of the higher education system. In sum, two-type models are widespread. The stability of two-type patterns varies: many French, Dutch, and German experts consider the existing distinctions in their country as more or less stable, but in the United Kingdom the traditional segmentation between university and other institutions of higher education continues to be blurred.[23]

Select Aspects Related to the Educational Tasks of Higher Education

Admission to Higher Education

In almost all Western European countries a clear vertical or track structure of secondary education existed until the 1960s whereby successful completion of academic secondary education—for example, by passing the "baccalauréat" in France or the "Abitur" in the Federal Republic of Germany—entitled one to enrollment at universities. Most nonuniversity institutions of higher education existing at that time or subsequently upgraded had their own individual admission criteria and selection procedures—a tradition that has been kept.[24] This system of open admission to universities for qualified school leavers was gradually shaken when, on the one hand, access to higher education from other types of secondary education was widened (comprehensive secondary education was only introduced partially in some countries, but not system-wide in any Western European country) and, on the other hand, capacities at least in some fields of study were not extended in accordance with the growing number of students.

The responses to those changes varied substantially by country.[25] In Austria, France, and Italy the old admission system to the universities survived, with some limitations and restrictions administered by some individual institutions or faculties. Very select admission systems continue in Greece and Turkey. In the Federal Republic of Germany and in the Netherlands the principle of open admission for qualified secondary school leavers has been preserved for the majority of course programs supplemented by nationwide systems of "numerus clausus" and "numerus fixus," respectively, for some fields of study, whereby school grades, waiting time after completion of secondary education, a lottery weighed according to school grades, tests, interview results, social criteria, etc., are taken into consideration.

The Swedish model of admission criteria and procedures to higher education became best known, for the Swedes tried to establish a deliberate compromise between opening higher education to greater numbers while securing advantages for high-achieving secondary school students.[26] In addition to those who have completed the "gymnasium" and altogether thirteen years of schooling, secondary school leavers who have completed only eleven or twelve years of schooling can in principle enroll at institutions of higher education, provided that the program includes two years of upper secondary education in Swedish as well as two years of English at an academic secondary education level. Moreover, those who are at least twenty-five years of age, have at least four years of occupational experience (or other recognized kinds of experience), and have similar secondary education credentials in Swedish and English as the above-named group are also qualified for tertiary education. For each field of study, additional subjects might be mandatory for admission. If the number of applicants surpasses the study places available, which is the case in most all programs, admissions are decided by a system in which students are awarded points for previous school achievements, admission tests scores, and work experience.

Contrary to the pattern in a majority of Western European countries, the individual universities in the United Kingdom and Ireland have traditionally selected their students by themselves. Whereas other countries favored open admission to universities following selective secondary education, the British model is selective both in secondary education and upon admission to higher education.[27] Admission procedures are centrally administered, but the individual universities set their own criteria (for each field of study).

Curricula, Teaching and Learning Modes, Examinations

Structures of curricula, teaching and learning modes, and the character of examination vary substantially in Western Europe according to field of study, type of institution, and national traditions of higher education. For example, medical science and engineering programs are more structured and standardized than programs in the humanities and social sciences. Nonuniversity-level institutions of higher education regard detailed curriculum regulations more favorably than university-level institutions. But across these differences, the British, German, and French university systems have cultivated different styles of curricula, learning, and examinations that continue to put their stamp on present-day higher education in Western Europe.

The traditional English universities stressed independent learning by students, individualized instruction by means of tutorials, and a substantial range of choice.[28] Contrary to the French and German traditions, British academic staff were expected to be educators in terms of being knowledgeable in teaching and learning modes, in emphasizing guidance and close contact with students, and in caring for the socialization process of the students in general. Only part of the course achievements are assessed, and written examinations form only one mode of assessment. Grading upon graduation is based on selected prior achievements, thus allowing authorities to disregard relatively bad grades in some courses.

The traditional German university stressed freedom of teaching and learning and the unity of research and teaching. Lectures and seminars are considered as opportunities for students to be directly involved in "Wissenschaft," not as part of a systematic process of transferring knowledge. Students, especially those in humanities, are free to choose courses and to organize their course program themselves. Professors are expected to involve students in scholarly dialogues. The duration of studies is individually determined: students begin to write the thesis when they feel sufficiently matured. Final grading is solely based on a final thesis and final written and oral examinations.

The French university traditionally offered highly structured programs. Academic staff are lecturers with the required knowledge. Neither educational care nor a close link between teaching and research is emphasized. Achievement is measured annually by means of written examinations; students who do not pass the annual examination must repeat the respective year of study.

For a long period, however, developments in the system of higher education and its societal surroundings have prompted a trend toward systematization of content, structures, and processes in higher education.[29] The advancement of scholarship made it necessary to establish sequences in learning and to secure the acquisition of basic knowledge. Knowledge needed by a highly qualified work force can be guaranteed more readily when detailed regulations are prescribed. In many countries experts came to the conclusion that the growing number of students from diverse educational and social backgrounds were better served if courses were highly structured, requirements were clearly specified, academic staff were trained in teaching techniques and put emphasis on the students' guidance, and examinations were stretched over the years rather than given only at the end of studies.

Most experts claim that the traditional low regard on the part of professors for educational skills continues in those countries more or less in the way it was customary until the 1960s.[30] For example, centers for Hochschuldidaktik were established at many German institutions of higher education around 1970, but a few years later most academic staff favored closing such institutions. Assessment of teaching plays at most a nominal role in recruitment of academic staff and any subsequent decisions affecting rewards, careers, and reputation. In France moves toward improving teaching and learning played even a lesser role than in the Federal Republic of Germany, the Netherlands, and the Scandinavian countries. But the trend toward systematization and formalization of teaching and learning obviously continues in all Western European countries.

Formalization certainly took place in terms of raising the numbers of required courses within course programs and increasing quantities of examinations and other ways of assessment.[31] Detailed guidelines and regulations became customary for the purpose of information and guidance in general, of explanation of the more highly structured curricula, and final-ly as a safeguard for legal challenges to decisions taken on the part of the institutions of higher education. Experts claim that study regulations and examination regulations in the Federal Republic of Germany are nowadays about ten times as long as two or three decades ago. The first and most visible change, however, has been the introduction of some elements of credit systems and/or the structuring of course programs according to stages. During the 1970s and 1980s France, Finland, and the Netherlands followed Sweden in introducing a system of "value units," "points," or "study load hours," etc., thus standardizing student work loads and putting more emphasis on assessment of individual courses, without, however, strictly copying the United States credit system. Second, stages of course programs have been more strongly emphasized in some countries. For example, Austria and the Federal Republic of Germany have introduced an intermediate assessment (Vor-Diplom, etc.) in all course programs. Third, efforts were made to structure graduate training and to reduce the time-span usually required for the award of a doctoral degree. In most Scandinavian countries the tradition of two levels of academic degree ("licentiatus" and "doctor") has been replaced by doctoral programs aimed to lead to a doctoral degree within four years upon completion of a regular university degree. Also, the "two phases structure" introduced at Dutch universities since 1982 and the "Graduiertenkollegs" established in the Federal Republic of Germany since the late 1980s are steps toward structuring doctoral training.

Seemingly similar directions of curricular innovations did not, however, lead to more or less the same styles of curricula, teaching, and examinations. The increased efforts since the 1970s to establish regular student exchange programs between specific faculties and departments hampered by their diversity. According to a survey on students participating in study abroad programs, British universities are conceived to emphasize the writing of essays and active participation of students in courses. Communication between teachers and students outside the classroom is considered to be frequent. But the individual search for research literature is less stimulated than in Germany. German institutions seem to stimulate, according to their guest students' views, understanding of theories, individual learning, and the search for research literature. Attendance at courses is seldom examined, and regular assessment of achievement is less frequent than in the other countries. Students who study in France view communication between teachers and students outside the classroom as infrequent. French institutions are considered to be teacher-centered. Written examinations are the dominant mode of assessment, and strong emphasis is placed on grades. Foreign students argue that students in France are not much encouraged to develop their own points of view. Altogether, British and French students assessed German higher education both before and after the study period abroad more positively than German students assessed British or French higher education. It is noteworthy that students studying for some time in the United Kingdom assessed the higher education system of that country more favorably upon return than they did before the study abroad whereas those studying in France assessed French higher education more negatively upon return.[32]

Transfer of Students Between Course Programs and Institutions

In most European countries, students are expected to complete a course program at an individual institution of higher education.[33] If students want to transfer from one institution to another or from one field to another, the receiving institution or department will decide about admission and recognition of prior studies. Transfer between universities in the same field of study is in principle eased in the majority of Western European countries by the fact that rules regarding access and admission are national. German students are traditionally encouraged to move from one university to another during their course of study in order to enrich their learning opportunities beyond the provision of the individual university. In open-admission subjects they are free to register in another university at any time; in highly selective fields they might trade a study place with a student wishing to make the reverse move. But available statistics show that less than 20 percent of German students move prior to being awarded a university degree.

As a rule, nonuniversity course programs in higher education in Western European countries are not considered to be linked to university course programs in terms of a stage structure. Only a few countries have systemwide regulations regarding the transfer from nonuniversity course programs to university course programs. In most cases the individual universities have substantial leeway in the degree of recognition of prior studies. Regular statistics on transfer are not available; estimates in various Western European countries range around 10 percent of graduates from nonuniversity higher education transferring to university programs.

In Spain, those successfully completing three-year course programs are in most fields entitled to transfer to the fourth year of corresponding university course programs. They are required to successfully take part in adaptation programs prior to or during the fourth year of study. In Norway two-year studies in economic and engineering fields as well as in some areas of humanities, social sciences, and natural sciences can be easily supplemented by a regular university degree. The traditional structure of university programs in which basic subjects (half a year of study), intermediate subjects (one or one and one-half years) and main subjects (two years) are combined to earn a degree eases the incorporation of short-course programs into regular university degree-programs. District colleges offer opportunities to combine two two-year programs for a regular four-year degree.

In Belgium students who complete two-year programs have to take a transitional year of courses before admission to the third year of a university program. In the Federal Republic of Germany the completion of a Fachhochschule degree is recognized in some Länder as equivalent to the first half of a university program in the same discipline (i.e., equivalent to the successful completion of a "Vor-Diplom"), but in other "Länder" the receiving university might require additional courses. Those Fachhochschule students who have not completed academic secondary education acquire this "maturity" to enroll in any field of university upon completion of the Fachhochschule degree. In the Netherlands all students who successfully complete the propedeutic year at HBO institutions are qualified for first-year study at the university in any field of study. Graduates from HBO course programs can transfer to the third year at universities in the corresponding field of study. Some advanced professional programs at Dutch universities are open to HBO graduates; in exceptional cases Dutch HBO graduates may be accepted by graduate programs at universities.

Duration of Study

The average duration of study varies more between European countries than overviews on the required length of course programs might suggest.[34] On the one hand, British and Irish universities try to ensure that almost all students complete their studies within the formally required period. This is achieved partly by strong emphasis on guidance and methods of instruction, but also by granting special kinds

of pass grades for low achievers, and by the introduction of course programs requiring one more year than usual, if a longer period of study might be necessary for some students—for example, due to a certain specialization, phases of work experiences, or phases of study abroad that cannot be integrated into typical course requirements in the home country.

On the other hand, a prolongation of study beyond the required period is a widespread phenomenon in most Western European countries. An average duration of study of more than 50 percent beyond the formally required period can be observed in Denmark, Spain, and Italy. An average prolongation by 50 percent seems to be customary, according to available information, in Austria, the Federal Republic of Germany, and Finland. Swedish experts estimate a 30–50 percent prolongation on the average. Estimates regarding the actual duration in France vary from five to seven years as compared to slightly more than four years required at universities.

The most detailed data regarding actual duration of study are available in the Federal Republic of Germany—a country in which concern about an increase in the average duration of study and about a high average age upon completion of studies was strongly expressed in the 1980s. The average age of new entrant students at universities rose by about half a year within a decade, to 21.3 years in 1987. Those graduating from universities in 1986 had spent on average 7.0 years since first enrollment—6.2 years in the respective field of study, 0.2 years for interruptions, and 0.6 years due to a change in field of study; again, the total time-span from first enrollment to graduation increased by about half a year within a decade.

In countries in which a prolongation of studies is customary, relatively high drop-out rates can be observed. By comparing data on new entrant students to data on graduates a corresponding number of years later, one discovers that only 50 to

70 percent of students in most Western European countries eventually graduate. If, however, research efforts are made to take into account all interruptions and changes of institutions and fields, estimates regarding the number of students not completing any course program at all are more likely to fall in the range of 15–30 percent.

The strongest efforts to reduce the actual duration of studies at universities were made in the Netherlands. When the "two-phases structure" was introduced in 1982, universities were required to outline course programs in detail according to "study load hours" in order to guarantee that students could complete the course programs within four years instead of the seven customary at that time. Students were not allowed to repeat the first propedeutic year more than once or to spend more than six years at universities; in the late 1980s a compromise allowed students to continue their studies beyond the sixth year on a special status, without any scholarship, and obliged them to pay three times the regular tuition fee. The lump-sum funding of universities was arranged in such a way that universities should have a financial incentive for weeding out during the propedeutic year those most likely to drop out, as well as for graduating students after a maximum of five years. Finally, the scholarship system was improved to a level at which at least half of study and living costs were covered for most students. In the late 1980s, statistics on the first cohorts of the new system led to estimates that the actual average duration of study was reduced to five and one-half years.[35]

Though concern is frequently expressed about prolongation of study and dropout, most European countries do not seem to want to reduce prolongation to less than half a year on the average or to reduce dropouts to about 10 percent of a cohort (i.e., as is the case in the United Kingdom and Japan). Rather, a certain degree of pro-longation (as well as certain degree of dropout) is taken for granted and even considered appropriate in order to cope with the expansion of academic knowledge, to safeguard freedom of learning, not to compromise quality standards for the sake of formally high "success rates," and to allow the students part-time studies in the formal framework of regular enrollment—for example, in order to earn their living costs. In Italy, "studenti furori corso," students who do not keep to the regular pace, are even entitled to pay lower tuition fees.

Academic Emphasis Versus Orientation Toward Practice

Traditionally in most Western European countries regular degrees conferred at institutions of higher education were conceived to indicate both the academic qualification and the acquisition of basic professional knowledge.[36] According to this principle, students solely interested in academic qualification could qualify for doctoral studies in some fields without having taken any prior degree in the Federal Republic of Germany until the 1970s, and in Austria until the 1980s. In Scandinavian countries, Austria, and some other countries the award of an academic degree in general implies an "effectus civilis," a right to practice certain professions (possibly after a period of initial training). In France, however, all graduates have to pass entrance examinations ("concours") in order to be admitted to corresponding (publicly supervised) professional training and careers. In the Federal Republic of Germany three types of university degrees exist, whereby the "Staatsexamen" in teacher training, law, and medicine entitles one for professional practice (this final examination is externally supervised and practitioneers are among the examiners); the "Diplom" is an internal university examination that confers basic professional qualification; and the "Magister" is a purely academic degree. In the United Kingdom and in Ireland professional associations—notably in engineering and business—control access to the profession through licensing and thereby exercise pressure on course programs by determining whether certain degree programs be exempt from a theoretical examination as part of the overall prerequisites for being licensed.

Since the late 1960s substantial criticism has been voiced that the university was too secluded from society. One of the major thrusts of the student protests in the late 1960s was their critique of the lack of social relevance of knowledge and of social responsibility on the part of the scholars. Additionally, many experts claimed that due to the higher education expansion a growing proportion of students needed a more direct occupational preparation for employment than previously under conditions of elite higher education. Finally, the increased economic and employment problems in general put pressure on institutions of higher education and notably on students to consider the utility of studies.

In Sweden and in the Federal Republic of Germany higher education legislation reforms during 1976 even foresaw a certain degree of professional emphasis for all course programs. Swedish institutions can establish, beside the "general" (allmänna utbildningslinjer, i.e., nationally approved) and the "local" course programs, "individual" course programs that were as rule academic in thrust. At German universities the "Magister" course programs were not discontinued in the wake of the new legislation, but on the contrary substantially extended.

Various other kinds of moves toward an increased direct professional emphasis of higher education could be observed in most European countries: a shift of resource allocation in favor of those fields of study whose graduates seemed to be most "employable," an "orientation toward practice" in terms of systematic confrontation of scientific approaches and professional problem solving in the teaching and learning process in higher education, the establishment of new fields of study combining knowledge from disciplines traditionally not linked to professions with those closely linked (for example "European Studies" as a combination of area-related humanities, social, and economic studies), the introduction of work experience or other work-related learning processes. Most experts conclude that some moves toward a stronger direct professional emphasis have taken place, but changes in this direction have been much more limited than what employers, some governments, and even some scholars had suggested. Many still argue that higher education can play a more meaningful critical role in society if students are actively prepared to confront practical problems with diverse scholarly concepts. A recent survey conducted in the United Kingdom, however, came to the conclusion that a substantial "vocational shift" has taken place in many programs traditionally considered to be "academic" programs or course programs traditionally occupying intermediate positions on a continuum between dominant "academic" and dominant "professional" emphasis.[37] Contrary to the widespread opinion that the universities hardly left the ivory tower, this study seems to suggest that the "epistemic drift" toward utility and employability might go so far as to endanger in many cases the distance from practice needed for pursuit of truth and for innovative and critical analysis. On the other hand, enrollment in nonuniversity higher education in Western Europe, traditionally considered to be "vocational," did not generally expand at a faster pace than enrollment at universities.[38]

Homogeneity or Diversity of Curricular Emphasis and Quality

In most European countries established patterns of communication, negotiation, and approval have ensured a certain degree of homogeneity of curricula within each field of study among all institutions of higher education. For example, almost all degrees conferred at French universities are called "national diplomas"; regular procedures setting frameworks for curricula by government and state approval of course programs suggested by the individual faculty ensure that differences between institutions of higher education are kept within bounds. In the Federal Republic of Germany framework regulations for "Diplom" course programs decided upon by the Standing Conference of the Ministers of Education of the States set guidelines for a certain proportion of required subjects. The ministry of the individual "Land" in charge has to approve the study regulations and examination regulations of the individual course program. In Sweden, "general" course programs tend to be almost uniform all over the country. Specific agencies were founded in the United Kingdom (Council for National Academic Awards) and in Ireland (National Council for Educational Awards), in the 1960s and 1970s, respectively, to be in charge of assuring a certain degree of homogeneity and quality of course programs at nonuniversity institutions of higher education. In various European countries scholars themselves are strongly in favor of quite homogeneous course programs.

Most experts agree that during the 1970s efforts grew in favor of national coordination of curricula. These efforts in part reflected intentions to carry through reforms on a broad scale, in part were a response to a growing heterogeneity of the academic community under conditions of higher education expansion, and in part reflected a confidence crisis in the traditional academic values. Efforts to make teaching and learning more transparent and more educational to the students contributed to more detailed regulations. During the 1980s, however, governments in various Western European countries favored a reduction of national coordination of higher education and increased leeway and responsibility for the individual institutions in shaping their course programs. Economic pressures on the individual institutions seem to have led to a growing diversity of course provisions.

It is noteworthy, though, that governments in some countries have changed their modes of supervision only to a limited extent. In the Federal Republic of the Germany the state governments' role in the approval procedures of study regulations has been reduced in the 1985 revision of the Framework Act for Higher Education, but the supervisory rights regarding examination regulations remain unchanged. In France universities are entitled since the mid-1980s to introduce university course programs leading to the "magistère" degree but not programs leading to national diplomas; the government provides financial resources and personnel only for the latter programs.

Various traditional measures continue to play a substantial role to ensure that quality differences are kept in bounds. For example, most research funding for higher education in the Federal Republic of Germany, the United Kingdom, and several other Western European countries continues to be channelled through the basic funding of universities. Also regulations such as the selection of new professors by national committees in France or the stimulation of mobility of professors in the Federal Republic of Germany (promotion to a professor position at the home university is almost impossible, and position and salary raises of professors can only be granted in the case of an external "call") serve as a counterbalance to steep institutional quality-hierarchies.

Higher Education and Employment

Changing Interpretations of the Relationships Between Higher Education and Employment

Expansion of higher education was accompanied in many Western European countries by the assumption that a growing number of graduates was instrumental in stimulating economic growth. The economics of education became very popular during the 1960s and contributed toward an optimistic interpretation of the rising student numbers. Substantial efforts were made to plan the quantitative and structural development of higher education according to perceived economic and social needs. Many Western European countries developed a "mixed type" of higher education policy during that period: whereas higher education in the United States was supposed to act under market rules in order to serve a society ruled by market economy, and higher education in the USSR was supposed to be centrally planned in order to serve a centrally planned economy and society, a certain degree of educational planning in Western Europe was expected to provide the necessary skills and abilities for the likely economic and social options within a social market economy expected in the near future.[39]

This does not mean, however, that higher education planning in Western European countries closely followed presumed manpower demands. For example, the first global manpower and higher education forecast in the Federal Republic of Germany, published in 1967, came to the conclusion that the supply of new university graduates in the early 1980s was likely to be twice as high as the demand.[40] Also, a considerable number of employers in Western Europe continued to voice concern during that period about a possible overqualification. Policies in favor of higher education expansion were based on the assumptions that it might help to reduce inequality of educational and social opportunities, contribute to personal and cultural enrichment, and stimulate economic growth by supplying graduates from higher education institutions to occupational strata traditionally filled by nongraduates.

Contrary to the United States and Japan, when such phenomena as "vertical substitution" and educational "upgrading" of careers had become widespread in the 1960s and early 1970s, the major impact of higher education expansion on the labor market in most Western European countries was not noted until the mid-1970s, when the oil crisis and subsequent economic problems led to substantial unemployment (ranging in Western European countries from about 2 to 10 percent). In the early 1980s general unemployment doubled again in most Western European countries and thereafter only declined moderately. Expansion of higher education slowed down somewhat in most Western European countries during the 1970s, but the number of graduates still rose. A comparative study of eight Western European university systems shows that the number of university graduates increased between 1975 and 1983 from 10 to 40 percent in all cases except Spain, where there was an increase of 88 percent.[41] In various countries the number of graduates from nonuniversity institutions of higher education increased at an even higher rate during that period. From the early 1970s until at least the mid-1980s debates on higher education and employment focused on the issue of a supply of recent graduates beyond the presumed demand, the problems and conflicts that resulted from this discrepancy, and possible adaptations or counteracting policies.[42]

Unemployed Graduates

In some Western European countries large-scale representative surveys are conducted annually or biannually describing the situation of new graduates six months or one year after graduation. In some countries regular labor force statistics are available indicating the educational credentials for persons at each occupational category as well as regular unemployment statistics according to educational background. Almost all Western European countries conduct at least occasional surveys on all graduates or on graduates from particular fields of study or from specific sectors of the higher education system. These data provide information on graduate unemployment, the time-span of transition from higher education to employment, links between fields of study and employment sectors, and the issue of "appropriate employment."

In most Western European countries unemployment of higher education-trained labor increased substantially in the early 1980s, but remained about half as high as unemployment in the total labor force. Not surprisingly, the unemployment ratio of recent graduates is somewhat higher than that of all college-trained labor. For example, the unemployment ratio of British university graduates six months after graduation rose from 7 percent in 1979 to 17 percent in 1983 and that of graduates from polytechnics from 10 to 20 percent.[43] The corresponding quota for Swiss university graduates one year after graduation were 2 and 5 percent.[44] In the Federal Republic of Germany the unemployment ratio of all higher education-trained labor increased during that period from somewhat more than 2 percent to almost 5 percent, whereas the unemployment ratio in the total labor force increased from slightly above 3 percent to almost 9 percent.[45]

Italy is an exception in various respects: in 1978 the unemployment ratio of university-trained labor (7.4 percent) was slightly higher than that of the total labor force (7.2 percent). Subsequently, graduate unemployment declined to 6.2 percent in 1983, whereas overall unemployment increased to 9.9 percent. In other words, job searches tend to be extraordinarily long in Italy. In 1983, 28 percent of university-trained persons aged under thirty were reported as being unemployed. But once regularly employed, there is little risk of becoming unemployed: among university-trained Italians aged thirty or over, the unemployment ratio was only 2 percent.[46]

Problems of Job Search

It is frequently assumed that the increased difficulties of graduates in various Western European countries in finding a job lead to extended job search periods after graduation. Available statistics, however, show that job search periods after graduation longer than six months have remained rare in some Western European countries, whereas long periods of job search already had been customary in some countries before the period discussed here. Job search periods increased less than is generally assumed. In Switzerland 47 percent of the 1984 graduates employed one year after graduation had started their job immediately after graduation and a further 30 percent within three months. In Sweden three-quarters of the 1984 graduates employed one year later had found employment immediately after graduation or after at most one month of search. Various German surveys indicate that a job search period of almost six months is now the average for graduates.

Statistics available about part-time work or contracts for a limited time-span do not indicate a worsening of employment conditions for recent graduates during the late 1970s and early 1980s. A Swiss survey shows that most part-time employment was voluntary and that contracts for a limited time-span do not necessarily indicate bad jobs. Also, available data do not confirm the widespread belief among experts that a continuation of study beyond the first higher education degree had increased in Western European countries during the period discussed here as a consequence of employment problems.

Employment Problems by Field of Study

All surveys that allow an analysis of change over time and all experts' assessments agree on the widening gap between employment opportunities depending upon the fields of study in Western European countries during the 1970s and 1980s. There are no indications that market mechanisms solve this problem. Certainly, the number of students opting for "marketable" fields seems to have increased in many Western European countries, but those adjustments remained small in comparison with the increased differences in employment prospects.

Not infrequently, generalizations are made that graduates from humanities, education, and social science fields not clearly linked to business or public administration careers face substantial employment problems, whereas graduates from science and engineering fields encounter few problems in getting jobs or are even in high demand. Available statistics for the early 1980s show that this might be true on average across all countries, but exceptions can be noted in each country. For example, among 1983 French graduates surveyed nine months after graduation the unemployment ratio of those graduating from humanities was lower than those from chemistry and earth sciences. In Austria graduates from all major science fields except mathematics and physics faced substantial employment problems. In Sweden the unemployment rates for 1984/85 graduates one year after graduation in biology (9 percent) and mechanical engineering (8 percent) were only half of those observed in general humani-

ties, but much higher than the average for all fields (3 percent).[47] British surveys report substantial unemployment six months after graduation for university graduates in life sciences. Finally, it should be noted that teacher unemployment was less visible in those countries in which prospective secondary education teachers graduate in specific subjects first and then take part in a specific teacher-training program; in France admission to subsequent teacher-training programs is strictly controlled according to prospective vacant positions.

Employment Problems by Type of Institution

It is frequently assumed that graduates from nonuniversity higher education have been less affected by the employment problems since 1973 and that they have faced fewer problems than university graduates. Available information, however, indicates striking differences between countries in this respect. In France graduates from universities traditionally have less favorable labor market prospects than graduates from *grandes écoles*. The increasing employment problems for university graduates during the 1970s contributed to the growing popularity of the IUTs. In Germany the fact that the unemployment ratio of university-trained persons surpassed that of Fachhochschule-trained persons around 1980 is frequently pointed out as an indicator of more favorable employment prospects for the latter. A detailed analysis, however, shows that Fachhochschulen do not offer most of the fields of study most negatively affected by the worsened labor market. If graduates are compared from fields of study offered both at universities and Fachhochschulen (engineering and business fields), unemployment quotas hardly differ and university graduates have shorter search periods and consider their work assignments less often as inappropriate or unsatisfactory.[48] In the United Kingdom, a lower proportion of recent university graduates are unemployed or in short-term employment than recent polytechnic graduates.

Inappropriate Employment

Various research methods have been employed to assess the percentage of graduates who are inappropriately employed. In some cases occupational categories as such are taken as indicators. In a French study university graduates whose jobs are classified as *employés* and *ouvriers* were considered as clearly downgraded. About 5 percent of university graduates and more than twice as many graduates from short-cycle higher education were registered in those categories.[49] Similarly, 5 percent of recent graduates from British universities in 1985 entered secretarial, clerical, and manual occupations, as did 6 percent of polytechnic graduates and 14 percent of those from other colleges. Most experts agree, however, that—notably for middle-level jobs—the occupational category as such is hardly a clear indicator of "appropriate employment." It might be added here that only a few Western European scholars have assessed the degree of over education through the calculation of rate of social return to educational investments; this method did not gain popularity because salaries are generally considered to be more strongly influenced by traditional reputation of professions, political decisions, long-term effects of bargaining, etc., than by the ups and downs of the demand-supply ratios regarding recent graduates.

Many surveys were conducted by Western European scholars in which graduates themselves were asked to rate linkages between higher education and employment. Graduates were asked about the extent to which they utilized the knowledge acquired during their studies, the credentials of their predecessors and the most suitable successors, the credentials considered indispensable for taking over the assignment, and the appropriateness of the position to the level of education and training reached. Depending on the kind of questions asked, researchers in Western Europe rated between more than 30 percent (in the case of a French-Italian survey)[50] and only 3 percent (in the case of a Swiss survey)[51] of recent graduates as inappropriately employed. These findings indicate the important role of the yardstick chosen, but are not suitable to show differences by country, because comparisons based on similar methods are lacking. In the Federal Republic of Germany some variations of questions employed led to similar results: about 60 percent of graduates take over positions and assignments considered typical for graduates, more than 20 percent note some limitations regarding the utilization of their knowledge or the appropriateness of their position, and less than 20 percent perceive little use of their knowledge or a position clearly below what is conceived to be appropriate for graduates from institutions of higher education. The proportions have not changed substantially since the late 1970s.

Recruitment Procedures and Criteria

The employment problems of graduates substantially raised attention concerning the employers' procedures and criteria in recruiting graduates and their expectations regarding higher education. In most Western European countries similar statements, which were partly contradictory, could be observed in this respect: students should more frequently opt for fields preparing for jobs in the private sector of the economy, studies should be more strongly oriented toward practice, curricula should be less specialized than in the past and emphasize the basic foundation of knowledge and problem-solving strategies, and personality and work-related attitudes played an increasing role in graduate recruitment at the expense of knowledge acquired.

Similar rhetoric among various European countries about changing expectations regarding higher education should not, however, lead to the conclusion that more or less similar relationships between higher education and employment emerged in this period. For example, a French-German comparative analysis of similar industrial enterprises showed that French firms had by far more positions above skilled workers but a smaller number of skilled workers with less responsibilities in their work assignments than German skilled workers.[52] This led the scholars to the conclusion that vertical substitution due to increasing numbers of graduates was likely to lead to very different consequences in the two countries concerned.

Two similar surveys conducted on employers' recruitment procedures and criteria in the Federal Republic of Germany and in the United Kingdom[53] in the early 1980s show similarities in some respects. The authors of both studies emphasize the great variety in the employing organizations in terms of both recruitment procedures and expectations regarding the graduates' competencies. They also show that an increasing weight has been placed on personality, work styles, etc. But a comparison of the two surveys shows substantial differences as well. British employers pay less attention to specific knowledge and skills, place more weight on the prestige hierarchy of institutions of higher education, and seem to be less critical about higher education, notably the traditional universities, than their German colleagues. These differences show that—among other factors—a traditionally strong orientation of German universities to government rather than to the private sector, more substantial prestige differences among British than among German universities, a lesser concern of British managers about the specific skills of engineers, and a high regard for generally educated persons continue to play an important role regarding the relationships between higher education and employment in the respective Western European countries.

Changing Views in the 1980s

Altogether, problems of graduate employment in Western Europe did not become as serious as the majority of experts had predicted in the late 1970s, although enrollment numbers continued to grow (though at a slower rate) and the total capacity of the higher education system was not geared to presumed manpower demand in any Western European country (though capacity of fields was modified in many cases according to presumed demand). Also, not a single one of the possible conflicts or adjustments in the face of the given discrepancy became dominant. Rather, various directions of change occurred alongside one another: increase of graduate unemployment, extension of the transition period, underutilization of the knowledge acquired, growing readiness among graduates of taking over less privileged assignments that allow a utilization of their knowledge, lowering of the standards regarding appropriate graduate employment both on the part of employers and graduates, upgrading of jobs, de-coupling of credentials and employment, etc.[54]

During the early 1980s experts' views differed about whether a gradual market-balance was likely to occur more or less according to traditional criteria, whether a worsening of employment prospects was only postponed and had be expected for the near future, or whether a new notion of a highly educated society was likely to develop in which graduate work is considered appropriate in a broader range of positions in the occupational hierarchy than in the past.[55] In the late 1980s, however, an increasing number of politicians and experts came to the conclusion that new demands emerged in the context of scientific and technological changes and that the demand for graduates from institutions of higher education in general was growing substantially. In the late 1980s the French and the British governments, for example, favored a further expansion of higher education.

Decision-Making Structures in Higher Education

Higher education in all Western European countries is by and large publicly funded. Almost all institutions are public institutions. British universities are officially independent institutions, but they are not to a lesser extent publicly funded than polytechnics. Private institutions of higher education in the Netherlands receive the same public support as public universities. The same is true of most church-related institutions of higher education in Western Europe.[56]

Except for the United Kingdom and Ireland, universities in Western Europe traditionally trained highly qualified persons for government (and possibly churches) as well as for publicly controlled services prior to industrialization. Close governmental supervision has remained a tradition in France and in some southern European countries predominantly influenced by the French model. According to the Humboldtian tradition that affected not only German universities but also those in many other European countries, government was supposed to be the enlightened sponsor of higher education. On the one hand, government was supposed to have many supervisory rights (at least regarding financial administration and many elements of training for civil service and other public-sector professions) but on the other was supposed to respect and safeguard the autonomy of the university regarding research and other academic issues.

Before 1980, very different modes of governmental influence on higher education in Western European countries were apparent. In the United Kingdom government handed over funds to a "buffer" organization, the University Grants Committee, which provided the universities with "block grants" accompanied by moderate advice regarding their utilization, but not by earmarked budget items. The universities hired staff themselves. In most public universities of other European countries professors are civil servants. Governments paid staff, destined funds for various purposes, and supervised the proper utilization of funds in a detailed manner. In some countries its influence on staff appointment was far-reaching. For example, German universities present government a ranked list of three candidates for a professor position: the government might appoint one of the three, might send the list back to the university for different names, or in exceptional cases might even appoint another scholar. In France academia has a stronger influence on the appointment of professors than in Germany through proposal by national commissions; but government earmarking of funds and supervision is far more detailed than in Germany. A comparative study came to the conclusion that governmental influence on higher education around 1980 was stronger in France than in Germany, but in the Netherlands less than in Germany.[57]

As Burton C. Clark points out, "authority has been distributed traditionally in most academic systems of the European continent in a combination of faculty guild and state bureaucracy."[58] The scholars aimed to secure the highest degree of autonomy possible regarding knowledge and research, regarding the content of what is taught within their area of expertise, and regarding the administrative supervision of teaching and research. In some countries curricula and the appointment of academic staff were areas in which universities strived for autonomy, whereas admission to higher education as well as routine administration was not considered in continental European countries to be an important issue of academic autonomy. From an Anglo-Saxon point of view, this might be a limited range of autonomy, whereas from the continental European point of view, this system secured more autonomy of scholarship than the market-driven, board-supervised higher education common to both public and private universities in the United States.

In the majority of Western European countries the central government is the supervisory agency. This is also true in the Federal Republic of Austria. In the Federal Republic of Germany the individual Länder governments supervise higher education, but the federal government provides a certain degree of coordination and financial support. The Swiss Kantone, as well as the governments of England, Wales, Scotland, and Northern Ireland are the European examples of decentralized government coordination. It should be added that local governments might play a role in supervision of universities. The British polytechnics were supervised until the late 1980s by Local Educational Authorities. In Sweden local higher education boards have substantial say regarding curricula. In various other countries a few institutions of higher education have been established by regional or local governments.

The involvement of more than one governmental level in decision making on higher education in the Federal Republic of Germany has completely different origins and functions from that in Sweden. In the Federal Republic of Germany the Länder supervise higher education and are in charge of the regular expenses. The Länder are responsible for education serving, in principle, cultural diversity. The federal government is in charge of international cultural relations as well as promotion of research as far as it is of national interest. The constitution (revised in 1969)

underscores "joint tasks" of the federal and the Länder governments in educational planning and research promotion in order to assure support beyond the potentials of the Länder and in order to maintain a certain degree of "homogeneity of living conditions." Some joint decisions are taken by the Länder (without involvement of the federal government), a common frame for state legislation is set by the Framework Act for Higher Education (since 1976), and federal legislation regarding the civil service standardizes salaries, tasks, and employment of staff in higher education. Federal-state cooperation in research promotion, funding of construction of higher education, student aid, etc., secures a certain degree of homogeneity within the system.[59] In Sweden the idea of centralization of higher education was introduced in order to reduce the power and influence of one major actor in higher education, the central government. The major features of the higher education system are expected to remain uniform, but institutions of higher education are expected to take into account diverse demands regarding research and curricula.[60]

Until the 1960s a university rector in most European countries was merely a symbolic "primus inter pares," elected for a period of one or two years, with little managerial power. The university senates were the major coordinating bodies, but in the majority of European countries they had little say regarding resource allocation, content of course programs, or research priorities. The regular administration was separately supervised in many countries by a head of administration appointed by the government. In the case of the Netherlands, no individual person heads the university; an administrative collegium ("college van bestuur") of three to five persons is appointed by the government, and one of these persons, the "rector magnificus," is elected for two years by the university council from among the professors. In France the individual faculties are the higher education establishments as such; the universities became formally the "établissements publics à caractère scientifique et culturel" only since 1968. In most Western European countries the underlying rationale for a relatively weak central administration of the university was that this system better serves the protection of academic autonomy than a strong one (which either could be more easily controlled by external powers or could aim to exercise control itself).

Legislation and practice substantially varies regarding the formal and actual power of the dean who is elected by the professor of the respective faculty. The power of the deans and faculty is relatively strong in France, where the coordinating function of the central level of the university is very weak. The power of the deans and the faculty is especially weak in the Federal Republic of Germany because major decisions on staff and other resource allocations are negotiated between the government and the individual professor prior to appointment (or upon a "call" from another university).

Reforms of higher education legislation in many Western European countries during the late 1960s and early 1970s primarily aimed to substitute new structures for the traditional internal decision-making structures within institutions of higher education. In most continental European countries the rule of the "academic oligarchy"[61] was replaced by participatory models. Professors—about 10 to 25 percent of the academic staff in most Western European countries—no longer had all or the clear majority of votes in the academic decision-making bodies; junior academic staff, students, and sometimes nonacademic staff and external representatives got a say as well.[62]

For example, during the 1970s, some university councils in Germany reserved 30 percent of the votes each for professors, junior academic staff, and students, with about 10 percent for other staff; in other cases up to 70 percent of the votes in such a body were reserved for professors. In central issues of teaching and research, the decision-making regulations had to guarantee at least 51 percent of votes for professors. Contrary to Scandinavian countries and France, participation models in Germany did not include external representatives. At Swedish universities during the 1970s external representatives, staff, students, and professors were represented in ratios of 6:3:3:4 at the central level. At Dutch universities one-third of the members of the university council are elected by the teaching staff (professors, senior lecturers, and lecturers, not including postgraduate research staff, assistants, etc.), by other staff, and by students, whereas at the faculty and department level the teaching staff (as defined above) holds one-half of the votes. Contrary to the German and French legislation, the Dutch legislation does not reserve any positions in the university council exclusively for professors.

In France all laws enacted and proposed since 1986 have aimed to change the representation of various groups. According to the "Loi Savary," enacted in 1984, three major councils have been established on the central level of the universities. Forty to 45 percent of the votes in the "conseil d'administration" are held by academic staff, in part elected by "professeurs" and in part by "autres enseignants," whereas 20 to 30 percent of the votes are held by "personnalités extérieures," 20 to 25 percent by students, and 10 to 15 percent by nonacademic staff. The "conseil scientifique"—in charge of research and junior academic staff—is predominantly (60–80 percent) comprised by academic staff, at least half of them professors, and in addition by graduate students (7.5–12.5 percent "étudiants du troisième cycle") and external representatives (10–30 percent). Finally, the "conseil d'études et de la vie universitaire," in charge of teaching, learning, and social affairs, has an equal number of members from academic staff and students (together 75–80 percent) as well as 10 to 15 percent of representatives each for external persons and nonacademic staff. The university president is elected by the members of all three councils; a majority of votes by the academic staff is required. In all central councils the votes held by professors are slightly more than 20 percent.

The participatory models were a major focus of controversial debates during the 1970s. Substantial conflicts arose in many cases—notably between professors and students, between the majority of professors and the majority of junior academic staff, or along different academic and sociopolitical views within the various groups. Some professors called for governmental intervention in order to reduce the influence of other groups. In various countries laws were revised in the late 1970s or during the 1980s in favor of a somewhat higher proportion of votes of professors without, however, returning to the decision-making structures prevailing until the mid-1960s. During the 1980s debates about internal decision making at institutions lost momentum, and the professors' influence at least informally increased to some extent. Major student protests during this decade in France focused on access to higher education or degrees and in Germany on the crammed universities due to shortages of academic staff, rooms, etc., rather than decision-making powers.

Available research in some countries shows that the majority of senior academic staff remained opposed to the participatory models the way they had been implemented. Also, complaint was widespread about additional work load for decision making. However, hardly any research has been conducted on decision-making structures in higher education that actually depicts the relative influence of government and university or the actual influence of students, junior staff, etc., on decisions.

Two French-German comparative research projects conducted in the late 1980s show that French universities are in a weaker position in negotiating with the government than German institutions, and that within French universities professors have a lesser say in major decisions than the German professors. The surveys also show that decision-making processes vary considerably between universities—for example, depending on institutional traditions, professors' motivation to act, or the degree of cooperation in faculties and departments.[63]

In addition to the introduction of participatory models, some efforts were made in the late 1960s and the 1970s to strengthen the managerial power of the central level of universities. For example, French rectors were elected for a period of five years and university senates for the first time got some say relative to the faculties. In the Federal Republic of Germany rectors' terms of office were increased from one to two years to four to eight years. In some German Länder the position of president was introduced; the president became the head both of academic administration and of personnel and financial administration. In various countries the authority of the central level increased substantially as compared to the past, but the number of administrative staff at this level remained much smaller than at United States universities, and also its power regarding academic issues and supervision of the faculties and departments (where deans and heads of department continued to be elected by the faculty) remained much more limited.

In the 1980s governments expected institutions of higher education to become more managerial entities. The most substantial efforts in this direction were made in the United Kingdom[64] and the Netherlands.[65] Both countries had experienced relatively high expenses in tertiary education by the early 1980s; cuts in funding for higher education were combined by government with efforts to change formal decision-making structures in higher education as well as the managerial rationales of the individual institutions of higher education. The rhetoric in both countries (as well as in other countries in which some more moderate changes in the same direction were implemented) was similar: institutions of higher education should establish a more efficient management, provide better evidence of the quality of "output," and become more market-oriented. To a certain extent, United States models of higher education management were expected to be adapted to the European context, although the academic profession was expected to retain a stronger position in decision making within institutions of higher education. The actual policies in the two countries were designed differently.

Experts agree that British universities faced a substantial loss of autonomy during the 1980s. Governmental policy was conceived as an "attack on higher education"[66]—among other reasons because of deep funding cuts and the government's new policies of steering higher education through tight priority-setting regarding costs. The University Grants Committee, most of whose members are professors, lost most of its "buffer" function as the government mandated differential financial cuts for certain institutions and certain fields of study. Administration of universities remained formally autonomous, but the government exercised more and more control over finances. Within a decade, public marketing of course programs, demonstration of quality and "efficiency" according to "performance indicators," etc.,[67] became a dominant element of British higher education. Most scholars criticized governmental policy and considerable controversy grew up regarding the opportunities and dangers in a higher education system experiencing substantial pressure to demonstrate its utility to government and "market" forces.

During the 1980s the Dutch government proclaimed its willingness to give up earmarked funding and bureaucratic supervision. Direct regulation by law would be replaced by a system of "steering from distance" ("sturing op afstand"). Resource allocation would be based partly on lump-sum funding (for example, according to the number of graduates) or on the results of evaluation. Government, under those conditions, would set a limited number of policy rationales and would try to see that funds are allocated in a way that serves as an incentive for quality of teaching and research, efficiency of resource utilization, economic and social needs, and the emergence of a certain degree of diversity in higher education. Many steps were taken in this direction, such as the establishment of various evaluation procedures, partial lump-sum funding, institutional discretion in deciding about the number of staff positions, introduction of new course programs, etc. The HBO institutions experienced a rapid change from being supervised like a secondary school to having more managerial leeway than most continental European universities. Experts' views vary, however, in assessing the effect of these policy changes on the academic autonomy of the Dutch universities.

In other countries, such as France and the Federal Republic of Germany, government tried to stimulate initiatives at the individual institutions of higher education by reducing its efforts of providing homogeneous curricula, for example, or by distributing a larger proportion of funds through competition-stimulating mechanisms. Research funding at German universities through basic institutional funding was gradually reduced but funds for research promotion schemes were slightly increased.[68]

Traditionally, nonuniversity institutions of higher education in Western Europe differed from universities in terms of a lesser autonomy regarding governmental supervision as well as in terms of a higher degree of internal centralization and control. In most Western European countries legislation during the 1970s or 1980s abolished or minimized those differences.

While the changes in the United Kingdom and the Netherlands seem to express most strongly the "Zeitgeist" of the 1980s, the substantial changes in higher education legislation in Spain are based on a different historical legacy and reflect different aims.[69] Higher education reform debates after the termination of the Franco regime focused on the issues of autonomy and decentralization. The law enacted in 1983 (Ley de Reforma Universitaria) introduced changes in the decision-making structure in a similar way as higher education legislation did in other countries in the 1960s and 1970s. The new law tried to reduce governmental control in various respects—for example, in the provision that all persons in executive positions at universities except for the rector should be elected from within the university. Emphasis on decentralization was placed in making the regions responsible for supervising most of the universities. A certain balance between university and external forces is guaranteed by two mixed bodies. First, the "Consejo de Universidades," comprised of the university rectors, representatives of the regions, and representatives of the central government and parliament, is supposed to be the highest higher education planning agency. It replaces a separate body composed only of university rectors that had no power for negotiating any policies with government. Second, the "Consejo Social," with 60 percent external representatives (from the central government, the regional government, cultural life, business, and unions) and 40 percent university representatives, is in charge of budget and financial planning. It replaces the "patronato," in which the university had only one to three out of twenty votes. Finally, the reform law provides some participation in internal deci-

sion making. In the university senate ("claustro universitario"), 60 percent of the seats are reserved for professors, and the other 40 percent of the votes are spread among other academic staff, nonacademic staff, and students.

Internationalization of Higher Education

Higher education in Europe tends to praise itself as being universalist as far as knowledge is concerned and international as far as the mobility of scholars and students are concerned. In various respects, however, national boundaries of higher education became the focus of debate during the 1960s and 1970s. National pools of research resources seemed to be too small in those areas of research that increasingly became dependent on large and costly resources. International communication in research lagged behind in those areas in the social sciences and humanities in which in-depth foreign language knowledge was indispensable. The existing differences between the national systems of higher education in terms of structures and course programs discouraged mobility of students. Higher education expansion seemed to increase the proportion of students showing little interest in international mobility. Finally, the national idiosyncrasies of what is taught in higher education have to be challenged and reconsidered if international mobility of graduates is to become a widespread phenomenon.

As far as teaching and learning in higher education in Western Europe is concerned, the most striking change in this respect during the last two decades has been the growing involvement of national and supranational agencies in stimulating, setting frameworks, and steering student mobility and transnational recognition of studies and degrees.[70] A select overview might serve to explain the major thrusts of those activities.

First, barriers of international mobility of students and graduates were considered to be too high as long as students wishing to enroll at an institution of higher education abroad could not be certain as to how their prior qualification related to higher education and employment in other countries. Except for the United Kingdom and Ireland, where admission to higher education in general is conceived to be the prerogative of the individual university, efforts were widespread in European countries to establish equivalences of studies and degrees that will ensure how qualifications acquired in one European country will be treated in another European country. In some fields of study efforts were made to standardize or "harmonize" curricula so that graduates could be easily accepted as equally qualified. Such activities have succeeded in medicine, but not in such fields as architecture and engineering.

Most activities regarding recognition of studies and degrees between European countries were based on the assumption that differences in the modes of learning, content of courses, institutional patterns, structures of course programs, and duration of study were part of the cultural diversity between European countries that ought to be preserved as a major asset. Several neighbor states in Europe concluded treaties regarding the recognition of entry qualifications to higher education, the institutions of higher education recognized, and the equivalence of first degrees. The Council of Europe was very involved in stimulating European conventions for mutual recognition of studies. In the late 1970s UNESCO aimed to take a lead in this respect in promoting a Convention on Higher Education Recognition in the European region. Finally, the Commission of European Communities intensified its activities in this area, aiming particularly at occupational mobility within the member states of the EC.[71] After complicated negotiations agreement was eventually reached that degrees awarded after at least three years of study in an officially recognized institution of higher education in any EC member state were to be accepted as a regular degree and a basic qualification for professional practice; however, individual countries could require additional studies and training for full professional qualifications according to the needs and traditions of the respective professions.

Substantial efforts were made to promote organized and integrated study abroad in Western Europe. Few faculties from different European countries cooperate in study abroad programs by coordinating courses, establishing preparatory provisions, assuring academic and administrative support for a study abroad period, and setting regulations for recognition. During the 1970s the EC Commission established the "Joint Study Programs" for institutions that created programs that emphasize curricular integration and mutual recognition. Similar national programs were created in Sweden and in the Federal Republic of Germany. The ERASMUS program was established in the European Community in 1987; it supports cooperating institutions, short visits by expert scholars, seminars, textbook development, etc., and supplies add-on grants for participating students (altogether about 30,000 in 1990) designed to cover the additional costs for studying abroad. A similar program was established between the Scandinavian countries. The COMETT program supports work placement of students in industry (again in another EC country). Many national grant schemes in EC countries now exist to cover costs of study periods abroad.

These examples indicate that efforts toward establishing equivalences have grown substantially in the recent past. Partial curricular coordination, improvement of information flow (through national information and recognition centers, handbooks, and possibly computerized information systems) and financial and administrative support for mobility have increased. During their course of studies about 4 percent of students in EC countries spend at least a few months studying in another EC country; proposals have been made to increase this proportion to 10 percent or even more in the not-too-distant future.

Altogether, cooperation of higher education institutions in European countries both in teaching and research has grown substantially in a relatively brief time. International cooperation has become a central part of activities at institutions of higher education. Still, views vary substantially regarding the degree of European integration expected to emerge and their implications for what are still individual, idiosyncratic national systems of higher education in Western Europe.

Notes

1. On quantitative and structural developments see T. Becher, "Higher Education System," in *The International Encyclopedia of Education*, ed. T. Husén and T. N. Postlewaite (Oxford: Pergamon, 1985); 2241–48; L. Cerych, S. Colton, and J. P. Jallade, *Student Flows and Expenditure in Higher Education* (Paris: Institute of Education, European Cultural Foundation, 1981); G. Neave, "Foundation or Roof? The Quantitative, Structural, and Institutional Dimensions in the Study of Higher Education," *European Journal of Education* 24, no. 3 (1989): 211–22; N. P. Eurich, *Systems of Higher Education in Twelve Countries: A Comparative View* (New York: International Council for Educational Development, 1981); see also the series "Systems of Higher Education" published by the International Council for Educational Development in 1987–88 and the respective literature named in P. G. Altbach and D. H. Kelly, *Higher Education in International Perspective: A Survey and Bibliography* (London: Mansell, 1985).

2. On higher education policies, see U. Teichler, *Changing Patterns of the Higher Education System* (London: Kingsley, 1988).

3. On the relationships between the issues of educational expansion and economic growth and issues of educational and social opportunities, see OECD, ed., *Education, Inequality, and Life Chances* 2 vols. (Paris: OECD, 1975); T. Husén, *Higher Education and Social Stratification* (Paris: UNESCO, International Institute for Educational Planning, 1987); U. Teichler, D. Hartung, and R. Nuthmann, *Higher Education and the Needs of Society* (Windsor, England: NFER, 1980).

4. Structural models and developments of higher education structures are discussed in H. Hermanns, U. Teichler, and H. Wasser, eds., *The Compleat University: Break from Tradition in Germany, Sweden, and the U.S.A.* (Cambridge, Mass.: Schenkman, 1983); see also R. A. de Moor, ed., *Changing Tertiary Education in Modern European Society* (Strasbourg, France: Council of Europe, 1978); G. Vedel, ed., *Reform and Development of Tertiary (Post-Secondary) Education in Southern Europe* (Strasbourg, France: Council of Europe, 1981).

5. See OECD, *Policies for Higher Education in the 1980s* (Paris: OECD, 1983); W. Wolter et al., *Planning in Higher Education* (Bucharest, Romania: CEPES, 1986); G. Williams, "Graduate Employment and Vocationalisation in Higher Education," *European Journal of Education* 20, nos. 2–3 (1985): 181–92.

6. L. Cerych and P. Sabatier, *Great Expectations and Mixed Performance: The Implementation of Higher Education Reforms in Europe* (Stoke-on-Trent, England: Trentham, 1986); see also Wolter et al., *Planning in Higher Education*.

7. Cf. M. Trow, "Elite and Mass Higher Education: American Models and European Realities," in *Research into Higher Education: Processes and Structures* (Stockholm: National Board of Universities and Colleges, 1978): 183–219; B. R. Clark, *The Higher Education System* (Berkeley and Los Angeles, University of California Press, 1983).

8. Cf. the overview in U. Teichler, *Convergence or Growing Variety: The Changing Organisation of Studies* (Strasbourg, France: Council of Europe, 1988); cf. also OECD, *Universities Under Scrutiny* (Paris: OECD, 1987); "Ten Years On: Changing Issues in Education, 1975–85," *European Journal of Education* 20, nos. 2–3 (1985); "Research on Higher Education in Europe," *European Journal of Education* 24, no. 3 (1989).

9. UNESCO, *Statistical Yearbook 1987* (Paris: UNESCO, 1987), 2–5.

10. V. Nicolae, R. H. M. Smulders, and M. Korka, eds., *Statistics on Higher Education* (Bucharest, Romania: CEPES, 1989).

11. Ibid., 59–66.

12. Cf. OECD, *Post-Graduate Education in the 1980s* (Paris: OECD, 1987); J.P. Massué and G. Schink, "Doctoral Training in Europe," *Higher Education in Europe* 12, no. 4 (1987): 56–67; "Post-Graduate Education," *European Journal of Education* 21, no. 3 (1986); see also Nicolae et al., *Statistics on Higher Education*.

13. Nicolae et al., *Statistics on Higher Education*, 58.
14. Ibid., 99.
15. OECD, *Education in OECD Statistics 1986-87* (Paris: OECD, 1989), 38.
16. Nicolae et al., *Statistics on Higher Education*, 67–81.
17. See OECD, *Education, Inequality, and Life Chances*, cf. also U. Teichler, "European Practice in Ensuring Equality of Opportunity to Higher Education," *Journal of Higher Education Studies* 3, no. 2 (1988): 2–11.
18. OECD, *Girls and Women in Education* (Paris: OECD, 1986); A. Cels-Offermanns, *Education of Opportunity for Girls and Women* (Luxembourg: Council of Europe, 1985).
19. See W. Isserstedt et al., *Das soziale Bild der Studentenschaft in der Bundesrepublik Deutschland* (Bad Honnef, West Germany: Bock, 1987).
20. P. Glancy, *Who Goes to College?* (Dublin: Higher Education Authority, 1988).
21. U. Teichler, *Convergence or Growing Variety.*
22. British Council, National Equivalence Information Centre, *International Guide to Qualifications in Education* (London: Mansell, 1984); H. Jablonska-Skinder and U. Teichler, *Higher Education Diplomas in Europe* (Bucharest, Romania: CEPES, 1989); Commission of the European Communities, *Student Handbook* (London: Kogan Page, 1988); U. Teichler, *Convergence or Growing Variety*; U. Teichler, *Europäische Hochschulsysteme: Die Beharrlichkeit vielfaltiger Modelle* (Frankfurt am Main, West Germany: Campus 1990).
23. On the nonuniversity sector, see OECD, *Short-Cycle Higher Education* (Paris: OECD, 1973); D. Furth, "New Hierarchies in Higher Education," *European Journal of Education* 17, no. 2 (1982):145–51; L. C. J. Goedegebuure and V. L. Meek, eds., *Changes in Higher Education: The Non-University Sector* (Culemborg, Netherlands: Lemma, 1988); U. Teichler, *Convergence or Growing Variety*; op. cit.; cf. also the mimeographed country reports of the OECD study on "Alternatives to Universities."
24. F. Bowles, *Access to Higher Education*, vol. 1 (Paris: UNESCO and International Association of Universities, 1963).
25. Developments of admission to higher education are summarized in W. Mitter, ed., *Hochschulzulassung in Europa* (Weinheim, West Germany: Beltz, 1979); UNESCO, *Access to Higher Education in Europe* (Paris: UNESCO, 1968); UNESCO/CEPES, *Access to Higher Education* (Bucharest, Romania: CEPES, 1981); OECD, *Policies for Higher Education*; P. Kellermann, ed., *Studienaufnahme und Studienzulassung* (Klagenfurt, Austria: Kärtner Druck- und Verlagsgesellschaft, 1984); B. R. Clark, ed., *The School and the University: An International Perspective* (Berkeley and Los Angeles: University of California Press, 1985); B. B. Burn, "Higher Education: Access," in *The International Encyclopedia of Education*, 2179–85.
26. L. Kim, *Widened Admission to Higher Education in Sweden: The 25/5 Scheme* (Stockholm: Almquist & Wiksell International, 1982).
27. O. Fulton, ed., *Access to Higher Education* (Guilford, England: SRHE, 1981).
28. On British higher education, see T. Becher, ed., *British Higher Education* (London: Allen & Unwin, 1987).
29. U. Teichler, "Higher Education: Curriculum," in *The International Encyclopedia of Education* 2196–2208; cf. also *Proceedings of the Third Annual Conference "Quality Assurance in First Degree Courses"* (London: Higher Education International, 1986).
30. On academic staff and attitudes toward teaching and learning, see B. R. Clark, ed., *The Academic Profession* (Berkeley and Los Angeles: University of California Press, 1987); L. Huber, "Teaching and Learning—Students and University Teachers," *European Journal of Education* 24, no. 3 (1989): 271–88; T. Becher, *Academic Tribes and Territories: Intellectual Enquiry and the Cultures of Disciplines* (Milton Keynes, England: SRHE & Open University Press, 1989).
31. Cf. the overview in Teichler, *Convergence or Growing Variety.*
32. U. Teichler and S. Opper, *Erträge des Auslandsstudiums fur Studierende und Absolventen* (Bad Honnef, West Germany: Bock, 1988).
33. See the overview in Teichler, *Convergence or Growing Variety.*
34. Overviews are published in U. Teichler and W. Steube, *Studiendauer und Lebensalter* (Bonn: Bundesminister für Bildung und Wissenschaft, 1989); M. Fries, "Differenzierende Analysen sind das Gebot der Stunde!" *Beiträge zur Hochschulforschung* 3 (Munich: Bayerisches Staatsinstitut für Hochschulforschung und Hochschulplanung, 1989): 112–81.
35. Cf. Ministerie van Onderwijs en Wetenschappen: *Richness of the Uncompleted* (The Hague, the Netherlands: State Printing Office, 1989), 136.
36. See the overview in Jablonska-Skinder and Teichler, *Higher Education Diplomas.*
37. C. J. Boys et al., *Higher Education and the Preparation for Work* (London: Kingsley, 1988).
38. See the recent OECD study on "Alternatives to Universities."
39. See K. Hüfner, "Higher Education in the Federal Republic of Germany: A Planned or Market System? Or Third Way?" In *Higher Education and Employment in the USSR and in the Federal*

Republic of Germany, ed. R. Avakov et al. (Paris: UNESCO, International Institute of Educational Planning, 1984), 185–96.

40. H. Riese, *Die Entwicklung des Bedarfs an Hochschulabsolventen in der Bundesrepublik Deutschland* (Wiesbaden, West Germany: Steiner, 1967).

41. G. Neave, "European University System," *CRE-Information* 75 (3rd quarter 1986): 3–142 (part I); *CRE-Information* 77 (1st quarter 1987): 5–115.

42. See the overview in U. Teichler, "Higher Education and Work in Europe," *Higher Education: Handbook of Theory and Research.* vol 4, ed. John H. Smart (New York: Agathon, 1988), 109–82; see also OECD, *Policies for Higher Education;* O. Fulton, A. Gordon, and G. Williams, *Higher Education and Manpower Planning* (Geneva: International Labour Office, 1982).

43. See J. Tarsh, "Trends in the Graduate Labour Market," *Employment Gazette* 93, no. 7 (1985): 269-73; see also J. Taylor, "The Employability of Graduates: Differences between Universities," *Studies in Higher Education* 11, no. 1 (1986): 17–27; A. Harrison and J. Gretton, eds., *Education and Training UK 1987: An Economic, Social, and Policy Audit* (London: Policy Journals, 1987); J. Brennan and P. McGeevor, *Graduates at Work* (London: Kingsley, 1988).

44. B. Morgenthaler, "Die Beschäftigungssituation der Absolventen der Schweizer Hochschulen: Ergebnisse der Befragung des Examensjahrgangs 1982," *Beiträge zur Arbeitsmarkt- und Berufsforschung* 90, no. 3 (1985): 229–46; B. Morgenthaler, "Die Beschäftigungssituation der Neuabsolventen der Schweizer Hochschulen 1985," *Wissenschaftspolitik* 34 (1986, Beiheft).

45. M. Tessaring, "Beschäftigungssituation undperspektiven für Hochschulabsolventen," *Aus Politik und Zeitgeschichte: Beilage zur Wochenzeitung Das Parlament* B 50/89 (1989): 14–24.

46. J.-P. Jarousse and C. de Francesco, *L'Enseignement supérieur contre le chômage* (Paris: European Institute of Education and Social Policy, 1984).

47. Statistiska centralbyran, *Högskolan 1984/85: Elevuppföljningar 1985* (Örebro, Sweden: Statistiska centralbyran, 1985).

48. U. Teichler, *The First Years of Study and the Role Played by Fachhochschulen in the Federal Republic of Germany* (Kassel, West Germany: Wissenschaftliches Zentrum für Berufs- und Hochschulforschung der Gesamthochschule Kassel, 1989, mimeo.).

49. J. Vincens, *Enseignement supérieur et marché du travail* (1986, manuscript).

50. Jarousse and de Francesco, *L'Enseignement supérieir.*

51. Morgenthaler, "Die Beschäftigung der Neuab-

solventen."

52. B. Lutz, "Education and Employment: Contrasting Evidence from France and the Federal Republic of Germany," *European Journal of Education* 16, no. 1 (1981): 73–86.

53. U. Teichler, M. Buttgereit and R. Holtkamp, *Hochschulzertifikate in der betrieblichen Einstellungspraxis* (Bad Honnef, West Germany: Bock, 1984); J. Roizen and M. Jepson, *Degrees for Jobs* (Guilford, England: SRHE and NFER/Nelson, 1985).

54. See U. Teichler, "Beziehungen von Bildungs- und Beschäftigungssystem-Erfordern die Entwicklungen in den achtziger Jahren neue Erklärungsansätze?" *Soziale Welt* (1987, Beiheft 5): 27–57.

55. See, for example, U. Beck, *Risikogesellschaft* (Frankfurt am Main, West Germany: Suhrkamp, 1986); P. Kellermann, *Arbeit und Bildung.* vol. 3 (Klagenfurt, Austria: Kartner Druck- und Verlagsgesellschaft, 1986); Teichler, "Higher Education and Work," J. Vincens, "Formation universitaire et emploi vus dans une perspective internationale," *Politique de la science* 32 (1985): 45–61; Williams, "Graduate Employment."

56. Cf. R. L. Geiger, *Private Sectors in Higher Education* (Ann Arbor: University of Michigan Press, 1986).

57. Frans A. van Vught, ed., *Governmental Strategies and Innovation in Higher Education* (London: Kingsley, 1989); cf. also G. Neave, "On the Road to Silicon Valley: The Changing Relationship between Higher Education and Government in Western Europe," *European Journal of Education* 19, no. 2 (1984): 116–36.

58. Clark, *The Higher Education System,* 125; see also J. H. Van de Graaf et al., *Academic Power: Patterns of Authority in Seven National Systems* (New York: Praeger, 1978); R. Premfors, ed., *Higher Education Organization* (Stockholm: Almquist & Wiksell International, 1984).

59. See U. Teichler, *Higher Education in the Federal Republic of Germany* (New York: Center for European Studies, Graduate School and University Center of the City University of New York: 1986), chapter 3.

60. B. Askling, "Structural Uniformity and Functional Diversification: Swedish Higher Education Ten Years after the Higher Education Reform," *Higher Education Quarterly* 43, no. 4 (1989): 289–305.

61. See Clark, *The Higher Education System,* chapter 5.

62. Little research is available on participatory models of higher education. For a collection of essays by scholars complaining about the introduction of those models, see H. Daalder

and E. Shields, eds., *Universities, Politicians, and Bureaucrats: Europe and the United States* (Cambridge: Cambridge University Press, 1982).

63. Erhard Friedberg and Christine Musselin, *En quête d'universités: Étude comparée des universitées en France et en RFA* (Paris: L'Harmattan, 1989).

64. See the overviews in Becher, *British Higher Education*; compare earlier accounts in T. Becher and M. Kogan, *Process and Structure in Higher Education* (London: Heinemann, 1980); C. Beckmeier and A. Neusel, "Decision-Making Processes in French and German Universities," *Higher Education Management* 2, no.1 (1990).

65. See P. A. M. Maassen and F. A. van Vught, eds., *Dutch Higher Education in Transition* (Culemborg, Netherlands: Lemma, 1989); U. Teichler, "Government and Curriculum Innovation in the Netherlands," in *Governmental Strategies and Innovation in Higher Education*, ed. Frans A. van Vught (London: Kingsley, 1989), 168–209.

66. M. Kogan and D. Kogan, *The Attack on Higher Education* (London: Kogan Page, 1983); D. Phillips, "A View from Oxford of Tradition and Reform of the British University," in *Tradition and Reform of the University under an International Perspective* (Frankfurt am Main, West Germany: Lang, 1987), 157–67.

67. Recent debates on the use of indicators and evaluation in Western Europe are summarized in M. Cave et al., *The Use of Performance Indicators in Higher Education* (London: Kingsley, 1988); M. Kogan, ed., *Evaluating Higher Education* (London: Kingsley, 1988); cf. also K. Hüfner, T. Hummel, and E. Rau, *Efficiency in Higher Education: An Annotated Bibliography* (Frankfurt am Main, West Germany: Lang, 1987).

68. See O. McDaniel, P. Gauye, and J. Guin, "Government and Curriculum Innovation in the Federal Republic of Germany," in *Governmental Strategies and Innovation in Higher Education*, 125–42; W.-D. Webler, "Externe Einflüsse auf die Hochschule," in *Das Hochschulwesen in der Bundesrepublik Deutschland*, ed. U. Teichler (Weinheim, West Germany: Deutscher Studien Verlag, 1990).

69. J. Villanueva, "Spain: Restructuring, Reform, and Research Policy," *European Journal of Education* 19, no. 2 (1984): 193–200; International Council for Educational Development, *La Reforma Universitaria Espanola: Evaluacion e informe* (Madrid: Ministerio de Educatión y Ciencia, 1988).

70. See the overviews in A. Smith, "Higher Education Co-Operation 1975–1985: Creating a Basis for Growth in an Adverse Economic Climate," *European Journal of Education* 20, nos. 2–3 (1985): 267–92; "Practice, Politics, and Function of Foreign Study in Higher Education," *European Journal of Education* 22, no. 1 (1987); "International Recognition of Studies and Degrees: Challenges and Perspectives," *Higher Education in Europe* 13, no. 3 (1988); S. Opper and U. Teichler, "European Community (EC): Educational Programmes," in *The International Encyclopedia of Education: Supplementary Volume One*, ed. T. Husén and T. N. Postlewaite (Oxford: Pergamon, 1989), 342–47.

71. Network of the National Academic Recognition Information Centres, *Adacemic Recognition of Higher Education Entrance, Intermediate, and Final Qualifications in the European Community* (Brussels: Commission of the European Communities, Task-Force Human Resources, Education, Training, and Youth).

Czechoslovakia

Jirí Kotásek

◆

The Czechoslovak Socialist Republic (CSSR) is a federal state of two republics, the Czech and the Slovak. A central European country, Czechoslovakia borders Germany, Poland, the Soviet Union, Hungary, and Austria. The basic geographical facts are given in Table 1.

The state is headed by a president. The supreme legislative power belongs to the Federal Assembly which consists of the House of the People and the House of Nations. Each republic also has its own legislative body—the Czech and the Slovak National Councils—and national government.

Historical Background

Czechoslovak higher education has a long history going back to 1348 when the first central European university was founded in Prague by Charles IV, king of Bohemia and Holy Roman Emperor. An-other institution of higher education, the Academia Istropolitana, was founded in Bratislava in 1467, and the University of Olomouc was founded in 1573. Although the Academia in Bratislava was abolished and the University of Olomouc in Moravia discontinued its activity, Charles University flourished and became an irreplaceable component of the European cultural heritage. In 1707 the Engineering Institute was founded in Prague; it became the polytechnic at the beginning of the nineteenth century. The year 1882 marks an important watershed in the history of Charles University for it was then divided into the Czech and the German universities. Thereafter, Czech higher education truly began to develop. However, only the establishment of an independent Czech state in 1918 enabled the systematic creation of national higher education. Besides the Czech and the German universities in Prague, another university in Brno and the first Slovak university in Bratislava were established. Technical colleges founded

---

Table 1

Geographic Facts About Czechoslovakia

Rep.	Czech Rep.	Slovak Rep.	Czechoslovakia
Territory	78,864 sq. km	49,036 sq. km	127,900 sq. km
Population	10,350,816	5,236,252	14,587,068
Population density	131	107	122
Capital	Praha	Bratislava	Praha

Nationalities: 63% Czechs, 31.6% Slovaks, 3.8% Hungarians, .5% Polish, .4% German, .3% Ukrainians, .1% Russians, .3% other

Table 2

Selected Statistical Data Concerning the Development of Higher Education in Czechoslovakia (1936–1987)

| | | | **Full-Time Students** | | |
Year	Higher Education Institutions	Faculties	Total Student Enrollment	Czechoslovak Citizenship	Female
1936	13	52	27,068	23,435	4,063
1946	17	54	60,285	60,285	12,232
1950	28	56	45,241	37,452	8,376
1955	40	106	72,426	48,534	12,300
1960	50	108	94,040	65,451	24,307
1965	38	102	144,990	91,720	37,355
1970	37	105	131,099	102,015	40,974
1975	36	103	154,645	119,264	48,927
1980	36	110	196,642	147,862	62,627
1985	36	110	168,699	136,944	60,224
1987	36	112	169,784	135,136	58,926

Source: Ministry of Education statistics.

in the nineteenth century continued to develop. Specialized colleges of agriculture, veterinary medicine, and commerce were also founded. All colleges assumed the features of higher institutions and became equal to the universities by statute.

In the period between the two world wars a fundamental network of Czech elite higher education institutions was developed. In the year 1937, thirteen higher education institutions with fifty-two faculties and more than 27,000 students and about 3,500 teachers were active. Although the development of Czech higher education in the period between the world wars was successful, it did not permit equal access to higher education for all students irrespective of social background and sex.

During the years of Fascist occupation (1939–45) Czech higher education institutions were closed; Slovak institutions of higher education were the only ones to remain open.

Development After World War II

After World War II, a new period in the development of the higher education system started, reflecting changing international and national conditions. In the beginning universities and colleges primarily enrolled students who had been prevented from completing their higher education during the Fascist occupation. In the first stage (1945–50) higher education faced a new challenge—to satisfy double the number of students than before the war. The Czech institutions renewed their educational and research activities, while the German universities were abolished. The network of Czech and Slovak institutions of higher education was enlarged. The University of Olomouc was reborn. New colleges of fine arts and new faculties of medicine and education were established, either at existing universities or elsewhere in regional centers.

Table 2 (continued)

Selected Statistical Data Concerning the Development of Higher Education in Czechoslovakia (1936–1987)

Foreign	Part-time Students	Students of other courses	Ratio of students per 10,000 inhabitants	Ratio of of students age 20–24	Faculty Members
1,530	—	—	16	2:6	3,521
—	—	—	50	5:8	—
1,432	6,357	—	35	4:3	—
975	21,662	—	54	7:9	7,143
1,849	26,740	8,104	67	10:6	10,504
3,303	49,967	8,092	100	13:5	15,388
3,619	25,465	5,061	89	10:0	16,402
3,363	32,018	5,679	102	11:8	17,009
3,642	45,138	7,273	126	17:1	18,320
4,160	27,595	10,149	109	15:0	19,131
4,792	29,856	9,377	109	15:0	20,391

In 1948 the Czechoslovak Communist party won power and assumed a leading role in the country, exerting a profound influence on further development. In higher education the challenge was to base research and educational activities on Marxist-Leninist ideology and to give all people, especially those who had been prevented before, access to higher education. The new policy in higher education, formed in compliance with the principles of a socialist society, was given a legislative form in the Higher Education Act of 1950 and in its 1956 amendment. These laws stated that "the Minister of Education administers higher education institutions from ideological, scientific, and educational viewpoints."

As early as the beginning of the 1950s new specialized colleges of technology, economics, and agriculture were established. In eastern Slovakia a new university and polytechnic started to operate. Parallel to the development of new institutions a major increase in student enrollment took place. Within a period of fifteen years after 1950 the number of students increased more than three times. This was due in part to the introduction of new forms of study: part-time study, evening courses, distance learning, and external courses.

The National Committee for Higher Education was established to be an advisory and coordinating center attached to the Ministry of Education. The Ministry itself linked leading representatives of higher education institutions. During this period the newly established Czechoslovak Academy of Sciences organized research institutes and academic collegiums to support coordination of research on a nationwide scale. Accordingly, this resulted in the fact that research was shared among universities and the Academy. A system of "aspirantura" was developed which was a program of individually controlled study for graduates who engaged in academic teaching and research.

Central management of the economy also included planning the rates of personnel involved in higher education. The government began to set the rates of enrollment in different fields of study and in individual institutions. A system of selective entrance examinations was also developed. A rapid upsurge in higher education took place in the 1960s. Further development in compliance with a new reality caused by ever more rapid advancement in science, technology, and economy throughout the world impacted on Czechoslovak higher education.

In 1966, a newly conceived Higher Education Act was launched putting high demands on the quality of teaching and learning and defining new principles of administration and management. For the first time there appeared a need to deepen the expertise of higher education personnel through a system of continuing education. More attention was paid to the research activity of university teachers because research was considered the necessary prerequisite to educational work of high quality. The question of taking care of gifted students and increasing their participation in research work with their teachers become a focus of debate. Higher education institutions became more independent in screening their staff and in deciding about curricula and syllabi for particular fields of study. But an attempt at the enhancement of admission procedures based on screening as well as reducing expenditures on higher education resulted in falling rates of students.

The Soviet intervention in Czechoslovakia in 1968 resulted in a period of adjustment of higher education to changed political conditions and a strengthening of the influence of Marxism-Leninism. The role of government and central political bodies in decision making in higher education, particularly in admission requirements and the assessment of college teachers, was ever more soundly expressed.

In the mid-1970s the regressive tendency in student numbers was stopped and enrollment increased. In this period global principles of educational policy were pronounced in the 1976 Scheme of the Development of the Czechoslovak Educational System. The main focus became the quality of ideological and political education of students and the development of a centrally based curricula and syllabi. There was a sound attempt to forge closer links between higher education and social practice and to improve teaching methods and aids.

All the above-mentioned trends of adjustment were reflected in the Higher Education Act of 1980. The participation of higher education institutions in conceiving the act was, however, very small. The act limited the jurisdiction of academic staff and their representatives. The initiative in the development of higher education was assumed by the Ministries of Education. Accordingly, the National Committee for Higher Education, the advisory body to the Ministry of Education, was abolished. Under these conditions the management of higher education by the ministries to a certain extent suffered from paperwork, and the activity of academic staff at departments and faculties was greatly interfered with. As a result of reducing courses of study from five to four years in many fields and the fear of high rates of unemployment of graduated specialists, student entrance rates fell again. Another critical symptom was stagnancy in material supply and technical equipment. The system of in-service education for specialists was never sufficiently developed. Since 1985 a way out of this stagnancy has been sought, and the tertiary system has faced new demands to accelerate social and economic development.

Figure 1

Development of Student and Faculty Numbers in Czechoslovakia Higher Education Institutions 1936–1988

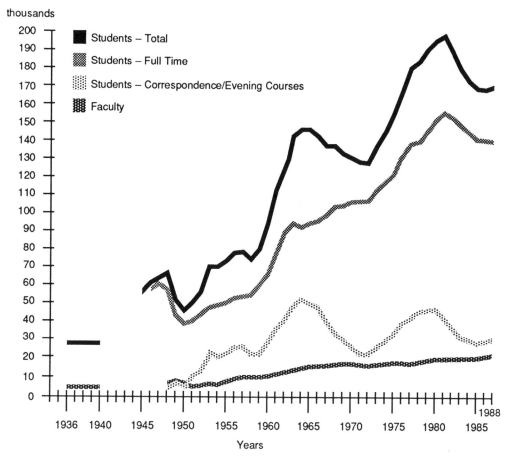

Source: Ministry of Education statistics.

Higher Education Institutions

The status, organization, and operation of higher education institutions are laid down in the Law of Federal Assembly of Czechoslovakia. According to the Higher Education Act now in force (No. 39, of April 10, 1980), tertiary institutions are defined as "educational, research and cultural institutions at the highest level." They "link educational and research (or artistic) activities together, emanating from the Marxist-Leninist ideology" and "promote the solution of current and progressive tasks of society." As for their educational role, which is considered primary and decisive, "higher education institutions according to the goals of Communist education and the recent outcomes in science and technology prepare politically and morally matured graduates, highly educated for work in the national economy, culture, science, administration, and other spheres of life of the developed socialist society."

Legally, all higher education institutions in Czechoslovakia have equal status. They can be established, consolidated, divided, or abolished by the Law of Federal Assembly. The majority of them are divided into faculties.

The network of thirty-six higher education institutions includes 112 faculties. Administered by the Czech and the Slovak ministries of education, youth, and sports, they are divided, according to their professional and academic orientation, into the following categories:

○ Universities (the five universities educate specialists in the fields of natural science, social science, humanities, medicine, pharmacy, law, education, journalism, physical education, and sports); seven independent pedagogical faculties that train the future teachers of primary and secondary schools;
○ Two veterinary colleges;
○ Technical colleges (four polytechnics, six specialized technical colleges);
○ Two economic colleges;
○ Four agricultural colleges including forestry;
○ Six arts colleges (for music, theater, film and TV, and fine arts).

Some other colleges are supervised either by the Czechoslovak Communist Party Central Committee (the College of Political Sciences), or by the Ministry of Defense (seven Army Colleges), or by the Ministry of the Interior (the College of the National Security Corps). Six independent faculties of theology are under the jurisdiction of the Ministry of Culture.

The higher educational system is unified and unitary. Following historical tradition, there are no substantial differences among universities and colleges in educational level, share of research and teaching, and quality and reputation.

Higher education institutions and their faculties have been established in twenty-three towns of Czechoslovakia. Four of them are large centers that include universities, polytechnics, and other colleges, and enroll high numbers of students (Prague, 52,426; Bratislava 27,347; Brno 25,276; and Kosice-Presov 12,063).

Table 3

Profile of Higher Studies in Czechoslovakia (1987–1988)

Sector of Higher Studies	Number of Fields of Study	Number of Students	Ratio in %
Natural Sciences	24	5,538	3:3
Technical Sciences	94	72,575	42:7
Agriculture, Forestry, Veterinary Medicine	14	15,736	9:3
Medicine, Pharmacy	8	13,340	7:9
Economics	16	20,557	12:1
Law	1	4,650	2:7
Humanities and Social Sciences	27	5,521	3:3
Teaching	7	20,789	17:5
Arts	8	2,078	1:2

Source: Ministry of Education statistics.

The Structure and Content of Higher Studies

Higher education studies are divided into 199 fields of study that have been laid down by the Czechoslovak government. Its regulations and duration of higher studies concerning the profile have now been valid since 1980. Higher education studies are from the outset specialized. The profile of higher education studies is exemplified in Table 3.

High specialization is obvious, especially in the technical sciences and economics sectors. These sectors also attract the most students.

The field of study is the basic structural and organizational unit of higher education. The aims, content, and timing of the teaching process within the particular field of study are laid down in "pedagogical guidelines" that are standard for all higher education institutions. They comprise the graduate's profile, field of study curriculum, and the syllabi of particular subject courses. They are worked out by advisory bodies of the ministries, nominated from among leading college professors and other experts.

The graduate's profile is a standard document that outlines the basic expertise necessary for a particular profession or academic discipline in a field of study. The required knowledge, skills, abilities, attitudes, values, and other personality characteristics of graduates are defined. The curriculum sets up the subject courses prescribed for each semester of studies and the number of teaching hours per week (max. thirty hours) or per semester. Furthermore, lectures, recitation, or seminars for each course are specified, as are the examinations for each subject. Curricula also include professional field practice, excursions, and training courses of several days or weeks duration. The calendar of studies for particular years is indicated so that it is clear when teaching, practice, and examination periods without teaching are to take place. Mandatory for all fields of study are the historical, philosophical, economic, and political aspects of Marxism-Leninism, Russian and one more foreign language, and physical training; these courses altogether form a common core for all fields of study.

Educational objectives in particular subject courses and their specific content are defined in syllabi that encompass a detailed system and range of knowledge, its structure, teaching methods, teaching aids, and other resources of study. On the basis of prescribed syllabi the ministries take over the elaboration and publishing of textbooks.

Different Types of Higher Studies

Higher studies are pursued in either "ordinary" or "extraordinary" ways. The basic type of study is ordinary study, after which students obtain a diploma or certificate of higher education qualification. Extraordinary study is provided in particular subject courses mainly for the purpose of extending one's knowledge. This form of study, however, does not provide complete higher education qualifications.

Ordinary study comes in two varieties: full-time or part-time, the latter including evening courses (max. 60 percent of a full-time teaching load) and distance courses (max. ninety-six teaching hours per semester). At present, part-time courses enroll about 17 percent of the total number of students.

Full-time study lasts for four years (120 fields of study—54 percent of all possible fields, five years (ninety-two fields of study, or 41 percent), or six years (ten fields of study, or 5 percent). Students enrolled part-time as a rule take one year longer to complete their studies.

Ordinary studies may be pursued in a slightly different way than that prescribed by the standard curriculum. An individualized curriculum is provided for those individual students or groups of students who are high achievers and who display a talent for research, technology, arts, or students in special sports programs, students who are permanently ill, or who have special family or community responsibilities. In interdisciplinary courses students may, apart from their main field of study, also undertake other fields of study either at the same faculty or elsewhere.

Higher studies are divided according to years and semesters. Each semester includes fifteen teaching weeks. Attendance is mandatory for students, except for lectures, where the dean of the faculty may grant students the right to decide about attendance. The basic methods of supervision for studies include: continuous supervision at seminars, in laboratories, and at recitation classes and examinations. The range and the level of knowledge required are given in the syllabus of a particular subject. Each semester, students take examinations in a maximum of five subjects. The vast majority of examinations are oral, but some oral exams are combined with written or practical parts. A student who fails an exam may ask the examiner for a reexamination twice; a third reexamination requires the dean's approval. On the fulfillment of all duties set up in the curriculum for a particular year of study, the student is allowed to enter the next year of study. It is possible to stay on probation for a year only twice during the course of study. Students may ask for deferment for a maximum of two years.

All the students in the same year of study have a leader who is nominated by the dean from among faculty members. He or she coordinates the teaching and learning process. Groups of fifteen to thirty students work together in seminars, recitation classes, and field practice. Another teacher is assigned to the group to coordinate and organize the students' moral, social, and cultural education, to respond to their problems and demands, and to generally assess their development. The group also has its student leader. The main purpose of this system is to promote an educational impact over the student's whole personality.

Admission and Leaving Requirements

The basic requirements for admission are stated in the Higher Education Act as follows: "The applicants for ordinary higher studies are admitted according to the needs of the socialist society, on the basis of their knowledge, skills, talent, interests, and health conditions with particular regard to their moral and social characteristics. Only those applicants may be admitted who have completed their secondary education and who have successfully passed the entrance examinations." Secondary education is completed after eight years of primary education and four years of secondary education. The applicants for higher studies are recruited mainly from gymnasia (i.e., general secondary schools) that are designed primarily to prepare students for the entrance to higher studies. Consequently, those who attend gymnasia are most successful at entrance examinations; they form three-fifths of the total number of college students. Secondary technical and secondary vocational schools also supply students for higher studies.

Since the number of applicants is usually twice the number of places available, the admission procedure must be selective. This is particularly true for arts colleges (only 10 to 20 percent of all applicants may be admitted), faculties of philosophy (e.g., social sciences and humanities) and law (24 to 35 percent), pedagogical faculties, faculties of economics and architecture (38 to 50 percent), and faculties of medi-cine (50 to 60 percent).

The dean of the faculty is responsible for the assessment of applicants and for the decision about their admission. An examination board screens applicants. Its decision is based on the student's results on an entrance examination, both oral and written (usually taken in two to three secondary school subjects, according to the desired field of study), and an interview that raises general political and cultural issues. The applicant's achievements at secondary school and his or her personal characteristics as described by the secondary school principal or by an employer are also taken into consideration. In the colleges of arts and of education practical examinations are held to ascertain a student's talent and disposition for studies. Students may be exempted from entrance examinations if, having fulfilled other requirements, they were high achievers during the whole course of study at secondary school, or if they have won first places in nationwide competitions in particular scientific, technical, artistic, or sports fields.

Higher studies in Czechoslovakia are free of charge. Social and achievement grants, scholarships, subsidized meals and board in students' hostels are provided. Health care is also provided free of charge. Students are treated like any other working person and are provided with sickness benefits and even pensions if they become disabled during their studies.

Higher studies in all fields, with the exclusion of medicine and veterinary science, end with a state final examination which includes the defense of a thesis, project, art work, or art performance, and an oral section. All of this is performed in front of an examination board. One of the three or more members of this board must be either a teacher at another faculty or an external specialist. The student's final thesis is devoted to a particular theme that is set in the last year of study. One of the staff in the student's department supervises the thesis and provides methodological assistance at special seminars held for this purpose. The state final begins with the defense of thesis during which the student responds to his teacher's written comments and to his opponent's comments. Following the defense the student takes an oral examination in a maximum of three subjects and in Marxism-Leninism.

After successful completion of the state final the student becomes a graduate, is awarded a diploma in higher education, and receives a particular degree: "inzenyr" (engineer, abbr. *Ing.* before name) at the technical, agricultural, and economic colleges, for example, and "academic architect," "academic sculptor," or "academic painter" at colleges of arts. Students at the faculties of medicine and veterinary colleges undertake the state rigorosum, very similar to final examination mentioned above, except for the defense of a thesis. On successfully passing it, graduates are awarded the degree "doctor of medicine" (abbr. MUDr. before name) and "veterinary doctor" (MVDr.). High achievers are awarded the so-called red diploma that testifies to their expertise.

Graduates of universities who have completed their studies in the state final may follow up by taking the state rigorosum. Then they are awarded the degrees JUDr. (doctor of law), PhDr. (doctor of philosophy), RNDr. (doctor of natural sciences), PaedDr. (doctor of pedagogy), PharmDr. (doctor of pharmacy), or RSDr. (doctor of sociopolitical sciences).

Higher education institutions also provide continuing education for former students. It is organized in the form of "postgraduate courses" in the approved curricula and is completed with a final examination including the presentation of the student's written project. Expenditures for continuing education are shared by the student's employer. Regrettably, due to the low interest of employers and some unsolved legislative and financial questions, the system of continuing education has not been very successful. It presently encompasses only 5 percent of all higher education students.

Graduates of higher education who seek qualifications to perform research and scientific work may enter the system of scientific education ("aspirantura") which has its legislative foundation in the Act of Education of Scientific Personnel (1977) and is coordinated by the Czechoslovak Academy of Science (CAS). It has been implemented at centers organized by the CAS, at universities, colleges, and other research institutes. The applicants are screened on a competitive basis. In the internal course applicants are exempted from working duties (three years of duration), in the external course (five years) applicants receive no exemption from working duties. The course of study is conducted in a tutorial style, and includes seminars supervised by outstanding professors or researchers. Studies end with examinations taken in the given discipline, in Marxism-Leninism, in Russian, and in one more world language. Scientific education is completed with the defense of a dissertation before a board of leading experts; the defense must take into consideration review by two opponents. The outcome of the defense is considered in academic councils of universities, colleges, or institutes of the CAS. The final verdict is expressed by the State Commission for Scientific Degrees, which awards the successful applicants the scientific degree "kandidát ved" (candidatus scientiarum, CSc. behind name). The highest scientific degree is "doktor ved" (doctor scientiarum, DrSc. behind name), which is awarded on the basis of the defense of a published dissertation.

Higher Education Staff

Academic teachers are not a large professional group; in 1987/88 they totaled 20,391, which was only 0.26 percent of the working population. Small as it is, the faculty is six times larger today than before World War II. Professors have a high social status, but society puts high demands on them, both professionally and politically.

Unlike other professional groups, academic teachers are highly differentiated. There are professors, associate professors ("docent"), lecturers ("odborny asistent"), and assisting teachers. The titles "professor" and "associate professor" may be awarded on the basis of nomination. Professors are nominated by the president of Czechoslovakia; associate professors are nominated by the minister of education. As a rule, would-be professors are recruited from doctors of science (DrSc.) and would-be associate professors from candidates of science (CSc). The suggestions for nomination are submitted by the rector of the university or college after a preparatory procedure during which a three-member commission of professors in the particular or related scientific discipline chooses candidates and academic councils of faculties and the whole institution vote on these candidates. Thirty-two percent of the faculty are professors and associate professors. Fifty-three percent of all academic teachers have achieved the degree CSc. Lecturers are the most numerous group, constituting 60 percent of staff. The complexity of the professional career as well as strict control by the state and political bodies have resulted in a situation in which the senior faculty tend to be old; the average age of a full professor is almost sixty. Academic teachers retire at age sixty-five, but some professors remain and work as consultants.

The structure of academic activity is also much more differentiated than in other professional groups. Its basic elements are educational and research activities, participation in college management, political and social activities, and participation in public activities in one's expert capacity out of school. Of the total working load (1,800 hours) five hundred hours are devoted to the teacher's mandatory scientific and research work. At present teachers are expected to perform an additional 25 percent of pedagogical activity for the same salaries. This burden has resulted in reduced research work and has lowered the level of teaching. In the 1980s a system for upgrading the professional qualifications of teachers was introduced. The instructional and personal development of the beginning assisting teachers have especially been upgraded because they are considered the linchpin for the necessary improvement of teaching at the higher education level.

Scientific and Research Work of Higher Education Institutions

The advancement of science and technology and the rapid introduction of its outcomes into the sphere of production and social practice is considered one of the priorities of state policy. Higher education is a fundamental part of scientific and technological progress and acts in accord with the developed system of research centers of the Academy of science as well as with the enterprise research institutes. An important feature of higher education is the creative research work of its teachers—a necessary prerequisite of quality and relevance of the profession at the tertiary level. Consequently, higher education covers all scientific disciplines in which students are educated. The multidisciplinary character of the research of higher education, therefore, enables it to solve problems in a more complex way then other sectors of research work. On the other side, however, academic personnel are to a great extent less concentrated on systematic research activity due to pedagogical duties. Accordingly, higher education institutions support establishing research units involving researchers exempted from wider pedagogical duties.

Most of the research work (66 percent) of universities and colleges lies in state schemes of fundamental research in which higher education institutions form 40 percent of the whole national volume. Higher education also takes part in state projects for technological advancement, economic research, and applied research in different fields (e.g., the spheres of health and education). Research tasks that are carried out by faculties and are not coordinated on a central basis involve only 5 percent of the research capacity of higher education institutions.

Recently, the role of research carried out jointly by higher education institutions and industrial enterprises has developed. This research comes about by means of direct requests to a higher education institution. Research outcomes are applied directly to the sphere of production. The organization that makes the order pays the higher education institution the amount stated in the joint agreement. Of this sum, part is paid to the higher education staff who took an active part in the research and the rest of the sum is supplied to the fund of the institution to cover further research activity and expenses.

The most recent form of linkage between science and practice has been the establishment of new corporations. Their purpose is to join the human and material resources of higher education institutions, research institutes, and enterprises in the solution of relevant research tasks that can be directly applied.

Current and Expected Changes in Higher Education

In the near future Czechoslovak higher education will enter a new state of development, which is generally considered complex and demanding because of socioeconomic conditions and demographic factors influenced by the population boom. An analysis and evaluation of the whole educational system was carried out by both Ministries in 1987/88. They decided to double the number of persons with complete secondary and higher education by the year 2000 and to increase educational expenditures from 5.5 percent to at least 7 percent of the whole gross national product.

In order to improve higher education, expand enrollment, enhance the quality of teaching, and promote scientific progress, it is necessary to amend the current Higher Education Act. One of the key principles of the newly drafted regulations is to eliminate overcentralization in decision making on higher education and any attempt at its unification. It is envisaged that universities and colleges will become more democratic; student and staff participation in and influence or institutional management and screening of academic personnel will be encouraged. Another important principle is to provide higher education institutions with the opportunity to take active part in socialist enterprises in the fields related to their educational and research tasks, which will enable them to obtain supplementary financial and material resources.

Hitherto scattered and overspecialized fields of study are now being revised. In the 1990s only eighty-one programs instead of the current 199 will be offered. Student specializations will be more soundly geared to employers' needs.

In the 1990s it is expected tertiary institutions will be entrusted with more control over development of their own curricula and syllabi, with only general coordination originating from central agencies. If Czechoslovak higher education is to meet the challenges of an upsurge of students and to satisfy increasing needs for the continuing education of its graduates, it will face completely new problems.

The need for democratization of access to higher education will make the Czechoslovak higher education system encounter reforms in vertical differentiation of study and in diversification of its institutional structure. Plans exist to gradually introduce short-cycle courses of two or three years' duration alongside the usual four- to six-year courses of study. The establishment of new institutes that would provide intermediate qualifications between secondary and tertiary education in some new vocations is being considered. Better legislative and material support for continuing education of graduates is being planned in order to promote specialization, refresh professional knowledge, or to extend qualifications. Some expenditures on continuing education are to be covered by employers who, moreover, will have more opportunity to influence the whole content of higher studies.

The necessary prerequisite to higher student enrollment is an ever more rapid increase in the number and quality of academic teachers. Introduction of a system of regular professional assessment of teachers, as well as concluding temporal teaching contracts, should lead to the improvement of teachers' research, educational, and organizational competencies. At the same time, the participation of external scientific personnel, namely those from the Academy of Sciences, should be stressed. In order to improve the quality and relevancy of teaching through the application of educational media, computer-based education, problem solving methods, simulations and games, and staff development programs are being implemented. To meet this challenge, Centers of Higher Education Pedagogy have been established at leading universities and colleges.

The text of the present study characterizes the development and the state of the art of the higher education system which existed in Czechoslovakia till the autumn of 1989. Forcible suppression of the demonstration of Prague students, who on the day of the 50th anniversary of their anti-Nazi demonstration on November 17 recalled democratic traditions and claimed their human and civic rights, triggered off a violent explosion of public disapproval with the existing political and economic system. The following massive demonstrations and general strike which most citizens partook of turned into a peaceful democratic revolution which in an incredibly short interval of time changed the political scene in the whole Czechoslovakia. Articles on the leading role of the Communist Party and Marxism-Leninism as the obligatory state ideology have been quashed in the existing constitution. Ideals of humanism and democracy have become the fundamental objectives of education. Immediately after the reconstruction of governmental bodies the formulation of the new Higher Education Act was begun with the participation of the students movement and Civic Forum as the representatives of statewide political efforts. This Act should come into force parallel with the new democratic constitution. Its determining principles should comprise freedom of research and instruction without ideological bias; autonomy of higher education institutions in relation to the state as well as their inner autonomy and democratic manner of vote in electing academic officials with and active participation of students; the possibility of establishing non-state higher education institutions; the updating of the system of instruction allowing each student to choose his or her own way of study; diversification of higher education structures; and promotion of such international contacts which would make it possible for the Czechoslovak higher education institutions to participate again in the European and world development of higher education. The launched process of democratic transformation will gradually change the existing system and it will most probably become the object of international comparative studies.

France

Alain Bienaymé

◆

The French higher education system is overwhelmingly under the control of the central government. Since Napoleon I launched the "Great Imperial University," French institutions of higher learning have been mainly divided into two subsets according to the two following criteria: the legal rules of student admissions and the major goals of the institution. The universities, which now number seventy-two, were and remain largely open to every baccalauréat-holder who wishes to apply to them. They were initially devoted to training future schoolteachers, professionals in law, civil servants, and physicians, but now offer training in a wide variety of disciplines. They are almost tuition-free; fees do not exceed one hundred dollars. In contrast, the grandes écoles, which now number just over 130, select their students through highly restrictive competitive tests. These tests generally require two years of preparatory courses taken at specific institutions called "classes préparatoires aux grandes écoles"(C.P.G.E.). The écoles train their students primarily in engineering. The students enrolled in écoles pay fees. Although the fees are higher than at the universities, they remain well below the real cost per student.

Universities are devoted to teaching, research, and training for research activities. The écoles used to be dedicated only to teaching and professional training, but research activities have begun to multiply very recently in a few "grandes écoles" such as the Polytechnique. The écoles are typically under the jurisdiction of the Ministry for Higher Education. A prestigious minority are controlled by other agencies: the Ministry of Defense runs the Polytechnique, the Ministry of Agriculture runs the Institut National Agronomique, and the Chambers of Commerce network run the business schools system.

The top-ranked baccalauréat-holders generally apply to C.P.G.E. according to their school marks in math. The écoles are ranked according to the quality of their applicants, the ratio of refusals to acceptances, and the career success of their alumni. Table 1 shows the relative "market share" of universities and écoles.

The higher education picture has grown in complexity since the mid-1960s. New kinds of institutions have grown up (Section de techniciens supérieurs [S.T.S.]) as the offspring of the secondary school system or have been invented afresh as sui generis institutes (Instituts Universitaires de Technologie [I.U.T.]) to expand options in postsecondary education. S.T.S.'s and I.U.T.'s were both intended to fill a gap in the system by offering two years of techni-

---

Table 1

Student Population Admitted

	Universities	Engineering Schools (in thousands)
1987/88	901.7	28.2
1989/90	931.2	30.6

Source: French National Assembly: Report on the Higher Education Finance Bill for 1989, 7 November 1988, p. 20 (38).

cal and vocational training in various job-related disciplines. Post-secondary training institutes for future primary school teachers were also created during this period. The I.U.T., after a slow start, have increased their enrollments considerably. And their graduates, as well as those from the S.T.S., are appreciated in the labor market. A significant percentage (30 percent) of the I.U.T. graduates go on to the university.

Thus, the Ministry of Higher Education does not have complete control over the whole system. It shares its power over business schools with the Chambers of Commerce and, through them, with the business community. The S.T.S. and C.P.G.E. are jealously kept under the control of the secondary school central administration. Some other ministries control their own specific institutions. This division of power causes endless controversies and struggles between lobbies, each of which claims to know what is best for their own institutions and constituents. Alumni associations, for example, have been very effective in keeping the grandes écoles largely separate from the university sector.

Table 2

Academic Years
Absolute Numbers—1960/1986
Thousands of Students in 1987/1988

	1960–61	1965–66	1970–71	1975–76	1980–81	1985–86	1987–88	Growth rates 1987–90
Universities (IUT excluded)	214,672	413,756	637,597	767,732	809,542	905,873	901.7	+11.4
I.U.T.	—	—	24,195	43,526	53,826	61,905	63.3	+17.7
S.T.S. (Higher technicians, two-year colleges)								
—Public	5,814	17,485	20,432	31,826	43,104	66,821	81.5	+89.1
—Private	2,200	8,255	6,408	14,390	24,211	50,528	63.1	+160.7
Preparatory classes to Grandes Ecoles								
—Public	18,452	24,814	30,641	32,104	35,385	39,904	45.2	+27.9
—Private	2,586	1,846	1,960	3,208	4,047	7,430	8	+98.2
Engineering Schools —Public —Private	20,770	26,609	30,512	33,788	36,952	45,095	48.3 (38.2) (10)	+30.6
Business Schools	5,286	7	9,394	10,929	17,730	28,633	30.3	+71.2
Private Universities	—	—	—	10,000	16,256	18,435	16.5	+1.3
Post-Secondary Primary School Teacher Training Institutes	9,709	9,875	14,520	15,981	11,354	17,452	13	+14.8
Totals (Double Counting Excluded)	259,489	446,640	721,659	900,044	987,407	1,166,067	1,196	+21.1

Source: French National Assembly: Reports on the Higher Education Finance Bills—1988 and 1989 (38).

Only a small proportion of students applying to institutions in the private sector, about 8 percent, is admitted, according to official data. But the real percentage would probably be much higher if all categories of postsecondary institutions, including private vocational training colleges, which are totally self-financed, were taken into account. But institutions that are completely funded by private sources are not accounted for in the official postsecondary education data pool. Thus, on the whole, although the French system is heavily centralized, it does not fit a single frame. Each component works according to different rules and has its own dynamics.

Table 2 shows that although the universities are still enrolling three-fourths of the student population in higher education, their relative enrollment significance has begun to decline in recent years. This is due to two main causes. First, freshmen are more and more attracted to institutions with lower teacher-student ratios, which lead to specific professional positions, even at the cost of a heavier work load. The French believe, rightly or wrongly, that there is a high correlation between the barriers to entry in a degree program, the quality of degrees awarded, and job opportunities. Faculties of law, humanities, and liberal arts suffer from poor faculties and a high teacher-student ratio. Second, some disciplines, such as law and business management at some Parisian universities (Paris II Assas, Paris IX Dauphine) have raised the level of school achievement marks they require from their applicants; this greater selectivity reduces the number of students enrolled. The proportion of students who are presently admitted in the selective subsystem of the public university is estimated at roughly 40 percent.

French higher education is facing the pressure of a growing overall number of admissions. This growth results from demography but also more and more from the higher rate of secondary school graduates who hold a baccalauréat. In 1988 12 percent more baccalauréats were awarded than in the previous year in the general education sector and 8 percent more were awarded in the technical sector. Today more than one-third of the relevant age group holds a baccalauréat degree. At present, 97 percent of the 206,000 general baccalauréat holders and roughly 75 percent of the 99,000 technical school baccalauréat holders are continuing their studies.

Slightly more than one-third of baccalauréat-holders are now applying to some postsecondary institution. This indicates, according to Martin Trow's terminology,[1] that France has established a mass higher education system clearly different both from its own past elitist system and from the United States's universal access system.

Current enrollment rates have stimulated debates regarding student-teacher ratios, staff resources devoted to higher education, and the problem of its productivity. In 1988 the total teaching staff reached 47,000, yielding an average student-teacher ratio of 24:1. This figure is significantly higher than in many other major industrialized countries. For 1982/83, the French student-teacher ratio was 30 percent higher than the average computed for a group of five leading developed countries: West Germany, France, Japan, the United Kingdom, the United States. Moreover, the disparities between France and its major partners are more pronounced at the level of higher education than at any other level of education. High student-teacher ratios could theoretically be interpreted in two ways: either as a sign of higher productivity in French postsecondary education or as a demonstration of a poor endowment in terms of teaching resources. The first interpretation seems unlikely. French student-teacher ratios vary from discipline to discipline (very low in sciences, very high in humanities and law), reflecting the mechanical consequences of massive enrollment in nonscientific disciplines rather than the results of a deliberate policy. The level of student dropouts is quite high, a situation that could be attributed to a poor endowment in human resources.

Recent data give an estimation of the overall yield of the system. In 1986 France granted 100,000 four- and five-year degrees and 75,000 two-year degrees. But the number who received degrees, something less than 200,000, must be compared to the numbers enrolled in degree programs from 1980 to 1982, an average of one million. The Centre d'Etudes et de Recherches sur les Qualifications has estimated that out of an intake of one hundred students in 1983, only sixty eventually finished their studies. Nearly forty students per hundred dropped out without receiving any public certification. These rather dramatic figures raise an important issue: what kind of policy should be implemented in order to improve the overall yield of the system, knowing that it suffers from significant understaffing and that French politicians have unanimously expressed the wish to see 80 percent of the eighteen-year-olds accede to the "level of baccalauréat."[2]

Main Historical Trends

The Sorbonne is one of the oldest institutions of higher learning in the Western world. It was founded in 1253, one century after Bologna (1119) and Oxford (1133), a few decades before Cambridge (1284), and one century before Heidelberg (1386). In those medieval times, the French university corresponded to the notion of "Universitas" and was a part of a global network with its own peculiar way of life. These academic brotherhoods had to provide jurists and professionals for administrations of church and state. But, according to recent historical records,[3] some universities were unable to maintain serious academic standards. Their discipline slackened. They suffered from teacher absenteeism and shallow curricula. Student registration was not kept thoroughly and the degrees awarded were unequal in quality. During the sixteenth century regional authorities began to react in order to promote fair competition between universities. The kings Henri IV and Louis XIV introduced new sets of regulations, so that Napoléon might be considered more as the heir of the ancien régime than the founder of a new university.[4]

Napoléon's intervention was inspired by systematic views on what a university was intended for and what it should not be.[5] Napoléon needed reliable artillerymen, engineers, and highly qualified professionals and was not very sensitive to the wishes of universities to continue as autonomous communities mainly dedicated to the free quest of truth. Realpolitik was not very far from Napoléon's schemes and purposes.[6] The Sorbonne was felt to be too politically unreliable and socially irrelevant. Therefore it underwent a drastic reform in 1806.[7]

The Great Imperial University that opened its doors in 1808/09 had to comply with very strict rules, most of which remained in effect until 1968. The university considered as a whole was subordinated to the central government. And, at the very beginning, it was even placed under the control of the Home Affairs Department. Napoléon's minister of education, L. de Fontanes, had to go through the minister of police in order to arrange an appointment with the emperor. Napoléon perceived the university as a major institution for training elites according to the economic goals of the nation as defined by its head of state.[8]

The system was redesigned to provide the country with the elite needed for theology, law, medicine, and school teaching in humanities, math, and sciences. A separate set of écoles was entrusted with the training of engineers. Neither the universities nor the écoles were considered to be primarily centers for free academic research or campuses for general education.

The tertiary system was geographically reorganized according to the principle that there should be as many universities as courts of appeal. Each of the twenty-seven universities contained a compartmentalized set of five faculties or more. Uniform curricula were taught throughout the whole country with the same methods. The rector, who served as ex officio president of the university, was designated by the government and represented the state. Faculty members became statutory civil servants, subject to nationwide career regulations and a uniform salary grid. Throughout the nineteenth and twentieth centuries new categories of teachers were created in order to cope with the specificities of new disciplines and budgetary constraints.

Although several laws (1850, 1854, 1896) and decrees corrected a few rather minor details, on the whole, the Napoleonic framework remained untouched up to 1968.

During the nineteenth century and the first half of this century, the French university was an ivory tower. Professors were required to teach just three hours per week to a limited number of students who were on a safe, guaranteed track leading to prestigious positions. Many professors were genuine scholars who contributed highly to maintaining France at the top rank of countries that have most contributed to literature, liberal arts, and basic sciences. But the imperial mold and individualistic behaviors combined to produce unanticipated and undesirable effects.

Higher education, with the exception of engineering, law, and medicine, was largely disconnected from the production sectors. The centralized system was unable to foster innovations or team research. Organized research activities took place elsewhere. The Ecole Pratique des Hautes Etudes, the Institut Pasteur, the Centre National de la Recherche Scientifique, the Institut National de la Recherche Médicale, the Commissariat à l'Energie Atomique, and other major French research institutions are not university offsprings. They were created externally by political fiat because the university structure had proven unable to stimulate innovation and scientific research from inside.[9] Although most public research laboratories and organizations are led by university professors, these individual links are too weak and tenuous to bind the academic world and the worlds of science, technology, and business. No wonder that French higher education proved ineffective in coping with the tremendous changes in its environment after 1950.

To sum up, on the eve of the 1968 outburst, the French university considered as a whole could neither move forward nor innovate. Each institution was, and still is today, surrounded by big outside research monopolies.

The University of Paris was nearing 200,000 students and could not be managed properly. The most important trend in the postwar French university is, as in many countries, the growth of the student population. The Great Imperial University enrolled 6,750 students in 1808/09, its birth year. France counted 30,000 students enrolled in public universities in 1900; 80,000 in 1939; 216,000 in 1960; 586,000 in 1968; and 821,000 in 1975.

Although student-teacher ratios are higher than the international standard in Western countries, the teaching staff has expanded greatly. In thirty years, less than the length of a career, from 1956 to 1986, the number of teachers in all categories has increased eightfold. Higher education offers a unique peacetime example of such a large institution experiencing such impressive growth rates. It is impossible to dissociate this dramatic period of student and faculty expansion from the fact that, since 1945, France has enjoyed one of the fastest economic growths of its history.

Conservatives believe that 1968 was the cause of the difficulties that now overwhelm French universities. But other observers think that the universities had already begun the process of decay and obsolescence after World War II.[10] In 1966 the Congress of Caen had demanded deep reforms. And forerunners like J. Plumyene and J. Lassierra[11] had expressed clear views on what would then become the core issues of the forthcoming intellectual stirring of 1968–73.

Yet, in order to dampen the student revolt, Edgar Faure, an experienced and broad-minded statesman newly appointed as minister of education, designed an orientation bill for higher education known as the 1968 law. He proved his exceptional skills in negotiation. The law was voted unanimously in spite of the reluctance of many members of Parliament to approve reforms that seemed to give too much elbow room to the student leaders. The Edgar Faure bill rested (and still rests to the extent that the 1984 Savary Law does not repeal it entirely) on three principles: autonomy, multidisciplinarity, and diversified participation. These three concepts serve to introduce the most important trends, developments, and recent controversies in French tertiary education.

The Controversial Development of French Higher Education Since 1968

I must first mention that the 1968 orientation law was more easily passed since it was intended to reform only the university system and kept the grandes écoles out of its purview. Both political wings agreed to protect the écoles subsystem from the turmoils of university reform.

The autonomy given to each university was real and substantial, but the system as a whole is still subject to a high degree of central government control and authority. Reform meant the death of the core institution of the former Napoleonic system, the Faculté. The biggest universities in Paris, Lyon, and other major cities were split into several autonomous universities (thirteen in Paris, three in Lyon, three in Aix-Marseille, etc.). Faculties were broken up; professors joined the new universities according to their selection of pedagogical programs. The small faculties located in cities like Dijon, Poitiers, etc., had to merge into one city university. Thus, the university has become the new core institution and exerts direct control on its components, called units of teaching and research. The government continues to designate an educational representative for each academic region but the rector of the academy no longer rules over the university. He can attend the university board meetings but each university is now led by an elected president.

France now has seventy-two universities. Their enrollments range from 5,000 to 35,000. The reforms resized the universities in an effort to render them more manageable. Some critics of reform believed that breaking up the larger universities enabled the ministry to regain its former political control. Certainly, the flood of detailed regulations issued by the ministry has not receded up to now. The complexity of university management has increased considerably as the result of efforts to diversify the curricula, the degrees, and the student admission and guidance procedures.

The combination of autonomy and multidisciplinarity was intended to generate synergies and to eliminate duplication in the core curricula. It was hoped that the universities could seize new opportunities to innovate by developing more professionalized degrees and new kinds of research programs. The goal of relevancy, however, did not always inspire the restructuring process. Many faculties preferred to choose the strategy of withdrawal to their tiny specialities. It was often a disguise for a kind of ideological apartheid instead of cooperation in new, carefully designed programs. Merging and splitting activities looked more like a politically biased process than the outcome of a thoughtful plan. Many "reformed" units of teaching and research simply replicate the older unidisciplinary faculties; this means that most of the college student population remains confined to four-year curricula that are still almost entirely designed according to the logic of a specific field of knowledge: economics, law, management, chemistry, and so on.

The political answer to student unrest has been to invite student participation. But under the pressure of trade unions and public opinion, participation was also extended to junior professors, administrative staff, and outside community representatives. Thus, without any transition, the universities that before 1968 were led entirely by senior faculties were plunged into an entirely different world. Now each university is led by an elected president; although he is normally a former faculty member, his constituency consists of different electoral bodies. He is elected by the university boards: the university board of administration, the scientific council, and the student life council, each of which numbers thirty or forty members. They are talkative miniparliaments more than effective boards. A university president has to be gifted in politics in order to establish his authority over such a diversified constituency.

Autonomy, multidisciplinarity, and extended participation have resulted in a patchwork of establishments. Those who feel nostalgia for the Napoleonic model regret the balkanization of the university. For others, the 1968 law represents a brilliant, bold, and swift reform of a system of higher education that had already dramatically revealed its incapacity to innovate by itself. But there is a lot to do in order to enforce and achieve the three-pronged policy that Edgar Faure outlined during his eleven months and eleven days of office as the head of the Ministry of Education.

The student generations since 1975 have been much less ideologically minded. They are hard workers and job-seekers. The university and the two-year technical colleges have displayed tremendous efforts in order to cope with growing numbers of students; enrollment has doubled during the last two decades. Graduate and postgraduate degrees have been widely diversified, mostly on the professional and vocational side. The Savary law improved student guidance procedures and the relevancy of curricula at the college levels. As a result of autonomy, several universities now compete with one another in every big city. Disciplines are taught in different programs and at different levels of difficulty. The higher education supply has grown and this has doubtless widened the span of students' choice and created more flexibility throughout the entire system.

But the negative side of the balance seems heavier. The reforms have multiplied the aims and goals of higher education but they have not been consistently implemented. This results from two main causes. First, beyond the repetitive political incantation concerning education as a national priority, the government actually provides diminishing real funds for tertiary students. As J. C. Casanova, a close disciple of Raymond Aron, put it: "The grandes écoles which are felt as the elite system in spite of their weak and young research experience are thriving and jealously put aside from the turmoil; the bright and wealthy students can afford to end their studies on U.S. campuses."[12] Second, in the same breath, the French passion for equality greatly hinders university endeavors to diversify degrees and outputs. Differences are seen as inequality and inequality as iniquity. Thus, a fiction of equality prevents the universities from granting new degrees and from diversifying their fundraising activities.

This collective schizophrenia entails many shortcomings, some very visible and close to the technicalities of education processes, other more deeply entrenched in the French mentality and culture.[13]

○ The higher the proportion of graduates who seek employment in private business, the more diversified degrees should become. Jobs outside public administration are much less standardized and more flexible. Thus it will hardly be possible in the future to keep the fiction of equality by maintaining national degrees approved and funded by the central government.

○ The need for equity and efficiency should prompt the public authorities to recognize that if the university is going to be enrolling increasing numbers of students, the student population is bound to become more and more diversified according to their cultural backgrounds, their skills, and their motivations. A changing student body requires new patterns of pedagogy, more systematic guidance, and a wide span of vocational curricula. In spite of benevolent efforts, freshmen and sophomores do not receive adequate guidance. As a result, too many applicants drop out and begin their adult life with a feeling of failure.

○ Mass higher education, for lack of forethought, has been created at the expense of academic excellence and basic research. It works as if democracy implied more of the same and/ or a general average downgrading of the culture transmitted. More subtle strategies that enhance the chances of intellectual development for every individual, including the brightest minds, are required. But there is no clear political will on this specific issue.

When higher education is primarily required to provide new skills in order to fill the needs of the production sector, and when, furthermore, access to higher education raises the chances to get a job ("only 14 percent of university graduates are still seeking a job one year after they leave university, whereas 28 percent of baccalauréat holders and more than 50 percent of those who leave school with lesser school achievements remain unemployed), then universities will be contaminated by a pervasive utilitarianism. But French society is still not ready to pay the cost of safeguarding and promoting areas of academic excellence and free research that appear to be economically unrewarding. For example, the proportion of students who receive the D.E.S.S., a professionalized degree awarded five years after the baccalauréat, instead of the D.E.A., which has a more theoretical and academic focus, has grown significantly during the last decade. Three significant testimonies from highly famed French intellectuals may be quoted at this point. Claude Levi-Strauss contends that even his generation could not stand intellectual comparison with the generation of Durkheim, Bergson, and Proust. The mathematician R. Thom[14] argues that French intellectual selectivity, manifested in a devotion to abstract mathematics and a fascination with computer techniques and data processing, is linked to the stagnation of scientific theory and the dormancy of fundamental thought. Finally, the philosopher M. Serres[15] stresses the idea that French society is closing its mind to progress because it tends to be subordinated to the power of management, mass media, and a certain type of highly specialized and technicized sciences. The takeover of French society by graduates of the Polytechnique and the Ecole Nationale de l'Administration is a by-product of the lack of countervailing powers within the French university.[16]

One of the most controversial issues concerns the level of knowledge and sophistication reached by French youth. Some argue that, according to the army instruction statistics and to sociological enquiries,[17] the French population is becoming better educated; others, such as J. de Romilly,[18] J.C. Milner,[19] A. Finkielkraut,[20] and

E. de Fontenay,[21] deny this conclusion. The statistical records on education obviously indicate that increasing numbers of students spend more time pursuing higher levels of education. The median marks obtained by young conscripts have been rising since 1967. But the gap between the educated elites and the illiterates is growing and the proportion of illiterates is not shrinking. One wonders what kind of intellectual wealth is accumulated during primary and secondary school time and during higher education studies. What kind of intellectual substance circulates within the campuses? Do mass information and computerized data lead to high intellectual achievements? What is the level of education of a school leaver who knows how to solve a problem in mathematics that his father is unable to solve, but who is ignorant of the conditional tense in which the problem is stated? After all, in spite of their "naïvetés" and their radicalism, the student leaders of 1968 were lucid on some of the traps in which modernity was bound to lock them later on, during their adulthood.

French Higher Education and the Political System

Two main observations should be stressed here. The first deals with logistics, finance, human resources, and staffing, that is to say the problem of implementing ambitious goals. The second is related to the significant new institution created in 1984, the "Comité National d'Evaluation des Universités," which is in charge of a periodical assessment of the higher education institutions.

The problem of implementing reforms is particularly hard to solve in the education sector,[21] and especially in France, where education raises passions and ideological controversies. There is a sharp contrast between the political world of words and the reality of "autonomy" and resource-funding. In the political sphere in the 1980s a wide consensus has emerged both on the Left and the Right according to which education should be recognized as one of the nation's two or three top priorities. Since 1983 the new political dictum in education is that 80 percent of the relevant age group should reach the level of baccalauréat within the next fifteen years.[22] But meanwhile, the financial situation of the universities continues to deteriorate to an extent that could be described as "pauperization." Because almost 90 percent of education funds are allocated by the central government, mainly through the Ministry of Education, the relationship between higher education and the political system is particularly tense and knotty.

As regards the aims and goals assigned to the university, the guideline law of 1984 is quite verbose. Every university should "enhance the scientific and cultural development of the nation and its citizens, contribute to the employment policy and regional development, and help to reduce social and cultural inequalities." It should "provide more opportunities for vocational and professional studies." "University 'teachers-researchers' should devote their full time to teaching, tutoring, counselling, research, management of the university, international cooperation, services to the community and dissemination of research results." Senior professors are only mentioned twice in that lengthy document. First, they are reminded of their specific responsibilities in curricula preparation, student guidance, and pedagogical coordination. Second, they are reduced to a small minority on the university governing boards. In fact, they are largely overwhelmed by the leftist unions that link together most of the junior faculty members, the administrative staff, many student associations, and a few outsiders designated by workers' unions.

The 80 percent goal for the year 2000 implies that, even if the baccalauréat does not provide automatic access to universities, some 40 to 55 percent of the relevant age group will probably be enrolled in the near future. The United States and Japan's examples are quoted explicitly in the foreword explaining the aims and goals of the 1984 law. But this goal is questionable on the following grounds:

○ Beyond some level, one might wonder why the residual fraction of the age group should be excluded from any postsecondary institutions. The figure of 80 percent raises the problem of the 20 percent left out who should also be taken care of by some adequate continuing education and apprenticeship facilities.

○ The 80 percent goal assumes that regardless of any gaussian statistical distribution of skills, the intellectual ability required to get university degrees is the same for the 25 to 55 percent of additional school leavers as for the former 5 to 25 percent, while we know that the present bracket from 5 percent to 25 percent displays lower intellectual talents than the 5 percent elites. This is a bold assumption, even if we can hope for some improvement in teaching-learning strategies by means of television and satellite communication networks.

○ Today, the share of upper-level and intellectual professions in the total labor force does not much exceed 10 percent. If we add to these professions the middle-level jobs (e.g., nurses, technicians, accountants, foremen, etc.), we reach roughly 30 percent of the labor force. These figures coincide with the rate of student participation for the relevant group aged nineteen to twenty-three years. It means either that university degrees give to the younger members of the labor force potentialities that remain underutilized in the country or that higher education delivers large numbers of irrelevant degrees that do not fit the

qualifications required by the job market. Both kinds of gaps will inevitably widen if the 80 percent goal is implemented without any major diversification of the postsecondary learning sector.

In spite of a real political effort demonstrated by the budget for the 1989 fiscal year, universities are still wondering how France will afford the cost of making higher education a major priority. They are still waiting for a scheme of renewal. The economic situation of French higher education seems to be one of the worst in the Western world as far as the university component is concerned. According to the statistical records of I.R.E.D.U., the higher education share of the GNP, which was 0.275 percent in 1960, reached a peak of 0.602 percent in 1969. Since 1970 it has dropped to a range of 0.45 percent/0.50 percent. This means that the real cost per student (excluding students enrolled in institutions whose budget is controlled by the secondary level administration or by departments other than the Ministry of Higher Education), which was 30,600 FF in 1968, has declined to 20,100 FF in 1985 ($2,300), according to J. C. Eicher.[23] In 1988 the corresponding figure is approximately 21,300 FF in 1985 francs. This means that a student costs, today, on average less than $3,000. If one excludes the student social entitlements, the research activities funded by the Ministry of Education, and investment expenditures, then the estimated direct costs per capita were the following in 1988/89:

○ 3,000 FF in Law ($500)
○ 4,000 FF in Humanities ($666)
○ 13,000 FF in Sciences ($2,166)
○ 16,000 FF in I.U.T. ($2,666)
○ 25,000 FF in engineering schools ($4,166) (Assemblée Nationale 1989)

These figures show that in spite of differences in methods of estimation and data collection between countries, France's higher education sector is treated like a poor relation, both when we compare it to the French secondary schools and to other higher education systems in Western countries. In the 1980s, the I.R.E.D.U.'s calculations show that while France's share of GNP allocated to higher education slightly exceeds that of Japan, it lies well below all other developed countries (West Germany and Sweden: 0.61 percent; Belgium: 1 percent; U.K.: 1.13 percent; U.S.: 1.17 percent in 1982). N. P. Eurich's report on continuing education in the United States indicates that a few years ago the United States spent almost two and a half times as much per student in their four-year universities as in France. These conclusions are illustrated by specific key items such as expenditures on libraries and documentation. According to a recent report, French university libraries are one of the "disaster-stricken zones of the higher education sector."[24] Too few seats, too little space per seat, too few books, and understaffing are the plagues of the university libraries. One could count 270 students per seat at Paris VII; France provides an average 0.65 square meters of library space per student instead of the standard 1.5. The per-student purchasing power of a French university library is one-fourth to one-ninth that in other Western countries. Only three out of sixty-five university libraries buy more than 15,000 books per year.

Since 1970 a steady share of the GNP has been devoted to higher education despite a 65 percent growth in the student population. Moreover, the steady share itself hides wide shifts within the budget structures. This shift has been shown by a French team of expert researchers, whose data are summarized in Table 3.[25]

Table 3 shows worrying tendencies. One notices the declining share for capital ex-

Table 3

Average Annual Growth Rates in Constant French Francs (1985)

From 1975 to 1985

Capital expenditures (Construction and maintenance)	-2.3%
Operating expenditues	+2.1%
Out of which: a) staff expenditures	+3.5%
b) other operating expenditures	-0.6%
Student welfare (Grants, scholarships and subsidies for housing and food)	+3.5%

Source: J. Guin et al. (28).

penditures and for operating funds other than teacher and administrative staff salaries. The physical environment and the working conditions in the higher education sector have steadily declined since the years of rapid economic expansion.

The growing proportion of funds devoted to staff expenditures is not due to the staff hiring and development but instead represents the mechanical effect of seniority. The increasing share of the budget allocated to student welfare is the result of a conscious political decision; without questioning the decision's appropriateness one may wonder why this additional burden has been taken on at the expense of capital and operating expenditures in the higher education budget. In the meantime the economic situation of the faculty staff has greatly deteriorated.

As Table 4 shows, the "greying of academia" is a reality. This reflects a deep loss of interest in higher education teaching and research careers. It finds its explanation in the mediocrity of working conditions and real-term income deterioration, as well as in declining opportunities for promotion and the lack of bonuses and allowances that are provided by other jobs that require a similar level of education. Today forty- to forty-five-year-old faculty members with fifteen to twenty years of seniority are earning 220,000 FF per year ($37,000), half as much as the head of the legal department of a medium-sized company. These salaries are even well below those earned by younger graduates who start their career in the production sector. If we compare this yearly income with the average salary of a British university professor—£28 820 ($50,416)—and if we compare the French and British salaries to GNP per capita in those two countries, we find that the relative economic position of the French professor is only 2.33 times the French GNP per capita whereas "Professor Pauper" in the United Kingdom earns four times the British GNP per capita.[26] Income gaps combine with a general loss of status and prestige to divert the brightest French postgraduates from teaching and research careers. The more professionalized the discipline taught, the more obvious is the decline in attraction to teaching. Law, business, management, technology, math, and many other disciplines are suffering from a teacher shortage. At the very moment when more professors are needed in order to cope with rising numbers of students, the pool of younger professors is running dry.

There are signs that the public authorities have recently begun to become aware of the gravity of the situation. The 1988 budget includes a 5.3 percent increase in current francs, a 2.1 percent increase in constant francs. But I must add that in 1988 the economic growth in the national economy was 3.6 percent. The 1989 budget increase represents an 8.4 percent increase in current francs over the 1988 allocation.

But what French higher education needs most is a long-term strategy that would help to attract more human resources, create facilities, and diversify the curricula. At present it is doubtful that the government will be able to afford it, for two main reasons. First, other priorities, such as jails, hospitals, and lower schools, seem more urgent. And second, France is spending huge sums on projects designed to maximize French national prestige, for example, great public works such as the Louvre, the new arch and tower in la Défense, a new Opera, and a "very big library." In order to find the resources to fund these projects, the government is beginning to urge the universities to sign contracts whereby state funds will be combined for the first time with regional and city community resources. These changes could give the universities some relief if the state does not provide them as a pretext for decreasing its share of the burden. Universities could find here a new way to diversify and increase their resources. But their financial autonomy will be restricted as long as each university is forbidden to allocate its resources more freely and to raise private funds by way of fees and tuitions. Fees and tuitions are presently less than one hundred dollars per year in a public university.

These gloomy statements should not stop me from stressing two positive observations. First, higher education in France, which has been the subject of ideological controversy, has become a field of positive thought and investigation.[27] Although the study of higher education is not a discipline in itself, the mass of data, figures, and reports devoted to this topic has grown

---

Table 4

Percentage of Faculty Staff Under 40 Years Old

	1977	1987
Junior Professors	51.1%	8.3%
Senior tenured Professors	16.4%	5.3%

Source: French Ministry of Education, 1987.

significantly in France during the last fifteen years. This new kind of literature contains arguments to cure a major disease of the French university—its deficiencies in marketing and communication—as well as suggestions for improving higher education policy.

Second, a new institution created in 1984 plays a new and increasing role in higher education. The Comité National d'Evaluation des Universités, chaired from 1984 to 1989 by Laurent Schwartz (who was awarded the Fields Medal in mathematics), is appointed directly by the president of the republic and not by the Ministry of Education, which clearly indicates that the committee stands free from the educational bureaucracy and its lobbies. This committee has been doing a good job. In five years it has elaborated an ad hoc method of audits and has completed audits on one-third of the universities.[28] Moreover, the prestige, the skillfulness, and the tact of the first committee has been a great help in order to:

○ Provide universities with sound advice, guidance, and a new taste for self-assessment.

○ Provide the administration and newspapers with deeper and thoughtful insights into the specific needs of each university.

○ Convey the idea that more autonomy could be granted to universities with the safeguard of an overall assessment procedure.

But the committee will be entirely renewed in 1989. This may entail a loss of experience. And the newly appointed committee will have to acquire its own experience.

France, like its other partners in the E.E.C., is entering a new era of intense economic competition and cooperation. The country participates in a host of programs in which students' and teachers' mobility will begin to grow, such as Comett, Pace, and Saturn. According to cost per student figures, France may appear to be a model of efficiency. But according to other standards, such as institutional autonomy and flexibility, campus facilities, research equipment, and working conditions of the faculty staff, France has a lot to do to close the gap between her tertiary system and the top university systems of leading Western countries. Its grandes écoles, as excellent as they may be, offer too narrow a base for this goal. France needs a few strong and leading universities in each major discipline. It still has the talent, but time is running short for saving a system at risk.

Notes

1. M. Trow, "Comparative Perspectives on Access" in *Access to Higher Education*, ed. O. Fulton (Guildford, England: Society for Research Into Higher Education, Guildford, 1981) and A. Bienaymé, *L'enseignement supérieur et l'idée d'université* (Paris: Economica, 1986).

2. Alain Bienaymé, "L'accès de 80 percent de la jeunesse aux portes de l'enseignement supérieur," *Chroniques d'Actualité de la S.E.D.E.I.S.* (15 January 1987).

3. J. Verger, C. Vuilliez, et al., *Histoire des Universités en France* (Toulouse: Privat, 1986).

4. G. Amestoy, *Les universités françaises* (Montpellier: Education et Gestion, 1968).

5. S. D'Irsay, *Histoire des universités françaises et étrangères* (Paris: Picard, 1935).

6. G. Gusdorf, *L'université en question* (Paris: Payot, 1964).

7. J. Drèze et J. Debelle, *Conceptions de l'Université* (Paris: Editions Universitaires, 1968).

8. Napoléon, *Vues politiques* (Paris: Fayard, 1939) and A. Aulard, *Napoléon Ier et le monopole universitaire* (Paris: Colin, 1911).

9. Conseil Economique et Social, *L'organisation et le développement de la recherche dans les éstablissements d'enseignement supérieur* (Paris: Documentation Francaise, 1978).

10. E. Faure, *Philosophie d'une réforme* (Paris: Plon, 1969).

11. J. Plumyène et J. Lasierra, *Le complexe de gauche* (Paris: Flammarion, 1967).

12. J. C. Casanova, "Célébrer mai 1968," *Commentaire* (Winter 1988), p. 1018.

13. Alain Bienaymé, "Materialism, not dialectics on the 'Rive Gauche,'" *Times Higher Education Supplement* (20 May 1988).

14. R. Thom, *Esquisse de sémio-physique* (Paris:

Flammarion, 1988).

15. M. Serres, Entretiens, *Dynasteurs* (October 1988).

16. Bourdieu, *La noblesse d'Etat: Grandes Ecoles et Esprit de corps* (Paris: Editions de Minuit, 1989).

17. C. Baudelot and R. Estabet, *Le niveau monte, réfutation d'une vieille idée concernant la prétendue décadence de nos écoles* (Paris: Seuil, 1988).

18. J. de Romilly, *L'enseignement en détresse* (Paris: Fayard, 1984).

19. J. C. Milner, *De l'école* (Paris: Le Seuil, 1984).

20. A. Finkielkraut et E. de Fontenay, "L'enseignement du mépris," *Le Monde* (10 February 1988).

21. L. Cerych and P. Sabatier, *Great Expectations and Mixed Performances* (Stoke on Trent, England: Trentham Books, 1986).

22. A. Bienaymé, "L'université dans les filets de la politique," *Chroniques d'Actualité de la S.E.D.E.I.S.* (15 August 1986); A. Bienaymé, "La mesure du problème universitaire," *Chroniques d'Actualité de la S.E.D.E.I.S.* (15 March 1987).

23. J. C. Eicher et al., "L'évolution comparée des coûts et des financements de l'enseignement supérieur dans quelques pays occidentaux développés," I.R.E.D.U. (24 September 1987).

24. A. Miquel, *Rapport sur les bibliotheques universitaires* (Paris: La Documentation francaise, 1989).

25. J. Guin, "How to Cope with Fund Restrictions?" (Paris: Organization for Economic Cooperation and Development, 1985).

26. M. Sollogoub, "La condition des enseignants de l'enseignement supérieur," *Revue d'Economie Politique* (December 1988).

27. See, for example, R. Ellrodt et al., *Pour que l'Université ne meure* (Paris: Le Centurion, 1977); P. Campus, *Reconstruire l'Université* (Paris: Albatros, 1986); A. Carpentier, *Le mal universitaire: diagnostic et traitement* (Paris: R. Laffont, 1988); J. Lesourne, *Education et société: les défis de l'an 2000* (Paris: La Découverte, 1988); L. Schwartz, *Sauver l'Université* (Paris: Seuil, 1983); H. Tezanas du Montcel, *L'Université: peut mieux faire* (Paris: Seuil, 1985); R. F. LeBris, *L'Université à la loupe* (Paris: Atlas Economica, 1985).

28. Comité National d'Evaluation des Universités, *Où va l'Université?* (Paris: Gallimard, 1987).

German Democratic Republic

Mark A. Ashwill

The guiding principles of GDR higher education are (1) equal access to higher education for every qualified citizen; (2) the unity of training and education, teaching and research, theory and practice; and (3) the right to suitable employment upon graduation. The Ministry of Higher and Technical Education is responsible for the policy, planning, and administration of higher education. Universities, colleges, and other institutions of equal rank are headed by rectors who are elected from a pool of full professors by the Academic Council (Wissenschaftlicher Rat) of the respective institution and appointed by the minister. Throughout its history, the GDR has looked to higher education to play a pivotal role in the development of socialism.

The GDR has six universities located in Berlin (East), Greifswald, Halle-Wittenberg, Jena, Leipzig, and Rostock, and forty-eight specialized institutions of higher education. Since 1951 the number of students attending these universities and colleges, including those engaged in correspondence (Fernstudium) and part-time study (Abendstudium), has increased from about 31,512 to 132,602 in 1987. In 1987, over three-fourths of all students were enrolled in technical courses of study, including chemical, mechanical, and electrical engineering and mining (31.8 percent), education (23.3 percent), economics (12.9 percent) and medicine (9.9 percent). Over half of all students are women; since the mid-1950s approximately 55 percent have come from the working and peasant classes of the GDR. (Note: the children of Communist party members are officially classified as working class.) The expansion of GDR higher education is also reflected in the rapid growth of the academic profession, which nearly tripled in size between 1960 and 1980.

University Admission

The GDR's integrated and unified educational system offers several ways to enter a university or college. The direct routes are successful completion of the two-year general-academic Extended High School (Erweiterte Oberschule) as evidenced by the Abitur (German secondary school completion certificate that entitles its holder to attend a university or college), and enrollment in a three-year course at a vocational school where, in addition to the Abitur, the pupil receives a skilled worker certificate.

Three indirect and less popular paths can also lead to higher education. Young workers can prepare for teacher education by enrolling in a one-year course in selected subjects (e.g., mathematics and physics). Qualified skilled workers have the opportunity to take specially designed courses at technical universities and engineering schools. Finally, working people who attend evening classes can eventually obtain a university entrance qualification. The vast majority (90 percent) of GDR students receive the Abitur through the Extended High School or the three-year course at a vocational school. About three-quarters manage to obtain a place of study in a subject of their choice.

Other Admission Requirements

Every GDR citizen in possession of the Abitur has the constitutional right to apply to a university or college. Other admissions criteria include references from the applicant's school and from the party organization to which she or he belongs, in most cases the Free German Youth (FDJ). Prospective applicants are expected to participate actively in the formation of socialist society, to protect the achievements of socialism as stipulated by the SED, to excel academically, and to enter a profession that is relevant to the individual's education and training and the needs of the collective.[1]

Academic Degrees

GDR universities and colleges award three academic degrees. The *Diplom*, the rough equivalent of an American master's degree, requires four to six years of undergraduate study, depending upon the subject. The *doctorate* is awarded to selected graduates who have spent three years in graduate study or served as a graduate assistant for four years, and who have produced and defended a dissertation under the supervision of an advisor. A *doctorate of science* (Dr. sc.) can be earned through the independent writing and defense of a second dissertation, usually after many years of experience and leadership in one's profession. The second Ph.D., which represents the GDR's highest academic degree, is a prerequisite to becoming a university professor.

Curriculum

The curriculum of GDR undergraduates falls into three categories: general education, specialized general education, and area of specialization. The general education courses, which are universal requirements, include Marxism-Leninism (dialectical and historical materialism, political economics, scientific communism, and the history of the Workers' Movement), Russian and one other foreign language, physical education, and military training for men and civil defense courses for women. Economics majors, for example, take 31 percent of their courses in general education, 42 percent in specialized general education (e.g., economic history, economic planning, cybernetics, mathematics), and 27 percent entirely in economics. By contrast, the program of a student enrolled in mechanical engineering consists of 19 percent general education, 47 percent specialized general education (e.g., physics, thermodynamics, law, socialist economics), and 33 percent in the area of specialization.[2] In addition to in-class work, a comprehensive examination, and the final thesis leading to the *Diplom*, students in many subjects gain practical experience through mandatory internships and summer work programs (*Studentensommer*) in industry, agriculture, construction, etc., which are organized by the FDJ.

Historical Trends

A directive issued in 1986 at the Eleventh Party Congress of the SED, outlining the party's expectations and goals for the higher education sector as an integral part of the 1986–1990 Five Year Economic Plan, focused on the acquisition of progressive and socially relevant knowledge and skills combined with thorough political-ideological training rooted in Marxism-Leninism.[3] These themes, which are woven throughout the historical fabric of GDR higher education, can best be illuminated through a general discussion of the three major higher education reforms of 1945/46, 1951, and 1968.

The period from 1945 to 1953 marked the transition from antifascist democratic reform to the creation of the socialist university. Higher education evolved from a set of progressive reforms in 1945/46, which traced their origins to the Weimar Republic, to the total reorganization instituted by the 1951 reforms, most of which bear the stamp of Soviet influence, to the changes implemented in 1968, reflecting the emphasis on academics and economics over ideology.

Unlike the Western zones of Germany, which opted against sweeping reforms and resolved to revive the pre-1933 system, the future GDR made the fateful decision to break with the past and commence the long and arduous process of constructing a socialist society modeled after the Soviet Union, but under distinctly nonrevolutionary circumstances. The GDR's present status as one of the world's leading industrial nations and the strong general identification of the majority of its young people with socialism attest to the ultimate success of the GDR in achieving these goals.

First University Reforms of 1945/46

The First University Reforms were heralded with the resurrection of a number of institutions in the 1945/46 academic year. From October 1945 to February 1946, universities in Berlin (East), Greifswald, Halle, Jena, Leipzig, and Rostock reopened their doors. In pursuit of their immediate goals, the authorities carried out a purge of all faculty members who could be linked to the Nazi party. At the University of Leipzig, for example, 170 out of 222 professors were summarily dismissed.[4] Some universities were forced to temporarily phase out certain faculties due to a shortage of teaching staff. Many members of the intelligentsia who had not been tainted in any way by National Socialism chose to emigrate to the Western zones, perhaps out a sense of foreboding over the imminent Soviet occupation.[5]

The German Administration for Education, a precursor to the Ministry of Higher and Technical Education, acted swiftly to abolish the bourgeois monopoly on education (*Bildungsprivileg*) identified with the stratified society of capitalist Germany. Efforts were made at all levels of the educational system to drastically increase the numerical representation of the heretofore excluded peasant and working classes. In higher education, schools were founded in 1946 to prepare qualified and politically reliable children of industrial workers and small farmers to enter a university. The stated purpose of these preparatory schools, later called Workers' and Peasants' Faculties (*Arbeiter- und Bauernfakultäten*) upon integration into the universities in 1949, was to compensate for the historically disproportionate representation of children from the middle and upper classes. (These institutes were abolished in 1962.) The hidden agenda of this particular reform was to create a new socialist intelligentsia by providing an education to those individuals who would be most politically sympathetic to and supportive of the new order.

As a result of the official elimination of class barriers to higher education, social class became an all-important factor in the university admissions process. Students of working- or peasant-class origins were preferred over those with a "bourgeois" background. (This trend continued until the 1960s, when pressing economic realities necessitated an official change of heart.) In addition, applicants who could prove that they had been victims of Nazi persecution were also given preference. This ideological affirmative action precipitated the mass migration of highly qualified, middle-class young people to universities in the Western zones of Germany. While this reaction surely retarded the economic recovery of the future GDR, it no doubt served also as a de facto homogenization process through which potential sources of opposition and dissent within academia and the larger society diminished. (The recent opening of the Hungarian border contributed to a minor brain drain with the emigration of thousands of well-educated GDR young people to West Germany via Austria.)

At the heart of higher education policy in the years 1945–49 was the preoccupation with the existing intelligentsia and the need to familiarize this special group with Marxist-Leninist ideology. The official documents of this transitional period reveal the growing pains of a nascent totalitarian system torn between the perceived need to win over key actors to its side, to persuade them of the righteousness of its cause, and to proceed in a timely fashion with the building of socialism with or without a broad-based consensus. The ultimate course of action endorsed by the SED led to a total reorganization and further regimentation of higher education. Out of the Second University Reforms of the early 1950s emerged the "socialist university" inspired by the Soviet model.

Second University Reforms of 1951

The Second University Reforms, which institutionalized the political socialization of university students, were consistent with the trend toward the exercise of control over every aspect of the educational system that had begun in earnest with the founding of the GDR. The reforms borrowed heavily from the Soviet Union and mirrored the exigencies of the cold war and, in particular, the intensified ideological struggle with West Germany. In the words of Professor Robert Havemann, who would later become one of the GDR's leading intellectual dissidents, these changes would replace the "principle of planlessness" with the principle of planning.[6]

The SED shifted the responsibility for higher education from the individual provinces (Länder) to the newly created State Secretariat for Higher Education. This change ushered in an era of rapid expansion and linked higher education with the Five Year Economic Plan. Within four years the number of students, including those attending the Workers' and Peasants' Faculties, more than doubled from 27,822 in 1951 to 60,148 in 1955. Aside from the introduction of set courses, a ten-month academic year, and a system of correspondence courses for working people, all based on the Soviet model, the key elements of this major overhaul were the creation of Free German Youth (FDJ) seminar groups, a general course of political/ideological training for all students, and a new program for the most academically talented graduates.

The FDJ study group, still an integral part of the contemporary academic scene in the GDR, was to consist of twenty to thirty students in the same field and the same year. The group was to be led by a FDJ group secretary who would act in a tutorial capacity. This individual, selected on the basis of academic excellence and a record of political activism, was to be an exemplary role model for the other students. The directive that later specifically addressed this innovation stated that the existence of the FDJ study group was a "decisive prerequisite for the education and political socialization [*Erziehung*] of the future intelligentsia into well-trained scholars who will use their capabilities and knowledge in a responsible and enthusiastic manner in the building of socialism in the GDR."[7]

The study groups were viewed as a direct means of extending the control of the SED. By organizing all students into units of twenty to thirty members, it would henceforth be possible to propagate and enforce a code of conduct prescribed by the SED, as well as to combat "antidemocratic" tendencies and root out "oppositional" elements among the student body. It would also enable the party to mete out punishment, when necessary, and to keep a record of the academic progress and political activity of each member of the group, thus ensuring that the majority of students would stay attuned to the policies and goals of the SED. Although academic achievement remained a high priority, the overall success of students would be determined ultimately by their ability to adapt and conform.

The second reform was the introduction of the Soviet-style "Studium Generale" (*Gesellschaftswissenschaften*), a mandatory program of general education courses in the foundations of Marxism-Leninism, political economy, dialectical and historical materialism, physical education, and Russian language and literature. In the courses of study for law, history, and philosophy from this period, these politicized general education courses accounted for 30 percent, 37 percent, and 32 percent, respectively, of the total program.[8] The requirement of such courses was a practical application of the official view that Marxism is the "science of sciences" and is therefore the basis of all political, societal, and intellectual endeavors.[9] From an academic perspective, these courses were intended as a counterweight to specialization.

The third reform, also a feature of Soviet higher education, was the implementation of a special program to train academically talented students (so-called *Aspiranten*, from the Russian) in their third year. This was a measure explicitly designed to contribute to the fulfillment of the Five Year Economic Plan. The best and the brightest were to be trained to take their place as professors and researchers after an additional three or four years of study that culminated in the writing and defense of a dissertation.[10] The short-term rationale for this initiative was the compelling need for "student instructors" who would have sufficient grasp of their subjects to produce and deliver lectures in a variety of courses. The *Aspirantur*, as it was termed, signaled a conscious effort to produce a highly educated and politically reliable elite who would one day replace the remaining bourgeois intellectuals.[11]

Third University Reforms of 1968

In 1965 the GDR Parliament (*Volkskammer*) passed the landmark "Law Concerning the Unified Socialist Education System" which dissolved all institutional barriers to higher education. By expanding educational opportunity for all pupils, regardless of class background, the party was not only attempting to realize its ideological mandate, but was also responding to the spiraling demand for a highly educated and well-trained legion of graduates. The deemphasis of class as a major admissions criterion is evidenced by the inclusion of the *Leistungsprinzip* ("performance principle" in reference to individual academic excellence) in Article 26 of the Constitution of 1968 and the decline in the number of working-class students from 51.4 percent in 1957 to 38.2 percent in 1967. (Since 1967, the government no longer publishes statistics on the social class composition of entering students.)

The demand for a technical intelligentsia is exemplified by a December 1964 speech to the SED Central Committee in which the GDR Minister of Education, Margot Honecker, highlighted the need to increase the number of university graduates with backgrounds in mathematics, the natural sciences, technology, and economics. She noted by way of comparison that 20–35 percent of all employees in the Japanese electronics industry possessed a higher education qualification while in the GDR that figure was closer to 10 percent.[12]

As delineated in the State Secretariat for Higher Education's "Principles for the Further Development of Teaching and Research at the Universities of the German Democratic Republic," later adopted at the Seventh SED Party Congress in 1967, the length of study leading to the first academic degree (*Diplom*) was shortened from five to four years in most subjects and divided into two parts: General education (*Grundstudium*) and major subject study (*Fachstudium*). Of two types of graduate study, specialized study (*Spezialstudium*), was a one-year period of study intended to prepare students for a narrow field of specialization and to shorten the time required for the student to enter his profession. (This reform was later abolished because it failed to adequately address the practical demands of the professions.) The other option, reserved for the more talented students, was research study (*Forschungsstudium*), lasting two to three years, during which the student writes and defends a doctoral dissertation.

The Third University Reforms also mandated major changes in the structure of the GDR university. The traditional German faculties and institutes were abolished and replaced with departments (*Sektionen*) that represented a single discipline or several related subjects. Each university was to be governed by a rector who would provide leadership based on the principle of democratic centralism (i.e., collective consultation and individual leadership). Three advisory bodies were also legislated into existence. The Council of Delegates (*Konzil*) consisted of representatives of various university groups and dealt with general questions relating to the university's mission. The Academic Council (*Wissenschaftlicher Rat*) was concerned with research priorities, the quality of education and training, the development of international cooperation, etc.; it is also endowed with the authority to confer degrees and appoint professors. The Social Council (*Gesellschaftlicher Rat*), the most influential of the three, oversaw the development of the socialist university and was concerned with the sociopolitical tasks of the university and staffing policy. The membership of all these councils was comprised of professors, party members, students, and representatives from industry.

The other noteworthy innovation of the 1968 Reforms was the special atten-

tion paid to the role of individual universities within the production process. In the interests of efficiency, the "profiling" of institutions was mandated to ensure an efficient division of labor. Each university was to invest its time and energies in applied research relevant to the local economy.[13] It was envisaged that a large portion of the funding for this research would be supplied by industry. Indeed, since the 1960s most of the research in the natural sciences, technology, and social sciences has been conducted on a contractual basis through cooperative agreements.

The reforms of 1968 represented a largely successful attempt by the SED to harness higher education for the technological and economic development of the GDR by aligning it more closely with long-term social and economic planning, streamlining the organizational structure, shortening the overall period of study, and more sharply defining the relationship between university research and its practical application in industry. Massive increases in spending during this period paralleled the SED's rhetorical support and legislated reforms, fueling the largest expansion in higher education in the GDR's history. In 1955 there were 42.1 students for every 10,000 GDR residents; by 1971 that figure had jumped to 83.9. In addition, total enrollment rose from 111,591 in 1965 to an unprecedented 143,163 in 1970.

However, the supply of qualified graduates exceeded the demand in many areas of the economy. One student of GDR higher education characterized the Eighth SED Party Congress (1971) as one of "disillusionment, of a sober and pragmatic reflection of its own limitations."[14] As the world entered a period of recession brought about by the oil embargo of 1974, the discourse of expansion shifted to one of consolidation with a view toward efficient management and planning. By 1975 the percentage of full-time students had increased from 70 percent to 76 percent with a decrease in total enrollment. The period of expansion had drawn to a close.

Important Trends and Developments

Differentiation

As a socialist society, the GDR takes pride in its legally sanctioned provision of equal educational opportunity. Therefore, it is not surprising that one of the major debates in higher education has revolved around the issue of equality versus meritocracy. In the GDR context, the principle of uniformity and differentiation means that although all students have the right to a uniform education and training of high quality, the most talented among them will receive special attention. As Kurt Sontheimer observed in his 1975 study of GDR society, "the socio-politically necessary uniformity of the school system on the one hand and the economically justified differentiation on the other shows once again that the GDR is neither a socialist state, set apart from general industrial development, nor an industrial state estranged from socialism."[15]

The selection process at the upper secondary and tertiary levels is intended to ensure that students are representative of the social class structure and gender of the population as a whole, and that they are academically deserving and politically reliable. However, educational authorities and related organizations make a conscious attempt to differentiate, or to "select out" those individuals who are judged to be especially promising. In universities and colleges, professors and the FDJ share the responsibility of recognizing, selecting, and promoting the very best or those who display potential, who are then able to take advantage of options outlined in a 1980 SED Central Committee "Resolution Concerning the Tasks of Universities and Colleges in the Developed Socialist Society."

These options include individually designed courses of study and research, the opportunity to transfer to another university, a double major, internships in the world of work and with other scientific establishments, study abroad, particularly in the Soviet Union and other socialist countries, and early graduation.[16] Selection criteria range from talent for creative scientific work and outstanding achievements in Marxism-Leninism and all other subjects, to political involvement and a variety of personal qualities such as discipline, modesty, and reliability.[17]

Engineering and Economics

A 1983 Politburo resolution laid the groundwork for a thorough reform in the education, training, and continuing education of engineers and economists for the remainder of the decade. To the extent that this measure has brought the education of economists and engineers more into line with the needs of industry and government, it represents a realization of one of the aims of the Third University Reforms of the 1960s. Under the new arrangement, the education of engineers has been raised to university status with a sharp distinction made between the occupations of engineer and technician. The former will henceforth be trained exclusively at an institution of higher education, while the latter will attend a technical college. The two basic tracks in the economics program consist of the following: one line of study trains students to become middle- and upper-level managers and administrators, and another course of study in socialist economics prepares managers to assume middle- and upper-level positions in collectives.

Central Institute of Higher Education

Under the administrative umbrella of the Ministry of Higher and Technical Education, the Central Institute of Higher Education was created in 1982 out of an array of smaller institutes of higher education. The purpose of this consolidation was to inject a greater element of planning and efficiency into higher education research and to ensure a more efficient utilization of research potential. More specifically, the decision to create the Central Institute resulted from the desire to establish a closer link between teaching and learning and research and to "make the links between the initial training of students and the in-service training of graduates more efficient."[18]

The Central Institute conducts and coordinates research on higher education within its own departments and in cooperation with partner institutions in the GDR and in the other socialist states. Research priorities are determined by long-term planning. Within the Central Institute, two related developments merit further attention. Both illustrate the attempt to look beyond the borders of the GDR in search of form and content that can be adapted to the internal needs of the GDR. First, the Central Institute created a department that deals specifically with higher education in other socialist countries and in capitalist industrialized countries and the developing world. Second, the Central Institute serves as a national clearinghouse on higher education research and information. The services it offers range from a computerized database and a special library to specific information aids for educational policymakers and researchers. A set of bibliographical resources, including reports on the development and structure of higher and technical education, and bigger education policies in foreign countries, is also offered.[19]

Distance Education

In the 1980s distance education (*Fernstudium*)[20] has received renewed recognition as an important form of continuing education. Twenty out of fifty-four GDR universities offer distance courses in 130 subjects. This type of higher education is intended primarily for intermediate specialists and qualified skilled workers who possess the university entrance qualification. Individuals enrolled in undergraduate distance education are an average of twenty-eight years old, have been recognized for their outstanding contributions to society and their superior work performance, have completed a course of vocational training in the chosen subject of study, and have several years of professional experience. One-quarter of all GDR university and technical college graduates received their education through distance education. The number of distance education students has been on the rise since 1985.

Subjects that are socially and scientifically relevant such as technical, social science, and economics predominate. The objectives for the first degree (*Diplom*) are identical to those of full-time students. The content differs, however, in that it takes into account the limited amount of study time available and the student's experience in the world of work. The emphasis is on improving the problem-solving capabilities of the students and on practical application. In order to meet the social and economic requirements of the 1980s and 1990s, degree programs in engineering and economics will be granted priority.

Higher Education and Employment

In accordance with the principles of a socialist economy, GDR university students are guaranteed employment upon graduation. Ideally, the nature and type of employment corresponds to the individual's qualifications and educational background. The allocation of university graduates is regulated at the national and local levels. The appropriate ministries (agriculture, industry, etc.) assess their need for university graduates and forward their requests to the Ministry of Higher and Technical Education, which proceeds to classify these requests according to economic areas and courses of study. This data is communicated to the State Planning Commission for inclusion in the Five-Year Plan. Students are notified of their future place of employment one year before graduation, whereupon the respective institution of higher education forwards their files to the employer. A three-year binding contract is then negotiated.[21]

Although this system places severe limitations on a student's freedom of choice, as it is conceived in the capitalist world, it also offers several advantages. First, it circumvents the often difficult transition from higher education to the world of work which is the hallmark of many corporate capitalist economies, eliminating the negative personal (e.g., insecurity) and economic (e.g., underemployment/unemployment) drawbacks inherent in such a system. Second, matching an individual's education and training with specific economic needs is in theory more efficient. It helps to ensure that GDR enterprises and institutions will have an adequate supply of labor.

Higher Education and Industry

In the GDR 90 percent of all scientific and technological research is conducted in combines (*Kombinate*), or large industrial production units. The remaining 10 percent of university research is used to link basic research to production through contracts negotiated between universities and combines. In 1987 there were 227 contracts that regulated such items as the conceptual work, the actual type of research being conducted, staffing, financing, and the provision of research technology for the cooperative partner. Approximately 60 percent of the university research potential in the natural sciences and technology is utilized by industrial and construction combines.

Research shared between institutions of higher education and industrial combines has a decidedly utilitarian bent. Its main purpose is to solve problems of a practical nature, make possible innovations in products, processes, and technologies, and produce research results that will expeditiously yield tangible benefits in order to contribute to the common welfare and the continued development of the GDR economy. But GDR officials have also become aware of the necessity of granting institutions of higher education the freedom of action to systematically pursue long-term basic research as well as exploratory research. At the Eleventh SED Party Congress, held in 1986, the SED general-secretary and GDR head of state, Erich Honecker, exhorted the GDR higher education establishment to focus more on basic research in selected fields, noting that it would be "short-sighted" to neglect this important area.[22]

From 1976 to 1980 the income earned by universities and institutions of higher education from commissioned research on behalf of the national economy rose by 149 percent.[23] This trend paralleled the increasing application of the results of scientific research to production as well as the proliferation of patent applications filed by universities and other research institutions. From 1980 to 1987 the number of patent applications nearly doubled. Given its lack of material and natural resources, and its limited productive capacity, the GDR will have to rely increasingly on the export of technology as a source of foreign trade exchange.

Higher Education and the Political System

For the last three decades the GDR has committed itself to the ideal of international cooperation as a means of furthering social, scientific, and cultural progress through exchange programs and study abroad. During that time the government negotiated treaties and agreements with institutions of higher education in the Soviet Union and other socialist countries, selected Western European nations, international organizations under the umbrella of UNESCO, and nongovernmental organizations such as the International Association of Universities (IAU). GDR universities and colleges presently have relations with over 300 partner institutions in all four corners of the earth.

The GDR's foreign student population, drawn mostly from the continents of Asia, Africa, and South America, accounts for between three and four percent of the total higher education enrollment. After completing a one-year preparatory course at the Herder Institute of Karl Marx University in Leipzig, foreign students enter undergraduate and graduate programs at an appropriate GDR university as fully integrated students with the same privileges and responsibilities as their GDR counterparts.

On a somewhat more modest level, a number of GDR universities and colleges sponsor short summer courses in German language and literature, among other areas, for students, scholars, and working people from socialist and capitalist countries. Such programs offer foreigners a rare and relatively inexpensive opportunity to gain firsthand insights into the official and unofficial workings of GDR society and to become acquainted with GDR citizens, even if the realities of a closed society often make it exceedingly difficult to maintain personal relationships. Since the early 1980s universities in Berlin (East), Halle-Wittenberg, and Jena have sponsored a study abroad program that permits students from capitalist countries to study in the GDR for a semester or a year at minimal cost. As instruments of policy, these programs represent both a contribution to international understanding and cooperation, and a public relations effort with mixed short- and long-term results.

Issues in Academia

Students: Trade-offs

GDR students live a privileged existence, unlike their counterparts in many capitalist countries. As of 1981 all students, regardless of parental income, receive a minimum monthly stipend of 200 GDR marks; additional grants are awarded to students on the basis of academic excellence, political commitment, and military service. Room and board and textbooks are heavily subsidized by the government. However, all of this security comes at a cost: academic and societal demands, as well as the organizational realities of higher education (i.e., scheduling, politicized extracurricular activities, etc.) act as constraints on independent thought and action. Most students respond by adapting themselves to their circumstances and surroundings.

In contrast to other countries, where students have stood at the forefront of movements for social, political, and economic change, students in the GDR have historically kept a rather low profile. For instance, with the exception of theology students, very few students participated in the unofficial peace movement of the 1980s.[24] Those who openly deviate from the party line and protest against perceived injustices within academia or in the larger society face possible disciplinary action or even expulsion. The latter action frequently results in the relegation of the individual to the fringes of society, effectively dashing any hopes the student may have had of pursuing a career in his or her chosen field.

As in other authoritarian societies, opposition, in all of its myriad forms, tends to express itself in subtle ways, often imperceptible to the uninitiated observer. These range from unenthusiastic participation in officially sanctioned activities to retreat into private life. GDR research findings that show that over 90 percent of all students are convinced of the moral superiority of socialism over capitalism must be tempered with the fact that many students publicly embrace the values and norms of Marxism-Leninism and SED policy aims, while reserving for themselves the right to privately disagree. Other students may subscribe to a variation on a theme of Marxism-Leninism, while taking issue with the manner in which the socialism of the GDR has been put into practice.

While most students have accommodated themselves to the constraints of the system, the fact remains that the formal and hidden curriculum of higher education presents them with the opportunity to measure that which they have been taught against the existing social reality, often with quite unexpected results. As Thomas Baylis notes in his study of the GDR's technical intelligentsia, "universities have been principal foci of political skepticism and revisionism and, on occasion, even outright opposition. For most of the young scientific and technical intelligentsia of the GDR, their university years are still those most likely to bring them into contact with such forms of political nonconformity."[25]

Marxist-Leninist Political Training

As a result of the 1951 reforms, Marxist-Leninist political training is a required course of study for all GDR students. These general education courses are defined as a means of helping students come to an understanding of the basic foreign policy goals of the GDR and to contribute to the real-

ization of the economic goals of the SED.[26] Identification with the concerns and aspirations of the working class (i.e., the SED) and the development of socialist moral qualities are consequently measured by the contribution of the GDR's university graduates to scientific, technological, economic, and social progress. In a speech to the Fourteenth Conference for Ministers of Higher Education in the Socialist Countries (1984), the GDR minister of higher and technical education unequivocally stated that the successful pursuit of SED policy goals would hinge upon the continuous improvement of the quality of teaching and the depth of Marxist-Leninist study.[27] Just as political education has been a chronic concern of the SED, it has also been a source of discontent for many students. A common complaint is that too much time is devoted to the study of Marxism-Leninism and other forms of ideological indoctrination at the expense of major subjects.[28]

The Status of Women

As in so many other countries, the gap between rhetoric and reality on the issue of equality for women is sizeable. Although GDR female university students are represented in proportion to their numbers in the general population (in 1987, 50.2 percent) and women comprise over half of the workforce, they are grossly underrepresented at the upper echelons of academia, industry, and government. In a 1985 five-country study of women who teach in universities, which included the GDR and West Germany, Margaret Sutherland discovered that women's minority position in academia is a result of factors common to all five countries: social attitudes, stereotypes, and prejudices.[29] Although women account for approximately 40 percent of all GDR university personnel, only 5 percent are professors and even fewer (2.6 percent) are chancellors, vice-chancellors, and department chairpersons.[30]

Despite the fact that the GDR has made great strides in the provision of equality of opportunity, and certainly compares favorably with other countries, it remains a patriarchal society in which the progressive tenets of socialist ideology are often subordinated to deep-seated attitudes of male dominance that mitigate against the advancement of women. Until societal attitudes and governmental policies concerning the division of labor at home and in the workplace change, women will continue to face formidable obstacles in the struggle for equality.

Conclusions

The GDR will continue to rely on higher education to make significant contributions to the further development of socialist society through the pursuit of a long-term plan for qualitative improvement rather than quantitative expansion.[31] One of the key elements of this ongoing process of reform is the notion of flexibility *as it relates to the status of the students.* According to official pronouncements, the role of the student of the 1990s and beyond will be transformed from that of a subordinate to a colleague who will play a more active role in the production and dissemination of knowledge as an important means of realizing his or her intellectual potential, becoming more receptive to innovations, and being able to react to changing conditions. The broader goal is to strengthen the relationship between higher education and society and, conversely, to narrow the gap between theory and practice by allowing students to apply their knowledge and skills in a practical setting.

The current and future trends of GDR higher education are indicative of the country's transition from an advanced industrial to a postindustrial society. First, the GDR intends to pursue policies that increase the flexibility of higher education and better enable it to respond to rapid changes in science and technology. These include modernization of the content, the integration of basic and specialized training as well as methodology, the development of independent student research, and continued differentiation of study corresponding to the differing talents, inclinations, and interests of students. Second, universities and colleges will become places of further and continuing education that build upon professional qualifications and skills and provide opportunities for lifelong learning. Third, it is hoped that the "profiling" of individual institutions and their integration into the regional and national network of scientific research institutions will ensure greater efficiency. Finally, the GDR plans to equip its universities and colleges with the most modern facilities and laboratories, especially in the areas of computer science and communications technology.[32]

In the final analysis, the long-term economic and political success of the GDR will depend in large measure upon the technical and behavioral quality and sophistication of its professional elite. The manner in which the GDR comes to terms with the internationally convergent social and economic challenges of postindustrialism will undoubtedly reflect its unique political and cultural context. With its reliance upon the principle of democratic centralism as the cornerstone of its system of higher educational policy, planning, and administration, and its stated commitment to a technicization and rationalization of intellectual work, the GDR might well come to typify one manifestation of the postindustrial society.[33]

Notes

1 Geoffrey J. Giles, "The Structure of Higher Education in the German Democratic Republic," *Higher Education* 7 (May 1978): 145.

2. Akademie der Pädagogischen Wissenschaften der DDR. *Das Bildungswesen der Deutschen Demokratischen Republik*, 2nd ed. (East Berlin: Volk und Wissen Volkseigener Verlag, 1983), 167.

3. "Zielstellungen im Hoch- und Fachschulwesen bis 1990," *Das Hochschulwesen* 34 (June 1986): 139.

4. Edwin Schwertner, *Zur Wissenschafts- und Hochschulpolitik der SED: 1945/46 –1966* (East Berlin: Dietz Verlag, 1967), 21.

5. Ernst Richert, "*Sozialistische Universität*": *Die Hochschulpolitik der SED* (West Berlin: Colloquium Verlag. 1967), 12.

6. Marianne Müller and Egon Erwin Müller, ". . . *stürmt die Festung Wissenschaft!*" *Die Sowjetisierung der mitteldeutschen Universitäten seit 1945* (West Berlin: Colloquium Verlag. 1953), 212.

7. Siegfried Baske and Martha Engelbert, *Zwei Jahrzehnte Bildungspolitik in der Sowjetzone Deutschlands: Dokumente 1. Teil 1—1945–1958* (West Berlin: Osteuropa-Institut, 1966), 221.

8. Paul Bodenman, *Education in the Soviet Zone of Germany* (Washington, D.C.: U.S. Office of Education, 1959), 88.

9. Kurt Sontheimer, *Die DDR: Politik. Gesellschaft und Wirtschaft* (Hamburg: Hoffmann und Campe, 1972), 179.

10. Baske and Engelbert, *Zwei Jahrzehnte Bildungspolitik*, 201.

11. Richert, "*Sozialistische Universitat*," 85.

12. Margot Honecker, *Zur Bildungspolitik und Pädagogik in der Deutschen Demokratischen Republik* (East Berlin: Volk und Wissen Volkseigener Verlag, 1986), 43.

13. John Page, "Education Under the Honeckers," in *Honecker's Germany*, ed. David Childs (London: Allen and Unwin, 1985), 56.

14. Gabriele Husner, *Studenten und Studium in der DDR* (Cologne: Verlag Wissenschaft und Politik, 1985), 13.

15 Kurt Sontheimer and Wilhelm Bleek, *The Government and Politics of East Germany* (London: Hutchinson, 1975), 132.

16 Sozialistische Einheitspartei Deutschlands, *Beschlüße und Erklärungen des Zentralkomitees Sowie Seines Politbüros und Seines Sekretariats: 1980–81,* vol. 18 (East Berlin: Dietz Verlag, 1982), 40.

17. Husner, *Studenten und Studium,* 74.

18. Hans-Joachim Richter, "Present Trends in Research in Higher Education in the German Democratic Republic," *Higher Education in Europe* 12 (January–March 1987): 95.

19. Richter, "Present Trends," 99–100.

20 Horst Möhle, "Higher Education and Postgraduate Studies in the GDR Organized as Distance Education," *Higher Education in Europe* 8 (July–September 1983): 26–33.

21. Bundesministerium für Innerdeutsche Beziehungen, DDR *Handbuch,* 3d ed. (Cologne: Verlag Wissenschaft und Politik, 1985), 1390.

22. Hans-Joachim Böhme, "Aufgaben und Erfahrungen bei der Vervollkommnung der Hochschulbildung mit ihren Entwicklungsperspektiven in den 90er Jahren," *Das Hochschulwesen* 37 (March 1989): 81.

23. H. Irmer and B. Wilms, "New Forms of Cooperation for Research in the German Democratic Republic between Higher Education and Industry," *Higher Education in Europe* 9 (October–December 1984): 36.

24. Husner, *Studenten und Studium,* 109.

25. Thomas A. Baylis, *The Technical Intelligentsia and the East German Elite* (Berkeley and Los Angeles: University of California Press, 1974), 59.

26. Fritz Göhring and Michael Brie, "Die Weiterentwicklung des marxistisch-leninistischen Grundlagenstudiums (MLG) an den Universitäten und Hochschulen der DDR nach dem XI. Parteitag der SED," *Deutsche Zeitschrift für Philosophie* 35, no. 4 (1987): 289–90.

27. Hans-Joachim Böhme, "Die Aufgaben der Hochschulen bei der Ausbildung und politisch-ideologischen Erziehung der Studenten und des wissenschaftlichen Nachwuchses," *Das Hochschulwesen* 32 (December 1984): 317.

28. David Childs, *East Germany to the 1990s: Can It Resist Glasnost?* (London: Economist Intelligence Unit, 1987), 40.

29. Margaret B. Sutherland, "The Situation of Women Who Teach in Universities: Contrasts and Common Ground," *Comparative Education* 21, no. 1 (1985): 24.

30. Radtke, Heidrun, "Frauen in Leitungsfunktionen der Wissenschaft," *Einheit* (October 1988): 980. Quoted in "Ergebnisse und weitere Aufgaben bei der Entwicklung und Förderung von Frauen zu Hochschullehrern," *Das Hochschulwesen* 37 (February 1989): 65.

31. Hans-Joachim Böhme, "Aufgaben und Erfahrungen bei der Vervollkommnung der Hochschulbildung mit ihren Entwicklungsperspektiven in den 90er Jahren," *Das Hochschulwesen* 37 (March 1989): 77.

32. Hans-Jürgen Schulz, "Auf dem Wege in das 21. Jahrhundert," *Das Hochschulwesen* 36 (April 1988): 99.

33. Daniel Bell, *The Coming of Post-Industrial Society* (New York: Basic Books, 1973), 12–45.

German Federal Republic

Jens Naumann and Beate Krais

✦

Broad Parameters of the System

Higher education in the Federal Republic of Germany consists of two classes of institutions. At the end of the 1980s there were about 120 universities, including twenty-nine arts academies, and also about 120 polytechnic colleges. The university stratum comprises the traditional universities and technical universities, sixteen theological seminaries, eight teachers colleges for the training of primary school teachers, seven comprehensive universities offering study courses at the university level as well as at the polytechnic college level, and the two universities for the armed forces (at Munich and Hamburg). Included among the polytechnic colleges are twenty-four internal polytechnic colleges of the state administration where state officials are trained. Access to these colleges, as well as to the universities of the armed forces, is limited to state officials or to officers, respectively.

Whereas the relative numbers might suggest a structural balance of the two types of higher education institutions, universities clearly form the upper stratum and polytechnic colleges the lower one.

The state plays a strong role in higher education. Virtually all universities are state universities. Only a small minority of polytechnic colleges are private, mainly church-affiliated, institutions (e.g., colleges for the social work professions). Whether private or not, all universities and polytechnic colleges are state-controlled and state-financed. Charges for tuition and fees, already moderate in the 1950s and 1960s, were further reduced to a symbolic enrollment fee in the early 1970s. Government supervision of polytechnic colleges extends to both administrative and subject/curricular matters but is restricted to the juridical supervision of academic self-governance of university-level institutions.

Given the authority and responsibility regarding cultural affairs of the individual states constituting the Federal Republic, "state" in matters of higher education usually does not refer to the federal government and the parliament in Bonn, but to the governments and parliaments of the eleven states (*Länder*). Staff at universities and polytechnic colleges are civil servants of the eleven state governments. Some 95 percent of total higher education expenditures are financed by the states, with the rest contributed by the federal government; the federal contribution is mainly earmarked for construction, research support, and student aid.[1]

Beside the parliaments of the eleven Länder, four major nationwide coordinating bodies contribute to higher educational policy debates. The Permanent Conference of the State Ministers of Culture (since 1945), with no participation from the federal government, requires unanimity for decisions implemented at the Länder level. The Federal and States Commission on Educational Planning and Research Support (since 1970) mediates, on the administrative level, the limited federal involvement possible after a constitutional amendment passed in 1969. The Science Council (since 1957) closely and effectively monitors the development of higher education through its statistical service, cooperatively develops expansion and restructuring plans, and provides inputs to the general public debate about higher education policies. Finally, the West German Conference of Rectors is the organized lobby of heads of universities vis-à-vis state administrations and the public.[2] The rectors of polytechnic colleges constitute a special Conference of Rectors of Polytechnic Colleges, but their influence lags far behind the influence of their university colleagues.

The university—with its old traditions and with the high social status accorded its graduates—still constitutes the core and, at the same time, the dominant model of higher education. Universities continue to be marked by the traditional values of "academic freedom" and "unity of research and teaching," which, inter alia, translate into a long and, in many cases, scarcely structured course of study. Of course, structuring varies over the different academic disciplines, ranging from such well-ordered disciplines as medicine and engineering with their tightly filled timetables to such loose disciplines as sociology, languages, or history. In the latter cases, academic freedom means the student's freedom to draw up his or her own course of studies and pursue it—perhaps at more than one university—as he or she sees fit, deciding for himself or herself when he or she is ready to be examined, and who the examiners will be. So far, no equivalent to undergraduate studies, so common in the United States, has emerged in any of the academic disciplines; the average length of university studies has reached almost eight years.[3]

Polytechnic colleges are recent institutions, dating from the early 1970s, but already well established today. Due to the historical roots of the polytechnic colleges in engineering and other higher vocational schools, which were deliberately transformed and upgraded to create a lower stratum of higher education, most of them are—in sharp contrast to the universities—unidisciplinary institutions (e.g., colleges

for the engineering professions, for administrative professions, for social work professions, or for business). The most important, quantitatively, are the technical colleges, which account for some 60 percent of the student body in the polytechnic colleges. The colleges for training in social work professions, the business schools, and the colleges for administrative professions account for another 20 percent of students. Polytechnic colleges are on average smaller than universities. Most of them vary in size between 1,000 to 10,000 students, while most universities range from about 20,000 to 40,000 students—the University of Munich, with 60,000 students, is the largest university.[4] The course of studies at polytechnic colleges is comparatively well structured, with an actual average length of about four years. Typically, the academic staff of the polytechnic colleges does not enjoy full academic privileges: teaching loads are twice as heavy as in universities (as a rule sixteen hours per week); research is not a formal, protected, and supported part of the staff role; advanced academic degrees cannot be conferred; academic self-government is limited. The degrees obtained at polytechnic colleges do give the right to continue university studies in corresponding fields, with some credits granted for courses in the introductory phase.

Students of the two strata of higher education differ in various socially relevant aspects. The student body of universities is more heterogeneous in social backgrounds, but at the same time includes a lower ratio of students coming from working-class families.[5] Ten percent of first-year students at universities are working class, but 19 percent of polytechnic students are working class. But for both types of institutions this ratio, as a rough measure for the social selectivity of institutions, has varied considerably over the past two decades. Enrollments of first-year students from working-class families in higher education rose up to 15 percent at universities and up to 28 percent at polytechnic colleges by the mid-1970s, when both the labor market and general political and social circumstances were favorable to higher education, but dropped again subsequently.

Polytechnic colleges are more "male-dominated" than universities: at polytechnic colleges the student body is 71 percent male and at universities the student body is 59 percent male. One has to bear in mind, however, the different kinds of academic disciplines offered by the two types of institutions, and the still different disciplinary preferences of female and male students. For example, disciplines traditionally chosen by women, such as teacher training studies, are found exclusively at the university level. And disciplines traditionally avoided by women, such as engineering studies, represent the majority of the student body at polytechnic colleges, but only 12 percent of the students at universities.

In educational background students of polytechnic colleges and universities differ less than could be expected in view of entrance regulations.[6] The Abitur certificate, first introduced in Prussia at the end of the eighteenth century, still provides the necessary and, as a rule, sufficient entrance qualification for university studies. After nine years of attendance at Gymnasium—thirteen years of schooling as a whole—and a successful Abitur examination the pupils of the Gymnasium obtain the so-called general qualification for university study. This gives the right to study any subject offered at any institution of higher education, no matter which type of Gymnasium the pupil had attended or which specialization he or she had pursued during the last three years of Gymnasium. And although the range of choices for pupils at the upper level of the Gymnasium has widened during the last decades, the Abitur certificate still is meant to be "qualitatively standardized" (without resorting to standardized achievement testing nor to nationwide homogeneous examinations).

There are two alternative paths to university studies. First, some states have a tradition of Fachgymnasien, which are specialized in fields such as the technical sciences and economics, and certify their graduates for admission to specific courses of study at universities. Second, certain institutions exist to prepare adults for university studies, either in evening courses or in special secondary schools. As these institutions follow essentially the educational program of the Gymnasium, including the Abitur examination, their graduates are entitled to pursue any course of university study. Both these alternatives to the traditional Gymnasium play but a minor role: the overwhelming majority of university students (85 percent of all German students in their first year at university at the end of the 1980s) come from the Gymnasium.

Access to polytechnic colleges becomes possible by completing ten years of general education and then continuing to the specialized technical secondary school. The specialized technical secondary school comprises the eleventh and twelfth grades and offers an educational program with a strong vocational orientation. Due to the historical roots of polytechnic colleges in the former engineering schools, which required previous vocational training for admission, many students complete a course of vocational training before entering a specialized technical secondary school or pursue part-time schooling simultaneously with vocational training. At the end of the 1980s about 60 percent of first-year students at polytechnic colleges had completed a course of vocational training before beginning their polytechnic studies. But many students of polytechnic colleges do not follow the special educational path that was set up for them. About 45 percent of them come with the Abitur certificate from a Gymnasium or Fachgymnasium.[7]

The general entrance requirements for polytechnic colleges also apply to students of internal state administration colleges;

these students also have to meet the requirements for state officials, as they acquire that status while matriculating at college. During their studies they are paid a salary that is actually about one-third higher than the maximum grant of the public student aid program.

The average age at obtaining the first university degree has climbed to above twenty-eight years; it is above twenty-six years for graduates from polytechnic colleges. Thus German graduates are, on the average, older than their peers in other nations. They tend to be older already at the time when they begin their studies. The average school-entrance age is seven; university-bound students complete a minimum of thirteen years of secondary schooling; and all young men have to serve in the armed forces. And, as already mentioned, students at polytechnic colleges often complete vocational training, mostly in the form of apprenticeships lasting three to four years, before going to the polytechnic college. And 20 percent of university students also complete some kind of vocational training before entering the university. In fact, university graduates are often about thirty by the time they enter the labor market. Graduates from the classical academic disciplines such as medicine, teaching, and law, after having obtained their first university degree, have to pass a so-called second phase of training that lasts between eighteen and twenty-four months in their future field of professional activity, with a second, state-controlled examination at the end of this phase, before they offically finish their studies. In some other cases, chemists, for example, a second university degree, the doctorate, is virtually required to obtain a job.[8]

Certain features associated with the social life of students and academics in Anglo-Saxon settings—campus universities with integrated residential areas for staff and students—never found parallels in post-World War II German universities,

even some twenty or thirty years ago when universities were still much smaller. As of 1986, some 10 percent of students lived in dormitories, slightly over 30 percent lived with their parents, almost 40 percent lived off-campus in private apartments, about 15 percent lived in (private) housing collectives, and about 5 percent lived in rented rooms.[9] Nevertheless, the existence of a substantial student population has always visibly influenced the sociocultural and political life of the cities where universities are located.

Historical Trends

The German university as it is known today has its origin in the social and political crisis of the late eighteenth and early nineteenth centuries. The French Revolution and the Napoleonic wars severely unsettled the monarchistic German states, confronting them with the problem of reorganizing and modernizing the institutional setting and administration of the state, and at the same time with strong pressures for abolishing feudal privileges. Prussia, which gradually emerged as the leading state among the multitude of separate kingdoms and fiefdoms on German soil, assigned a central position in this transformation process to higher education.[10] Due to the then influential ideas of reformists such as Wilhelm von Humboldt, universities began to be thought of as institutions that might guarantee appropriate selection procedures as well as education for high administrative functions. Yet, in order to fulfill these demands the university still had to find its modern character; this happened first at the new university of Berlin (1810), which subsequently served as a reference and model for the path-breaking reform conception of Wilhelm von Humboldt, a Junker from Tegel to the north of the Prussian capital.[11]

Within an aristocratic environment and in the face of an absolutist regime, von Humboldt argued for the university as a harbor of freedom and independence from state and church, yet still fully sustained by the aristocratic state. Furthermore, he interpreted higher education as an integral part of the general education system, in principle open to everybody, regardless of his estate or origin.

In actual fact, the extension of access to and the expansion of secondary schooling and higher education remained extremely limited (but was not smaller than in other Western countries). By 1880 higher education attendance had slowly reached 1 percent of a birth group. It reached about 2.5 percent for those born between 1900 and 1915 (graduating between 1925 and 1940). For those born between 1915 and 1930 (graduating between 1930 and 1960) attendance reached an average of a little over 3 percent per birth group. Parallel to this slow process of expansion was the growth of the higher education participation of, mainly, upper and middle bourgeois and of middle and lower civil servant strata, besides the heavy overrepresentation of students from the landed aristocracy, the military establishment, and high civil servants.[12] Only since 1908 have women had access to university studies.

In the last third of the nineteenth century the growth to prominence of the natural and engineering sciences stimulated formation of higher level technical schools. Today, the former technical "high schools" have acquired full university status, regardless of whether they are named "university" or "high school," and offer, in addition to engineering studies, a wide range of studies in various academic disciplines. This evolution of the higher-level technical schools may be regarded as an example of a pertinent feature of German higher education. Professional schools begun as separate institutions, specializing in one or a few neighboring disciplines, in the manner of the French "grandes écoles," in Germany, unlike in France, gradually became integrated in the university system, either by growing into

a university or by being incorporated into existing universities. The same thing happened with new disciplines, whether the economic disciplines prominent in the first decades of this century or informatics today. The transformation of the former higher vocational and engineering schools into polytechnic colleges (around 1970) and their inclusion into the academic system, if only as lower-class members, and the process of upgrading teachers colleges and including them in universities, together with a strong push for institutionalization of the social sciences in the upper and in the lower class, probably mark the major structural transformation of the German academic system after World War II. In fact, the university that originated in Humboldt's concept continues to provide the model par excellence for higher education institutions, despite its well-developed inner differentiation.

In 1911 the Kaiser Wilhelm Society was founded as a state-financed association of independent research institutes in the natural sciences (to be continued, after 1948, as the Max Planck Society for the Advancement of the Sciences). For a long time this research society remained the only institution in the German system of higher education and research that was established on the *national* level. Throughout the nineteenth century the multitude of separate kingdoms and fiefdoms on German soil—which are the historical source of the constitutionally guaranteed educational federalism in the German Federal Republic—continued to exist; only after the establishment of the Second Reich (1871) under the leadership of Prussia and its capital, Berlin, did a political and cultural center emerge. Both the Second Reich and the Weimar Republic (1918–33) maintained the educational autonomy of their constituent parts—often referred to up until the 1950s as different German tribes. The pronounced political and ideological centralization during the fascist Third Reich (1933–45) led, as a response, in the three zones occupied by the Western Allies to the conscious effort to continue the basically federalist structure of the Weimar Republic in the Federal Republic of Germany (since 1949). The impetus for a federal structure was reinforced by the socialist centralism practiced in the Soviet Eastern zone (mainly consisting of the heartland of Prussia) which became the German Democratic Republic in 1949.

From about 1890 to 1945 German academics in general, and the professorial class in particular, were held to be unusually conservative and nationalistic.[13] Whether this was really the case up to the Third Reich is hard to say, due to the lack of valid international comparisons. Although possibly true in relation to the United States, doubts concerning this idea are justified when comparing Germany to other European countries. After all, neither the social class basis, nor the dominating ideologies (rising nationalism, strong remnants of monarchism, rising organistic/racist social theories, and relatively weak republican and socialist leanings) were different in Germany. There can be no doubt, however, that the majority of German academics had strong conservative leanings and did not—after World War I—support the republic but instead, either directly or indirectly, the rising National-Socialist tide.

Even before the beginning of World War II, the impact of fascism on higher education was traumatic.[14] Between the winter semester of 1931/32 and that of 1938/39 more than 3,100 academic staff, some 40 percent of the total, were forced to give up their positions (and emigrate) because of their Jewish background and/or political leanings. The number of students dropped from a high of 138,000 in 1931 to 57,000 in 1939. At the same time, tightening political and ideological control forced the universities into line with the political system in those few cases when they did not cooperate fullheartedly. This fact, though widely negated and belittled in the West

German public and higher education system, was finally admitted after the student unrest of 1968.

In 1937 Germany had twenty-four universities and fourteen technical schools at the university level, the majority of which were located in the territory of the later German Federal Republic. Higher education, in the first decade of the Federal Republic, consisted of sixteen universities and nine higher-level technical schools, about eighty teachers colleges, sixteen theological seminaries, and twenty-six art academies. As a reaction to the challenge of educational reform and expansion in the German Democratic Republic, and as a response to the educational interventions of the Western Allies in the years preceding the establishment of the Federal Republic of Germany, the first decade after World War II was essentially marked by a lack of reforms and overall structural stability in the effort to link up with the educational traditions of the Weimar Republic.

In the early 1960s, in close connection with the international debate on higher education, the forces of reform and expansion gathered momentum, rallying around the banners of modernization and expansion to face economic challenges and improve chances for the lower social strata and women as a civil right. In the decade of the 1960s it was common—and fully justified—to point out that the Federal Republic of Germany was far behind a number of Western and socialist industrial countries in terms of the openness of advanced secondary and higher education.[15] The response of the German public was immediate, enhanced and permitted by burgeoning building and staffing programs of the eleven Länder and the federal government, especially between 1965 and 1975 (see Figure 1 for the development over time of the enrollment rates for beginners in the major forms of secondary schools and first-year students in the two forms of tertiary education).

Figure 1

Enrollment Rates in Secondary and Tertiary Education
1960 – 1987

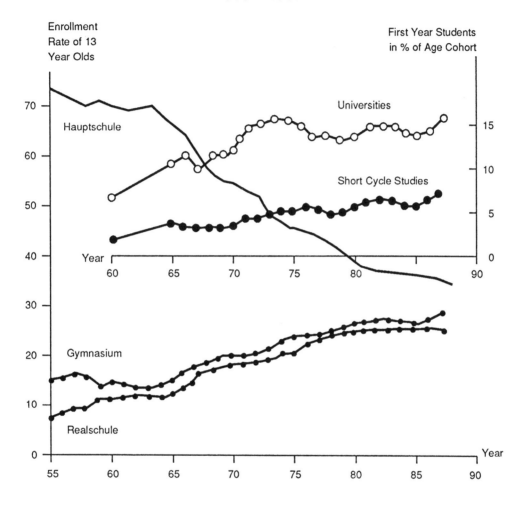

After 1975—in the wake of the oil price shocks, world economic turmoil, and rising unemployment—the drive for expansion of higher education slowed down somewhat. In fact, the pattern of the percentage of first-year students in universities (somewhat less so in polytechnic colleges) mirrors the impact of the economic crises following 1973 and in the early 1980s. It should be pointed out that since the end of the 1960s the number of secondary school graduates qualified to pursue tertiary education began to be substantially higher than those actually beginning higher studies. Thus, surveys of school graduates show that the propensity to continue studies declines from about 90 percent of those qualified around 1970 to somewhat less than 60 percent in 1985, with a noticeable upswing in the most recent years.[16]

While primary schools began to feel the slackening of the demographic demand component—and eventually its sudden and permanent drop—after 1973, the Realschule and the Gymnasium continued to grow rapidly—because of the rising attendance rates—until the early 1980s, when they were hit by the dramatic decrease in the size of their clientele age-cohorts. As a consequence, the total number of teachers grew rapidly for more than a decade until 1975, reached a peak in 1980, and then began to decline, demonstrating a swift and lasting downturn in the demand for young teachers after the middle of the 1970s.[17]

With a time lag, the same demographic dynamic reached higher education, with moderately growing cohorts of the average entrance age during the decade 1965 to 1975 and rapidly rising cohorts for the following decade. Thus, in spite of the overall stability of the age-specific percentage of first-year students, their absolute number grew consistently until 1983. This meant a continued increase in the absolute size of the student population, expected to reach its peak only in the early 1990s.

Figure 2

Students in Higher Education and 18 Year Old Resident Population in the FRG 1965–2010

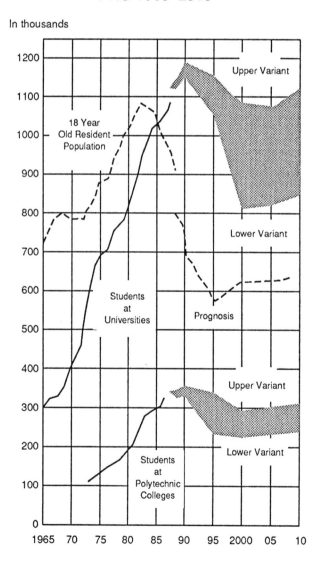

In thousands

Flashpoints of Crisis and Controversy

Tremendous growth in the absolute number of students (see Figure 2) necessitated the introduction of centralized administrative measures to channel and curb excess demand for study places; these measures included republicwide allotment of the limited number of study places on the basis of average Abitur marks, special tests, waiting lists for those courses of study, like medicine, that suffered from a particularly high overdemand, and geographic redistribution of students to enable balanced utilization of the available capacities in the (changing) subsets of subjects experiencing a milder excess demand.

In 1977, after about two years of heated public debate, the prime ministers of the eleven Länder of the Federal Republic of Germany decided to keep the system of higher education wide open in spite of the foreseeable rapid decline of public sector demand for graduates to assure—albeit at a reduced level—a reasonable opportunity to study for the exceptionally large cohorts of prospective students expected until the end of the 1980s. In the background of this decision loomed, of course, the old controversy about the relative merits of elite versus mass education in the German educational system. The decision to continue on the path of mass education was, in a sense, politically and ideologically facilitated by the official proclamation and recognition, since 1970, of the upper and the lower class of higher education institutions.[18] Still, the general political consensus held that the overall long-term capacity of higher education should be kept constant at about the level reached by the mid-1970s, implying that the strains of growing overcrowding should be faced by accepting heavy overloads for about a decade to come and, at best, by short-term relief measures (see Figure 3 for the development of scientific staff positions).

This limited support for a policy of "keeping the system open" was accentuated in a restrictive manner once the Christian-Liberal coalition took over the federal government from the Social-Democratic-Liberal coalition in 1982/83. In a general sense, this change of government symbolized the overall public reassessment

Figure 3

Scientific Staff Positions at Universities and Polytechnic Colleges in the FRG 1960–1988

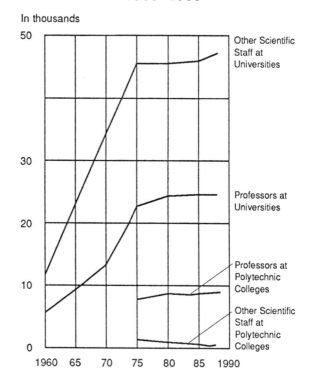

of priorities and needs—with education as one of the losers. More specifically, it meant continued low-key federal support for building and investment measures in higher education but a substantial cut in the public financial support scheme for students. In terms of space and equipment available and academic and nonacademic services rendered per student, these developments led, until now (1989), to a bare maintenance, if not a net deterioration, of the rather poor standards reached in the late 1970s.[19] Not surprisingly then, the first drop, after more than twenty years, in the absolute number of first-year students, in 1984, was hailed by the government as the first light at the end of the long tunnel of coping with the demographic mountain of excess demand. Yet, mainly because of the response-lag in the system, the total number of students continued to grow and exerted increased pressure. Finally, student unrest all over the country shattered hopes of a smooth transition to the slope of rapidly decreasing demand in the 1990s. The government response consisted of rather swift—but still insufficient—provision of some additional resources to ease the last few years of extraordinary demographic pressure. But the conference of state ministers of finance maintained—even at the end of 1989—their old position of refusing to increase tertiary-level training capacities beyond the mark of 800,000 places reached in the early 1980s. Opposition circles claiming the need for—in the extreme— 40,000 additional posts for scientific personnel have not yet made a substantial public inroad beyond the sphere of the higher education scene.

As a corollary to dynamic growth in absolute student numbers a variety of issues and controversies arose. We shall address the external issues, relating to the wider economy and the sociopolitical system, first, and then cover the internal problems of differentiation and policy.

Higher Education and Employment

Throughout the last century and up to the 1960s in this century, university graduates formed part of the thin social stratum occupying elite positions in German society. Typically, and consistent with the social functions assigned to a "modern," transformed university in the historical context of the early nineteenth century, the state official in high positions became the model after which the German *Akademiker* as a social type was patterned— not, as in the United States, the self-employed professional (e.g., doctor or lawyer).[20] University graduates in the nineteenth century became judges, high-ranking

state officials, professors, priests in the (Protestant) established church, and teachers at the Gymnasium. Of course, there were also doctors, lawyers, and, at the end of the century, engineers, chemists, and other scientists, who were to be found in the growing industry, but these professional groups did not have, at the time, the modeling power of the state-employed academic groups. Two circumstances should be kept in mind: Germany was, relatively, a latecomer among the industrialized nations, and throughout the nineteenth century participation in political power even for the bourgeoisie was basically limited to participation in the bureaucracy of the monarchic state.

The privileged socioeconomic situation of university graduates over the last 150 years did not, however, translate into a situation of stability over the whole period: crises of oversupply have been a recurring phenomenon in the history of higher education.[21] Therefore, when it became apparent in the middle of the 1970s that the current expansion of higher education would reach unprecedented dimensions, catastrophic visions of the academic labor market and fears of an emerging "academic proletariat" were reborn. It should be noted that the number of higher education graduates per year—from both universities and polytechnic colleges—has risen steadily during the last twenty years, from about 55,000 in 1965 to 139,000 in 1987, and will continue to rise, following actual previsions, up until the mid-1990s.[22] Severe employment problems for higher education graduates appeared to be inevitable, so much the more as overall unemployment in the Federal Republic of Germany clearly rose during the 1970s to reach the so far highest unemployment rate of 9.3 percent in 1985.[23]

In fact, unemployment has become a serious problem for graduates from universities and polytechnic colleges. Their unemployment rate is about 5 percent (i.e., about 140,000 graduates) at the end of the

Table 1

Unemployed Higher Education Graduates by Fields of Study, 1975, 1985, and 1988

Type of Institutions/ Field of Study	1975 Persons	1985 Persons	1988 Persons	1988 in Percent
Universities				
Teaching	2,623	28,954	29,092	20.9
Economics, Business Administration, and Social Sciences	3,525	11,189	13,622	9.8
Humanities	614	7,480	10,374	7.5
Engineering	2,960	7,373	8,048	5.8
Medicine, Pharmacy	907	5,702	10,665	7.7
Law	1,349	3,224	4,490	3.2
Chemistry, Physics, Mathematics	1,058	3,032	3,782	2.7
Others	2,455	14,630	19,251	13.9
Total Universities	15,491	81,584	99,324	71.5
Polytechnic Colleges				
Engineering	8,261	13,189	12,559	9.0
Social Work	923	9,860	10,650	7.7
Fine Arts	1,505	3,423	3,004	2.2
Economics, Business Administration, and Social Sciences	1,676	2,256	2,832	2.0
Others	2,552	7,223	10,500	7.6
Total Polytechnics	14,917	35,951	39,545	28.5
Grand Total	30,408	117,535	138,869	100.0

Source: *Amtliche Nachrichten der Bundesanstalt für Arbeit* (January 1976, March 1986, March 1988).

1980s, with a slightly lower rate for polytechnic colleges graduates than for university graduates. Although lower than unemployment rates for the unskilled (18 percent) or even for skilled workers (7 percent), unemployment among higher education graduates has been rising since the end of the 1970s, even at times when unemployment for skilled workers decreased. Between 1975 and 1985 unemployment among higher education graduates rose by a factor of four, while it only doubled for the active population as a whole.[24]

Apart from global trends, unemployment among higher education graduates presents no clear features over time. Graduates from different academic disciplines are affected differently and at different times. In 1975, when the oil-price shock and world economic turmoil weighed heavily on the Federal Republic's economy, 37 percent of all unemployed academics were engineers. Ten years later, the absolute number of unemployed engineers had multiplied by 16, but they made up for no more than 16 percent of the whole group of unemployed academics (see Table 1). From the early 1980s on, the most serious problem has been teacher unemployment, especially for new entrants into the labor market. At the end of the 1980s even medical doctors, an otherwise well-protected professional group, were struck by unemployment.

Typically, unemployment in the academic segment of the labor market affects different social groups differently. First, unemployment clearly is more frequent among the younger generation (i.e., among people having just finished their courses of studies and applying for a first job) than among the older ones. This, however, is not valid in the same way for all disciplines: whereas, in 1988, about 90 percent of all unemployed teachers were younger than forty, only half of the unemployed engineers were in this age group. In general, the higher the percentage of graduates of a discipline employed in private enterprise, the less unemployment is a problem for newcomers to the labor market. Whatever the discipline may be, however, to get out of unemployment is more difficult (i.e., takes a longer time) for academics

Table 2

Employment by Sector of Economic Activity, 1976 and 1987

	1976			1987			Changes from 1976 to 1987		
	Total In Thousands	Higher Education Graduates Ratio[1] (%)		Total In Thousands	Higher Education Graduates Ratio[1] (%)		Total In Thousands	Higher Education Graduates Ratio[1] (%)	
1. Agriculture and Forestry	1,682	10.3	0.6	1,185	22.4	1.9	-497	+12.1	+1.3
2. Energy and Mining	507	27.0	5.3	219	34.5	6.6	+12	+7.4	+1.3
3. Manufacturing	8,915	294.8	3.3	8,790	499.4	5.7	-125	+204.6	+2.4
4. Building	1,974	58.1	2.9	1,772	70.6	4.0	-202	+12.5	+1.1
5. Commerce	3,365	84.2	2.5	3,355	133.3	4.0	-10	+49.1	+1.5
6. Postal Service, Railways	878	26.9	3.1	810	43.5	5.4	-68	+16.6	+2.3
7. Other Transport	584	12.5	2.1	730	32.9	4.5	+146	+20.4	+2.4
8. Banking, Insurance	767	34.1	4.4	979	75.3	7.7	+212	+41.2	+3.3
9. Hotels, Catering, Cleaning	1,104	11.4	1.0	1,621	39.8	2.5	+508	+28.4	+1.5
10. Sci., Ed., Media, Sports	1,158	623.5	53.8	1,584	814.7	51.4	+426	+191.2	-2.4
11. Health Services	1,033	187.5	18.2	1,471	246.2	16.7	+438	+58.7	-1.5
12. Consulting, Other Srv.	677	123.0	18.2	1,050	243.8	23.2	+373	+120.8	+5.0
13. Non-Profit Organizations	394	70.4	17.9	487	107.1	22.0	+93	+36.7	+4.1
14. Public Admin., Social Sec.	2,492	242.3	9.7	2,720	418.6	15.4	+228	+176.3	+5.7
Total	25,530	1,806.0	7.1	27,073	2,782.3	10.3	+1,543	+976.3	+3.2
—of which Primary and Secondary Sector (Sum of Rows 1 to 7)	17,905	513.8	2.9	17,161	836.6	4.9	-744	+322.8	+2.0
—of which Services[2] (Sum of Rows 8 to 14)	7,625	1,292.2	16.9	9,912	1945.5	19.6	+2,278	+653.3	+3.0

[1] Higher education ratio: Economically active persons holding a degree from a university or polytechnic college in percent of the labor force of an economic sector.

[2] The sum of economically active persons in the various service sectors is the same as in the GNP accounting, the distribution among the individual sectors follows the structure of micro-census results.

Source: Special analysis of the micro-census 1987, *Jeschek/de la Chevallerie 1988*, p. 131.

over forty than it is for their younger colleagues.[25]

Second, unemployment among the highly educated, just as is the case for all other levels of education, affects, above all, women. One reason for this situation is gender-specific disciplinary preferences: women are more often engaged in those courses of studies that actually show the highest unemployment rates (teaching professions, humanities). But a closer look at the statistics reveals high unemployment rates for women in all disciplines. At the end of the 1980s, almost two-thirds of all unemployed female graduates had graduated from the humanities (including teaching), but in these disciplines the unemployment rate for women was only 1.6 times higher than that of males. Differences in unemployment rates of men and women were most pronounced in those disciplines with the lowest overall unemployment: engineering and business studies had unemployment rates for women of 12 percent and 6 percent, respectively, but those for men were only 3 percent and 2 percent, respectively.[26] Women are not only much more affected by unemployment, they also have to struggle harder to get a first job. Thus, the virtual closure of the public sector labor market at the end of the 1970s struck female graduates much harder than their male colleagues because this segment of the labor market—with the important exceptions of the male-dominated health services and the academic sector—in contrast to the private sector, had provided relatively equal opportunities for women.

However, any assessment of the employment situation of the highly educated that focuses exclusively on the unemployment issue would be not only incomplete but also misleading. The remarkable expansion in higher education during the 1970s and 1980s has translated into an expansion of graduates' employment that is no less remarkable. In 1970, just 1.5 million of the total labor force (5.7 percent) had obtained their professional training at universities or engineering schools; six years later the highly educated accounted for 7.1 percent of the total labor force; and in 1987 they accounted for 10.3 percent of the labor force (see Table 2). This growth in graduate employment between 1970 and 1987 corresponds to an 85 percent increase in seventeen years, in a period of general labor market contraction or stagnation. Whereas during the 1970s higher education graduates found employment mainly in the public sector, thus following traditional patterns of academics' employment in Germany, from the early 1980s on the private sector has absorbed graduates from universities and polytechnic colleges in hitherto unseen quantities: more than half of the increase of about 1 million gainfully employed higher education graduates between 1976 and 1987 found employment in the private sector. Certainly, the public sector still is the most important employer of the highly educated at the end of the 1980s, but the private sector has almost reached the same proportion for the overall stock of graduate employees, and has even surpassed the public sector in its importance for new entrants into the labor market. The impact of this continuing structural change on industrial innovation and productivity, or on the professional roles of graduates, remains, so far, unclear, as empirical research on these issues is only beginning.

As to the socioeconomic situation of academics in the Federal Republic of Germany today, it may be stated that they undoubtedly still form part of the upper 20 percent-stratum of this society, with the highest incomes and the highest social status. Unfortunately, income information is one of the most guarded secrets in the Federal Republic. The income data collected in Table 3 may serve to give a rather general view of income differences between graduates and other social groups, and between graduates of different social status or from different disciplines.

More than half of the graduate labor force is to be found in positions whose focus is on technical competence and professional skills as, for example, teachers and medical doctors in the public services and technical experts in industry. About 14 percent of the highly educated occupy positions that emphasize power and management, and another 14 percent are self-employed.[27]

A historical trend in the social situation of the highly educated is not clearly evident, as the data base is both poor and inconsistent over time. Referring to a "new class," consisting mainly of higher education graduates,[28] remains ambiguous and possibly misleading in the sense that the differentiation of the social anchoring of graduates has even increased over time. No longer does higher education lead almost automatically to positions of power in the public and in the private sectors. Positions focusing on technical competence and professional skills (but with a lack of corresponding authority aspects) are typical for the majority of academics, and increasingly represent the only perspective for an entire working life, for more and more graduates. Furthermore, during the last decade, many graduates from universities or polytechnic colleges have taken over jobs formerly held by people from lower educational levels. Usually, these substitution processes have resulted in a clear upgrading of working tasks and a modest raise of salary. From an overall perspective, the minimum income level of graduates has dropped, and entrance into the labor market has become more difficult. But these changes cannot be characterized, so far, as anything close to a "breakdown" of the labor market or a total disruption of social

Table 3

Yearly Gross Income of Economically Active Persons by Profession and Employment Status, 1983

Profession/Sector	Self-Employed[1]		Employees[2]	
	Persons	DM	Persons	DM
Services	—	181,547	—	—
Manufacturing Firms	—	161,238	—	—
Medical Doctors	55,789	179,592	70,000	ca. 67,000
Public Accountants	942	177,455	—	—
Lawyers/Judges	23,000	135,983	16,000	ca. 67,000
Architects	28,605	90,698	—	—
Engineers	10,670	84,098	—	—
Teachers	—	—	467,000	ca. 57,000
Memo Item: Skilled Industrial Worker (Male)	—	—	—	35,000

1 Average income, computed on the basis of income-tax statistics.
2 Income refers to the modal remuneration category of the public service sector for the respective professional groups; yearly income of a married employee/civil servant, 40 years old with one child.

Sources: Einkommenslage und -entwicklung der freien Beruf. Deutsches Institut für Wirtschaftforschung, Wochenbericht 55, 22, 287–294 (1988); Statistisches Bundesamt, Fachserie 14, Reihe 6: Personal des öffenthchen Dienstes 1983; and relevant remuneration schedules of the public sector.

standards concerning graduate employment. The correspondence between competences acquired and defined by education and working tasks, an issue of high importance in the debate, has been preserved. The lowering of standards concerning income and stability of employment has been, on the whole, modest, limited by regulations, and, most important, confined to specific fields. Moreover, traditional domains of graduate employment—power positions in the private as well as in the public sector—have remained completely unaffected by labor market troubles. A university degree has become more than ever before in German society a precondition for access to such positions.[29]

The political system of the Federal Republic of Germany in the 1950s was "traditional-democratic" in the sense that the party system and the forms of political participation and mobilization were predominantly structured along religious and social class lines and rather hierarchically organized.[30] More specifically, the voting behavior and political involvement of graduates—a small minority of not more than 3 percent of the population older than forty at the time and not more than 5 percent of those between twenty and forty—also clearly followed the traditional pattern. A strong majority was oriented toward the great Christian parties located in the middle and to the right of the center of the political spectrum, while a minority leaning toward the small, centrist Liberal Party was actually stronger than that voting for and active in the parties of the left (mainly the Social Democrats). The 1960s and 1970s were a time of transition, during which the consequences of the post-World War II educational upgrading of society and the replacement processes of the pertinent generations have led to the "modern-democratic" structures of the 1980s and beyond.

The student unrest of 1968 can be interpreted as a forerunner of the rising tide of "new social movements" of the late 1970s and early 1980s. The establishment of the Greens as a fairly successful political party can be interpreted as the consolidation of "new" patterns of political involvement and participation by the highly educated.

The 1970s witnessed the emergence of so-called new social movements focusing on peace and disarmament, atomic energy, and ecology, human rights, and third world issues. For a number of years these movements stood outside of and even against the mainstream, including even the leftist mainstream of political parties and trade unions. Due to the fact that the element of proportionality (with a 5 percent hurdle) is decisive in the voting system of the Federal Republic of Germany, originally diffuse currents that represented the "new politics" coalesced and managed to establish themselves in the course of the 1980s, as did the Green party, mainly at the expense of the traditional left, the Social Democratic Party (see Table 4).

Empirical evidence exists to suggest that, hidden underneath the surface of changed party preferences, the traditional cleavages continue to have a major, and surprisingly stable, impact on voting "right" or "left."[31] But to emphasize this overall structural stability would certainly not do justice to the topical, dogmatic-ideological, and stylistic innovations brought to German political life by the well-educated "new-politics generations." The better education of the younger generations has enlarged the small pool of people who value highly individualism and independence, yet who are committed to and sensitive to a wide range of public issues and instrumentally capable of creating and participating in (political) associations.[32] Irrespective of the fate of the Greens as a party, their (potential) voters and their activists will continue to be a discernible force to be reckoned with in the public discussions and in the processes of interest and commitment accommodation.

Issues of Internal Differentiation

Until the 1970s, higher education was almost synonymous with "universities," and universities were considered to be more or less equal in quality and standards. The institutional history of higher education may even be described, for a long period, as one of reducing institutional differences, mainly by widening the range of disciplines and study courses offered by institutions that originally had been founded as specialized "high schools," such as university-level technical schools or the medical academy of Düsseldorf. When, in the mid-1960s, the debate about the need to build up a mass higher education system was opened, the structural differentiation of higher education was one of the options to be adopted. Nevertheless, equalizing trends within the university sector was never ruled out completely.

The most evident line of differentiation, introduced by establishing the polytechnic colleges, has already been mentioned, as well as the main characteristics of this new type of higher education institution. The establishment of polytechnic colleges had important consequences, as it introduced a new principle into higher education: the recognition of demands coming from the social world outside the higher education sector. Whereas universities traditionally have functioned on the principle of science production and communication (and continue to do so), and on these grounds have acquired a status of autonomy toward the outside social world, polytechnic colleges are related more directly to "external" needs and to developments in the economic and professional structures. Their legitimation consists of responding quickly to externally formulated demands regarding certain professional qualifications.

But the university sector has also become more diversified. During the 1970s new universities were founded, former teachers colleges were transformed into universities, and a university working by correspondence courses (at Hagen), and comprehensive universities were established. The comprehensive university was to merge different levels and types of higher education into one institution. Its proponents hoped that this new model of higher education institution with its greater internal differentiation would allow for the cre-

Table 4

Political Preferences by Educational Background and Age Group, 1987 (in Percent)

First Preference	Total	Younger than 35			Older than 35			
		Basic Secondary	Realschule	Abitur (incl. higher)	Basic Secondary without Apprenticeship	Basic Secondary with Apprenticeship	Realschule	Abitur (incl. higher)
CDU-CSU	44.4	34.1	37.0	20.9	47.3	47.3	57.3	55.0
SPD	37.3	42.3	30.2	27.4	41.8	44.8	27.7	22.4
FDP	6.5	6.5	8.5	6.5	4.0	4.2	7.5	21.8
The Greens	9.2	13.9	20.9	45.2	0.9	2.3	5.4	0.8
Others	2.6	3.2	3.4	0.0	5.9	1.4	2.1	0.0
	100.0	100.0	100.0	100.0	100.0	100.0	100.0	100.0
Total (N)	1,043.0	130.0	119.0	78.0	179.0	329.0	157.0	51.0

Source: Forschungsgruppe Wahlen e.V., Mannheim, ZDF-Politbarometer, January 1987, Frage 7.

ation of a link between the research orientation of the universities and the vocational/professional orientation of nonuniversity institutions of higher education, and enable better utilization of resources and a more feasible transfer between courses of study. This concept, though it met with wide support around 1970, finally lost its persuasive power, and gave way to the institutional division between universities and polytechnic colleges. The revised Framework Act for Higher Education of 1985 considers comprehensive universities as an exception; but seven still exist and offer study courses leading either to a university or a polytechnic college degree.[33]

Many of the new universities opted for a special profile. The universities of Konstanz and Bielefeld, for example, accentuated a strong research orientation and the social sciences (including law, in the case of Konstanz, and mathematics, at Bielefeld). The university of Bremen emphasized interdisciplinary study courses and the community of students and teaching staff. Often, the new universities opened with a relatively small range of disciplines, mostly prestructured by the institution that had served as the point of departure for the new university, be it a teachers college, as in most cases, or the hospitals of the armed forces at Ulm, which formed the nucleus for the medical university. In general, the new universities focused on the humanities and the social sciences, rather than on the natural sciences with their costly requirements in modern technology.[34] Thus, the vogue of new foundations clearly was a step toward more diversification within the university sector.

But it would be misleading to read the history of German universities during the last twenty years only in the perspective of increasing differentiation. Institutional differences that were relatively marked just after the foundation have consequently been leveled out, to a certain degree, by the mere force of student masses, but also

by political decisions concerning such things as examination regulations (which were used to narrow the range of curricular experiments) and new appointments of teaching staff. At the same time, the dominant principle of the university system (i.e., science production and communication) and the subsequent emphasis on disciplinary differentiation also worked in the direction of leveling out institutional differences, because in the German setting it is quite normal for a university to have a number of strong or relatively strong departments along with some weaker ones.

But formal institutional diversification is not the only dimension of differentiation in higher education. Another one—and a controversial issue—is the quality of research and teaching at universities. A few years ago the Science Council responded to fears that the expansion of the tertiary sector in the preceding two decades had produced pressures toward dedifferentiation and a corresponding decrease in the quality of academic teaching and research. The response was a recommendation on the strengthening of academic competition in the upper tier of the system,[35] which clearly accepted the American pattern as a normative reference of academic modernity.

The council stressed that the forces of tradition and recent political pressures for democratization had produced a public higher education regime largely in accordance with the ideology of institutional equality, and forms of bureaucratic personnel and resource management inconsistent with individual independence and responsibility, the prerequisites for the search for efficiency and excellence at different organizational levels. A strengthening of individual responsibility and competitiveness—so the council argued—would eventually:

○ On the level of students and study organization, reduce study lengths and improve standards

○ On the level of scientific staff and departments, improve efficiency and productivity in teaching and research

○ Raise the overall efficiency and (international research) competitiveness of the whole system

A recent set of studies has tried to illuminate some of the basic assumptions of the competition debate, focusing on the issue of the existence and acceptance of qualitative institutional differentiation—now supposedly inexistent or insufficient—in the fields of physics, economics and business administration, sociology, political science, and education.[36]

Policy Issues

In late 1988 governments and universities were confronted with a completely unexpected wave of student unrest throughout the Federal Republic. Independent of—but parallel to—these events, the Science Council published a voluminous report assessing a wide array of dimensions of the development of higher education and university-based research.[37] The Science Council report is couched in technical terms, but it points out many of the problems that were raised by the students' protests and furnishes, to a large extent, the data basis for it. It does not at all reflect the blood, sweat, and tears of the ongoing decision-making and political debate. Read as what it is meant to be, a common meeting ground on a very abstract technical level, it conveys a general impression of some major issues animating the "real debate." We will, therefore, in our account of policy issues concerning higher education and the related field of research rely mainly on this report.

The net public expenditures for the tertiary sector decreased in real terms by some 2 percent between 1975 and 1986, mainly due to substantial cuts in the federal government's support for two major student aid programs, the construction of

facilities and student housing. On the other hand, federal support for university-based research increased in real terms. Expenditures for the tertiary level as a percentage of the GNP decreased slightly since 1975 and as a percentage of total public budgets since 1980 both at the federal and the state level. These overall expenditure trends signify drastic reductions in investments (in 1987 about 46 percent of the [highest] 1974 level), especially in construction, whereas the share of technical equipment increased strongly. Current expenditures in real terms decreased since 1980 by some percentage points, and per student expenditures dropped dramatically. The volume of competitively awarded research funds increased in real terms by almost 30 percent between 1975 and 1985. These dry figures translate into the worst living and studying conditions students have faced since the immediate postwar period. Not surprisingly, then, their protest focused on these two problems: living and studying conditions.

Public programs for student housing were cut back radically at the end of the 1970s; during the 1980s the housing shortage has become more and more of a problem, especially in the big cities and most especially in the university cities. The public student aid plan (B*afög*) which, in the early 1980s, had been changed from a subsidy system to a loan system, offered financial support at a relatively low level. Thus, in 1988, just 23 percent of all students obtained a loan from the public student aid program (other forms of student aid such as scholarships from firms or foundations traditionally play a marginal role, with only 2–3 percent of students getting such a scholarship). Overall, the financial volume of Bafög loans made up just one-eighth of the whole sum of students' living expenses in that year, while they had covered one-fourth of expenses in 1982. Employment was the only or the main source of funds for 46 percent of all university students—the highest percentage since 1956, when the first survey of the social situation of students was made.[38] This figure may be read as indicating nothing more than the lower social selectivity of higher education. But it has to be stated that just because of the greater social heterogeneity of the student population, the restructuring and economizing of the public student aid scheme had immediate, drastic consequences. The percentage of students from working-class families has dropped markedly, almost to the level of the period before higher education expansion. Moreover, if the social background of the so-called education renouncers (i.e., graduates from the Gymnasium who either choose to go to a polytechnic college—despite their Abitur certificate—or renounce higher education completely) is examined, it is shown that students from working-class families are overrepresented, and the same is true for women.[39] Thus, the issue of social inequality in access to higher education, which was one of the main issues of the reform debate in the 1960s, is again on the political agenda.

The Science Council's report from 1988 pointed out the financial difficulties of students and called for an increase in per capita support and a gearing of the repayment and bonus structure to time-efficient studies and examinations. A law redressing some of these shortcomings enters into force in 1990.

The decrease in public expenditure for higher education over the past decade translates, as far as general conditions are concerned, into overcrowded universities and polytechnic colleges, poorly equipped libraries, a shabby exterior and interior for many buildings, especially those constructed in the early 1970s, and, most visible for students, too few and overburdened teaching staff. The Science Council, elaborating the lack of growth and even drops in the numbers of jobs for scientific personnel since 1975, despite ever-growing student numbers, stresses the point that the expected demographically induced decrease in student numbers should not be interpreted as an opportunity to cut down personnel capacities proportionately, but, rather, to maintain them in order to be able to return to the quality level of the mid-1970s in research, in the teaching of first-degree courses, graduate training, and the services rendered to the communities and society. The poor operating conditions of the system in the 1980s, politically accepted as a transitory phase some fifteen years ago, should not become the plausible norm of the 1990s and beyond. It should be noted that the council's argument is based on the assumption of very low numbers of (beginning) students, old assumptions of the statisticians of the Standing Conference of the Ministers of Culture, substantially revised in an upward direction in 1989 (and used for Figure 2). As has been mentioned already, as of late 1989 the federal and state governments still seem unwilling to substantially increase higher education resources.

Length of studies is another issue that has been discussed repeatedly over the past fifteen years.[40] The issue was first raised as a means of relieving the overstrained capacities of universities and polytechnic colleges by a substantial reduction in length of studies. More recently, facing the consolidated European market in 1992, some concerned observers have argued that the long duration of studies in the Federal Republic and the corresponding relatively high age of graduates will handicap German graduates in international labor markets. The Science Council, in its assessment of the performance of the higher education system, discusses the trend toward longer studies—as well as the rising drop-out rate (now about 20–30 percent)—as one of the major problems of higher education in the Federal Republic. It is characterized as partly due to conditions of overcrowding, inadequate financial aid, and the poor labor market, and partly due to institutional mismanagement in terms of course organization and unduly long and difficult examination procedures (especially for diploma theses). The council calls for target length of studies of "4 years plus," and suggests that the law on higher education statistics concerning final examinations be changed to include not only the marks (and the distribution of marks awarded to a graduating group from a particular institution), but also the length of time required to graduate as an essential criterion to assess both the individual student's performance and the performance of institutions and their departments. The council also criticizes the recent innovation of formalized "programs of graduate studies"—which exist alongside the diffuse and loosely structured traditional German forms of individual preparation for the Ph.D.—for having been established "on top" of unreformed, unduly lengthy diploma studies. In the future, formalized graduate programs should only be institutionalized if institutional proof of the existence of time-efficient basic diploma studies is available.

Many issues in the current debate can be seen as variations on a more general theme: improvement of the efficiency of higher education and university-based research. During the ten years from 1965 to 1975 the problem of efficiency was dealt with (or hidden) mainly under the heading of a more explicit commitment of higher education to society—that is, was presented in terms of adequate forms of public control over universities, of decision-making structures inside universities, and between universities and government agencies, etc.—but in the 1980s the problem of improving the performance of the higher education system is seen to hinge on strengthening the competition between institutions. Ideas and instruments that have been suggested as means to increase competitiveness focus mainly on the research aspect of higher education; these solutions imply that the problem concerns, above all, universities, and only to a lesser degree polytechnic colleges or the competition between them and the universities. Thus, for example, the debate on the repu-

tation and productivity of professors and university departments (mentioned above) focuses on research criteria but ignores other aspects of higher education, including efficient organization of study courses, teaching success, and the like. In the same way, the emphasis on research financing during the last decade was on competitive project financing (instead of basic budget financing), to guarantee more flexibility, competitiveness, and, finally, efficiency of public resources utilization.

The proportion of research performed by the higher education sector has decreased from above 18 percent in 1975 to 13 percent in the late 1980s, reflecting, essentially, a disproportionate growth of research and development performed and financed by industry. The Science Council warned that cuts in funding for scientific and technological research damaged the infrastructure built up during the 1960s and early 1970s and endangered the international competitive position of the Federal Republic of Germany. It called for substantial reductions in spending in the field of medical clinical facilities and training (suggesting that clinics should increase their own revenues by charging public health insurance for their medical services), underlined the urgent need for the modernization and expansion of the technical research infrastructure in all fields, and expressed doubts that the states will be able to meet the financial requirements of the decade to come. As a consequence, the Federal Government is called upon to partially redirect its growing research and development support to the tertiary sector and to use its constitutional possibilities and responsibilities to participate substantively in strengthening the training and research capacities of the tertiary level.

In its report on the perspectives for higher education in the 1990s, the Science Council also tackles the problem of more competition in the field of academic teaching and studies. The Science Council suggests that the current practice of central, republicwide allocation of scarce study places reformed so that the individual polytechnic colleges and universities can decide locally about the size of and the criteria for enrollments as demographic pressures ease in the next few years. In late 1989 this suggestion is meeting strong resistance from state legislatures that fear local imbalances caused by students' pronounced preference either for institutions close to their place of origin or to university cities with their animated culture and student life.

Notes

1. See Horst Weishaupt, Manfred Weiß, Hasso von Recum, and Rüdiger Haug, *Perspektiven des Bildungswesens der Bundesrepublik Deutschland. Rahmen- bedingungen, Problemlagen, Lösungsstrategien.* (Baden-Baden, West Germany: Nomos, 1988), 102–21. For basic statistical information, see Bundesminister für Bildung und Wissenschaft, ed., *Grund- und Strukturdaten 1988/89* (Bad Honnef, West Germany: Bock, 1988).

2. See Max Planck Institute for Human Development and Education, *Between Elite and Mass Education: Education in the Federal Republic of Germany* (Albany, N.Y.: State University of New York Press, 1983), chapter 3.

3. See Wissenschaftsrat, *Empfehlungen zur Struktur des Studiums* (Cologne: Wissenschaftsrat, 1986).

4. See Statistisches Bundesamt, *Fachserie 11: Bildung und Kultur. Reihe 4.1, Studenten an Hochschulen. Sommersemester 1989. Vorbericht* (Stuttgart: Metzler-Poeschel, 1989).

5. For the following information, see Bundesminister für Bildung und Wissenschaft, *Grund- und Strukturdaten 1988/89* (Bad Honnef, West Germany: Bock, 1988). It must be mentioned, however, that in recent years the percentage of nonrespondents to the question concerning social origin has risen to almost 20 percent. Yet, the general trend of a marked decrease in higher education enrollment by students with a working-class background is confirmed by other sources, such as Bundesminister für Bildung und Wissenschaft, ed., *Das soziale Bild der Studentenschaft in der Bundesrepublik Deutschland. 12. Sozialerhebung des Deutschen Studentenwerkes* (Bad Honnef, West Germany: Bock, 1989).

6. For an overview of entrance regulations, see Christoph Führ, *Schulen und Hochschulen in der Bundesrepublik Deutschland* (Bonn: Inter Nations, 1988), 112–20, 133–40, 157 f.

7. See Karl Lewin and Martin Schacher, *Studienanfänger im Wintersemester 1988/89—Trend zum Studium hält weiter an-* (Hannover, West Germany: HIS GmbH 1989), 20, 46 ff., 71–78.

8. See Wissenschaftsrat, *Empfehlungen zur Struktur des Studiums* (Cologne: Wissenschaftsrat, 1986); and Dirk Hartung and Beate Krais, "Studium und Beruf in der Bundesrepublik Deutschland," in *Das Hochschulwesen in der Bundesrepublik Deutschland,* ed. Ulrich Teichler (Weinheim, West Germany: Deutscher Studien Verlag, 1990).

9. For the socioeconomic situation and living conditions of students, see the regular reports (Sozialerhebungen) of the Deutsches Studentenwerk; the most recent one is Bundesminister für Bildung und Wissenschaft, ed., *Das soziale Bild der Studentenschaft in der Bundesrepublik Deutschland. 12. Sozialerhebung des Deutschen Studentenwerkes* (Bad Honnef, West Germany: Bock, 1989).

10. See Ludwig von Friedeburg, "Bildung als Instrument etatistischer Gesellschaftsorganisation. Notizen zur Geschichte des deutschen Bildungssystems," *Zeitschrift für Sozialisationsforschung und Erziehungssoziologie* 6 (April 1986): 173–91.

11. See Daniel Fallon, *The German University: A Heroic Ideal in Conflict with the Modern World* (Boulder, Colo.: Colorado Associated University Press, 1980), 5–36.

12. Based on census data.

13. See Konrad H. Jarausch, *Students, Society, and Politics in Imperial Germany: The Rise of Academic Illiberalism.* Princeton: Princeton University Press, 1982.

14. See Dietrich Goldschmidt, "Hochschulpolitik," in *Die Geschichte der Bundesrepublik Deutschland,* ed., Wolfgang Benz (Frankfurt on Main, West Germany: Fischer, 1989), 354–89, and Hartmut Titze, "Hochschulen," in *Handbuch der deutschen Bildungsgeschichte, Vol. 5: 1918–1945, Die Weimarer Republik und die nationalsozialistische Diktatur,* ed. Dieter Langewiesche and Heinz-Elmar Tenorth (Munich, West Germany: C. H. Beck, 1989), 209–40.

15. See Max Planck Institute, *Between Elite and Mass Education,* chapter 2.

16. See Hochschul-Informations-System-GmbH (Hannover), *HIS-Ergebnis-Spiegel 1987* (Hannover, West Germany: HIS GmbH, 1987), 40 ff.; and Karl Lewin and Martin Schacher, *Studienanfänger im Wintersemester 1988/89—Trend zum Studium hält weiter an—* (Hannover, West Germany: HIS GmbH, 1989).

17. See Bundesminister für Bildung und Wissenschaft, ed., *Grund- und Strukturdaten*, various issues.

18. See Max Planck Institute, *Between Elite and Mass Education*, chapter 2.

19. See Wissenschaftsrat, *Empfehlungen des Wissenschaftsrates zu den Perspektiven der Hochschulen in den 90er Jahren* (Cologne: Wissenschaftsrat, 1988); and Claudius Gellert, "The Limitations of Open Access to Higher Education in the Federal Republic of Germany," *Higher Education Policy* 2 (1989): 32–34.

20. See Werner Conze and Jürgen Kocka, eds., *Bildungsbürgertum im 19. Jahr-hundert. Teil 1: Bildungssystem und Professionalisierung in internationalen Vergleichen* (Stuttgart: Klett-Cotta, 1985), and Hannes Siegrist, ed., *Bürgerliche Berufe. Zur Sozialgeschichte der freien und akademischen Berufe im internationalen Verzgleich* (Göttingen: Vandenhoek und Ruprecht, 1988).

21. See Walter M. Kotschnig, *Unemployment in the Learned Professions: An International Study of Occupational and Educational Planning* (London: Oxford University Press, 1937; re. ed. 1977); and Hartmut Titze, "The Cyclical Overproduction of Graduates in Germany in the Nineteenth and Twentieth Centuries," *International Sociology* 2 (December 1987): 349–71.

22. See Wissenschaftsrat, *Zur Lage der Hochschulen Anfang der achtziger Jahre. Quantitative Entwicklung und Ausstattung. Statistischer Anhang* (Cologne: Wissenschaftsrat, 1983), 85–95; and Statistisches Bundesamt, *Fachserie 11: Bildunz und Kultur. Reihe 4.2, Prüfungen an Hochschulen 1975, 1980, 1987* (Stuttgart: Metzler-Poeschel, 1975, 1980, 1987).

23. See *Amtliche Nachrichten der Bundesanstalt für Arbeit* (1988): 726. For an overall view of unemployment and education in the Federal Republic of Germany, see Manfred Tessaring, "Arbeitslosigkeit, Beschäftigung und Qualifikation. Ein Aus- und Rückblick," *Mitteilungen aus der Arbeitsmarkt- und Berufsforschung* 21 (1988): 177–93; for the university graduates labour market, see Martin Baethge, Dirk Hartung, Rudolf Husemann, and Ulrich Teichler, *Studium und Beruf. Neue Perspektiven für die Beschäftigung von Hochschulabsolventen - Denkanstöße für eine offensive Hochschul- und Beschäftigungspolitik* (Freiburg: Dreisam, 1986).

24. See *Amtliche Nachrichten der Bundesanstalt für Arbeit* (1988): 739–46.

25. See *Amtliche Nachrichten der Bundesanstalt für Arbeit* (1988): 390 ff.

26. See Dirk Hartung and Beate Krais, "Studium und Beruf in der Bundesrepublik Deutschland," in *Das Hochschulwesen in der Bundes-republik Deutschland*, ed. Ulrich Teichler (Weinheim: Deutscher Studien Verlag, 1990).

27. Ibid.

28. Discussed by Alvin Gouldner, in *The Future of Intellectuals and the Rise of the New Class. A Frame of Reference, Theses, Conjectures, Arguments, and an Historical Perspective on the Role of Intellectuals and Intelligentsia in the International Class Contest of the Modern Era* (New York: Seabury Press, 1979).

29. For the general trend in the relation between social background, education, and status in the Federal Republic, see Karl Ulrich Mayer and Hans-Peter Blossfeld, "Die gesellschaftliche Konstruktion sozialer Ungleichheit," ed. Peter A. Berger and Stefan Hradil, *Ende der Schichtungssoziologie*. Sonderband 7 der *Sozialen Welt*, forthcoming; for elite groups, see Ursula Hoffmann-Lange, "Aufstiegsbedingungen in die Eliten," in *Kreativität und Leistung. Wege und Irrwege der Selbstverwirklichung*, ed. Konrad Adam, 229–36 (Cologne: Hanns-Martin-Schleyer-Stiftung, 1986).

30. See Wilhelm Bürklin, *Wählerverhalten und Wertewandel* (Opladen: Leske and Budrich, 1988).

31. See Lutz-R. Reuter, *West German Social Democrats in Transition: Shifts in Agendas and Their Effects Upon Party Ideology and Strategy*. Beiträge aus dem Fachbereich Pädagogik der Universität der Bundeswehr Hamburg (Hamburg: Universität der Bundeswehr, 1988).

32. Heinz-Ulrich Kohr, Hans-Georg Räder, and Ralf Zoll, "Soziales und politisches Engagement in der Bevölkerung," *Politische Vierteljahresschrift* 22 (1981): 210–29.

33. See Ulrich Teichler, *Changing Patterns of the Higher Education System: The Experience of Three Decades* (London: Jessica Kingly, 1988), chapters 3 and 5.

34. See Christoph Oehler, *Hochschulentwicklung in der Bundesrepublik Deutschland seit 1945* (New York: Campus, 1989), 87–110.

35. Wissenschaftsrat, *Empfehlungen zum Wettbewerb im deutschen Hochschul-system* (Cologne: Wissenschaftsrat, 1985).

36. Jürgen Baumert, Jens Naumann, and Peter Martin Roeder, "Reputation—A Hard-Currency Medium of Interchange. A Structural Equation Approach," *Scientometrics* 15 (1989); Jens Naumann, Jürgen Baumert, Peter Martin Roeder, and Luitgard Trommer: "Leistungshierarchien, Reputationsdif-ferenzen und Fachkulturen," in *Leistungshierarchien, Reputationsdifferenzen und Fachkulturen*, ed. Michael Buttgereit (Frankfurt on Main, West Germany: Campus, 1990); Jürgen Baumert and Peter Martin Roeder, "Expansion und Wandel der Pädagogik. Zur Institutionalisierung einer Referenzdisziplin," *Zeit-schrift für empirische*

Pädagogik 3 (1989), Beiheft; Peter Martin Roeder, Jürgen Baumert, Jens Naumann, and Luitgard Trommer, "Institutionelle Bedingungen wissenschaftlicher Produktivität," Hans-Dieter Daniel and Rudolf Fisch, eds., *Evaluation von Forschung* (Konstanz: Universitätsverlag Konstanz, 1988), 457–94.

37. See Wissenschaftsrat, *Empfehlungen des Wissenschaftsrates zu den Perspektiven der Hochschulen in den 90er Jahren* (Cologne: Wissenschaftsrat, 1988).

38. See Bundesminister für Bildung und Wissenschaft, ed., *Das soziale Bild der Studentenschaft in der Bundesrepublik Deutschland. 12. Sozialerhebung des Deutschen Studentenwerkes* (Bad Honnef: Bock, 1989).

39. See Wolfgang Böttcher, Heinz Günter Holtappels, and Ernst Rösner, *Wer kann sich Studieren noch leisten? Die Wende in der staatlichen Ausbildungsfinan- zierung und ihre sozialen Folgen* (Munich 8: Juventa, 1988); Hochschul-Informations-System-GmbH (Hannover): HIS-*Ergebnis-Spiegel* 1987 (Hannover: HIS GmbH, 1987), 46–65; Karl Lewin and Martin Schacher, *Studienanfänger im Wintersemester 1988/89 - Trend zum Studium hält weiter an -* (Hannover: HIS GmbH, 1989), 71 ff.

40. See *Studienzeiten auf dem Prüfstand. Dokumentation des HIS-Colloquiums am 18. und 19. Mai 1988 im Wissenschaftszentrum Bonn-Bad Godesberg* (Hannover: HIS GmbH, 1989).

◆

Hungary

Gábor Halász

◆

The Basic Characteristics of the System

The system of higher education in Hungary, according to the typology of Burton R. Clark,[1] is a *single public system with multiple sectors*. On the one hand, this means that, apart from a few exceptions, all institutions of higher education are controlled by the state; on the other hand, it means that the system is divided into two tracks: lower-level higher education institutions and the universities. The few nonstate institutions, owned by churches and serving exclusively to train members of the priesthood, do not offer publicly recognized diplomas (in 1987 there were about 650 students studying in postsecondary church schools). The military schools form part of the state system but the official reports and statistics do not deal with them. There are also a few other postsecondary institutions with special training goals; Communist party schools, for training cadres and a recently founded international manager training school, for example, are not integrated into the state system.

The public system consists of nearly one thousand basic teaching and research units (departments, groups of departments, and institutes) which function in fifty-four separate institutions, nineteen identified as universities and thirty-five as colleges or institutes of higher education. In fact, of the nineteen universities, only four can be considered as *universitas* in the strict and traditional sense of the word (these are the universities of Budapest, Pécs, Szeged, and Debrecen). Only these four offer teaching in more than one disciplinary field. The other fifteen institutions are specialized: four in medicine, four in technology, six in agriculture, and one in economics. The four traditional universities are also incomplete institutions because they have no more than two or three faculties. The whole university sector enrolls 46 percent of the tertiary student body and employs 64 percent of the teachers in higher education.

The thirty-five institutions in the nonuniversity sector consist of fourteen teachers training colleges (four for the ten to fourteen age group and ten for the six to ten age group), seven colleges of technology, five art colleges, and seven other institutions. Generally, the university and the nonuniversity sectors are not linked with each other. In some disciplinary fields, colleges have been attached to universities, but this attachment is only a formal linkage without true integration. Students, when entering higher education, must decide whether to choose the longer and more prestigious university studies or the shorter and more specialized training offered by the colleges.

In the middle of the 1980s 9.6 percent in the eighteen to twenty-two age group was enrolled in higher education. In 1987 the number of full-time students for every 100,000 inhabitants was 629, a low figure when compared to other European countries. Despite the low level of enrollment, the proportion of graduates in the working population is relatively high: in 1984 the number of people with a diploma of higher education for every 100,000 inhabitants was 5,512. This high ratio is due to the great number of graduates from evening and correspondence courses, and to the relatively low level of student wastage (75–80 percent of full-time students entering higher education leave with a diploma). In 1987 the total number of teachers was 15,300, with a teacher/student ratio of 4.5 to 1.

Only students who possess a certificate of final examination from secondary school can be admitted to higher education. In addition, every applicant has to pass an entrance examination. Each institution organizes its own entrance examination, but the procedure and the scoring system are defined centrally. Admittance depends partly on secondary school results, and partly on the score obtained on the entrance examination. In 1987, out of 53,768 secondary school leavers, 52,434 (that is about 36 percent of the eighteen-year-old age group) passed the examination. This gave them the right to apply for admittance to higher education, but out of this total only 18,227 (about 12 percent of the eighteen-year-old age group) were eventually admitted to a higher education institution.

Historical Background

Hungary, like other countries in Central Europe, has experienced a rather stormy history. Its national sovereignty was threatened several times, its territory was partly or entirely occupied by neighboring powers, and its population has continuously been divided on religious, national, or ethnic lines.

The origins of Hungarian higher education go back as far as the fourteenth century. During the 1300s three medieval universities were founded but none of them has survived. The development of schooling was given an impetus in the sixteenth century when the Protestant churches, following Western models, set up schools mainly in the eastern part of the country,

Table 1

The Expansion of the System
(Number of Students and Institutions)

	Number Of Students			
Year	Full-time	Evening and Correspondence	Total	Number Of Institutions
1937/38	11,747	—	11,747	16
1946/47	24,036	1,216	25,252	n.d.
1950/51	26,509	5,992	32,501	19
1955/56	30,665	14,766	43,431	32
1960/61	29,344	15,241	44,585	43
1965/66	51,002	42,955	93,957	92
1970/71	53,821	26,715	80,536	74
1975/76	64,319	43,236	107,555	56
1980/81	64,057	37,072	101,166	57
1985/86	64,190	35,154	99,344	58
1987/88	66,697	32,328	99,025	54

including Transylvania. The counter-reformation led by the Hapsburg kings impeded the development of these institutions but, at the same time, contributed to the creation of new Catholic schools. The first university that survived the vicissitudes of history was founded by the Jesuits in 1635. It is considered to be the predecessor of the present "Eötvös Loránd University" in Budapest.

The development of higher education was inspired by rapid economic and social development in the second half of the nineteenth century when the country gained relative national independence within the framework of the Austro-Hungarian Empire. Three new universities were founded in this period. After World War I Hungary lost two-thirds of its territory, and with it two universities and other higher educational institutions. The governments of this period tried to compensate for the loss by setting up new institutions; the teaching personnel for these were recruited from the universities in the lost territories. However, by means of *numerus clausus* (enrollment restrictions) the government prevented the expansion of the higher education system. Thus it kept its elite character, with a higher proportion of students enrolled in law and theology faculties.

After World War II Hungary became part of the socialist block led by the Soviet Union. The system of higher education, with the building of socialism, underwent profound changes. The following discussion focuses on some of the most significant features of the postwar period.

Rapid Quantitative Expansion of the System

Between 1946 and 1976 the total number of students rose from 25,252 to 110,528. A particular feature of this growth was the huge proportion of students enrolled in evening and correspondence courses. While in 1946 this group represented a mere 5 percent of the students in higher education, by the early 1950s and on to the 1970s it represented 40 percent of the total. Thus, the expansion and the democratization of the system was achieved mainly by opening up lower-quality channels. The process of expansion was extraordinarily uneven, and this factor demonstrated the influences of direct political interventions. The number of higher education institutions in 1946 was eighteen; by 1965 this number had grown to ninety-two. Since then, as the result of a policy encouraging organizational mergers, the number has been steadily decreasing. The huge increase had been achieved mainly by transforming secondary level technical and teachers training institutions into higher education institutes. Later on, many of these newly created schools were attached to other institutions or simply transformed back into secondary schools. (For the expansion of the system, see Table 1.)

Reorientation of the Whole System Toward Technical and Practical Fields

While prior to World War II nearly 50 percent of all students were enrolled in law or theology faculties and only 20 percent were studying in industrial, agricultural, or economic branches, by 1960 about 40 percent of all students were enrolled in these latter branches and only 8 percent in law. (For the present professional structure of higher education, see Table 4.)

Radical Changes in the Composition of the Student Body in Favor of the Manual Worker Strata

Prior to World War II only 4 percent of students came from manual worker families. By the mid-1960s this figure had risen to 50 percent; it has since been decreasing. The changes in the proportion of students of manual worker origin are an excellent indicator of the shifts of education policy, one of the main goals of which has often been to influence this factor.[2] At the same time, these changes also reflect the fluctuations of general internal politics. (See Figure 1.)

The Spread and Development of Direct Political Control Over Curricula and the Internal Life of Institutions

During the 1950s the former autonomy of the universities was removed and the organizational framework of direct political and ideological control of higher education was established. As a consequence of political purges and the expansion of the system the teaching body was almost totally changed. The internal organization and curricula of universities and colleges came under direct control of the central authorities. The government prescribed, in detail, the content of teaching, the timetables, the texts, and the requirements to be met for every special field of study. New compulsory subjects—Marxist philosophy, political economy, Russian language, etc.—were introduced in every institution; these were designed to increase the general political education of students. Compulsory subjects sometimes accounted for more than 20 percent of the learning time.

The main organizational and political features that took shape during the 1950s survived until the end of the 1960s, when some measures were taken to loosen the government's administrative and political control over higher education. In this period, when universities became the focus of public interest in many developed countries, higher education in Hungary did not excite particular interest: the public was mainly concerned with lower-level education. However, by the end of the 1970s higher education became a policy field full of controversies; most of those within the system (teachers and students) and out of it (politicians, administrators, and professional experts) agreed that the system was suffering from many dysfunctions and needed major reforms.

The 1980s: A Decade of Crisis

Since the end of the 1970s a number of expert committees and social organizations have prepared reports concerning the state of the higher educational system and proposing new policies. These reports stimulated public debates, which in turn led to several governmental measures designed to improve the higher educational system. As a result of these measures, important changes have been introduced into the system, but many problems still remain to be solved in the 1990s.

Deteriorating Material Conditions

During the 1970s and the first part of the 1980s state expenditure on education increased constantly, but higher education spending in this period fell from 17 percent to 12 percent of the total educational budget (see Table 2). The state of buildings and equipment has deteriorated steadily and the living conditions of university and college teachers have also suffered. The salary of university teachers has often been lower than that of their secondary school colleagues, and professors complain that their earnings are less than that of certain categories of skilled factory workers. In 1987 the regular monthly salary of a university professor was 12,673 Ft, the equivalent of about $280.

Figure 1

The Percentage of Children of Manual Worker Origin Among First Year Full-Time Students

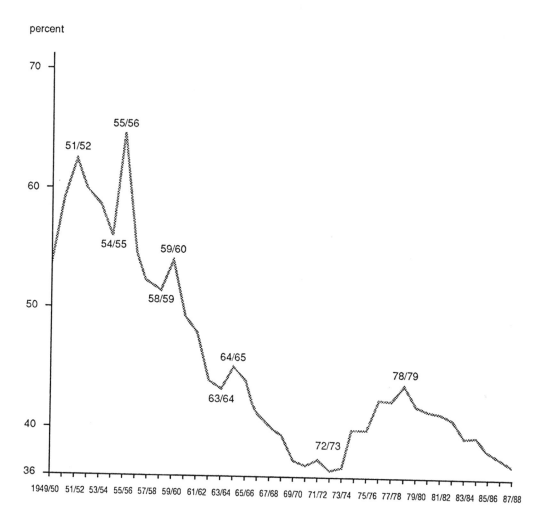

The Low Number of Secondary School Leavers Entering Higher Education

One of the main topics of public debates on higher education concerns the extension of the system. Many experts say that Hungary is lagging behind the developed world in terms of the number of students moving from secondary to higher education. In 1987, for example, only 35 percent of pupils with secondary certification were admitted to universities and colleges as full-time students. Others argue that, due to the high retention rate, the number of graduates entering the labor market is relatively high, and thus there is no need to expand the system.

Loss of Talented Young People Due to the Rigidity of the System of Access

Tough selection at the entry-point, together with a lack of linkage between the higher and lower prestige sectors, can make the choice of higher education institutions highly risky for secondary school leavers. If a pupil with relatively high achievement fails the severe entrance examination of a prestigious institution he or she may be lost from higher education for good, while his or her fellow with lower achievement may be admitted to the low-prestige sector and become a graduate. Access to higher education is based on a kind of "double or nothing" game.

Flaws in the selection process can be traced back to the rigid quotas for admission established by the central government. Until 1989 the central authorities mandated exact numbers for each institution. In 1988 the total provision officially authorized for 44,757 applicants was only 16,533; in other words, the implication being that the institutions were supposed to refuse more then 60 percent of their applicants. (The provisions are, in general, slightly surpassed.)

Low Academic Quality

The most frequently criticized feature of higher education in Hungary is the low academic achievement of students and the insufficient professional knowledge of the teaching body. Although some institutions of the traditional sector offer high-quality teaching and do successful research, many institutions do not meet the quality requirements of higher education. The reports of the 1980s identified several causes underlying this situation.

Lack of internal selection is often mentioned as an important reason for the low academic achievement of students. Those who manage to enter the system will almost certainly be able to stay on until they reach the graduate level, regardless of their performance. Student mediocrity is encouraged by their knowledge that they cannot really fail or be ejected from the system.

The low academic quality of the teaching body is related to several factors: the dispersal of traditional academic com-

---

Table 2

Expenditure on Higher Education as a Percentage of Total Educational and Total State Expenditure

Period	Higher Education Expenditure	
	% of all educational expenditure	% of all state expenditure
1956–60	13.7	2.1
1961–65	15.5	2.4
1966–70	17.2	2.5
1971–75	17.1	2.4
1976–80	15.7	3.3
1981–85	13.7	2.8
1986–87	12.6	2.7

munities following political purges after World War II; rapid expansion of the system during the 1950s and the 1960s; selection of teachers often based on political or bureaucratic rather than academic criteria; Hungary's long-lasting isolation from the international academic community; lack of knowledge of foreign languages; the internal hierarchy of academic organizations that promotes and grants more on the basis of conformist and bureaucratic attitudes than scientific creativity or academic achievement; budgetary restrictions which, since the mid-1970s, have impeded the hiring of younger, better-trained teachers; and lack of competition both between professors and between institutions.

Other frequently mentioned reasons for low quality include the high proportion of evening and correspondence courses, the lack of freedom for students to choose between different courses and teachers according to their quality, the lack of connection between academic achievement and labor market position and, last but not least, the large amount of time spent on political-ideological education.

The Separation of Teaching and Research

The low academic quality of university education is often imputed to the separation of teaching and research, this being a basic characteristic of the Hungarian system. During the 1950s and 1960s, following the Soviet model, a large framework of research institutes was set up as part of the Hungarian Academy of Sciences

Table 3

Demographic Conditions

Year	Number of Births Per Thousand Inhabitants
1965	13.1
1966	13.6
1967	14.6
1968	15.1
1969	15.0
1970	14.7
1971	14.5
1972	14.7
1973	15.0
1974	17.8
1975	18.4
1976	17.5
1977	16.7
1978	15.8
1979	15.0
1980	13.9
1981	13.3
1982	12.5
1983	11.9
1984	11.8
1985	12.2
1986	12.1

(Magyar Tudományos Akadémia [MTA]). The highest authority in scientific matters, MTA has no direct linkage with higher education. The most prestigious and most expensive researches, both in natural and social sciences, are conducted in MTA institutes. In 1985 the expenditure of higher education institutions on research and development was only 13 percent of the total national expenditure on research and development. In the same year universities and colleges employed only half of the holders of scientific degrees (awarded not by the universities but by the MTA). Creative people with academic ambitions are more often attracted by MTA institutions because they offer better conditions for scientific work.

Organizational and Curricular Rigidity

This factor is usually regarded as a key reason for the mediocrity of Hungarian academic achievement. The system permits few individual choices. Most young men or women who enter higher education in a special field do not face any situation requiring individual choice on his or her way through the system until graduation. There is not much room for individual planning of studies according to individual interest. All the significant choices are made by the central manpower planning authorities. Lack of choice is compounded by overloading the curricula. In some institutions and some specialities students are obliged to attend forty or more classes weekly, a situation that certainly is not favorable to in-depth study. The rigid course of studies is often compared to that of secondary schools, which have a highly structured curriculum. In the university sector institutions have more curricular freedom than in the nonuniversity sector but curricular guidelines, elaborated by expert bodies and confirmed by the central administrative authorities, must be followed even by universities.

Student Unrest

The main causes of increasing student activism during the 1980s have been the worsening of living conditions and the rejection of paternalistic political control. Attempts to form independent student organizations have multiplied. During the 1970s almost every student was a member of the official and only youth organization (KISZ), but by the end of 1988 this organization had practically ceased to exist in many institutions. Independent student organizations had replaced it. The main demands of the new organizations usually center upon the following: the increase of allowances, more freedom to choose between alternative courses, the reduction of the numbers of compulsory lessons, and the abolition of the compulsory study of Marxist ideology and the Russian languages.

Government and Control

One of the main issues in the recent debates on higher education concerns the problems of government and control. The constantly criticized low quality of the teaching staff is often blamed on strong governmental control over the selection of professors and the frequent use of political criteria instead of professional ones when hiring or promoting faculty. Although since 1985, when a new educational law was enacted, universities have gained a certain degree of autonomy, the shaping of their internal organization and operation, as well as the appointment of administrative leaders and heads of departments, are directly controlled by governmental agencies.

The universities and lower-level institutes of higher education are supervised by a variety of ministers. Only two-thirds of the institutions (the traditional multidisciplinary universities, the universities of technology, the institutions of teacher training, and the art colleges) are supervised by the Ministry of Education and Culture. The others are controlled by different ministries (e.g., agricultural universities and colleges by the Ministry of Agriculture, and medical universities by the Ministry of Health).

The universities are led by rectors who are appointed by the government from among the faculty. Each faculty is headed by a dean. Each college is headed by a director. Directors, like rectors, are appointed from among the professors, with the appointment being made by the minister supervising the given institution. The supervising ministers appoint the heads of basic teaching and research units as well.

Universities and colleges have only a limited freedom in determining their internal organization. The supervising minister has the right to decide on the creation and abolition of teaching or research units.

The degree of autonomy in the university and nonuniversity sectors differs significantly with regard to the freedom of the respective institutions to determine the content of their teaching. While universities and university faculties can make independent decisions about their programs, the programs of colleges are determined by their supervising ministries. Though he or she does not interfere directly in the shaping of university curricular programs, the minister has a veto that he or she can use if he or she thinks a program contradicts the principles of state culture policy.

The administrative power in higher education is divided between three important agencies: the supervising ministers, the heads of institutions, and the governing councils of the institutions. The latter, which have gained important new rights since the 1985 Educational Act, are made up of elected representatives of the teaching and student body, as well as ex officio members (the three parts having equal representation).

Although, during the 1980s, universities became more independent from central control, the autonomy question seems to remain the most significant issue of higher education policy. But the rising demand for independence from governmental interference is not without contradictions. The rejection of the direct interventions of the local and central political apparatus, and of the organizational rigidity imposed by incompetent central bureaucrats, often goes together with the rejection of all kinds of external control, blended with illusions of reviving the medieval model of autonomy.

Many participants in the recent public debates maintain that higher education is best served not by total rejection of governmental control but by reforms concerning aims, content, and means. Instead of being political watchdogs or pursuing short-term goals, central authorities should learn to play a new strategic role that aims at the improvement of quality and the modernization of the system. According to this logic, it would be a mistake to give wide-ranging autonomy to a teaching body characterized by low professional competence and self-protecting attitudes. Thus, the appointment of professors by the government must represent a pledge for quality selection. Others claim that quality improvement is based upon the assertion of market principles. Therefore, governmental agencies, instead of exercising direct quality control, should create conditions in which teachers are encouraged to compete and urged to evaluate themselves; in addition, students should be given more freedom to choose the teachers from whom they want to learn.[3]

Higher Education and Employment

The expansion of the system during the 1950s and the 1960s was mainly a response to the growing needs of the national economy for skilled manpower.[4] Until the end of the 1970s economic growth generated a corresponding shortage of manpower; one of the main goals of state policy was the elimination of this shortage. In order to fulfill the manpower needs of particular economic sectors, extremely specialized training branches were created.

The main problem with this system of the meticulous planning of manpower needs was how to make students choose a job in their special professional field after graduating. Several attempts were made to push young people toward those training fields where the shortage seemed to be the greatest (e.g., heavy industry or lower-level education) and different compulsory employment schemes were implemented in order to compel graduates to accept jobs in the field corresponding to their original specialty. However, the national census of 1980 found that, in certain fields, more than 50 percent of graduates had left their original profession and had taken jobs in fields not corresponding to their training (30 percent was the average number).

Until recently students leaving higher education would be certain to find a job broadly corresponding to their qualification. It was a common view that if the state provided a qualification it must also provide employment. However, since the mid-1980s this common view has tended to fade as market principles have taken the place of central planning in all sectors of the economy. At one time enterprises were interested in employing as many graduates as they could; and, even if they did not want more graduates, the central authorities could order them to take them. Now enterprises are interested in decreasing the number of their employees to increase profits. Because of budgetary restrictions the social services and the state administration are also reducing the number of jobs available for graduates. All these factors, coupled with the intention of the government to let more people enter higher education, combine to indicate employment difficulties in the 1990s when a particularly populous generation will enter the labor market.

The imbalance of demographic conditions is a special source of tension for employment in Hungary. In the mid-1970s, after a period in which the birth rate was low, the number of births grew extremely high, and remained so for a few years. This created a demographic wave that reached the school system at the beginning of the 1980s (see Table 3). This demographic wave has produced serious difficulties at the elementary and secondary levels and will create new ones at the tertiary level in the 1990s.

The relative certainty of employment over the past few decades has been accompanied by relatively low salaries in most graduate professional groups. In 1984 the salary of an industrial engineer was only 1.3 times higher than the salary of a skilled worker, and that of a teacher for the fourteen to eighteen age group was only 1.2 times higher. Low salaries often compel graduates to give up their original profession or look for a second job.

The internal professional structure of higher education is often mentioned as a potential source of tension for employment in the future. The technical and agricultural fields are overrepresented, while the proportion of professions in the service sector (health, business,

Table 4

The Professional Structure of the System

Branches of Studies	Number of Students (1985)
Engineering	24,044
Agriculture	5,534
Economics	11,096
Medicine and Pharmacy	7,422
Other Sanitary	2,780
Veterinary	524
Arts and Philosophy	6,450
Law	5,836
Natural Sciences	4,580
Teacher training for the 10–14 age group	14,541
Teacher training for the 3–10 age group	13,347
Sport Teacher Training	1,065
Fine arts	2,125
Total	99,344

arts, and sciences) is low (see Table 4). As a consequence of this training structure, inherited from the period of rapid expansion, a surplus of graduates is foreseen in the industrial and agricultural sectors and a shortfall of graduates in the service sector. However, these tensions will appear only if the employment conditions of the different sectors change. During the 1980s state policy and the behavior of individual employers have both encouraged over-employment in the so-called productive industrial sector (with a great number of engineers employed in jobs requiring lower-level qualifications) and underemployment in the service sector (with teachers and doctors obliged to take on a huge quantity of supplementary working hours).

Changes and Plans for Reform

Since the end of the 1970s several plans for reform have been formulated and some governmental measures have been taken in order to solve recognized problems. In 1981 the political committee of the ruling party made a decision on the development of higher education.[5] In 1984 the parliament adopted an overall development plan for education, including higher education,[6] which was followed by the enactment of a new Education Act in 1985. At the end of the 1980s further initiatives were taken to elaborate reform proposals.

Although new funds were allocated for research and institutional development, faculty salaries were raised, and universities were granted more freedom to look for external resources, none of these measures has significantly improved the financial conditions in higher education. Recently, the questions concerning finance have come to the center of public discussions. The policy proposals formulated in this field suggest that the direct financing of institutions should be replaced by more flexible forms, including special funds controlled by elected or expert committees and distributed through individual applications, concrete agreements between institutions and industry, student loans, etc.

Although their financial problems have not been solved during the 1980s, institutions of higher education have gained more freedom. According to the provisions of the 1985 Education Act the governing bodies of the institutions of higher education can now define their own internal regulations, can develop their own curricula, and can set the requirements to be met by their students. These factors imply that there has been a redistribution of power between the central authorities and the institutions. The government has not given up its power of control in such fields as the setting up of new teaching and research units, and the appointment of professors and heads of institutions, but even these decisions cannot be taken without negotiating with those concerned.

A recent, and very important, policy aim has been to give more freedom to higher education institutions in relation to the formulation of their admission procedures. Centrally prescribed provisions are to be loosened or abolished so that individual institutions will be able to admit more students by extending internal selection procedures.

Recent governmental policies aim to make the system more flexible on two levels: that of institutional structure and that of individual choice over different subject options. Efforts are being made to change the monolithic institutional structure into a multilevel one that will permit students to modify their course of studies or to leave the system with lower- and higher-level diplomas. These changes are in addition to those that are intended to make access to the system easier, to reinforce internal selection, and to set up postgraduate training forms (which so far exist in a only a few fields). Students have been given more opportunities to follow individually defined paths through the system. They have been allowed to follow, simultaneously, different courses in different institutions or to negotiate individual curricula with their teachers. In several fields of study attempts have been made to introduce modular structures into the curricula, thus permitting an increase in the range of choices.

Notes

1. Burton R. Clark, *The Higher Educational System* (Berkeley and Los Angeles: University of California Press, 1983).

2. Peter Lukács, *Changes in Selection Policy in Hungary: The Case of the Admission System in Higher Education* (Paper presented at the American-Hungarian Seminar on Comparative Educational Policy, Esztergom, Hungary, May 1988, Hungarian Institute for Educational Research, 1988).

3. Béla Pokol, "Az egyetemi-tudományos szféra," *Kutatások a felsooktatás köréböl*, no. 3 (1988).

4. Andor Ladányi, "A magyar felsöoktatás fejlödése a felszabadulás után," in A *felsöoktatás távlati fejlesztésének Kérdései*, ed. Ladanyi; (Budapest: Hungarian Institute for Educational Research, 1985).

5. János Palovecz, ed., A *magyar felsöoktatás helyzete* (Budapest: Hungarian Institute for Educational Research, 1983).

6. János Palovecz, ed., Dokumentumok a felsooktatás fejlesztési programjának elökészitö szakaszából (Budapest: Hungarian Institute for Educational Research, 1984).

Italy

Roberto Moscati

◆

Since the unification of the country and the birth of the nation in 1860 higher education in Italy has been affected by requests and pressures of various kinds. As in almost all centralized systems, education has been used either for social purposes (reproduction of the elites), or for economic reasons (training of labor forces at upper levels), or for political ends (legitimation of the existing ruling class). The alternate prevalence of these purposes has affected the structuring of the higher education system and especially access to it from the upper secondary level, as I will later demonstrate. At the present time, the pressures of social demand for higher education which developed in the 1960s, as in many other European countries, is still visible in the working of the university in Italy.[1]

The booming period of enrollments started out in the early 1960s and was facilitated by the introduction of an open-door policy, which allowed admission to the university without entrance examinations for all students holding a upper secondary degree of any kind (from the lycee, technical or vocational diplomas, or educational certificates.) University enrollments increased dramatically but were accompanied by a visible decline in productivity level. A series of dysfunctional phenomena found a more favorable ground to develop:

1. The number of dropouts increased; so, too, did the rate of delays (students officially behind in their scheduled curriculum).

2. The number of degrees granted every year increased at a much lower rate than the rate of new enrollments; for years now it has been basically stable.

3. The new wave of enrollment distributed the students along different disciplinary tracks in a casual manner, in part because of the absence of any sort of orientation or counseling service before university admission. Some tracks seem to appeal to students solely because of the pro-

Table 1

General Trend of University Population in Italy: 1960–1987

Academic Years	A	B	C	D	E
1960/61	59,708	268,181	21,886	61.3	8.2
1970/71	194,280	681,731	65,414	85.5	8.3
1980/81	244,071	1,047,831	74,118	74.2	7.1
1986/87	246,942	1,085,900	75,810	64.9	7.0

Note: A—1st year enrollment; B—Overall student population; C—Degrees awarded; D—Ratio of first-year enrolled over upper-secondary output ("diploma" owners); E—Ratio of degree owners over total enrollment in the university.

fessional fields they are related to (as in the cases of medicine or law); others are chosen because they are considered to be easier and shorter (social sciences and the humanities in general).

Another relevant phenomenon that has affected the Italian university has been the growth of the number of women among its students, with particular geographical growth in the southern regions (which is remarkable keeping in mind the general underdevelopment of the area) and disciplinary track growth in humanities and the natural sciences.

The productivity of the higher education system in Italy has been traditionally low, but the fast growth of enrollments in the last two decades has made this problem more evident than ever. The total number of students who receive degrees each year has kept basically stable (between 70,000 to 78,000) while student enrollment has jumped from 680,000 in 1970/71 to 1,000,000 in 1987/88.

The distribution of degree holders among different fields shows an impressive increase in medicine and a strong decline in the humanities. Natural sciences, mathematics, physics, engineering, and law have remained basically stable, with negative implications for scientific re-search, the development of higher technology, and further modernization in Italy.

Official attitudes and public opinion regarding the drive to mass higher education has changed substantially over the years. After a long period of general criticism about excess enrollment, held responsible for mismatches between supply and demand and for the creation of unemployment among the university graduates, now higher education is being blamed for not producing enough graduates, especially in some key fields like engineering and business administration. As I will point out later, this contradictory attitude regarding the role of education and the adequate or inadequate production of graduates seems to be traditional both for the governing class and the public. Neither group will commit itself to using education for economic purposes (emphasis on the output of higher education) or for social purposes (emphasis on the access, that is to say the input, to higher education). Neither government nor the public at large will commit itself to a single vision concerning the mission of higher education.

Historical Trends

The educational system in Italy was created during the political unification of the nineteenth century. The main task of

Table 2

Dropouts and Degrees Awarded
(1960–1985)

Academic Years	A Dropouts	B Graduates	A/B
1960/61	19,078	20,842	91.5
1970/71	60,614	47,520	127.5
1980/81	157,218	74,118	212.1
1984/85	150,000	72,148	207.9

the ruling class involved in the process of unifying the different small states into a unified Italy was to generalize the Piedmontese system of administration, which was heavily influenced by the French model.[2] Little wonder that the resulting government turned out to be a very centralized and hierarchical system, with the central power represented directly in all provinces, leaving practically no room for local autonomy. The educational system followed this same trend and was structured as a pyramid, reproducing the structure of the social classes, although with a special emphasis on the upper secondary level.

Since the aim of the ruling class was to politically and culturally socialize the new citizens, and also to create a new strata of middle-level technicians and public administrators, the possibilities for entering and progressing through the school system were kept wider and larger than in other European countries.

The secondary level was structured along two basic tracks, leading respectively to university (gymnasium/lycée), or to the labor market (technical and vocational school). The task of training (socially and politically rather than technologically) a new middle class made the system of education relatively open: transferring from one type of institution to another was encouraged. As a result, in a matter of years, a surplus of trained people flooded the labor market. The Fascist regime had to deal with the latter problem and at least twice (with a school reform at the beginning of its hegemony, in 1923, and a would-be reform near the end, in 1938/39) tried to reduce the pressures of social demand for education, differentiating tracks at the secondary level and even at the primary level (at least on paper).

Table 3

Rate of Transfer from Upper-Secondary to University[1]

Years	Percent Values
1970–1971	87.7
1980–1981	72.5
1982–1984	68.3
1984–1985	67.0
1985–1986	63.6
1986–1987	63.7
1984–1988	67.5

[1] Ratio between first-year enrollment and upper-secondary degrees.

Source: Italian Institute of Statistics—I.S.T.A.T.

The alternative between a system of tertiary education aimed at creating "citizens" with a common cultural background and a system designed to meet the needs of the economy and the labor market has constantly influenced the Italian policy toward education. As a consequence, the entire educational system (of tertiary education especially) has moved between closed and open, between "professionalized" and "deprofessionalized."

Of course, Italy is not unique in this respect; closed versus open educational systems has always been a problem for the European countries. What makes the Italian scenario perhaps unique has been its resistance to the introduction of the "numerus clausus" (enrollment restrictions) at university. No Italian government has ever been able to introduce such a measure—just as no Italian government has been able to close down a single university, even one of those lost up in the mountains and attracting practically no students, which are remnants of former small Renaissance states merged eventually in the kingdom of Italy).[3]

The Italian elite have had a constant concern about the function of legitimation (of the public administration, the state, and thus the ruling social class itself) arising from the system of education. Their only formal "defense" against a growing social demand for higher education turned out to be the differentiation of tracks at the secondary level, with only some tracks enabling students to continue their studies at university. These conditioning elements are still present in the framework of the Italian system of education, even if in an indirect way: when the social demand for higher education grew suddenly in the 1960s (a demand common to all Western countries), the Italian system was less prepared to resist it and the ruling class less able to deal with the problem. The pressure toward establishing a more egalitarian system was exerted both in the economic sector (thanks to the power of the unions at that time), and in the educational sector (thanks to the student movement, which in Italy from the beginning was much more related to the political domain outside the school world than was the case elsewhere). In the university milieu, internal and external issues were unified by a new wave of young people who turned out to be much more politically experienced than any previous generation. The general situation was favorable because of the "momentum" the unions had already obtained (they supported the student movement much more than any political party). The main target became, more or less consciously, the social division of labor and the class structure in society. As a consequence, in the school system the quest was for equality, at all levels. For years political forces discussed several options without reaching even the cultural level of debate that events required. In the end, the situation in the political and administrative domains (mentioned above) led to a "compulsory" solution, equalizing all tracks at the upper secondary level, as far as admission to university was concerned; this perfect example of an open-door policy came into being practically overnight (in 1969).

In the middle of the 1970s, when the impact of the mass drive for higher education, together with the ideological and political push toward a more egalitarian society, began to slow down, the Italian sys-

Table 4

Rate of Women Per Field of Study

Field of Study	1982–83	1984–85	1985–86	1986–87
Sciences	52.9	51.7	50.0	50.6
Medicine	36.9	38.8	41.4	41.0
Engineering	15.8	17.3	18.8	19.4
Agriculture	22.9	25.2	27.2	32.8
Economics[1]	34.8	37.1	38.4	39.1
Law	43.9	45.6	47.7	47.4
Humanities	78.4	78.8	79.5	80.1
Short-Cycles	52.7	52.8	53.7	51.7
Total	44.6	45.9	46.8	47.2

[1] Political and Social Sciences enclosed.

Source: Census and I.S.T.A.T. data.

Table 5

Trends of Higher Education in Italy

Granted	No. of Students	1st year Enrollment	Degrees
Upper Secondary			
1962–1963	929,033	302,488	133,089
1983–1984	2,508,800	715,889	488,563
1984–1985	2,550,147	726,538	491,881
1985–1986	2,607,749	749,789	491,491
1986–1987	2,658,588	760,517	492,300
1987–1988	2,719,334	766,763	—
University			
1962–1963	312,334	75,058	23,973
1972–1973	802,603	213,226	62,944
1983–1984	1,054,768	256,611	73,208
1984–1985	1,106,661	253,778	72,148
1985–1986	1,112,898	241,250	75,810
1986–1987	1,085,300	240,992	77,869
1987–1988	1,096,205	258,837	—

Source: Census and I.S.T.A.T. data.

tem of higher education had a secondary level subdivided into four tracks: classical and scientific studies and teacher training; technical education; vocational education; and artistic education.

Differences concerning admissions possibilities to secondary school in terms of social origin are more clear-cut for females than for males, due to cultural factors and/or to choice based on economic roles. Class distinctions are clearly noticeable in a comparative analysis of the different types of secondary schools. The middle class is traditionally inclined towards the *licei* (the traditional secondary school leaving examination) especially the *classico*; the lower-middle and working classes tend, according to the information available, to enroll in technical and teacher-training institutes. Children of businessmen, professionals, and executives made up approximately 34 percent of the students in technical schools, but more

than 40 percent in the *licei scientifici* and 70 percent in the *licei classici*.

Any of these tracks can now lead to university. University-bound students need only complete five years of secondary studies and pass a final exam leading to a formal qualification (diploma). At the tertiary level, there were no longer any differentiations, either in terms of tracks (inside and outside the university) or in terms of level of exit: one type of course led (after four, five, or six years) to one kind of degree, the *laurea*.[4]

The actual working of the system went against the hopes and the official aims of the egalitarian forces. The "perverse" results[5] of the open-door policy together with the formal equalization of all tracks at the secondary level allowed concentration of the collective quest for social mobility in the "channel" of formal instruction. Education became the easiest and in many cases the only visible path to escape from manual work, and/or from a proletarian condition. This trend was obviously supported by a number of social and economic factors, from the process of urbanization to the need for a new kind of labor force at all levels in industry and in the services. It also revealed an additional, and very Italian, belief in an academic degree as passport to a better job and a higher standard of living.

Italian government policy was to grant what was being asked for. For a number of years the only measure taken—although with traditional delay—was related to the number of teachers (at different levels) which rose substantially and became for a period a central focus for the output of the school system (reproducing itself) on the labor market.

Higher Education and the Labor Market

As in many other European countries, Italy experienced rapid economic development and an equally rapid social transformation after World War II, particularly during the 1950s and the 1960s. The impact of these two phenomena on the system of education has been rather peculiar. On the one hand, the economic development did not necessarily require a growing number of workers with higher levels of education; on the other hand, the process of upward social mobility was largely based on increased education and the acquisition of degrees (credentialism). As a result, a surplus of degreeholders both at the upper secondary and at the university level affected the labor market, and the rate of unemployed persons with higher education grew quite rapidly.

The system of higher education, on its part, was not ready to face the growing social demand and tried at first to resist change.[6] The only policy enacted—as already mentioned—was free access to university granted to every student who

had completed five years of upper secondary school and had received any type of degree. As a consequence of this new policy, the rate of transfer from the upper secondary school to university increased substantially.

But since the demand for degreeholders did not enjoy a simultaneous increase in the labor market, the number of unemployed degreeholders (those with a secondary diploma or a university *laurea*) grew accordingly.

In recent years (the late 1970s and the 1980s) the number of university degreeholders among the unemployed has declined; total unemployment stood at about 11 percent in 1988, but unemployment for university graduates was only about 3 percent. A number of factors contributed to this decline. First, the growth of temporary jobs at low levels of qualification has increased supply flexibility. In the modern economy, degreeholders have accepted low-qualified jobs made available on the market, in Italy as in other industrialized countries. Together with this phenomenon of overeducation/underemployment of the labor forces, the gap between developed and underdeveloped areas has increased. In particular, professional opportunities have become increasingly diversified for university graduates both in terms of the quantity and the quality of jobs available. Recent research shows 2.5 percent of university degreeholders among the unemployed in northern Italy, and 10 percent unemployed in southern Italy. The percentage of degreeholders in temporary jobs was less than 15 percent in the north, but over 27 percent in the south.

Periods of unemployment after the acquisition of a degree and before acquiring stable occupation vary. Graduates in engineering, statistics, and the natural sciences must wait an average of twelve months before finding a permanent job; graduates in the social sciences and the humanities must wait more than twenty-four months before finding permanent employment.

Even if the flexibility of supply helped to ease tension in the labor market, the demand for university graduates did not show any substantial change regarding the traditional resistance to absorbing large numbers in industrial and agricultural sectors. This resistance has been a rather peculiar aspect of the Italian economy throughout the years. Indeed, even many sectors of the service economy are late in modernizing and continue to ignore labor forces with higher levels of education. Only very recently has the need for a substantial number of engineers and other technicians become visible. But the introduction of higher technology in Italy has not been a labor-intensive process as it has been elsewhere. Moreover, applied research, always a marginal factor in the Italian economy, provides few job opportunities.

In this framework of large social demand for higher education but little increase in occupational opportunities for the better educated, the higher education system worked, and is still working, as an informal filter. This filter is created by differences between the high school tracks, all of which provide access to the university but also provide students with uneven cultural backgrounds. Lack of orientation and counseling services reinforces the filtering effect. Thus the drop-out rate and the rate of students falling behind schedule is constantly increasing: every year only about 75,000 students out of the 250,000 enrolled as freshmen actually receive their degree (*laurea*). Such a low level of productivity is actually functional, considering the needs of the economy and the stability of demand in the marketplace.

However, changes in work organization, modernization of several significant economic sectors, and growing competition at the European level with a stronger economic integration inside the EEC have combined to create a demand for a new kind of professional figure with different levels of postsecondary training. As a consequence, the system of higher education in Italy must strive to keep up with the others in the European community. In more specific terms, Italian universities must produce more graduates with new and different levels of knowledge. The need for differentiation among tracks and levels is especially keen. The Italian university has traditionally operated with just one degree level; only very recently has a timid reform been passed that introduces short-cycle courses and a third level of degrees (doctorate). In other words, programs both for introductory and highly advanced levels of professional training in Italian universities lag far behind other European university systems.

Crisis and Development: (1978–88)

Since the unification of the country, universities in Italy have been under the direction of the Ministry of Education. The centralized structure of the Italian system of education reproduces features of the French and German school systems, although with some peculiar differences. Like the French, the ruling class who unified the country tried by means of national legislation and national administration to establish detailed policies and procedures for the system of education at all levels. The university structure was designed in the shape of a pyramid, composed, from the top down, of (1) the minister of education, aided by an advisory structure originally called the "Superior Council of Instruction," and later renamed the "National University Council (C.U.N.), consisting of representatives from academia; (2) the ministry's Division of Higher Education, headed by a bureau chief and consisting of ten staff sections; (3) the university rectors, serving as chief campus officers at the different universities, and the administrative directors, serving as chief business officers; (4) the deans of the various faculties; (5) chair-holding professors and institute directors; and (6) several levels of nontenured professors and assistants.[7] This organizational structure linked the central power at the state level directly to each university no matter where it was located.

The Italian system of universities, a system that remained largely unchanged until the beginning of the 1980s, was based on a national agency created with the aim of coordinating all universities across the country by means of a large body of laws and rules. But this agency was never able to operate in an effective bureaucratic manner because of internal fragmentation of control and weak techniques of integration. The result was a sort of balkanization caused by the combination of a bureaucratic overstructure and a guild understructure, which—according to Burton Clark's view—helped to strengthen the hegemony of the chaired professors.[8]

This peculiar form, with its fragmented bureaucratic and centralized structure, lasted—with some minor changes and much debate on the need for change—until 1980. In that year a reform law was finally introduced.

The Presidential Decree dated July 2, 1980 n. 382, entitled "Reorganization of university teaching, of related training, as well as experimentation with new types of organization and didactics," introduced a number of innovations within the general framework of an educational philosophy dedicated to making higher education open to the masses and not limited to the elite.

1. The first innovation concerned scientific research. A new fund for research was created for projects at both the local and the national levels. All members of the professoriate have the right to apply for grants from this fund. Opening this research fund to *all* members of the faculty was very important because it went against an Italian tradition of research carried out in an individual manner only by the most prominent members of the professoriate. It was also hoped that the new fund would stimulate joint projects between universities.

2. Another innovation designed to counteract the traditional power of the university "barons," the tenured and chaired professors, was the introduction of departments. Departments are collective, horizontal structures; their power is meant to balance the hierarchical, vertical organization of power represented in Italy by the holding of a "chair." Moreover, departments as a unit for organizing teaching and research were badly needed in order to keep up with the rapid development of knowledge in different fields.

3. The education reform law mandated diversification in levels of curricula and degrees. In addition to the traditional level leading to the *laurea*, the law introduced a higher level, the "research doctorate," similar to the Ph.D. in American universities. A limited number of places were made available to students who want to pursue an academic career. Often working at a coordinated group of universities, these future academics take seminars and pursue independent research.

In the same spirit, a new kind of "schools for special purposes" was created in 1982. Their task is to train middle-level professional figures, such as nurses, who previously required only secondary level instruction for their work. These courses, which include two years of instruction, were inspired by the proliferation of private schools that were teaching all sorts of "new professions." The schools for special purposes have introduced short-cycle professionalized instruction at the university level.

4. The reforms recognized the need to adapt the university to the diversification of professions in the modern economic world. Thus, they opened up teaching activities to "experts" from different fields who earned their livings and mastered their professional subject area outside the walls of academia. This innovation was designed to subvert the old view of the university as an independent, autonomous, self-sufficient stucture. Not only did the reformers mandate closer connections between the university and the outside world by inviting outsiders to come inside the university to share their knowledge with members of the university community, they also encouraged the universities to reach out and sign research contracts and engage in consultation activities for private and public customers. The reforms also enabled universities to sell educational opportunities to nontraditional students for retraining purposes and/or lifelong education activities.

These innovations represent an overall change in the conception and working of the university in Italy. They represent a serious effort to make the Italian university system relevant to modern Italian society.[9]

The reform law passed in 1980 has had a more limited impact on the university than its supporters had originally hoped. Compromises forced on progressives by conservative forces have weakened some reforms and slowed down the enactment of others. Today, deterioration of the working conditions inside the university, and the growing pressures from outside to improve the quality of higher educa-

tion output, have again made the problem of what to do with the university system an important political issue.[10]

Reforms and Changes in Higher Education: The Present Situation

At present, three reform projects are under discussion, with two of them on the verge of passage in Parliament. For a very conservative system this is a very peculiar phenomenon.

The new season of reform projects began in mid-1987 when the new national government called for the creation of a new ministry, the Ministry of University and Scientific Research. The idea of detaching the section of the Ministry of Education devoted to the university and transferring it to the Ministry of Scientific Research was not greeted with universal praise. This project had to be justified by the government and debated by political forces in relation to a crucial point: the autonomy of the university. Almost at the same time, a parallel discussion began concerning reform of the university curricula. These issues eventually became intertwined in a general debate over the direction a process of university reform ought to follow.

The creation of the new Ministry of Universities and Scientific Research has been hailed as a way to unify all programs of scientific research supported by public authorities, and to maximize the efficiency and productivity of the country in several fields where the international competition is becoming tougher and more challenging. Supporters believe that the university has to be more closely connected to the economy and to society in general; they also believe that teaching activities will benefit from close contact with research. Detractors fear that the appeal of research activities (not to mention monetary rewards) will cause university professors to neglect teaching duties. Other critics argue that the separation of the secondary and tertiary levels of education will damage the former (especially in respect to teacher training), and that increased university involvement in applied research will occur at the expense of pure academic research.

Independence and the right of self-government for every university are expressly laid down in the Italian constitution but do not exist in practice. All details of organization are imposed uniformly by the central authority, not only by means of law and regulations but also by other, more subtle methods through which the ministry makes known its own interpretations of the laws in force.

Recent debate on this topic has pitted supporters of the autonomy of the university system as a whole in relation to the patronage (and control) of the Ministry of Education against those more inclined to support the concept of autonomy for the individual university. The former group aims at reducing differences (and avoiding new differentiations) between universities (which are already uneven for a variety of reasons, many of which are historically related); the latter group is more concerned with connecting the university to the real world. One position is supported by those political forces that are more inclined to believe that public services should and could be improved, but should remain public and continue to provide ad hoc services in order to reduce differences among the representatives of demand. The other position believes in competition and the free market in order to improve services (including higher education).

The reform of university curricula also represents an area in which conservative and progressive forces confront each other. The conservative position is represented by the attitude taken by all the commissions for curricula reform created by the former minister of educa-tion. Their general approach to reform —intended to modernize university studies—has been characterized by an increase in the length of studies (with almost all moving from four to five years), and by the elimination of subjects not strictly belonging to the specific field in question. Conservatives want to cut the links between similar or related fields, but do not want a move toward specialization in professional terms. A large majority of the professoriate continue to abhor the idea of a professionalizing university.

The progressive position is represented by those who support a growing flexibility within the curricula, through the introduction of short-cycles and a differentiation of possible university tracks. Progressives want to encourage more university participation by adult learners through projects of recurrent education. They also want individual universities to have the right to emphasize a specific field of studies and to give it a specific structure.

Conservatives oppose short-cycles on the grounds that they will become a second-rate kind of studies, penalizing those who will attend them. Inside the university professors oppose short-cycles because they fear they will have to teach in second-class institutions. Conservatives both outside and inside the university seem blind to the situation of the university in other countries, and to the needs of modern professionals in Italy.

Conclusions

If one looks at the Italian system of higher education, its shaping and its practical working through the years, the general impression one receives is of a conservative milieu that has been able to successfully resist mass social demand, and that has refused even to experiment with some of the innovations frequently introduced in other countries.

Italy has made no attempt to create a truly comprehensive system of higher education. The structure of the upper-secondary school, with its different paths and varying quality of education, continues to be maintained. An emphasis on selectivity at the university level continues to reflect the ideological character of the prewar period which defined the university as an institution for social selection as well as for teaching and learning.

Second, no attempt has been made to make education regionally relevant. As a result, the gap between culturally rich and culturally poor areas in Italy has been constantly widening.

Third, no real attempt has been made to develop any kind of short-cycle education nor to vocationalize, in general, higher education (as has happened in so many other countries).

To understand this general resistance to innovations it is crucial to go back to the process of political decision making as practiced in Italy. The polity in Italy is characterized by a coalition of heterogeneous forces: the government consists of Catholics and lay forces of different kinds (Socialists, Republicans, Liberals). Traditionally, the Christian Democrats have conceived of education as a tool and a channel for ethical socialization, while the Socialists support state intervention in education, and the Liberals and to some extent the Republicans support private lay initiatives, taking into special account the needs of the economy and the market. The opposition is basically represented by the Communist party, which is too weak to take power or to represent a real alternative, but too strong (in terms of veto power) to be ignored.

As a consequence, political decisions concerning reforms in education have to be taken in two basic stages. First, the various forces within the government coalition have to make an agreement. During this process the different agendas of the various parties in the coalition gradually merge into a government proposal. Second, parliamentary debate in the special committee for education begins. Eventually the governing coalition reaches an agreement (after some adjustment of the project) with the opposition parties, which in the end will not prevent passage of the bill (although they might continue to oppose it). The result of this procedure is incoherent, heterogeneous law that allows a degree of experimentation and leaves room for not very clearly defined changes. Implementation of the law is left to the central administrative power (which, as a traditional bureaucracy, is inclined to resist all changes), and to local power (in some cases the universities) where conflict now erupts between vested (corporate) interests and advocates of change. In higher education the local interests—the administration and/or the professoriate—are highly likely to be oriented toward maintaining the status quo.

Italy is run by compromise. Because Italy has such a variety of political parties representing such a variety of interests, mediations always end by satisfying no one. "Reforms" are adopted but then fail to show expected results. Nobody is really in a position to check the results or to fight over them.

Traditionally, a diffuse interest in politics and its ideological components gives more room in Italy than in other countries to values and general principles; the best example in education is the endless debate on diversification and the need for equality. The basic contradictions between the system of education and social and economic organization (social justice vs. division of labor) in capitalist societies have more relevance in Italy and make it more difficult to follow some general trends. Obviously, this ideological relevance complicates the process of "political exchange" between social forces and interests.

In fields not conceived of as central—and education is not central in Italy—this situation represents a powerful obstacle in the path of all kinds of real change, and also prevents the complete development of a parallel private sector organized according to different rules.

The higher educational establishment in Italy has been successful for decades in making the system work as if it were intended for an elite. An informal (although very effective) process of selection prevents most students from the mid- to lowest social strata from attending elite institutions. Meanwhile, various political forces have pursued different ideological goals; have not faced the social demand for mass higher education; and have not introduced real reforms nor provided the universities with the needed structures and personnel. Economic forces seem to find the limited level of productivity of the university system barely acceptable; one can detect islands of efficiency and high quality in a sea of generally poor performance. At present the system of higher education maintains a precarious balance. Two crucial questions remain to be answered in the near future: how long will this precarious equilibrium continue; and who pays (and will pay) the heavy cost engendered by the current situation.

As far as the first question is concerned, the equilibrium is already becoming unstable in the face of progressive deterioration of the labor market (for medical doctors, in particular), and in the operational quality of the few "happy islands" (like the departments of engineering and architecture in Milan and Turin). As far as the second question is concerned, costs are particularly high for students living in less developed regions (mostly in the south). Students from lower cultural origins, because of the decline of peripheral universities, also pay higher costs.

The rapidly growing distance between central and peripheral universities affects the quality of teaching and research activities both for internal and external reasons. On the one hand, growing demand for individual expertise in different fields of knowledge is concentrated in the major cities and keeps professors and researchers where the "market" is more rewarding: thus a growing number of university professors spend a large part of their time far from their home universities. On the other hand, the social and economic demand on the universities for expertise in research and consulting is also most visible at the economic core of the country—basically the same urban areas where the demand for individual expertise is most apparent. As a consequence, specific departments in large universities located in key urban areas are very efficient and have top-quality personnel (Engineering in Milan and Turin, Physics in Rome), while departments of the same kind found in universities located in other parts of the country are terrible. It is worth noting here that the university system has not contributed substantially to the development of the poor areas of the country, with the exception of the awarding of a number of degrees, though even these are often of inferior quality.

People in privileged positions, both inside and outside the university system, continue to resist essential change in the system. They continue to ignore their society's needs in a postindustrial world and the cultural necessity for a general upgrading of the levels of education. Higher education bureaucrats and academics continue to look to the past; their conservatism prevents a real modernization of the system. Thus, Italy's desire to keep up with other leading countries, basically the European partners in the EEC, will be hampered by its failure to modernize its higher educational system.

Notes

1. In Italy higher education largely coincides with university, since different aspects of diversification (such as short-cycles or postdoctorate courses) have been experimented with only recently and only in a few places.

2.   Marzio Barbagli, *Educating for Unemployment: Politics, Labor Markets, and the School System—Italy, 1959–1973* (New York: Columbia University Press, 1982).

3.   Only in recent years has the "numerus clausus" been introduced for medicine, due to the large surplus of medical doctors in the labor market.

4.   Robert L. Merritt and Robert L. Leonardi, "The Politics of Upper Secondary School Reform in Italy: Immobilism or Accommodation?" *Comparative Education Review* 25 (July 1981): 369–83.

5.   Raymond Boudon, *Effets pervers et ordre social* (Paris: Presses Universitaires de France, 1977).

6.   Massimo Paci, "Education and the Capitalist Labor Market," in *Power and Ideology in Education,* ed. Karabel and Halsey, 340–55 (New York: Oxford University Press, 1977).

7.   Burton R. Clark, *Academic Power in Italy: Bureaucracy and Oligarchy in a National University System* (Chicago: University of Chicago Press, 1977).

8.   Clark, *Academic Power in Italy.*

9.   Sergio Bruno et al., *Le politiche dell'istruzione superiore negli anni '80: L'Italia in un contesto internazionale* (Rome: Ministry of Education Printing Office, 1983); Roberto Moscati, *Universita': fine o trasformazione del mito?* (Bologne: Il Mulino, 1983); Guido Martinotti and Roberto Moscati, *Lavorare nell'universita' oggi* (Milan: F. Angeli, 1981); Clark, *Academic Power in Italy.*

10. Giunio Luzzatto, "The Debate on the University and the Reforms Proposals in Italy," *European Journal of Education,* 23 (June 1988): 216–56; Roberto Moscati, "Reflections on Higher Education and the Polity in Italy," *European Journal of Education* 23 (June 1985): 127–39.

The Netherlands

Frans A. van Vught

◆

General Features of the Higher Education System

The higher education system in the Netherlands consists of three main branches: the universities, the schools for higher vocational education (*hoger beroepsonderwijs*, often called the HBO-institutes), and the Open University. Each branch has its own characteristics and history.

Generally speaking, the tertiary system in the Netherlands is oriented toward students aged eighteen and upwards. Higher education is accessible to anyone who has earned the appropriate type of secondary education diploma. The diversified system of secondary education, with its various streams and levels and its variety of diplomas, provides an adequate selection of candidates for the higher education system. (Figure1 offers a diagram of the complete Dutch education system.)

Traditionally, the universities and the HBO-institutes have existed as two separate worlds. Recently, however, these two worlds have moved closer together, especially because of government policies with respect to the HBO-sector. The Open University is a relative newcomer to the system. Established by the Open University Act of 1984, the Open University offers fully accredited university and HBO degree programs, as well as other (mainly short-cycle) courses, all in the form of distance learning.

A new Higher Education and Research Bill has recently been introduced in parliament. This new law, which will probably come into force in the academic year 1990/91, encompasses all branches of the higher education and research system in the Netherlands. The law will introduce important reforms in Dutch higher education, especially deregulation in higher education policy making. The new law will take the place of the six existing acts on higher education as well as the nearly fifty orders and decrees.

Universities

There are thirteen universities in The Netherlands, three of which are universities of technology (the universities of Delft, Twente, and Eindhoven), one of which is a university of agriculture (the University of Wageningen), and nine of which are "general universities" (the University of Amsterdam, the Free University of Amsterdam, the University of Groningen, the University of Leiden, the University of Maastricht, the University of Nijmegen, the University of Rotterdam, the University of Tilburg, and the University of Utrecht). Of these thirteen universities, ten are public bodies. The Universities of Nijmegen and Tilburg are Roman Catholic. The Free University of Amsterdam is reformed Protestant. These three universities were founded under private law. However, except for the differences in foundation, hardly any differences exist between private and public universities.

The largest university is the University of Amsterdam (23,000 students). The smallest is the University of Maastricht (4,000 students). The average enrollment is 12,000 students.

At present all universities are governed by the University Education Act of 1960, which makes them all eligible for govern-ment funding. The general conditions and the objectives of the universities are stated in the Revised University Education Act (1986). According to the general conditions, university education is a form of higher education and comprises training for the independent pursuit of scholarship; com-prises preparation for the performance of professional functions for which academic training is required and desirable; promotes understanding of the field of science and scholarship as a whole. The objectives of the universities are indicated as: teaching

---

Figure 1

The Dutch Education System

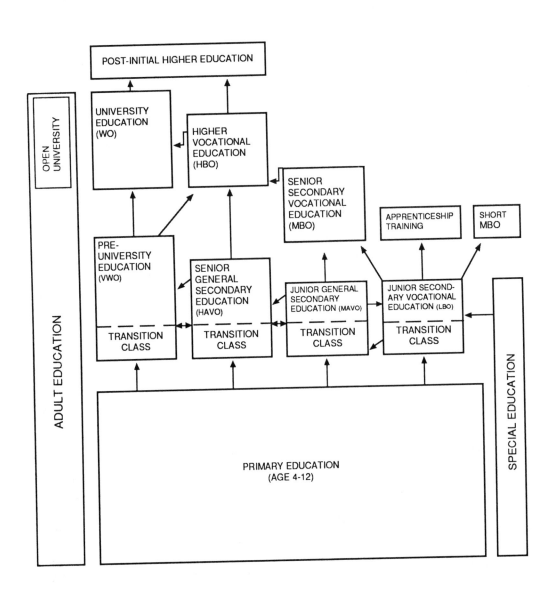

and research; the promotion of the transfer of knowledge acquired through research for the benefit of the community; the promotion of a sense of social responsibility; the provision of postgraduate training.

To obtain government funding the universities must adhere to the national statutory regulations and conform to the governmental systems of planning and funding. The University Education Act provides government regulation on a variety of subjects, including the procedures to be followed prior to the establishment of curricula, the administrative organization of the universities, and the specific rights and duties of both the government and the universities. Constitutional orders in the form of the University Statute, an Implementation Decree, and a few regulations with respect to budgets and investments supplement the University Education Act.

Presently there are about 170,000 students enrolled in the universities in The Netherlands. As Figure 2 indicates, the number of students has generally been rising. However, because of the demographic situation in the Netherlands, the estimates indicate a decline in student numbers in the years to come.

All thirteen Dutch universities do not offer the same range of courses. The two largest universities (Utrecht and Amsterdam) provide most of the 104 degree courses that are officially recognized. The other general universities offer a more restricted range. The establishment of a new degree course by a university has to be preceded by a government decision as to whether the new course will be eligible for government funding.

HBO-Institutes

Schools for higher vocational education (the HBO-Institutes) have undergone some far-reaching changes since the early 1970s. Originally the HBO-sector consisted of more than three hundred small- and medium-sized institutes. Government-imposed mergers have changed this variety of relatively small schools into a group of approximately fifty large institutes. This merger operation will be described in more detail below.

Most HBO-institutes were officially governed by the Secondary Education Act, instead of a form of higher education legislation, until 1986, when the Higher Vocational Education Act was passed. In this act the general conditions and objectives of the HBO-institutions are described as follows: HBO is a form of higher education and is designed to give a theoretical and practical training for the practice of professions for which higher vocational training is required or desirable; it promotes the personal development and functioning in society of its students; it is directly accessible to school-leavers from the higher form of secondary education.

The objectives of the HBO-institutes are: to provide teaching; in some cases to perform (applied) research; to contribute to the development of the professions for which they provide training; to provide postgraduate courses.

The HBO-institutes offer a wide range of courses in a number of categories. These categories include teacher training, agriculture, technical training, health care, commerce, social work, and the performing arts.

Unlike the universities, most HBO-institutes are privately run. But private status does not mean that the institutes do not have to conform to the national regulations and the national systems of planning and funding. To be eligible for government funding private institutes, like the private universities, must follow government guidelines. The degree of detail in the government regulations with respect to the HBO-institutes is comparable to that of the universities. HBO-schools do have more autonomy than universities regarding their internal administrative organization.

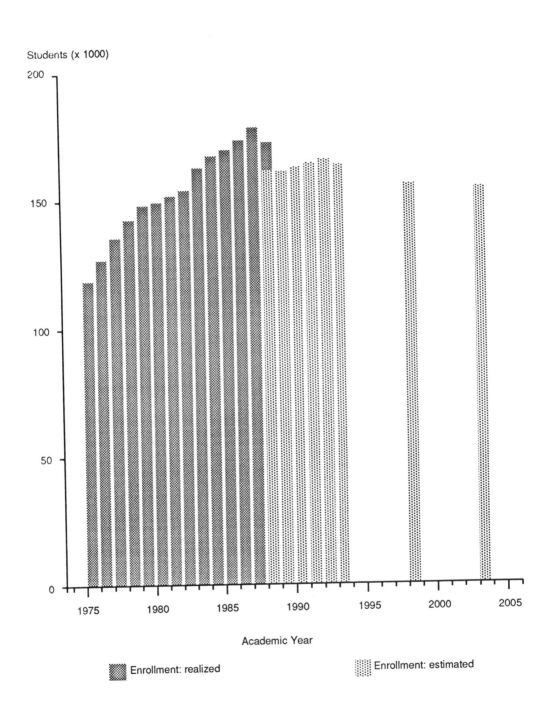

Figure 2

Number of Enrolled University Students

More students attend the HBO-institutes than attend the universities. In 1986/87 more than 220,000 students were enrolled in the HBO-sector. The number of enrolled students has been steadily rising. (See Figure 3.) The number of students enrolled was 31 percent higher in 1987/88 than in 1975/76. With the exception of "teacher training," this change is reflected in all fields.

Individual HBO-institutes offer a differentiated set of study programs. In total about 175 full-time or part-time study programs are offered at present. As is the case with the universities, the establishment of a new degree course requires government approval.

The Open University

The Open University started its activities on September 1, 1984, after ten years of preparation. The Open University has its offices in a city in the southern part of the Netherlands. It also has eighteen regional study centers spread over the country.

The Open University Act of 1984 regulates the Open University. The Open University is a provision of higher education through the medium of distance learning, with the following features: no admission requirements; freedom for students to choose their own courses; freedom for students to study at their own pace. The Open University Act mandates that the Open University will offer teaching that:

○ Is designed to prepare students for the independent practice of a profession;

○ Is designed to give training for the performance of functions in which research skills or scholarly insights and methods are required or desirable;

○ Contributes to the promotion of personal development;

○ Helps foster a sense of social responsibility with regard to the practice and application of science and scholarship;

○ Is a follow-up to the higher forms of secondary education.

As these descriptions indicate, the Open University offers courses that are comparable to those offered by the universities or those offered by the HBO-institutes. It can also provide courses that combine elements of both university and HBO courses.

The Open University offers courses in law, economics, management and public administration, engineering, sciences, social sciences, and arts. By the end of 1987 forty-nine courses had been developed and nearly sixty more were planned.

The start of the Open University brought some unexpected problems. An intensive advertising campaign for the Open University attracted far higher numbers of entering students than expected, which led to the decision to proclaim a "numerus clausus" because of insufficient capacity. Also, the development of the curricula took much longer than originally planned, leading to higher costs per course and longer waiting times for students.

On November 1, 1987, there were about 35,000 students enrolled in the Open University. Of the applicants approximately 50 percent are between age twenty-six and age thirty-five. Males outnumber females by a ratio of 2:1. It also appears that more than 50 percent of the students enrolled intend to obtain a diploma.

The Research System

In the Netherlands scientific research is undertaken by the universities as well as by specialized institutes outside the universities. Government research policies are based on the assumption that the universities are the most important places for scientific research. Recently the government has indicated that the following criteria are crucial with regard to government research policies:

Figure 3

Number of Enrolled HBO-students

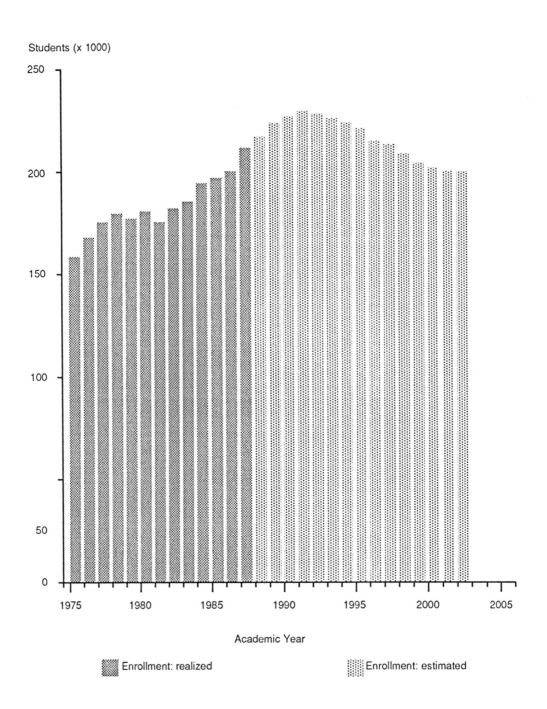

○ Research is, in principle, at home in the universities. Accordingly, the role of research institutes outside the universities needs to be justified on special grounds.

○ The research system must form a coherent whole, but administrative and organizational conditions should also enable the setting of priorities.

○ The role of government should be limited.

With regard to the universities, the so-called conditional financing plan was introduced in 1983. This plan indicates that a certain part of the total budget for a university must be earmarked for research. A university designs its own research programs but before implementation programs must be assessed by independent national committees (since 1987 these committees have been organized for each discipline). Each program must undergo a new assessment every five years. Positive assessments lead to guaranteed funding. Universities are free to initiate new programs and to alter existing programs as long as they remain within the earmarked budget.

The nonuniversity research institutes are attached to either universities, to the Netherlands Organization for the Advancement of Academic Research (NWO), or to the Royal Netherlands Academy of Arts and Sciences (KNAW). NWO plays an important role in the Dutch research system. It operates as an assessing body in the conditional financing system; it is in charge of various nonuniversity research institutes; and, perhaps most importantly, it disburses funds (the so-called "second flow of funds") for research projects. The KNAW was founded in 1808 by King Louis Napoleon to promote the pursuit of learning. It acts as an advisory body to the government on all possible subjects in the field of research and higher education. It also performs assessing tasks in the conditional financing system and it is responsible for a number of nonuniversity research institutes.

Historical Note

The first university in the Netherlands was founded in Leiden in 1575. It was a gift of Prince Willem van Oranje, the founder of the Dutch republic (later monarchy), who wanted to reward the city for resisting the Spanish. The University of Leiden was followed by the University of Groningen (1614), the University of Amsterdam (1632), and the University of Utrecht (1634). The newest universities are the University of Twente (1961), the University of Rotterdam (1973), and the University of Maastricht (1976).

Throughout its four hundred years of history, Dutch higher education has been able to maintain high academic standards while at the same time adapting to changing societal demands. Traditionally the Dutch universities have followed the continental model of the "Humboldt university." In this model the basic philosophy of W. von Humboldt (1767–1835) prevails, implying a close relationship between academic training and scientific research as well as a strong orientation toward disciplines. At present a shift can be witnessed toward a more Anglo-Saxon (especially U.S.) type of institution, with a greater accent on mass education and an increasing market-orientation.

Higher vocational education in the Netherlands is much younger than scientific education. Although a few lines can be traced back to a growing awareness of the importance of vocational education in the seventeenth century, the introduction of vocational education in general and of higher vocational education in particular took place in this century. Since World War II especially, both the number of vocational training schools and the kinds of courses they offer have expanded rapidly. In 1963 this differentiation resulted in the Secondary Education Act, in which higher vocational education was formally acknowledged as a new category of higher education. The introduction of the Higher Vocational Training Act of 1986 marked the government's awareness of the significance of vocational education in the tertiary system.

Generally speaking, the HBO-institutes offer practical and applied course programs that enable students to prepare themselves for specific professional careers. As such, these institutes represent the French "Napoleonic" tradition in higher education, in which, from the nineteenth century on, professionalism has always been an important value.

Admission, Tuition, and Financial Assistance

Admission

There are no entrance examinations for newly enrolling students in Dutch higher education. In principle, all qualified secondary school graduates are allowed to enter higher education.

At present there are, however, two kinds of "numerus clausus": a numerus clausus based on capacity and a numerus clausus based on an estimation of the labor market. The "capacity numerus clausus" is supposed to be an exception in Dutch higher education. The Ministry of Education and Science can proclaim such a numerus clausus for a specific university degree course when the universities convincingly argue that sufficient capacity cannot be realized on short notice. The "labor market numerus clausus" can be used by the ministry when it thinks that the prospects of employment in a specific profession are not too good. Since the introduction of this regulation in 1985, it has only been applied in a few medical and teacher training courses.

Admission policies are based on the general policy-objective of "higher education for the many," an objective that has dominated the general development of the higher education system since its introduction in 1978. "Higher education for the many" implies the aspiration to make (and hold) the higher education system accessible to as many persons as possible.

Tuition

All students enrolled in higher education institutions have to pay a tuition fee. Tuition fees for HBO-institutes were introduced in 1981. In 1988 the fees were harmonized for universities and HBO-institutes. This meant an increase for HBO students and a (small) reduction for university students. At present the fees are the same for all courses at a university and for all courses at a HBO-institute, 1,500 Dutch guilders.

Tuition fees have constantly increased during the last few years. An important consideration with respect to this constant increase relates to the budget deficit of the Ministry of Education.

Financial Assistance

Since the beginning of the 1960s the government has been providing financial assistance to students. In 1986 a new Financial Aid to Students Act was introduced. In the new financial assistance system every student is entitled to a basic grant provided by the government. This grant does not have to be paid back. In some cases the basic grant can be supplemented with an extra grant or loan, up to a certain maximum. Decisions regarding extra grants or loans take into account factors including the student's expected costs of living, his/her parents' ability to pay, and whether the student is living with parents, with a partner, or independently.

Recently the financial assistance system has become an object of sometimes heated political debates. The administration of the system appears to be quite difficult. To reduce these difficulties a new agency for financial assistance has been set up. Also, a discussion has started about the advantages and disadvantages of a voucher system in higher education.

Higher Education Staff

The university sector of the Dutch higher education system employs nearly 39,500 people, about 18,500 as academic staff. During the last few years these numbers have hardly changed. The HBO-institutes employ approximately 13,000 persons, of which nearly 10,000 are on the academic staff. Staff numbers in the HBO-institutes have gradually increased during the last years.

All staff members of all higher education and research institutions have the status of civil servants. As government personnel, their salaries and secondary conditions of employment are to a large extent centrally determined. Generally speaking, the regulations laid down by government for personnel in government service can only be formalized after consultation with the civil service trade unions. Next to the general civil servants regulations, higher education organizations also have their own national legal status regulations, which sometimes contradict the general regulations. These more specific regulations are supposed to enable processes of fine-tuning in the employment conditions for higher education institutions.

Debate continues about whether government personnel policies have a detrimental effect on flexibility and innovation in higher education institutions. Well-known problems such as an aging staff, limited accessibility for young people and, in a few cases, a brain drain to the private sector have intensified these discussions. However, as of now no structural changes are foreseen with respect to personnel policies in higher education.

Higher Education and Employment

In the Netherlands, forecasts about the future employment situation of graduates leaving the higher education system have been produced since the end of the 1950s. The forecasts for 1980, made in 1958, 1968, and 1975, have all been more or less incorrect. The 1958 forecast predicted a shortage of academics in the labor market. The 1968 and 1975 forecasts predicted an unemployment figure of 6,000 and 20,000 respectively (and a figure of employed academics of 126,000 and 140,000 respectively). The actual academic unemployment figure in 1980 was 5,000 (with 165,000 employed academics).

It appears that the societal demand for academics and the absorption capacity of the labor market are very hard to predict. In the older forecasts no attention was paid to the effects of graduates with higher degrees driving out people with lower-level degrees or to the explosive growth of some specific-sector labor markets. Recent forecasts tend to be more cautious. Instead of singular forecasts, alternative scenarios are presented. Also, differentiations have been developed according to disciplines and fields.

The present unemployment figure (1988) for the overall higher education labor market is approximately 6 percent. This number is lower than the years 1987 (7.1 percent) and 1984 (8.3 percent). However, there appear to be large differences between the various disciplines and fields. Presently, in the university sector, the unemployment numbers range between a high of 11.5 percent for language and culture graduates and a low of 2.2 percent for law graduates. The HBO-sector shows numbers ranging from 18 percent for language and culture to 1.9 percent for economics. The technical and economic disciplines and fields appear to have particularly low unemployment numbers. The various forecasts for these fields predict attractive future employment perspectives. The forecasts for the year 2000 predict an overall unemployment figure of ± 5 percent for the university sector and ± 4 percent for the HBO-sector.

Structural Reforms and Retrenchment Operations

In the 1970s and the beginning of the 1980s the higher education system in the Netherlands was confronted with some major structural reforms and a few severe retrenchment operations. These rather comprehensive processes of change are sometimes described as corrective reforms. The government refers to the structural reforms and retrenchment operations of the 1970s and the 1980s as necessary corrective policies. The new governmental strategy toward higher education in the Netherlands, introduced in 1985, differs widely from the reform-oriented strategy followed before 1985. It is understandable that from its own point of view the government likes to define the reforms and budget cuts as necessary corrections. However, it should not be forgotten that these "corrections" have left a major negative impression in the minds of many academics employed in the higher education system.

The Introduction of Two-Tier Structure in the University Sector

The Two-Tier Act was passed in parliament in 1981. This act sought to introduce into the university a number of innovations that would solve two important problems that arose in the 1960s and 1970s.

The first problem was the enormous growth of the student body. In 1960 the number of registered university students was 40,727, but this number had increased to 116,359 by 1975. The problem of how to adapt the university system to this growing number of students, particularly in the face of severe pressures on governmental budgets, demanded solutions. The increase of the number of students seemed to demand an automatic increase in the higher education budget. But the national budget could no longer afford such an increase.

The second problem was the rather low level of efficiency in the university system. Before 1982 the mean intended length of the university study programs was about five years. However, the average student took 7.2 years (in 1982) to complete his/her studies. Also there was a substantial group of "eternal students," who apparently felt no obligation to finish their studies. A second aspect of this efficiency problem was the rather large drop-out rate. Although enrolling students were assumed to be qualified to complete a university study program, 40 to 45 percent of the students nevertheless failed to do so. This situation was considered to be unacceptable in light of the increasing tight governmental budgets.

In 1975 the Dutch government had already proposed some radical reforms for the university system. But the proposals were confronted by strong opposition from the universities. However, although the universities' resistance seemed to be successful in the short run, in the long run it had the opposite effect. Because the universities did not want to face the problems of mass education and low efficiency, the governmental policymakers developed solutions on their own. Once these solutions were designed, parliament remained as deaf to the universities' complaints as the universities had been to the politicians.

In 1978, the then minister of education suggested introducing a two-tier structure in the university system. In 1979 he published a draft bill. One year later he sent his final bill to parliament where it was easily passed. In less than four years a comprehensive reform of the Dutch university system was realized.

The most important features of the Two-Tier Act are the following:

○ University study programs now have a first tier (or phase) with a duration of four years. In other words, former programs were reduced by about a year. This reduction was supposed not to affect the qualification of the graduates.

○ A maximum period of six years was set as the time limit for completing studies. Students who exceed this six-year period are excluded from the opportunity to participate in a university study-program.

○ Selected students who have successfully finished a first-tier program are enabled to follow a specific course in the second tier. Four kinds of programs are offered in this second tier:

   ○ Professional courses in the medical disciplines with a duration of two years; in practice all medical graduates from the first tier proceed to the second tier;
   ○ one-year teacher-training courses;
   ○ specialized professional courses in various fields with a maximum duration of two years, to be financed by government or the private sector;
   ○ research fellowships with a maximum duration of four years; these fellows are expected to do research and write a dissertation; because they are offered specific research training courses, they are appointed as university staff members at a restricted salary level.

The introduction of the two-tier structure led to heated debates which continue to the present day. The two main points of discussion are the level of the qualification of the graduates of the first tier and the number of students that are allowed to enter the second tier.

In 1987 an evaluation-study of this comprehensive structural reform was published.[1] According to this study, the implementation of the two-tier structure has not increased the level of efficiency of the university system. Hoped-for reduction of the drop-out rate for first year students of 20 percent was not achieved; actual drop-out rates ranged between 26 and 30 percent. The number of students finishing the first tier was estimated at a maximum of 67 percent (optimistic) or 62 percent (realistic), which is below the government's objective of 70 percent. As good news, the average period of study had dropped to 5.4 years, which is much shorter than the 7.2 years of the 1970 cohort of students. Also, the limitation of the period a student is allowed to stay in the system apparently has created an efficiency increase of 25 percent. Student workloads have increased; the obligation to shorten study programs in the first tier has induced many faculties to compensate with an increase in student workload.

The study also notes that the capacity of the second tier is limited. Although the second tier is still in a developing stage, its potential capacity seems to be smaller than had been expected. During the discussions in parliament on the Two-Tier Act a target had been established which implied that 30 percent of the graduates of the first tier could enter the second tier. The evaluation-study shows that the actual percentage appears to be 19 percent. Taking into account the fact that 100 percent of the medical graduates automatically enroll for the second tier, only 12 percent of other first tier graduates continue on to the second tier.

All in all, it may be concluded that, although the two-tier structure has certainly provided an answer to the problems the university system encountered in the 1960s and the 1970s, it cannot be called a complete success.[2]

The Merger Process in the HBO-Sector

In 1983 the government published a thirty-page policy document on "scale-enlargement, task-allocation, and concentration" in higher vocational education. The objectives of this comprehensive reform policy in the HBO-sector were: a considerable enlargement of the size of the HBO-institutes by means of mergers; an enlargement of the autonomy of the institutes with regard to the use of resources, personnel policies, and the structuring of the educational processes; a greater efficiency in the use of resources by using larger groups, concentration of expensive equipment, coordination, and, where possible, combination of course elements. The objectives were oriented toward strengthening the HBO-institutes, both in an educational and a managerial sense. Apart from this basic goal, there was also a retrenchment objective. The operation had to result in a financial reduction for the HBO-sector, amounting to Dfl. 68 million in the year 1988 and beyond.

As was indicated before, the HBO-sector in Dutch higher education started from a somewhat peripheral position. And although during its development some initiatives were taken to ameliorate this position, for several decades the HBO-sector remained a kind of second-rate higher education. The comprehensive merger operation has drastically changed this situation.

The organization of the whole operation was carefully planned. The merger process was supported by a new legal structure (the Higher Vocational Education Act of 1986) and by a new financing system. Moreover, a tight time schedule was laid out. Final agreements about the mergers had to be reached by August 1986. A complete organizational restructuring of the HBO-sector had to take place in a   period of two-and-one-half years.

As Goedegebuure et al. indicate, one of the most remarkable features of this restructuring process was the way it was organized. The mergers were not centrally imposed by government, but to a large extent were left to the institutes themselves. The HBO-council was asked to coordinate the whole merger process. "The results of the merger operation are remarkable and surpass the expectations of many who were involved. To refer to the legend of the phoenix might be too much of an exaggeration, but there can be little doubt as to the success of the operation in terms of merger. By July 1987, 314 of the 348 had merged into fifty-one new institutes, while thirty-four remained independent . . . the mergers have resulted for the most part in multi-sectoral mergers."[3]

Retrenchment Operations

In the university system in the Netherlands, the 1980s are probably marked above all by the two major retrenchment operations of 1982/83 and 1986.

The first retrenchment operation started with a letter from the minister of education and science to parliament. The minister declared that a severe cutback in the funds for the university system was inevitable. A retrenchment would take place by reallocating tasks between universities. The minister indicated that the budget cuts would rise from Dfl. 20 million in 1983 to Dfl. 60 million in 1986. The minister also offered the universities a choice: they could either try to defend the then existing situation, forcing the minister to impose budget cuts, or they could themselves develop a reallocation plan.

The universities chose the latter option. They established a reallocation committee to develop a plan. The minister meanwhile published his official document (called *Task Reallocation and Con-*

centration in Scientific Education) in which he pointed out that the cuts would have to rise to approximately Dfl. 258 million in 1987. Parliament supported the minister's general policy.

The rest of this story is easily told. The universities published their plan after half a year. The minister praised the committee for its good work, but he also indicated that the proposed concentration of activities did not go far enough and he developed some alternative proposals. The universities were disappointed, but could only accept the final "policy intentions" formulated by the minister. The minister sent his final task-reallocation plan to parliament, which to a large extent agreed with the various proposals.[4]

The second retrenchment operation was a solo performance by the minister. In 1986 he imposed his "Selective Contraction and Expansion" proposals for the years 1987–1991. The universities had no choice about accepting these cuts. But bitterness and apathy in the universities grew. By the second half of the 1980s the Ministry of Education and Science seemed to many academics in the university system to be the enemy, rather than the advocate of higher education. The ministry appeared to sense this basic mistrust and then embarked upon a completely new governmental strategy toward higher education.

A New Governmental Strategy Toward Higher Education

In 1985 the Dutch Ministry of Education and Science published an important policy document called HOAK (*Hoger Onderwijs: Autonomie en Kwaliteit* [Higher Education: Autonomy and Quality]) in which a new governmental strategy regarding higher education was presented. This new attitude indicates an important break with the traditional governmental strategy.

Under the old strategy the government practiced detailed planning and control. The government tried to steer the higher education system with stringent regulations and extensive control mechanisms. The government saw itself as an omnipotent master able to guide the higher education system according to its own objectives.

The new strategy marks an important change. By strengthening the autonomy of higher education institutions, the government hopes to create fruitful conditions for increasing the adaptive power and flexibility of higher education institutions. The government hopes that more freedom will enable the university to better respond to the needs of society. By strengthening institutional autonomy the government also hopes to stimulate the levels of quality and differentiation in the higher education system.

The new governmental strategy is based on the idea that increased institutional autonomy will result in an improvement of the performance of the higher education system. Higher education institutions will now have more freedom to shape their own activities. The institutions will be allowed to assume responsibility for themselves in the fields of education and research. Detailed governmental regulations concerning these activities will be dropped.

Another basic idea of the new governmental strategy is that instead of an ex ante control of the performance of the higher education institutions, an ex post evaluation of quality will be institutionalized. For this kind of ex post evaluation government claims to need a quality control system, consisting not only of the monitoring and evaluation activities of the institutions themselves, but also of an independent quality assessment by government.

Government has indicated its willingness to step back. But it also still sees itself fulfilling the tasks of coordinating the higher education system and trying to stimulate it to higher levels of performance. The enlargement of the institutional autonomy is first and foremost seen as an instrument for trying to reach a higher degree of societal usefulness. Government remains the central authority for the guidance of the system.

Recently the HOAK paper has been followed by another important policy document: HOOP. HOOP is the acronym for *Hoger Onderwijs en Onderzoek Plan* (Plan for Higher Education and Scientific Research). HOOP is the next operational step in the development of the new Dutch governmental strategy toward higher education.

The new strategy gives a great deal of prominence to planning by means of dialogue. The dialogue is supposed to be based on the objectives for the future of both government and the higher education institutions. These objectives will be written down in the two central documents of the planning system developed as a consequence of the new strategy: the governmental plan called HOOP and the development plans of the institutions.

The HOOP document will bring together all the governmental higher education documents that previously were issued separately. It offers an image of the future of the higher education system as desired by government. The institutions' development plans are to be a reflection of the intentions of the institutions, of the influences from their environment, and of their internal activities and developments. The new planning system has a two-year cycle, with the HOOP document being published in the first, and the institutional development plans in the second year. The first (draft) HOOP document was published in September 1987; the first development plans appeared in the spring of 1988.

The New Dutch Governmental Strategy: An Evaluation

In its new strategy government envisions steering the higher education system by means of "steering-networks." A steering-network is defined as a combination of actors (particularly the Ministry of Education and Science and the higher education institutions), of issues at which the steering-activities are aimed, and of instruments that are used by the actors to try to reach their objectives. It is the opinion of the ministry that, as a consequence of the new governmental strategy towards higher education, the characteristics of the steering-networks will change. In the past, government was very much involved in activities such as the approval of degree courses and the detailed control of all kinds of institutional decisions and processes. Under the new strategy government wants to limit itself to general frame-setting and general control processes.

The new strategy has been characterized as an "intriguing Janus-head."[5] In the new strategy the institutions have a certain amount of autonomy, but government has the power to influence the behavior of the institutions. Higher education institutions are confronted with more freedom, but this freedom is, in part, only a freedom to act according to the wishes of government. The newly emerging strategy appears to be a combination of two different conceptions of system dynamics. If government really accepted the idea of institutional autonomy, it would also have had to accept, and, if necessary, to optimize the working of the market mechanism in higher education. This would have meant reconceiving the higher education system as a system characterized by complete, open competition. The "producers" of higher education (the institutions) should be able to compete for the favors of the "consumers" (e.g., students choosing an education; organizations giving out contracts for research projects). Every producer would try to find his own specialized niche while offering his goods at the market. But he could not attempt to control the market by forming a monopoly or an oligopoly. Competition is a crucial characteristic of this model.

The role of government in this model would be to try to guarantee competition. On the one hand, government would attempt to protect the sovereignty of the consumers. On the other hand, government would prevent the formation of monopolies and oligopolies. Government would have no role in coordinating the system or trying to optimize its performance.

However, the new Dutch governmental strategy, as presented in the HOAK and the HOOP policy papers, shows quite another role of government. Certainly, under this strategy the autonomy of the producers of higher education is increased and the competition between these producers is stimulated. But in the new strategy, government is not primarily the protector of the sovereignty of the consumers and the fighter of monopolies and oligopolies. Government in this strategy tries to steer the higher education system. Government apparently thinks itself capable of formulating overall targets for the higher education system. And the government will continue to influence the behavior of the institutions to try to reach these targets. By doing this, however, government has to restrict the behavior of the higher education producers. Certain forms of behavior by the institutions will not be allowed. And because of such restrictions government creates a situation in which the institutions cannot develop certain adaptations to their environment. Because government wants to coordinate and steer the system from its own position, it will have to exclude some forms of adaptive behavior by the institutions.

Under the new strategy the autonomy of the institutions is a restricted autonomy. Higher education institutions may operate as self-steering organizations to the extent government lets them. Higher education institutions will have more autonomy than they used to have, but the dynamics of the higher education system are restricted by the coordinating and steering activities of government. The specializations and the structural order in the system can only partly be the result of the institutional profiles that are being developed because the institutions try to find their own niches. The structural order and the specializations in the system are to a large extent an outcome of the various decisions and actions of government, aimed at the optimization of the system from the government's point of view.

Conclusions

The new Dutch governmental strategy toward higher education is a combination of two fundamentally different theoretical conceptions. In the new governmental strategy aspects of the classical model of detailed planning and control are combined with aspects of the natural selection model.[6]

The newly developing governmental strategy toward higher education in the Netherlands is an important innovation in higher education policy-making. It indicates a fundamental change in the traditional governmental attitude regarding higher education. It reveals a loss of confidence in the government's capabilities to centrally plan and control a higher education system and a willingness to take the self-regulating capacities of higher education organizations seriously. Other European countries have introduced innovations similar to the developments in the Netherlands.[7] It may very well be the case that in the near future the new governmental strategy toward higher education in the Netherlands will appear to have been the herald of a new general governmental approach to higher education.

Notes

1. F.A. van Vught and A.M.L. van Wieringen, eds., *Evaluatie-Onderzoek Wet Twee-fasenstructuur* (The Netherlands: Ministry of Education and Science, 1987) (in Dutch).

2. R.J. Bijleveld, *The Two-Tier Structure in Dutch University Education* (Enschede, The Netherlands: Center for Higher Education Policy Studies, 1987).

3. L.C.J. Goedegebuure and H.J. Vos, "Blown on the Steel Breeze: Institutional Mergers in Dutch Higher Vocational Education," in *Change in Higher Education: the Non-University Sector*, ed. L.C.J. Goedegebuure and V.L. Meek (Culemborg, The Netherlands: Lemma, 1988), 116, 117.

4. F.A. van Vught, "Negative Incentive Steering in a Policy Network: The Case of the Policy Development Process Concerning the Retrenchment Operation in the Dutch University System in 1982 and 1983," *Higher Education* (1985): 593–616.

5. P.A.M. Maassen and F.A. van Vught, "An Intriguing Janus-head: The Two Faces of the New Governmental Strategy for Higher Education in the Netherlands," *European Journal of Education*, nos. 1, 2 (1988): 65–77.

6. H.E. Aldrich, *Organizations and Environments* (Englewood Cliffs, N.J.: Prentice-Hall, 1979); H.E. Aldrich and J. Pfeffer, "Environments of Organizations," *Annual Review of Sociology*, no. 2 (1976): 79–105; R. Birnbaum, *Maintaining Diversity in Higher Education* (San Francisco: Jossey-Bass, 1983); M.T. Hannan and J. Freeman, "The Population Ecology of Organizations," *American Journal of Sociology* (1977): 929–64.

7. F.A. van Vught, *Governmental Strategies and Innovations in Higher Education* (London: Jessica Kingsley, 1989).

Poland

Jan Sadlak

◆

Poland is the second largest Eastern European socialist country, with a present population of 38 million. For the past forty years the development of higher education has taken place within the context of a centrally planned socioeconomic system whose ideological roots are Marxism-Leninism. Nowadays, Poland is a country in transition in which major political, economic, and ideological issues, including those related to higher education, are subject to reinterpretation and change.

At present, there are ninety-two higher education institutions in Poland[1]: eleven universities, including the only private but state-recognized university in Eastern Europe, the Catholic University of Lublin (KUL); eighteen higher technical schools, of which fourteen have a status equivalent to the "technical university"; five academies of economics; ten higher pedagogical colleges; six physical education and sport academies; two theological academies; and one social sciences academy (ANS) associated with the Polish United Worker's Party (PZPR). All of these, except KUL, which is mainly administered by the Roman Catholic Church, and to a lesser degree ANS, are subordinated to the Ministry of Education. There are also eleven medical academies (subordinated to the Ministry of Health); seventeen arts schools—eight music academies, six schools of fine arts, and three theater and film schools (subordinated to the Ministry of Culture); and two merchant marine officers training schools (subordinated to the Office of Maritime Economy). Some of these establishments have units in other towns; "branches" function like affiliated colleges and "consultation centers" mainly serve part-time students. Their number has declined because only some of them can provide appropriate university-level education and research programs. Still, in the academic year 1988/89 there were twenty-four "branches" and forty-two "consultation centers."

Higher education institutions are situated in twenty-four localities. The major academic centers, those with some seven to thirteen higher education institutions, are Warsaw, Crakow, Wroclaw, Gdansk, Katowice-Gliwice, and Poznan. More than 70 percent of all academic staff work in those seven centers. These cities also have many other institutions that substantially enrich and enhance academic activities and supplement the research infrastructure of higher education establishments. Some of them are part of the institutional network of more than seventy units run by the Polish Academy of Sciences (PAN) which employ about 15 percent of the country's research staff and which are engaged mainly in basic research. The others are research institutes linked to various ministries (there are more than 120 such institutes), some of which have the legal right to grant doctoral degrees in their field of research expertise.

The composition of the academic staff in Polish higher education—whose categories originate mainly from the German academic model with various postwar modifications—is as follows: 1) "senior" or "independent" scientific workers—"ordinary" professors, "extraordinary" professors, and *docents*; 2) "junior" or "assisting" scientific workers—adjuncts, lecturers, senior assistants, and assistants; and 3) "other teachers"—lectors, sport coaches, laboratory assistants, etc. At present, the proportion in each category is 16 percent, 67 percent, and 17 percent, respectively. Only those belonging to the first category are tenured.

The statistical information presented in Table 1 shows that student enrollment in Poland, even though it slightly increased in the academic year 1988/89, was substantially lower in the 1980s than in the previous decade. As a result of the present decline in the number of study places, less than 10 percent of the nineteen-to-twenty-year-old age group now enters higher education; this figure stood at about 15 percent in the mid-1970s. The number of students per 100,000 inhabitants has declined from 1,369 in the academic year 1975/76 to 842 in the year 1988/89. This decline has been particularly severe among part-time students and graduate

students (both represent some 23 percent of the respective totals).

In the academic year 1988/89 the number of part-time students dropped by about 55 percent in comparison with the academic year 1975/76. The decline in the number of graduate students is even more pronounced, showing how this segment of the student population is influenced by general economic conditions as well as by their prospects of advancement in professional careers after completion of studies. Other basic statistical data presented in Table 1—concerning academic staff, foreign students, and Polish students studying abroad—shows that after a drastic decline in the early 1980s the trend has been gradually altered. Particularly noticeable is a steady growth in the number of foreign students. Their estimated number in 1989 is already about seven thousand.

Table 1

Basic Statistical Parameters of Polish Higher Education, 1975–76, 1980–81, and 1988–89

	1975–76	1980–81	1985–86	1988–89
Number of Higher Education Institutions	89	91	92	92
Number of students	468,129	453,652	329,686	356,400
Full-time	283,159	299,048	254,786	272,500
Part-time	184,970	154,604	74,900	83,900
Foreign students	2,438	2,913	2,850	3,447[1]
Polish students abroad	2,680	3,542	2,400	2,749[1]
Number of graduates	63,236	83,955	59,919	49,700
of full-time studies	37,046	50,145	41,765	38,300
of part-time studies	26,190	33,810	18,154	11,400
Academic staff	48,837	54,681	57,280	59,003
Number of students per 100,000 inhabitants	1,369	1,269	998	842[2]

[1]   Figures for academic year 1987/88.
[2]   Figures for 1988.
Source: National Statisitcal Yearbooks, various years.

As a result of bilateral cooperative and assistance agreements the total cost of study, inclusive of cost of living, for approximately 75 percent of the foreign students is covered by the Polish state. Some 25 percent pay "full cost," on average about $4,500 (US). Some 45 percent of the foreign students are studying engineering, about 30 percent are in medicine, and about 15 percent are studying humanities and natural sciences.

Historical Trends

Higher education has a long tradition in Poland. Poland's first university, Jagiellonian University in Crakov, was founded in 1364 and is one of the oldest universities in Central Europe. In the sixteenth and seventeenth centuries, when Poland was one of the major European powers, two new universities were founded: Stefan Batory University in Wilno (1578) and Jan Kazimierz University in Lwov (1661). The cultural atmosphere of the Enlightenment, combined with nationalist pressures from the Polish part of the Russian Empire, led to the creation of another new university, the Warsaw University, in 1816. The emerging industrial development of nineteenth-century Poland resulted in a growing need for technical and commercial professions. It also brought forth new academic institutions, such as the Warsaw Polytechnic (1826), to provide these types of studies.

Academic institutions, in particular universities, played an important role in the development of scholarship and research and in educating the Polish intellectual and political elite. They also contributed to the maintenance and enhancement of links with the larger European cultural tradition and its humanistic values. The higher education community—students, professors, and institutions—played a significant part in the preservation of the Polish national and cultural identity during the period when the Polish state ceased to exist at the end of the eighteenth century as a result of its partition between czarist Russia, Prussia, and the Austrian Empire.

The reemergence of the various higher education institutions after World War I was considered one of the important confirmations of Polish statehood. Prior to World War II thirty-two institutions of higher learning existed. Thirteen were state institutions, which at that time contained more than 60 percent of the student population and the majority of the academic staff. The largest private academic institutions were the Catholic University of Lublin and the Independent University in Warsaw with its four-faculty campus in Lodz. In the prewar period the largest academic center was Warsaw, with almost one-third of all higher educational institutions and more than 40 percent of the total student population of some 49,550 persons. The next largest was Lwov (with 19 percent), followed by Crakov (some 16 percent), Poznan (about 12 percent), Wilno (more than 7 percent), Lublin (about 3 percent), and Lodz (1.1 percent).[2]

Higher education used to be elitist and costly. Only 10 percent of the students received financial aid, mainly in the form of loans. Some 14 percent lived in the student dormitories. In the academic year 1937/38 some 9 percent came from worker's family backgrounds and some 9 percent from peasant or farmer's families.[3]

Academic institutions enjoyed, generally speaking, a high degree of academic autonomy, especially with regard to admissions policy, teaching content, topics of research, and nominations for the faculty. Organizationally, they embodied a kind of "federation of chairs." This corporate form of academic institution, based among other things on the experience of the Polish universities in the Galician province of the Austro-Hungarian Empire, and Humboldtian ideals of freedom in search of knowledge, was criticized for its lack of accountability; it was argued, for example, that the excessive independence of chairs prevented their integration within an overall institutional structure. Despite various attempts in the mid-1930s to limit academic autonomy and enhance the prerogatives of the government, liberal academic traditions were soon restored. Academic autonomy, a corporate system of governance with dominant power held by the faculty and the academic senate, and the right of student self-organization were, despite periodic restrictions, important features of the Polish model of higher education.

The functioning of higher education during World War II was very much affected by Nazi Germany's strategy of destroying Polish intellectual life. The Germans followed a general policy of "Germanization" in the territories incorporated into the "The Thousand-Year Reich."

From September 17, 1939, until June 1941 two major academic centers—Lwov and Wilno—were in that part of prewar Poland that was incorporated into the Soviet Union's territory. Whatever the motives for this action, there should be little doubt that this situation could not contribute to the functioning of these institutions as *Polish academic institutions*, even if they were not closed down by the Soviets.

The loss of human life as a result of World War II was enormous. One-third of the Polish intelligentsia perished and only about 40 percent of professors at university-level institutions survived. In 1938 there were 13,200 registered engineers in Poland, but only some 4,000 lived through the war—and some of these survivors remained in the West after the war because they were discouraged by the change of political system in Poland. Material losses were equally substantial. But from the point of view of the postwar development of Polish higher education the human losses were slightly compensated for by those who had benefited from secret underground teaching, nicknamed "the flying university." Not less significant was the moral commitment of students and faculty as well as the representation in the occupied Polish territor-

ies of the Polish-Government-in-Exile which provided the overall organizational and financial structure for underground education. The speed with which higher education establishments were either reopened or created following the gradual liberation of Poland shows that such actions were often regarded as a symbol of the rebirth of the Poland's statehood and an important prerogative of the new state administration. Altogether, the war years and the first postwar years showed that, like in other times and other countries, academic institutions gained a new dimension in addition to their "usual" tasks of preparation of an educational elite and knowledge development—they also symbolized national continuity and the state power.

Higher education functioned within the same institutional structure until near the end of the 1940s. Academic institutions enjoyed almost the same degree of autonomy as in the prewar years, although not all academic bodies were reactivated, such as, for example, the Rectors Conference of the Academic Institutions (*Konferencja Rektorow Szkol Akademickich*), which had played an important role in the representation of higher education interests before the war. But soon higher education became an arena of intensive political struggle, which resulted in the direct introduction of external political and social organizations into its internal governance and administration process. On October 28, 1947, a decree on the organization of science and higher education introduced the state-coordinated national system of higher education. The new law also founded a central advisory body, the Main Council on Higher Education (*Rada Glowna Szkolnictwa Wyzszego*). The roles and prerogatives of this body have been extended or curtailed almost each time new legislation on higher education has been passed but, ever since it was created, it has been an important element in the Polish higher education system.

The next important step in the remodeling of the Polish academic system toward what had begun to be called a "socialist model of higher education" came on December 15, 1951, with the Law on Higher Education and Scientific Workers. This law has to be seen in the context of another important act for Polish academic life that was adopted on October 30, 1951, creating the PAN. This newly created academy replaced the three prewar academies. The new law also introduced other major structural changes. Some of them, as was a usual practice in those years, were adopted from the Soviet Union's system of higher education and its organization of science. The most important consequence of this bill was the initiation of the restructuring of the higher education institutional framework and the introduction of basic changes with regard to academic personnel. Another element of this process was the development of the so-called socialist model of the university mandating concentration on theoretical research and teaching in such disciplines as philosophy, law and other social studies, mathematics, and natural sciences. At the same time, the following disciplines were removed from the university's structure: agriculture, theology, physical culture, medicine, and pharmacy. All the above faculties were reestablished in separate academic schools.

Changes concerning academic personnel were equally profound. Top-level positions in the academic institutions became part of the system of *nomenclatura*. New terms were introduced into Polish higher education: "scientific worker" (*pracownik nauki*), for example, a person professionally preoccupied with scholarly research and possessing a scientific title, and "independent" and "assisting" scientific workers. All these changes were very similar to those introduced, more or less in the same period, in other socialist Eastern European countries. Another common element was the creation of a central screening body for academic staff; this body takes into ac-

count not only academic merits but also the political soundness of the candidate. The Polish version of this screening group is called the Central Qualification Commission for Scientific Personnel of the Chairman of the Council of Ministers (CKK).

The early 1950s also witnessed major changes in the forms of studies. In the context of a policy for social equalization of participation in education and the growing need for a qualified workforce, new forms of part-time study—evening, correspondence, and extramural courses—were introduced. All these forms continue as part of the existing model of higher education in Poland.

Intensive de-Stalinization after 1956 and the new political climate associated with it brought significant changes to Polish academic life and, generally speaking, liberalized educational policy. However, the basic elements of the Law of 1951 remained in effect; these elements, together with the dogmatism of the Stalinist years, caused considerable damage to Polish academic development. A new law on higher education was adopted by the Polish parliament on November 5, 1958, but this law introduced only slight changes. A more repressive policy regarding higher education began following the "March Events" when a deteriorating economic situation and growing restraints on intellectual life sparked a wave of student strikes. The government reacted with brutal measures toward students, professors, and other intellectuals. The government's policy was accompanied by an anti-intelligentsia, anti-Semitic, antiliberal campaign which, among other things, led to complaints about "overproduction" of intelligentsia, calls for acceptance of a utilitarian approach to science, and demands for intensification of ideological indoctrination of students.

Legislative measures adopted in December 1968 again gave almost unrestrained control to the Communist Party, strengthened state administration of academic institutions, and reiterated the

Table 2

Students Per Major Group of Disciplines in Polish Higher Education
(Selective Academic Years 1960/61–1987/88)

Discipline	Engineering		Agriculture and Veterinary		Economics and Management		Law and Public Administration	
	I	II	I	II	I	II	I	II
1960/61	54,816	33.1	12,063	7.3	21,477	13.0	10,234	6.2
1965/66	85,967	34.2	24,295	9.6	50,002		19.9	
1970/71	129,533	39.2	27,707	8.2	37,117	11.2	22,729	6.9
1975/76	150,272	32.1	34,055	7.3	48,791	10.4	32,101	6.9
1980/81	145,900	32.2	40,548	8.9	54,459	12.1	32,037	7.1
1985/86[1]	84,900	24.9	23,200	6.8	34,800	10.2	19,900	5.8
1987/88[1]	77,600	22.7	22,600	6.7	33,400	9.7	21,000	6.1

I—Total number of students in the given discipline.
II—Percentage of students in the given discipline to the total student number.

[1] Figures for academic years 1985/86 and 1987/88 in ('00).

Source: National Statistical Yearbooks and author's calculations.

Marxist-Leninist context of university-level teaching and research. "Chairs" (*katedra*), formally the basic unit of the academic institution, were abolished. The process of determining professorial appointments was modified, mainly by abolishing a compulsory postdoctoral examination (*habili-tacja*). These changes opened up the possibility of politically motivated but academically unjustified nominations, especially at the rank of docent.

The 1970s were years of rapid, practically uncontrollable, economic growth based mainly on foreign credits. It was also a period of great expansion within higher education. The policymakers of that time expected that both research and a highly qualified workforce would be needed for the realization of their policies. Student numbers increased from some 330,800 in the academic year 1970/71 to 468,100 in 1975/76. A similar trend could be observed with regard to the number of academic staff: staff rose from 31,320 in 1970/71 to 48,837 in 1975/76. Most of this rise was achieved by increasing the number of positions for two midlevel categories of academic staff: docent and adjunct. In the second half of the 1970s, when it became clear that without rapid fundamental modifications of the socioeconomic system the government's ambitious plans would fail, the relations between the academic community and the central governing bodies became strained again. However, the reactions of the government were less repressive this time, at least with regard to the academic community, than they had been in previous periods of crisis.

Growing reformist tendencies in economic and political life dominate the Polish political scene in the 1980s. Pressure for reforms that would create more academic autonomy in Polish higher education, one of the principal issues in the whole postwar history of Polish higher education, continues to grow.

Major Trends and Developments of the Past Decade

Until the end of the 1970s the major direction of development for Polish higher education was fairly clear: the government

Table 2 (continued)

Students Per Major Group of Disciplines in Polish Higher Education (Selective Academic Years 1960/61–1987/88)

Medicine		Humanities and Teacher Training		Mathematics and Natural Sciences		Fine Arts		Others		Total
I	II	I	II	I	II	I	II			
23,728	14.3	23,305	14.1	15,160	9.1	3,712	2.2	1,192	0.7	165,687
24,962	9.9	35,295	14.0	26,528	10.5	4,815	1.9	—	—	251,864
22,851	6.9	51,672	15.6	31,717	9.6	5,237	1.6	2,726	0.8	330,789
29,707	6.4	107,729	23.0	54,842	11.7	7,210	1.5	3,422	0.7	468,129
35,143	7.7	97,829	21.5	36,598	8.1	7,772	1.7	3,400	0.7	453,652
34,200	10.1	99,400	29.2	32,700	9.6	7,600	2.2	4,000	1.2	340,700
35,700	10.4	107,200	31.4	33,200	9.5	7,700	2.2	4,300	1.3	342,600

encouraged expansion of student enrollment designed to respond to manpower needs; promoted the role of higher education as an agent of social change; increased the number of higher education graduates in order to meet needs for highly qualified manpower; and expanded the institutional network in order to increase opportunities for higher education, stimulate regional development, and respond to local ambitions stimulated by new administrative divisions of the country to have their own academic institutions. Each of these objectives brought a set of positive results. The breakdown of the country's centrally planned socioeconomic system entirely changed the final outcome of the 1970s strategy for Polish higher education. In this section of the chapter I will focus on educational developments that could be perceived as being "controversial," including policies related to student enrollment and admissions regulations at university-level institutions. Other developments that affected Polish higher education in the 1980s and that were often a source of dispute between political authorities and the academic community were restrictive legislation on higher education, discussed in the next segment of this chapter.

Table 2 and Table 3 show that until the beginning of the 1980s there had been a substantial growth in student enrollment in almost all disciplines except medicine. Engineering has been developing faster than other disciplines, but quantitative growth—number of students and graduates—in other disciplines was also substantial. As a result of the massive influx of graduates the proportion of the workforce possessing a higher education degree or diploma has been steadily growing. It has increased from about 200,000 persons in the mid-1950s (at the time some 3 percent of those employed in the socialized—state-owned or state-funded—sector of the economy) to more than 1 million in 1984 (some 9 percent of the total workforce in the socialized sector). This growth can be considered both as an achievement of Polish higher education and a long-term human capital asset in a country on the verge of restructuring its economy and its social institutions.

The goals and tasks of Polish higher education have been—as in other countries

Table 3

Graduates Per Major Group of Disciplines
(Selective from 1960 to 1987)
of Polish Higher Education Institutions

Discipline	Engineering		Agriculture and Veterinary		Economics and Management		Law and Public Administration	
	I	II	I	II	I	II	I	II
1960	7,877	38.6	1,671	8.0	2,358	11.5	1,039	5.1
1965	8,189	32.5	1,849	7.3	2,707	10.8	2,282	9.0
1970	16,883	35.8	3,554	7.5	7,150	15.3	3,603	7.6
1975	20,589	32.6	4,256	6.7	7,570	12.0	5,813	9.2
1980	24,904	29.7	7,210	8.6	9,713	11.5	7,456	8.9
1985	16,325	27.3	5,749	9.6	8,069	13.5	4,307	7.2
1987(1)	15,600	28.2	4,200	7.6	6,100	11.1	3,100	5.6

I—Total number of students in the given discipline.
II—Percentage of students in the given discipline to the total number of graduates.

[1] Figures for 1987 in (00's).

Source: National Statistical Yearbooks and author's calculations.

with centrally planned socioeconomic systems—dominated by national manpower considerations. The government has attempted to foresee manpower needs and to establish study place quotas to fill these needs. Inspired by Socialist ideology, the government has also tried to achieve a "suitable" social composition within the student body. Close analysis, however, does not allow us to conclude that the existing system of student admission has been successful in increasing representation in the student population of those from working-class or peasant families. The overall admission system to higher education is known as the Preferential Points System (PPS). PPS has been operational since 1965. Subject to intense controversy, it has been reformed on several occasions—1968, 1972, 1979—and since the academic year 1984/85 survives only in a modified form and only for some fields of study. Generally, the additional points given for "social origin" helped only 1 percent of applicants from working-class or peasant backgrounds to gain admission into higher education institutions. The remainder are either admitted anyway on the basis of their entrance examinations results alone, or fail to score high enough to benefit from the social point system.

The main reasons for the unsatisfactory social composition of the student body in higher education can be traced to problems lower down in the educational system. First, only 40 percent of the graduates of compulsory primary education can be admitted to the three types of school that give a foundation for the next step in educational and vocational development: general secondary schools (*liceum ogolnoksztalcace*), technical schools (*technikum*), and vocational lycées. Second, selection is also related to the number of places, geographical location, differences in curriculum, and quality of learning in the above schools. Third, it appears that the educational attitudes of parents and their financial ability to provide their children with supplementary educational experiences plays some role in the social composition of the student population. The relevant data indicate that 58 percent of the students admitted to higher education have fathers who received higher education, 27 percent have fathers who finished secondary edu-

Table 3 (continued)

Graduates Per Major Group of Disciplines
(Selective from 1960 to 1987)
of Polish Higher Education Institutions

Medicine		Humanities and Teacher Training		Mathematics and Natural Sciences		Fine Arts		Others		Total
I	II	I	II	I	II	I	II	I	II	
3,148	15.3	1,570	7.6	1,710	8.3	522	2.5	640	3.1	20,535
3,135	12.4	3,195	12.7	2,371	9.4	715	2.8	775	3.1	25,218
3,873	8.3	5,630	11.9	4,665	9.9	908	1.9	851	1.8	47,117
3,487	5.5	13,811	21.9	4,746	7.5	1,035	1.6	1,929	3.0	63,236
5,469	6.5	15,921	19.0	8,162	9.7	1,429	1.7	3,691	4.4	83,955
5,272	8.8	11,787	19.8	4,345	7.3	1,302	2.2	2,559	4.3	59,715
5,100	9.2	12,800	23.2	4,700	8.5	1,300	2.3	2,400	4.3	55,300

who received higher education, 27 percent have fathers who finished secondary education, 5 percent have fathers whose education ended with primary school, and only 2 percent had fathers who never completed primary education. There are also some socially based differences with regard to choice of higher education institutions. The majority of the student population from working-class and peasant backgrounds are enrolled in less prestigious academic institutions, the higher schools of engineering (WSI), and the higher pedagogical schools (WSP) in which studies are shorter (up to four years), predominantly vocationally oriented, and their graduates receive a "diploma of studies" but not a *Magister*, which requires longer studies (up to six years plus a thesis), and which enables students to continue to doctoral-level studies.

Finally, research findings of the Consultative and Research Center for Recruitment for Higher Education (which functions, since 1984, at the Institute of Science Policy and Higher Education in Warsaw), reveal a quite clear public preference

for giving priority to meritocratic criterias for entry selection to higher education and undertaking long-term policy measures to eliminate selectivity at the secondary level and reduce the disproportionate quality of educational provision.[4] Some of the proposed solutions are already reflected in the present admission system. It is still based on a points system but it now gives greater importance to results obtained during an entry examination (a maximum 70 out of a total of 100 points). Other points can be obtained for grades on the secondary-graduation certificate (maximum 20 points) and evaluations received from school, place of work, or, in the case of recent military service, from a candidate's military unit (maximum 5 points). Actual admission takes place when a "point list" is correlated with the number of study places allocated by central planners to a given institution and its faculties. In the process of enhancing academic autonomy some of the higher education institutions can establish their own admission quotas. It remains to be seen whether a more cohesive policy of access to higher persistently low salaries for most professions that require university-level education, and greater autonomy of higher education institutions, which should allow individual institutions to have their own policy with regard to student admissions.

Higher Education and Employment

Higher education institutions in Poland, as in many other countries, are called upon to contribute to the country's socioeconomic development. The centrally planned socioeconomic system creates a general framework in which this task of the higher education system is closely linked with narrowly interpreted manpower needs. Until the end of the 1970s one of the main prerogatives of the central administration, in particular the Planning Commission at the Council of Ministers, was determining the number and type of higher education graduates needed and projecting from this data the number and kinds of study places to be allotted. Postwar manpower shortages as well as the ideologically motivated responsibility of the state to assure employment meant that the state gained control over the free movement of the labor force and professional development, eliminating "market forces" within the job "market."

An interesting characteristic of the Polish situation is that while an employment policy did exist and did lead to a centrally established student enrollment plan and number of graduates targets, central planning in the strict sense was never really implemented in Polish higher education. Thus, it should not be surprising that the overall results of manpower planning in higher education were at best mixed, with only some positive correlation between plans and target fulfillment.[5] The centrally administered system of placement of higher education graduates has not been successful either. According

to the evaluation of the last comprehensive system of planned graduate employment (as outlined in a law adopted in February 1964 and which intended to secure a more equitable geographical distribution of graduates through such methods of graduate employment as sponsored study grant contracts, preengagement agreements, and direct job placement), only about 60 percent of graduates directly placed at the end of 1970s stayed in their jobs after the first three years of obligatory employment. Other difficulties have been reported in providing employment suited to the level and structure of skills and knowledge of the graduates. At present, under conditions of deep economic crisis and facing the urgent need to restructure the country's economic system, close correlation—quantitative as well as qualitative—between higher education and employment is even less likely to be achieved.

It is difficult to predict how much time it will take to establish a proper labor market in Poland; it is already evident that the present employment situation for higher education graduates requires a major overhaul. The existing deformation of the salary structure in the socialized sector of Polish economy (i.e., the relative salary scale between engineers and unqualified workers, for example, has declined from 1.6:1 in 1960 to its present level 0.8:1), even if counterbalanced by the generally high prestige of some professions that require university-level education (e.g., doctors and teachers), makes this task even more urgent. Thus, it is not surprising that large numbers of highly qualified people search for employment abroad or that applications continue to decline in those fields of study that are intellectually demanding but not adequately rewarded. Another controversial situation exists in regard to graduates of medical studies. In addition to some eight hundred medical doctors, representing 1 percent of all practicing doctors in Poland, who work officially abroad for a limited period of time, in the last seven years some 25 percent of the recently graduated doctors emigrated from Poland.[6] Such developments do not go unnoticed in Poland. Most students of the problems agree that measures must be taken to improve employment conditions, compensation, and professional development perspectives for higher education graduates.

Higher Education and the Political System

The very nature of countries ruled by Communist parties, their governance principle of "democratic centralism," and their concept of centrally planned development, implies a greater involvement of central political institutions in issues of higher education than is absolutely necessary, from a policymaking and administrative position, to run a higher education system. Poland is a country in which the Communist party, the Polish United Worker's Party (PUWP), played until mid-1989 a dominant role in formulating and implementing policy for most institutions, including higher education.

The PUWP and the state administration controlled by it have, on a number of occasions, demonstrated both ignorance and arrogance in their relations with the academic community. Only in the last decade have they had to recognize the limits of their power and their ability to introduce, without facing opposition, policy measures that are not approved by society at large or its various constituencies, including the academic community.

Traditional factors in Poland such as strong adherence to national and democratic values, diversification within the political structure, the social status of the Roman Catholic Church, an intellectual identification with European culture, and a significant percentage of the population who consider themselves "intelligentsia" who value intellectual freedom and are ready to express critical views on policy and social issues—all these represent, especially nowadays, important elements to be reckoned with in Polish politics and higher education. Thus, even if not free of political manipulation and opportunism, Polish academics and students have suffered fewer deprivations and have held on to more academic freedom than is the case in some other socialist countries.

The political struggle over reform of Polish higher education in this decade therefore has to be seen as a reflection of the above framework. This is particularly evident when one looks at how the Polish universities serve as the perennial source of calls and actions for reinstatement of the principles expressed in probably the most democratic legislation in the postwar history of Polish higher education, adopted by the Polish parliament on May 4, 1982.

The bill, which reflected a compromise between the expectations of the academic community and the restrictive demands of the state administration, stressed the importance of academic freedom, institutional self-management, acceptance of differences in worldview, multidirectional versus the previously dominating Marxist-Leninist doctrine in research and teaching, as well as greater organizational freedom for student activism. But the bill's implementation was suspended in the climate of general restriction brought about by the imposition of martial law in December 1981. A formal modification was introduced on July 25, 1985, by the same basic constituency in the Polish parliament that had passed the previous law, but the modified bill practically eliminated the democratic character of the above legislative act. It reinstated some repressive measures with regard to academic staff that had previously existed in Poland only in the early 1950s, and reinforced political criteria for personnel decisions by requiring, for example, the taking of an ideologically framed oath. It also greatly limited the prerogatives of academic collective bodies, and reduced student rights for self-organization and their participation in university management. These measures weakened the legal standing of Polish academic institutions and seriously damaged morale inside the academic community, particularly among its younger members.[7]

Implementation of the new measures was not very successful. Many institutions, including PAN's Institute of Nuclear Research, openly resisted the new regulations. Open opposition, especially among students, was widespread. Calls to "separate education—Polish, socialist, and nondominational—from political struggle and desintegrative attempts" led to the introduction of gradual and rather pragmatic institutional liberalization of higher education as formulated, for example, in February 1986 by the 24th Plenary Session of the Central Committee of the PUWP.[8]

The material conditions of higher education deteriorated as spending on higher education declined—from 1.16 in 1975 to 0.5 of the GNP in 1988. Student discontent continued to grow. The Polish academic community continued to call for change. Recent major political changes (sometimes described as a "peaceful revolution"), in which the PUWP no longer plays the "leading role" but is replaced by a "citizens' society," in which state organization is based on parliamentary democracy and the rule of law, in which there is a functional and institutional separation of political parties from executive power and administration, reflect the concerns of the Polish academic community. These changes have brought about conditions that are favorable to a general democratization of the political and administrative framework in which Polish higher education can function.

Internal Trends in Higher Education

Before describing the internal governance of higher education institutions I must point out that the centralized character of the state and its control of financing makes higher education establishments almost totally dependent on the state's budget. It also implies that not only major policy direction but a significant number of administrative decisions are taken outside academic institutions. However, such a body as the Main Council on Science and Higher Education allows, especially recently, for more collaboration between the academic community and the state. The Main Council is composed of a representative of almost every higher education establishment, elected by his/her respective academic senates. However, nominations for membership, made by the prime minister, require prior approval of the minister of education. The membership of the other important academic policy central body—CKK—consists of more than two hundred representatives of academia. They are nominated for a three-year period by the prime minister at the suggestion of the minister of education and in consultation with the candidate's academic institution. Even if CKK is still a vital institutional element for administrative supervision of the Polish academics, scholarly factors are more important and the administrative process itself is much more open. CKK's present role is as an agency of "quality control" over academic nominations. Recent creation of rectors conferences for the various types of higher education institutions (e.g., polytechnics) is another sign of increasing democracy in the governance of Polish higher education.

The formal basis for the structure and functioning of each higher education establishment are specified in its statutes, drawn up by its senate. However, they become legal documents only after the approval of the minister responsible for that particular institution. Traditionally, at the top of the administrative hierarchy in higher education institutions stand the rector and the senate, which is in part a collective decision-making body and in part an advisory body. Senate members serve for three years with a possibility for reelection. The rector, who must be a tenured professor, is elected by the senate. But the candidate has to be approved by the appropriate minister. The rector, whose status is a combination of *primus inter pares* in the academic community and principal administrator, is assisted by the pro-rectors for specific tasks (e.g., research, student affairs, international cooperation, etc.). Higher institutions also have an advisory body called the Rector's Kolegium, whose members include the leaders of the political organizations functioning in the particular institution and the administrative directors of the establishment. The senate membership is 70 percent professors and docents and 30 percent representatives of the junior rank of academic staff, political parties, trade unions, and student organizations.

The present internal structure of higher education institutions was established in 1968. Each establishment is divided into "faculties" which in turn are subdivided into "institutes." Institutes are relatively independent in their research activities. Faculties, primarily concerned with teaching and student affairs, are run by a dean in collaboration with the Faculty's Board (*Rada Wydzialu*). A majority of the Polish academic institutions are relatively large enterprises. Besides such support services as libraries and archives, without which hardly any academic institution can function, quite frequently the Polish establishments also administer various auxiliary units such as workshops, printing presses, vacation and conference centers, as well as residence halls for students and academic staff. All these units are subordinated to the rector but their management is carried out by separate administrative bodies.

With regard to study programs, there is a constant concern with such issues as linking curricula to the changing needs of science, the economy, and culture; all these issues have to be determined in the appropriate proportions between general education, professional training, and practical experience. Curricula decisions are no longer subject to a monolithic educational doctrine promulgated by the central government; some leading higher education institutions can now decide their own study programs. As a consequence, such objectives as the need to enhance scientific criticism, to nourish respect for true social and cultural values, and to raise the level of study motivations are frequently emphasized. However, these ideal educational goals remain a long-term objective in view of the present low quality of the academic staff, the low position of teaching as a criteria for promotion and other academic rewards, the substantial deterioration of the material conditions of students and their families, the limitations of corresponding studies to employment expectations of university graduates, as well as the low level of available funding for higher education in general.

Reforms in Polish Higher Education

Generally speaking, Polish higher education has been the subject of at least one major change each decade. There are even proponents of the view that many of the present difficulties in Polish education (e.g., the admission system) are an outcome of too many reorganizations, and the disorganizations usually associated with far-reaching reforms. Some of the reforms in Polish higher education—for example, those related to new laws adopted in 1956 or 1982—were an expression of major political reforms carried out nationwide. Deterioration of the political and economic climate has also brought "reforms"—in the form of new legislation—as was the case in 1968 and again in 1985, when liberal regulations were subverted or overturned. But it should be pointed out that even if the centralized system of Polish higher education allows central authorities to initiate reforms, these authorities have also to deal with a characteristic common to all academic systems: its own inertia. This inertia can reduce unfavorable effects, but it can also reduce the system's own ability to innovate. The present anachronistic system of academic staff development, which is too lengthy and too bureaucratic, demonstrates academic inertia at its worst. The actual procedure for a given academic nomination can involve not less than ten academic, political, social, and governmental institutions, from the level of the faculty up to that of the state council.[9] It also requires seeking approval from the CKK three times during an academic career, at habilitation, at nomination for "extraordinary" professor, and at nomination for "ordinary" professor. This is one of the problems on the agenda of the recently created Legislative Commission at the Main Council on Science and Higher Education, whose task is to prepare the new law on higher education. The draft version of the new law also indicates that Polish higher education should be based on principles of academic freedom formulated in the *Magna Charta* of European Universities (adopted by a majority of the European universities in Bologna in September 1988), the Polish academic traditions, and the constitutional principles and legal norms of the Polish state.

Polish higher education is experiencing a reformation. The present non-Communist-led government has already called for a return to full academic autonomy, enhanced self-governance of science and higher education, a shorter path for academic nominations, promotion of international academic relations, and many other

reforms. But there is also a recognition that there are numerous problems to be reckoned with, in particular the present dismal economic situation of the country, which quite likely will also require new concepts for financing studies and research activities. Healthy skepticism is called for. Only those reforms that will meet societal expectations, win the approval of the authorities and the support of the academic community, and that are economically feasible have a real chance to be carried out.

Factors Affecting Students and Academic Staff

As in other countries the Polish student community is socially and economically diversified. Certain factors affecting almost all students such as the rapidly increasing cost of study—mainly related to cost of living—are causing growing concern. Some degree of student pessimism with regard to professional employment prospects helps to explain negative attitudes toward learning and the timely completion of studies. Students complain about bad organization and a workload that is too heavy. It is estimated that, depending on the field and year of study, students are required to spend from twelve to sixty hours a week in classes and laboratories.

Judging by comments coming from the student community a recent structural change in their right for self-organization has caused student morale to rise. Until September 1988 there were only four national organizations allowed to function in the Polish higher education institutions: Polish Students' Association (ZSP), Union of the Polish Socialist Youth (ZSMP), Union of the Rural Youth (ZMW), and the Polish Scouting Organization (ZHP). At present, the proliferation of student organizations is almost impossible to follow. Many of the new student organizations espouse Catholic and liberal principles. The present diversity of student organizations is probably greater than that in Polish society as a whole. There are anarchist, monarchist, radical communist, liberal, pacifist, and ecological student organizations, among others. The most popular group is the pro-Solidarity organization, the Independent Students' Association (NZS), which was banned after the imposition of martial law in December 1981, but was legalized again in September 1989.

The majority of issues affecting academic staff—conditions and regulations concerning its development, participation in governance and administration of higher education, etc.—were already discussed in previous parts of this chapter. Here I can add, however, that significant issues pertaining to faculty, especially over the long term, include the small number of starting positions for the academic staff, the status and professional perspectives for the adjuncts who, at present, are the largest group among academic staff, and most of all the quite rapid decline of the financial and professional attractiveness of an academic career.[10] Unionization within the Polish universities will probably accelerate and become organizationally more diversified.

Conclusions

As in the past, during the whole postwar period Polish higher education has been vital for educating the country's professional and intellectual elite and for developing research. If some policy measures brought only exiguous results (e.g., modification in the social composition of the student population) overall, its quantitative and intellectual growth has been substantial. Its presence in the international academic and research community is evident and visible. Often under adverse conditions, Polish higher education has made efforts to preserve its intellectual integrity and values. But as the whole vision of Polish society changes so, too, do the tasks and functions of the Polish higher education system. It has to cope with paramount material problems under conditions of austerity. Under such circumstances it is rather difficult to foresee a spectacular expansion of the system. However, despite present difficulties, it has a potential to show that it is still an important and constructive element in the process of coping with the country's coming challenges.

Notes

1. As one of the results of the recent bill regulating the public and legal status of the Polish Roman-Catholic Church, the so-called papal faculties and pontifical academies of theology have been recognized by the state as higher education institutions. In addition, the Bialystok branch of Warsaw University is going to be upgraded to an independent institution. These changes of the formal status of the concerned institutions will affect the institutional network and a number of higher education institutions in Poland.

2. J. Zerko, "Structural Changes in the System of Higher Education in Poland in the Years 1918–1973," in *Higher Education and Society: Historical Perspectives. Proceedings of the 7th International Standing Conference for the History of Education* (Salamanca, Spain: Universidad de Salamanca, 1985).

3. A. Swiecki, ed., *L'instruction et l'education en Pologne Populaire* (Warsaw: Ministerstwo Oswiaty i Wychowania/Ksiazka i Wiedza, 1974).

4. B. Witkowska, "Doskonalenie systemu rekrutacji na studia wyzsze," *Zycie Szkoly Wyzszej* 37, no. 4 (1989):165–77.

5. J. Sadlak, *Planning of Higher Education in Countries with Centrally Planned Socioeconomic Systems: Case Study of Poland and Romania* (Ph.D. diss., State University of New York at Buffalo, 1988).

6. Z. Lazowski and J. Machowski, "Emigracja lekarzy," *Polityka*, 4 February 1989, 17, 19.

7. "Oswiata w kryzysie," in *Raport—Polska 5 lat po Sierpniu* (London: Aneks, 1986).

8. W. Jasinski, "XXIV Plenum KC PZPR o problemach szkolnictwa wyzszego," *Zycie Szkoly Wyzszej* 34, no. 3 (1986): 3–14.

9. "Stanowisko Komitetu Nauk Zootechnicznych PAN w sprawie stanu kadr naukowych w dysciplinach zootechnicznych w Polsce," *Zycie Szkoly Wyzszej* 37, no. 3 (1989):40–43.

10. M. Gmytrasiewicz, "Problemy zatrudnienia nauczycieli akademickich," *Zycie Szkoly Wyzszej* 35, nos. 7, 8 (1987):33–48.

◆

Romania

Jan Sadlak

✦

Romania was until the end of 1989 a socialist country with a dominant Marxist-Leninist ideology which since mid-1970 has a specific national form embodied in the concept of a "multilaterally developed socialist society" (*societate socialista multilateral dezvoltata*). The Romanian educational model puts strong emphasis on the close relation of higher education to manpower needs, and on ideological concerns, particularly the formation of a "socialist/working intelligentsia." This form of higher education, seeing education, research, and production as a unitary process, has existed in Romania since the late 1960s. As this chapter goes to press, the direction of Romanian higher education in the newly established non-Communist republic is unclear, although significant change is likely.

Through all its history Romania has remained a multiethnic state. Besides Romanians, there were two major national minorities, called in contemporary Romanian writings "coinhabiting nationalities" (*nationalitati conlocuitoare*).[1] These are Hungarians, representing about 8 percent of the total population of more than 23 million, and German-speaking Saxons, who constitute about 2 percent of the country's population. The ability of these or any other national minority to influence in any significant way the educational policy in the areas of their particular concern has diminished in recent years. The institutional network, for minority ethnic populations has been reduced or eliminated. Out of three Hungarian higher education institutions, the "Janos Bolyai" University in Cluj, the Medical and Pharmaceutical Institute in Tirgu-Mures, and the "Szentgyorgyi Istvan" Institute of Dramatic Art in Tirgu-Mures, only the last is still functioning in its original institutional form. However, the national minority students are still allowed to take entry examinations for those institutions in their mother tongue.

The basic statistical information presented in Table 1 shows that there are forty-four higher education institutions in Romania: seven universities, five polytechnic institutes, one institute of architecture, twelve engineering colleges that provide training mainly for "sub-engineers," four agricultural institutes, five medical and pharmaceutical academies or institutes, one economics academy, two fine arts institutes, three musical schools, two drama and film schools, nine teachers training institutes, one physical education and sport institute, one social sciences academy—"Stefan Gheorghiu" Academy, which is the Communist party's school, and one merchant marine officers training institute.[2] The major academic centers are Bucharest, Cluj-Napoca, Jassy, and Brasov.

Since the years of continuous growth in student enrollment, particularly through the second half of the 1970s, there has been a substantial decline in the student population, from 192,769 students in the 1980/81 academic year to 157,174 in 1986/87. The decline in student enrollment was highest, by some 60 percent, among full-time students. It should also be noted that foreign students in Romanian higher education establishments represent a substantial part of the total student population. In the course of the last few years it was about 7 percent, which is the highest percentage of foreign student enrollment for all Eastern European socialist countries.

As foreign students are allowed to pursue only full-time studies, the number of Romanian full-time students is at present relatively low and similar to the level in the mid-1960s.

Historical Trends

Institutional forms of university-level higher education only emerged in Romania in the second half of the nineteenth century. However, Romania did have educational and scientific institutions such as St. Sava Princely Academy, founded in 1694 in Bucharest, and *Academia Mihaileana*, established in 1714 in Jassy, that were similar in their scholarly activities and study requirements to institutions offering higher education in that period in other European countries.[3] The first true "university" was established in October 1860 in Jassy, in large measure as an expression of the state power acquired by the newly formed independent Romanian state—the Union of the Romanian Principalities. This new university was comprised of four faculties: law, philosophy, theology, and medicine. A similar internal institutional structure was adopted in 1864 when the University of Bucharest was established.

Both institutions, together with other educational and academic organizations, most of them having the status of "research societies," played a significant role in the state and nation building process as well as facilitating industrial development in nineteenth- and early twentieth-century Romania.

Prewar Romanian higher education, as well as its secondary level education, was modeled mainly on the French, and to a lesser degree the German, educational systems. Institutional governance, organization, and certification of studies, names of degrees and academic titles, the admission system, as well as the elitist character of such institutions as polytechnic institutes, give strong evidence of this influence. Some of the names of degrees   and academic titles (e.g., *Bacalaureat*, *Licentiat*— a degree awarded upon completion of four to five years of studies at a university or university-level institution—*Conferentiar*, etc.) are still used in Romanian education.

In the period between the two world wars, there were sixteen higher education institutions. Four were universities,[4] located in the academic centers of Bucharest, Cluj, Jassy, and Cernauti. The interwar years, particularly the 1930s, were a period of

Table 1

Basic Statistical Dimensions of Romanian Higher Education, 1975–76, 1980–81, 1985–86, and 1986–87

	1975–76	1980–81	1985–86	1986–87
Number of higher education institutions	42	44	44	44
Number of students	164,567	192,769	159,798	157,174
Full-time	115,769	161,110	110,040	——
Part-time	48,798	31,659	59,758	——
Foreign students	4,971	15,888	10,774	8,897
Number of graduates	30,839	38,615	30,643	——
Academic staff	14,066	14,592	12,961	12,504
Number of students per 100,000 inhabitants	775	868	720	690

Source: National statistical yearbooks.

academic excellence and fierce struggle to protect the university's autonomy and its separation from direct political interference.[5]

The aftermath of World War II brought major changes for the political, economic, and social order of Romania together with a significant modification of state borders. All these changes impacted on and served to modify Romania's system of higher education institutions. The process of remodeling Romanian higher education—often referred to as the dividing line between the old "bourgeois education" and the new "socialist education" that would correspond to the needs of a people's democracy—was initiated by the Educational Reform Act of August 1948 after the communists took total control of the country's political as well as its economic system. This act was designed to achieve a uniform and centralized educational system that would establish a strong link between higher education and the needs of the centrally planned economy. The reform also foresaw the creation of a new access policy and a centralized system of research supervision and staff policy that would comply with approved ideological doctrine. The reform called for substantial changes in admission and staff development criteria, in order to comply with class perspectives on education, to combat stratification of the student population and to establish an ideologically sound intellectual and professional elite. The reform act was an important part of the "cultural revolution" organized by the communist Romanian Worker's Party.[6] Similarly, a revision of the content of social sciences courses and a modification of the orientation of research in natural and technical sciences was initiated for both utilitarian and ideological reasons.

Soviet higher education and its academic policy served as the role model for reforms concerning education in all the newly socialist countries of Eastern Europe. In restructuring their educational system, the Romanians became dependent on Soviet study programs, scholarly literature, textbooks, etc. The Soviet model led to the introduction of new academic titles such as candidate-in-sciences, the reorganization of the academies of sciences, and major changes in staffing procedures, among many other things.

The Education Law of 1948 also modified the institutional structure of the Romanian higher education system and substantially reduced the academic autonomy of the faculty and their role in the university's governance. All private and religious organizations were prohibited from providing formal education. Particularly substantive were modifications carried out in the Romanian universities. Consequently, the faculties of medicine, pharmacy, and veterinary medicine were separated from the university structure and reintegrated into academic establishments known as "institutes," some of which, mainly in medicine, later became "academies." The remodeling of the universities also resulted in the elimination of all faculties of theology.

As in all other Eastern European socialist countries, Romania introduced, at the level of governance, a new body— the High Commission on Diplomas (*Comisia Superiora de Diplome*). This commission, which functions organizationally under the Ministry of Education and Instruction, enables political and administrative authorities to control major academic appointments and screen the awarding of doctoral-level degrees. The possession of an advanced academic degree, a doctorate, which has been confirmed by the commission was, and still is, a precondition to entering the two highest academic positions: "Professor" and *"Conferentiar,"* which corresponds to an associate professorship. The lower positions of "Lector," "Study Supervisor" (*Sef de lucrari*), and "Assistant" do not require this competitive procedure.

An important feature of Romania's higher education is the system of part-time studies that can be carried out in evening and correspondence courses. It was introduced in the academic year 1949/50 to bring about an improvement in the social class composition of the student body and to contribute to the formation of a new, workers' intelligentsia. The significance of part-time studies, particularly those carried out in evening courses, has increased greatly in the 1980s. Students pursuing part-time studies represent about one-third of the present student population. The original ideological objectives for promoting part-time studies have been superseded by manpower concerns.

If the end of the 1940s and the early 1950s was a period of structural change in the objectives of higher education, it was also marked by the development of the institutional network. This took place not only in the traditional academic centers of Bucharest, Cluj (since the end of the 1970s called Cluj-Napoca) and Jassy, but also, in view of the state policy of equitable regional development, in cities with little or no previous academic tradition, such as Brasov, Craiova, Galati, Tirgu-Mures, Petrosani, Arad, Constanta, Brad, and Cimpul Moldovenesc. The profile of the newly established institutions was linked with the particular economic activity of the town's region. Some of the newly created institutions were amalgamated in the mid-1950s with other institutions of a corresponding profile (e.g., the Institute of Economic Sciences and Planning in Jassy was combined with the similar institute in Bucharest to become the present Academy of Economic Sciences). Some institutions were even closed, such as those in Brad and Cimpul Moldovenesc. Amalgamations and closings were prompted mainly by shortages of academic staff.[7] The expansion and subsequent shrinking of the system explains why universities located in cities without polytechnic institutes or medical academies have a variety of faculties, often including everything from natural sciences and humanities to medicine, engineering, and agriculture.[8]

Toward the end of the 1950s, unlike some Eastern European socialist countries, Romania did not experience a rigorous de-Stalinization, but neither was it immune to self-criticism and calls for changes. With regard to higher education such criticism pointed to excessive centralism, rigidity in policy implementation, insufficient consideration of Romania's own experience in education and research, and staff incompetence and the breech between content and methodology of research, caused giving more importance to political considerations than academic excellence, particularly in the social sciences and biology.

In the late 1950s the multiethnic character of Romania also played a role in the institutional changes within its higher education system. The most profound change led to the redefinition of the functioning of the Hungarian "Janos Bolyai" University in Cluj. When the Hungarian uprising of 1956 began on October 23, 1956, the Hungarian political security forces opened fire on the unarmed student demonstrators. The events that followed motivated the students of the "Janos Bolyai" University to stage a demonstration in support of their compatriots. This demonstration, labeled as a "show of bourgeois nationalism," prompted the Romanian authorities to reconsider the principles of the functioning of the higher education institutions, particularly those serving the national minorities. As a result of the measures taken by the government, the above-mentioned Hungarian university was merged with its Romanian counter-part, the "Victor Babes" University in Cluj. In July 1959 the "Babes-Bolyai" University in Cluj was formed, with Romanian as a dominant language.

Two other major legislations—the Educational Law of 1968 and the Educational Law of 1978—substantially influenced the developments which led to the formation of the present structure, organizational form, and governance system of higher education in Romania.

First, the Law of 1968 introduced a shorter form of technical studies (three years for full-time students and four years for part-time ones), in order to train technical cadres of subengineers (*subinginer*) who would function at an intermediate level between engineers and foreman. For organizational reasons admission to this form of technical training started only in the academic year 1970/71. Because such courses emphasize a vocational type of training with only a limited amount of theoretical study, their graduates are excluded from admission to doctoral programs. The Law of 1968 also reinforced admission requirements based on academic and meritocratic criteria. Since then, admission to higher education has been by a competitive written and oral examination for those who also have a secondary-school-leaving certificate, the *bacalaureat*. Since 1968, neither political nor socially disadvantaged criteria have been used in student admissions.

Second, the Law on Education and Instruction of 1978 reiterated "polytechnization" as one of the major objectives of the whole educational system and indicated that higher education should provide society with highly qualified specialists in all fields of activity. This law also modified a system-level policymaking framework by giving a prominent role to central political institutions, particularly the State Council (*Consiliul de Stat*). For example, it is the State Council that, at the behest of the Ministry of Education and Instruction, establishes the student enrollment figures and the duration of studies. It also decides about the conditions for obtaining the doctoral degree and the rules regulating the rights and obligations of the teaching staff in all types of higher educational institutions.

Any analysis of policymaking and governance in Romania, including higher education, particularly since the beginning of the 1970s, has to draw attention to the central role in Romanian political life of two persons: Nicolae Ceausescu and his wife, an academic by profession, Elena Ceausescu. Ceausescu came to power at the 9th Congress of the Romanian Communist Party (RCP) in July 1965, and until his recent downfall and execution, his power increased from year to year. He was both the general secretary of the RCP and the president of the republic. His wife's role in higher education and science policy was even more direct than his. For many years she was a member of the Permanent Bureau of the Executive Political Committee of the RCP, where she was mainly in charge of personnel policy, including academic nominations. Until the early 1980s she was also the director general of the National Institute of Chemistry (*Institutul National de Chimie*), and at the time of her execution she was still a chairperson of its Scientific Council. She also held powerful positions as the first vice-prime minister, chairperson of the National Committee "Scientists for Peace," and chairperson of the National Council on Science and Education (*Consiliul National al Educatiei si Stiintei*). The Ceausescus' concentration of power made the actual formulation and implementation of policies concerning higher education noticeably different in Romania from that existing in other Eastern European socialist countries, even if it was carried out within the same formula of the dominant Communist party's power and control mechanism in academic affairs.

Major Trends and Developments of the Past Decade

Calls for improvement in such areas as training, teaching methods, and research carried out in academic institutions have been quite frequent in the discussions on development in Romanian higher education during the last decade. But specific

Table 2

Students Per Major Group of Disciplines in Romanian Higher Education 1960/61–1985/86)

Discipline	Engineering		Agriculture and veterinary		Economics and Management		Law and Public Administration	
	I	II	I	II	I	II	I	II
1960/61	22,190	30.8	8,306	11.5	5,085	7.1	3,101	4.3
1965/66	42,304	32.4	9,961	7.6	12,866	9.8	4,534	3.5
1970/71	44,518	29.3	9,074	6.0	21,016	13.8	5,901	3.9
1975/76	64,088	38.9	11,962	7.3	22,854	13.9	6,820	4.1
1980/81	113,323	58.8	10,683	5.6	21,919	11.4	3,863	2.0
1985/86	99,779	62.4	7,005	4.4	16,485	10.3	2,380	1.5

I—Total number of students in the given discipline.
II—Percentage of students in the given discipline to the total student number.

Source: National statistical yearbooks and author's calculations.

criticisms must be seen in the light of a dominant opinion that Romania has witnessed overall advancement in higher education since the new policy framework was adopted in 1968.

Scholars agree that Romanian education at all grade levels meets the expected needs of the national economy, social services, and culture. This assessment is common to both official and academic Romanian writing on the state of higher education system.[9] Although this positive view is generally justified, certain trends in the development of Romanian higher education in the course of the last decade invite a critical analysis.

For example, a policy of rapid enhancement of industrial and technological development put special emphasis on engineering studies. In consequence, as can be observed from the figures in Table 2 and 3, the number of students and graduates in engineering has grown steadily throughout the last quarter of a century. Their percentage representation in the total number of students and graduates in Romania has increased in the last de-

cade by some 20 percent. It is now reaching the unusually high proportion of some 60 percent of all students and graduates. Engineers and graduates in economics and management now represent more than 70 percent of all graduates. The relatively high numbers of students and graduates in medicine are deceiving because many of the students pursuing medical studies are foreigners. Thus one can draw the conclusion that a substantial part of resources available to Romanian higher education have been devoted mainly to the technocratically understood needs of industry and other sectors of the national economy. The decline of students and graduates in such fields as the humanities, teacher training, mathematics, and natural sciences is very substantial. This trend, if continued, will create serious qualitative obstacles to the realization, for example, of the introduction in the years 1991–2000 of the twelve-year compulsory primary and secondary education mandated by the last Congress of the RCP.

The issue of social/individual demand and access to higher education in Roma-

Table 2 (continued)

Students Per Major Group of Disciplines in Romanian Higher Education 1960/61–1985/86)

Medicine		Humanities and Teacher Training		Mathematics and Natural Sciences		Fine Arts		Total
I	II	I	II	I	II	I	II	
7,825	10.9	14,615	20.3	9,137	12.7	1,730	2.4	71,989
9,345	7.2	38,208	29.3	10,977	8.4	2,419	1.8	130,614
9,898	6.5	43,207	28.5	14,901	9.8	3,370	2.2	151,885
17,008	2.0	21,568	13.2	17,487	10.6	2,780	1.7	162,567
23,381	12.1	8,720	4.5	8,673	4.5	2,207	1.1	192,769
18,833	11.8	6,261	3.9	8,156	5.1	899	0.6	159,798

nia also merits some attention. Without doubt, Romania has a particularly strong formal mechanism, even by comparison with other European countries with centrally planned socioeconomic systems, for matching the quantitative developments of higher education with centrally established manpower plans and projections.[10] Such plans are elaborated on the basis of reports submitted by various economic and planning institutions in which they formulate their needs for highly qualified specialists. Recent statistical data (see Tables 1 and 3) show that those needs are diminishing quite rapidly. Leaving aside the eventual long-term consequences of an inadequate supply of highly-qualified personnel for Romanian culture, agriculture, and the service sector of the economy, it should be noted that the overall potential number of persons eligible to seek access to tertiary education is growing as a direct result of the development of Romania's primary and secondary education as well as its present demographic policy. Since university-level education in Romania still carries considerable prestige value and a certain degree of material advancement, the social/individual demand for higher education is high—up to ten candidates compete for each study place in a majority of subjects. The inability of the educational system to respond to such demands will only reinforce the discrepancy in the "rural" versus "urban" composition of the student population. At present some 65 percent of the Romanian student population comes from urban regions.[11] A policy of reducing the number of students proceeding to higher education is also rather out of tune with the official Romanian concepts of seeing education as a determining factor of socioeconomic development, of successfully building a multilaterally developed socialist society, and of building ideal communism in Romania.[12]

Two other developments in Romanian higher education also deserve discussion in this part of the chapter. These are the role of the National Institute of Chemistry and the government's educational repayment plan.

Table 3

Graduates Per Major Group of Disciplines in Romanian Higher Education (1960–1985)

Discipline	Engineering		Agriculture and veterinary		Economics and Management		Law and Public Administration	
	I	II	I	II	I	II	I	II
1960	2,851	27.7	1,263	12.3	967	9.4	893	8.7
1965	6,434	28.5	1,629	7.2	1,275	5.7	553	2.4
1970	8,540	29.6	1,894	6.6	4,408	15.3	1,072	3.7
1975	12,955	42.0	1,756	5.7	4,111	13.4	1,309	4.2
1980	19,929	51.6	2,691	7.0	4,779	12.4	1,270	3.3
1985	20,627	61.2	1,595	4.7	4,103	12.2	536	1.6

I—Total number of graduates in the given discipline.
II—Percentage of graduates in the given discipline to the total number of graduates.

Source: National statistical yearbooks and author's calculations.

The National Institute of Chemistry, created in 1973 from an idea of Elena Ceausescu, is unique, even by its size, from any other academic or research establishment in Romania.[13] It includes twenty-seven specialized research centers and production units of the Ministry of Chemical Industry as well as others functioning within the organizational framework of the Academy of the Socialist Republic of Romania. It also coordinates all the chemistry departments functioning in higher education institutions. Though the creation of the National Institute of Chemistry enabled a concentration of research potential, it also had certain questionable effects on the institutional structure of higher education establishments. At the University of Bucharest, for example, the Faculty of Chemistry was dissolved and chemistry as a field of study was replaced by chemical engineering.

Finally, the Romanian government's decision of November 6, 1982, requiring that would-be emigrants repay the entire cost of the last two years of secondary school and higher education before leaving the country has caused controversy. Payment must be made in convertible currency, which Romanian citizens are not allowed to possess. The introduction of this law, which has stimulated sharp criticism in the West, was justified by the fact that by providing "free education" Romanian society allocates substantial resources. Therefore, those who received such education, but who leaving the country would no longer serve it, should repay the cost of their education.[14] There is no statistical evidence but the desire to emigrate has been quite high in recent years in Romania, particularly among German and Jewish ethnic groups. So far no cases have been recorded of emigrants actually having to repay their education costs, but the regulation has not been formally cancelled.

Higher Education and Employment

All Romanian higher education is seen in the context of productive activities and manpower needs which are considered by central planning and policymaking bodies as being essential for an overall strategy of economic and social development. It is considered inefficient and socially unjustified to provide expensive higher education provisions and its research facili-

Table 3 (continued)

Graduates Per Major Group of Disciplines in Romanian Higher Education (1960–1985)

Medicine		Teacher Training		Natural Sciences		Fine Arts		Total
I	II	I	II	I	II	I	II	
1,796	17.4	1,394	13.5	879	18.5	253	2.5	10,296
1,473	6.5	8,635	38.2	2,174	9.6	416	1.9	22,589
1,569	5.4	8,626	29.9	2,157	7.5	574	2.0	28,840
1,978	6.4	5,084	16.5	2,938	9.5	708	2.3	30,839
3,822	9.9	2,846	7.3	2,419	6.3	859	2.2	38,615
3,528	10.5	1,452	4.4	1,547	4.6	281	0.8	33,669

ties for programs and courses leading to degrees and qualifications for which there is no clear economic or social policy justification. A medium level of economic development (Romania still considers itself to be a developing country), provides additional reasons for the adherence of higher education to the foreseeable needs of society at large.

To allocate graduates—a function played by the labor market in free market economies—and to avoid regional shortages of specialists with university-level training, Romania has (since 1968) adopted regulations that require every first-year student to sign a contract with the higher education institution in which he/she has been enrolled. One of the most important conditions for undertaking studies is the acceptance of work after graduation, for a certain number of years (generally two or three), in jobs and places assigned by the state, or else repayment of the cost of one's studies. The conditions and amount to be repaid are not specified in the contract. As virtually all professional positions that require a university degree are allocated by the state or remain under its strict control, a graduate who refuses to take up a designated position has little chance of finding another more desired job. Therefore, cases of students refusing to accept assigned postgraduation employment are extremely rare. In the process of matching a graduate with a particular job assignment, consideration is given to marks received during the course of study. Therefore, good students have some degree of choice in the first steps of their professional career.

In view of the substantial differences in the level of social and cultural provisions between urban and rural settings, after a period of compulsory job assignment, a substantial number of graduates leave those positions and seek employment in other places, mainly the large urban areas. This tendency is likely to be reinforced because the majority of Romanian students come from urban families. In some professions the problem of those seeking jobs not related to their previous area of studies, but which better meet their nonprofessional expectations, has reached proportions that required additional regulations for graduate employment. For example, special legislation had to be introduced in 1981 to ensure that graduates of agricultural faculties would actually work on the land in jobs directly related to agricultural production enterprises or institutions, instead of using their diplomas to search for jobs not related to agricultural production in urban settings.

Higher Education and the Political System

In Romania the relationship between the political system and higher education is directly related to an issue of control over various aspects of policymaking vital for the functioning of the academic system, such as governance and financing, organization, accountability, and autonomy. It should be kept in mind that it is a dominant feature of a state governed by the Communist party to possess optimal control over political, economic, and cultural life. Thus it is logical that the Romanian government considers higher education to be an integral part of the state socioeconomic system. In essence, these principles of relations between higher education and political institutions are similar to those of many other Eastern European socialist countries. But since the mid-1970s, Romania's party and state governance over various aspects of policymaking regarding higher education and science was modified and further centralized as the apex of the leadership and power in the party was concentrated in the hands of Ceausescu. A similar process took place in various top-level state institutions. As a result of this process such bodies as, for example, the Council of State and its chairman became involved in the policymaking process to a much greater extent than was the case in previous years.[15]

It can be argued that in all socialist countries governed by the Communist party all governmental bodies function as the extension of the party's controlling powers, mainly through the mechanism of "democratic centralism" that governs relations between the party and its members and keeps most of the top-level positions within its direct or indirect control—the *nomenclatura* system. But in a majority of those countries some degree of formal separation between the "zone of political bodies" and the "zone of government" is preserved. But in Romania, in the mid-1970s, a process of direct subordination of certain state bodies, including those relevant to higher education and research, was initiated. Thus such organizations as the National Council for Science and Technology and the Academy of Social Sciences have a double status of "Party and State organs."

One of the characteristics of the Romanian system of policy-formation and governance of education is the institutionalization of bodies that are neither political parties, constitutionally legislative organs, nor governmental bodies. They are usually called a "congress" and are attended by several thousand delegates. They were created in the spirit of direct participatory democracy which has been practiced in Romania since the mid-1970s. The congress most relevant for present developments in Romanian higher education is called the Congress of Science and Education. It was organized in November 1985 and meets every five years. Related to it, even if formal linkage is not clear, is the National Council of Science and Education. One of the council's four commissions—the Commission on Higher Education and Further Training of Highly Qualified Personnel—plays some role in the development of higher education policy.

As state institutions Romanian higher education establishments are mainly dependent upon state/government funding which is combined with governmental control of the budgeting as well as spending process. In addition, educational institutions are supported by "other socialist units," usually the industrial (also state-owned) enterprises, which, under collaboration plans, supply them with equipment, installations, and, if needed, some technical assistance. The direct scope of this support, carried out in the context of the policy of integration of higher education and academic research with production, is the mutual utilization of the facilities for realization of the jointly undertaken small-scale production or applied research programs in which both students and academic staff usually participate. The general and system-wide objectives of these combined—academically and economically relevant—activities is better economic use of new knowledge and greater relevance of student training for the future job environment. In some institutions, like the Polytechnic Institute in Bucharest, such contractual relations with industry represent over a third of the annual funds for its research activities and scientific equipment.[16] However, there is little evidence that this external form of financing Romanian higher educational institutions makes them any more independent or less vulnerable to the financial supervision of the central state administration. Having said that, I should note that a view prevails that close state supervision is basically conflict-free and wholly beneficial to the academic institutions because the socialist/communist state itself is believed to be the promoter of progressive development; therefore the state or party direction does not clash with the spirit of university autonomy.

Internal Trends in Higher Education

The organizational structure and governance of the higher education institutions is based on the principle of "collective governance" (*conducerea colectiva*) characterized by the existence of a Professorial Council (*Consiliul profesoral*) at the faculty level and a Senate (*Senatul*) at the institutional level. The size of these bodies depends on the number of teaching positions: in the case of the Senate, 53–55

members in the institutions with 501–1,000 teaching positions; 61–63 members in those with 1,001–1,300 positions; and 89–91 members in cases where the number of teaching positions exceeds 1,300. Academic staff holds a clear majority: two-thirds of the members of the Professorial Councils and the Senates have to come from this group. Student members represent between 6 and 15 percent of the total number on these two governing bodies. If the representatives of the academic staff in Professorial Councils are elected by the general assembly of the faculty, the members of the Senate are elected from the members of the Professorial Councils. However, a significant contingent of the members of these governing bodies, especially the Senate, are ex officio representatives, functionaries of the party organization, members of the trade unions, members of the student organization—Association of the Communist Students in Romania (*Asociatia Studentilor Comunisti din Romania*, [A.S.C.R.])[17] as well as those who are responsible for the ongoing governance of the whole institution, the rector and deans of the various faculties. Besides these "internal" members, there are also "external" members representing various ministries or other governmental bodies, the people's council (organs of local administration), and representatives from industrial enterprises and research organizations. The composition of the Senate and the very fact that it normally meets only once a trimester requires that day-to-day governance and administration be carried out by its Executive Bureau. The bureau is composed of the rector, who serves also as its president, prorectors, a scientific secretary, a secretary of the party's organization, and the chairman of the institution's chapter of the A.S.C.R. The term of office for these bodies of academic institutional governance is four years. Unlike many other elective positions in Romania's societal organizations, there is a limit on total term of office in Romanian academic institutions, which for rectors and deans is two consecutive four-year terms. Rectors and deans are appointed and dismissed by the minister of education and instruction.

The composition of the bodies that govern academic institutions, particularly that of the senate and its bureau, demonstrates that in Romania the system of institutional governance is hierarchically centralized; despite significant faculty representation, a substantial influence on institutional decision making is assured for administrative and political bodies.

Reflecting Romania's educational doctrine of integration of education with research and production, study programs are organized not only according to the needs of traditional, academic curriculum but also in view of the practical requirements of productive activities. It is often argued in Romanian scholarly writing concerning these issues that teaching staff and students, in close cooperation with experts from industry, have managed to deal with a series of tasks that were vital for the country's economy. Cooperation between academia and industry has also enhanced multidisciplinary approaches to research and study programs. At the same time, the transition period needed to integrate the graduates, particularly engineering, into the workforce has been shortened.[18]

Factors Affecting Students and Academic Staff

The limited number of study places and the very competitive selection of candidates obliges students to make their choice concerning a field of study to a great extent according to their perception of the possibility of being admitted. Almost half of Romanian students make such a decision without taking into consideration the educational aspects of their future studies. Therefore, about 30 percent of all

students would not apply for admission to the faculty of their present study if they were given another choice or if multiple registration was allowed. This disequilibrium between the field of study and individual educational aspirations could have negative consequences for students' academic performance as well as the future professional performance of higher education graduates. However, it is believed that the system of study guidance, together with a policy of planned graduate employment and relatively small number of persons with university-level degrees, creates numerous possibilities to reduce such shortcomings of the admission system in Romania's higher education.

One of the principles of the "socialist model of education" is no tuition.[19] However, education is not entirely free. Despite heavy state subsidies, particularly for student hostels and student canteens, maintenance and expenses related to studies can be a problem for some members of the student population and/or their families, particularly those in full-time courses. The number of students using academic residence halls is not high; at present, only some 55 percent of the full-time students benefit from this form of student aid. Some 55 percent of the Romanian full-time students get means-tested study grants, called a *bursa*. Little part-time work and few summer jobs are available. Thus living expenses and other study-related expenses have to come from students' families. Students can receive financial remuneration for their work on a research or production contract signed by their institution; officially up to 20 percent of monies received can be distributed among students. But how much they are actually paid is difficult to determine from available sources or official publications.

As mentioned earlier, there has been, since the academic year 1980/81, a continuous decline in the number of academic staff. Even if the rate of this reduction were smaller than that of student numbers, little new hiring might create a problem of continuity of academic work and vitality of higher education institutions. The primary teaching and research obligations and tasks of the academic staff working in Romanian higher education institutions are similar to those in other academic systems, even if teaching and research is more practice-oriented. However, there is quite an important difference in the organizational discipline Romanian academics must face. According to the legislation now in force, the work obligations for all categories of academic staff are calculated on the basis of an eight-hour working day, and a forty-hour work week, which they must spend *in* their respective institutions or in other places *closely* linked to their academic activities. At the same time it is expected that weekly work time be spent as follows: eighteen hours for teaching, tutoring, examinations, etc.; twelve hours for research and related activities; four to six hours for other activities related to student work and instruction.[20] To what extent these regulations facilitate the organization of faculty work or increase its productivity and to what extent they are only a formal, bureaucratic, and difficult-to-execute tool of administrative control over academic staff is one of the issues worth looking at when sufficient and relevant data become available.

Conclusions

After the years of expansion Romanian higher education is confronted with a substantial contraction, reflected in significant decline in student enrollment and the number of faculty. Certain areas of higher education, particularly those related to engineering and medicine, continue to show excellence both in teaching and research. Overall, the present economic situation and austerity measures in budgetary spending seem to be less favorable to the policy of quantitative growth in higher education or democratization of access

to higher education, despite assumptions, deriving from the Marxist interpretation of the theory of human capital, concerning the role of education in economic growth, and despite political declarations about the vital role of higher education and research in turning Romania into a multilaterally developed socialist country. For the time being, even if a general vision of the role of higher education in socioeconomic development goes beyond merely fulfilling manpower needs, narrowly interpreted manpower considerations form the foundation and main objectives of policy and functioning of higher education in Romania.

Notes

1. The replacement of the term "national minority" by "co-inhabiting nationality" is not, at least in contemporary Romanian political theory and official declarations, purely a matter of semantics. It is argued that the term "national minority" is out of step with present-day realities in Romania and the transformations that supposedly brought about, among other things, the settling of the country's nationalities question. See also E. Florea, *Natiunea—realitati si perspective* (Bucharest, Romania: Editura stintifica si enciclopedica, 1982).
2. See "Romania" in *World List of Universities*, 17th ed., ed. F. Eberhard (Paris: International Association of Universities, 1988).
3. L. Jilek, ed., *Historical Compendium of European Universities* (Geneva: Standing Conference of Rectors, Presidents, and Vice-Chancellors of the European Universities, 1984).
4. According to some historians there were five universities in Romania in the period between the two World Wars. See S. Stefanescu, "Romania," in *Historical Compendium of European Universities*, ed. L. Jilek (Geneva: Standing Conference of Rectors, Presidents, and Vice-Chancellors of the European Universities, 1984).
5. L. M. Imangulova, "Partidul Muncitoresc Romin—organizatorul revolutiei culturale din R.P.R.," *Revista de Pedagogie* 7 (June 1958): 1–8.
6. One of the most outspoken defenders of the university's autonomy in Romania and separation of universities from direct political in-

terference was Nicolae Iorga, professor of history at the University of Bucharest and Jassy, and in the early 1930s also prime minister and minister of public instruction. See: "Cuvintarea d-lui Prof. Neculai Iorga, rostita in Senat in ziua de 5 martie 1937, cu prilejul discutiei proiectului de lege pentru com-pletarea unor dispozitii din legea invata-mintului universitar," *Revista de Pedagogie* 7 (March 1937): 54-69.

7. Gh. Platon and V. Cristian, eds., *Istoria Universitatii din Iasi* (Jassy, Romania: Editura Junimea, 1985).

8. "Romania—Universities and Technical Universities," in *International Handbook of Universities*, 10th ed., ed. D.J. Aitken (Paris: International Association of Universities, 1986).

9. N. I. Brinzei, "Invatamintul Romanesc in Concordanta cu cerintele progresului multilateral al Patriei," *Revista de Statistica* 36 (September 1987): 1–10.

10. J. Sadlak, *Planning of Higher Education in Countries with Centrally Planned Socioeconomic Systems: Case Study of Poland and Romania* (Ph.D. diss., State University of New York at Buffalo, 1988).

11. C. Schifirenet, *Pregatirea pentru profesie a tinaretului universitar—Raport de cercetare* (Bucharest, Romania: Centrul de cercetari pentru problemele tinaretului, 1982).

12. C. Prisacaru, "Invatamintul—factor de civilizatie si izvor de cultura pentru intreaga populatie," *Revista de Statistica* 36 (September 1987): 43–50.

13. M. Florescu, "The Romanian School of Chemistry and Petrochemistry," *Journal of the National Commission of Romania for Unesco* 25 (February 1983): 243–49.

14. "Decret privind obligatiile persoanelor care cer si li se aproba sa se stabileasca definitiv in strainatate de a plati integral datoriile per care le au fata de stat, organizatii socialist si persoane fizice, precum si de a restitui unele chieltuieli suportate de stat cu scolarizarea lor," *Scinteia* (6 November 1982): 1.

15. Ministry of Education and Instruction, *The Education and Instruction Act* (Bucharest, Romania: Editura didactica si pedagogica, 1978).

16. C. Bala, "University-Industry Relations: Romanian Case Study," *Higher Education in Europe* 8 (October 1983): 17–25.

17. The Association of the Communist Students in SRR (A.S.C.R.) is an integral part of the Union of the Communist Youth (Uniunea Tinaretului Comunist). Its central governing body, the Council of A.S.C.R., is subordinated to U.T.C's Central Committee.

18. T. Voicu, "Modernication of Polytechnic Higher Education," *Journal of the National Commission of Romania for Unesco* 25 (January 1983): 91–95.

19. Contrary to the general assumption that the "socialist model" of education implies free studies for those undertaking them, enrollment, examination, and certification fees were charged in Romanian secondary as well as higher education until the beginning of the academic year 1961/62. These fees were not particularly high; the amount the student paid was based on political, economic, and academic performance criteria. See also R. L. Braham, *Education in Rumanian People's Republic* (Washington, D.C.: Department of Health, Education, and Welfare, 1964).

20. S. Ghimpu, "Characteristic Traits of the Status of Higher Education Personnel in the Socialist Republic of Romania," *Higher Education in Europe* 10 (April 1985): 28–36.

Soviet Union

George Avis

♦

Broad Parameters

Official Soviet age-group data for 1987 suggest that approximately one-quarter of the young people between the ages of fifteen and twenty-four receive a higher education, and about 15 to 16 percent do so in full-time courses. In 1987 five million or so Soviet *vuz* students were taught by 370,000 academic staff, a gross staff-student ratio of 1:13–14.[1] The number of Soviet higher education establishments (*vuzy*)[2] increased in the Brezhnev era (1965–82) from 756 to 891, that is, by some 18 percent, in order to cope with a 38 percent rise in enrollments over the same period.[3]

Total student numbers rose rapidly in the 1950s and 1960s, slowed down in the 1970s, and began to drop in the early 1980s—the first real decline since World War II. Between 1983 and 1987 enrollment fell by 5 percent to 5,026,000. This occurred in both full-time day and part-time evening course enrollments. Official policy after the fall of Khrushchev gave priority to the full-time form of higher education in order to raise standards. Accordingly, the proportion of full-timers rose from 41 percent in the mid-1960s to nearly 57 percent at the beginning of the 1980s. Since 1983, however, full-time numbers have dropped both in absolute terms and as a proportion (53 percent) of overall enrollments. The number of evening-course students began to decline even earlier, from 1980, and is now no higher than in 1966, although their share is down only marginally at 11.6 percent. A countertrend of steady growth is to be observed in admissions to correspondence-extension higher education courses, which now serve more than one-third of all Soviet students. This increase demonstrates the popularity of this form of higher education among qualified technicians who are encouraged to gain superior qualifications in their field of work in order to meet the challenge of rapidly changing technologies.[4]

The general retrenchment in enrollments in recent years may be attributed in part to the much-discussed demographic downturn caused by wartime losses and decreasing birthrates in European Russia. Falling enrollments can also be attributed to the Soviet government's intention to correct the overproduction of *vuz* graduates in certain fields—especially engineering—and to intensify tertiary training with a stress on quality rather than quantity. These factors certainly play a role in the trend. But an examination of recent intake data does not as yet indicate any marked impact on numbers; indeed, overall figures for new entrants rose continuously throughout the 1980s, dipping a little only recently.[5] It appears more likely, therefore, that numbers in the system have started to drop as a result of a sudden and large increase in dropouts.

Enrollments have also fallen in the 1980s in most of the economic branch groups into which Soviet *vuzy* are officially categorized. An exception is the education sector, represented by pedagogical institutes and universities, which experienced steady but unspectacular growth till 1982/83, a decline for two years, and then a resurgence to a record 1,573,000 students in 1987, thereby accounting for 31.3 percent of all students in higher education. This rising trend is clearly a consequence of the school reform of 1984 that created a need for more staff by lowering the school starting age from seven to six years and improved teachers' salaries and conditions. The steepest drop in enrollments has been experienced by the largest and, until recently, the most prestigious category of *vuzy* among young people, namely industry and construction, resulting in its lowest representation (37.3 percent) for student population since the Khrushchev years.[6]

Saturation rates have worsened, too. From a peak in 1979/80 of 196 students in higher education per 10,000 inhabitants for the Soviet Union as a whole the figure dropped to 177 per 10,000 in 1987, and the USSR lost its once proud position as one of the leading countries in the world in this respect. Nevertheless, by any standard, the rates for all areas of the Soviet Union are very impressive, particularly in the Central Asian republics which were so backward socially and economically before the revolution. This record is not vitiated by some slippage in recent years.[7]

The 1980s have seen continuous cutbacks in the proportion of state expenditure devoted to higher education. To be sure, in money terms the appropriation actually rose from 3.75 to 4.17 billion rubles between 1980 and 1987. But higher education's share of the allocation for education and science has declined from 9.4 to 7.6 percent over the same period. As a proportion of the total state budget this represents a drop from 1.27 percent to 0.97 percent. At a time when the physical plant and equipment of *vuzy* require urgent modernization, this reduced government funding represents a serious development and may, indeed, underlie new proposals for financing courses contained in the latest reforms.[8]

Until recently higher education was administered by the USSR Ministry of Higher and Secondary Specialized Education which exercised its authority through corresponding ministries or departments in the fifteen union republics of the Soviet Union. The broad functions of the ministry were: to develop the system of higher and secondary specialized education with the aim of supplying the national economy with fully qualified specialist personnel in accordance with state plans; to maintain standards of undergraduate and postgraduate training; to develop and monitor teaching methodology; to promote research in *vuzy*; to recruit and train academic and research staff, and develop their qualifications; and to improve living conditions and cultural facilities for students and staff.[9] In March 1988 the USSR ministries and state committee concerned with education were abolished and their responsibilities transferred to a new State Committee for Public Education under the chairmanship of former higher education minister Gennadiy Yagodin. The new controlling body for the whole of Soviet education comprises thirteen main administrations including one for higher education. In order to provide leadership in the development of curricula and teaching methods, the State Committee has direct jurisdiction over some thirty-seven leading universities and institutes, most of which are located in Moscow and other major cities.[10]

Historical Trends That Have Shaped the System of Higher Education

From the first years after the revolution, Soviet higher education has pursued two principal aims: the professional training of specialists who are meant to establish the economic basis of a communist society, and the formation of well-rounded harmonious personalities, activists of high moral principles who are ideologically committed, politically reliable, and patriotic fighters for the cause of communism. Both aims are essentially utilitarian. Even the elements of humanistic and liberal education implied in the above formulations are harnessed to a specific ideology and are designed to impart qualities and attitudes useful to party and state. The notion that higher education is essentially a means of personal development and fulfillment or an intrinsic good, worth acquiring for its own sake, has played little part in official Soviet educational thinking.[11]

From the outset, then, economic and ideological goals have been fundamental features of Soviet higher education. And the course of its development since the late 1920s leaves no doubt that the dominant function is the economic one. An early major decree, "On the Work of the Higher School" (1925), states this priority unequivocally: "The basic task of higher educational establishments should be the training of workers for practical activity and production in the wide sense of the word in all its branches. Therefore the whole organization and structure of teaching, and the whole life of higher educational establishments should be linked as closely as possible with practice, and moreover this link should increase from year to year."[12] The same emphasis is to be observed in all major party and government reports and decrees on higher education since that time.

The structure of the nascent higher education system in the 1920s reflected economic imperatives. The small prerevolutionary system of higher vocational training was developed and expanded. Further specialized *vuzy* were formed from faculties detached from existing universities and other multifaculty institutions. At the beginning of the first five-year plan in 1928 higher education adopted the "branch" principle from the structure of the various branches of the national economy. Virtually all higher education establishments were transformed into specialized institutes providing professional training for specific occupations. In this way higher technical education, in particular, was boosted dur-

ing the first years of industrialization. The numbers of students recruited for different fields of study (specialties) and the content of their curricula and syllabi conformed to the requirements of the national economic plan. Specialties corresponded broadly to the official listing of jobs requiring highly qualified personnel which was adhered to in all branches of production and the nonproduction sectors. This remains the practice today.[13]

Since 1928 the administration of higher education has mirrored the branch grouping of *vuzy*. Legal jurisdiction for many types of *vuz* was removed from the then People's Commissariat of Education and vested in various economic ministries and organizations that employed graduate manpower. The benefits these arrangements brought for higher vocational training were counterbalanced by a division of authority in higher education that has tended to multiply bureaucracy and to hinder efficient planning and policy implementation. And the self-reinforcing relationship between the content of education and the division of labor eventually led to rigidities and imbalances in graduate employment.[14]

Operating within a planned economy, Soviet higher education was inevitably subject to a considerable degree of centralized control. This feature became more marked as the industrialization of the country's economy got underway during the first five-year plans. There is certainly some diffusion of power at the top between educational, industrial, and other ministries, and certain functions are delegated to various national organizations and to republican ministries. But lower echelons of the system, individual establishments, administrators, and teachers are deprived of any real autonomy. Virtually all aspects of *vuz* life are regulated in minute detail by directives from controlling central and republican ministries and the party.[15]

Centralized planning and control were, no doubt, necessary in order to mobilize the nation to match the capitalist world in material production and to build up military strength in as short a time as possible. But they made the achievement of quantitative targets the dominant criterion of success, a feature which has come to hinder the development of higher education in recent years. Decision making from the center also tended to stifle initiative and self-reliance, resulting in uniformity and rigidity of administration and course content, and in resistance to change—a state described by Buttgereit as "institutional automatism."[16] And it has fostered merely formal or superficial compliance, and sometimes an attitude that regulations are made to be avoided or broken.

The party has always viewed the political and ideological formation of the future leaders of Soviet society as a major function of higher education. As early as March 1919 the program adopted by the party at its Eighth Congress speaks of education as a tool for the communist transformation of society and a means for "exerting the ideological, organizational, and educational influence of the proletariat" in order to "form a generation capable of finally establishing communism." One of the tasks it was expected to carry out was "to develop the widest propagandizing of communist ideas and for this purpose to utilize the resources and machinery of state power."[17] In the 1920s and early 1930s student recruitment to *vuzy* was based on the class principle in order to exclude the children of "class enemies" and to ensure dominant representation of the working class. So-called workers faculties were established in this period to provide basic preparation for higher education courses. Bourgeois teaching staff were replaced or made to conform. All students were obliged to undergo compulsory ideological instruction. Party organizations were enjoined to see that this instruction, as well as regular social science courses, was given by communist teachers. V*uz* party members supervised the work of their institu-

tions to ensure that the policy of central party authorities was carried out. By 1936, when the new Soviet constitution declared that antagonistic classes officially no longer existed in the Soviet Union, the active class struggle in higher education was deemed to be over. However, a sizable proportion of curricula in all *vuzy* continues to be given over to a cycle of compulsory classes in Marxist-Leninist theory and practice, and students are expected to devote much of their spare time to sociopolitical activities.[18] In the formation and implementation of educational policy the party still plays the leading role.

The Most Important Trends and Developments of the 1980s

The 1980s have been a decade of dramatic upheaval in all areas of Soviet life. The death in 1982 of CPSU general secretary Leonid Brezhnev, followed by a rapid succession of party leaders, heralded the beginning of a process of national reappraisal and change. This gained momentum after 1985 as the current leader, Mikhail Gorbachev, embarked upon a frank reassessment of past policies and a radical restructuring of the economic, political, and social life of the country.

In the tertiary sector of education the need to find solutions to chronic and deep-seated problems had become urgent. Several adverse trends combined to bring about a crisis during the 1980s (some of which are discussed in sections devoted to employment, the political system, and recent reforms). Here I shall examine particular controversial issues that have dominated much of Soviet public and academic debate on the quality and effectiveness of higher education in recent years, namely the shortcomings of planning, student recruitment, and wastage.

The weaknesses of Soviet higher education planning have long been acknowledged and criticized. As part of national manpower planning its decisions and targets, such as the size and mix of entry and graduation cohorts, are legally binding for all ministries and *vuzy*. Yet the methods used have remained essentially unchanged since they were described by DeWitt in the 1960s.[19] At that time their inherent lack of accuracy in forecasting the long-term graduate requirements of the economy and their general ineffectiveness were of less consequence. The scarcity of specialists was then so great (Yelyutin speaks of a 46.7 percent shortfall of specialists needed in the economy in 1963) that surplus highly qualified personnel in a given field could usually be assigned suitable employment at the specialist level in another.[20]

By the 1970s, however, planned saturation figures for specialists in the economy as a whole were achieved. Horizontal substitution was no longer possible and serious underutilization of graduates ensued. A superfluity of this type in the nonmarket economy of the Soviet Union is considered to be a serious planning failure and an investment loss. Western scholars have attempted to identify underlying causes. Balzer argues that industrial managers, who ensure themselves against future labor shortages by submitting inflated estimates, are, in fact, acting quite rationally.[21] In a similar vein but using a more convoluted argument, Granick regards the state's overproduction of specialists as a means of reconciling two contradictory goals: the need to achieve sufficient labor mobility to maintain a vigorous economy, and the deep-seated ideological imperative to guarantee job security. A higher level of education is given to more of the work force than is economically necessary because this tends to develop a greater psychological preparedness to change jobs.[22] Buttgereit, on the other hand, questions the notion of "adequacy of employment." He embraces the thesis that the high proportion of graduates in the Soviet economy stems from the historically determined organization of Soviet production and management. While deliberately leaving aside considerations of efficiency, he readily acknowledges the distorting role played by social demand in the way graduate manpower is distributed within the economy.[23]

Soviet planners and economists do not share these views. They have strongly criticized both the expansion in engineering higher education and the movement of specialists away from work for which they have been expensively trained. Their solution, therefore, is a reduction in the number of engineering students and broader courses to make *vuz* graduates more adaptable.[24]

Planning errors had also been compounded in the post-Stalin decades by the rapidity of scientific and technological changes that have made certain types of expertise and specialties obsolete and created new ones. Imbalances in territorial patterns of employment of *vuz*-trained specialists and in the ratio of their numbers to those of technicians, together with labor shortages due to a demographic downturn and the unpredictable career orientations of young people, began to have a deleterious effect on the higher education system and graduate employment.[25] Frequent decrees and instructions were issued in an effort to correct faults and to improve the assignment and use of graduates. Branch ministries and organizations, for example, were directed to produce up-to-date lists of jobs requiring higher education training and to establish saturation norms for the proportion of specialists who should be employed in different spheres of work. But the normative nature of Soviet planning and its long-standing emphasis on physical indicators make it resistant to change, and these measures were generally not implemented.[26]

A relative swing away from higher education in the career plans of Soviet school leavers has been well chronicled since the early 1970s. It is reflected most noticeably in a decline in the popularity of engineering. Here the social demand for higher education has obviously worked against state economic plans. At the same time an acute shortage of specialists developed in particular industries, especially mining, gas and oil extraction, heavy construction, and metallurgy, and in certain regions of the country. Even elite engineering institutes had difficulty in meeting their intake targets. Figures for 1971 prepared by the Ministry of Higher and Secondary Specialized Education record a ratio of 2.87 applicants per place for Soviet *vuzy* as a whole. In 1983, however, the ratio had slumped to below 2:1 in all forms of higher education. Universities and humanities courses that usually experience the fiercest competition for entry among applicants were also affected by this trend. These problems have been a matter of serious concern for nearly two decades among government planners, education authorities, and economic managers. Despite special measures to attract recruits to these fields with easier *vuz* entry procedures, the problem remains.[27]

This change in demand coincided with an official policy of setting ever-higher intake targets; so, proportionately fewer applicants were chasing a greater number of places. In order to meet their admissions targets *vuzy* were compelled to lower entry standards and consider less well qualified and motivated applicants. Similarly, graduation quotas were met by relaxing course assessments and by giving priority to the maintenance of cohorts at all costs. The phenomenon of the "grey" student who does the minimum amount of work to achieve barely passing marks for assessments became increasingly widespread judging by frequent castigation in the literature.[28]

The recruitment of less able students, however, did not lead to a greater number of dropouts as might have been anticipated. Graduation targets had also to be met and these seemingly did not take into account academically less able intakes. Hence wastage rates remained comparatively stable for full-time students. Available data indicate an average course attrition of 12 to 13 percent for full-time cohorts throughout the 1970s—a level that had remained relatively unchanged for two or more decades with the exception of the years of the abortive Khrushchev reform (1959–64).[29] In short, student numbers were maintained at the expense of academic standards. This had serious repercussions for the status of higher education, the morale of staff and students, and the employability of graduates. The persistence of these shortcomings aroused public concern, and party criticism of the Ministry of Higher and Secondary Specialized Education intensified.[30]

Then, in the 1980s, the wastage rate among full-time students began to move upwards, initially to 14.2 percent for the 1980–85 cohort. Graduations slumped by a total of one hundred thousand in the years 1985 to 1987, representing a steep rise in dropouts to 18.2 percent in 1986, and then to an unprecedented 29.9 percent among students due to graduate in 1987.[31] These sudden extremely high rates are possibly connected with withdrawal for military service and nonreturn of students during the Afghanistan campaign. But other explanations include voluntary abandonment of their studies by large numbers of students or increased expulsions as a result of the tightening up of standards urged on *vuz* staff by party and government in the 1986–87 reform debate.

Higher Education and Employment

As already observed, Soviet higher education is essentially vocational in character; its development and direction have been dictated by the needs of the economy. *Vuzy* are officially grouped in the following categories: industry and construction, transport and communications, agriculture, economics and law, medicine (including health, physical culture, and sport), education, and the fine arts. Two types of establishment—universities and polytechnical institutes—offer a broader range of specialties than most *vuzy*. The former, designated the leading *vuzy* of the system, provide a more fundamental and theoretical training in the humanities and natural sciences for future teachers, lecturers, and researchers. (Some universities also offer more specific professional courses in faculties of medicine, law, and technology.) Polytechnical institutes offer a variety of applied science and engineering subjects.[32]

Higher education is thus inextricably bound up with the occupational structure, a nexus that has shaped most aspects of its organization and administration from the planning of the *vuz* network to the allocation of students after graduation to compulsory employment for three years in particular branches of the economy. Important decision making affecting higher education is shared by the state planning authorities, the Ministry of Higher and Secondary Specialized Education, and the consumers of highly qualified manpower. Most ministries, for example, have a legitimate interest in the number and quality of graduate specialists produced for their branches of the economy, and in the structure and effectiveness of the training given. They also provide periods of practical work experience for students during their courses and permanent job placements when they graduate. A number of them, moreover, as noted above, exercise direct jurisdiction over *vuzy* that offer specialties relevant to their industries.[33]

Vuz-enterprise cooperation has been particularly stressed since the 1950s. In 1959 special entry arrangements were established for production workers to be seconded by their enterprises to take higher education courses. At the same time an initiative began to bring higher education

to the workplace with the setting up of technical *vuzy* at large plants (*zavody-vtuzy*). This experiment has been lauded as a prototype for higher education in the future but its scope continues to be restricted. In 1969 special preparatory divisions were set up at most *vuzy* to offer full-time revision courses to leading workers and demobilized servicemen recommended by their work collectives or unit commanders with the added bonus of nonexamination, noncompetitive entry to the first year of the regular course. Up to 20 percent of a *vuz* intake can consist of this sort of privileged entrant.[34] Contract research is another increasingly common feature of direct links between enterprises and *vuzy*. And, in general, enterprises and economic ministries are expected to provide some capital funding and equipment to the *vuzy* they are connected with, but this obligation lacks a legal basis and hence is frequently ignored.[35]

These forms of cooperation are not universal, nor are they systematically maintained. Based mainly on goodwill, they rarely affect the main activities of the partners. Higher education authorities complain that enterprises profit more from this mutual dependency than *vuzy*, getting a free supply of highly trained personnel but giving little in return. Indeed, they receive their quota of fresh graduates via centralized agreements between the Ministry of Higher and Secondary Specialized Education and the relevant ministry or organization, irrespective of whether they have direct links with a *vuz* or not.[36] Moreover, branch ministries and enterprises have tended not to regard higher education as a major concern and have been reluctant to help equip and modernize the *vuzy* for which they are responsible, or to provide funds for research. In 1986 higher education minister Gennadiy Yagodin rather pointedly revealed that the thirty leading universities and technical institutes directly controlled by his ministry did as much research as five hundred or so institutes under the aegis of branch ministries.[37]

Changes in these traditional arrangements are difficult to effect because of the labyrinthine structure of the administration of the higher education system: seventy-four different ministries and organizations exercise some degree of direct control of higher education. Their failure to coordinate adequately with each other has led to disparate standards, course duplication, waste of resources, and unnecessary bureaucracy. Particularly contentious issues include the need to update official lists of enterprise posts that call for *vuz* training, inflated forecasting by industrial managers of their future manpower requirements, and the employment of *vuz* graduates in work not compatible with their qualifications.[38]

By the late 1970s it had become clear that a serious situation had developed in the training and employment of graduate manpower. Particular blame was attached to the Soviet economy's traditional emphasis on extensive development and the attainment of ever-rising quantitative targets.[39] The low quality of graduate manpower, inadequate professionalism, and lack of vocation were the object of continuing complaint. Examples were highlighted in the educational press of huge discrepancies between advance estimates for specialists and the numbers eventually employed.[40] New graduates frequently managed to avoid official job placements or simply failed to arrive at their designated workplaces. A major party and government decree in 1979 included proposals to put an end to the inefficient use of specialists and to improve the training of students for their future careers by assigning them to particular enterprises well in advance of graduation.[41] But these provisions remained a dead letter because of lack of cooperation between the ministries concerned.

Not all Western observers detected the dimensions of the problem now revealed. Gruson and Markiewicz-Lagneau, writing in 1983, rightly describe the Soviet preoccupation with quality in higher education as an old concern. But their view that the higher education system was a stable one, which was vigorously implementing coherent policies and which had avoided inflation of numbers, is hardly supported by the available evidence.[42] Buttgereit, on the other hand, is certainly aware of the shortcomings, but fails to see any reference in the Soviet literature that they signaled a need for adjustments.[43] Yet, the fact that the signals were there to be seen is underlined by other German scholars who, in 1984, noted that change of a structural nature had become essential.[44]

Higher Education and the Political System

The dominance of the Communist party in the political process is enshrined in the Soviet constitution of 1977 which designates it as "the leading and guiding force of Soviet society and the nucleus of its political system and of all state and public organizations."[45] Policy-making in all spheres of national life therefore originates in party pronouncements and decrees, which have generally been rubber-stamped and enacted by government.

Because of its importance for the economic progress of the country and the ideological formation of the future leaders of Soviet society, higher education receives special attention and close monitoring from the party. In this respect it may be said to be highly involved in the political system. At the top party level of the Central Committee Secretariat all education matters have since 1989 come within the purview of the Ideological Department.[46] Higher education policy is elaborated in speeches by party leaders, reports and decisions of party congresses, plenary sessions of the Central Committee, and special party conferences and commissions.

Its implementation in day-to-day administration and decision making is monitored by the party in various ways: (1) through party committees that largely parallel and shadow the functions of state bodies, public organizations, and workplace administrations at all levels; (2) by controlling appointments to senior government and managerial positions (the *nomenklatura* system)—a powerful instrument; and (3) by giving party officials and ordinary members legal authority to supervise the work of *vuz* managements. Not surprisingly, the party maintains a high level of representation in *vuzy*. The proportion of party members among higher education staff is much higher than in the population at large; some sources suggest as many as one in two overall, and between 75 and 96 percent for social science teachers.[47]

It should not be assumed that a political system of relative longevity that can boast undoubted economic and social achievements under the leadership of a single highly organized party necessarily conforms to a monolithic totalitarian model. The record of attempts to impose change and reform on Soviet higher education tends to suggest that a pluralist perspective might be more appropriate. Lane speaks of "endemic tension between the party and other sources," the most powerful of which he identifies as the economic and military hierarchies. These can offer most resistance to party control because of the overriding importance and legal basis of the functions they perform. Organized professional groups—managers, scientists and technologists, and quasi-institutional groups such as the Academy of Sciences and *vuz* staff—also possess expertise that gives them greater bargaining power.[48] But it is educational bureaucracies, notably in the Ministry of Higher and Secondary Specialized Education, that have played a crucial "political" role in the success or failure of party and government policies.

The evidence of opposition to the implementation of party plans for higher education since the 1950s testifies to a considerable degree of factual autonomy enjoyed by the various bureaucracies involved in higher education. A graphic illustration of this autonomy is provided by the conflict between the party and both central and republican higher education ministries that came to the fore in the early 1980s and culminated in 1986–87 in the most radical proposals for reform since the Khrushchev era.

From the early 1970s the party had urged the higher education authorities to adapt to the demands posed by the scientific and technological revolution and manpower shortage. In particular, the Twenty-fourth and Twenty-fifth CPSU Congresses in 1971 and 1976 stressed the need to improve the quality of *vuz* teaching and research and of student academic performance. But little concrete progress was made. Charges of neglect and complacency with regard to the country's higher education system that were later directed at the Brezhnev administration are not entirely justified. Indeed, by the end of the decade it had clearly recognized that faulty planning, declining academic standards, and inadequate material support for higher education were causing serious problems. Efforts were made to solve them through wide-ranging legislation such as the January 1978 decree of the USSR Council of Ministers, "On the Improvement of the Planning of Specialist Training and of the Use of Graduates of Higher and Secondary Specialized Educational Establishments in the National Economy," and the joint decree of the Central Committee of the CPSU and the USSR Council of Ministers of 1979, "On the Further Development of Higher Education and the Improvement of Quality in the Training of Specialists."[49] But such enactments produced few tangible improvements.

At the Twenty-sixth Party Congress in 1981, and most of the party plenums in the years following, concern was forcefully expressed at the failure of the Ministry of Higher and Secondary Specialized Education to implement these party and government directives. Ministry officials blamed the cumbersome and fragmented machinery of higher education administration and accused other ministries of failing to cooperate in providing essential data, information, and views. Ministries of higher education in several republics (Uzbekistan, Kirgizia, Tadzhikistan, Lithuania, Latvia) were singled out for special castigation for their backsliding and corruption, and for putting local interests before those of the country as a whole. Notwithstanding the powerful political pressure exerted over a long period by these various party measures and decisions, the decline in the performance of the higher education system continued beyond the Brezhnev era and through the short terms of office of his successors, Andropov and Chernenko.[50]

Recent Reforms

The long-awaited major shake-up of higher education was initiated by extensive legislation promulgated in March 1987. The reform constitutes an integral part of Gorbachev's ongoing campaign to accelerate and intensify the social and economic development of the Soviet Union through more extensive and rapid application of scientific and technological achievements. Radical changes were outlined in a joint document of the Central Committee of the CPSU and the USSR Council of Ministers entitled "Fundamental Guidelines for the Restructuring of Higher and Secondary Specialized Education in the Country."[51] The preamble to the document catalogues the numerous shortcomings that had accumulated in the previous decade and a half. They might more accurately be described as inherent in the system, for, in fact, they feature in many of the major decrees on higher education since the 1920s.

The "Guidelines" are very wide-ranging—ten detailed sections that cover most aspects of the higher education system and that are designed to ensure that higher education plays a crucial role in the revitalization of the Soviet economy. At the same time, five decrees of the Central Committee and the USSR Council of Ministers were enacted implementing various provisions of the reform. One dealt with the main proposals; two concerned improvements in staff pay, training, and conditions of work; another was devoted to expanding research within *vuzy*; and the fifth gave details of better grants, accommodations, and facilities for students.[52] Since 1987 the Ministry of Higher and Secondary Specialized Education (now incorporated into the State Committee for Public Education) has issued a stream of orders and regulations detailing specific measures that give effect to these decrees.[53]

Key words to identify important objectives of the reform should include the following:

Acceleration—of social and economic development

Intensification—of economic production

Modernization—of curricula, methods, plant

Unification—of the overall control of higher education

Decentralization—of decision making to promote independence and initiative

Democratization—of educational administration

But two words that best sum up the principal aims of the reform are *integration*—that is, much closer links between higher education, production, and research—and *quality*—in teaching, research, and learning.

Integration of Higher Education, Production, and Science

One of the prime purposes of integration is to bring into play for the first time a direct external economic lever to improve the recruitment and training of students and the way they are employed after qualifying. Essentially, integration is to be realized through the establishment of real economic mutual dependence between *vuzy* on the one hand, and enterprises and research institutes (both academic and industrial) on the other. This is to be done through legally binding contracts whereby these outside parties will pay a sum of three thousand rubles toward the costs of training each student they subsequently employ as specialists. They will also contribute funding, equipment, premises, and researchers for sponsored or joint research projects. Postexperience training for existing enterprise graduate personnel will be offered on a contract basis. Such arrangements, it is claimed, constitute a sort of market mechanism based on a direct customer-supplier relationship. They will promote three things: (1) more efficient forward labor planning by enterprises and branch ministries; (2) more relevant and practical undergraduate courses with an emphasis on producing high-quality specialists; (3) a doubling or trebling of research output by higher education staff. Henceforth industrial managers wishing to get value for their money should be more sensitive to the quantity and quality of the graduates they take on. In their turn, *vuzy*, hitherto rather divorced from production and the practical application of academic disciplines, will have to take more interest in customer requirements by improving teaching and research performance.

Other forms that integration will take include the following:

1. The promotion of special-purpose job training (*tselevaya podgotovka*) for employees seconded to *vuzy* by enterprises. Part of their courses, leaving aside the usual industrial practice periods, will be taught at the sponsoring enterprises themselves. It is envisaged that eventually one in two of all Soviet students will be trained in this way. And 15 percent of *vuz* teaching time may be set aside for training geared to specific jobs in specific workplaces.

2. Enterprises and research institutes are to be encouraged to set up training centers (*uchebnye tsentry*) which can incorporate branches (*filialy*) of *vuz* faculties. Or such *filialy* may form part of larger joint ventures involving enterprise or research institute laboratories and experimentation-testing units. These go under the name of UNPK (*uchebno-nauchno-proizvodstvennyy kompleks*), that is, "teaching-production-research complexes," one hundred of which were already set up by the end of 1987.

3. Every Soviet student will be instructed in a manual skill connected with the area of his specialty. It is argued that a graduate engineer should be able to perform some of the operations that the manual workers under his control carry out. During work experience periods in industry students will be expected to use such skills (clearly, official acceptance of an existing practice).

4. Staff are to be seconded for up to a year to enterprises or to research institutes in order to get practical experience. Conversely—and this is a controversial matter—leading outside experts will be encouraged to teach for up to four hours a week in higher education establishments.

Many of these initiatives had already been tried out on an experimental basis before the reform was finalized.

Integration is the key to the success of the whole reform. It may be argued, however, that it could also be the source of major difficulties. Certain Soviet educators see this type of development as wrong in principle because it allows enterprises to exert undue influence on the academic process and to distort the graduate assignment system. Objective factors have been cited as evidence that the reform is impracticable or should be delayed. For example, there is no gainsaying the fact that when the reform bills were passed in 1987 the national budget for the period 1986–90 had already been settled; so the sort of investment and funding implied by integration cannot be found until the thirteenth and fourteenth five-year plans in the 1990s. And the question has been asked: how are workplaces in the nonproduction sector of the economy—education, medicine, and culture—going to pay for the graduates they need?

Many interest groups who are affected by the proposed new order for higher education have entrenched attitudes and traditional ways of doing things. There are indications that it is here that difficulties have already been encountered.[54] Despite the amalgamation in 1988 of the two USSR education ministries and the State Committee for Vocational Education into a single State Committee, the edifice of multiple controlling bodies in higher education remains largely intact. The reactions of branch ministries to the changes appear so far to be somewhat halfhearted, while *vuz* staff have expressed dismay and alarm at particular proposals that alter their professional roles and work conditions.

It is obvious that a universal positive attitude to the reform on the part of economic managers could not have been, and cannot now be, taken for granted. Enterprises and branch ministries may prefer to keep costs down by reducing the number of graduates they employ to dangerously low levels that will hinder the loudly proclaimed aim of intensification of the economy. (By the beginning of 1989 only 135,000 students had been "ordered" by branch ministries under the new payment arrangements, and less than one-third of the projected amount of income from this source had been received.)[55] Graduates, though paid for, may well be inefficiently employed, as before, in order to fill immediate urgent vacancies for scarce manual workers or technicians.

The relative indifference of enterprises to the material needs of *vuzy* has not disappeared overnight. It was not surprising that at the February 1988 Central Committee plenum, party secretary Ligachev made a particular appeal to economic managers and work collectives to show concern for higher education because in so doing they would be showing concern for the future of their own enterprise and industry, and for the economy as a whole.[56]

In fact, direct economic relations between *vuzy* and enterprises are still very much circumscribed, which raises doubts about the outcome of the reform. State planning priorities such as intake targets and graduate assignment quotas will remain. The state, too, will continue to meet major *vuz* costs such as staff salaries and student stipends. Payments for training will be made to the State Committee for Public Education from branch ministries' allocations earmarked for enterprise development funds.[57] Thus the economic mechanism will operate *indirectly* and be mediated by the old bureaucracies.

The proponents of the reform point out that, in the past, attempts to bring higher education and industry closer together were voluntary and spasmodic, and always subject to arbitrary interference from above. Now, they insist, there is a clear legal and administrative basis for integration and this gives the present reform teeth. Ultimately, however, it must be recognized that there is no consensus that *vuzy* can, or should, be run on a full self-financing basis. Many educators believe that they should not enter into direct economic relations or compete, as it were, in an academic market.[58]

The Pursuit of Quality in Higher Education

The second principal objective of the higher education reform is to bring about a radical improvement in the quality of both teaching and learning, and to boost the research output of academics. At the institutional level quality will be pursued by regular inspections and appraisal of *vuzy*. Already some have been closed down or amalgamated, and others have been warned or face repeat inspections.[59] Higher education, it is decreed, will now produce what are termed "broad-profile" specialists rather than narrow ones. A broader training will make them professionally more mobile and adaptable. To further this aim the range of individual specialties on offer throughout the system has been significantly reduced by grouping. At the same time the network of *vuzy* is expected to be somewhat rationalized to cut out duplication and waste.[60]

Soviet pedagogy has traditionally placed great reliance on formal methods, lecture courses, the assimilation of huge amounts of factual material, and rote learning. Students are obliged to attend a large number of compulsory classes per week. Inevitably, this has fostered passivity and dependency in the learning process, and discouraged creative, independent thinking and initiative. Young Soviet engineers, it is now admitted, are simply not capable of exploiting and designing modern technology.

The Soviet student, hitherto overloaded and overorganized, has been ostensibly liberated by the reform. Class hours have been cut, and the proportion of those devoted to lectures has also been reduced. These changes are intended to provide much more time for private study and individual tutorials with the aim of promoting better learning and more effective social and political training. Active methods of teaching are now widely being advocated. Discussion, role-play, business games, student participation in real research projects, and more practical classes are gaining popularity. The size of seminar groups has been halved. The average staff-student ratio is to be improved appreciably. Staff are exhorted to treat students from now on as colleagues.

Student ability and performance will be rewarded differentially. The brightest students will be offered individual study programs, special assignments to research institutes, and longer courses of up to six years to prepare them as elite specialists. Higher stipends will be awarded for outstanding academic attainment, and enhanced initial salaries after graduation will be paid to the best graduates.

Students have also benefited greatly from reform provisions for increased democratization within *vuzy*. Their opportunities to participate in the administration of their institutions have been greatly extended through a guaranteed 25 percent representation on academic councils and one-third representation on assemblies that elect rectors and deans.

On the other hand, assessment standards have become more stringent. Expulsion for academic failure is now encouraged. (In the past, when staff establishments were tied to student numbers, the consequence of student wastage was a reduction in staff. This pernicious connection, which led to *protsentomania* [mania for high pass rates], is now abolished and staffing will be calculated on the number of students at entry.) Widespread abuse of the rules on repeat examinations and carrying over academic obligations from year to year are to be stamped out.[61]

The "carrot-and-stick" nature of these measures to raise student performance does seem rather crude. It remains to be seen whether student behavior will be influenced. Some Western scholars have speculated that students may resent the increased vocationalism of *vuz* courses.[62] It is an intriguing question as to how far the authorities would be prepared to go to alienate the large number of students whose motivation is primarily social rather than vocational. In fact, the system has not really come to terms with social demand and with the notion that higher education is a right for all who are capable of benefiting from it. Even less acceptable at present to the education authorities would be the suggestion that course structure might be influenced by student preference. Where the reform may err is in the assumption that the new work-oriented higher education with its broad-profile training will alter the career behavior of future graduates. The latter are quite likely to continue to prefer to take manual work, if necessary, in Moscow to avoid mental work in Siberia! Certainly, student reaction to the proposals so far has been skeptical and unenthusiastic.

Without the cooperation of academic staff the above measures for raising quality will prove fruitless. Yet for them the reform has brought confusion and upset. Despite timetable cuts they face heavier loads thanks to the new system of tutorials and individual supervision of students. At the same time they must dramatically increase their research productivity. They are being urged to abandon familiar time-honored teaching methods and materials. Even more alarming is the loss of their former job security. Every five years their posts will be declared vacant and they will obliged to reapply for them in competition with others. During this process their records will be discussed publicly at meetings of their colleagues and students. Finally, one of the most resented innovations is the introduction of annual student assessment of teaching which will form part of periodic salary reviews. The compensation for all this is higher pay, better pensions, and improved accommodation. And a promise

that the new regime will raise the prestige of learning among students and restore the high status formerly enjoyed by *vuz* academics among the public.[63]

The point must be made that these internal reforms, unlike legal contracts, rely wholly for their success on the human factor. If they are not accompanied by "restructuring" of the hearts and minds of staff, then they will at best be honored in the letter but not the spirit. Staff and student response to the reform so far has been pessimistic. The psychological adjustment urged upon them by the political authorities is a painful and slow process.[64]

There is a dearth of detailed Western comment on the reform or, indeed, on trends in higher education generally in the 1980s. A particular focus of published work here has been the effect on access. The reform is seen by some as a contraction of higher education opportunity designed to channel young people into lower-level vocational training.[65] This view was no doubt influenced to some extent by similar vocational emphases in the 1984 reform of secondary and vocational schooling, which have subsequently been modified. To be sure, some contraction is planned and tougher admission and assessment standards may act as a deterrent. But the reduction in numbers is unlikely to be substantial—more a transference of student numbers from certain specialties to others and between full-time and part-time modes. This has been the trend in any case. In other words, there is no reason to doubt the declared basic goals of improved quality and productivity in higher education. The reform is more radical than a mere cut in numbers, which could have been carried out by simple fiat. It seeks to shake up outmoded thinking and practices within the system that hinder economic progress, and to prepare it for the twenty-first century.

The same commentators imply that social discontent will be aroused among young people denied *vuz* places.[66] Yet higher education has already lost some of its prestige, and demand could be dampened by recent proposals to issue school graduation certificates of differing academic weight. The present meritocratic procedures for *vuz* entry, which are regarded as fair by the bulk of the Soviet public, have not been basically altered. Now that corruption and privilege in admissions is being tackled vigorously under Gorbachev and part-time courses have been made more accessible to graduates of vocational schools, the danger of serious discontent seems unlikely and has not been broached in the Soviet literature.

Conclusions

Throughout its history Soviet higher education has suffered from certain inherent dichotomies that find expression in changing emphases and trends in policy-making and legislation:

○ Centralized control and administration of higher education have had to contend with powerful centrifugal pressures exerted by industrial, territorial, and nationalist interests, and by bureaucracies.

○ Forecasting and regulation essential in the planning process are vitiated by the unpredictability and perversity of demographic change and social demand.

○ The branch principle of organization has come into conflict with the principle that there should be equitable provision of higher education throughout the USSR.

○ The traditional values of academic scholarship, learning and enquiry for its own sake, and high attainment have clashed with the principle that higher education should be available to all and organically linked with the world of work. When quality becomes the focus of policy, basic egalitarian aspirations have often suffered.

○ The parochial concerns and short-term immediate solutions of economic managers, politicians, and educational administrators have often obscured the importance of longer-term goals.

Particular features and tendencies are, of course, interconnected; they come to the fore or recede into the background in association with each other. Yet the tensions they engender do not wholly disappear, and as a consequence Soviet higher education legislative reform tends to exhibit a recurring, cyclical pattern, as former concerns and emphases reemerge. It is therefore banal, but necessary, to observe not only that many of the problems contributing to the present upheaval in Soviet higher education have afflicted the system in the past, but that the solutions now being attempted are similar in intent to those in the past that failed.

The current reforms were long overdue but given past experience their success is problematical. They will not necessarily eliminate underlying dichotomies. Indeed the general process of glasnost and democratization now taking place may give prominence to historical contradictions and tensions. Nor can they remedy basic inadequacies in the economic and social life of Soviet society.

Can the reforms then succeed? At the time of this writing their progress is slow, and constant difficulties are being encountered.[67] Everybody agrees that change is essential, but old habits die hard. Government and party legislation has been resisted or ignored in the past. Most of the participants in this reform recognize the need for change, but many are gripped by a deep conservatism or skepticism. They have to be moved and cajoled to persevere with the new to a point where there can be no going back. The cajoling and encouragement is the task facing party and trade union organizations within higher education. Yet, paradoxically, it is they who must bear much of the responsibility for past inertia. More persuasive, of course, would be additional investment in the system and greater financial rewards for individuals. But the economy cannot provide these tangible results for some time. Ultimately, change in higher education can only come about if economic and social perestroika as a whole can be made to succeed.

Notes

1. *Narodnoye khozyaistvo* SSSR (hereinafter *Narkhoz*) *v* 1987 *godu*, 346, 496; *Vestnik statistiki* 1988, no. 8: 72.
2. The Russian acronym *vuz* (plural *vuzy*) denotes any higher education establishment, whether university, institute, or academy. Following accepted convention I shall use it throughout this chapter in both nominal and adjectival senses.
3. *Narkhoz v* 1982 *godu* (Moscow, 1983), 462; *Narkhoz v* 1985 *godu* (Moscow, 1986), 508; *Narodnoye obrazovaniye, nauka i kul'tura v SSSR. Statisticheskiy sbornik* (Moscow, 1977), 218.
4. *Narkhoz v* 1983 *godu* (Moscow, 1984), 494; *Narkhoz v* 1987 *godu*, 496.
5. *Narkhoz v* 1982 *godu*, 468–69; *Narkhoz v* 1984 *godu* (Moscow, 1985), 525–26; *Narodnoye khozyaistvo* SSSR *za* 70 *let* (Moscow, 1987), 550, 552; *Narkhoz v* 1987 *godu*, 504, 506; N. E. Golubeva, comp., *Narodnoye obrazovaniye v SSSR: Sbornik normativnykh aktov* (Moscow, 1987), 248.
6. *Narkhoz v* 1982 *godu*, 465; *Narkhoz v* 1987 *godu*, 499.
7. *Narkhoz v* 1987 *godu*, 502–3; *Izvestiya* (2 July 1988), 8.
8. Estimates from *Narkhoz v* 1987 *godu*, 496, 591–93; M. N. Rutkevich and L. Ya. Rubina, *Obshchestvennyye potrebnosti, sistema obrazovaniya, molodezh'* (Moscow, 1988), 122; Julian Cooper, "Industry and Higher Education under Gorbachev: On the Move Again, " *Industry and Higher Education* 2, no. 4 (1988): 217–21.
9. *Byulleten' Ministerstva vysshego i srednego spetsial'nogo obrazovaniya* (hereinafter *Byulleten'*) 1968, no. 8: 2.
10. *Byulleten'* 1988, no. 5: 1, and 1989, no. 4: 4–7, 14.
11. Nicholas DeWitt, *Education and Professional Employment in the* USSR (Washington, D. C.: National Science Foundation, 1961), 30, 225, 302.
12. A. A. Abakumov, N. P. Kuzin, F. I. Puzyrev, and L. F. Litvinov, comps., *Narodnoye obrazovaniye v SSSR: Obshcheobrazovatel'naya shkola: Sbornik dokumentov* 1917-1973 *g.g.* (Moscow, 1974), 413.
13. V. P. Yelyutin, *Vysshaya shkola obshchestva razvitogo sotsializma* (Moscow, 1980), 68–79, 82–83, 123–25.
14. Yelyutin, *Vysshaya shkola*, 124, 478; D. Chuprunov, R. Avakov, and E. Jiltsov, "Higher Education, Employment, and Technological Progress in the USSR," in *Higher Education and Employment in the* USSR *and in the Federal Republic of Germany*, ed. R. Avakov, B. C. Sanyal, M. Buttgereit, and V. Teichler (Paris: IIEP, 1984), 49–50; Michael Buttgereit, "Higher Education and Its Relations to Employment in the USSR and in the Federal Republic of Germany—A Comparison," in Avakov et al., *Higher Education and Employment*, 297–98, 311; *Pravda* (21 March 1987), p. 1.
15. Yelyutin, *Vysshaya shkola*, 476–79; DeWitt, *Education and Professional Employment*, 40–41, 207, 224–25; N. S. Barabasheva, *Pravovoi status vuzov v* SSSR (Moscow, 1979), 58.
16. Nicholas DeWitt, "Educational and Manpower Planning in the Soviet Union," in *The World Yearbook of Education* 1967, ed. George Z. F. Bereday and Joseph A. Lauwerys (London: Evans Brothers, 1967); 220–21; Buttgereit, "Higher Education," 311.
17. Abakumov et al., *Narodnoye obrazovaniye*, 18–19.
18. Abakumov et al., *Narodnoye obrazovaniye*, 405–6; Yelyutin, *Vysshaya shkola*, 69–73; Mervyn Matthews, *Education in the Soviet Union: Policies and Institutions Since Stalin* (London: Allen & Unwin, 1982), 123–26.
19. DeWitt, "Educational Planning"; Chuprunov, Avakov, and Jiltsov, "Higher Education," 64–77; Yelyutin, *Vysshaya shkola*, 399–404.
20. Yelyutin, *Vysshaya shkola*, 210–17, 405–16.
21. Harley D. Balzer, "Education, Science, and Technology," in *The Soviet Union Today: An Interpretative Guide*, ed. James Cracraft (Chicago: University of Chicago for *Bulletin of the Atomic Scientists*, 1983), 240.
22. David Granick, *Job Rights in the Soviet Union* (Cambridge: Cambridge University Press, 1987), 219–21.
23. Buttgereit, "Higher Education," 279, 285.
24. Golubeva, *Narodnoye obrazovaniye v SSSR*, 248, 250.
25. Yelyutin, *Vysshaya shkola*, 210–17, 405–16. See also E. N. Zhil'tsov, "Vysshaya shkola v usloviyakh intensifikatsii narodnogo khozyaistva," in *Effektivnost' ispol'zovaniya resursov vysshei shkoly: Sbornik nauchnykh trudov*, ed. M. K. Shermenev (Moscow: 1985), 11–13; Harley D. Balzer, "The Soviet Scientific-Technical Revolution: Education of Cadres," in *The Status of Soviet Civil Science*, ed. Craig Sinclair (Dordrecht, Boston, and Lancaster: Martinus Nijhoff,

1987), 6–8.

26. Zhil'tsov, "Vysshaya shkola," 12–13; Yelyutin, *Vysshaya shkola*, 409, 412–14; Buttgereit, "Higher Education," 311.

27. George Avis, "Access to Higher Education in the Soviet Union," in *Soviet Education in the 1980s*, ed. J. J. Tomiak (London: Croom Helm, 1983), 203–4; O. I. Karpukhin and V. A. Kutsenko, *Student segodnya—spetsialist zavtra* (Moscow, 1983), 44–49; Zhil'tsov, "Vysshaya shkola," 12; *Byulleten'* 1972, no. 3: 23; and 1984, no. 11: 6.

28. D. I. Zyuzin, *Kachestvo podgotovki spetsialistov kak sotsial'naya problema* (Moscow, 1978), 43, 65–66; Karpukhin and Kutsenko, *Student segodnya*, 15–19; George Avis, "Soviet Students: Lifestyle and Attitudes," in *Soviet Education under Scrutiny*, ed. John Dunstan (Glasgow: Jordanhill College Publications, 1987), 93–95; Rutkevich and Rubina, *Obshchestvennyye potrebnosti*, 125–26.

29. Estimates based on *Narkhoz v 1980 godu* (Moscow, 1981), 468–69; *Narkhoz v 1983 godu*, 500–501; *Narkhoz v 1984 godu*, 511–12; *Narkhoz za 70 let*, 550, 552; *Narkhoz v 1987 godu*, 504, 506; Mary Ghullam and George Avis, "Student Wastage in Soviet Higher Education Under Khrushchev and Brezhnev: A Review of Materials in the Educational and National Press," in *Soviet Higher and Vocational Education: From Khrushchev to Gorbachev*, ed. George Avis (Bradford, England: University of Bradford, 1987), 121–23.

30. Rutkevich and Rubina, *Obshchestvennyye potrebnosti*, 125–26; Chuprunov, Avakov, and Jiltsov, "Higher Education," 57; *Pravda* (21 March 1987), p. l.

31. See n. 29.

32. DeWitt, *Education and Professional Employment*, 208–20; Yelyutin, *Vysshaya shkola*, 82–83, 112–13, 129.

33. G. I. Ushakov and A. S. Shuruyev, *Planirovaniye i finansirovaniye podgotovki spetsialistov* (Moscow, 1980), 155; G. Yagodin, "Vyssheye obrazovaniye: sostoyaniye i perspektivy," *Kommunist* 1986, no. 16: 66; Barabasheva, *Pravovoi status*, 58–60, 101–4.

34. Chuprunov, Avakov, and Jiltsov, "Higher Education," 42–43; Zhil'tsov, "Vysshaya shkola," 8; George Avis, "Preparatory Divisions in Soviet Higher Establishments 1969–79: Ten Years of Radical Experiment," *Soviet Studies* 35, no. 1 (1983), 14–35.

35. *Byulleten'* 1968, no. 8: 4; *Vestnik vysshei shkoly* 1987, no. 4: 10; Ushakov and Shuruyev, *Planirovaniye i finansirovaniye*, 188–89; Chuprunov, Avakov, and Jiltsov, "Higher Education," 49–51.

36. I. E. Tarapov, "Imet' vozmozhnost' vybora," *Vestnik vysshei shkoly* 1988, no. 6: 6; V. Zuyev, "Ekonomicheskiye problemy reformy vysshei shkoly," *Ekonomicheskiye nauki* 1988, no. 1: 111.

37. *Pravda* (21 March 1987), p. 1; *Sovetskaya Rossiya* (3 June 1986), p. l, and (18 July 1986), p. 2; G. A. Yagodin, "Potentsial vysshei shkoly," *Nauka i zhizn'* 1986, no. 9: 7.

38. Ushakov and Shuruyev, *Planirovaniye i finansirovaniye*, 62; Zhil'tsov, "Vysshaya shkola," 11–13; Tarapov, "Imet' vozmozhnost'," 7; *Sovetskaya Rossiya* (18 July 1986), p. 2. For the administrative subordination of Soviet higher education establishments, see Balzer, "The Soviet Scientific-Technical Revolution," 6–7.

39. Zuyev, "Ekonomicheskiye problemy," 111; *Sovetskaya Rossiya* (6 June 1986), p. 2.

40. Tarapov, "Imet' vozmozhnost'," 7; Rutkevich and Rubina, *Obshchestvennyye potrebnosti*, 125–26; *Pravda* (21 March 1986), p. 1.

41. *Byulleten'* 1979, no. 9: 4.

42. Pascale Gruson and Janina Markiewicz-Lagneau, *L'Enseignement superieur et son efficacite: France, Etats-Unis, URSS, Pologne*. La Documentation francaise, Notes et Etudes documentaires, no. 4713/14 (Paris: La Documentation francaise, 1983), 112, 122, 124.

43. Buttgereit, "Higher Education," 289.

44. Wolfgang Mitter and Leonid Novikov, "Tendenzen der Hochschulpolitik in der Sowjetunion," in *Bildungssysteme in Osteuropa: Reform oder Krise?*, ed. Oskar Anweiler and Friedrich Kuebart (Berlin: Berlin Verlag, 1984), 273–74.

45. Cited in David Lane, *Politics and Society in the USSR*, rev. ed. (London: Martin Robertson, 1978), 162.

46. *Izvestiya TsK KPSS* 1989, no. 1: 84. For the functions of party bodies responsible for higher education affairs, see Lane, *Politics and Society*, 210; and Jerry F. Hough and Merle Fainsod, *How the Soviet Union Is Governed* (Cambridge: Harvard University Press, 1979), 416, 493–95.

47. Peter Kneen, *Soviet Scientists and the State: An Examination of the Social and Political Aspects of Science in the USSR* (London: Macmillan, 1984), 64–81, 86–89, 103–4; Barabasheva, *Pravovoi status*, 205–6.

48. Lane, *Politics and Society*, 227.

49. *Byulleten'* 1978, no. 5: 2–5, and 1979, no. 9: 3–11.

50. *Vestnik vysshei shkoly* 1983, no. 4: 9–13, 31–33, and no. 5: 3–7; Zhil'tsov, "Vysshaya shkola," 12–13; *Byulleten'* 1981, no. 11: 3–8; 1982, no. 6: 1–5, no. 8: 17–23, no. 9: 17–21, and no. 11: 4–9; 1984, no. 6: 2–9; 1985, no. 9: 19–22, and 1986, no. 2: 3–7.

51. *Pravda* (21 March 1987), pp. 1–3. For an English translation of the Guidelines and of authori-

tative Soviet commentaries on them, see Richard Dobson, ed., *The Restructuring of Soviet Higher and Secondary Specialized Education: Phase 1. Soviet Education*, vol. 29, nos. 9–10 (Armonk, NY.: M. E. Sharpe, 1987). For detailed Western scholarly comment, see Dobson, *Restructuring*, 5–25; Balzer, "The Soviet Scientific-Technical Revolution"; Stephen T. Kerr, "The Soviet Reform of Higher Education," *Review of Higher Education* 11, no. 3 (1988): 215–46; and Julian Cooper, "Industry and Higher Education."

52. Golubeva, *Narodnoye obrazovaniye v SSSR*, 246–57, 264–75, 287–89, 298–301.

53. See, for example, *Byulleten'* 1987, no. 8: 2–4, and 1988, no. 3: 2–21.

54. E. K. Ligachev, "O khode perestroiki srednei i vysshei shkoly i zadachakh partii po eye osushchestvleniyu," in *Materialy Plenuma Tsentral'nogo Komiteta KPSS, 17–18 fevralya 1988 goda* (Moscow, 1988), 13, 16–28, 35, 50–51, 56, 62; *Izvestiya* (21 December 1988), p. 2; F. I. Peregudov, "Uspekh zavisit ot kazhdogo," *Vestnik vysshei shkoly* 1988, no. 8: 3–10; *Izvestiya TsK KPSS* 1989, no. 4: 89–92; Kerr, "The Soviet Reform," 241; Dobson, *Restructuring*, 22.

55. *Izvestiya TsK KPSS* no. 4 (1989): 90. See also Balzer, "The Soviet Scientific-Technical Revolution," 16.

56. Ligachev, "O khode perestroiki," 25. See also *Pravda* (9 June 1986), p. 3, and (7 January 1987), p. 3.

57. Zuyev, "Ekonomicheskiye problemy," 114; "Ekonomicheskiye aspekty perestroiki vysshei i srednei spetsial'noi shkoly (obmen mneniyami v redaktsii)," *Ekonomicheskiye nauki* 1987, no. 9: 118–19.

58. Zuyev, "Ekonomicheskiye problemy," 110–11; *Vestnik vysshei shkoly* 1989, no. 3: 85, 88.

59. Peregudov, "Uspekh zavisit," 5.

60. Ibid., 9; Golubeva, *Narodnoye obrazovaniye v SSSR*, 246; G. A. Yagodin, "Perestroika: stat' normoi zhizni," *Vestnik vysshei shkoly* 1987, no. 4: 3.

61. Golubeva, *Narodnoye obrazovaniye v SSSR*, 247–49; *Byulleten'* 1987, no. 8: 2–4.

62. Kerr, "The Soviet Reform," 241; Balzer, "The Soviet Scientific-Technical Revolution," 14.

63. Ligachev, "O khode," 23, 62; Yagodin, "Perestroika," 5; *Pravda* (29 April 1987), p. 1; *Byulleten'* 1987, no. 8: 2–4, and 1988, no. 3: 2.

64. Yagodin, "Perestroika," 7–20; *Vestnik vysshei shkoly* 1987, no. 9: 21–25; 1988, no. 3: 16–19, and no. 9: 4; 1989, no. 3: 83, 88.

65. Kerr, "The Soviet Reform," 226; Dobson, *Restructuring*, 20; Harley D. Balzer, "Is Less More? Soviet Science in the Gorbachev Era," *Issues in Science and Technology* 1, no. 4 (1985): 42; Balzer, "The Soviet Scientific-Technical Revolution," 13–15.

66. Kerr, "The Soviet Reform," 241; Dobson, *Restructuring*, 22, 29; Balzer, "The Soviet Scientific-Technical Revolution," 15.

67. Ligachev, "O khode," 62; *Vestnik vysshei shkoly* 1988, no. 9: 4.

Spain

José Luis Garcia Garrido

◆

In Spain, for several reasons that I will examine below, the concept "higher education" has come to be synonymous with the university. As the first article of the Law of the University Reform (Ley de Reforma Universitaria) declares, "the public service of higher education corresponds to University, which performs it by means of teaching, study and research." Outside the university system there are few higher study options; for the military and the church have their own institutions of study, and there are specialized schools for music and art training, but even these few exceptions tend to be considered "university level" or a part of university training.

Access to higher or university education begins at age eighteen, after, as a rule, twelve years of primary and secondary studies divided into two basic periods. The first period, lasting eight years, from six to age fourteen, is compulsory for all children. The second period is voluntary and includes the Bachillerato, a three-year period of secondary higher education, and the so-called Curso de Orientación Universitaria (University Orientation Form), of one year. This educational structure, established by the General Law of Education of 1970, is now in the process of revision.

There are thirty public and four private (belonging to the Catholic Church) universities of several different types:

○ University Faculties (Facultades Universitarias), in which studies corresponding to three university degree programs can be taken; the first two are directed to the obtaining of the Licenciado degree, while the third one leads to the Doctor degree. These studies encompass all the fields of knowledge (health sciences, physical-natural sciences, social and human sciences, etc.), except the technologies.

○ Higher Technical Schools (Escuelas Técnicas Superiores), in which studies corresponding to three university cycles are taken in engineering (in several specialities) or architecture. The degree, therefore, is not that of Licenciate, but Engineer or Architect. The third cycle leads, as in the case of the University Faculties, to the degree of Doctor.

○ University Schools (Escuelas Universitarias), in which only the first cycle of university studies exists (usually a period of three years), at the end of which the Diploma, Technical Engineer, or Technical Architect degree is obtained. The studies taken at these schools are of a professional nature (teachers of basic education, technical engineering, nursing, management and business, etc.). Some of these centers are private, though they may be attached to public universities.

○ University Colleges (Colegios Universitarios), in which only the first cycle of the university studies (those of the University Faculties, as mentioned above) can be taken. These centers are registered in a certain university, where students later pursue studies in the corresponding university faculty. The University

Colleges can be public or private, and the latter can be attached to the former.

The thirty public universities include four polytechnic universities (in Madrid, Barcelona, Valencia, and Las Palmas de Gran Canaria), made up of higher technical schools and university schools of a technical nature. The Distance Teaching Spanish National University (*Universidad Nacional de Educación a Distancia*, UNED), which has its headquarters in Madrid, also belongs to this network of public universities.

The university student population has grown spectacularly in the last 20 years. Today it includes almost a million students, of which approximately 50 percent are women. This student population is distributed unequally among the universities. The greatest number of students are enrolled at the Universidad Complutense in Madrid and the Universidad Nacional de Educación a Distancia (UNED)—each has more than 100,000 registered students. The Universidad Central in Barcelona has 80,000 students, and the Universidad of Valencia more than 50,000. Ten more universities have enrollments of more than 25,000 students: Universities of the Basque Country, Polytechnic of Madrid, Santiago de Compostela, Sevilla, Granada, Autonomous University of Barcelona, Autonomous University of Madrid, Zaragoza, Valladolid, and Oviedo. Another eleven—Polytecnic of Barcelona, Salamanca, La Laguna (Canary Islands), Málaga, Murcia, Extremadura, Polythecnic of Valencia, Córdoba, Alcalá de Henares, Cádiz, and Alicante— have enrollments of between 10,000 and 25,000 students. Only five public universities have fewer than 10,000 students: León, Cantabria, Baleares, Castilla-La Mancha, and Polythecnic of Las Palmas (Canary Islands). Of the private universities, Deusto and Navarra, each with more than 10,000 students are the largest.

Pontificia in Comillas enrolls about 6,000 students and Pontificia in Salamanca enrolls about 2,000 students. The private university sector accounts for only 7 percent of the university students.

The university academic staff has also grown, though not at the same rate as the student population. In 1989 there are approximately 48,000 teachers, of whom 28 percent are women. Most of these teachers serve on the public university faculties; approximately 10 percent of the teachers work in the private sector. The average teacher/student ratio is 1:21, although noticeable differences exist between some universities and others.

The legal rules by which the higher education system in Spain is regulated at present are the Spanish Constitution of 1978, the Law of University Reform of 1983, Royal Decrees, rules issued by six Autonomous Communities that make independent decisions in the matter of higher education, and the statutes of each of the universities.

Historical Development

Spain has a long tradition of university life. The University of Salamanca was opened at the beginning of the thirteenth century. It received confirmation on behalf of King Alfonso X, "The Wise," in 1254 and on behalf of the pope, Alexander IV, a year later. Other universities were subsequently created in Valladolid, Toledo, Alcalá, Valencia, Sevilla, and elsewhere. The fifteenth and sixteenth centuries were times of great splendor for university studies and for knowledge in Spain. In the sixteenth century (the "Golden Century") there were more than thirty institutions defined as universities,[1] besides a noticeable number of *Colleges*, institutions of a residential nature which served as a basic support for university life.

Although the number of universities grew—to forty—in the seventeenth century, their quality generally declined. Most attempts at reforming Spanish higher education during the Age of Enlightenment took place outside the university. To sidestep the Catholic church and its control of educational institutions, reformers established "Academies," "Economic Societies of Friends of the Country," etc., as they searched for ways to improve Spain's educational system. The expulsion of the Jesuits in 1767, in the kingdom of Carlos III, marked another stage of reform which, however, did not have spectacular results.[2] The state government moved to increase its power over the universities and to decrease ecclesiastic power. Many existing universities were eliminated or reduced in size, leaving the surviving institutions with greater uniformity in their organization and function. In short, principles were promoted which decades later would succeed all over Europe after the appearance of the Napoleonic university.

However, it was still not possible to apply wholesale reform because the individual universities continued to retain strong autonomy. Reform of study plans went forward slowly in the main universities (beginning with Seville, in 1769). New learning was introduced (for example, study of the national law began to replace the study of Roman law, and interest in the experimental sciences increased) and the state gradually asserted its power (the rector in every university basically became a representative of this power).

Reforms continued into the early nineteenth century. The liberal Constitution of 1812 paved the way (with great opposition) for a conception of the university as an institution of the state, which now assumed the monopoly over higher education that the church had previously held. A rule of 1821 created, in the capital of the kingdom, a *Central University*, as a model for all the other universities.

But the legal document that eventually had more impact on the Spanish university, and on the structure and functioning of the entire educational system, was the so-called *Moyano Law* of 1887 (Claudio Moyano was the minister who obtained its approval). This law mandated a comprehensive structure for higher education in Spain. Henceforward there were to be three different sources for higher studies: the university, made up of the traditional faculties; the "higher education," which grouped together new studies of a technical nature (such as engineering) and the training of high officials; and, finally, the field of "professional learning," which trained students for veterinary medicine, foremanship, master building, surveying, primary teaching, etc. All the institutions in these three categories, according to the law, "will be supported by the state." The new law recognized ten universities (the Central University in Madrid and another nine), and granted each a specific university district.

The structure of higher education introduced by the Moyano Law remained in force for more than a century. The Free Education Institution (Institución Libre de Enseñanza) in the last decades of the nineteenth century and in the first years of the twentieth promoted a series of reforms, and the Second Republic (1931–36) also elaborated an ambitious program of reforms, but the basic structure, however, remained little changed. During the Franco period the Catholic church's role in education once again became important, but the field of higher education continued to be a state enterprise. In fact, it was not until 1964 that the first private Spanish university, the University of Navarra, promoted by Opus Dei, was officially recognized.

The 1960s witnessed great expansion of the university student body. Between 1961 and 1968, it increased from 81,721 students to 176,428 students. Like other countries during these years Spain suffered the effects of overcrowding in the classrooms, which, together with the curtailment of freedoms by Franco's regime, led to frequent student conflicts.[3] The extension of the number of universities and other university centers, already begun in 1968, served as preparation for the reform of 1970. This reform, though timid in some respects, was a considerable step forward. The principle of "university autonomy" was finally consecrated, a considerable expansion and diversification of the number of centers occurred, and the tertiary structure that is still substantially in force today was adopted. The number of students once again increased spectacularly, reaching 450,000 university students registered in 1980, ten years after the approval of the law. A similar increase has taken place over the past decade.

The transition from dictatorship to democracy, culminating in the Constitution of 1978, led to some basic changes in higher education. The new state territorial order transferred control of many universities from the central government to new regional authorities. Spain today is divided into seventeen Autonomous Regions. Six of these have already assumed full control of higher education within their areas.

Higher Education and Employment

It has almost become a cliché to define the Spanish universities as "unemployed factories."[4] In fact, especially during the last decade, Spanish higher education institutions have given up trying to give their graduates that "employment certainty" they used to endow. In many professional sectors, university graduates have run into remarkable difficulties trying to find a stable job; many have had to give up their initial aspirations and dedicate themselves to tasks that have little or nothing to do with their specific professional training.

However, higher studies continue to attract many young people in Spain because they still offer prospects of well-paid employment and of upward social mobility significantly more ample than those offered by professional schools or schools of a lower academic level. The rate of youth unemployment in Spain today is alarming, with nearly 50 percent of the postschool population between sixteen and twenty-five years out of work. This rate is the highest for all the countries in the European Community. (So, too, is the general rate of unemployment in Spain—about 20 percent.) In 1986 the total rate of unemployment for graduates of higher education (that is to say, in proportion to the total of higher graduates) was 15.6 percent. Graduates in such areas as humanities or social sciences often spend two or more years looking for relatively permanent employment.

A more detailed analysis of the numbers demonstrates the limited suitability that higher studies keep with respect both to the employment market and to the predictable needs of economic development in Spain. In 1986, in all the higher education institutions, a total of 90,393 students graduated.[5] Of that number, almost 57 percent (52,343 students) graduated from the University Faculties (Humanities, Sciences, Law, Medicine, and so on), after five or more years of schooling. Only 3.3 percent (3,031 students) had fulfilled long-term studies in the Higher Technical Schools (Architecture and Engineering studies). The Technical University Schools, with their three-year short-term programs of studies, graduated only 6 percent (5,516 students) of the total. Finally, in the nontechnical University Schools, with short-term programs of studies for teaching, nursing, enterprise management, etc., 29,053 students, or 32 percent of the total, graduated.

These statistics immediately generate two important conclusions: first, Spain produces an unbalanced body of graduates with far too many (some 60 percent) pursuing long-term university studies (five or more years); and second, Spanish students give limited attention to studies of a technical nature, whether short- or long-term, with little more than 9 percent of the graduates demonstrating mastery of technical subjects.

One should also note that the majority of graduates from the universities majored in the humanities and social sciences. Humanities graduates numbered 15,378, almost 17 percent of all the Spanish graduates in 1986. Law graduates numbered 8,947, or almost 10 percent of the total, and a number higher than the total sum of graduates from all the technical studies, both short term and long term. Economics, psychology, and other social sciences attract equally high numbers of students. The health sciences, and more specifically medicine, constitute another of the favorite fields. In 1986 more than 7,000 students, more than 8 percent of all the Spanish graduates for that year, received medical degrees. For experimental and mathematic sciences, the number of graduates exceeded 6,000, almost 7 percent of the total.

With regard to the nontechnical, short-term courses of studies, the number of graduates in the Teacher Training Schools stand out; in 1986 these schools graduated 19,687 students—more than 21 percent of all Spanish graduates.

All these data emphasize an important malfunction of the higher education institutions with regard to the professional world and to what should be a stable development of the Spanish economy. The Spanish university produces more lawyers than technicians. Almost half of the graduates of the higher institutions end up devoting themselves to teaching, at some level, at a time when there are already too many teachers and the numbers of the school-aged population are going down. The production of medical doctors, psychologists, journal-ists, and other professionals grossly exceeds real needs. Meanwhile, there is a criminal lack of technicians, and studies aimed at new and necessary professions have not even been organized.

Concern about ways to remedy this terrible imbalance between the kinds of students higher education produces and the kinds of professionals Spanish society needs continue to grow. Interesting ideas and innovations appear, both in the public sector and in the private sector. In this regard, the University-Enterprise Foundation (*Fundación Universidad-Empresa*) is performing an important function; their main objective is to facilitate contact between university institutions and the productive and working field.

Politics and the University

The Spanish Constitution of 1978 completely recognizes university autonomy. This does not mean, however, that universities have lost all dependence on political and governmental organs. The sixth article of the Law of University Reform clearly establishes that "the Universities will be governed by the present Law, by the rules issued by the State and the Autonomous Regions in the exercise of their respective competencies and by their Statutes." The same Law of University Reform includes an extensive set of regulations which, in certain matters (teachers' appointments, internal government of the university, general structure of the study program, kinds of centers, etc.) leaves small margin for university autonomy. Both the central government and the respective regional governments can issue, and in fact have issued, other complementary rules of arrangement and functioning, thus developing the precepts of the law related to teachers, university departments, etc. Moreover, we must not forget that the financing of the public universities is the responsibility of the state. So university autonomy has very clear limitations.

As for the central government, there exists within the Ministry of Education and Science a State Secretary for Universities and Research which, through its state offices, constitutes the highest governing organ of higher education. There also exists a Board of Universities which consists of the university rectors and members appointed by the central government. The Board of Universities is not limited to giving advice, but, (as article 23 of the Law of University Reform specifies), it assumes "order, coordination, planning, proposal and advice functions." It is, in short, an instrument of government in the hands of the central power, though it is, undoubtedly, also a forum for open discussion and study of common problems.

The central government has transferred responsibility for higher education to six Autonomous Communities or regions (Catalunya, Basque Country, Galicia, Andalucía, Valencia, and the Canary Islands). In them, both their own parliament and the regional government can elaborate certain guidelines and coordinate the actions of the local universities. Concrete exercise of this responsibility is strongly limited, however, by the regulations and financial support originating with the central government, and by the aspirations of the universities themselves to exercise without more interference their own autonomy.

Autonomy can be exercised to a certain extent in certain fields. Specifically, the universities have full autonomy to elaborate their "Statutes and other rules for internal operation" and to control "the election, designation and reform of the government and administration organs"; they also have the power to establish relations with other Spanish or foreign institutions. In other matters university autonomy can be exercised only in a par-

tial way. That is the case with "the elaboration, approval, and management of their budgets"; "the establishment and modification of their staff" (teaching and nonteaching); the "selection, training, and promotion of the staff"; the "elaboration and approval of the study plans," etc. In all of these and in many other important matters, the state lays down operational norms that restrict the field reserved for university autonomy. The existence in the core of each university of a Social Council whose composition is mainly nonacademic also constitutes—as many academics think—an obstacle for the exercise of autonomy.

Article 20 of the Constitution of 1978 expressly includes the recognition and protection of academic freedom (*libertad de cátedra*, "freedom of chair"). The second article of the Law of 1983 establishes that "the activity of the University, as well as its autonomy, is based in the principle of academic freedom, which is shown by the freedom of chair, of research and of study." As for teachers, this academic freedom is established by article 33 of the same law, in which it is admitted that all the university permanent teachers have "full academic and research capacity" (the last conditional to the possession of the doctorate). Consequently, all teachers can and do resort to the freedom of chair guaranteed by the constitution. Both the ordinary courts and the Constitutional Court have already had the opportunity of reaffirming the importance of this right, which includes not only the free oral and written expression of ideas, but also the free adoption of programs, methodologies, texts, etc.

Government and the Operation of Tertiary Institutions

All public universities are forced to have an identical structure of governance, of which both the collegiate organs and the individual ones are a part. The first group includes the Social Council, the University Assembly, the Governing Body, the Faculty or School Boards, and the Department or Institute Councils.

The Social Council is defined by the law (article 14) as "the organ of the participation of society in University." Three-fifths of it is formed by "representation of the social interests," decided by the law of the respective Autonomous Community (Region). The law specifically states that none of the "social interest" members can be a member of the university community. The rest of the Social Council is made up of "a representation of the Governing Body, chosen by this among its members, and of which the Rector, the Secretary General, and the Manager will necessarily be part." It is not the rector who presides over the Social Council but a person appointed by the corresponding Autonomous Community (Region). So, to a certain extent, the Social Council can be considered as the control organ external to the university, to which such very important competencies as the approval of the budget and the university pluriannual programming, as well as the "supervision of the activities of economic nature" and "of the rendering of its services" correspond.

The University Assembly, generally made up of a large number of members, is strictly a university organ, of which at least three-fifths must be teachers. The Assembly also includes representatives of students and nonacademic staff. Its three essential assignments are the elaboration of the university statutes, the election of the rector, and the approval of the general lines of action of the university. The Assembly is presided over by the Rector.

The Governing Body is defined in the law as "the ordinary governing organ of the University." It is presided over by the rector. Besides the principal team as a whole, representatives both of the University institutions (deans, department directors, etc.) and of the different levels (teachers, students, and nonacademic staff) sit on this body.

Each of the institutions or centers which make up the university (Faculties, Schools, Departments, and Institutes) also has its own Board or Council, which, among other duties, elects a person to lead them (as dean or director).

In the individual governing organs, the first university authority is the rector, who is chosen by the Assembly, according to the rules that their statutes establish, always from among "full professors" (*catedráticos*) of the same university. Once appointed, it is the rector who in turn appoints the members of his team (vice-rectors, secretary general, and manager).

The main centers (Faculties, Schools, University Colleges, etc.) that constitute the internal structure of the university were already mentioned and described at the beginning of this chapter. This structure may also include university institutes, exclusively dedicated to research tasks. The main organs of the university, "in charge of organizing and developing research and teaching," are the university departments, which are constituted according to the different areas of scientific, humanistic, technical, or artistic knowledge. Subsequent to the Law of 1983, the government has issued extensive regulations about the organization and operation of the university department, considered today as a basic part of the university.

Let us now turn to the structure of higher studies in Spain. Such studies are divided into three cycles, respectively leading to the degrees of "diplomate" (bachelor), "licenciate" (master), and "doctor." The traditional length of time for the first cycle has been three years; since 1970 there have been attempts to introduce changes so that at the end of this first cycle students could obtain a degree of a practical nature that would entitle them to go into a profession. But the attempt has failed again and again, in such a way that (except for the so-called University Schools) the first cycle continues to be regarded merely as the first step in a minimum two-step process. The second cycle, of two years, leads to the degree of "licenciate," which is the traditional sign of competence to enter a profession. This system means that the length of university studies is at least five years (six in the case of medicine and of some higher technical studies). After receiving the licenciate the student can choose to enter the third cycle, leading to a doctorate; this cycle lasts at least two years, generally three or four.

Access to higher studies is, in principle, open to all those students who have the degree of *Bachillerato* (title given at the end of secondary education); who have taken the so called University Orientation Course (COU); and, lastly, who have passed a general entrance examination, usually known as the "selectivity examination." The University Orientation Course (COU) was an interesting innovation of the General Law of Education of 1970, but it has been severely impaired almost from the beginning. The COU has become little more than another year of secondary studies, not the true preparation for higher studies it was intended to be. The "selectivity examination" was created some years later, with the intention of weeding out poorly prepared and weakly motivated students. But it too has failed to fulfill the task planned for it in a satisfactorily manner.

The General Law of Education also established that all persons over twenty-five could enter the university directly even without vouching for previous primary and secondary education, provided they passed a special entrance exam. All the public universities today offer these examinations, though it is the Spanish National Distance Teaching University (UNED) that has done it most systematically and with the greatest number of candidates. In the academic year 1988/89 the UNED had about 25,000 students registered in the Foundation Course for people over twenty-five.

Current Reform Efforts

It has already been suggested that even though the Law of University Reform (LRU) of 1983 introduced important modifications, it has not brought to the field of higher education important structural changes. The institutional structure of the Spanish university is still, in essence, the same as the one established in 1970 by the General Law of Education, which was already at that time accused of an excessive policy of continuity. The most important modifications introduced by the LRU are in the areas of structure, the selection of university teachers, precisely defining what "university autonomy" means, and promoting democratic participation in the governing organs of the university.

With regard to the structure of higher studies, considerable efforts are being made to attain what up to now has been impossible: creating programs of study for the first cycle (two or three years) that will really interest the majority of students and really lead to a professional activity. The Board of Universities is immersed in the preparation of new plans and programs of study that avoid the excessive traditionalism of the Spanish university system and that really prepare students for new professions. This effort is in line with what is being developed by institutions in other industrial countries, especially in Europe. In fact, the European Community has mandated, as of 1992, the free circulation of students, teachers, and professionals, which demands from all the member states the adoption of homogeneous degree and graduation criteria. In Spain, due to the prevailing traditional structure, this effort is complicated.

Also, in the last four years, greater attention has been given to the need of encouraging research tasks. At this time, a comparison of the Spanish universities with their European equivalents would be quite unfavorable. Spanish educators are conscious that, in a few years, it will be necessary to improve both resources and teachers, in such a way that the universities will be able to compete suitably with industrial countries in Europe and other continents. Already several legal and financial provisions have been made and are in preparation to help attain this objective.

Basic Problems of Higher Education in Spain

It is necessary to summarize briefly the main problems that Spanish higher education faces in the immediate future.

1. The first of these problems is the considerable imbalance existing between the field of higher education and the field of employment, imbalance which results in a high rate of unemployment for university graduates (especially in the period immediately after the end of studies). In the long run, the solution to the problem of unemployment in Spain lies in a restructuring both of the economy and of the higher education standard or model. If Spain decides to try to reach higher levels of industrialization, and at the same time develops a more improved agriculture and a more dynamic service sector, including tourism, it will be essential that it implants technical education more solidly and extensively. If Spain intends to reach a higher goal and decides to become an advanced society in the fields of information, communication, and high technology, all the universities will have to emphasize basic research and advanced technology."[6]

2. Spain has no nonuniversity sector in postsecondary education. All institutions of postsecondary education have become, in Spain, "university" ones. This has meant that young people consider the university as the only means to acheive cultural, social, and economic advancement. The creation of a prestigious nonuniversity sector such as exists in other developed countries will help, to a great extent, to clarify the present situation and to make feasible the attempts for a qualitative reform of higher education institutions as a whole.

3. Obviously, it is not only necessary that there exist different options for nonuniversity higher education, but that the students are motivated by them and that society as a whole learns how to value them properly. The traditional lack of systems of vocational guidance in Spanish secondary education is one of the main problems that has repercussions in higher education. The reform of the educational system, now in an advanced stage, is considering this important deficiency, but it will not be easy to remedy it unless important human and material resources are summoned to the fight. At the same time, it will be necessary to define more properly the selection procedures to ensure that those who enter higher education institutions have the proper training, and that the quality of teaching is guaranteed.

4. It is also of great importance to find the right balance as regards the autonomy of the universities within the new territorial structure in Spain. For the moment, despite advances,

there still prevails a mentality of state centralism, which causes the majority of university decisions to be strongly controlled or pressed by the state organs. This old tradition of a "Napoleonic" character also has its influence on the behavior of the new regions or Autonomous Communities, which often tend to reproduce, within their borders, a smaller version of the centralist model. Even within the universities themselves the view that the state is the institution that can solve even the smallest of problems frequently prevails. Universities must develop a real desire to face their problems with a responsible autonomy.

5. Adopting a previous policy (which failed) in the matter of the selection and recruitment of the teacher body, the Law of 1983 has decided to try out new reforms in this area. These reforms, however, are being strongly criticized because they lead to situations of indiscriminate recruitment, of endogamy, and of a lack of prospects for young talents. In the immediate future, younger professionals have very limited possibilities of obtaining an academic post in the university. Though there are many excellent professors, universities have been flooded—since passage of the Law of 1983—by a teacher body that on many occasions leaves a lot to be desired and that can be replaced only slowly and with much difficulty.

6. Some of the problems mentioned combine to impede the effort of homologation that Spanish higher education must realize in order to prepare for the European integration. For example, the pressures that teachers and students are already exerting on revised study plans do not seem to favor the effort of making studies, degrees, and diplomas homogeneous with regard to other countries of the European Community. Other obstacles also hobble this effort of homologation. One of the first and most significant challenges which the integration of Spain in the EEC raises is "that of adding a strong international dimension to its study plans, up to now relatively provincial, as an integral part of the general education of all and sundry students."[7]

Conclusions

Spanish higher education is passing through one of the most delicate moments of its already long history. Among the numerous phenomena that testify to this special situation, the following ones must be included: the considerable number of students registered in the institutions, the new political and administrative structure of the country, the search for current models of governing and operational autonomy, the effects of the reform of 1983 on the selection of the teacher body and on the government of the university, the need to be properly integrated in the whole of European higher education, and the need to answer the challenges of the economic, social, and cultural order raised in a country during a period of rapid evolution.

Notes

1. La Fuente recognizes it so. V. La Fuente, *Historia de las Universidades, Colegios y demás establecimientos de enseñanza en España*, 4 vols. (Madrid: Fuentenebro, 1884–89). For historical matters, see especially A. Jiménez Frau, *Historia de la Universidad española* (Madrid: Alianza, 1971).

2. The main reforming efforts are collected in A. Alvarez de Morales, *La Ilustración y la reforma de la Universidad en la España del siglo XVIII*, 3rd ed. (Madrid: Pegaso, 1985).

3. More details of the Franco period can be found in J. L. García Garrido, "Universidades durante el franquismo," *Historia de la Educación en España y América* (Madrid: Fundación Santamaría, 1990), as well as in R. Montoro Romero, *La Universidad en la Espana de Franco* (1939–1970) (Madrid: CIS, 1981).

4. See J. Martín Moreno and A. de Miguel, *Universidad, fábrica de parados* (Barcelona: Vicens Vives, 1979).

5. Consejo de Universidades, *Anuario de estadística universitaria* 1988 (Madrid: Ministerio de Educación y Ciencia, 1989).

6. ICED (International Council for Educational Development), "La reforma universitaria española: Evaluación e informe," in *La educación postsecundaria* (Madrid: Santillana, 1988), 161.

7. Ibid., 48.

Sweden

Jan-Erik Lane

✦

Swedish higher education is basically a public system. Only one major private institution remains after vast structural changes in the 1960s and the 1970s. The higher education system includes a huge state sector and a small local government sector. Table 1 indicates the elements of the system.

The present structure is the outcome of two processes, organizational growth in the 1960s and political reforms in the 1970s. Before the decade of organizational expansion the Swedish system was quite heterogenous, including a large number of different institutions, as Table 2 demonstrates.

Coping with the sudden and drastic increase in student enrollment in the late 1950s and early 1960s involved both the enlargement of already existing institutions and the foundation of new institutions. Comparison of the number of Swedish colleges and universities today, as shown in Table 1, with the pregrowth number, as shown in Table 3, illustrates how the higher education system grew.

Organizational expansion was managed by means of a comprehensive higher education reform policy that involved most aspects of the higher education institutions.[1] The well-known U68 Commission initiated the attempt at a major institutional reform in 1973; its recommendations led to the 1975–77 reform decisions. They were implemented in a carefully designed process that was monitored in terms of a series of evaluation studies. Policy performance was mixed: some objectives achieved success whereas others failed, because of the occurrence of unintended outcomes.[2] Higher education policy during the 1980s has been different from that of the 1960s and 1970s because it aims at acheiving institutional consolidation after the period of radical reform.

History

Typical of the system of higher education prior to the 1975–77 reform was a combination of external political control

---

Table 1

Structure of the Reformed System of Higher Education in 1980

	State Principal	Private Principal	Local Government Principal	
			Counties	Municipalities
Units with research resources	11	1	—	—
Units without research resources	23	—	42	31

Source: National Board of Universities and Colleges.

and internal academic governance based on a collegial model. Swedish universities and professional schools with permanent research facilities were run by the tenured faculty. This faculty elected its own governing board; this board, in turn, elected its chairman, the rector, who served as chief administrator of the institution. Academics elected their own decision-making boards in accordance with professional criteria.[3] Colleges without permanent research resources had less autonomy; they were administered by a rector or a board appointed by the government.

Internal academic governance was offset by a low level of institutional autonomy. The government and its central agencies made decisions in a large number of crucial domains, including the appointment of tenured staff on the basis of proposals from the university, the orientation of the curriculum, the construction of physical facilities, and student enrollment. Swedish universities and colleges have never had a *legally* autonomous status in the manner of English or German universities. The members of the Swedish academic profession have long been regarded as state employees rather than as an independent professional group.

Two important policies introduced in the major institutional reform of 1977 involved extensive decentralization and the introduction of external participation in the decision-making bodies. The 1975–77 higher education reforms returned many major policy decisions to the local level including certain decisions about the curriculum, establishing graduate programs, creating nonpermanent professorships, and determining the structure of departments and basic units. An investigation in 1979 called for a "decentralized higher education system," resulting in changes in the composition of central and regional bodies. Decentralization was enhanced by the 1983 reform which gave the universities and colleges more autonomy to determine the structure of their internal decision-making structures. Decentralization has stimulated more variation throughout the system, from top to bottom. Everything from the general character of whole institutions to the organization of basic departments was affected by decentralization.

Table 2

Structure of the System of Higher Education Before the 1977 Reform

	Public Principal		Private Principal
	State Principal	Local Gov. Principals	
Universities	6	—	—
Professional schools with research	10	—	1
Professional schools without research	80	41	7

Source: National Board of Universities and Colleges.

Table 3

Structure of the Pre-Growth System of Higher Education

	Public Principal		Private Principal
	State Principal	Regional and Local Governments Principals	
Universities	2	—	2
Professional schools with research	9	—	5
Professional schools without research	12	19	2

Source: National Board of Universities and Colleges.

The policy to decentralize higher education has been continued in the reforms of 1987 and 1988, in particular with regard to financial decisions. The appropriations system used to be highly centralized, consisting of narrow line item expenditures, but it is now of a program budgeting type comprising broad program functions with much local discretion with regard to the use of the resources.

Increased external participation within universities and colleges has been the counterweight to their increased autonomy. The 1977 reform abolished academic self-governance restricted to the tenured professors; often the reform participants on various boards within these institutions were to be recruited from among all kinds of staff. Moreover, the government now assumed the power to appoint the rector on the basis of proposals submitted from the local governing board; no longer would the rector be recruited strictly from within the institution's own tenured faculty. The 1983 reform strengthened this development still further by mandating that roughly one-third of the members of the local governing board of eighteen people would be nonacademics, representative of external interests, appointed by the central government.

There is also external participation on the line committees at the intermediate level. The 1983 reform called for external participation at this level and indicated that one-fourth of committee members should be recruited from "occupational life." A university or a college that sets up a comprehensive board for both education and research at the intermediate level must include at least one external participant for every three institutional members. Typically only line committees have external participants; faculty committees that deal with research and graduate instruction include only internal participants. The 1987 reform also changed the overall composition of the institutional board so that external participants now number six of the eleven board members; people from outside academia now constitute the majority on the highest policy-making body at each university and college.

Recent higher education policy has reflected deep concern about the complex nature of internal higher education planning. The government stated in the 1983 reform that organizational complexity had to be reduced and the relative scale of the administrative element decreased, and that enhanced local discretion would be conducive to greater flexibility and adaptability in the higher education system. Thus, a strictly regulated system was to be transformed into one with fewer rules and a greater degree of latitude in local decision making, a principle that has been applied to both the structure of the decision-making system within the universities and colleges and to the new structure of the academic profession itself.

An important part of the antibureaucratization policy conducted since 1979 was the decision in 1986 to abolish the entire system of regional coordinating bodies, six in all. The decision in 1975 to introduce a totally new regional level of higher education planning was severely criticized from the beginning and the results of this system never matched the hopes of its creators.

Structure

Although the Swedish higher system, after the extensive political reforms of the 1970s, is an almost exclusively public system, there is complexity and variation. Table 4 presents data that indicate the diversity of the Swedish postsecondary education system.

The state sector of the higher education system consists of thirty-six universi-

---

Table 4

Basic Data About the Swedish Higher Education System (1988)

Number of Universities	7	
Number of Colleges	19	
Number of Art Schools	8	
Number of Local Government Higher Education Units	54	
Number of Employees at Universities and Colleges	33,000	Full-time equivalents
Number of New Entrants into Universities and Colleges	64,000	
Number of New Entrants into Local Government Higher Education	12,000	
Number of Students Enrolled in Basic Training at Universities and Colleges	147,000	
Number of Students Enrolled in Local Government Higher Education	17,000	
Number of Students Enrolled in Graduate Training	13,300	
Number of Basic Examinations at Universities and Colleges	23,300	
Number of Basic Examinations at Local Government Higher Education	7,800	

Source: National Board of Universities and Colleges Report 1986: 15: 19, Statistics Sweden.

Table 5

The State Higher Education Sector (1987)

Unit	Number of Undergraduates	Number of Employees	Number of Faculties	Number of Educational Sectors
Stockhom U	20,385	3,545	4	5
Royal Techno In.	6,880	2,895	1	1
Caroline Medical In.	2,370	3,165	1	2
Stockhom Teacher In.	3,750	635	1	1
Uppsala U	14,370	4,825	8	5
Linköping U	10,140	2,220	3	5
Lund U	22,740	7,135	8	5
Gothenburg U	18,000	4,910	6	5
Chalmers'	6,255	2,335	1	1
Umeå U	7,790	3,155	5	5
Agricultural U	2,530	3,600	1	1
Luleå College	3,625	895	1	3
Eskilstuna/Västerås	1,680	140	—	3
Falun/Borlänge	1,320	145	—	3
Gävle/Sandviken	1,690	215	—	2
Örebro	4,450	450	—	4
Jönköping	1,740	140	—	3
Halmstad	705	70	—	1
Kalmar	1,380	310	—	—
Kristiansstad	1,450	125	—	3
Växjö	3,825	337	—	4
Borås	1,545	160	—	3
Karlstad	3,380	355	—	4
Skövde	820	60	—	1
Sundsvall/Härnösand	1,710	250	—	3
Östersund	1,180	105	—	1
Schools of Artistic Training (8 Units)	1,695	810	—	—
Other	—	575	—	—
Total	147,405	43,562	—	—

Source: Statistics Sweden 1988: 8; 13.

ties and colleges. The bulk of the student body is enrolled within the state sector, but a considerable portion of the new entrants go to the local government sector where shorter, vocationally oriented courses are offered. The number of students has not increased much since 1970, but the total number of employees has expanded considerably.

The thirty-six universities and colleges differ quite substantially in a number of aspects: size, orientation, and research facilities. Table 5 indicates the overall structure of the state system. The formal organization is based upon a distinction between research and graduate instruction on the one hand and undergraduate training on the other. Faculty boards are responsible for the planning of graduate

Table 6

Occupational Structure of the Higher Education System 1969–84: Various Occupational Groups in Percentages of the Total Number of Employees

	Number of Students	Teachers	Researchers	Academic Assistants	Engineers
1969	131,359	18.1	11.6	18.7	3.7
1977	127,784	17.8	10.1	18.6	4.8
1978	141,593	21.3	8.8	15.4	4.7
1980	138,023	20.6	9.2	16.8	5.6
1981	143,396	22.4	9.3	15.1	5.8
1984	150,886	23.8	10.7	13.8	5.9

Note: The total number of employees includes full-time and part-time staff divided by two.

Source: Statsjänstemannastatistiken.

training and research. Educational boards handle the undergraduate training. Each board is recruited on the basis of representative criteria that provide various groups with a legitimate voice: teachers and researchers, students, the trade unions, external interests. The division into faculties follows the traditional international model. Basic education is divided into five major educational sectors: technical training; administrative, economic, and social training; health care training; educational training; and cultural and informational training.

The state sector includes eleven institutions that have both research and educational programs: seven universities, three technological institutes, and the Caroline Medical Institute. In principle, the colleges provide only for undergraduate training programs, with the exception of the Stockholm Teacher Training School at which there are permanent professorships. However, while the colleges lack the permanent resources to conduct research and maintain a graduate training program, they do search eagerly for ways to get hold of the resources for research and advanced training. Colleges have created non-permanent professorships as a way to break down the boundaries that

separate them from the universities. The small schools for artistic training in Stockholm also have some professors on their faculties. But these schools are very small; the number of students enrolled ranges from thirty-five at the Opera School to 505 at the School for Music.

Academic Work

Undergraduate training is conducted in terms of educational "lines" and single courses. A line of training is a set of courses oriented toward vocational preparation; a line may last from one to five and a half years. There are three types of educational lines: general lines (120), local lines (45), and additional lines (25). The system of single courses applies to a liberal arts type of education. These courses vary considerably in length, from one week to one semester. Screened admissions, based on general competency as well as special competency for some lines and courses, is used for entrance to all types of higher education training. A general competence may be acquired by means of a gymnasium leaving certificate or work experience; the latter is determined by means of the 25/4 rule—the applicant has to be twenty-five years old

Table 6 (continued)

Occupational Structure of the Higher Education System 1969–84: Various Occupational Groups in Percentages of the Total Number of Employees

Adminis-trators	Secretaries	Technicians	Librarians	Other Personnel	Total
2.6	8.3	15.2	2.5	19.2	18.5
5.1	11.5	13.8	2.3	16.1	26.4
4.6	10.2	11.8	2.3	20.9	30.9
8.3	8.8	11.5	2.6	16.7	30.9
8.7	8.9	11.9	2.7	15.1	32.3
9.9	8.1	11.3	2.6	15.0	34.1

and have been occupationally active for at least four years.

Although the central authority, the National Swedish Bureau of Universities and Colleges (NBUC), is responsible for the identification of educational lines and single courses, the universities and colleges may introduce courses on their own. The relevance of single courses has increased at the same time as the gulf between educational lines and single courses has narrowed. In 1982 it was decided to change the admission system to the advantage of young students by narrowing down one-third of the beginners to students under age twenty-five. About 40 percent of the new entrants go to single courses, which means that the reform attempt in 1977 to push most of the students into vocationally oriented lines of education partly failed.

Among the beginners, the relative proportion of older students (i.e., students older than twenty-five) is larger than the proportion of young students, although it is going down. This situation applies in particular to the single courses. Females outnumber males in a ratio of 60 percent versus 40 percent. Study preferences for the two sexes are very different: men dominate the technically oriented lines and courses whereas women are more numerous in nursing and teacher education. Women take more basic degrees than men. The number of degrees within the health care sector and the teacher education sector is far higher than that of any other sector, and in these two sectors women dominate.

Graduate training attracts roughly 2,500 entrants each year. The total number of graduate students is about 12,500, most of whom are males (roughly 70 percent). A graduate program formally lasts four years, but few students are able to reach the examination level within that time interval. In order to increase the number of higher-level graduates, a two-year graduate degree was reintroduced in 1981; this degree was based on an earlier form of degree that had been abolished in 1969 after a new kind of Ph.D. degree had been introduced. About 850 students receive the Ph.D. each year; about 18 percent of the recipients are women.[4]

Staff

The number of people employed in higher education has increased at a more rapid rate than the student increase. Table 6 presents data about the overall devel-

Table 7

Full-Time Equivalents

Year	Teachers	Researchers	Academic Assistants	Adminis- trators	Secretaries	Engineers
1975	4,732 17.8%	2,645 10.0%	4,140 15.6%	1,551 5.9%	3,246 12.2%	1,056 4.0%
1984	6,114 18.4%	3,631 10.9%	4,357 13.1%	3,193 9.6%	3,229 9.7%	2,061 6.2%
1985	5,937 19.1%	3,808 12.2%	4,232 13.6%	3,270 10.5%	3,163 10.2%	2,067 6.6%

Source: National Board of Universities and Colleges.

opment of higher educational employment.

From about 1970, when the higher education system moved toward a steady state, the number of staff has grown at a more rapid rate than the number of students. Whereas the student body grew from 131,300 in 1970 to 151,000 in 1985 the total number of people employed in the system increased from 18,550 to 34,186. In terms of full-time equivalents the growth between 1975 and 1985 was not as striking. Table 7 has the information about the full-time equivalents.

There has been substantial growth in the number of administrators at both the local and central level. Thus, the central coordinating body expanded from 197 to 419 employees between 1968 and 1980. The growth in administrative personnel within the universities and colleges was strong enough to set off a debate about the bureaucratization of the entire system. When the number of supervisors expanded by almost 100 percent it was feared that the basic functions of academia, research and instruction, would be swamped by various administrative systems for planning and evaluating performance and decisions.[5]

The male dominance among teachers and researchers is overwhelming:

ninety-five percent of the full professors are male; 85 percent of the associate professors are male; 84 percent of the university lecturers are male; 79 percent of the assistant professors are male; 72 percent of the university teachers are male; and 54 percent of other teachers are male. This pattern stands in strong contrast to employment in positions other than teaching and research, where women dominate.

Autonomy

The Swedish education system is a public administration system in which centrally placed public bodies exercise some authority over the local units. In higher education, the local institutions are primarily state universities and colleges. Above the local level there is a national agency, the National Swedish Board of Universities and Colleges, and a Unit for Higher Education in the Department of Education. The basic thrust of the present policy is to decentralize the education system, meaning that decision-making power is transferred from the national level to the local level.

Since 1986 there have been four types of faculty positions: full professor, associate professor, lecturer, and assistant

Table 7 (continued)

Full-Time Equivalents

Tech-nicians	Librarians	Cleaners	Porters	Other	Total
3,626 13.7%	589 2.2%	1,290 4.9%	425 1.6%	3,216 12.1%	26,516 100%
4,015 12.1%	932 2.8%	1,524 4.6%	505 1.5%	3,714 11.2%	33,275 100%
4,016 12.9%	945 3.0%	1,463 4.7%	481 1.5%	1,747 5.6%	31,129 100%

professor. Full and assistant professor-ships are research posts; the remaining two positions are oriented toward teach-ing. A full professorship and an associate professorship are tenured posts; lecture-ships and assistant professorships are untenured. The government appoints the full professors on the basis of proposals submitted from the institutions; the uni-versity or college board of the higher education unit makes other appointments. Reform has meant that universities and colleges themselves fill all levels of posts except full professorships. Various deci-sion-making bodies within the local units also have more discretion to plan man-power resources; for example, the institu-tion itself can decide to give an associate professor a grant to carry on full-time research for an extended period. Planning the manpower resources of the individual department is a task of the departmental head.

The government decides on the over-all size of the higher education system by controlling the number of entrants. It also decides on the structure of general lines and the broad outline of the system of single courses. However, the ongoing de-centralization of both the financial sys-tem and educational planning has meant that the universities and colleges exer-cise real power in relation to both fi-nances and educational planning.

Although the government still ap-points full professors, defines subject ar-eas, allocates a large share of money, and plans the overall structure of the curricu-lum, considerable steps have been taken to increase local discretion and initiative. A real recognition exists among the cen-tral authorities concerning the value of decentralization, both as an end in itself and as a means to other ends. The ideol-ogy of decentralization derives its sup-port from various sources.

First, it may be regarded as a reaction against the expansion of the public sec-tor in combination with the typical cen-tralized model of Swedish planning and administration. People no longer believe that the center always knows the best solutions to all kinds of problems. Many now argue that local initiative should be encouraged and that local adaptation is desirable. There is more confidence in what the market may accomplish and it is believed that public sector performance would be greatly improved if decision making was devolved structurally. Sec-ond, there is the fiscal aspect. According to one view, the state is using decentrali-zation in order to relieve itself of extensive financial obligations by allowing local institutions more discretion. The central authorities now maintain fewer and less conspicuous mechanisms of control (for example, by means of the central evaluation of the performance of local operations). Third, the growing importance of regional and local identities in general is bound to have an impact on the structure and functions of the higher education system. The regional and local environment previously served the universities and colleges; the ideology of decentralization has reoriented this relationship. Higher education institutions are now considered as crucial resources for regional development. These educational resources are considered an asset of the locality that should be employed to serve regional and local needs.

The relevance of the decentralization model must also be interpreted in the perspective of political power. The expansion of the public sector at the local government level means that municipalities and county councils are powerful enough to successfully demand that decision making be moved to that level from the center. The ideology of decentralization reflects the weakening of the state and the strong expansion of local government organizations. It also reflects a resurrection of a professionalism that is highly critical of central administration in educational and research matters. It is increasingly difficult for central planners and administrators to claim that they know enough about the internal life of the higher education institutions to allow them to regulate in detail what is going on at the local level.

Efficiency and Productivity

Efficiency in higher education refers to *quality* on the one hand and *productivity* on the other hand. The role of the central authorities has been redefined, from planning in advance to evaluation later. The internal functions of the universities and colleges are considered more important than the external tasks of academia. Gone is the ambition to govern education and research in terms of comprehensive social goals.[6] The prevailing theory is that the universities and colleges themselves have to identify their own means for the accomplishment of their own basic tasks, education and research.

The combination of organizational decentralization and a quality orientation means a larger scope for planning and decision making at the university or college in order to enhance its attractiveness and status. Locally, there is much

---

Table 8

Proportion of Students with an Examination

	After 3 years		After 5 years		After 7 years	
	Men	Women	Men	Women	Men	Women
Technical Sector	5	7	30	37	42	46
Administrative & Economic Sector	10	9	42	57	53	65
Health Care Sector	43	45	71	88	—	—
Educational Sector	85	78	93	90	—	—
Culture & Information Sector	12	10	27	30	38	35

Source: National Board of Universities and Colleges Report 1987: 12.

activity going on to develop educational lines and research projects that are adapted to regional needs. Nonpermanent professorships, funded by external sources other than the state budget, are proliferating. The ivory tower characteristics of Swedish academia are fading away as the universities and colleges enter into joint efforts both among themselves and with industry and local governments. There now exist several development centers to encourage cooperation between academia and society in a broad sense.

Student achievement is not altogether easy to measure. There has been a long and sustained debate in Swedish educational planning about how to interpret data about student performance. It is now considered vital to make a distinction between capacity utilization and the passing of tests. Whereas the first measure relates to how educational opportunities are used by the students, the second measure indicates how they score on tests within a certain time limit. The basic lesson is that capacity utilization as measured by the actual number of students in relation to the planned number of seats, as well as test scoring as measured by the proportion of students who take a certain number of points within one year, vary depending on the educational line.

In some educational lines, including those for musicians, librarians, doctors, and civil engineers, all seats are utilized and more than 90 percent of the students pass their tests on time. In other educational lines, such as public administration, law, and social studies, less than 70 percent of the seats are utilized and only about two-thirds of the students pass their final tests on time. In liberal arts, journalism, and systems science the situation is worse; here capacity utilization is a high 90 percent, but only 50 percent of the enrolled students complete their studies and pass their final tests on time.

The standard measure of student performance, however, is the frequency of examinations. The data on examinations show that student performance is a problem, at least with regard to certain educational sectors. If one looks at the proportion of students having passed an examination on an educational line intended to take 3–3.5 years after certain time intervals, then the following picture emerges (see Table 8).

These figures have not changed much over the years, but what they actually mean has been much debated. To some they indicate poor student performance, particularly within technology, social science, and the arts. Others interpret the data differently, arguing that there are valid causes for study interruptions: change to another training, leaving higher education, starting graduate training without passing an examination. And these changes may not indicate poor performance. In any case, there is now much more sensitivity about student performance than in the 1970s.

Measurement of productivity in the higher education sector proceeds from a model that relates output measures to the costs for the input of resources. The difficulty is to identify quality improvements on the output side. The focus in the Swedish debate has been on yearly productivity comparisons over longer time intervals. Table 9 indicates productivity changes in higher education from 1960 to 1980.

Negative productivity seems to characterize the present Swedish higher education system, with costs outpacing the number of students taught or the number of degrees passed. In a sense it costs more each year to produce the "same" output in the system of higher education. So far productivity measurements have not entered policy making as planning stops in front of simple per capita measures of the cost of various kinds of education. Attempts have been made to cut back on excessive seats in some educational lines and move the resources saved to meet real student demands in other lines. Moreover, per capita costs are compared between various institutions in order to hold costs back. Basically, however, the budgetary system for higher education is not as advanced as it should be: it begins with negotiations within the institutions and thereafter moves to negotiations with the central authorities, when it should move in the opposite direction.

Resources

The state universities and colleges receive three basic types of resources: a state grant for education, a state grant for research, and variable monies for research projects from the national research councils among other bodies, public or private. Whereas the first two items are allocated in the yearly budgetary process, the size of the last item depends on how proposals for research projects are handled by various research councils or how much commissioned research there will be from public authorities or private companies. A variety of national research councils or agencies for commissioned research provide the universities and colleges with "soft" money that is crucial as a complement to the faculty appropriations in the national government budget. Local government education is paid for by the municipalities and county councils.

The overall development of the resources of Swedish higher education cannot be described as one of fiscal stress. In real money terms there has not been retrenchment because all the political parties generally consider higher education a promising area where money invested will pay off in the near or distant future. At the institutions with permanent resources for research, "soft" money usually makes up about 30 percent of the total budget; institutions that lack research resources have to manage with a smaller share of roughly 10 percent. It should be pointed out that the distinction between these two types of units is not clear-cut. Although the colleges without permanent research resources do try to attract "soft" money it is on a far smaller scale than that of the universities.

In 1986/87 the higher education sector spent almost 10 billion Swedish crowns ($1.4 billion), of which more than one-third went to undergraduate instruction, and one-third to permanent research. The grant for undergraduate education has shrunk in real money terms, but the grant for permanent research has increased considerably. This shift indicates the faith government places in possible benefits from advanced research. New professorships

Table 9

Productivity Changes in Higher Education 1965–80

	65–70	70–75	75–80	65–80
Overall productivity development	-10.8	-3.8	+0.7	-4.5
Adjusted productivity measure (part-time students)	-13.0	-2.11	-4.5	-4.5
Productivity with regard to undergraduate examinations	-3.8	-4.7	+2.3	-2.1
Productivity with regard to graduate examinations	-5.4	-5.9	-11.3	-7.8

Source: Stenkula, 1986.

are being added each year as well as many new junior research positions. And the amount of "soft" money granted for commissioned research has not gone down. The strong commitment to joint ventures between academia and various external interests continues to grow.

The single most expensive item on the higher education budget is salaries. Since salary increases have tended persistently to be high during the 1980s, it is all the more obvious that the higher education sector has not suffered from any fiscal retrenchment. The budget of each institution has kept up with inflationary pressure.

Conclusions

At present the emphasis is on local adaptation to the needs of the environment of the university or the college. Planning functions have been moved from the national level to the local level. Decentralization in combination with a quality concern has meant that the initiative now rests with the local institutions. Higher education engages in innovative activities in both the supply of training and the structuring of research. A number of new local educational lines have been introduced, meaning that the centrally governed system of general educational needs and lines has been complemented by locally defined educational needs. Several centers for various kinds of research have been created by local intiative. Each university and college may introduce temporary professorships supported by their own budget, in particular six-year professorships in order to attract external people with some special competence to academia. In order to enhance the interaction between the community at large and academic research and training, special research villages have been built up: Ideon (Lund), Stuns (Uppsala), Teknikhöjden (Stockholm), Uminova (Umeå), Centek (Luleå)

and Teknikbyn (Linköping). At the regional level the universities and colleges have joined various research and development councils in order to promote the development of regional areas.

The creation of new nonpermanent professorships has rested with the institution itself since 1982; this innovation has become very important in emerging local planning. One may speak of a new entrepreneurship at the local level where various interests have joined forces in order to develop the vicinity on the basis of higher education activities. A large number of new professorships, extrapermanent ones as well as time-limited adjunct professorships, have been created—mainly in engineering, the natural sciences, and medicine.[7] The developments at the local level have been rapid since central coordination gave way to decentralized planning. The number of new professorships created by the institutions themselves, for example, far outnumber the number of professorships introduced by the central authorities. Both the policies conducted in the 1980s and the locally initiated developments have moved the Swedish system of higher education away from the integration model that dominated the U68 attempts at a major institutional reform and toward a diversified model as it is conceived of in the United States system of higher education.[8] Most probably, the future path will include further diversification and decentralization.

Notes

1. B. Lindensjö, *Högskolereformen* (Stockholm: Stockholm University Press, 1981).
2. J. E. Lane, *Institutional Reform* (Aldershot, England: Dartmouth, 1989).
3. R. Premfors and B. Östergren, *Systems of Higher Education: Sweden* (New York: International Council for Educational Development, 1978).
4. UHA materials.
5. UHA materials.
6. G. Ström, *Erövra universiteten åter* (Stockholm: Liber, 1985).

7. B. Wittrock and S. Lindström, *De stora programmens tid* (Stockholm: Akademilitteratur, 1984); R. Premfors, *Svensk forskningspolitik* (Lund: Studentlitteratur, 1986).

8. G. Richardsson, "Den frigjorda högskolan—ett oberäkneligt inslag i den statliga forskningspolitiken." *Forskning om utbildning*, no. 16 (1989).

United Kingdom

Graeme C. Moodie

◆

When people in the United Kingdom talk of higher education they primarily have in mind what goes on in a relatively small number of institutions: the universities (ancient and modern), the recently established polytechnics, and the most recent colleges of higher education. It is convenient, as well as customary and only slightly misleading, to refer to the universities as the "private" or "autonomous" sector and the two latter categories together as the "public" one. Higher education is thus only a part (and the smaller part) of tertiary or postsecondary education and is usually sharply distinguished from "further" education, the general term given to organized provision for most of those who continue their education beyond the school-leaving age of sixteen. Even to begin to understand British higher education, some figures must be attached to these labels; more will then be said about their meanings.

Organization

No one who knows Britain should be surprised that it is not a straightforward matter to decide how many universities there are. In 1989 there are, it is true, forty-six legally independent degree-granting institutions that bear the name "university," but of these only forty-two are on the list of recipients of money from the University Grants Committee (UGC) and its successor the University Funding Committee (UFC). The four exceptions are: the two Northern Ireland universities, financed directly by the central government (on the advice of a subcommittee of the UFC); the Open University, funded directly by the Department of Education and Science (DES) and con-

cerned only with distance learning; and Britain's newest university, Buckingham, which receives no government money as a uniquely private institution. The index of universities in that authoritative reference work the *Commonwealth Universities Yearbook*[1] contains two other degree-giving institutions, Cranfield Institute of Technology and the Royal College of Art, which receive grants directly from the DES. Realistically, the number needs to be further expanded to include the larger components of the federal Universities of London and Wales which, though not formally awarding their own degrees, are for most intents and purposes autonomous institutions that are more like universities than (say) Oxford or Cambridge colleges. If these are separately counted, then the university sector contains about sixty members (which is, not entirely coincidentally, virtually the same number as there are members of the Committee of Vice-Chancellors and Principals—the committee of the executive leaders that correspond roughly to American university and college presidents or continental European rectors). In that sector, according to the latest official published figures, some 273,000 full-time and nearly 45,000 part-time UK students were enrolled in 1986/87[2]; these figures do not include Buckingham nor overseas students.

A comparable number of full-time students, some 282,000, were enrolled in the thirty polytechnics, fifteen Scottish central institutions, and over four hundred colleges at which at least some degree-level courses are offered, but none of which may confer its own degrees. In addition, there were over 234,000 part-time students (not including the 80,000 who were enrolled with the Open

University). Altogether, counting both sectors, a little over 14 percent of the relevant age-group (eighteen- to nineteen-year-olds) enter full-time education. The total enrollment in further education, however (i.e., in non-degree-level education) further to secondary education in a virtually limitless range of subjects available to any age of student beyond school-leaving, was just under 4,000,000 in 1986/87. The courses are provided in hundreds of colleges and thousands of adult education centers throughout the country. Almost all of their students are part time. A small proportion, however, will be engaged in work for subdegree but "advanced" qualifications (i.e., more advanced than the school-leaving examinations, GCE and GCSE, which are used to define the minimum entry into higher education). As already suggested, however, higher education is normally taken to exclude most of these students and institutions. Certainly, within the public sector, the great bulk of full-time work for degrees takes place within the polytechnics and the fifty-nine larger colleges which, under the Education Reform Act of 1988, have been given the legal status of self-governing higher education corporations (the other colleges continuing, like most of further education, to be under the control of local government authorities). It should be added, in the interests of complete accuracy, that this ostensive definition of higher education is not entirely watertight. Some students at polytechnics and the higher education colleges are engaged in subdegree work and some few who pursue a higher education can be found in further education institutions. But in what follows I will largely ignore these minorities as well as the Open University and Buckingham.

The division between the private and the public sectors, the so-called binary system, is rooted in history and politics as much as in educational or even organizational principles. The university sector is the older. In England and Wales Oxford and Cambridge trace their origins back to the twelfth century, and in Scotland the four ancient universities date from the fifteenth and sixteenth centuries. But no additional universities were established until Durham and London in the 1930s, and of the rest only a handful are much over a hundred years old and some no more than a quarter of that. The sector as a whole is thus quite modern. The earliest were founded (Edinburgh apart) on royal or ecclesiastical initiatives. The nineteenth- and twentieth-century institutions evolved, typically, from local colleges founded and financed by a mixture of private and local government enterprise to satisfy a variety of local needs and ambitions.[3] The most recent, dating only from the 1960s, owe their origin primarily to national policy (and finance), though local initiative and support were among the criteria by which the location (not the existence) of these new universities was determined. Also in the 1960s, however, the ten former Colleges of Advanced Technology (CATS) and two Scottish central institutions achieved university status; these all had their roots in the world of technical and further education.

Governance

Whatever their origins, all universities are legally independent corporations whose status is conferred by royal charter or statute law; self-governing; empowered to confer their own degrees (both first and higher); and responsible in fact for most basic civil and much other research. Although private in these respects, they are heavily dependent on central government funds for recurrent and capital expenditure, for particular research projects and programs (through the government-financed research councils), and indirectly through government grants to students (for fees and maintenance, the amount varying between individuals according to parental income). The proportion of recurrent expenditure covered by government grants (about which more will be said below) was about 30 percent between the two World Wars, rose to 50 percent in 1946, and by 1980 was between 75 percent and 90 percent for most universities. From less than £10 million annually before World War II government grants rose to a total of £25 million in 1956/57 and by 1980/81 it had reached £1000 million. (During the same period student numbers rose from 50,000 in 1939, an increase of 30,000 since 1920, to about 90,000 in 1956/57, and to over 200,000 [including overseas students] by 1981. Academic staff numbers rose more than proportionately from 5,000 in 1939 to about 44,000 in 1981.) Despite this financial dependence on central government, however, in 1980 it was still reasonable to include "academic rule" among the distinguishing features of the university sector.

By their formal constitutions British universities (other than Oxford and Cambridge whose internal government follows a slightly different pattern) are run by relatively small bodies (the Council in England and Wales, the Court in Scotland) on which the majority of members are laymen (usually local notables from business, elected local authorities, and others in various forms of public service). Nevertheless, largely by convention, decisions on all academic matters (including resource allocation) are normally taken by academic bodies or on their advice, the main bodies being, typically, the Senate (representing all academic staff) and its committees, the Faculties (of Arts, Science, Medicine, etc.), and the Department or similar subject-level basic unit. The focus for day-to-day university-wide decision making is the vice-chancellor (or Scottish principal) who has few formal powers other than those inherent in the role of chairing senates and their main committees, but his place at the center of communications, both internal and with the outside world, his position as effectively the summit of the administrative hierarchy, and sheer functional necessity combine to confer upon an able person a strong leadership position lying somewhere, in terms of real power, between European rectors and American presidents. Most vice-chancellors come from the academic world and, historically, have "ruled" for, rather than over, the academics.

Until well into the 1950s this "civic" model of university government gave pride of place to the professoriate, and especially the professorial head of department, but by now professorial power, like professorial authority, has been considerably diluted by the very large numbers of specialist nonprofessorial staff and, even, since the late 1960s and in some areas of decision making, by students. But it has remained the case that almost all important decisions taken within universities are taken by or on the advice of committees which, however hospitable to student representatives, and however well briefed (even steered) by full-time officials, consist of academics.[4]

The University Grants Committee

The most striking aspect of academic rule, however, lay in the relations between the universities and their state paymaster as mediated by the UGC (1919–89), particularly in its "golden age" when the UGC dealt directly with the Treasury, but even after 1964 when the DES added higher education to its formal responsibility for all other levels of education.[5] The UGC's task was, in essence, threefold: to advise the government about the financial needs of universities, which it did in the light of consultations with the universities; to collect and publish information about the universities; and, once the government had decided upon the total sum to be granted to the universities, to apportion the grant between individual institutions, which it did entirely independently in the light of its knowledge of universities (i.e., government had no part in the decisions about funding to individual universities, but only about the general purposes for which public money would be made available). This is the main sense in which the UGC was a "buffer" between politics and academia.

The UGC system could properly be seen as safeguarding university autonomy in two crucial respects: the bulk of UGC subventions for recurrent expenditure took the form of a "block grant," leaving to each university the responsibility for using it wisely and apportioning it among the approved purposes for which it was given; and (until the mid-1970s) these grants were given for five-year periods (quinquennia), so that universities could plan in relative security over an appropriate time-span—though supplementary grants were often given for special needs. The UGC itself could also be seen as an extension of academic rule (in the form of collective self-government) because the great majority of its members were retired academics, or, after 1943, active senior academics, and its full-time salaried chairman was always a former academic. It also had a civil service staff, seconded from the Treasury or, later, from the DES, but the crucial decisions (like those within universities) were always taken by the preponderantly academic Committee. (Among these crucial decisions, it may be noted, were the establishment of the criteria for recognition as a university and agreement that a particular candidate had or had not crossed the threshold and qualified for grant aid.) At the same time, as adviser to the Treasury and DES, and articulator of the universities' long-term interests, and as the wielder of the main instrument of public policy (which it had helped to shape), the UGC was also the major link between the universities and the state—though the universities always had their own links with society. For long and to many people the UGC seemed the ideal model for the relationship between government and higher education. But in Britain it was not the only model, even if it

was the best-known one, and from the late 1960s governments began to show signs of disenchantment with it and the universities, as we will see.

The Robbins Report and Its Impact

The early sixties, however, were a high point in the recent history of the universities. Thus, it is worth looking at that period before charting the immense changes and challenges that have occurred since. The great symbol of that peak in the universities' fortunes and prestige was the publication in 1963 of the report of the official Committee on Higher Education chaired by Lord Robbins[6] and the immediate government acceptance of its recommendations for considerable expansion of higher education, through the creation of new institutions as well as the expansion of existing ones. That this was the central and most urgent practical issue was undeniable. World War II had demonstrated the practical value for national survival of higher education and university research, and peace brought a possibly inflated belief in their potential contribution to prosperity; the postwar period saw the introduction of universal compulsory free secondary education, with its consequent impact on the numbers qualified for university admission; and more people were showing an interest in obtaining higher education. The Robbins Report took full account of the strains upon both universities and secondary education caused by the increased competition for scarce places and proposed the appropriate remedy, but in other respects it was not particularly radical (or so it seems in retrospect). In most respects it did little more than endorse the existing system, including the UGC, with some exhortations to think about and review certain aspects. But "its vision was a traditional university system vastly expanded,"[7] and its impact was even less radical, as things turned out. Only one new university was created after that time, at Stirling in Scotland, and most of the other major proposals of the committee—except for the increased numbers, the elevation to university status of the CATS, and the creation of the Council for National Academic Awards (CNAA) to award degrees to students in further education institutions—were sooner or later either reversed or ignored. Even in its proposals for expansion it was not entirely innovative: student numbers in 1963 were already more than double the prewar number and the UGC had already approved initiatives to create six new universities in England and seemed sympathetic to Scottish pressures to create a new one there. But the report marshalled the evidence and arguments with immense cogency and authority and it secured general acceptance of its principle that places be found for all applicants who were "qualified by ability and attainment" to enter higher education. Its "real achievement . . . was to make increased public expenditure on higher education politically respectable."[8] But, only two years later, the general identification of the universities with higher education was undermined by new government policy.

In speeches delivered at Woolwich in 1965 and Lancaster in 1967 Anthony Crosland, then secretary of state for education, announced and explained the decision to institute (he would have said "maintain") what came to be known as the binary system.[9] The crux of the new policy was to divert a sizable proportion of the university expansion envisaged by Robbins to new polytechnics to be created from existing teacher training colleges, technical colleges, art schools, and other further education institutions where advanced work was taking place. A vital corollary was that no other institutions from further education should be allowed to follow the former CATS into the university sector as soon as they reached the highest standards. This, Crosland held, would prevent the "residual public sector" from becoming "a permanent poor relation . . . with a permanently and openly inferior status." The binary system was designed also to serve part-time students, to retain local (as well as local authority) involvement in higher education, to provide for more "vocational, professional, and industrially based courses," and to strengthen that area within higher education that came "under more direct social control" than the universities. Two other factors were also important, one explicit and the other not. The explicit factor, to quote from Crosland's Lancaster speech, was "that we did not start off *tabula rasa*; we started off with a given historical situation. A plural system already existed." (In 1961, which was before the CATS were promoted, there had been over 126,000 students taking advanced courses leading to recognized qualifications at publicly assisted further education establishments, of whom over 9,000 were taking a first degree.)[10] The other factor, it is reasonable to believe, was the fact that it was much less expensive to provide places in the public sector, and it still is; but this has never been officially acknowledged as a reason for the binary system. In 1969, in consequence, thirty-one polytechnics were designated by the DES and fifteen "central institutions" in Scotland were identified for similar status.[11]

The Binary System

The polytechnics and other public sector institutions differ from universities in certain important respects, though less so after twenty years than initially. Until 1989 they were all under close financial and administrative control from their parent city or county council and were not fully self-governing even over all academic issues. Internally, too, the academic staff had less leeway individually and less collective influence over decision making than their university colleagues—though there was continuous and effective pressure from central government to move to greater autonomy. None of the institutions award their own qualifications, though they do initiate their own courses and curricula. But the latter must be approved by (in the main) the CNAA or the Business and Technician Education Council that actually confer the degrees and diplomas gained by the students and oversee the assessment procedures. In practice this has led to an elaborate system of regular peer review by colleagues within institutions and from elsewhere (including universities), following procedures and guidelines prescribed by the appropriate national organization. Both in subject matter and approach, the public sector ventures beyond the conventional views about what are "proper" university courses, typically in the more practical and work-oriented directions Crosland envisaged. As matters of fact rather than principle, the public sector has lower levels of amenity (libraries, laboratories, etc.) than the private and its students on average are less well qualified at entry (in terms of formal grades) as well as being more likely to live in the immediate locality. Initially at least the academic staff were also less well qualified, formally, but the differences between entrants to the two sectors have steadily lessened as universities (since the mid-1970s) have had drastically to reduce their levels of recruitment to match lower funding and as the reputation of the public sector has risen. But the most research-minded still are drawn to the universities where both the opportunities and expectations for research are greater.

The gap between the sectors has narrowed, however, particularly in the 1980s. From the start polytechnics have concentrated increasingly on full-time degree-level students (now forming some 70 percent of the total) and have catered to student demand for courses in the humanities and social sciences as well as the "practical" areas. In other ways, too, including the growing use of the title of "professor," they have striven to attain university status. Their internal system of government has given widening roles to academics. The CNAA, in the 1980s, relaxed its monitoring and now, in the case of the majority of polytechnics, restricts its role to accreditation of the institution (and its internal procedures for review and the maintenance of standards) rather than the earlier and more pervasive task of validating individual courses and curricula. The 1988 Act has made the most radical changes, however. The polytechnics and those colleges most extensively engaged in higher education have been removed from local government management, have been made legally autonomous self-governing corporations, and from April 1989 are financed by the central government through the newly created Polytechnics and Colleges Funding Council (PCFC), the powers and composition of which are laid out in the act in terms identical to those used in setting up the new UFC which began to operate at the same time.

From the point of view of the outside observer, however, the differences between the sectors are less striking than the broad characteristics of the system as a whole. In particular the outsider is likely to be impressed by its emphasis on quality (somewhat restrictively defined), its selectivity, its costliness, and its effectiveness—and by the current state of flux and uncertainty. To these we must now turn our attention.

Admission and Study

No one in Britain is entitled to higher education, but anyone may be admitted who has two advanced-level passes in the General Certificate of Education or its equivalent (the examinations are usually taken at the age of seventeen-plus in the last year of secondary education), and a few (usually much older) who have not. In principle, therefore, the student body could be very varied, but in fact there is something close to a standard pattern. This "normal" or "standard" full-time student will have passes at more than the minimum grade in at least three A-level subjects; will be between eighteen and nineteen years old at entry (slightly younger in Scotland); will be enrolled in a "professional" faculty (e.g., medicine or law) or will be taking an honors degree in no more than two subjects; will end up with a degree labeled second-class (in a three-class system) at the end of three, or at most four, years; is now (though not formerly) almost as likely to be female as male (more likely in further education); is still very much more likely to have parents in middle- than working-class occupations; and is increasingly likely to be the child of at least one graduate.[12]

Another dimension to this standard pattern is the existence of definite notions about what is "degree-level work" and, though this is beginning to fray at the edges in the public sector, about what subjects can be studied at that level (the conventional wisdom suggests that physics and philosophy can; nursing, catering, and brass band musicianship are on or near the borderline; brick-laying, undertaking, and hairdressing cannot). Significantly, by its Statute 9 (1) the CNAA is charged with ensuring that its awards "are comparable in standard with awards granted and conferred throughout higher education in the United Kingdom including the universities," and there is a widespread belief, expectation, or aspiration that degrees from different institutions are of the same standard (even if the facilities, teaching, and reputation are thought not to be). Indeed, in the private sector, the universal use of examiners from other institutions in all forms of assessment is in part designed to maintain that uniform standard (as well as to safeguard individual students from discriminatory treatment, to provide a check against staff corruption or incompetence, and to ensure that justice is seen to be done: in the UK no degree grade is left entirely to a student's individual teacher). This "gold standard," as it has been called, is defined, but seldom explicitly, by reference to such academic and scholarly attributes as intellectual difficulty, basicness, generality of application, and use in training the mind (as well as, in some cases, by unavowed reference to social convention and the market): hence science rather than technology and, in some universities, anatomy, physiology, and biochemistry but not clinical medicine. This same gold standard lies behind the informal pecking order that coexists with the assertions of comparability of degrees and thus helps to sustain something like a single academic hierarchy. Even in face of the binary divide there is a widespread belief that all those engaged in higher education are "playing the same academic game," that all the institutions can be ranked on the same scales of quality and prestige, and that they all should be judged by the same standards rather than be seen as different kinds of institution each with its own distinctive form of excellence. Some in the public sector challenge this consensus, but the process of assimilation or "academic drift" already referred to shows how strong the consensus is.

The pursuit of academic quality also underlies the selectivity of the system and helps to define the kind of elite that it represents. The formal requirements of two A-level passes applies to all sectors but, in practice, this minimum will not secure entry to the most sought-after subjects and institutions nor will it suffice to pass in just any two subjects. Since there is no right of entry—in effect there is a *numerus clausus* in all subjects and institutions—competition has forced secondary education to become specialized at a relatively early age (at fourteen, with more intense specialization at sixteen) for potential entrants into higher education and created strong pressures to distinguish potential entrants from the majority of children for whom it is not deemed to be a realistic ambition.

(Until the 1960s this initial selection was effectively made, at least negatively, because children were selected at age eleven-plus for different kinds of secondary school. This system has now largely disappeared, but different schools still reflect their history in their sifting and preparation of children for higher education.) One consequence of this pre-entry winnowing is that relatively few qualified entrants do not enter higher education—any very serious attempt to widen access must therefore either begin in the schools or entail a radical change in entry qualifications (for which there is much else to be said).[13]

The selection process as a whole, if only because of its emphasis upon attainment rather than potential, transmits into higher education the differences in quality of education and achievement that seem built into the secondary system, not only in the existence of an expensive, and in some cases superior, private sector, but also through the fact that the state schools reflect both their differing traditions and the stratified neighborhoods from which their pupils are drawn. These social biases are compounded by the extent to which the admission process has become national, with limited scope for institutional variation. Not only, as already indicated, do the standard minimum entry qualifications apply across both sectors, but each sector now has a central "clearing house" for applications and, particularly in the university sector but also to an increasing extent in the polytechnics, students in every institution come from all parts of the country in which they are located. In seeking to recruit an academic elite, British higher education therefore also recruits disproportionately from the social elite—least so in the case of the Open University and other part-time students, most markedly so in Oxford and Cambridge because of the links they formed with those secondary schools that flourished during the Oxbridge duopoly. To give one index only: in 1977 the age participation rate in higher education for students in the top occupational class (Registrar General's Class I) was 43 percent and of the lowest 3 percent, while, also in the 1970s, 20 percent of the university students came from the top class as compared with 12 percent of full-time students at polytechnics and 8 percent at the Open University.[14] And this despite the existence of government grants which, for the poorest students, cover full maintenance as well as all fees; these grants are automatically available to university students and are usually paid to other full-time students, but at the discretion of local authorities (which have lately come under strong pressure to cut all forms of expenditure). These are signs, however, of a greater willingness by institutions to admit students with "nonstandard" entry qualifications.

Partly because access to higher education is so selective, but partly also because it is an expensive system in which there are very favorable staff-student ratios (the national average in 1986 was about eleven students for each member of staff; it has slightly worsened since) that permit a significant amount of personal attention and small-group teaching, the system is remarkably efficient, at least in terms of first-degree completion rates (less so at the graduate level, for which the British system has been relatively less well organized). Thus, according to a study carried out by the Organization for European Cooperation and Development, some 16 percent of the relevant age group entered British higher education (excluding the Open University) in 1977, as compared with 18 percent in West Germany, 25 percent in the Netherlands, 37 percent in Japan, and 57 percent in the United States; but the figures for those obtaining a degree (including the Open University) was over 14 percent for Britain, placing it in the next highest position to Japan's 20 percent and the United States's 25 percent.[15] The fact that most graduates find suitable employment within six months of graduation and almost all within three years, even during a period of high unemployment, perhaps serves as another index of competence.[16]

Its efficiency has not, however, saved higher education from a period of change and acute uncertainty introduced by the economic crisis of 1973/74 and the subsequent rises in the rate of inflation, and continuing with the election in 1979 of a government dedicated to reducing public expenditure, stimulating efficiency through competitive markets, and strengthening the power of the state in its dealings with other organizations and, especially, trade unions and professional "guilds" (like doctors, lawyers, estate agents, and teachers). Higher education, with annual costs by 1982/83 of around £3000 million and its system of academic rule, was an obvious target for cuts and reform. The 1970s had seen the funding per student reduced by over 7 percent as the real value of grants no longer kept pace with inflation; the 1980s have seen additional cuts even in money income of close to 20 percent (including the effects of the government's decision that overseas students be charged full-cost fees) as, in a radical change of direction, policy for higher education became "cash-led" instead of being influenced primarily by effective student demand. The consequent need to reduce staff numbers, worsen staff-student ratios, close down courses and even whole departments, switch resources between areas of study (at UGC instigation), and reduce the funds available for research have been the most painful and immediately demoralizing features. However, it is the consequent loss of young scholars who could not be given appointments in higher education and of research foregone that may turn out to be the most damaging. But the cut in funding is by no means the only important aspect to the current crisis of confidence both within and about British higher education.

The creation of the binary system was, of course, one early sign of limited confidence in the self-governing universities; an earlier one was the opening of UGC and university accounts to inspection by Parliament's comptroller and auditor-general. The student disorders that began in the late 1960s further lessened public confidence and may well have encouraged governments to reduce the level of funding in the 1970s. From 1980 onwards government ministers have repeatedly stressed the need to ensure "value for money" and to be assured about the "quality" of the education being provided. The first of these is a clear and understandable objective, if difficult to measure, but the second is more complex and less defined. It seems to cover a number of different concerns: that inadequate teachers have excessive leeway (which is probably true), that students, especially at university, are "turned off" industrial and business careers (for which there is only very slight evidence, at most),[17] that too many students study the humanities and social sciences (by their own choice), and that too many courses, again especially at universities, are nonvocational or unpractical or insufficiently related to the "world of work."[18] The changes resulting from these economizing and instrumental attitudes are far-reaching.

Recent Changes

The most recent and conspicuous of these changes are contained in the Education Reform Act of 1988. As we have already seen, it conferred corporate status and independence from local government on the polytechnics and on colleges that satisfy certain criteria (about size and the weight of degree-level work). Of greater significance, however, are the new Funding Councils for the universities (UFC) and for the polytechnics and independent colleges (PCFC). The latter has replaced an elaborate scheme whereby the public sector was financed from a "pool" (contributed by local and central government) which was allocated among the institutions by the DES on the advice of a National Advisory Committee, chaired by a minister and representing a variety of interested parties, which in turn leaned heavily on the detailed proposals prepared by a smaller board. Under the old scheme but not the new, local authorities were free to add to the allocations to their own institutions. The new arrangements thus threaten to reduce the support available to the public sector just when it is undergoing extensive internal upheavals in preparedness for full self-government. The former has replaced the UGC and, in so doing, has killed any hope of returning to quinquennial budgeting and ended the last vestige of the original notion that university grants were designed to make up deficiencies in income in the face of the necessary costs to a university of performing its functions satisfactorily—the change in title from "grants" to "funding" is more than merely terminological. The composition has changed. The members are part time (with one exception, not the chair), are reduced in number to fifteen from over twenty, and need not have an academic majority—though the first appointments by the secretary of state comprise nine academics, five businessmen, and one polytechnic director. They are clearly intended to make fewer decisions themselves and to leave most of the detailed work to a reformed and probably enlarged staff headed by one of the members who is full-time chief officer (the first being the last chairman of the UGC). They are also given more explicit powers to attach conditions to grants and to require universities to return money received if the conditions are not met. The secretary of state, moreover, is empowered to give directions to the councils on virtually anything except the individual allocations to particular institutions. It is unclear how far or how often these powers will be used, but the context of the new legislation and the speeches of government ministers and supporters have given rise to anxious uncertainty.

Before its demise the National Advisory Board and Committee had become increasingly *dirigiste* and the UGC had already, since 1981, become more discriminating in the level of support given to different institutions on the basis of judgments about relative quality—judgments which led, in the worst cases, to cuts in support of some 30 percent in three years. Since 1984 these have been supplemented by somewhat less impressionistic ratings of departments' research performance as a basis for discrimination. In the background for both councils—and possibly in the realm of accomplished fact by the time this is published—is official talk of replacing grants with "contracts" (possibly awarded on a competitive basis), of departing from the former UGC practice of including a routine element of support for unspecified research in universities, or raising student fees (with compensating reductions in direct government funding) so that universities must compete for students to obtain income (instead of being told by the UGC how many students to admit and receiving grants more or less in proportion), and of expecting institutions in both sectors to find more money from private sources, by appeals for donations or in payment for specific services rendered. Simultaneously, all institutions have had to convince their paymasters that they are becoming more managerial and businesslike in their internal decision making; they have also been urged to give larger roles to businessmen in their governing bodies and to give those bodies (Councils or Courts in universities, Governing Councils elsewhere) a greater say in internal government.

Meanwhile, reductions in the general level of funding continue, further staff reductions are still needed, the student grant system is under review, disputes about salaries become more bitter, security of tenure for university academic staff is to be reduced under other sections of the 1988 Act, and the secretary of state urges wider access to higher education (it would seem mainly to assure an adequate supply of graduates despite a major drop in the size of the normal age group during the 1990s) without promising more money or sanctioning (yet) a departure from the "gold standard" of degrees or a radical change in the types of courses offered or the entry qualifications demanded.

Conclusions

For many working in higher education the main problems are thus insecurity and uncertainty. The events of the 1980s and, especially, the 1988 Act are seen as the entering wedges of a system of higher education subject both to closer control by central government and to the unpredictabilities of the open market (for funds and students). But no one can be sure how far these wedges will be driven home, how far the universities will lose their academic autonomy and the polytechnics their local roots and greater openness,[19] and how far considerations of public expenditure limits will continue to dictate educational policy, let alone how higher education can escape from under the present clouds of suspicion. Also unresolved are the longer-term tensions: between maintenance of the "gold standard" and of highly selective entry on the one hand and, on the other, the social and economic arguments for wider access; between the traditional homogeneity of the national system and the hankerings for diversity only inadequately satisfied by the binary system; between pride in the effectiveness of the system in turning entrants into graduates and the impossibility of persuading governments and taxpayers to pay for the further expansion (or even survival) of such a costly provision of higher education. One price for the pursuit of academic quality is now becoming apparent (though not to all the affected interests). Selectivity goes hand in hand with exclusiveness and higher education is therefore not yet a dream, let

alone a concrete aspiration, for the great majority of people in the UK; as a result of its remoteness, higher education seems also unresponsive. The upshot of all these is that at a time of change, even crisis, higher education lacks the support of a large public constituency. British higher education has preferred academic quality and selectivity to wider access and a variety of forms of excellence; at the end of the 1980s it needs to find a way of combining these goals or it may well end with less both of quality and of access. The predicament and the tension seem likely to continue well into the foreseeable future.

Notes

1. *Commonwealth Universities Yearbook* (London: Association of Commonwealth Universities, annually).

2. Central Statistical Office, *Social Trends* (London: Her Majesty's Stationery Office, 1989). This is also the source of the other statistics to be given shortly.

3. An excellent account of the early history of three typical nineteenth-century foundations can be found in David Jones, *The Origins of Civic Universities: Manchester, Leeds, and Liverpool* (London: Routledge, 1988).

4. For fuller accounts of internal government, see Graeme C. Moodie and Rowland Eustace, *Power and Authority in British Universities* (London: Allen and Unwin, 1974); John van de Graaf et al., eds., *Academic Power: Patterns of Authority in Seven National Systems of Higher Education* (New York: Praeger, 1978); and Graeme C. Moodie, "The Disintegrating Chair: Professors in Britain Today," *European Journal of Education* 21, no. 1 (1986): 43–56.

5. See John Carswell, *Government and the Universities in Britain: Programme and Performance 1960–1980* (Cambridge: Cambridge University Press, 1985); Christine Helen Shinn, *Paying the Piper: The Development of the University Grants Committee, 1919–1946* (Lewes, England: Falmer Press, 1986); R. O. Berdahl and M. L. Shattock, "The British University Grants Committee: Changing Relationships with Government and the Universities," *Higher Education* 13 (1984); 471–99; and Graeme C. Moodie, "Buffer, Coupling, and Broker: Reflections on 60 Years of the UGC," *Higher Education* 12 (1983): 331–47.

6. Cmnd. 2154 of 1963 (London: Her Majesty's Stationery Office).

7. Gareth Williams and Tessa Blackstone, *Response to Adversity* (Guildford, England: Society for Research into Higher Education (SRHE), 1983), 15.

8. Williams and Blackstone, *Response to Adversity*, 15.

9. Key extracts from the speeches were reprinted in the *Times Higher Educational Supplement* for 7 March 1975.

10. Ministry of Education, *Statistics of Education*, Part I (London: HMSO, 1962), tables 14 and 29.

11. For a full account, see Paul R. Sharp, *The Creation of the Local Authority Sector of Higher Education* (Lewes, England: Falmer Press, 1987).

12. See Central Statistical Office, *Social Trends*; O. Fulton, ed., *Access to Higher Education* (Guildford, England: SRHE, 1981); E. Rudd, "Students and Social Class," *Studies in Higher Education* 12 (1987), 99–106; and "The Educational Qualifications and Social Class of Parents of Undergraduates Entering British Universities in 1984," *Journal of the Royal Statistical Society*, Series A, vol. 150 (1987), 346–72.

13. See Oliver Fulton, "Elite Survival? Entry 'Standards' and Procedures for Higher Education Admissions," *Studies in Higher Education* 13 (1988); 15–25.

14. See J. Farrant, "Trends in Admissions," in Fulton, *Access to Higher Education*.

15. Cited in L. Cerych, "Appendix," to Williams and Blackstone, *Response to Adversity*, 133–46.

16. Chris J. Boys and John Kirkland, *Degrees of Success: Career Aspirations and Destinations of College, University, and Polytechnic Graduates* (London: Jessica Kingsley, 1988).

17. See Boys and Kirkland, *Degrees of Success*, 43–59.

18. For a nongovernmental version of this last point, see Tyrell Burgess, ed., *Education for Capability* (Windsor, England: NFER/Nelson, 1986); and Patrick Nuttgens, *What Should We Teach and How Should We Teach It? Aims and Purposes of Higher Education* (Aldershot, England: Wildwood House, 1988).

19. See the editorial comment in the *Times Higher Education Supplement* for 31 March 1989.

Yugoslavia

Niksa Nikola Soljan

◆

Historical Background

The Beginnings of Higher Education

The history of higher education in different parts of what is now Yugoslavia has been far from uniform. In some of the nations making up Yugoslavia it is more than three centuries old. For instance, the earliest institution of higher learning in Croatia was established as far back as 1669, when the Croato-Hungarian King Leopold I issued a decree recognizing the Jesuit Academy in the Croatian capital Zagreb as an institution of higher learning.[1] Over the next two hundred years the Croatian people strove to develop a modern university along the lines of the universities in other Central European centers of culture and learning. The transformation of the Jesuit Academy into a full-fledged university came in the second half of the nineteenth century, at the height of the struggle for Croatian national rights and national identity. In 1874 the University of Zagreb was inaugurated as an academic institution with all the characteristics typical of contemporary European universities. Croatia was at that time still part of the Austro-Hungarian Empire, and its legal status in the empire determined the position of Zagreb University until the end of World War I. Following the collapse of the the Austro-Hungarian Empire, Croatia joined the newly formed Kingdom of the Serbs, Croats, and Slovenes on December 1, 1918. (The name of this state was changed to the Kingdom of Yugoslavia in 1929.) That day marked the beginning of a new historical period in the life of the University of Zagreb.

The roots of higher education in Serbia are to be sought in the College in Belgrade, which opened in 1808, but closed in 1813. Between 1838 and 1863 the Kragujevac Lyceum kept the idea of higher education alive in Serbia; it then moved to Belgrade and continued as the Belgrade College until 1905. These two institutions can be regarded as forerunners of the University of Belgrade. The University Education Act of 1905 created the University of Belgrade as a modern academic institution. The entry of the Kingdom of Serbia into the newly formed Kingdom of the Serbs, Croats, and Slovenes in 1918 marked the beginning of a new era for the University of Belgrade as well.[2]

The beginnings of higher education in Slovenia go back to the Jesuit Grammar School of Ljubljana, established in 1597, and the Jesuit College, which continued operation until 1773. However, the modern University of Ljubljana was established only in 1919, several months after the unification of the South Slav nations in the Kingdom of the Serbs, Croats, and Slovenes.[3]

All three universities were built on the traditional model of Central European universities, particularly those in the Austro-Hungarian empire. The leading academic disciplines were law, theology, philosophy, medicine, and natural sciences. Compared with other Central European universities of that time, the universities of Zagreb, Belgrade, and Ljubljana were somewhat less developed. Thus, the best developed among them, Zagreb University, had only twenty-four teachers when it became a modern university in 1874/75, and 108 teachers on the eve of World War I (1914). The number of students had risen during that time from 290 to 1,123.

Higher Education between the World Wars

In this period higher education in Yugoslavia developed under the dominant influence of social, political, cultural, and ethnic contradictions in the country. Social inequalities were quite sharp; confrontations among the leaders of the bourgeois parties were the cause of severe and constant fighting; cultural identity was allowed to legitimize itself only up to a point, with a tendency to project the culture of the dominant nation as the culture of all the Yugoslav nations and ethnic groups; the question of national identity remained unresolved. In this situation access to higher education was more freely open to members of the ruling classes, representatives of the dominant nations, and urban dwellers. Numerous members of the underprivileged classes, including women, found it much more difficult to pursue higher education.

Throughout the interwar period traditional disciplines (law, theology, philosophy, medicine) dominated the universities, while natural and engineering sciences developed more slowly. The institutional network of higher education remained pretty much as it was at the beginning of the period. On the eve of World War II the three universities included a total of eighteen faculties, four arts academies, two four-year colleges, and two two-year postsecondary schools. A certain amount of institutional dispersal took place during this time, with the opening of the Law School in Subotica and the Faculty of Pharmacy in Skopje in 1920 and the Faculty of Forestry in Sarajevo in 1940 (all of them as parts of the University of Belgrade).

Enrollments did not increase dramatically either in the interwar period. In 1938/39, 15,505 students (3,498 of them women) were enrolled in all the eighteen faculties of the three Yugoslav universities and 228 students (86 of them women) in the four arts academies. In addition, the two four-year colleges enrolled 986 students (224 of them women) and the two two-year postsecondary schools enrolled 259 students (148 of them women). The total number of graduates in all three universities that year was 2,594 (526, or 20 percent, of them women).[4]

Higher Education During World War II and in the Early Postwar Years

The war years were a distinctive period in the life of all three of the Yugoslav universities. The University of Belgrade remained for the most part closed during the Fascist occupation (1941–45). The universities of Zagreb and Ljubljana continued to operate, though under very unfavorable circumstances. Many students and a certain number of teachers took part in the Liberation War.[5]

It was during the war, in 1943, that the "new" Yugoslavia was established as a federally organized state. After the liberation in 1945, the new state was proclaimed a republic. Its first constitution in January 1946 gave it the name the Federal People's Republic of Yugoslavia. This name was changed to the Socialist Federal Republic of Yugoslavia in 1963. The new state had six constituent republics: Bosnia-Herzegovina, Montenegro, Croatia, Macedonia, Slovenia, and Serbia, with the Autonomous Province of Voivodina and the Autonomous Region of Kosovo-Metohia (subsequently renamed the Province of Kosovo). New Yugoslavia opted for socialism in its socioeconomic and political relations, for the brotherhood and unity of its nations, and for the full equality of all the Yugoslav peoples and national minorities. All schools were declared state institutions, separated from the church. The three universities existing at that time became state institutions in the service of the new socialist system. Faculties of theology were abolished because the communist view of the world, which the new authorities favored, was incompatible with religious beliefs and thus also with the institutional forms of their communication. The present chapter will make no attempt to deal with that segment of higher education in Yugoslavia that is conducted in religious institutions of higher learning. Similarly, the relatively well-developed system of military postsecondary education, including the military colleges, military academies, and two-year postsecondary schools, will be omitted from the present analysis.

The central task of higher education institutions in the early postwar years was defined by the developmental objectives of the Yugoslav society at that time. These objectives focused on the reconstruction of the war-devastated country, its economic (primarily industrial) growth, and the improvement of the general cultural and political standards of the Yugoslav people. In order to achieve these objectives, large numbers of highly educated young people were needed in all areas of social life. The three universities were unable to cope with swelling enrollments, and in 1949 two new universities were established: the Kiril and Metodij University of Skopie (Macedonia) and the University of Sarajevo (Bosnia-Herzegovina). The emergence of the new universities was motivated also by the desire of each of the Yugoslav republics to have a university of its own. Thus, Montenegro remained the only republic without a university until 1974, when the University of Titograd was established.

Higher Education in Yugoslavia: Main Characteristics

Institutions

Two types of institutions can be distinguished in the higher education system in Yugoslavia in the postwar period: (1) university institutions and equivalent arrangements, (2) other third-level (postsecondary) institutions. Faculties are by far the most common type of university and equivalent institutions, together with art academies and four-year colleges. Undergraduate studies at such institutions normally take four years, with the exception of medical schools, where the course of study takes six years. Other third-level institutions are two-year postsecondary schools (vise skole), some of which are also incorporated in universities (depending on the legislation of each constituent republic or province).

Faculties in Yugoslavia are built on the traditional Central European pattern. They teach a variety of disciplines, the variety being particularly great at Faculties of Philosophy (or Liberal Arts). Unlike some other European countries, Yugoslavia has not adopted the departmental model of university organization, though the advocates of this type of organization have become increasingly vocal in recent years, particularly in certain fundamental disciplines.

Most of the university and equivalent institutions also offer postgraduate courses for a duration of two years. Postgraduate programs are for the most part completed as part-time study for students already in employment. Following the completion of the course and the presentation and successful defense of a dissertation, the graduates receive the appropriate academic degree, the M.A. or M.S. The precondition for the doctoral degree is the presentation and successful defense of a Ph.D. dissertation. No full-time or part-time doctoral courses are run by Yugoslav universities. The doctoral candidate prepares the dissertation on his or her own or under the supervision of a mentor. This means that no graduate schools of the kind found in the United States exist at Yugoslav universities. Also, there are no postdoctoral studies in Yugoslavia as there are in some countries with a better developed and more diversified tertiary education.

It can generally be said that there is a high degree of uniformity among the institutions of postsecondary education in Yugoslavia. In the 1970s and 1980s, even two-year postsecondary schools were in many cases obliged by law to "merge" with Faculties and join the universities. In the process they lost their primary function, which had been the development of practical skills. New legislation, currently under preparation, is expected to increase the diversification of institutions of tertiary education.

As already noted, Yugoslavia had three universities at the end of World War II—in Zagreb, Belgrade, and Ljubljana—to which two more were added in 1949: in Skopje (Macedonia) and Sarajevo (Bosnia-Herzegovina). The expansion of the university network was particularly rapid in the 1960s and 1970s, as fourteen new universities opened in the following sequence: University of Arts in Belgrade, Serbia (1957); University of Novi Sad, Province of Voivodina (1960); University of Nis, Serbia (1965); University of Prishtina, Province of Kosovo (1970); Vladimir Bakaric University of Rijeka, Croatia (1973); Veljko Vlahovic University of Titograd, Montenegro (1974); University of Split, Croatia (1974); University of Osijek, Croatia (1975); University of Maribor, Slovenia (1975); Djuro Pucar Stari University of Banja Luka, Bosnia-Herzegovina (1975); Svetozar Markovic University of Kragujevac, Serbia (1976); University of Tuzla, Bosnia-Herzegovina (1976); Dzemal Bijedic University of Mostar, Bosnia-Herzegovina (1976); and finally the University of Bitola, Macedonia (1979).[6] No new

university was established during the 1980s, nor are there any plans for the expansion of the university network in the 1990s.

The newly established universities have helped to reduce regional educational disparities in the country. They have made higher education accessible to large numbers of students in the "periphery" and to young people with different social backgrounds. At the same time, however, they have not fulfilled the expectations of many people: the long-awaited innovativeness has failed to materialize. Instead of offering fresh ideas and innovative approaches, the new universities have done their best to emulate the traditional university centers in which many of their member institutions had their roots. Unfortunately, they have been less than successful in their efforts to duplicate the older institutions: the new universities remain for the most part pale copies of their traditional models.

Unlike many universities in the rest of the world, the Yugoslav universities, both old and new, are rather large institutions with massive enrollments. Thus, in 1989, the University of Belgrade had 43,014 full-time students, the University of Zagreb 36,334 students, and the University of Prishtina 21,989 students.[7] The size of the universities is just one reason why they appear as loose associations of the member institutions, lacking firm organizational or curricular linkages.

As the number of universities grew over the past decades, so also did the number of institutions of higher learning. From twenty-six institutions in 1938, the number rose to eighty-one in 1955, 204 in 1960, 246 in 1970, 294 in 1975, and 356 in 1980. The numbers began to decline in the early 1980s, dropping to 330 in 1985 and to 322 in 1987. The increase has been particularly marked in the total number of Faculties, which reached 203 in 1988 (according to preliminary data). The number of two-year postsecondary schools rose rapidly between 1970 and 1975, so that there were 131 such schools in 1975, but then the numbers began to decrease and there were 124 such schools in 1980 and 103 in 1985. According to preliminary data, ninety-one two-year postsecondary schools were in operation in 1988.[8] The marked drop has been due primarily to the integration of such schools into Faculties as a result of the 1974 educational reform.

Enrollments

During much of the postwar period university enrollments grew steadily; it is only since 1980 that a downward trend can be observed. The enrollments were particularly large when the postwar baby boom generation reached the universities. In the early postwar years there were only several thousand students, but their numbers rose dramatically in the 1960s and 1970s. In 1960, for instance, there were a total of 140,574 students (40,700, or 28 percent, of them women); ten years later, in 1970, there were 261,203 students (103,011, or 39 percent, of them women). In 1975 enrollments reached 394,992 (157,514, or 40 percent, of them women). The peak was reached in 1980 with 411,995 students (186,991, or 45 percent, of them women). Enrollments began to decrease in 1980, dropping to 350,334 in 1985 (160,494, or 46 percent, of them were women) and to 348,068 in 1987 (165,210, or 47 percent, of them women).[9] According to preliminary data for 1988, enrollments were down to 339,577 (146,821, or 48 percent, of them women).[10] The drop in enrollments in the 1980s was due to unfavorable population trends, as well as to the effects of the economic and political crisis that set in at the beginning of the decade and to the inappropriate educational legislation introduced in the latter part of the 1970s (the legislation limited part-time study to workers sent to the university by their firms). A further drop in enrollments can be predicted for the years ahead, primarily caused by the economic difficulties that Yugoslav society will face in the 1990s.

A breakdown of enrollments by types of tertiary institutions reveals significant differences. Thus, enrollments in universities and equivalent institutions have continued to grow in most cases. For instance, institutions of this type had 108,381 students in 1960 (31,213, or 28 percent, of them women) and 180,129 students in 1970 (69,225, or 38 percent, of them women). In 1975 the number rose to 271,517 (109,450, or 40 percent, women), and ten years later, in 1985, it stood at 287,907 (132,421, or 46 percent, women). Finally, in 1987, enrollments in universities and equivalent institutions numbered 296,289 (141,448 or 48 percent, of them women). In other third-level institutions, however, two opposite trends can be observed: first, in the early postwar decades enrollments rose steadily, only to decline drastically between 1975 and 1987 . Here are the statistics to prove this: in 1960, such institutions enrolled 32,193 students (9,407, or 29 percent, of them women); in 1970, their enrollments rose to 80,074 students (33,786, or 42 percent, women), and in 1975 to 123,475 students (48,064, or 39 percent, women). From 1975 to 1987 there was a marked decline in enrollments in such institutions: 1980 —101,345 (44,474, or 44 percent, women); 1985—62,427 (28,073, or 45 percent, women); 1987—51,079 (23,762, or 47 percent, of them women).[11] Such a drastic drop in enrollments in nonuniversity tertiary institutions was due to two main factors: merger of two-year postsecondary schools (vise skole) with university-type institutions (Faculties) and a general decline of part-time studies (a favorite form of study at two-year postsecondary schools).

The data given here show a steady rise in the proportion of women students in the student population. The rise has been as much as 10 percent during the past fifteen years, and in the 1990s—for the first time in the history of Yugoslav higher education—women will represent a majority in the total student population. In certain disciplines, such as medicine, teacher training, and foreign languages, women already outnumber men by a considerable margin.

As regards the number of students per 100,000 inhabitants, it first went up significantly in the 1960s and 1970s, and then in the 1980s it dropped markedly. In 1970, for instance, Yugoslavia had 1,282 students enrolled in higher education per 100,000 inhabitants; in 1975 the number was 1,850; in 1980, 1,848; in 1985, 1,515; and in 1987, 1,491.[12] This decline should be viewed against the background of unfavorable economic, social, and political developments in the country during the 1980s.

The same developments could not but have an effect also on the third-level enrollment ratios for the twenty- to twenty-four-year-old segment of the general population. The ratio stood at 15.9 percent (including both men and women) in 1970, 20.0 percent in 1975, and 20.8 percent in 1980. Then it dropped by a few points during the 1980s to 18.5 percent in 1985 and to 18.6 percent in 1987.[13]

Interesting changes can be observed also in part-time enrollments, again showing a marked increase during the 1960s and 1970s and a sharp decline during the 1980s. There were 45,814 part-time students in 1960, representing 32 percent of the total student population. Ten years later, in 1970, their number rose to 77,065, which was 29 percent of the total enrollments. The 1970s were the golden years for part-time study: part-time enrollments reached 152,746, or 38 percent of the total enrollments, in 1975. The negative effects of the legislation passed in the second half of the 1970s began to be felt in the early 1980s: there were 148,641 part-time students (36 percent of the total student population) in 1980, 95,616 (27 percent of the total) in 1985, and 89,947 (26 percent of the total) in 1987. Preliminary data for 1988 point to a further drop in part-time enrollments—to 83,912, or 24 percent of the total enrollments that year.[14]

Working adults have always formed the majority of part-time students in Yugoslavia.[15] As the system of education increasingly favored full-time study, the opportunities for working adults to pursue higher education gradually diminished. This trend is contrary to developments in a number of the more developed countries, in which the proportion of adult students over twenty-four years old, has actually grown in recent years. Negative trends in part-time enrollments can be reversed primarily through the removal of the restrictive legislation, which allows only people already holding jobs and sponsored by their employers to enroll as part-time students. If the legislation is revised in the early 1990s, positive effects can be expected by the mid-1990s.

Teaching Staff

At the end of World War II Yugoslavia had a very limited supply of university teachers—mainly those who had taught at the three existing universities in the country and who had not "politically compromised themselves" during the war (to use the ideological language of that time). Immediately after the war the new Yugoslav authorities sent a certain number of promising young academics to the Soviet Union for further study. However, such cooperation was brought to an end when Tito clashed with Stalin in 1948. A new generation of teachers came on the scene during the 1950s and 1960s, but their numbers were still inadequate. The total number of teachers in 1955 was 3,007, of whom 310, or 10 percent, were women. The number rose to 5,123 in 1960, 607, or 12 percent, of them women. The massive expansion of postsecondary education in the 1970s necessitated large numbers of teachers for the existing and new higher education institutions. Thus, in 1970, the postsecondary institutions in Yugoslavia taken together employed 16,783 teachers (3,492, or 20 percent, of them women). Ten years later, in 1980, that number rose to 24,449 (5,785, or 24 percent, of them women). In 1987 the number of teachers in higher education stood at 25,927 (6,968, or 27 percent, of them women).[16]

The expansion of the teaching staff showed different patterns in different types of third-level institutions. The growth was continuous in the universities and equivalent institutions: in 1960 they employed 3,346 teachers (266, or 8 percent, of them women); in 1970 there were 12,830 teachers (2,730, or 21 percent, of them women); in 1980, 19,981 teachers (4,799, or 24 percent, of them women); and in 1985, 22,204 teachers (5,943, or 27 percent, of them women). It is interesting to note that the number of teachers in institutions of this type continued to grow even after 1980, and that it did not decline with the declining enrollments in the 1980s.[17]

Unlike the universities and equivalent institutions, other third-level institutions recorded a rise in the number of teachers until 1980 and a sudden drop since that time. In 1960 such institutions employed 1,777 teachers (341, or 19 percent, of them women); in 1970, 3,935 (762, or 19 percent, of them women); in 1980, 4,468 (986, or 22 percent, of them women). In 1985 the number dropped to 3,658 teachers (841, or 23 percent, of them women), and in 1987 it dropped further to 2,963 teachers (644, or 22 percent, of them women). The declining trend continued also in the late 1980s.

The statistics presented here point to another interesting trend—namely, the growing proportion of women among postsecondary teachers. The trend can be observed equally in total numbers of postsecondary teachers and in the teaching ranks they occupy in universities and equivalent institutions. Taking all third-level institutions together, the percentage of women grew from 20 to 27 percent between 1970 and 1987. The same increase was recorded in universities and equivalent institutions during that period: the proportion of women in the teaching staff

of such institutions rose from 21 percent in 1970 to 28 percent in 1987. In other third-level institutions, however, the proportion of women in the teaching staff was 19 percent in 1970, 23 percent in 1980, and 22 percent in 1987.[18]

In the context of the present discussion it should be noted that the teaching staff at institutions of higher learning in Yugoslavia appears also in the statistics of R & D personnel. In 1987 25,402 teachers were also active researchers, which was 33 percent of the total number of R & D specialists in all the sectors (76,246), exclusive of the military and defense-related research and development. However, the number of R & D scientists and engineers working in higher education was considerably smaller—10,533 in 1987.[19]

Educational Policies: Reexamination of the Successes and Failures

Objectives, Curriculum, and Technology: Certain Qualitative Aspects of Higher Education

The objectives of higher education in Yugoslavia during the last few decades have focused mainly on the preparation of young people for work and for life in an industrial society with a socialist orientation. The changes brought about by the information revolution and postindustrial society have only recently begun to make an impact on the objectives of higher education in the country. Life in an active society, rich in information and offering ample opportunities for self-fulfillment, demands a respect for social and technological change and a renunciation of political dogma. In this respect, it can be said that Yugoslav higher education has yet to face the future.[20]

Changes will be needed not only in the objectives, but also in the very nature of the curriculum. Higher education curricula are still dominated by a subject matter that is becoming obsolete. Besides, a shift toward the acquisition and development of metacognitive skills and abilities will become increasingly important in higher education, too, in the future. In a world characterized by rapid change, the task of higher education is not to prepare an individual for a lifelong career. Rather, it should provide initial professional education and prepare the student for lifelong learning and recurrent education. In addition, the purpose of higher education is not merely to provide knowledge and develop skills in a particular area. Particularly in postgraduate studies and in doctoral dissertation work, the emphasis should be placed on the development of research competence. However, many postgraduate curricula are at present no more than slightly advanced copies of the undergraduate curricula. Instead of stressing the methodology of research, they merely repeat the subject matter of undergraduate courses, only at a "higher level."

As for educational technology and style of teaching, it can be said that the Yugoslav educational institutions—with some notable exceptions—have for many decades relied on obsolete methods, with teaching still being understood as one-way communication. Inadequate attention has been paid to the improvement of the pedagogy of university teaching and teachers. The potential of the new information technologies has remained largely unused in higher education. Computers are used mostly for research and hardly at all for computer-assisted and computer-managed instruction. This is due both to a shortage of hardware and the resistance of teachers to the use of unfamiliar technology. Computer search, access to foreign data bases, use of expert systems—all these are utopian exercises for most students and many of their teachers in Yugoslavia. The ecology of the Yugoslav institutions of higher learning remains uncultivated and deprived of the content that should make for pleasant study and life in these institutions. After years of financial deprivation, teaching is still done with nothing much more than "blackboard and chalk." If the unacceptable financial treatment of education continues into the 1990s, no change can be expected in the technology of higher education, or in the individualization of instruction and educational efficiency.

Higher Education Links with the Social Environment

In every country higher education institutions are part of a large social and cultural setting. The links that the Yugoslav universities have established with their social environment during the past decades have been rich and varied, though not always successful. I shall focus here only on the most important links: (1) those between higher education and research institutions, and (2) those between higher education and the world of work.

In the first case, I have in mind primarily the research institutions that are part of the university organization. There are many reasons why the Yugoslav universities have failed to develop an active, working relationship with research institutions (institutes and centers) outside the university, in spite of the government's verbal support for the idea that leading researchers should be "brought into" teaching. Equally rare have been the cases of university teachers being engaged on projects run by research institutes outside the university. The reason for this is to be sought in the inadequate organization of research and teaching and in the rigid system of their financing.

The lack of good links between the universities and independent research institutions is easier to understand in view of the fact that such links are equally poor between the university teaching institutions and research institutes incorporated into universities.[21] Many university research institutes have excellent specialists, who, however, have no chance to participate in teaching and working with students. This is another reason why the principle of integration of teaching and research in higher education is realized only to a limited extent in Yugoslavia.

As for its relationship with the world of work, Yugoslav higher education now faces a new challenge. Over the past two decades institutions of higher learning have all too often been treated as a direct service of self-managed business organizations. Higher education is expected to obey the dictate of the short-term, not infrequently also short-sighted, demands of the world of work, particularly those of material production. Subjecting higher education to the daily needs of business (industrial) organizations and placing them in a position of direct financial dependence on the good will of worker-managers was an experiment that produced negative results and distorted the subtle relationship that should exist between the two partners.[22]

What the relations between higher education and the world of work will be in the new, market-oriented rather than self-management-based economy remains to be seen. The Yugoslav institutions, of higher learning cannot, in this respect, draw on rich historical experience. They may choose to follow well-known forms of cooperation, such as providing for a greater transfer of knowledge and personnel, sponsoring joint projects in science parks, continuing professional education and improvement schemes, offering short refresher courses for continuing education. If the country does indeed proceed in the direction of the market economy and reprivatization of the socialized sector, qualitatively new relations between higher education and the world of work are expected to emerge in the early 1990s. Though these relations will certainly be different, this does not in itself guarantee that they will therefore be better and more successful than those that preceded them.

Management, Planning, and Finance

In the early postwar decades educational policy in Yugoslavia was the responsibility of the state authorities. It was only in the 1960s that higher education began to gain a measure of independence from the state. In the 1970s and 1980s, a radical attempt was made to free higher education from state controls through self-management and socialization of education. "Self-management" was taken to mean free decision making by those employed in higher education in all relevant matters affecting the work and development of such institutions. "Socialization," on the other hand, represented an attempt to involve a number of social bodies in the management of the subsystem of higher education. Thus, the intervention of the government bodies was to be replaced by the action of the social bodies. Also, those employed in postsecondary education, in direct cooperation with those employed in the economy and other public service sectors, were meant to manage the totality of higher education.[23]

On the macrolevel the last decades have seen the process of decentralization of management of higher education. It should be noted that Yugoslavia consists of six constituent republics and two autonomous provinces and encompasses a considerable number of nationalities and ethnic groups. Respecting the federal organization of the state and the multinational composition of the country, a decision was made in the early 1970s to abolish the federal Ministry of Education. Instead, each of the republics and autonomous provinces has its own Ministry of Education, eight of them altogether. The coordination of educational policies in the whole country is entrusted to a variety of federal commissions on which all the republics and provinces are represented. Also, the institutions of higher learning are organized in associations of universities on the republic level and in the Association of Universities of Yugoslavia for the whole country. These associations help to coordinate higher education policies nationally, but they do not significantly affect the way that individual institutions are run.

The processes of decentralization, self-management, and socialization of education have affected not only management and decision making in higher education but also the nature of planning. Thus, central planning for the whole country has been replaced by planning on the level of the constituent republics and provinces. Instead of the (republic and provincial) governments taking the key role in the planning of higher education, planning over the last two decades has been conducted by the Self-Managed Communities of Interest made up of delegates representing institutions of higher learning and those representing the world of work (whose needs the system of higher education was called upon to meet).[24]

The influence the universities and their member institutions have on the self-managing planning process has weakened considerably, with individual institutions acting as separate parts of a disintegrated university organism. But the influence of the nonuniversity bodies, such as the Self-Managed Communities of Interest and the world of work in material production, has greatly increased. However, the educational needs of the world of work have not infrequently been viewed in the perspective of short-term and pragmatic interests of the economy. To make matters worse, the dominant role in planning has often been played by the professional and administrative staff of the Self-Managed Communities of Interest rather than the delegates of the institutions of higher learning and of the economy. Initially established as professional backup services, these bureaucracies gradually acquired a degree of "autonomy" that enabled them to decisively influence the planning process and its outcome. Thus, the republican and provin-

cial government bureaucracy has been replaced by a large and well paid apparatus in the Self-Managed Communities of Interest, which makes decisions not only on the general plans of development of higher education but also on such matters as enrollment policies and curricula for individual institutions of higher learning.

To complete the picture, it should be said that the process of socialization of education has been reduced in practice to direct interference by different social and political bodies and corporations in purely academic affairs. Thus, the development plans for higher education have been debated, with equal (in)competence, by the Communist party, the trade unions, the Socialist Alliance, the Youth Organization, and various other state, parastatal, and self-management bodies. All this has made the process of planning and decision making in higher education unwieldy and inefficient. The situation has been further aggravated by the fact that, following the 1974 educational reform, higher education has been planned only in the context of postelementary education as an integral whole, rather than being treated as a relatively independent educational sector.

The financing of higher education has followed the same pattern as management and planning.[25] This means that in the early postwar period it was financed through the state budget, then through the so-called Social Funds, and during the last two decades through the Self-Managed Communities of Interest for Postelementary Education and for Science. Institutions of higher learning also generate part of their income through direct cooperation with industry and by charging tuition fees to part-time and postgraduate students.

The funds contributed for higher education as a fixed proportion of wages and salaries have accumulated in the Self-Managed Communities of Interest for Postelementary Education, and their allocation should in theory be decided by the delegates representing higher education institutions and those representing the world of work, meeting together in the assemblies of the Self-Managed Communities of Interest. In practice, however, the greatest power in deciding on the allocation of the available money was exercised by the bureaucratic apparatus of the Communities of Interest. Though firm criteria had been established for the financing of higher education, they were practically ignored during the 1980s. In addition, the runaway inflation in the second half of the 1980s mercilessly decimated the value of the money set aside for higher education. In this situation securing money for teacher salaries became the main concern. Strikes became a common feature of the higher educational scene. There was just enough money to keep the institutions of higher learning afloat, but not to make any qualitative improvements.

As we enter the 1990s new solutions are being sought for the financing of higher education. These will essentially depend on the broader options that will be chosen for the country's general social, economic, and political development. It is certain, however, that the existing system of financing, through the Self-Managed Communities of Interest, is no longer tenable, and more stable sources of funding will have to be found. There is a growing tendency to seek alternative sources of financing for higher education, including tuition fees, while budgetary provisions are being arranged through the Ministries of Education. In the current changes the universities are striving for greater autonomy, which in this case also implies greater influence on the allocation of funds and independent decision making in all matters affecting their development.

It can be expected that educational policies in the 1990s will be more directly influenced by the state on the one hand and by the university establishment on the other. The scope of authority of the Ministries of Education will be increased, but at the same time the universities are looking forward to a greater degree of autonomy. The influence of the numerous parastatal bodies that have interposed themselves— especially in the form of the Self-Managed Communities of Interest—as intermediaries between those contributing money for higher education and those receiving this money as payment for their services is expected to decline. In short, the 1990s will in all probability see a major change in the country's educational policy. The administration of education will shift from self-management to government administration, with greater or lesser centralization, while planning will move from self-managed planning to a combination of administrative and market planning. In keeping with the new development, an increasing role in the financing of higher education will be played by the institutions of higher learning from sale of their services. Private payments will also become an increasingly important source of revenue for these institutions. The actual effects of these changes on the efficiency, democracy, and quality of higher education will not be known before the mid-1990s.

Future Development

The future of higher education in Yugoslavia will decisively depend on the path that Yugoslav society takes in the crucial early 1990s. Though it is not easy to forecast social developments, I shall review three possible options that now stand before Yugoslavia.

First Option

The first option is one of the market economy, parliamentary democracy, political pluralism, and law-based state. If this option is chosen, Yugoslavia will have to give up the statal, parastatal, and self-managing forms of regulation of economic life, the predominance of politics over economics, the single-party political system, the monopoly of the ruling party, and ideological rigidity.

Assuming this course of social development, a number of rather drastic changes can be expected in higher education. These will affect in particular the relationship between higher education and employment and, more generally, the relationship between higher education and the world of work. Though the labor market is perhaps not an ideal solution, it would certainly evaluate the human resources with appropriate skills and abilities more adequately than is the case in the present system characterized by the principle of egalitarian wage-leveling. The effect will be a faster restructuring of the Yugoslav economy and greater mobility of the labor force. Closer links will be established between higher education and the world of work, with greater respect for the mutual interests of the two partners.

Another consequence that can be expected as a result of this option is that a premium will be put on the quality of higher education. This will stimulate competition among the universities and affect also the students' choices of the institutions at which they would prefer to study. This option will also favor the autonomy of the universities in academic matters and the increased responsibility of both teachers and students for educational success. The responsibility will be all the more direct if tuition fees are introduced and if parts of the higher education system are privatized. Closer cooperation between Yugoslav and foreign universities will be a natural consequence of the adoption of this course. A greater internationalization of higher education, with an emphasis on teacher and student exchanges, will stimulate the integration of Yugoslav society in the current processes in Europe. Apart from these, a number of other challenging developments can be expected in Yugoslav higher education if the first option is chosen.

Second Option

This option involves a possible shift toward the kind of socioeconomic and political relations characteristic of state socialism. Put differently, this is an orientation toward centralized state planning in the economy and the command role of the Communist party not only in the political and economic sphere but also in culture, science, and education. This model of socioeconomic and political relations, known as "administrative socialism," prevailed in Yugoslavia in the years immediately after World War II, officially until 1950. However, since social relations are not easily abolished by proclamations, the model survived much longer, and some of its anachronistic aspects are visible to this day. The choice of this option could be induced by the very serious economic situation which the country has endured for close to ten years and by national conflicts that transcend purely political antagonisms. This option could receive further support from those social forces that oppose the first option. However, recent developments in the countries of the so-called real existing socialism, particularly those occurring in 1989 and 1990, provide evidence of the collapse of a system that for a long time stopped at nothing to maintain itself in power.

If, hypothetically speaking, the second option were chosen in Yugoslavia, higher education would develop in accordance with the well-known pattern, with the state administrative and ideological apparatus playing the main role in organizing and implementing a system of higher education. Everything would be strictly planned and controlled: what is studied, who studies, under what conditions, who is politically suitable to be a teacher, and who to become a student.

The university would slowly lose its autonomy. The power of decision making would devolve upon the obedient bureaucratic and party apparatus. Ideological indoctrination would form part of any higher education curriculum. Education would be considered worthwhile only in so far as it served the high collective goals, far above any individual goal of an individual person. Considerations of the quality and excellence of education would be replaced by empty talk of "true democracy" in education under the socialist system and claims of "social equality" and "justice" always illustrated by impressive statistics that impress only those who do not quite understand what the figures stand for.

Events that took place in Eastern Europe in 1989 and 1990 and the promising integration processes in Western Europe diminish the chances of the second option being chosen. This option would certainly not take today's young Yugoslavs into tomorrow's united Europe without borders. Instead, it would leave them unprepared to participate actively and fully in the creation of new relations in the world.

Third Option

The third option for Yugoslavia as it traces its path into the twenty-first century is to stick to the self-management model of development, "enriched" with elements of the first two options. Self-management, after all, is the *differentia specifica* of the Yugoslav socialism in contradistinction to socialism in other countries. Heralded as a genuine alternative to Stalinist-style state socialism in the 1950s, the Yugoslav "experiment" aroused high hopes in the country and throughout the world. During the 1960s and 1970s, the entire socioeconomic and political life of Yugoslavia, including higher education, was organized in line with the theory of self-managing socialism. According to this theory, workers and citizens were to be the chief makers of their own subjectivity. The same applied to teachers and students in higher education. However, as has happened so often in modern political history, an easily visible gap appeared between the attractive theory

and its less-than-ideal practical implementation. In the early 1980s, the overall balance of the Yugoslav self-managing experiment was seen to be disastrous. The causes of the failure were many. Rather than trying to list them all, I will pose a single question: can self-management have a chance at all in a monistic political system and in a party-controlled state in which all key decisions are made independently of the worker-managers, yet in their name? In this situation, self-management is just a facade behind which the games of life are played according to non-self-management rules.

Some elements of self-management can be expected to continue in Yugoslavia, including within the sphere of higher education. However, they will probably blend with elements characterizing the other two options. The introduction of the market economy and political pluralism will tend to reduce self-management to different forms of participation, not unlike those that we find in some developed Western societies, for instance in Scandinavia. Whether it takes the form of worker participation in management or citizen self-organization in alternative movements and parties, it will cease to be the concept of "self-managing" socialism. It is an open question as to how much room for real participation is left in the so-called new socialism now advocated in the country. Many of the changes now being introduced in the public-service sector, including education, eliminate the earlier forms of self-managing decision making, replacing them with greater government competences. Given the inadequately developed political pluralism in the country, this may mean the strengthening of the old administrative and bureaucratic apparatus, particularly in those parts of the country in which the longing for a party-controlled state is still quite strong. It is not impossible, in this situation, that instead of an efficient state that would competently stimulate the development of higher education, we may get a system that will not need self-management in education even as a mere facade.

Regardless of which of the three options is chosen for Yugoslavia's future social, economic, and political development, we can expect important changes in its educational policy, especially in higher education. The 1990s will certainly be the years of challenge for the educational policymakers. They will also be lean and difficult years for all those involved in higher education. As we approach the twenty-first century, Yugoslavia cannot avoid radical changes—the problem is that they will have to be made in a situation characterized by a weak economy, the absence of a social and political consensus, and the lack of good will to reach such a consensus.[26]

Notes

1. For a historical overview, see Borivoj Samolovcev, "Higher Education in Yugoslavia: A Historical Overview," in *Higher Education in Yugoslavia*, ed. Niksa Nikola Soljan (Zagreb: Andragogical Center, 1989), 13–43.
2. Ibid., 16–18.
3. Ibid., 22–23.
4. See Nikola M. Potkonjak, "Educational Reforms in Yugoslavia and Changes in Higher Education," in *Higher Education in Yugoslavia*, 45–56.
5. Borivoj Samolovcev, "Higher Education in Yugoslavia: A Historical Overview," in *Higher Education in Yugoslavia*, 26–30.
6. Ibid., 32–40.
7. Data source: The Association of Universities of Yugoslavia (Belgrade).
8. *Statisticki godisnjak Jugolsavije* 1989 (Statistical Yearbook of Yugoslavia 1989) (Belgrade, Yugoslavia: SZS, 1989), 378.
9. UNESCO *Statistical Yearbook* 1989 (Paris: UNESCO, 1989), 3-263.
10. *Statisticki godisnjak Jugoslavije* 1989 (Statistical Yearbook of Yugoslavia 1989).
11. UNESCO *Statistical Yearbook* 1989.
12. Ibid., 3–231.
13. Ibid., 3–65.
14. *Statisticki godisnjak Jugoslavije* 1989, 378.
15. See Ana Krajnc, "Adult Studies in Yugoslav Higher Education," in *Adult Education in Yugoslav Society*, ed. Niksa Nikola Soljan (Zagreb, Yugoslavia: Andragogical Center, 1985), 84–88. See also Milan Matijevic, "Part-Time Study in Institutions of Higher Learning in Yugoslavia," in *Higher Education in Yugoslavia*, 69-77.
16. UNESCO *Statistical Yearbook* 1989, 3–263.
17. Ibid. p. 7.
18. Ibid. p. 7.
19. Ibid., 5–82.
20. See Niksa Nikola Soljan, *Yugoslav Education Under Examination: Educational Reform, Policy, and Theory* (Zagreb, Yugoslavia: University of Zagreb Institute for Educational Research, 1988).
21. See Miroslav Pecujlic, *The University of the Future: The Yugoslav Experience* (Westport: Greenwood Press, 1987).
22. See Niksa Nikola Soljan and Hans Georg Schütze, eds., *Higher Education and the World of Work: An OECD/CERI—Yugoslav Report* (Zagreb, Yugoslavia: Andragogical Center, 1989). See also Niksa Nikola Soljan, ed., *Recurrent Education in Yugoslavia* (Belgrade, Yugoslavia: Jugoslovenski Pregled, Newspaper and Publishing House, 1983).
23. Milenko Nikolic and Tomislav Bogavac, *Educational Policy in Yugoslavia* (Belgrade, Yugoslavia: Jugoslovenska Stvarnost, 1980).
24. OECD, *Conditions, Problems, and Policy of Education in Yugoslavia* (Paris: OECD, 1980).
25. OECD, *Reviews of National Policies for Education: Yugoslavia* (Paris: OECD, 1981).
26. See Niksa Nikola Soljan, "Yugoslavia," in *Student Political Activism: An International Reference Handbook*, ed. Philip G. Altbach (Westport: Greenwood Press, 1989), 297–312.

LATIN AMERICA

Latin America

Orlando Albornoz

◆

There are several ways to study the university in Latin America and the Caribbean. But whatever method is chosen, the institution is undergoing a severe crisis and seems to have lost the chance to promote and sustain scientific and technological development in the region. As in other areas of the third world, the university is having a real problem functioning. In the *Arab World*, for example, Ahmed has written that "Higher education, which has an insufficient capacity to receive students, is in addition contested in its methods and its ability to promote and sustain scientific and technical development. The near nonexistence of serious research structures and efficient documentation makes the situation worse. Thus assimilation and technological creation are made difficult while the Arab region inexorably undergoes a considerable brain drain."[1]

The university in Latin America and the Caribbean is mostly a teaching institution that trains people for the professions. But that common goal does not mean that all universities in the region are the same. In fact, there is a good deal of difference among them, even within the same country. Public urban universities are different from small public universities in provincial cities. In the private sector one finds quite a difference between those institutions that cater to the upper classes and those universities that work to fulfill the educational needs of the middle and working class.

Most studies of Latin America and Caribbean universites analyze the larger university systems in the region, in countries such as Argentina, Brazil, and Mexico. Some studies, however, examine elements of university life across the region, like students, or faculty life, or even the physical conditions of the campuses and university buildings, and compare the topic across all or a sample of countries. For this chapter I have taken another approach that needs to be justified. I have taken university models as the unit of analysis.

By "university models" I mean the economic and political approach to the institution. I find three very different models of universities in the region: (1) those controlled by the state—in this case I have taken the most representative case, Cuba; (2) those where market forces prevail, for example, in Chile; (3) those where both the state and the private sector share important segments of university life—countries like Argentina, Brazil, and Mexico are in this category, as well as Colombia, Peru, and Venezuela. Any of these countries could be used in my analysis. Since the Venezuelan university has been little studied, and since I am Venezuelan, I focus on this country for category three.

It must be pointed out that Brazilian higher education has been by far the most studied. The three-volume study of the university in Brazil written by Luiz Antonio Cunha is the best and most complete study of the university in any country in the region. Due to historical processes higher education came late to that country but it is at present the best and most sophisticated network of higher education in the region, followed by Mexico. These two countries would be on top of any list if one were to classify in terms of quality.

The reader should be aware that no single approach to the study of higher education in Latin America and the Caribbean would be totally satisfactory. Country analysis lacks the comparative perspective while the variable approach can be too general. Model analysis has an advantage, in that it offers a theoretical framework and a comparative country analysis at the same time.

My aim in this chapter is to give the reader a full understanding of the university in Latin America and the Caribbean, in terms of three different institutional models as they operate in the region. Within each model I will try to examine some common variables, although I am concerned above all with political issues and with university organization. I also describe the complexities of the region and the diversity of the institution in this part of the world. To the Western reader the region is a homogeneous area, but the closer one gets to it the more complex and diversified it becomes.

The university came into being during the Spanish conquest. During the long period of Hispanic hegemony the university was an appendix of the colonial power. It was not until the late 1910s that the so-called Latin American model of the university emerged, first in Argentina and later in the rest of the region. After 1945 universities based on the American model came into being. The Soviet model of the university came to Cuba during the early 1960s. What we have in the region is a multiple university model; the way the university should be analyzed is through the study of the different university models prevalent in the region.

It is not possible to generalize about higher learning in Latin America and the Caribbean. If we understand higher learning as any schooling after the secondary level of education, then we will be speaking about more than a thousand institutions. They generate a multinational school map that is very complex and about which any broad definition or general conceptualization should be rather cautious and limited. Higher education, of course, is bound to reflect, to some extent, the soci-

ety in which it is situated. For this reason, higher education in Latin America and the Caribbean comprises an unwieldy mass of institutions as varied in quality as in size. Like the region itself higher education is full of contrast, by turns outstanding and incompetent, regimented and chaotic, futuristic and antiquated, internationally minded and parochial, idealistic and complacent, and even corrupt. Indeed there is no way to analyze higher learning in the region through simple concepts, just as it would not be possible to do so about any other region in the world. However, in this chapter I am going to try to give a general analysis of higher learning in Latin America and the Caribbean, and to identify general problems throughout the region through reference to specific countries as examples of certain institutional trends.

Historical Background

Institutions are part of a society, but they are created by a culture under specific historical circumstances. In the case of the university in Latin America and the Caribbean it is necessary to make a historical survey in order to see the evolution of the institution in the different subareas of the region. In successive stages a number of colonial powers came to the region, first the Spaniards, later the Portuguese, later still the British and the French, and more recently the Americans and the Soviets. With each successive historical step the universities coming to the region became a part of the regional map.

In spite of the Cordoba Reform that took place in Argentina in 1918 and created what is probably unique about the university in the region—a public institution ruled by both the faculty and the students—higher education in the region is still a nonnative institution devoted to the needs of the elite. A number of institutions dedicated to mass higher education in Latin America and the Caribbean do exist. But generally the Latin American University is still an academic institution in a largely nonintellectual society; that is, the university, to refer to the typical unit of post-secondary education, trains people in intellectual ways in societies where such a life is quite remote from the daily life of the masses, who live in poor conditions and are intent on survival.

The university in the region follows a colonial model and is mainly a teaching institution. As such, it has not become an instrument to nourish the process of modernization; rather, it is still an institution that reproduces and perpetuates a given social order. As in many other areas of life, the region must reconcile the needs of an emerging industrial power with those of a predominantly rural, uneducated, and poor population.

I should emphasize that the universities in the region are mostly new institutions created after 1945. That is to say, they are not the result of an indigenous elaboration, like universities in Europe. The history of the rise of the universities is one of the most exciting chapters in the annals of world civilization; this effort, however, was not replicated in Latin America and the Caribbean because the institutions were not born of these societies but rather were transferred there from the educational systems of the metropolitan powers.

So, to understand Latin American and Caribbean higher learning, a long and careful analysis of the historical process that has led to the development of those institutions, from the colonial Spanish times to the colonial present times, should be done. However, this is not the purpose of this chapter since I am attempting to make a more contemporary analysis. But it should be kept in mind that the higher education system we have now is the result of a historical process that has taken almost five centuries.

The Classification of Universities

Before doing a contemporary analysis of universities in the region, it is worth discussing a possible classification of Latin American and Caribbean universities. These universities are ordinarily classified by their raw size. The Universidad Autónoma de Mexico is one of the largest universities in the world in terms of population, with almost 400,000 students. Statistics in the region show a national pattern: the largest state university is located in the capital city of the country; fashionable small elite private institutions are located in the main provincial cities; most tertiary institutions are concentrated in and around the capital city.

If one wanted to classify universities in the region according to more technical criteria, it would be difficult to do so since statistics are not collected with technical purposes in mind. The 1987 Carnegie classification of universities, for instance, shows several categories that would be inadequate to use in the region I am discussing. The Carnegie classification refers to research universities, doctorate-granting institutions, and comprehensive universities. In Latin America and the Caribbean most universities would be in the weakest category of institutions, for the majority are no more than liberal arts colleges. The region lacks the fine European and American universities that are primary centers for scientific and technological innovation. Nonetheless, some institutions could be classified in the first category of the Carnegie classification, including the Universidad Nacional Autonóma de Mexico and the Universidade de São Paulo, two of the finest universities in Latin America and the Caribbean, granting at least fifty Ph.D. degrees each year.

In general, however, research, the main function of the university in the industrial world, is done only marginally in the region. Teaching is the main function of the university. In some cases, teaching is the only function, particularly in those small public and private universities opened only to train people for the professions but not to advance knowledge through research.

The university in the region is a place of employment for the faculty and staff or the way to obtain a professional degree for the student. Rarely is there a link in the region between day-to-day life and the institution. This situation helps to explain why sometimes the universities are closed down, either by the action of political regimes, or by strikes, or simply because of long holiday periods, without any real effect in the society at large. Daily life is dependent on products and services that are acquired through the international market of ideas or provided by international organizations. This is a key point in understanding the role of the university in Latin America and the Caribbean: the institution is very important in the region, but for the wrong reasons.

What we have in the region is a complex network of national systems of higher education, made up of parallel institutions, private and public, governmental and autonomous. These institutions do not compete but live independently from each other. As Graham puts it: "Most are virtual monopolies run by the ministry of education or a national grants committee, and their faculty members are civil servants."[2]

There is indeed a strong difference between universities in the region and those in industrial countries:

> In the United States an enormous number of quite similar institutions compete fiercely for students, faculty members, and prestige. Their distinctive personalities and reputations are derived not from being specialized by function or mission but from the internal leadership of each institution in the highly competitive pursuit of excellence. Indeed, the superiority of American higher education is due in large part to decentralized governance by lay boards that protect the institutions' freedom to compete with one another.[3]

Each national system of higher education in Latin America and the Caribbean is highly centralized and in the public sector also highly bureaucratized, with almost zero interuniversity mobility of members of the faculty or students. Since members of the faculty are not rewarded by performance but because of different levels of seniority, members of the faculty tend to stay all their academic lives in a given academic institution in a given country. If they do move to another institution, the move is a result of poor economic conditions or political problems, not because they are recruited on the basis of academic achievement.

What Allison and Scott Longe analyze, in their comments on interuniversity mobility of academic scientists in the United States, would not be applicable at all to Latin America and the Caribbean where research productivity does not affect prestige. In fact, many public universities, either controlled by political leaders, as in the autonomous universities, or by governmental bodies in what we call "governmental" universities, appoint members of the faculty by ascription criteria, be it political, group, or even personal interest. In many countries faculty members are paid independent of their performance. They maintain very powerful pressure groups to obtain their salaries and fringe benefits on a group basis and not on an individual basis, which takes away any possibility of recognizing personal merits.[4]

The lack of competition as a principle, both personal or institutional, eliminates the criteria of excellence. The leader of the powerful faculty union of the Universidad Central de Venezuela, later elected rector, recently said that the "Venezuelan universities are the only institutions in Latin America that have been able to maintain *acceptable* (my italics) academic conditions and that has been possible thanks to the teachers and the students who have stood to defend it. We guarantee that every time we are going to have a better university."[5]

"Acceptable" is not the best but a quality level that shows a middle-of-the-road expectation. To generalize, concepts of efficient performance, competition, and excellence are virtual strangers to the university in the region.

The institutional stratification of universities in the region is due not to factors related to quality in terms of the talents of individuals but to social selection and political interference. In some countries faculty members and students are chosen because of their wealth and social origins. Elite private universities in many countries only cater to the sons and daughters of the rich and do not accept any member of ethnic minorities. In politically centralized regimes, no members of the political opposition are accepted at the university; an ideological criteria is used to filter out candidates who do not adhere to acceptable political views. Very few universities are able to impose academic criteria in order to choose their members, whether faculty or students; intellectual selection is very much against the current in the region. Social selection is the accepted model although opposed in the official liberal political discourse.

The Cognitive Complex

In general terms it could be said that in Latin America and the Caribbean it has not been possible to build what Parsons and Platt mention as the "two principal features of the American university: (1) that it, and with it the institutionalized cognitive complex, has become a differentiated part of a complex society, and (2) that it has become upgraded in prestige and in-

fluence within the society to the point . . . as the central institution in the society."[6] Parsons and Platt use Weberian concepts to illustrate how in American culture there was a special affinity "between the ethic of Protestantism and a high valuation of economic productivity," contrary perhaps to an ethic in the Latin region that has given form to what could be described as a hedonistic set of values. According to Parsons and Platt, "The primary focus of the university is the cognitive complex, which is grounded in the cultual system and institutionalized in the structure of modern society. Higher education, in general, and the university in particular, represents institutionalized concerns with cognitive matters."[7]

In my view, neither higher education in general nor the university in particular is grounded in cognitive matters in Latin America and the Caribbean. Education at the advanced level has a cognitive importance in the region, of course, but according to my view the main focus of the university is the political and bureaucratic culture developed at the higher learning institutions in the region. In fact, it could be said that universities in the region are noncognitive institutions within a nonlearning society, although this does not mean that universities are not important. They just do not play the role common to a properly developed cognitive complex.

When I say a "nonlearning society" I mean that, generally, universities in the region are "higher learning" simply because of the enormous differences between the culture at the university and the general culture of the population. But because of its double bureaucratic and political role, the institution is not alien to the needs of society. The university in the region trains professionals for the needs of the ruling classes and for the needs of both the public and private bureaucracies. It also provides prestige and reputation from the social point of view. The university provides a necessary symbol of social status. In Latin America and the Caribbean almost any kind of postsecondary education is automatically recognized as a doctoral level of schooling. Actually, in many countries in the region university graduates are addressed as "doctor" as a matter of course.

After five hundred years, in spite of any historical justification, the fact is that the region does not have "scientific institutions (that) are the envy of the world."[8] The region lacked a concept of what was desirable for the development of society. People in the region have excelled in sports, arts, and literature, but not so much in science and technology. This is the main point I would like to make in this chapter: universities in Latin America and the Caribbean are institutions that exist within the national context in each country of the region but they do not contribute in a substantial way to the production and dissemination of knowledge, on a worldwide scale. The material and general well-being of the region's people still depends very little on what is done at the universities and higher learning centers throughout this part of the third world.

Universities in Latin America and the Caribbean are still essentially teaching institutions and they do not produce knowledge as a basic goal. "Knowledge is the type of cultural object with respect to which the cognitive-designative meaning of symbols and codes have primacy. Knowledge, though a product of action, is, as a cultural object-type, independent of any particular actor."[9] Knowledge, then, is a cultural object-type alien to the cultural development in the region, whose universalistic orientation moves away from the rationality of that search for knowledge. Teaching is, therefore, objectively accepted because it has an intrinsic goal: to train a person to occupy a place in the labor market or to legitimize one already obtained.

As I see it, the region has developed a "tendency," favored by the activist components of the value system, to emphasize "political concerns." Universities in the region have mainly political concerns and their preoccupation is with the utilization of cognitive resources more than the institutionalization of a cognitive complex. For this reason, the whole educational system in the region is oriented toward professional studies without the component of any kind of general or basic studies. Graduate studies have not been developed in the region except in a primary stage. The higher education system is almost strictly oriented toward training for the applied professions and not for the pursuit of knowledge either "for its own sake" or for "problem-solving." Graduate studies are not really part of the educational system of the region, since the whole process ends with the professional degree. It is not continued to the level at which the objective would be the search for knowledge.

Because there is not a cognitive complex through which education is rationally separated from the rest of society, taking to itself specific functions concerning the pursuit of knowledge, the university is linked to political power, both within and outside the university. Political strategies can assume different forms, from gentle persuasion and logical reasoning through bribery and intimidation to physical violence. I will offer a few examples that may give a clear idea of where the university stands in the region. To do so, I will use the concepts expressed by Kirkpatrick, when she provided an analytical scheme to study political systems as well as her criticism of the modernization of the region. She argues that "although the modernization paradigm has proved a sometimes useful as well as an influential tool in social science, it has become the object of searching critiques that have challenged one after another of its central assumptions."[10] The same could be said of the other very popular analytical tool to study the region, dependency theory, which says that institutions in dependent countries should always be seen more as international phenomena, that is to say, explained by reference outside the national system.[11]

I could also use the economic analogies of state-controlled societies vis-à-vis market-controlled societies. In this case I could use three examples: Cuba as an example of the state-controlled society, Chile as an example of a market-controlled society, and Venezuela as an intermediate case. Whatever way we choose, the idea is to try to demonstrate how in the region the politics of the government define the institutional role of the university.

Whatever the method of analysis, there is little empirical research on universities in the area. One can find some statistics but these are different in kind from research. So, to provide a general view of the university in Latin America and the Caribbean I will take the relationship between education and politics in specific countries in order to work out a kind of typology, because it would be quite difficult to discuss every country in the region. I may say, nevertheless, that when native authors do analyze the region, they seem to prefer the two extremes: either the macroanalysis of studies of modernization and dependency or the microlevel of country analysis.[12]

University Models

There are three university models in the region: the state-controlled university, the market model, and a combination of the two. Cuba is an example of the first, Chile an example of the second, and Venezuela an example of the third. Cuba is a unique case of the socialist university influenced by the Soviet model, the only example in Latin America and the Caribbean, though Nicaragua is following that pattern. No country in the region has been more willing to open itself to the forces of the market than Chile under Pinochet's regime. It must be said that in Chile the public sector of the university is also quite important. However, Venezuela represents the combined model, with both public and private interests having strong parallel university institutions, in a pluralistic society, from the political point of view. This model is also found in countries like Mexico, Colombia, Brazil, Argentina, and Peru, any of which could be taken as a unit of analysis.

The State-Controlled University: The Cuban Case

The Cuban Revolution in 1959 opened the opportunity for the Soviet Union to participate in Latin America and the Caribbean. In the education sphere, it meant an important addition to what was already a complex set of different educational models that were associated with different colonial powers. The Cuban university can be described as being under complete state control, without the traditional Latin American concept of autonomy. It follows the Soviet model.

The Cuban position on the development of their educational system is that it can be divided into two clear periods, before and after the Revolution. This argument can be read in a document prepared by Cuban experts for UNESCO in 1985. According to the document, prerevolutionary higher education, and university education in particular, was quite weak:

> Common features characterized the three state universities which, closed after the Gramma, began classes again shortly after the triumph of the Revolution in January 1, 1959. Enrollment hardly reached 15,000 students, humanities dominated other branches of science, and content, forms, and methods of teaching were traditional and obsolete. There was little and almost nonexistent scientific research work on the part of teachers and students.[13]

The same document written for UNESCO establishes that 25,295 students were enrolled at Cuban universities in the academic year 1959/60.[14] Valladares presents the argument that the educational system in Cuba before the revolution was in fact one of the best developed in the region; indeed, data from international organizations at the end of the 1950s show that higher education after the revolution did not start at zero point.[15] The opposite view, however, is taken not only by Cuban officials but also by authors like Carnoy and Werthein. In their book on Cuban educational reform they stated the following:

> In 1959 Cuba had many of the social and economic problems of the other Latin American countries of the same size and climate, and was not much different from other larger Latin American societies. In fact, in the second half of the decade of 1970, Cuba had not solved these problems. It is not a country with high incomes and a high style of life: it is a highly productive country where there is complete participation in the decisions at the factories, urban areas, and the nation. But in Cuba, differently from the Dominican Republic, Jamaica, Central America, and even Venezuela with its petroleum wealth, one has the feeling that all problems are going to be solved, that in ten years' time everybody will be well fed, children will attend secondary education, everybody will live in a decent house and will have complete medical attention.[16]

This is typical of the naive view about Cuba and its revolution, the idea that all problems will be solved. Carnoy and Werthein actually ended their book by saying that "The role of the Cuban educational reforms . . . will be . . . an important lesson for other countries." Suchlicki, more recently, has interpreted the present feeling about the Cuban situation: "Cuba as a model of economic development has lost its appeal for Latin Americans."[17] Actually, these days, at the beginning of the 1990s, only those with very extreme views or those who are ignorant about the evolution of the Cuban educational system would be able to share the view expressed in 1978 by people like Carnoy and Werthein. The ideals about the Cuban Revolution were based upon the aspiration to get away from foreign dependence. The fact is that in 1990 Cuba's foreign dependence is perhaps even higher than before. Cuba's dependence on the USSR has actually washed away many hopes not only about Cuba but about the whole idea of independence from foreign dependence and domination in the region.

The transfer of the Soviet educational model to Cuba has been completed, including ideological aspects and full dependence on Soviet knowledge. Of course, it is not a question of taking sides in the political situation in Cuba. What I am trying to do in this chapter is to show how this penetration of the Soviet educational model took place and the consequences for the university in Cuba. The university is totally under the political and ideological control of the state. The institution has lost its traditional capacity to negotiate a certain specific role. In less centralized societies, and even in countries where repressive political governments have strongly intervened in the university, like in Chile under Pinochet's regime, universities have more freedom. The university in the region is a political institution, often in conflict with both the government and within its own community. Jaksic has pointed out, for instance, that:

> Numerous events corroborate the view of the Latin American university as a highly politicized institution. The Cordoba reform in

1918, the students' role in the overthrow of dictatorships in the 1920s and 1930s, and the Tlatelolco tragedy of 1968 in Mexico, to mention only some of the major events of the twentieth century, all underscore what seems to be a pattern of political unrest in the region's institutions of higher learning. Particularly during the 1960s, vigorous scholarly attention brought this pattern to the status of a predominant view. The Latin American university is, by almost all accounts, largely political in nature.[18]

The university is a highly politicized institution in such a system as the present Cuban social structure where all institutions are part of a political project that leaves no room for independent institutions. In the rest of the region the relationship between the university and the government reveals different degrees of independence, according to the political system. But everywhere the institution has to deal openly in the political arena as a political institution.

Intellectual activity needs a cultural context to grow in. Education is not a technique only but a device to build a person. The most persistent ideal of Western civilization has been that man should be built for freedom, political participation, and the pursuit of truth in intellectual matters. In Latin America and the Caribbean, universities and whole educational systems are working toward cooperation and accommodation with political powers and not actually searching for truth and freedom. In the case of Cuba excessive party control severely limits the activity of Cuban universities. Cuban universities are so dependent on a single educational model that they are isolated from the main intellectual currents, particularly in social sciences. Political opposition is banned in Cuba and so the university cannot promote

the critical role it has to play, particularly in growing societies. Epstein has written about this problem: "The thought that scholarship may not be wholly invulnerable to ideology profoundly disturbs the academic world. Science is supposed to discover truth, it seeks to scrape the veneer of subjective judgment to achieve wisdom, insight, and understanding. Systematic methods are painstakingly devised to serve this goal. Entire tomes are devoted solely to advancing objectivity in procedure and to avoiding ideological deception. Such fear of ideology is well justified, for a science contaminated by partisan beliefs diminishes intellectual activity."[19]

In Cuba we have the example of an educational system entirely controlled by the state and ideologically part of a political complex where dissent and opposition are out of the question. Curriculum design, textbooks, mass media, access to education and its facilities, access to employment, not to mention access to travel, and the ability to keep some contacts with the outside world are all politically controlled activities, monitored by the party and the government. Free intellectual inquiry in Cuba is a diminishing activity, according to several reports and personal observations. Marxism-Leninism is the ideology against which every political activity in Cuba is measured and anything outside that ideological line would be considered as against the revolution.

Chile: The University within a Market Economy

The opposite takes place in Chile where we have the other side of the coin as far as rationalization of university life. That is, in Chile the official doctrine is simple: to "fight communism" and to extirpate the Marxist ideas that supposedly erupted during the years of Allende's government. The purpose and main goal of the educational system in Chile has been to get rid of any idea that could have the slightest possibility of being a Marxist idea, though this will change, of course, when a new elected government takes over in 1990.

"Chile has long been considered to have one of the most advanced educational systems in Latin America," says Farrell in his book about educational reform under Allende. It is in fact commonly believed throughout the region, by almost all interested parties, that the countries of the South Cone of South America—Argentina, Chile, and Uruguay—have developed much better educational systems than many of the countries in the rest of South America, Central America, and the Caribbean.

The development of the Chilean educational system can be divided into clear periods. In Chile there are three very clear recent periods in the evolution of the educational system. First, the years of the Frei government (1965–70); second, the very intense years of the Allende period (1970–73); and since 1973, the dictatorship of Pinochet.

What is fascinating about the Chilean case is that the struggle for the control of the educational system became a real political issue. The fall of Allende's regime was at least in part a consequence of the conflict between the traditional values of Chilean society and those of the socialist government. In other words, the conflict grew between the liberal point of view on education, which advocated educational pluralism, and the strong interest of the socialist government to have an educational system completely controlled by the state. Allende's regime was never able to gain control of the whole educational system. His government lost elections to choose university leaders, both at the level of the students and at the level of the authorities of the main public university in the country where the government candidate was defeated by the most potent political force among university people, the Christian Democrats.

When Allende's government was toppled by the army in Chile, they took immediate measures to "dismantle" Marxist ideologies within the university. Antiintellectualism is one of the key elements of military coups and Chile was not the exception in 1973. Within days after the coup the government moved to intervene in all public universities. All campuses were occupied by the army, authorities changed, autonomy was ruled out, and both faculty members and students had to leave the university, with many of them going abroad to avoid further political repression.

The new government acted against the university because "the university had been transformed into centers of dogmatism and Marxist propaganda often promoted by undesirable aliens who occupied lecture hall seats that belonged by right to young Chileans." Anyone suspected to have any relationship with Marxist ideas was expelled from the universities. A member of the junta that was ruling the country said that the universities could not be used in a way contrary to national interest but that the junta was going to respect the concept of autonomy, with the provision that "This does not mean that we can allow delinquents to continue their courses or, in our lecture rooms, train professionals to undermine the security of the nation."

It is a well known fact that the monetarist theories of certain conservative American scholars had a large impact in the design of Chilean society and its institutions after 1973. But in the realm of education the influence of the American model was still clearer, as the government tried to create an institution, the university, linked to the market like any other unit of the economy of the country. All the principles of what I call the market university were implemented in Chile under Pinochet: charging fees to students even in public institutions, diversifying the whole higher educational system by creating several alternatives to the universities, opening the field for new private institutions. These objectives, however, have to be linked in Chile to the political ideology of repression, of anti-Marxism as an ideological paradigm. This situation works against knowledge, though it can also be said that due to the nature of the political regime in Chile there have been certain opportunities for intellectual dissent and discussion through academic alternatives financed by international sources. In other words, there is room for some political opposition in Chile, but on the whole an authoritarian culture suppresses free intellectual activity, particularly at the universities. Brunner has done a detailed analysis of this question. According to him, the authoritarian design of the Pinochet regime in Chile was a global political project articulated through three axis: (1) privatization of the educational system; (2) adaptation of the educational development of the market economy; and (3) forcing of the educational and cultural system to become a part of a disciplinarian and authoritarian society.[20]

The University between the State and the Market: The Venezuelan Case

Venezuela is an intermediate example of many things happening in the region. It is one of the very few stable democracies on the continent. It is a showcase of dependent capitalism in action. It has one of the most diversified higher educational systems, one copied from the American model. Political dissent is quite open and autonomy has been preserved through a complex set of political negotiations. Private interests have grown rapidly in the last two decades, in spite of the fact that there are a limited number of people able to pay for their university studies, due to the unequal income distribution in the country. The size of the private sector at the university level is small, but growing in importance. Within the complex map of the Venezuelan universities we find, in the private sector, the best and the worst in terms of educational quality.

The Venezuelan universities are typical of the region in many respects. From the early 1950s to the present an enormous expansion has taken place. Tertiary institutions have gone from almost nonexistence through an intense diversification process, that now encompasses all types and sizes of institutions. There are traditional Hispanic-model universities, institutions under the influence of the American model of education, and open commercial universities about which it is said that it is more difficult to park a car nearby than to obtain a degree. There are several types of universities: (1) large public autonomous universities, which cater to more than half of the university population of the country, (2) institutions created after 1970, which are controlled by the government, (3) private universities, where the members of the elite are trained, and (4) private mass institutions that do not care about their academic standards but offer access to university degrees to people of low social origins. In terms of their knowledge stock, they are almost all teaching institutions. Scientific research is conducted almost exclusively at large state autonomous institutions. Graduate studies are still in their infancy; the main university in the country, with some 60,000 students, only granted eleven doctoral degrees in 1986.

Between 1950 and 1989 the university system expanded so much that today the society has financial problems keeping all of them going—though the political cost of trying to stop their growth would be too risky to any government, at least concerning the public sector. The private sector is expanding beyond reason and logic. In Venezuela a very complex political negotiation is taking place through which public control is co-opted by private interest. This is indeed a quite interesting phenomenon. The private sector has responded to demand for places in universities by creating new institutions that lack even the elementary ingredients of a higher education institution. They are usually controlled by private entrepreneurs linked to former civil servants from the public educational area; in this way they manage to obtain the necessary influence to be approved by the institutional bodies that control the growth and expansion of higher education.

In terms of Archer's analysis one could say that Venezuelan universities took off but that they expanded without coming to the point of real educational growth. What has taken place in Venezuela is a shift from public control of the universities to a private ideology and control. Public funding became too diversified in Venezuela because of the expansion of all types of universities. Now the state is virtually unable to support such a large number of institutions. Even private universities are partially under state subsidies. However, through political manipulation, a negotiation process has taken place in Venezuela, and university expansion has been rationalized under the democratic principles of the regime.[21]

There are private institutions both for elite and mass demands. Even the new experimental universities, controlled by the government, follow this social class distribution of their population.

Venezuelan universities are very politicized. Through the institution of *gremialismo* University faculty have become a powerful pressure group.[22] *Gremialismo* means that all people teaching or doing research at Venezuelan universities are paid the same and given the same fringe benefits, through political negotiations between the faculty organization and the government. The faculty members define their own working conditions, fix detailed norms concerning the number of hours to teach per week, the number of free days every year, and the different fringe benefits to be paid to all members of the faculty, including full pay when they retire, a benefit that is paid to the children of those

faculty members who die until their last child becomes twenty-one years old. *Gremialismo* is maintained through faculty strikes to press the government. It does not have a place in the private universities because these institutions work under a different pattern, hiring their faculty members on a nonpermanent basis. In Venezuelan universities *gremialismo* protects the academic career of each member; each faculty member has a given rank and is paid according to that rank regardless of performance.

Meritocracy has no place in Venezuelan universities. Knowledge is not the main search of the institution. Power is the main activity of this highly politicized institution. The authorities in the autonomous universities are appointed through elections and their positions are hotly disputed. In governmental universities the Ministry of Education makes appointments and the academic merits of the person are not relevant at all—only political affiliation counts. In private universities authorities are appointed mainly to guarantee ideological continuity. In the propietary universities families and political cronies control the institutional government without any outside interference.

The social expectations of Venezuelans are very high concerning universities. They like the state to provide for educational need by keeping university education free. They would like not only free education but free meals, free sport facilities, free health care, free travel, and so on and so forth. People who pay quite high school fees for private primary and private secondary education would be incensed if they were asked to pay for public universities. They do pay, however, at local private universities or when they send their children to American colleges and universities. Providing free university education is considered to be part of the democratic duties of the state.

As I have already said, we cannot generalize about universities in Latin America and the Caribbean. We have already come across three types of universities, trying to relate them in three countries to their political environment and see them mainly as political institutions. But none of the three big countries in the region, Mexico, Argentina, and Brazil, has been analyzed. The three big countries in the region fit into the three types of universities already discussed in this chapter. Argentina has been a society fractured by internal political problems. After President Alfonsin came to power he had to respond to a social demand for university places long repressed by the army government that had been in power in that country. By opening the doors of Argentinian universities he created a further deterioration of their academic standards.[23] Brazil is another case of both state and private interest sharing the same goals. Brazil is a relative newcomer to the university scene in the region, but is one country with the capacity to create the cognitive complex I have spoken about. Brazil has perhaps the finest universities in the region.[24] And Mexico also fits the pluralistic model found in Venezuela. Both the state and the market play substantial roles in university life. Mexico shares a border with the United States; that means an enormous influence by American education. After Puerto Rico, Mexico is the country with the most visible debt to American ideas on education.[25]

According to the *International Handbook of Universities* (Paris: International Association of Universities, 18th ed., 1990), there are approximately five hundred universities in Latin America and the Caribbean, with a rate of growth of 5 percent each year. Brazil has seventy-six universities, Mexico forty-one, Argentina twenty-nine, Peru twenty-four, Venezuela twenty-four, and Chile twenty-one. In each case and in each country what is a university depends on subjective criteria. If we were to use international criteria for definition, very few universities in the region would be considered full universities because very few of them are research institutions. Most would be no more than comprehensive universities and colleges or liberal arts institutions, to use the American standard for types of institutions of higher learning. In most countries there exists an enormous difference between the universities located in the capital city of the country and those in the provinces. Most universities in the region are quite poor quality institutions. Some cannot go beyond a very low level of teaching. The average institution is located in a provincial city, is middle-sized, conducts no research, has a very poor library and poor laboratory facilities, and has a faculty ill-trained to stimulate learning beyond those concepts appropriate to obtain a professional degree. Many people who have studied the university in the region are appalled to see how rapidly Latin America and the Caribbean are slipping behind other regions in terms of the quality of tertiary education offered.

Conclusion: Unequal Development at the University Level

The university map in Latin America and the Caribbean is consistent with what is known as unequal development. On the average, the university in the region is only a professional school with teaching as the main and perhaps its sole objective. But some universities are coming along in terms of the modernization process. These institutions are opening up new academic programs, are trying to do research, and are cooperating with local and international industry. But the main thing one can observe in the region is the extreme between fine universities and poor institutions scattered through the continent, and how the complexity of the region makes it difficult to generalize about the university in such a large geographical and historical area.

Vargas Llosa, the well-known Peruvian writer and politician, said that the "Latin American state and public universities have put aside any academic interest to become institutions full of fanaticism that only promote hate and violence." This is a typical generalization that does not do justice to the fact that among the several hundred universities in the region many are struggling to become institutions able to promote knowledge and in fact to become modern institutions.

One aspect of this tendency toward academic innovation is the private university, which is a recent development in the region. Some of these are taking steps to become the modern university demanded by growing local and international industry. Unhappily the best private institutions recruit students only among the members of the elite. They are closed institutions, closed both in terms of access and in terms of their academic goals. This privatization process has been carefully studied in the region by Levy, who says that "The scope of documented change brought by privatization is such that once valid ways of thinking about Latin American higher education no longer suffice."[26]

There are excellent individual scholars and fine institutions of higher education in the region, but, unfortunately, they exist in an intellectual environment of mediocrity. This intellectual mediocrity helps to explain the limited role of the university in the development of the region.

Notes

1. Abdelkader Sid Ahmed, *The Arab World by the Year 2000*, Synopsis of the Studies and Work of the Tunis Workshop (Paris: UNESCO, 1988).
2. Hugh D. Graham, "We Don't Need Superboards," *Chronicle of Higher Education*, 4 November 1987.
3. Graham, "We Don't Need Superboards."
4. Paul D. Allison and Scott Long, "Mobility of Scientists," *American Sociological Review* (October 1987): 643–52.
5. In fact the Venezuelan case is rather interesting. The faculty union has taken over the leadership at Venezuelan universities, so much so that the leader of the faculty union at the main autonomous university managed to have himself elected as rector. The point to be made here, however, is how in Venezuela, at least, there is a working rule for the faculty: avoid accepting personal and individual responsibility and behave only according to the rules of the faculty union.
6. Talcott Parsons and Gerald M. Platt, *The American University* (Cambridge: Harvard University Press, 1973), especially chapter 3, "The Core Sector of the University: Graduate Training and Research," 103–62.
7. Parsons and Platt, *The American University*, 33.
8. "America's Scientific Institutions Are the Envy of the World," *Time*, 16 June 1986.
9. Parsons and Platt, *The American University*, 33.
10. Jeane Kirkpatrick, *Dictatorship and Double Standards: Rationalism and Reasons in Politics* (New York: Simon & Schuster, 1982), 73.
11. One of the best analyses of the situation in the region from the theoretical framework of dependency is by Peter Evans, *Dependent Development* (Princeton: Princeton University Press, 1979). The foreword by the Brazilian sociologist Florestan Fernandez is also well worth reading. For a critical view of this theory, see Harold J. Noah and Max A. Eckstein, "Dependency Theory in Comparative Education: Twelve Lessons from the Literature," in *Theories and Methods in Comparative Education*, edited by Jurgen Schriever and Brian Holmes, 165–96. (Frankfurt am Main, West Germany: Peter Lang, 1988).
12. A recent example of this type of national analysis is the book edited by Fernando Calderón Gutierrez, *Latinoamerica: Lo político y lo social en la crisis* (Buenos Aires: Consejo Latinoamericano de Ciencias Sociales, 1987).
13. *La educación superior en Cuba* (Caracas, Venezuela: UNESCO-CRESALC, 1985).
14. Armando Valladares, "La Educación en Cuba," *Diario de Caracas*, 17 March 1986.
15. *United Nations Statistics*, 1960–1962.
16. Martin Carnoy and Jorge Werthein, *Cuba, Cambio Económico y Reforma Educativa: 1955–1978* (Mexico: Editorial Nueva Imágen, 1980), 133.
17. Jaime Suchlicki, "Soviet Policy in Latin America: Some Implications for the United States," *Journal of Interamerican Studies and World Affairs* 29, no. 1 (Spring 1987).
18. Ivan Jaksic, "The Politics of Higher Education in Latin America," *Latin American Research Review* 20, no. 1 (1985): 209–21.
19. Erwin H. Epstein, "Current Left and Right: Ideology in Comparative Education," *Comparative Education Review* 27, no. 1 (1983): 3.

20. José Joaquín Brunner, *La cultura autoritaria en Chile* (Santiago, Chile: Facultad Latino-americana de Ciencias Sociales, 1981). See also his *Informe sobre la educación superior en Chile* (Santiago, Chile: Facultad Latinoamericana de Ciencias Sociales, 1986).

21. Margaret Archer, *The Sociology of Educational Expansion: Take-off, Growth, and Inflation in Educational Systems* (Beverly Hills, Calif.: Sage Studies in International Sociology, 1982), particularly her "Introduction: Theorizing About the Expansion of the Educational System." In the same book also see David P. Ericson, "The Possibility of a General Theory of Educational System."

22. On this topic, see my analysis of Venezuelan student political activism, in Philip G. Altbach, ed., *Student Political Activism: An International Reference Handbook* (New York: Greenwood Press, 1989).

23. For Argentinian universities, see Augusto Perez Lindo, *La educación superior en Argentina* (Caracas, Venezuela: UNESCO-CRESALC, 1985), *Universidad, politica y sociedad* (Buenos Aires: EDUDEBA, 1985), and paper, "La universidad sin futuro y el futuro de la juventud," in *Proyecto*, no. 3–4, Buenos Aires, 1987.

24. There is widespread acceptance in the region that the universities in the area of São Paulo, both the University of Campinas and University of São Paulo, are among the best on the continent, which should be no surprise at all since that area is one of the richest in the region. Brazil also has the best graduate studies already organized and the best nonuniversity research centers in the region. Finally, there is an effort in that country to link the university with the production sector. Books on education and universities in Brazil are quite extensive. The UNESCO-CRESALC monograph on Brazil, *La educación superior en Brasil* (1985) offers some good information. From the historical point of view the best source is Luiz Antonio Cunha's three-volume book on the development of Brazilian higher education: *A Universidade Tempora* (Rio de Janeiro: Francisco Alves, 1980); *A Universidade Critica* (Idem, 1982); and *A Universidade Reformanda* (Idem, 1988). For a critical view, see Dermeval Saviani, *Ensino publico e algunas falas sobre universidade* (São Paulo: Cortez Editora, 1984).

25. The literature on the Mexican university is very large. *La educación superior en Mexico* (UNESCO-CRESALC, 1986) is good and provides an excellent bibliography. Mexico is quite an interesting country from the university point of view with the whole spectrum of institutions and political and ideological ideas. I have the impression that the Mexicans are at a disadvantage vis-à-vis the Brazilians in their efforts to improve their universities. Mexico is an old established democracy while Brazil is just emerging from twenty years of military government. But, somehow, the Brazilian universities have been able to develop an institutional project of their own, while Mexican universities are still attached to the old traditional Latin American model. Private universities are expanding but with the same conservative outlook that seems to be typical of private interests when they look more to their own interests than to the national interest. The Universidad Nacional Autónoma de Mexico is one of the largest universities in the world in terms of population, but the authorities have been unable to put forward plans to modernize it. In a personal interview in August 1987, Rector Carpizo mentioned the fact that if UNAM could be modernized it would have a positive effect on the whole educational system in Mexico and that otherwise Mexico would not be a competitive factor in the world economy in the next century. Still, there is no doubt that today Brazil and Mexico have the most advanced universities in Latin America and the Caribbean.

26. Daniel Levy, *Higher Education and the State in Latin America* (Chicago: University of Chicago Press, 1986).

◆

Argentina

Carlos Alberto Torres

◆

Politics, Education, and Society

Argentina is the second largest country in Latin America, with an area of 2,781,000 sq. km. (1,073,700 sq. mi) and a population close to thirty million. Its annual rate of population growth is low, only 1.3 percent, with a decreasing rate in the rural areas of –0.9 percent and an increasing rate in the urban areas of 1.8 percent, the second lowest rate after Uruguay. The rate of population growth for the entire region in 1980 was 2.7 percent, with 3.8 percent growth for the urban population and 0.9 percent growth for the rural population. Rich in natural resources, including oil, Argentina is well developed industrially. Its principal exports, however, are still beef and wheat.

The population is predominantly of European origin; less than 170,000 people are of indigenous descent. In 1970 73 percent of the population resided in towns and cities with two thousand inhabitants or more. By 1980 82.7 percent of the population resided in urban settings, compared with 64.4 percent for the rest of Latin America. The Argentinean labor force is employed primarily in the secondary and tertiary sectors of the economy.

During the second half of the last century and the first quarter of this one, Argentina was an attractive land for immigrants and foreign capital. Between 1857 and 1914 it welcomed 3,300,000 immigrants, mostly from Europe. The total foreign capital in the country at that time reached almost ten million dollars (1960=100), representing 8.5 percent of the total amount of foreign investment in the world, 33 percent of the total amount of foreign investment in Latin America, and 42 percent of the total investment of the United Kingdom in the region.[1]

Argentina has experienced considerable political instability that has led at times to an almost complete breakdown of its democratic tradition. On average, the country has had one president every thirty months. It has had twenty-nine presidents in seventy-three years; according to the constitution, there should only have been twelve presidents in that period, or fifteen at the most, allowing for resignations and deaths. Similarly, the powerful minister of finance and economy, who is in command of the process of economic development, has been changed sixty-one times in the same period; such turnover drastically undermines any attempt to plan stable economic growth and development. Military coups are common features of Argentinean politics. The short period during which a president usually remains in power affects the formulation of public policies—including education. Only four presidents have completed their terms since 1916,[2] and in the last two decades military regimes have controlled the government twice, 1966–73 and 1976–83. The latter, by far the most repressive regime ever installed in the country, changed the head of the executive branch four times, removed several cabinet members, and made drastic shifts in its policy decisions. A case in point is the surprising decision to invade the Malvinas (Falkland) Islands that led to the war with Great Britain in 1982 and to the subsequent military defeat.

Educational System: Historical Background

Argentina has a federal system of education, with significant financial participation also from the provinces and municipalities. A considerable portion of primary and secondary education for the middle and upper classes is under private control (mainly church or church-related organizations). However, the educational system is highly centralized, with many decisions made by the central government. Teachers are mainly trained in the teacher colleges, which follow the "école normale" model; a key element in teacher training is the liberal ideology of compulsory, free, nonreligious, public education advocated for over a century. There are five main teachers' unions, who continuously bargain (and strike) over salaries and labor conditions. In spite of government shifts and instability, an important share of Argentina's national budget has always been allocated to education.

The ruling groups in Argentina have historically assigned education primarily a political rather than an economic function. The economic growth that occurred in the second half of the nineteenth century did not call for large-scale training of human resources, so the structure of the educational system only changed in those aspects suiting the political interest of the ruling alliance. In short, the development of the educational system can be seen as a function of the political desires of Argentina's conservative elite, who, because of Argentina's export-oriented economy, felt no need to develop highly trained human resources.[3]

Argentina, like Uruguay, Costa Rica, and Chile, was a Latin American country that became part of the world market as an exporter of raw materials and an importer of manufactured goods. These countries developed a social and juridical organization that called for the cultural integration of the masses. Their educational systems were conceived as systems of socially restricted distribution of knowledge that would prevent the majority of the population from obtaining access to more than a minimum of basic instruction. Mass compulsory schooling at the primary level would guarantee the cultural homogeneity of societies that were receiving at that time large stocks of immigrants from Europe. But only the elites in these societies would have access to the upper levels of the educational system (e.g., secondary and higher education). In other words, primary education was designed to be inclusive, while secondary and tertiary education was designed to be exclusive.

The educational system in Argentina was organized in the nineteenth century without linkages to the most production-oriented sectors in the country. No matter which ruling alliance was in control of the government, the educational system was divorced from industry and the demands of the labor market. From 1880 onwards, immigrants with diverse levels of training and qualifications supplied the country's labor needs for manufacturing.

A good example of the way the system worked was the orientation given to the secondary schools in the provinces.[4] The *colegios nacionales* (national colleges) were created as the conduit for access to the universities. They were not created to expand scientific knowledge or to develop a body of scientists or technicians for the country. On the contrary, their explicit purpose was to create and sustain a ruling elite, an elite that would have a homogeneous view, identified with the objectives of the politically dominant groups, and would be able to overcome the peculiarities and the cultural and political fragmentation of parochial life in the provinces. In 1884 National Law 1420 established free and compulsory schooling for children between the ages of six and twelve. This law, although explicitly directed at the primary schools of the Federal District and the National Territories, was in fact highly influential in the provinces, and it was quickly adopted by the provincial legislatures. Thereafter, in accordance with the federal political organization of the country under which the provinces have political autonomy, four types of schools came into being: national, provincial, municipal, and private. All were subject to regulation from either national or provincial laws. By 1890, however, it was evident that the provinces by themselves would not be able to handle the cost of financing public education. Thus, National Law 2737 provided a subsidy to the provincial schools. This law was insufficient, so in 1905 the so-called Láinez Law (National Law 4874) created the National Council of Education with the purpose of promoting the establishment of national schools in the provinces. This brought about a notable imbalance in the development of the school system: by 1965 16,200 schools were in operation in the provinces, of which 6,700 were national schools.[5]

Despite these imbalances and shortcomings, advances in Argentinean public primary education after 1853 were astonishing. The illiteracy rate fell from 80 percent to less than 35 percent by 1947, in spite of the fact that the population had doubled three times between 1869 and 1947.[6] By 1970 the illiteracy rate had fallen to 7.1 percent, one of the lowest in the region. However, due to the policies followed by the military dictatorship that ruled Argentina between 1976 and 1983, the new democratic government has had to launch a national, massive literacy campaign to return to the previous standards in literacy.[7]

Higher Education: Historical Trends and Legal Foundations

The Universidad Mayor de San Carlos was founded in Córdoba in 1613. This was the beginning of the colonial university era in Argentina. This university was organized into two main faculties: arts and theology. Three principal degrees were conferred: bachelor, licenciate, and master. In addition to these three, a Ph.D. degree in theology was also offered. The colonial university in Argentina was modeled on the University of Salamanca in Spain.

The university structure in Argentina by the mid-1850s was designed to follow the post-Napoleonic model, thus differing in its objectives and content from the colonial university. When Napoleon created the modern French university by decree in May 1806, the university became the highest level of the educational system. Its goals were to train teachers for public education, and professionals to serve the government bureaucracy and society. After Napoleon, the French university became a powerful instrument at the service of the state, especially in charge of training the higher cadres for the public sector. This model has predominated in Argentina throughout modern history. However, some aspects of the colonial university still remain, such as the qualifying examination to appoint professors, their participation in the designation of university authorities, the elaboration of a university constitution by the academic community—subject to the approval of the government, and the organization of the university by faculties instead of departments.[8]

The University of Buenos Aires, the largest and most prestigious tertiary institution in Argentina today, was created in 1816 with three faculties: preparatory studies, law and jurisprudence, and medicine. In 1870 a faculty for mathematical sciences, physics, and nature was created. By 1910, the university had 1,100 law students, 2,500 medical students, 600 engineering and architecture students, 250 students of philosophy and humanities, and 200 students of agronomy and veterinary science.[9] Today, it has grown to thirteen faculties, with an academic staff of 18,098 members, that currently enrolls

175,216 students (See Table 1).

Between 1900 and 1960 the Argentinean universities conferred a total of 150,000 university degrees in programs requiring four or more years of study. Half of these degrees were conferred by the University of Buenos Aires. The distribution by careers was as follows: 32,500 medical doctors, 21,100 lawyers, 17,700 engineers, 11,800 dentists, 11,700 pharmacists, 9,700 public accountants, and the rest other disciplines and careers.[10]

There are twenty-six national (public) universities in Argentina, one provincial university (the Universidad de la Rioja, created on June 2, 1972), two universities linked to the armed forces and police, including the Superior Academy of Police Studies (created December 26, 1977), and the School of Aeronautic Engineering (created August 19, 1971), and twenty-three private universities, a total of fifty-two universities.

Avellaneda's Law of 1885—namely after the senator and former president who proposed it—proclaimed that the state was in charge of financing education and overseeing its performance. Only national (public) universities were able to confer professional degrees. The provincial and private academic centers conferred degrees that did not grant credentials for the exercise of a profession. A turning point in university affairs occurred with the promulgation of National Law 14557 in 1958. This law authorized the creation of private universities and endowed them with the capacity to issue titles and degrees that, af-

Table 1

University of Buenos Aires: Students and Staff (1988)

Faculty	Students	Professors*	Total Academic Staff**	1/2	1/3
Agronomy	2,649	156	775	17	3.4
Architecture	12,089	575	1,831	21	6.6
Economics	24,003	890	1,368	27	17.5
Exact Sciences	6,636	370	1,556	18	4.3
Social Sciences	5,382	320	676	17	8
Veterinary Sciences	2,854	71	545	40	5
Law	23,185	1,329	1,572	17	14.7
Pharmacy and Biochemistry	5,436	100	706	54	7.7
Philosophy and Literature	7,543	425	1,108	17.7	6.8
Engineering	10,130	467	1,842	21.7	5.5
Medicine	20,344	327	1,366	62.2	14.9
Dentistry	2,959	143	766	20.7	3.9
Psychology	10,142	142	841	71.4	12
Common Basic Level (1st-year students)	41,864	396	3,146	105.7	13.3
Total	175,216	5,711	18,098	30.7	9.7

* Includes all Full Professors (*Titular*), Associate Professors, and Adjunct Professors (*Adjunto*).

** Includes all of the above and Head of Practical Studies (*Jefe de Trabajos Prácticos*), Teaching Assistant Category No. 1, and Teaching Assistant Category No. 2.

Source: Censo de Rematriculación General de Alumnos, 1988, Cifras provisorias. Dirección General de Planificación Educacional en base a planta de cargos, Marzo de 1988. Servicio de Procesamiento de información administrativa, Universidad Nacional de Buenos Aires, mimeographed.

ter a professional examination at a designated national agency, would qualify the candidates for professional status. After 1958 twenty-three private universities were created, nine of them in the Federal District, four in the Province of Buenos Aires, and the rest in the provinces of Córdoba, Mendoza, San Juan, Santa Fe, Santiago del Estero, Tucumán, Entre Rios, and Salta. Almost half of the private universities are controlled by the Catholic church; as of 1974 they were serving 14.28 percent (54,127 students) of the total number of university students in the country. A decade later, in 1986, enrollment in the twenty-three private universities had reached 71,824 students (10.1 percent of the total enrollment). Private universities employ 33.5 percent (14,023) of the total academic staff in the country.

The University Reform Movement of 1918 greatly influenced the university atmosphere throughout Latin America. Starting in Córdoba City on March 13, 1918, as a violent strike of university students, the reform movement had a number of specific goals: the implementation of a new system of teacher appointments and their terms on the job; modernization of teaching methods; participation of students and alumni in university government; creation of endowed chairs for invited professors; exemption of students from the obligation to attend theoretical classes; and the opening up of examination dates. The reform movement quickly spread beyond the university environment. Starting as a way of democratizing the university, it soon made a significant contribution to the political and socioeconomic democratization of a society still dominated by conservative, oligarchical parties. The reform movement was an expression of the new-born middle class of Argentinean society. Its new program tried to modernize the university, a fief of oligarchical and conservative forces.

A setback for the gains made during the University Reform Movement was the passing of National Law 13031 by the Peronist government on October 9, 1947, later complemented by Law 14297, passed on January 11, 1954. These laws practically proscribed the participation of scholars and university students in politics and annihilated university autonomy through a tight political control by the executive power. The government that overthrew Perón in 1955 abolished the Peronist-sponsored laws and reinstated the Avellaneda Law of 1885. Several decrees were promulgated in 1955, 1956, and 1957 to update the legal corpus of Avellaneda's law, and in 1958 all these legal conditions were consolidated in National Law 14507. Through these laws some of the main prescriptions of the reform of 1918 came into being, and national universities obtained their autonomy.

In 1966 the military dictatorship that overthrew the government of Dr. Illía, of the Radical party, cancelled university autonomy with Law 16912 of July 29. This law suspended all preceding legislation and a new university was promulgated on April 21, 1967. This law restricted many of the reforms advocated by the reformist movement of 1918, and the overall university establishment was repressed, with thousands of academics quitting their jobs, and many of them emigrating to other countries.

In 1973 the newly elected democratic government, under Peronist leadership, created new legislation with National Law 20654, which did not grant autonomy to the universities. On March 24, 1976, the military dictatorship that overthrew the civilian Peronist government abolished the preceding legislation and created its own university law 21276 of April 1, 1976. In fact this law partially modified National Law 20654 but it did not abrogate laws 17604 and 17778 that established norms for the private and provincial universities, respectively.[11] National Law 21260 was used to discharge all scholars and university workers or employees suspected of any connection with "subversive activities."[12] A great number of professors as well as public servants were dismissed; many were killed, kidnapped, or exiled.[13]

In summary, since 1884 there have been thirteen laws or decrees concerning the university. And since the Peronist government of 1947 almost every government has promulgated its own university law abolishing, totally or partially, the preceding ones. At the time of writing this article, seven drafts of a new law for higher education are under consideration in the National Congress.

In 1989 the Argentinean universities offered 312 course programs. Their distribution is as follows: architecture, six; agronomic sciences and basic and technological sciences, thirty; engineering sciences, seventy-five; exact and natural sciences, thirty; biochemistry, pharmacy, and chemistry sciences, fourteen; defense-related, seven; social science, including administration, organization, and economic sciences, forty; social science, including law, political science, and diplomacy, sixteen; other social sciences (i.e., social work, sociology, etc.), sixteen; humanities, philosophy, and letters, three; science of education and psychology, twelve; other human sciences (i.e., foreign languages, theology, history, etc.), fifteen; arts, music, and crafts, sixteen; health sciences, thirty-two.

Higher education comprises university education and nonuniversity education. The latter includes teacher education, artistic education, and other minor disciplines. The length of these courses of study is between one and four years, while the length of university undergraduate programs is between four (but more commonly five) to six or more years. By 1986 there were 1,457 establishments providing higher education in Argentina: 479 are university establishments and 978 are nonuniversity. Table 2 shows the evolution of this nonuniversity modality within higher education in Argentina.

The academic year usually starts in mid-March and ends by early December. Some universities use the quarter or semester system. There has been an accelerated process of decentralization of universities. Between 1971 and 1975 sixteen new national universities were created. By 1986 there were fifty-two national, provincial, and private universities in the country.

Higher Education and the Political System

Five main periods of university development can be singled out of the recent past. The years between 1958 and 1966 constituted a period of full university autonomy, with a flourishing university environment and a consolidation of teaching and research at high levels. The years between 1966 and 1973 constituted a period of government intervention in the university and the loss of university autonomy. In addi-

---

Table 2

Higher Education: Student Enrollment at the University and Nonuniversity Levels (selected years)

Year	Total	University	Nonuniversity level
1970	293,302 (100%)	86.4%	13.6%
1976	600,768	88.6%	11.4%
1981	525,688	76.5%	23.5%
1986	902,882	78.3%	21.7%

Source: Ministerio de Educación, Secretaría de Justicia, Centro Nacional de Información. *Estadísticas de la Educación: Establecimientos, Alumnos, Docentes (por Jurisdicción),* several years.

tion, there was an expansion of national universities in the provinces (but with an important centralization of decisions) and of a government policy to promote professional studies. Between 1973 and 1975 the university became, as never before, an arena of struggle for political projects, struggle characterized by political violence with a disastrous effect upon university practices and structures. After 1975, the Argentinean university suffered one of its most dismal periods, with strict limitations on student enrollment and ideological control and repression of scholars, students, administrative staff, and university workers.[14]

With the government of the Radical party in 1983 a new democratic period began. This period has been characterized as the passage from the democraticization of the university to its full autonomy.[15] By means of Presidential Decree 154/83 the government of the Radical party declared its purpose of normalizing academic life. Law 23068 of June 1984 established a period of one year for the total normalization of the universities and the reestablishment of university autonomy following the principles of the 1918 University Reform. The main principles of this change were: (1) limited renewal of the academic staff with appointments made by the higher council after competitive examination based upon credentials before a search committee. Only those professors appointed after this competition can enjoy professional security, and academic tenure can only be lost after an academic trial;[16] (2) full university autonomy, with the highest single administrative authority vested in the president of the university (rector) who has to be elected, and with the Superior Council, composed of elected professors, students, graduate students, and some professional officers of the university, as the highest administrative body; (3) open policy with no restriction to students' admissions[17]; (4) a pedagogical reform creating a common basic level (for

first-year students). The purpose of this first common year was to create a common system of training with diverse options to allow students to gather better information about the diverse disciplines, careers, and options, and to be able to switch careers easily after the first year.

University enrollment grew consistently between 1958 and 1981, tripling from 138,000 to 402,900 students. In 1981 324,458 students were enrolled in national universities, 823 in provincial universities, and 77,612 in private universities. Student enrollment slowed down during the military regime but increased to unprecedented levels after 1984. By 1986 higher education institutions had 902,882 students enrolled, 78.3 percent in universities (707,016) and 195,866 in nonuniversity postsecondary education. This is more than double the 1981 figure. Enrollment in public universities (national and provincial) accounts for 89.85 percent of the total enrollment.

The restrictions on university enrollment during the military dictatorship pushed a substantial number of secondary graduates to postsecondary but not university studies. Teacher education represented 83.3 percent of student enrollment in nonuniversity higher education. The participation of private education at this level is growing. In 1970 it enrolled only 14,000 students; in 1981, 46,000 students; and in 1986 61,281 students (31.2 percent of the total enrollment in nonuniversity higher education in the country).

Higher Education, Students' Social Background, and Employment

Although higher education in public institutions is entirely subsidized by the state and there are no students' costs beside supplies, transportation, and living expenses, the lower classes are not widely represented in the student body. Higher education is a preserve of the middle and upper classes—although the concept of the middle class in Argentina embodies professionals, some self-employed people, several categories of white-collar workers, and middle-level entrepreneurs and farmers. A study of the social background of university students in three major universities (University of LaPlata, University of Buenos Aires, and University of del Sur) conducted in 1960 by a government institution found that 82 percent, 87 percent, and 89 percent of students enrolled in the three universities, respectively, were middle- and upper-class students.[18] A more recent survey taken in the mid-1970s that looked at the occupation of the fathers of university students reported that less than 20 percent were blue-collar or lower-level white-collar workers.[19]

Accurate information and empirical research on the relationship between education, work, and employment in Argentina is scarce,[20] and all the more so for higher education graduates. By 1980 approximately 5 percent of the economically active population (i.e., ten million) had completed a diploma in higher education. According to Pérez Lindo three occupational strata (i.e., professionals, managers of enterprises and higher officials in the public administration, and teachers-educators) accounted for almost everyone at the higher education level.[21] There were 281,187 professionals (2.8 percent) of the economically active population), 67,114 entrepreneurs and high functionaries in the

Table 3

University Students: Faculty and Type of University
(Public and Private)

Year	Total	Medical Sciences	Physical Sciences and Engineering	Social Sciences	Humanities
1973	377,773	52,914	140,643	131,440	52,776
1974	487,661	104,813	142,317	174,710	72,821
1975	536,956	85,178	193,340	194,058	64,183
1976	535,525	75,390	202,953	198,982	55,289
1977	465,167	73,663	175,179	171,777	44,548
Public University					
1973	327,637	51,746	129,607	100,688	45,596
1974	431,781	63,679	162,460	142,450	63,192
1975	481,155	83,916	181,399	160,299	55,541
1976	473,612	73,965	189,646	164,856	45,115
1977	403,204	72,026	160,679	136,769	33,730
Private University					
1973	50,136	1,168	11,936	30,752	7,180
1974	52,880	1,134	9,857	32,260	9,629
1975	55,804	1,262	12,141	33,921	8,642
1976	58,913	1,425	13,181	34,133	10,174
1977	61,963	1,637	14,500	35,000	10,818

Source: Ministerio de Cultura y Educación, *Estadísticas de la Educación, Síntesis,* Buenos Aires, 1978.

public administration (0.67 percent of the economically active population) and 358,417 teachers-educators (3.58 percent of the economically active population). Overall, looking at the three national censuses conducted in 1960, 1970, and 1980, the occupational categories that include professionals, teachers, and technicians represented 6.32 percent, 7.5 percent, and 10 percent of the labor force, respectively.[22] Clearly there has been an increase in the educational levels of the labor force. Further evidence of this fact derives from comparing the educational level of entrepreneurs and high functionaries in the public sector. In 1960 only 9.1 percent had acquired some measure of higher education, but by 1980 38.05 percent of people in those categories had a university diploma, a higher education diploma, or had spent some time in a tertiary-level institution.

However, the employment of higher education graduates in the predominantly service-oriented Argentinean economy is less than perfect. Many higher education graduates have emigrated to other labor markets. Numbers are indeed impressive. For instance, Pérez Lindo has argued that "It seems reasonable to calculate close to 100,000 persons with a university degree working abroad. This figure is equal to the total of four annual promotions of the university system. If we estimate that the cost of production of a university undergraduate is between twenty and twenty five thousand dollars, the loss resulting from the exodus of highly qualified persons is close to two billion dollars."[23]

Perhaps this is too high an estimate. Noting that between 1954 and 1984 547,000 Argentineans have emigrated to the United States, Israel, Venezuela, Spain, and neighboring countries, recent studies have estimated 50,000 of these were university graduates.[24] Unfortunately, it is impossible to discern whether they emigrated because the political instability of Argentina undermined institutional development and hence

their own professional prospects, or because they suffered concrete persecution during the years of dictatorship, or because they sought better economic and employment opportunities.[25]

Internal Trends in Higher Education and Problems Affecting Students and Academic Staff

Males and females are not evenly represented in the student body in higher education. In 1986 46.9 percent of students enrolled were males, and they were slightly overrepresented at the university level (53.8 percent). But due to the predominance of females in teaching careers, males were underrepresented at the nonuniversity level (22.2 percent). Male professors in 1986 comprised 52.7 percent of the total (69,985) staff in higher education institutions but 67.3 percent of the university staff (as opposed to 31.1 percent of the 8,771 teaching staff working in nonuniversity higher education).

Table 3 shows the distribution of university students by faculty and public or private university for the periods 1973–77 and 1978–86. The public universities have approximately 58 percent of their students enrolled in medical sciences, physical sciences, and engineering, while the private universities have almost 75 percent of their enrollment in social sciences and the humanities. The superior equipment of the public universities in "hard sciences" and the higher prestige of their programs in these disciplines attract a large number of students.

Pérez Lindo analyzed the real duration of undergraduate studies in three Argentinean universities. Using data provided by graduates from 1969, architects took between seven and eleven years to conclude their studies, engineers took be-

Table 4

Graduates in Higher Education (1963–1969 and 1972–1979)

	1963	1964	1965	1966	1967	1968	1969
University Medical, Basic and Technological Sciences	6,038	6,478	7,218	7,399	7,899	8,197	9,168
Social Sciences and Humanities	3,472	3,812	4,902	4,619	6,055	6,782	6,987
Sub-Total	9,510	10,290	12,120	12,018	13,954	14,979	16,155
Nonuniversity	3,168	3,456	4,136	4,208	4,478	4,577	5,211
Total	12,678	13,746	16,256	16,226	18,432	19,556	21,366

* This figure reflects the first promotion of teachers resulting from the upgrading of teachers' education to a higher education, nonuniversity modality.

Source: Ministerio de Educación, Departamento de Estadistica *Egresados, Educación Superior no-Universitaria* (several years); Ministerio de Educación, Departamento de Estadistica, *Egresados; Educación Superior Universitaria* (several years).

tween seven and ten years, medical doctors took between nine and ten years, public accountants took seven to eight years, and lawyers took between seven to nine years on average.[26] Such slow progress can be traced to the fact that more than 50 percent of undergraduates work full time while pursuing their university studies. In a recent unpublished survey of 493 students that enrolled in 1988 in the Faculty of Social Science at the University of Buenos Aires, 397 of whom were males and 196 of whom were females, 19.4 percent did not work, 28.7 percent worked part time (i.e., less than eight hours a day), and 51.8 percent worked full time (eight or more hours a day).[27]

The number of graduates produced by Argentinean universities is high compared to the total population. In the periods 1963–69 and 1972–79, 345,363 students graduated, distributed as follows: 181,884 graduated in medical sciences and basic and technology sciences, and 163,479 in social sciences and humanities. If nonuniversity graduates in higher education were to be included, the total between 1963–69 and 1972–78 would amount to 441,055 (see Table 4).

University graduates and total higher education graduates in that period represent approximately 1.33 percent and 1.70 percent of the total Argentinean population in 1980, respectively. The number of graduates in social sciences and humanities has been growing consistently since the establishment of modern social sciences in the Argentinean universities in the late 1950s. By the mid-1970s social science graduates became comparable to the number of graduates in the more traditional areas of medicine, sciences, and technological sciences. When, in 1970/71, the training of elementary school teachers was upgraded by adding two years of further training to secondary education, and thereby leading to a postsecondary diploma, the number of students (and therefore graduates) in nonuniversity higher education almost doubled. This change does not, however, account for the overall expansion of higher education that has

Table 4 (continued)

Graduates in Higher Education (1963–1969 and 1972–79)

1972	1973	1974	1975	1976	1977	1978	1979
12,069	13,475	15,513	16,647	21,776	15,221	16,775	18,010
11,725	12,883	14,081	16,674	20,777	15,200	16,900	18,611
23,794	26,358	29,594	33,321	42,553	30,421	33,675	36,621
12,221*	13,768	13,059	15,269	14,257	17,873	16,632	—
36,015	40,126	42,653	48,590	56,810	48,294	50,307	—

mainly taken place in the universities. In 1970 there were 293,302 students in higher education, and 86.4 percent were university students. By 1986 there were 902,882 students in higher education, and 78.3 percent were university students.

As of 1989 the quality of education in Argentina is deeply affected by several variables, among which is the lack of proper buildings. The majority of Argentinean universities do not have distinct campuses; they usually operate out of a variety of buildings scattered around cities. Other problems include the lack of proper computing facilities for students and staff, general underfunding, poor salaries and benefits for academic staff,[28] lack of proper libraries, and the absence of a consistent policy in higher education after so many years of military intervention in the university. Three main university problems deserve to be highlighted. First, by March 1989, the annual salary of a senior full professor, someone at the top of the scale with twenty-four years of seniority, in a public university was $5,428.[29] The salary of an adjunct professor was $4,187 at the senior level and $2,260 at the beginning level (i.e., equivalent to a beginning assistant professor). These salaries are not sufficient to attract the best qualified people, dedicated to working on a full-time basis (see Table 5).

Second, in addition to the low salary problems that have undermined any attempt to develop a stable body of full-time professors, the years of repression wiped out a whole generation of scholars, those that would now be serving in the intermediate ranks of the academic profession. Table 6 shows the distribution of the university staff by rank and dedication (full time, part time, hourly) at the University of Buenos Aires. It is clear that the majority work on a part-time (hourly) basis: 82.9 percent of the total staff is classified under the simple dedication category. Only 6.6 percent are full-time, exclusive dedication professors. It is important to note how the intermediate generation of associate professors is virtually absent from the academic ranks: they represent only 3.23 percent of the total academic staff: the distribution is basically binomial, with a surprising high number of both full and adjunct professors. In practice, full professors rarely teach but are in charge of running a very large course that is attended by thousands of students distributed sometimes in several dozen sections. This system, of course, shifts the burden of teaching toward the lower ranks of the teaching staff. Full professors count on the support of associate and adjunct professors who have more regular contact with students through the so-called theoretical classes (or lecture sections). By and large, most work with students takes place in the "practical studies sessions" with the junior faculty, particularly the head of practical studies and teaching assistants; it is not unusual that a student could finish his or her course work without ever having met the chair of the course (or "cátedra" in the old Spanish tradition).

Table 5

University Staff Yearly Salary Scales (Beginning and Senior Levels) March 1989

US dollars
(Rate of Exchange $US1=400 Australes)

Rank	Full-time Exclusive Dedication	Part-Time Semi-Exclusive Dedication	By the Hour Simple Dedication
Full Professor			
Beginner	2,859.48	1,049.88	470.21
Senior	5,427.50	2,309.84	1,034.41
Associate Professor			
Beginner	2,614.95	972.40	434.73
Senior	5,037.89	2,139.80	956.54
Adjunct Professor			
Beginner	2,260.31	811.59	363.87
Senior	4,187.56	1,785.55	800.67
Head of Practical Study			
Beginner	1,893.58	676.26	302.64
Senior	3,500.25	1,487.98	665.99
Teaching Assistant Category 1			
Beginner	1,622.79	582.92	260.78
Senior	3,011.45	1,282.45	573.95
Teaching Assistant Category 2			
Beginner	na	na	218.92
Senior	na	na	481.78

Source: Calculated from the *Salary Scale,* University of Buenos Aires, February 1, 1989, mimeographed. By May 1989, the rate of exchange was US$1=400 australes, and with the new government, the *australes* were changed for a new currency, *federales,* and the exchange rate reached 600 federales per US dollar by August 1989.

Table 6

University of Buenos Aires: Distribution of University Staff by Category and Dedication (1988)

| | Professoriate | | | | Assistants | | |
	Full	Associate	Adjunct	Head of Practical Study	Teaching Assistant Category 1	Teaching Assistant Category 2	Total
Full-Time (Exclusive Dedication)	205	104	248	374	258	00	1,189
	15.5%	17.8%	6.5%	10.6%	4.3%	—	6.6%
Part-Time (Semi-Exclusive Ded.)	313	123	383	500	580	—	1,899
	23.6%	21.1%	10.1%	14.1%	9.8%	—	10.5%
Hourly (Simple Dedication)	805	357	3,173	2,668	5,080	2,927	15,010
	60.8%	61.1%	83.4%	75.3%	85.8%	100%	82.9%
Total	1,323	584	3,804	3,542	5,918	2,927	18,096
	100%	100%	100%	100%	100%	100%	100%

Source: Dirección de Plantificación Educacional en base a planta de cargos —Marzo 1988—Sevicio de Procesamiento de Informacíon Administrativa (unpublished).

A third problem can be added to low salaries, lack of highly qualified associate professors, and the complexities of the organization of teaching activities in Argentinean universities: the lack of library resources and/or the interest among the students to consult on a regular basis the materials placed in the reserve rooms of the libraries. In a survey carried out by the Faculty of Social Science at the University of Buenos Aires in 1989, 92 percent of the students reported that they did not spend even one hour a week in the libraries.[30] This is due partly to the scarcity of library materials, which makes it very difficult for students who work fulltime to have access to books, journals, etc., when they want to, and partly to a common practice in Argentinean institutions by which students study using the recorded or transcribed lectures delivered by the professors of a particular course. These recorded and transcribed notes ("apuntes") are usually made available to all students by the different student centers at nominal costs.

Conclusions

Nobody will deny the need for a profound reform in higher education in Argentina—an educational reform that would tackle the need for modernization of universities' organizational structures, laws, finances, and the teaching-learning process itself. The University of Buenos Aires, for instance, cannot function properly with 175,000 students, and needs to be split into several universities, perhaps following the University of Paris model. In addition, the concentration and centralization of academic resources needs to be evaluated. By 1986, 38.8 percent of the universities and 36.4 percent of the nonuniversity higher education institutions were located in the Province of Buenos Aires and in the Federal District. That is to say, a region with approximately 25 percent of the total population is served by almost 40 percent of the total number of higher education institutions.

Similarly, problems concerning equality of access to higher education in the context of equality of opportunity need to be addressed. So, too, do the related problems arising from growing expansion (massification) of higher education and the quest for excellence in the context of job availability for graduates. These issues of excellence and equality have to be incorporated into the rationale for a new and comprehensive Law of Higher Education in the country. More fellowships must be made available to needy students in order to alter the predominantly middle-class composition of the universities. Moreover, the need for a better balance between undergraduate and graduate studies has to be considered—on average, less than 7 percent of all graduates from universities have completed postgraduate programs.

The organization of research activities in the country deserves careful scrutiny. Currently, the National Council of Scientific and Technological Research (CONICET) sponsors, subsidizes, and controls research. Researchers are placed within universities and research centers (many of these centers are financed by, and administratively dependent upon, CONICET). CONICET finances the work and pays the salaries of university researchers—with the exception of few universities, such as the University of Rosario in Santa Fe, which has organized its own Council of Scientific Research. Hence, research and teaching are not integrated into a single academic role within universities.

A substantive reform of higher education in Argentina depends upon the political stability of the country, and upon the economic stabilization of an economic system besieged by external debt, the action of powerful financial sectors that speculate in nonproductive financial markets, and the traditional power of the large agricultural producers who control the main products for export and hold the state's policies continuously in check. University development has been historically associated to state-building, and hence the limits of university autonomy have been constrained by the goals and purposes of the state and the nature of the political regime.

Notes

1. Aldo Ferrer, *La Economía Argentina* (Buenos Aires: Fondo de Cultura Económica, 1963), 104.

2. In May 1989 presidential elections took place in Argentina. When President Raúl Alfonsin (1983–89) handed over the office to his successor, the Peronist Carlos Menem, President Alfonsin became the first democratically elected president to conclude his term of office in a normal fashion since 1952, and the fifth president to complete his term during this century.

3. Juan Carlos Tedesco, *Educación y Sociedad en la Argentina* (1880–1900) (Buenos Aires: Pannedille, 1982).

4. Emilio Fermín Mignone, "Relación entre el sistema político y el sistema educativo en la Argentina (1853–1943)" (Buenos Aires: FLACSO, 1978, Mimeographed).

5. Jorge Padua, *El Analfabetismo en América Latina* (Mexico: El Colegio de Mexico, 1979), 61.

6. Argentina, between 1853 and 1954, received a net increment in population of 7,166,000 immigrants, mostly from Europe. This is a very significant factor, since Argentina becomes the world's second largest receiver of immigrants from Europe after the United States. Between 1821 and 1954 the United States received 33,958,000 immigrants, Canada received 6,318,000 immigrants, Brazil received 4,842,000 immigrants, and Australia (between 1861 and 1954) received 3,810,000 immigrants from Europe. See Alfredo Lattes, "La migración como factor de cambio de la población en Argentina" (Buenos Aires: Instituto Torcuato Di Tella, no. 76, 1972), 72.

7. George Kurian and Carlos Alberto Torres, "Argentina" in *World Education Encyclopedia*, ed. George Kurian (New York: Facts-On-File, 1988), 58–68.

8. Emilio Fermín Mignone, "Universidad y poder político en Argentina (1613–1978)" (Buenos Aires: FLACSO, 1979, Mimeographed), 13.

9. Ibid., 13–25.

10. Ibid., 13.

11. Ibid., 57.

12. The then-governor of the Province of Buenos Aires, Gral. Ibérico Saint Jean, stated that: "First we will kill the subversive people, after that their collaborators, after that their sympathizers, after that all those that will remain indifferent, and finally, we will kill the timids" (my translation, quoted in Richard Gillespie, *Montoneros. Soldados de Perón* [Buenos Aires: Grijalbo, 1987], 304).

13. The National Commission for the Disappearance of Persons (CONADEP), appointed by the democratically elected government of Dr. Raúl Alfonsín in 1983, concluded in its report entitled "Never Again" that of the documented 8,960 persons who were reported as "disappeared" between 1976 and 1983, 40 percent were connected with the educational world, including 21 percent students, 10.9 percent professionals, 5.7 percent teachers, and 1.6 percent journalists—the list is completed by 30.2 percent blue-collar workers, 17.9 percent white-collar workers, 5 percent self-employed people, 3.8 percent housewives, 2.5 percent members of the armed forces and police, 1.3 percent actors and actresses, and 0.3 percent members of religious organizations.

14. Jeffrey M. Puryear, *Higher Education, Development Assistance, and Repressive Regimes* (New York: Ford Foundation, 1983).

15. Augusto Pérez Lindo, *Universidad, Política y Sociedad* (Buenos Aires: EUDEBA, 1985), 187–94.

16. Emilio Fermín Mignone, "Argentina Republic," in *The International Encyclopedia of Higher Education*, ed. Asa S. Knowles (San Francisco: Jossey-Bass, 1977), 470.

17. A measure taken to modify the restrictive enrollment policy pursued during the military dictatorship. For instance, while in 1982 the University of Buenos Aires had 12,700 new students enrolled, by 1984 there were 42,757 students enrolled in the common basic level. Geometrical rates of growth seem to be in operation; in the academic year 1985/86, 81,831 applicants applied for enrollment in the common basic level at the University of Buenos Aires.

18. CONADE, *Educación, Recursos Humanos y Desarrollo Económico-Social* (Buenos Aires: CONADE, 1968).

19. Augusto Pérez Lindo, *Universidad, Política y Sociedad*, 209.

20. Maria Antonieta Gallart, *Educación y Trabajo: un Estado del Arte de la Investigación en América Latina* (Ottawa, Canada: IDRC, July 1986).

21. Augusto Pérez Lindo, *Universidad, Política y Sociedad*, 270.

22. Ibid., 273.

23. Ibid., 290.

24. *Página 12*, 22 December 1988, p. 18 (newspaper).

25. Estimates by Inés Izaguirre show that with each change of government thousands of employees working for the public sector and the universities either were fired or were asked to resign, including 84,807 in 1969–70; 79,366 in 1971–72; 128,896 between 1973 and 1975; and 85,611 after 1976 (cited by Pérez Lindo, *Universidad, Política y Sociedad*, 269).

26. Pérez Lindo, *Universidad, Política y Sociedad*, 232.

27. The author wants to thank Mrs. Lilita Puig de Stubrin, director of the School of Social Science, University of Buenos Aires, for providing this information.

28. That accounts for the tiny portion of full-time professors entirely dedicated to teaching and research—professionals and university staff usually hold several part-time jobs.

29. Faculty ranks are full professor ("Profesor Titular"), associate professor ("Profesor Asociado"), adjunct professor ("Profesor Adjunto"), and head of practical study ("Jefe de Trabajos Prácticos"). This last category also includes various ranks of auxiliary teaching staff. In this rank, there are three types of dedication to teaching: exclusive dedication or full-time (which forbids any other salaried activity), semiexclusive dedication or part-time (which allows other salaried activities, although limited), and simple dedication (professors who are paid by the hour). The ranks of special professors include honorary professors, emeritus professors, and visiting professors.

30. Students were asked to distribute their weekly hours between attendance at lectures, attendance at practical study classes, consulting library resources, exchanging or interacting with academic staff, and other student activities (i.e., political activities, activities in the student centers, etc). Regarding lectures, 33 percent of the students never attend any, 28 percent attend between one to three hours of lecturing, and 39 percent attend more than four hours of lecturing a week. Practical study sessions are not attended by 32 percent of the students, 30 percent attend between one and six hours of these sessions a week, and the rest attend more than seven hours of practical study a week. The majority (92 percent) do not spend time consulting books in the libraries, nor consulting with academic staff (92 percent never approach the professors). Curiously enough, these students do not spend much time with extracurricular student activities either (88 percent declared that they do not even spend one hour a week).

Brazil

Robert E. Verhine

◆

Brazil's system of higher education is a complex, nationwide network consisting of universities, school federations, and isolated (or single-purpose) institutions distributed within both public and private domains. As of 1987, Brazil had 853 tertiary institutions, eighty-two of which could be classified as universities. More than 70 percent of upper-level institutions are private, but most of the universities are publicly run. Within the public sphere, the dominant force is the federal government, which through its Ministry of Education operates thirty-five major universities (in general, one per state), that account for 21 percent of Brazil's higher education student body, 35 percent of its faculty members, and a major portion of the nation's scientific output. State universities tend to be recent creations, with the notable exception of those in the country's richest state, São Paulo. Private-sector universities include thirteen religious and sixteen secular institutions. Private control is particularly evident among institutions not having university status. Three-fourths of the entities so classified are privately operated, in many instances for the purpose of profit making.[1]

Brazil, of course, is a very large country—the fifth largest in the world—exhibiting much disparity in socioeconomic development across its regions. The distribution of higher education reflects this diversity. The three richest states—São Paulo, Rio de Janeiro and Minas Gerais—account for over 60 percent of the total number of institutions; if other indicators are used, such as total expenditures or scholarly production, this imbalance becomes even more apparent.[2] Courses of study at the undergraduate level are professional in nature and vary from three to six years. Medicine, for example, is a six-year undergraduate program; law and engineering take five years to complete; and journalism and physical education usually take only three.

Brazil's higher education student body currently numbers about 1.5 million, a figure representing about 1 percent of the country's population. About half of the students are enrolled in universities and, as with the distribution of institutions, the private domain is responsible for about 60 percent of the total. After growing enormously in the 1960s and 1970s, enrollment levels have remained fairly constant throughout the 1980s, reflecting a continuing national economic crisis.[3] Business administration and economics are currently the most popular courses of study, a distinction that once belonged to law.

Admission to higher education institutions is via entrance examination (*vestibular*). In 1987 approximately 400,000 of the 2.2 million vestibular takers gained higher education admittance, with the candidate/admission ratio substantially higher at universities (6:1) than at other tertiary institutions (4:1). An upper secondary degree is required to take the admissions exam; it is customary to prepare for the test by way of a prep course, known as *cursinho*.[4] These intensive, fact-cramming courses are private, profit-oriented programs; their prevalence in all major urban centers is testament to the notoriously poor and/or inappropriate quality of Brazilian secondary schools.[5] The cursinhos, together with the selective nature of secondary instruction (only about 14 percent of the fifteen- to nineteen-year-old age co-hort are in school and most high-standard establishments are private) contribute to the fact that the higher education student body is principally of middle- and upper-class origin. This socioeconomic bias is especially apparent at the most influential institutions (most notably the federal universities where, paradoxically, no tuition is charged) and in the most prestigious fields of study (i.e., medicine, engineering, and law).[6]

The number of students per faculty member is estimated at 12.1 for the system as a whole and at 7.6 and 6.9 for federal and state universities, respectively. Factors contributing to these relatively low figures include the presence of part-time instructors, legal/institutional barriers to faculty dismissal and forced retirement, and a tendency for faculty members, including full-time ones, to hold other jobs. In other words, the low ratios do not mean that class sizes are necessarily small or that many professors do not have heavy teaching loads.

The above-mentioned multiple-job tendency continues to prevail despite a major effort in recent years to prioritize full-time staffing. Whereas in 1974 only about 20 percent of higher education professors worked full time, the corresponding figure for 1987 was 75 percent.[7] However, low salaries compared to those of other professionals[8] and the absence of an effective system for faculty evaluation, especially as relates to out-of-class activities in research and extension, combine to cause many faculty members to seek alternative employment.

The faculties at all public and most private establishments are organized into the categories of full, associate, assistant, and auxiliary professor. Since 1981 advancement from the auxiliary to associate level has been based on formal credentials and time of service. A federal decree in 1987 stipulated that academic productivity, as defined within each institution, should also

be taken into account.[9] Attainment of full professor status is via a public examination that involves, among other things, the submission of a dissertation.

Career entry is also based on public examination, although many of the country's current faculty members did not submit to this procedure. Changes in employment policy over time, past flexibilities in hiring due to burgeoning enrollments, and a 1981 nationwide faculty strike settlement in which the federal government agreed to incorporate all short-term contractees (collaborating and visiting professors) into the federal university career hierarchy help account for this distortion. These factors also explain another distortion, in this case related to official dictates concerning career level/degree attainment linkage. Whereas federal legislation mandates that assistant professors have master's degrees and associate and full professors a doctorate, exceptions to this requirement are commonplace. Only 12 percent of the nation's higher education teaching staff have doctorates, and only 21 percent have a master's degree. If federal universities alone are considered, the corresponding figures improve, but only slightly.

The low qualification of Brazil's higher education personnel has long been recognized as a major problem by Brazilian authorities. Since the early 1950s federal organs such as CNPq (National Research Council) and CAPES (Campaign for Improving Higher Education Personnel) have offered scholarships for graduate study abroad. Since the late 1960s the Ministry of Education has promoted an ambitious program of establishing and supporting master's and doctoral programs at Brazilian universities. These programs are, in large part, based on the United States model and require both the attainment of credits via the taking of graduate-level courses and the defense of a thesis (for the master's level) or dissertation (for the doctoral level).[10] By 1987 there were a total of 831 master's programs and 354 separate doctoral offerings, serving, respectively, 31,719 and 7,759 students.[11]

In addition to the preparation of higher education personnel, the graduate network has the expressed purpose of promoting scientific and technological development. Traditionally the Brazilian university has been essentially a teaching institution. As in France, on whose model the Brazilian system was originally based, serious research has historically been conducted in specialized institutes supported by public funds.[12] Scholarly output has tended to be of only secondary importance in faculty hiring, even at the most prestigious universities. The graduate programs, however, have played a major role in increasing the university's participation in knowledge production. They have provided a safe haven for those who are research oriented. By linking program funding from CAPES to the scientific contribution of faculty members, the government has created research incentives that do not exist on the undergraduate level. As a result, scientific output in Brazil tripled between 1973 and 1980 and, according to one estimate, the country now ranks second on this indicator among third world nations (behind India).[13] Of course, this output is highly concentrated: São Paulo alone accounts for nearly 50 percent of all research articles published. Thus, although since the late 1960s the Brazilian university has ostensibly emphasized scientific and technological development, advances in this direction have been obtained on only a very limited scale (primarily on the graduate level and mainly in the most prestigious universities).

Organization and Governance

Institutions of higher education (IHEs) in Brazil are organized in accordance with national legislation. To offer valid diplomas, an institution must be accredited by the Federal Council of Education, a twenty-four-member board appointed by the republic's president. Structure and administration are much the same in all tertiary institutions, although numerous interinstitutional differences do exist. The Brazilian system is characterized by dichotomies between public and private establishments and between universities and colleges (integrated and isolated). Moreover, federal universities are divided into autarchies and foundations, while private institutions include those that have a religious affiliation (mostly Catholic) and those that are secular. Two other factors have contributed to differences in institutional organization. First, a major reform instigated in 1968 was superimposed on existing structures; the resulting compromises between the old and the new were not uniform across establishments. Second, since 1980 a nationwide faculty union movement has brought about a number of changes in the name of institutional democracy and autonomy. Again, the adaptation of reforms has not been uniform. Most recent modifications exist in practice but not in law. Thus, offering a coherent picture of a "typical" Brazilian IHE is difficult, a fact that should be kept in mind when reading the paragraphs that follow.

The Ministry of Education (MEC) runs the large federal university system through its Department of Higher Education (SESU). Since primary and secondary instruction is essentially a state and local responsibility, at least two-thirds of the ministry's budget goes to supporting the tertiary level.[14] All federal establishments are tuition free; dormitory and campus food services are heavily subsidized. In the autarchies, which are usually the oldest and most traditional entities, the ministry's control over institutional expenditures is extensive. Foundations, which are dominant among institutions created after 1960, have greater institutional flexibility in both raising and dispensing funds. Until recently these latter entities could provide incentives to promote employee performance that autarchies, locked into the federal civil service system, were unable to offer. However, in the last couple of years some of this autonomy in setting pay scales has been curtailed in response to pressure from the professors' association (culminating in a prolonged strike in 1987) to standardize salary levels within the public sector. Also, although the foundations have been actively encouraged to seek alternative funding sources, very few have exercised this option to any substantial extent.[15]

MEC subsidies are tied to fixed incremental allotments. A very high percentage of dispersals go to pay personnel. Federal assistance is also channelled to private institutions, but this money is usually earmarked for special items, such as student aid, graduate program maintenance, and faculty research. Most of the routine operating costs of private universities are financed through tuition.[16] Catholic institutions (PUCs) receive a disproportionate amount of federal funding both because of their graduate programs and research involvements and because of the political clout of the Catholic church.

Within the university major power rests with the rector, the institution's chief administrator.[17] For federal universities the rector is chosen by the president of the republic from a list of six names submitted by an electoral college composed of the institution's faculty, administrators, and students. In recent years these six candidates have often been selected via universitywide direct elections based on a corporate model that gives equal voting weight to professors (as a class), students, and functionaries. At state universities the governor makes the final choice of rector; at private entities a board of trustees makes the choice—except in the case of Catholic institutions, where the list is submitted to the church authority (i.e., cardinal or bishop) who acts as the university's chancellor.

The rector's power within each institution is evidenced by the fact that at public institutions his or her selection often involves both local and national politics, with major political parties participating in the fray. The rector governs with the aid of prorectors (universitywide deans) for administration, planning, undergraduate affairs, graduate study and research, and extension studies. The rector controls the purse strings at the institutional level and thus has major influence over program development, construction, hiring, and the like. His or her actions, however, are monitored by both the Ministry of Education and the Federal Council of Education. The former determines total institutional funding and tags monies for specific purposes. It also specifies the number of faculty and student slots available. The latter organ, in turn, has the right to intervene in university governance in cases of proven misconduct and/or incompetence.[18] The rectors as a group can exert pressure on these national entities (and government policy in general) through a voluntary organization known as the Council of Rectors of Brazilian Universities (CRUB).[19]

At the bottom of the university hierarchy are *colegiados*, composed of professors who manage the academic affairs of specific courses of study and departments which offer related disciplines and monitor the teaching and research activities of their members. The department is legally denoted as the smallest, most basic unit of the university; as will be discussed shortly, its existence is a relatively recent phenomenon, the product of efforts to "modernize" the nation's system of higher education.

The structure just described is marked by the presence of competing and overlapping decision-making bodies, and lines of authority and communication are often unclear.[20] In this context, centralization tends to prevail. The rector not only controls spending policy, he or she also has the right to convoke and preside over the university-wide councils and determines, either directly or indirectly, many of their members. However, in recent years the relative influence of the bottom-up representative organs has probably increased as faculty, functionary, and student associations have increased in strength and militancy during the 1980s. The organization of students (UNE) is mandated by federal law and has existed, with varying degrees of autonomy and influence, since 1938. The faculty and functionary associations are more recent, essentially products of the political relaxation that occurred in the late 1970s. ANDES, which represents the faculty, is the strongest of the three groups and has recently obtained the status of a union, a status made possible by Brazil's new constitution that grants public employees the right to strike. Illegal strikes, though, have been commonplace since 1980 and, as will be noted later in this chapter, have had major consequences. All three associations are structured according to principles of participatory democracy, although reliance on assemblies for decision making has been criticized because low attendance and nonsecret voting have tended to facilitate domination by the most militant.[21]

Historical Development

Whereas universities appeared elsewhere in Latin America as early as the sixteenth century, Brazil's first university was not established on an accredited basis until 1920.[22] This retarded development has its origins in the country's status as a Portuguese colony. Portugal was dedicated to maximum, immediate exploitation of its largest colony; this policy and Brazil's slave-based plantation economy meant that investment in higher education was seen as not only unnecessary but also counterproductive. Other factors mitigating against university formation during this period included the relative economic poverty of the mother country, the fact that even in

Portugal higher education was poorly developed, and a desire on the part of the Portuguese crown to integrate Brazil into the kingdom rather than create separate institutions.

The only opportunities for advanced study in colonial Brazil were offered by the Jesuits and Franciscans who established seminaries and colleges where courses in philosophy and theology were given. These religious orders made a number of efforts to have their programs accredited by the crown but were not successful. Circumstances changed in 1808 when the Portuguese royal family, fleeing from Napoleon in Europe, moved the seat of the government to Rio de Janeiro. This created a need for trained administrators, military leaders, and professionals (e.g., physicians) to support and defend the royal court. Thus, by the time the country gained independence in 1822, programs in the fields of medicine, military science, and economics had been established; shortly thereafter law schools appeared to meet state needs for bureaucrats, legislators, and diplomats.

The nation's first constitution (1823) called for the creation of universities in appropriate places, and the Imperial Act of 1834 reserved for the federal government the right to promote and regulate higher education throughout the nation. However, despite these legal initiatives, no universities were established during the Imperial period (1822–89). Brazil remained dominated by a rural oligarchy who feared that the presence of universities might generate challenges to traditional structures and values. Interestingly, progressive elements in society were also against the creation of such institutions. Military leaders and intellectuals, many of whom were adherents of the philosophy of positivism espoused by Frenchman August Comte, argued that universities would serve reactionary interests (in the manner of the University of Paris) and that science would be retarded by centralizing its production. Others noted that single-purpose colleges were more conducive to knowledge specialization and that universities would require resources better spent on mass education.[23] As a result, the only advances in the field of higher education made during the latter nineteenth century were the creation, in 1874, of Brazil's first engineering school (in Rio de Janeiro) and of a school of mines (in Ouro Preto).

The Republican period (1889–1930) was marked by changes in Brazil's socioeconomic structure. The success of coffee on world markets generated financial capital for industrialization, which in turn provoked urbanization and public and private bureaucratization. In this context educational credentials became increasingly important in the new process of social stratification, and, as a consequence, opportunities for higher education expanded. Enrollments increased from 2,000 students in 1890 to 20,000 forty years later, and between 1890 and 1910 twenty-seven colleges—both public and private—were created, primarily in the fields of law, medicine, and engineering.[24] Beginning in 1910, the federal government began to take measures to more carefully regulate higher educational development and actively sought to preserve the status of higher education diplomas by ensuring selectivity in student admission. Hence, entrance exams were mandated by a decree in 1910, a secondary level credential was made a prerequisite for advanced study in 1915, and a national limitation on admission openings was set by legislation in 1925.

Finally, the federal government bowed to growing pressures to create a national university and in 1920 established the University of Rio de Janeiro by joining three existing colleges under a single administration. Importantly, in founding this university, the government sought to put forth a model for any and all later initiatives and thus ensured the institutionalization of two tendencies that characterized the Brazilian university for the next fifty years:

the presence of semiautonomous faculties linked by a weak central administrative apparatus and an almost exclusive emphasis on professionalization, thereby minimizing the importance given to general knowledge and scientific research. Another aspect incorporated into the original model was the so-called chaired professorship (*catedratico vitalicio*), whose position was first mandated by the 1915 decree and then sanctified in the Constitutions of 1934 and 1946. The chaired professor served for life, was guaranteed total academic freedom, and had complete decision-making power over a given area of knowledge and those who taught it. Rule by these "feudal lords" was often autocratic; in the opinion of many students, educators, and public officials, these individuals came to represent a major impediment to university modernization.

In 1930 a governmental takeover by Getúlio Vargas gave urban interests an upper hand in national policy-making, and economic development became a major state concern. A year later the Statute of Brazilian Universities was elaborated in which the university was made the keystone of the higher education system. The first university based on this law was the University of São Paulo (USP), founded in 1934 as a political response on the part of São Paulo oligarchs to a loss of national influence during the Vargas regime.[25] USP had as its expressed purpose the production of modern, intellectual elites, and, aided by the region's wealth and a large number of visiting professors from Europe and the United States, it quickly established itself as the country's finest institution of higher learning, a status that it enjoys to this day. However, as with other Brazilian universities, USP was essentially an agglomeration of preexisting colleges, and its much touted integrative organ, the College for Philosophy, Letters, and Sciences, which was designed to provide a core course of basic studies and to promote pure research, soon became just another professional school, preparing secondary school teachers. Thus, even in São Paulo the model of semiautonomous colleges linked by a weak administrative apparatus prevailed.

Brazil's first accredited private university, the Catholic University of Rio de Janeiro (PUC/RJ), was created in 1941. The university was a consequence of the Catholic church's desire to regain a long-lost foothold in the field of higher education and of an effort on the part of the Vargas regime to secure church support for its centralized, corporate state.[26]

In 1945 Brazil had five universities, 293 isolated colleges, and a total higher education enrollment of about 25,000. The system expanded markedly over the next two decades and by 1964, the year of the military takeover, the network included thirty-seven universities, 564 single-purpose colleges, and nearly 150,000 matriculants.[27] During this period the federal government played a particularly active role, federalizing at a rapid pace state, municipal, and private institutions. Demand for higher education during this period was provoked not only by a growing urban/industrial economy and an increasing number of secondary school graduates, but also by a series of initiatives designed to facilitate access. A sequence of laws augmented the types of secondary schools whose graduates were eligible to take the vestibular, and, at the same time, the fees at public institutions were progressively lowered until, by the early 1950s, these institutions had become free to users.

Meanwhile, as a nationalistic-developmentalist ideology became dominant in official circles, the university was increasingly attacked for its lack of relevance to modern society. There appeared a generalized demand for a more integrated university whose courses and programs would be directly related to modern social and technological circumstances. Whereas the political right tended to want the university to better serve labor market needs, the political left, dominated by the students, advocated using the university as a resource for social criticism and eventual social transformation.[28] Both groups, however, were united in demanding a real merger of the semiautonomous colleges and the elimination of the all-powerful chaired professors. The Technological Institute for Aeronautics (ITA), created in 1947 by the federal government, and the University of Brasília (UnB), opened in 1962 in the nation's new capital, had many of the attributes then assumed to be essential features of a modern university. Both institutions were characterized by departments, a core curriculum of general studies, full-time professors with research obligations whose academic position was linked to a career ladder, and a credit system designed to eliminate course duplication and give students latitude in determining their program of studies. UnB also allowed for ample faculty and student participation in university decision making, and, unlike other federal universities at that time, was built in accordance with an integrative plan and organized as a foundation, meaning that it had flexibility with respect to budgetary matters.[29]

During this period university students were a major political force, not only within the university community but also in society as a whole. Organized in the late 1930s under government auspices as part of Vargas' corporate model, the students quickly turned against the government and during the 1950s constituted a militant, politically experienced element in national left-wing politics.[30] From the outset this group fought for university reform, favoring, above all, democratization of access (e.g., more openings, tuition-free instruction, reduced entrance exam rigor) and greater student participation in university decision making. Student protest intensified in the early 1960s, in part because of tacit encouragement given by Goulart's populist government in its efforts to effectuate major structural change and in part because of the frustration generated by a higher education system unable to meet demands for access and a labor market incapable of responding to the job and status expectations of recent graduates. Aggravating the situation was the fact that the vestibular was eliminatory rather than classificatory, which meant that each year the number of students who passed the exam invariably exceeded the number of university places available.

Thus, pressure for reform was great at the time the military took over the government. Devoted to promoting national development and internal security through a political dictatorship and an economy linked to international capitalism, the new regime sought to integrate higher education into the modernization process and, at the same time, diffuse and control radical movements on campus.[31] Beginning in 1966 it issued a variety of decrees mandating major changes in the higher education system. The process culminated in November 1968, with the passage of Lei 5540/68, a wide-ranging reform law pertaining to all universities and colleges, public and private.[32] As a result of these measures, the chaired professor system was abolished, departments became the fundamental unit of the institution, and each university was to promote not just teaching but also research and extension. The use of credits, enrollment by discipline, adoption of a semester system, incentives for full-time faculty employment, the adoption of a career ladder, the development of graduate programs at both master's and doctoral levels, the creation of a cycle of basic studies followed by professional preparation, the unification of entrance exams within institutions and, eventually, within regions, and the making of the vestibular classificatory rather than eliminatory (thus solving the problem of more people passing than slots were available) are examples of the reforms introduced.

From an administrative standpoint, the reform clearly favored increased centralization, both to ensure greater organizational rationality and efficiency and to guarantee effective control of potential subversive activity. Thus, budgetary powers were transferred from college deans to the rector, a central organ to coordinate teaching and research was mandated, and the Colleges of Philosophy, Sciences, and Letters were broken up into distinct schools, institutes, and departments.[33]

Centralization went beyond the institutional level, however. At federal establishments, control over certain personnel matters was transferred from the university to the central government, the president of the republic kept the right to nominate rectors and college deans, a representative from MEC was given a seat on the Curator Council, and powers of the Federal Council of Education, created in 1962 to accredit and establish core curricula, were expanded to permit its intervention into the affairs of specific institutions in cases of law infringement.

Thus, whereas the effort incorporated many of the innovations utilized earlier at ITA and UnB and met many of the demands that had been set forth in previous decades by a variety of groups, both within and outside the university, it also had a decidedly authoritarian character consistent with the interests of a right-wing military government. The resulting framework reflected the military's concern for administrative rationality, for meeting the labor market needs of a modern, industrial economy, and for maintaining social order. With regard to this last point, it should be added that during this period all political activity on the part of students and faculty was expressly outlawed and federal intelligence-gathering agencies infiltrated the campuses. Academic freedom was seriously curtailed, professor firings and student dismissals became commonplace, and a general climate of fear and distrust prevailed at many of the country's institutions of higher learning.[34]

In this respect, mention should be made of the participation of United States consultants in the Brazilian university reform process. In 1964 a USAID team evaluated the Brazilian university system, found it highly deficient in both quantitative and qualitative terms, and recommended that the United States government assist Brazil in planning and implementing major reforms. A year later MEC and USAID signed the first of several accords which developed two distinct lines of action. The first involved establishing a planning committee composed of an equal number of United States and Brazilian specialists to make reform proposals, and the second provided United States financial and technical assistance for the modernization of Brazilian university administration.[35]

The North American involvement has led many to assert that the new university model in Brazil was imposed by the United States as a form of cultural imperialism. More careful scholarship, however, suggests that the United States model was sought out by a variety of Brazilian groups in the name of modernization. And, too, it should be remembered that the adoption of these reforms on the various campuses was not uniform; a number of adjustments were made on the institutional level as a consequence of local traditions and power arrangements. Thus, what finally emerged from the late 1960s reform effort was a complex, not altogether consistent reflection of historical experience, current circumstances, and future expectations. The laws formulated during that period govern Brazilian higher education to the present day.

Recent Trends and Future Prospects

Whereas during the 1970s Brazil was characterized by economic growth and political dictatorship, the 1980s have witnessed both economic stagnation and political democratization.[36] Developments in higher education over the past two decades reflect this changing climate. For example, as already indicated, until about 1975 academic repression, including censorship, arrests, and even torture, was a dominant component of the scene. Then, as part of the political "opening" of the latter years of the decade, academic freedoms were gradually restored. One consequence was an outpouring of critical, Marxist scholarship; another was the formation of ANDES, the nationwide faculty association whose militancy can be, in part, attributed to the fact that many of its members were student activists in the 1960s.[37] A similar (but weaker) organization for federal university functionaries was also created, and UNE, initially suppressed by the military government, reappeared, although with less clout than in the pre-1964 days. The various nationwide strikes promoted by these three groups since 1980 have produced some tangible gains, including cost-of-living adjustments, a standardized career plan, and equivalent pay across all federal IHE entities. The associations have also achieved the de facto right to elect deans and rectors, although, as noted earlier, final appointment remains the responsibility of the central authorities. On the other hand, the strikes have caused severe losses in classroom and teaching time and have generally disrupted the normal routine of academic life. Also, the strikes with the elections of chief administrators have combined to politicize the institutional atmosphere, making the choice of leaders a popularity contest and, in many instances, bringing national political parties into university affairs.

These events, together with the generally low qualification of teaching personnel, the lack of effective faculty evaluation, the virtual impossibility of employee firing, the absence of incentives for research and publishing, and the need for many in the IHE ranks to hold down additional employments to meet income expectations have led to a major internal crisis. A number of recent critiques produced by leading scholars have railed against corporatism, populism, incompetency, and irresponsibility in the Brazilian academic community and have noted that declining quality is not only a function of funding stringency but also of a nonproductive intrainstitutional dynamic related to the attitudes, goals, and commitments of those involved.[38]

These problems in quality, of course, are complemented by those of quantity. In the 1970s there was a significant expansion in enrollments, especially in the private sector. Public sector enrollments doubled during the decade, while private sector enrollments quadrupled. Whereas at the time of the military takeover only 43 percent of IHE matriculants were in private establishments, in 1980 the corresponding figure had risen to 63 percent. Part of the growth represented an effort on the part of public authorities to meet manpower needs for highly specialized personnel. Much of it, however, was a response to burgeoning demand made by a government actively seeking middle-class support.[39] In response to this second concern and, also, reflecting an evident proprivate bias within the ruling group, the state directly promoted private sector growth through the very loose sanctioning of new private institutions and through tax exemptions, credits, and direct dispersals. Five percent of the National Higher Education Fund was distributed to private higher learning establishments, and, when a monitored student loan program was initiated in 1976, private programs were the chief beneficiaries.[40] Public expansion, on the other hand, tended to stress enlarging existing institutions rather than creating new ones. A number of federal universities were transferred to integrated campuses, in line with a recommendation much emphasized by the United States advisors.

During the 1980s, in contrast, IHE enrollments have increased very little. Expansion began to tail off in the latter 1970s, partially the result of a political decision by the federal government made in light of evidence of low academic quality (especially in the private sector) and mounting higher education costs.[41] Thus, the accreditation process for new establishments was made more rigorous and, in 1979, steps were taken to raise the difficulty level of the vestibular. The tendency for reduced growth was fortified in the 1980s as the nation's economic woes (closely linked to a huge public debt burden) led to major governmental cutbacks in nonpriority areas. Thus, at federal universities funds for operation and capital investment were reduced and hiring freezes were mandated. Private institutions also suffered, victims of the reduction in user purchasing power. Thus, with both sectors stalling, the private/public enrollment ratio has remained fairly constant over the present decade.

The pattern of higher education expansion just described has had important implications for the relationship between this schooling level and employment. In the past two decades there have been a number of governmental efforts to more closely link the university and the economy, including investing heavily in academic fields related to science and technology and creating, in conjunction with private enterprise, programs for in-company student internships. However, these initiatives have been undermined by the proliferation of demand-absorbing private institutions that have sought to maximize profits by offering only the least costly courses of study. Thus, from a manpower standpoint Brazil has an overabundance of graduates in such areas as business administration, accounting, and pedagogy and scarcities in the fields of medicine, engineering, and agronomy.[42] Although relatively few college graduates are unemployed, many work on a level below that for which they prepared and/or pursue a nonrelated occupation. But, despite these problems, research confirms that higher-level schooling in Brazil is a good investment for the student.[43] The relative paucity of higher education opportunities and the fact that many of those who study also work (thereby minimizing foregone income costs) contribute to the high rates of individual return. These payoffs, however, vary substantially from one academic field to another, and, needless to say, they tend to be greater for public institutions than for private ones.

The coexistence of both public and private domains in Brazilian higher education is far from tranquil. For years a heated national debate has raged as to how these two sectors should relate to the state. The propublic faction has received articulate support from a number of known scholars (public university faculty members) as well as from ANDES and leftist political parties. It argues that public funds should go exclusively to public institutions and favors restricting the private school alternative. This group contends that since 1964 the Brazilian government has sought to privatize higher education to both guarantee an access limited to the elite and relieve the state of a costly responsibility. Advocates of this position complain about the quantity of public monies channeled to the private sector as well as about efforts by MEC to change autarchies to foundations (the latter being quasi-public rather than totally public) and to implement techniques of business management into university administration.[44] Proprivate proponents, on the other hand, contend that the private sector deserves public support because it is helping to meet important social demand and that its clientele (generally the least privileged among IHE enrollees) merits both quality instruction and affordable tuition costs.[45]

A closely related controversy concerns the question of charging fees at federal establishments.[46] As already noted, public institutions became tuition free in the early 1950s, but this policy was never sanctioned legally. Since the late 1960s, a number of high ranking officials have made statements favoring the reinstitution of fees for those able to pay. The debate intensified in the early 1980s when a leading advocate of tuition became the minister of education. Arguments in favor of user charges are that such a policy would generate needed funds and also serve purposes of equity since now the rich, who gain entrance by attending high-quality private primary and secondary schools, receive a free ride to credentials that confer an elite status at the cost of society as a whole. Antituition forces respond that fees would further solidify existing class lines (only the rich would be able to pay), that efforts to provide scholarships to the needy would be undermined by patronage and corruption, and that charging students would be merely a first step toward privatization.

Both the tuition and public versus private issues were hotly contested during the 1987/88 constitutional convention. Progressive forces won the former by having included in the constitution an item declaring that all public institutions must be free of charge. They were unsuccessful, though, in efforts to guarantee that public funds be used exclusively for public institutions. According to the new document, community, confessional, and philanthropic schools are also eligible. Other items in the constitution pertaining to higher education establish a minimum percentage of tax receipts that federal, state, and municipal governments must apply to education, guarantee to universities didactic-scientific, administrative, and financial autonomy, and call for the "insolubility" of teaching, research, and extension.[47] It should be noted, however, that the last three dictates already existed in Brazilian law and, as the contents of this chapter should suggest, none has been effectively implemented. Indeed, both within and outside the academic community there is little consensus as to what terms like "autonomy" and "indissolubility" really mean.[48]

As Brazil embarks on the last decade of the century, its higher education inadequacies are widely recognized and actively discussed. Proposals for reform abound, although no clear agreement on appropriate approaches is evident. ANDES, representing most faculty members at major universities, offers a plan calling for, among other things, more institutional control over MEC allotments, decentralization of power and participatory decision making within establishments, and restriction and closer supervision of the private sector.[49] A publication by three university rectors in São Paulo adopts a different orientation, arguing for abandoning the "single model" approach that has characterized federal higher education policy since 1920 and, instead, promoting system diversity and fortifying the private IHE network.[50] Other writers have emphasized the need for effective faculty evaluation, for research and performance incentives, and for strengthening the general education component of university instruction.[51] In the final analysis, however, it is clear that the difficulties confronting Brazilian higher education reflect deeper troubles that permeate the wider society. Such problems include poverty, income inequality, regional disparity, pervasive public bureaucracy, and a school system notoriously poor on the lower levels. Rapid modernization and a recent transition from dictatorship to democracy add to the complexity of finding acceptable, workable remedies. Clearly, the crisis in Brazilian higher education reflects a wider social crisis and solutions to the former require major improvements with respect to the latter.

Notes

1. For recent statistical information on Brazilian higher education, see Ministério da Educacão, *Sinopse estatística de ensino superior: graduacão* (Brasília: Servico de Estatística da Educacão e Cultura, 1988). All current figures in this chapter are from this source, unless otherwise specified.

2. For regional comparisons of scholarly output, see Claudio de Moura Castro, "Ha' producão científica no Brasil," in Simon Schwartzman and Claudio de Moura Castro, eds., *Pesquisa universitária em questão* (Campinas: Editora da UNICAMP, 1986; São Paulo: Ícone, 1986), 190–224.

3. For enrollment comparisons over time, see Daniel Levy, *Higher Education and the State in Latin America: Private Challenges to Public Dominance* (Chicago: University of Chicago Press, 1986), 180.

4. These "cursinhos" are discussed in Fay Haussman and Jerry Haar, *Education in Brazil* (Hamden, Conn.: Archon, 1978), 87–88. See also Levy, *Higher Education*, 191–92.

5. For a recent critical analysis of Brazilian secondary schools, see Acácia Kuenzer, *Ensino de 2o. grau: O trabalho como principio educativo* (São Paulo: Cortez, 1988).

6. See Florestan Fernandes, *Universidade Brasileira: Reforma ou revolucao?* (São Paulo: Alfa-Omega, 1975), chap. 5; Luis Navarro de Britto and Inaiá Carvalho, Condicionantes sócio-econômicos dos estudantes da Universidade Federal da Bahia (Salvador: CRH/UFBA, 1978).

7. Comparisons made based on figures in Haussman and Haar, *Education in Brazil*, 93, and Ministério da Educacão, *Sinopse: Graducão*, 21.

8. In recent years most professors have earned substantially less than U.S. $1,000 per month (information based on paychecks received by author as professor [now Adjunto III] in Brazilian federal university system since 1978).

9. For details concerning career structure at federal universities, see Decreto No. 94.664, reprinted in *Textos APUB* (Salvador: Associacão dos Professores Universitários da Bahia, 1987), 11–22.

10. The nature of graduate study in Brazil is discussed in Claudio de Moura Castro, "O que esta' acontecendo com a educacão no Brasil," in *A Transicão incompleta: Brasil desde 1945* ed. E. Bacha and H. S. Klein (São Paulo: Paz e Terra, 1986), especially pp. 148–51. Also see Haussman and Haar, *Education in Brazil*, 92–94.

11. Ministério da Educacão, *Sinopse estatítica do ensino superior: Pos-graduacão* (Brasilia: Servico de Estatística da Educacão e Cultura, 1986).

12. Background on research in Brazil and the contribution of universities and their graduate programs are provided in Simon Schwartzman, *Formacão da comunidade científica no Brasil* (Rio de Janeiro: FINEP, 1979); Schwartzman and Castro, *Pesquisa universitária*; Edmundo Campos Coelho, *A Sinecura acadêmica: A ética universitária em questão* (São Paulo: Vertice Ed. Revista dos Tribunais, 1988).

13. Castro, "Ha' producão científica," especially 220–1.

14. Castro puts the estimate at 70 percent in "O

Que esta' acontecendo," 126. Alírio Fernando de Souza suggests a figure of 80 percent in "Higher Education in Brazil: A Short Note" (1989, Mimeograph).

15. The financing of Brazilian higher education is reviewed in Levy, *Higher Education*, 184–93. Also see José Carlos de Araujo Melchior, O *financiamento da educacão no Brasil* (São Paulo: E.P.U., 1987); and David Plank, "Issues in Brazilian School Finance," *Journal of Educational Finance* (in press).

16. This point is argued by Levy in his well-documented analysis in *Higher Education*, 184–85. Others, though, claim that more public funds go to private entities than is commonly recognized. See Luis Antonio Cunha, "Ensino superior brasileira nos anos 80: Divergências e paradoxos," in *Nova realidade, novos desafios*, ed. José Augusto de Lima Rocha (Salvador: Washington Estúdio, 1986), 25–38; and Jacques Velloso, "Política educacional e recursos para o ensino: O salário-educacão e a universidade federal," *Cadernos de Pesquisa*, 60 (1987): 3–29.

17. The organizational structure of the Brazilian university is described by Maria Stela Santos Graciani in O *Ensino superior no Brasil: A estrutura de poder na universidade em questão* (Petropolis, R.J.: Vozes, 1982); and Antonio Gaspar Ruas, "O Ensino superior no Brasil e sua estrutura básica," in *Educacão brasileira contemporânea: organizacão e funcionamento*, ed. Walter E. Garcia (São Paulo: McGraw-Hill, 1978), 126–64. Also see Haussman and Haar, *Education in Brazil*, 80–84.

18. For a critical treatment of MEC's control over the university system, see Pedro Lincoln Carneiro Leão Mattos, *As Universidades e o governo federal: Politica de controle do governo em relação as universidades federais autarquias e suas consequências sobre as estruturas administrativas destas instituicões* (Recife: Universidade Federal de Pernambuco, 1983).

19. For a scholarly study of CRUB, see Georges Fréderic Mirault Pinto, *Caracterizacão de Conselho de Reitores das Universidades Brasileiras como poder intermediário* (Brasília: Conselho de Reitores das Universidades, 1983).

20. See Graciani, O *Ensino superior*, especially 115.

21. ANDES is discussed critically by Castro in "O Que esta' acontecendo," 135–9; and by Eduardo Portela in "Desempenho docente na universidade brasileira," *Educación* 30 (1986): 79–81. A balanced, analytical account of the organization and activity of the university employee and student associations in the 1980s has not yet been produced.

22. Histories of higher education in Brazil are provided by Vera Regina A. Canuto, *Políticos e educadores: a organizacão do ensino superior no Brazil* (Petropolis, R.J.: Vozes, 1987); Luis Antonio Cunha, A U*niversidade temporã* (Rio de Janeiro: Civilizacão Brasileira, 1980), A U*niversidade crítica* (Rio de Janeiro: Francisco Alves, 1983), A *Universidade reformanda* (Rio de Janeiro: Francisco Alves, 1988); Maria de Lourdes Fávero, *Universidade e poder: Análise crítica/fundamentos históricas: 1930–1945* (Rio de Janeiro: Achiame', 1980); Otaiza de Oliveira Romanelli, *História da educacão no Brasil (1930-1973)*, 11th ed. (Petropolis, R.J.: Vozes, 1989); Jose' Antonio Tobias, *História da educacão brasileira* (São Paulo: IRASA, 1986). Histories in English are dated but informative. See Fernando de Azevedo, *Brazilian Culture* (New York: Macmillan, 1950); and Robert J. Havighurst and J. Roberto Moreira, *Society and Education in Brazil* (Pittsburgh: University of Pittsburgh Press, 1965). This section draws from all of these sources. Specific contributions of some of the above and additional, more specialized literature are referenced in notes numbered 23–36.

23. For analysis of forces mitigating against the creation of a Brazilian university in the latter nineteenth century, see Roque Spencer Maciel de Barros, A *Ilustracão brasileira e a idéia de universidade* (São Paulo: Convívio/Editora da USP, 1986).

24. Figures from Cunha, *Universidade temporã*, 148.

25. For in-depth treatment of the founding of USP, see Irene de Arruda Ribeiro Cardoso, A *Universidade da comunhão paulista: O projeto de criacão da Universidade de São Paulo* (São Paulo: Cortez: Autores Associados, 1982).

26. For the creation of PUC/RJ, see Levy, *Higher Education*, 176–8.

27. Figures from Cunha, *Universidade crítica*, 253.

28. This point is developed in Cunha, *Universidade crítica*, 207–52.

29. Details on the creation of UnB are furnished by Darcy Ribeiro, the institution's first rector, in A *Universidade necessária* (Rio de Janeiro: Paz e Terra, 1969) and *UnB: investigacão e descaminho* (Rio de Janeiro: Avenir, 1978).

30. The history of the student movement in Brazil from 1938 to about 1970 is provided by Cunha in his three volumes: *Universidade temporã*, 322–28; *Universidade crítica*, 48–71, 207, 213–16, 227–34; *Universidade reformanda*, 30–31, 47, 55–69.

31. See Canuto, *Políticos*, 76-113; Romanelli, *História*, 228–33; Cunha, *Universidade reformanda*, 240–316.

32. For the text of Law 5540/68 and complementing decrees (numbers 53/66, 252/67, 464/69), see Guido Ivan de Carvalho, ed., *Ensino superior: Legislacão e jurisprudência*, vol. 1 (São Paulo:

Ed. Revista dos Tribunais, 1975), 77–103.

33. See, for example, Luis Antonio Cunha, *Qual universidade* (São Paulo: Cortez/Autores Associados, 1989), 53; Dermeval Saviani, *Política e educação no Brasil: O papel do Congresso Nacional na legislação do ensino* (São Paulo: Cortez Autores Associados, 1987), 24.

34. See especially Cunha, *Universidade reformanda*, 39–115, 307–16.

35. Cunha, in *Universidade reformanda*, 167–226, provides balanced analysis of USAID involvement. Key USAID recommendations are included in Rudolph Atcon, *Rumos a reformulação estrutural da universidade brasileira* (Rio de Janeiro: Ministério de Educação e Cultura, 1965). For critical treatment, see Ted Goertzel, "MEC-USAID: Ideologia do desenvolvimento americano aplicado a educação superior brasileira," *Revista Civilização Brasileira*, 14 (1967): 123–37.

36. For information on recent developments in the Brazilian economy and political situation, see articles in Alfred Stepan, ed., *Democratizing Brazil: Problems of Transition and Consolidation* (New York: Oxford University Press, 1989). Also see Werner Baer, *The Brazilian Economy: Growth and Development* (New York: Praeger, 1989); and Wayne A. Selcher, *Political Liberalization in Brazil* (Boulder, Colo.: Westview Press, 1986).

37. See Cunha, *Qual universidade*, 27.

38. For example: Coelho, *Sinecura*; Portela, "Desempenho docente"; Jose Arthur Giannotti, *A Universidade de ritmo de bárbarie* (São Paulo: Brasiliense, 1986).

39. See Levy, *Higher Education*, 179–82.

40. See Levy, *Higher Education*, 182; Cunha, "Ensino superior brasileira," 29–30.

41. See Levy, *Higher Education*, 182–83.

42. See Luis Aranha Corrêa do Lago, Fernando Lopes de Almeida, and Beatriz M. F. de Lima, *Estrutura ocupacional, educação e formação de mão de obra: Os países desenvolvidos e o caso brasileiro* (Rio de Janeiro: Instituto Brasileiro de Economia, Fundação Getúlio Vargas, 1983), 264–76. Also, Seminário Internacional sobre Educação e Trabalho, *Educação e trabalho* (Rio de Janeiro: Instituto Euvaldo Lodi, 1982).

43. See Lago, Almeida, and Lima, *Estrutura ocupacional*, 321; and Cândido Alberto Gomes, "Curso superior e mobilidade social: Vale a pena?", *Educação Brasileira* 10 (1988): 63–84.

44. For a defense of public schooling, see articles in Luis Antonio Cunha, ed., *Escola pública, escola particular e a democratização do ensino* (São Paulo: Cortez/Autores Associados, 1986).

45. For a defense of private schooling, see articles in Cândido Mendes and Claudio de Moura Castro, eds., *Qualidade, expansão e financiamento do ensino superior privado* (Brasília: Educam ABM, 1984).

46. The debate over tuition is summarized in Levy, *Higher Education*, 190–93. The references in notes 45 and 46 also apply.

47. Constituinte, *Constituição: República Federativa do Brasil, 1988* (Brasília: Senado Federal, 1988), Articles 202, 207, 212.

48. For historical treatment of the question of university autonomy, see Cunha, *Qual Universidade*, 9–32. For discussion of the teaching/research relationship at Brazilian universities, see Edmundo Campos Coelho, "Ensino e pesquisa: Um casamento (ainda) possível," in Schwartzman and Castro, *Pesquisa universitária*, 95–113.

49. "Proposta para a universidade brasileira," *Cadernos ANDES*, no. 2 (1986): 17–28.

50. Jose Goldemberg, Paulo Renato Sousa, and Jorge Nagle, "O Ensino superior: Contribuição ao debate sobre os fundamentos de uma nova Lei de Diretrizes e Bases," *Educação Brasileira* 10 (1988): 13–25.

51. See, for example, Cunha, *Qual Universidade*, 68–85; Coelho, *Sinecura*; Giannotti, *Universidade de ritmo*.

Chile

Joseph P. Farrell

◆

This chapter focuses on the recent and current state of higher education in Chile, as influenced by a series of postsecondary policy changes introduced by the military government that has been in power since 1973. These policies cannot be properly understood without considering (1) the previous development of postsecondary education; (2) the ideological framework from which they were derived; and (3) several related, and consistent, changes in other parts of the educational system. Thus the following discussion will begin with that broader context and then move on to a detailed consideration of the recent changes and current conditions regarding postsecondary education. It should be noted that this is being written in April 1989. In late 1988, the Chilean military government lost a plebiscite through which it had hoped to confirm General Pinochet as president for eight more years. The government appears to have accepted the results of the plebiscite, and the nation is now thoroughly involved in a political campaign leading to an election to be held in December 1989. Recent opinion polls indicate that currently opposition forces will win that election and bring a very different government to Chile. Since the higher education policies discussed here have been very controversial, any new government may substantially alter the postsecondary system. The description and analysis of the current situation found below is written in the present tense. By the time this is published, it may be more appropriate to read it in the past tense.

Chile has long been considered to have one of the most advanced educational systems in Latin America. After independence from Spain was achieved early in the nineteenth century, successive governments recognized the importance of education to the consolidation and development of the new nation, and that recognition was converted into policy and action much more rapidly than was typical in Latin America. In 1842 Chile became the first Latin American nation to formally establish a system of public instruction. Before 1850 the University of Chile had been established, on the Napoleonic model, and it became a major focal point for bringing the "liberal" political philosophies of non-Mediterranean Europe into the nation. In 1860 primary education was made free, for all who wished to attend; enrollments at all levels grew steadily thereafter. Later in the century, Chile became the first Latin American nation to admit women to the university and to allow them to practice the professions to which the university provided access.

Throughout the first half of the century there was a steady expansion of educational opportunity, particularly at the primary level, and more slowly at the postsecondary level. In 1940 there were just under 8,000 students enrolled in university, representing 1.7 percent of the eligible age-group, almost all of whom came from the small socioeconomic elite of the society. The postwar epoch saw a significant expansion of university enrollment, reaching 76,979 students by 1970, which constituted 9.0 percent of the eligible age group. The female enrollment ratio was only slightly lower at 7.1 percent, continuing a long-standing pattern of providing almost equal university access for females. A major university reform was introduced in the late 1960s which focused principally on democratization of internal governance, allowing for participation by all sectors of the university community (academic staff, nonacademic staff, and students) in the election of university authorities at all levels. The resulting elections were fought almost entirely along political party lines. In a politically highly polarized society, almost all decision making within universities became highly politicized, and a period of great turbulence and internal disruption ensued. In 1970 the socialist government of Salvador Allende was elected; part of its platform was the slogan "University for all." During the following three years a massive expansion of university enrollment occurred; it grew by 89 percent between 1970 and 1973, reaching an enrollment ratio of 16.8 percent in the latter year. A wide array of measures were adopted to increase access to university resources for the children of workers and peasants, and political fights within the universities became increasingly disruptive and paralyzing.

The military coup in September 1973 which eliminated the Allende government, ended a long tradition of elective parliamentary democracy in the nation. It also marked the introduction of a reigning political ideology very different from anything experienced in Chile's recent past, which was rigorously used to reorient almost all areas of national policy. In education, it resulted in a series of major reforms that represent a very significant break with national tradition. These new educational policies are particularly interesting for three reasons: (1) they represent an unusually close correspondence between an official government ideology and educational policy; (2) but at the same time they present the ironic situation in which some policies long advocated by the political left in Latin America have been implemented by an authoritarian right-wing military government for its own, quite different, purposes; and (3) they reflect an

inherent contradiction between two major strands of the reigning ideology.

A central aspect of the military government's policy toward education has been to systematically purge the universities (and lower-level schools as well) of any potential sources of "dissident" thought. This policy has, however, had one unintended consequence. It led to the creation of a large network of nonofficial research and teaching institutes, here called the "counter-academy," which have kept alive outside of the state-controlled universities Chile's long tradition of critical scholarship. This appears to be a unique development within an ideologically repressive regime.

The New Ideology

In one sense, the Pinochet government in Chile can be seen as a modern embodiment of the Mediterranean corporatist philosophy of the state, which arrived in Latin America with the Spanish and Portuguese colonizers. This philosophy has been a fundamental strand of Latin American political thought since the earliest colonial epoch. In twentieth-century Europe, this political philosophy undergirded the Mussolini and Franco regimes in Italy and Spain. It includes a strong stress on patriotism based on a sense of emergent national destiny, depoliticization of the society, a belief in a relatively fixed and immutable class order with opportunity for individual economic advancement based upon personal ability or initiative, strict authoritarian rule, and an emphasis on order, discipline, efficiency, and sobriety in all areas of national life. In the words of Kathleen Fischer: "Society is viewed as an organic entity, in which man exists in a complex, hierarchical network of social structures, of which the State is the ultimate manifestation. . . . The embodiment of the nation is her leadership, an elite that is the expression of the will and purpose of the people. A primordial task of the government, through its military and internal security apparatuses, is to protect the nation from internal and or external subversion and to eliminate from national life all vestiges of 'foreign' ideologies identified as subversive of the national destiny, particularly 'Marxism-Leninism.'"[1]

In its recent manifestations in Latin American military dictatorships, this political philosophy has incorporated, primarily due to the influence of United States military advisors and trainers, a strong strain of anticommunism (under what is often referred to as the "National Security Doctrine"). But in this sense "communism" is only the most recent of the "foreign" ideologies seen as potentially "subversive of the national destiny." For example, in the previous century the ideas of the classical English liberal philosophers, such as John Stuart Mill, Jeremy Bentham, Nassau Senior, Malthus, etc., and a few decades later the French and Italian radical socialists, played a similar role. To identify a regime such as the Chilean military government as only, or fundamentally, "anticommunist" or "antisocialist" is to miss the fact that the basic conception of the state, and the individual's relation to it, resonates deeply with a very ancient element of Latin American cultural history.

In post-1973 Chile this traditional corporatist model was melded with a commitment to the principle that economic activity should be, to the greatest extent possible, governed by the free play of market forces, both internally and externally, with the national government playing the minimal possible role in the regulation of free competition between individuals and private enterprises. This economic doctrine, which was brought to Chile by a cadre of young economists who were trained at the University of Chicago under the influence of Milton Friedman (in Chile they are called the "Chicago boys"), has been generalized to all areas of government activity under the doctrine of the "minimal" or "subsidiary" state. In this view, the state should undertake only those roles essential to the well-being and integrity of the nation which demonstrably cannot be handled effectively by private individuals or agencies.

While the corporatist aspect of the government philosophy is part of a very old tradition, the emphasis on a minimal state role represented a major shift from previous Chilean history. All Chilean regimes during the several decades preceding 1973, including the most conservative, placed a high value on government intervention, initiative, and regulation, not only in the economy, but in most areas of public policy. Indeed, by the late 1960s, in Latin America as a whole, only Cuba exceeded Chile in the degree of direct or indirect state intervention in the national economic system.

As should be evident, there was in the post-1973 Chilean political condition a built-in contradiction between the demands of the traditional corporatist model for a maximal state role in the ideological sphere—primarily carried by the military governors—and the demands of the civilian "Chicago boys" for a minimal state role in most areas of government policy. This contradiction has never been fully resolved, and it can be seen in the development of educational policy after 1973.

Immediate Post-Coup Changes in Education

Official statements regarding education during the first year after the coup contained not positive declarations of new policy directions but allegations regarding the condition in which the military government had found the educational system in September 1973. It was claimed that the previous government had "launched a sustained campaign against the substantive values of our nationality and tried to penetrate into the consciousness of Chilean children and youth with a Marxist-Leninist ideology far removed from the idiosyncrasy of our people." Moreover, it was claimed that within the Ministry of Education there was found "a high degree of disorganization, inefficiency, and structural anarchy" and that the primary and secondary schools and universities had been semiparalyzed throughout the previous year, operating irregularly because of strikes, occupations of buildings, and confrontations.[2] Accordingly, the first educational measures of the military regime were aimed at these problems. Plans for administrative simplification and decentralization were announced, aimed at transferring many aspects of educational control and decision making from the level of the national ministry, where they had always resided in a highly centralized system, down to the level of the provincial authorities. Educators at all levels were instructed to emphasize order, discipline, patriotism, exaltation of the military, and complete dedication to academic studies. A massive campaign was undertaken to purify the educational system of anything seen as reflecting Marxist-Leninist infiltration. This involved such measures as elimination from the schools of teachers who were in any way politically suspect; closing or suspending the activities of schools or faculties that had a history of left-wing political orientation, including particularly many university faculties; close military supervision of schools at all levels—military rectors were appointed for all universities, and all civilian school directors were made directly responsible to local military authorities; selection and control of the content of textbooks and other teaching material; careful supervision of who, other than teachers and students, could enter educational premises; elimination or tight control of student organizations; and severe sanctioning of any "political" activity, particularly in universities but also in secondary schools.

Within the universities it has been estimated that the early period of military intervention resulted in the purging of approximately 25 percent of the teaching faculty, 10 to 15 percent of the nonacademic staff, and 15 to 18 percent of the students (totalling more than 20,000 expelled students). Twenty-three academic departments or faculties in five of the eight national universities were closed. The disciplines most affected were the social sciences and political science, and to a lesser degree, psychology, social history, anthropology, and economics.[3] Counteracting the democraticization of university governance which resulted from the reforms of the late 1960s, and which provided students and nonacademic staff, as well as faculty, access to control over decision making, universities under the new regime were governed with a mixture of managerial principles appropriate to private-sector economic organizations and military notions of efficiency and discipline. One observer has described the internal situation as follows: "Professors of even the highest rank . . . had to sign attendance registers, they could not speak with university authorities without following the 'chain of command,' they were not consulted regarding academic decisions which directly affected them, and they did not dare voice a discordant opinion even in the most respectful and measured terms."[4]

In December 1975, statements regarding the educational objectives of the new government were included in an official proclamation outlining the "National Objectives of the Government of Chile." The document first noted: "Education should deepen and transmit love of country and national values, respect for the free and transcendent vocation of the human being and the rights and duties derived therefrom, appreciation of the family as the basic cell of society, loyalty to the concept of national unity, and valuation of wisdom and virtue as the elements of progress for man and society."[5] It emphasized the preferential right of parents to educate their children and to have the freedom to choose the education they wished for their children, so long as this would not involve the transmission of any idea or doctrine that would threaten "tradition or national unity" or "the integrity of the family or the nation." Specifically excluded from the concept of freedom or teaching was the use of education for day-to-day political purposes.

One of the most essential functions of the state would be "assuring that compulsory primary education is a reality for all Chileans, providing it without cost, at least for those who cannot finance it themselves. Moreover, it is the state's role to establish and maintain educational institutions at all levels, to the extent that private initiative is insufficient to meet all the needs of the nation, and to provide subsidiary financing to education in general."[6] The other major role of the state would be to establish effective mechanisms to control the quality of education provided in both public and private institutions.

During the next several years no major structural alterations in the educational system were introduced. University enrollments were curtailed (they fell by 17.76 percent between 1974 and 1980) and university matriculation fees were increased markedly, on the ground that most students were from relatively prosperous families whose education should not be subsidized by the state.

The Reform Begins

In 1979 a set of Presidential Directives regarding education were issued, accompanied by a public letter from the president to the minister of education and a nationally televised presidential speech on educational policy. These initiated a series of major educational changes that have since been reshaping almost all aspects of Chilean education. With respect to philosophy and objectives, these presidential declarations represented an amplification of the "National Objectives" statement issued four years before. In particular, the "subsidiary" role of the state in education

was emphasized. The president indicated that it "should be considered improbable" that the state would further expand its own educational role. Rather, "it will energetically stimulate the assistance that the private sector can provide."

The primary objective of state policy was to ensure as quickly as possible that all Chilean children receive a complete and adequate primary education, sufficient to make of each child "a good worker, a good citizen, and a good patriot, and to have options open for further education." Secondary education, and particularly university education, were to be considered "exceptional situations" for youth, earned solely through academic effort. Those who received such education should pay for it, or, if their studies were supported by the state, through subsidies to institutions or through loans or grants to the student, they should repay the community when they entered the work force. The most important substantive changes introduced in higher education as a result of the Presidential Directives follow.

Postsecondary Reform

Structural Changes

Between 1973 and 1981 no major structural changes were introduced into the university system. State subsidies were decreased (from 49 percent of national educational expenditures in 1974 to 30 percent in 1981), and student fees were increased. At the beginning of 1981 there were eight universities in the nation, with forty-three regional campuses, offering postsecondary education in more than 650 specialties and subspecialties. In 1981 a massive change in the postsecondary system was introduced. The primary objectives of the new system were:

1. To administratively rationalize and simplify the existing system (for example, by collapsing the regional

campuses of several national universities in a city or region into a single local university).

2. To convert universities from institutions that combined professional training with general humanistic or liberal arts education and critical scholarship and research, into centers devoted wholly to training for professional certification.

3. To improve the quality of instruction by submitting postsecondary institutions to the rigors of free-market competition.

Under this system, these institutions are to ultimately thrive or fail depending upon their ability to attract students because of the quality of their programs and their salience to the job market.

Under the new system three types of postsecondary institutions are available. The broadest and most prestigious are *universities*. Only universities can grant the academic degrees of licenciatura, magister, and doctor (approximately equivalent to bachelor's, master's, and doctoral degrees). In addition, there are twelve identified professional titles, with appropriate training programs, that can be offered by universities only: lawyer, architect, biochemist, dentist, agronomist, civil engineer, commercial engineer, forestry engineer, medical doctor, veterinary doctor, psychologist, and pharmaceutical chemist. Universities may also offer professional certification and academic degrees in other fields if they choose. If new universities are formed, they must offer at least three of the professional titles noted above, and (originally until 1986 but extended to 1988) be authorized by the Ministry of Interior "which will judge the real or presumed danger that such an entity could represent to public order or national security, . . . avoiding the creation of universities by currently dissolved political parties and especially Marxist sectors in general."[7]

Professional Institutes may offer any professional certificates except the twelve reserved for universities. They cannot grant academic degrees to their students, but their graduates may be enrolled in master's or doctoral programs in universities. Both universities and professional institutes may receive state subsidies under a scheme described below. *Technical Institutes* are wholly private institutes offering middle-level technical certification in whatever fields they wish, subject to the control and supervision of the Ministry of Education.

Funding Policy Changes

The structural change was accompanied by a new policy for state financing of universities and professional institutes. The new policy was to be phased in between 1981 and 1986. However, due to what were seen as academically counterproductive responses of many institutions, and the effect on government finances of a severe economic recession in the early to mid-1980s, several significant changes were introduced in subsequent years. Consequently, the original policy and its justification will first be described, and the later changes then noted.

This new funding policy had three principal objectives. The first was to continue to gradually reduce the overall level of state subsidization of postsecondary education, shifting more of the cost burden to the students or their families. This was justified on the grounds of social justice. In the words of a policy document produced by the Ministry of the Interior:

So-called free university education which some still demagogically defend has meant during many years that the education of professionals was supported by the state, using the money of all Chileans. In this fashion low-income sectors, whose children rarely enter university, have been supporting the education of children from high-income sectors. The situation was even worse, from the point of view of justice, when one considered that such professional education enabled its recipients to gain throughout their lives income levels well above the average of those who paid for the education.[8]

The second objective was to allow for and stimulate modest enrollment increases without corresponding increases in state fiscal responsibility. The third objective was to stimulate the academic development of universities and professional institutes by making them compete for the academically most talented students in the nation.

The level of direct state subsidy of the postsecondary sector was to be reduced by 50 percent between 1981 and 1986 (and to remain constant, adjusted for inflation, thereafter), and to be redistributed among the eight existing universities and new institutions derived from them (i.e., new professional institutes under their supervision and new regional universities formed from existing local campuses of the traditional universities) through a formula established by law. This reduction in direct institutional subsidies was to be replaced by a nationwide system of per-student grants that would gradually increase through 1986. These per-student grants were, however, to be available only for the 20,000 new students each year who scored highest on the national university entrance examination, and were to be weighted by field of study according to the estimated costs of providing the training (with a weight of 2.5 for medicine and dentistry; 1.8 for biochemistry, civil engineering, agronomy, forestry engineering, chemistry, pharmacy, and veterinary medicine; 1.0 for all other fields). Any student beyond this 20,000 (in 1983 approximately 38,000 new students were admitted to universities and professional institutes) would not provide their institutions with the per capita subsidy.

Individual student fees were markedly increased, but differentiated with reference to the cost to the institution of providing a particular field of study and the projected lifetime earnings of students in the field of study. This new fee policy was accompanied by an expanded system of state scholarships and loans granted in accord with the student's family income. State-supported institutions would receive an additional grant based on the number of their students (among the "20,000 best") who required such individual financial support.

The immediate effect of this new funding policy was to produce what many observers referred to as "savage competition" among postsecondary institutions as they attempted to maximize their income in response to the new "market signals." For example, new enrollments in some of the more highly subsidized fields of study increased sharply (between 1981 and 1982 new enrollments in the engineering fields increased by 380 percent).[9] Moreover, to attract new students (especially the 20,000 best) institutions created new fields of study for which they did not often have adequate teaching resources (fifty-four new fields were proposed by March, 1984, including such exotica as "preschool education with specialization in German") and to lower admission requirements. Strong complaints from postsecondary institutions and from politically powerful national organizations of university-educated professionals became increasingly public.

Among the changes which resulted were the following. In 1983 the differential weighting of per capita grants by field of study was eliminated. In 1984 the "20,000 best" policy was changed, so that *all* admitted students brought a state subvention to their institution. To preserve some competition for the most academically qualified students, however, the per capita grants are now weighted on a five-level scale according to the level of the student's score on the university entrance examination. The proportion of total state subsidy granted on a per-student basis was reduced from the intended target of 50 percent by 1986. By 1987 such indirect support was only 14.1 percent of total public funding for higher education.

Two further unanticipated outcomes of the 1981 changes were the formation of more provincial universities from regional campuses of the "old" universities than had been expected; and very slow development of new private (i.e., without public support) universities—by 1986 only three very small such institutions had been established. Accordingly, in 1987 the direct public support to "old" universities was reduced by 10 percent, with the funds redistributed to new regional institutions. This was accompanied by a "rationalization" of academic offerings in various regions. In the same year, with reference to the private university sector, "political" approval of new universities by the Ministry of the Interior was removed, such universities were allowed to compete for government research funding (see below), and private donations to universities were made tax-exempt. During the following year, 1988, four new private universities were either established or in the process of being established.

Cutting across the effects of the funding policies discussed earlier was the effect of the severe economic recession experienced at the same time. It had originally been anticipated that the reduction in total public support for higher education would be gradual, accomplished mainly by keeping the rate of growth of state support below the anticipated rate of inflation. However, the economic crisis produced a much sharper decrease. By 1987 total state support for postsecondary education, in constant currency, was approximately half of that provided in 1980. This has made higher education much more dependent upon student fees, which have been steadily rising. Between 1980 and 1987 the proportion of total postsecondary sector revenue derived from student fees increased from 29.4 percent to 51.6 percent.[10]

One final aspect of the 1981 reform, relating to university research funding, is worth noting. Traditionally, university-based research had been funded through competitions within each university for research funds set aside by the university in its own budget. The 1981 reform established the National Science and Technology Fund (Fondecyt) which provides research support via national level discipline-based and peer-reviewed competitions.

Table 1

Changes in Number of Postsecondary Institutions, 1980–1987

Type of Institution	1980	1982	1984	1986	1987
University with public support	8	17	17	20	20
University without public support	0	1	3	3	4
Professional institute with public support	0	7	7	4	2
Professional institute without public support	0	13	19	19	19
Technical institute	na	na	102	112	na

Source: Maria Jose Lemaiter, "Caracteristicas generales de las instituciones privadas de educacion superior en Chile," in *La educacion superior privada en Chile*, ed. Viterbo Apablaza and Hugo Lavados. (Santiago, Chile: Corporacion de Promocion Universitario, 1988), p. 3, and Maria Jose Lemaitre, Ivan Lavados and Hugo Lavados, "Desajustes y perspectivas le la educacion superior en Chile," in *Educacional chileno*, eds. Hugo Lavado et al. (Santiago, Chile: Corporacion de Promocion Universitario, 1986), p. 369.

Between 1982 and 1988 the number of research projects funded by this national agency tripled, from 115 to 381, and the funds available, in constant pesos, increased steadily (for example, the increase in constant pesos between 1986 and 1987 was 75 percent). However, this significant increase in direct state support for research in universities was accompanied by an approximately equivalent decrease in the amount of research funds and the number of projects financed by the universities from their own funds. Thus, there has been little change in the amount of research conducted, but an almost complete shift away from university-based funding to the nationwide funding supplied by Fondecyt. This has had the indirect effect of freeing up the funds the universities previously devoted to research for teaching and administrative purposes. In a very tight fiscal situation this has been important—in 1987 Fondecyt research funding amounted to just over 6 percent of all state financing of postsecondary education under the mechanisms discussed previously.[11] It has also broadened the national research base beyond the traditional universities. As noted, new private universities are eligible for Fondecyt support, and nonuniversity research institutes (see the discussion of the "counter-academy" below) are able to compete for and do receive Fondecyt financing.

Structural and Enrollment Consequences

Table 1 displays the changes in the number of types of postsecondary institutions since 1981. Table 2 shows enrollment changes for the system as a whole and by type of institution. To interpret these data it must be noted that prior to 1981 all of the eight existing universities received direct state support, although six of them were formally (owned "private" and administered by nongovernmental entities such as the Catholic church). Before the 1981 reform there were no professional institutes, but there was a large system of private proprietary technical training schools operating at the postsecondary level. In 1980 these institutes enrolled 65,706 students compared to 118,978 in the university system, but they were not formally recognized or regulated by the Ministry of Education.

From Table 1 we see that by 1987 twelve new publicly supported universities but only four new privately financed universities had been established. Immediately following the new policy seven publicly supported professional institutes were formed, but five of these subsequently closed, while nineteen privately financed professional institutes were operating in 1987. By 1984 more than one hundred technical institutes had been recognized and approved by the Ministry of Education. Thus, institutional diversification did occur.

The enrollment data in Table 2 show a somewhat different picture, however. Although there was modest overall enrollment growth between 1982 and 1986 (12.9 percent increase), the postsecondary enrollment ratio did not change. Total enrollment growth was just sufficient to keep up with growth in the age-eligible population. Some shifts in the composition of that enrollment did result. Universities, overwhelmingly publicly supported universities, which offer the traditionally prestigious professions, maintained their predominant position within the system, increasing slightly their share of all postsecondary enrollment. This is where most of the enrollment growth centered. Previously unrecognized technical schools almost entirely converted themselves into technical institutes approved by the Ministry of Education, and some new technical institutes were created, but the total enrollment in this sector declined markedly. It is not clear whether this decline is due to market forces (e.g., changes in student perception of the quality or job relevance of the programs offered relative to their cost) or to the overall economic crisis in the society. The one wholly new type of institution, professional institutes, accounted for 13 percent of all postsecondary enrollment by 1986. There is no indication whether the enrollees in professional institutes were prospective university entrants who were not admitted to (or who did not believe they would be admitted to) universities, or students who would otherwise have attended technical institutes. (It may be instructive that the decline in technical institute enrollment is almost identical to the increase in enrollment in professional institutes).

Table 3 displays the postsecondary enrollment for 1986 by type of institution and by the occupation of the household head of the student's family, in three categories (roughly the upper class, middle class, and working class). Considering the

Table 2

Postsecondary Enrollment Change 1982–1986 by Type of Institution

Type	1982 N	1982 %	1983 N	1983 %	1986 N	1986 %	Total Increase
University with public support	102,050	51.4	105,154	49.4	122,127	54.4	20,077
University without public support	400	0.2	2,708	1.3	6,295	2.8	5,895
Professional institute with public support	14,230	7.2	16,796	7.9	10,443	4.7	-3,747
Professional institute without public support	3,690	1.9	7,524	3.5	18,717	8.3	15,023
Technical institute approved by Mined.	33,221	16.7	39,702	18.3	57,852	25.8	24,631
Technical institute other	45,117	22.7	41,022	19.3	8,900*	4.0	-36,217
Total postsecondary	198,708	100.0	212,906	100.0	224,334	100.0	25,662
Postsecondary enrollment ratio (age 20–24)		17.3		18.2		17.3	

Total change by type of institution:

University	+25,972
Professional Institute	+11,276
Technical Institue	-11,586

Total Change by Source of Funding:

with public support	+16,330
without public support	+9,332

* estimated

Source: Andres Sanfuentes, "Desarrollo de las universidades privadas en Chile; 1981–1988," in *La educacion superior privada en Chile*, eds. Viterbo Apablaza and Hugo Lavados. Santiago, Chile: Corporacion de Promocion Universitaria, 1988), p. 198; Luis Eduuardo Gonzalez, "Privatizacion y redistribucion de la educacion terciaria en Chile," in Apablaza and Lavados, p. 54 and p. 65; unpublished Ministry of Education data.

three types of institutions, there are only small differences among social classes in enrollment patterns. The percentages of students from each social class who are in universities and in technical institutes vary only slightly. The proportion of upper-class students in professional institutes is somewhat higher than that of middle- or working-class students. When publicly supported institutions are compared to those without public support, however, the differences are striking. Sixty percent of all upper-class students are enrolled in institutions without public support, while the same percentage of middle-class students are in publicly supported institutions. Fully 70 percent of working-class students are in institutions that receive public support, and almost all of those in private institutions are enrolled in technical institutes. Clearly, as one would expect, the "new" private sector—universities and professional institutes—(as noted above, technical institutes are a newly regulated form of an existing institutional sector)—are drawing students whose families can afford their high fees.

Table 4 presents the enrollment data in a different form. Here one finds the percentage of the enrollment within each institutional type which is derived from each occupational group, and the percentage of each occupational group in the total labor force. With these data one can calculate "selectivity indexes" that indicate the degree of over- or underrepresentation of each occupational group in each type of institution and in the system as a whole. (An index below 1.0 indicates underrepresentation; an index above 1.0 indicates overrepresentation; the farther away from 1.0 the greater the degree of under- or overrepresentation compared to a condition of perfect equity in which each population group would be represented in universities in proportion to its representation in the total population.) In the system as a whole upper-class students are overrepresented by a factor of 3.7 and

middle-class students by a factor of 2.4, while there are only 30 percent as many working-class students as one would expect if they had equitable access to postsecondary education. The patterns by type of institution and source of financing seen in Table 3 are naturally evident here as well. Working-class students are better represented (but still well below the equity an index of 1.0 would show) in publicly supported institutions. It is hardly surprising that poor youngsters are significantly underrepresented in postsecondary education and that middle- and upper-class youngsters are overrepresented—this is a worldwide pattern. What may be surprising is the comparatively high representation of working-class students—higher than one typically finds in developing nations. Chile has long had more equitable access to all levels of education than most developing nations provide, and major educational reforms in the late 1960s significantly increased the flow of working-class children through the educational system.[12] It is difficult to determine with certainty whether the general fee increases, or the reforms of 1981, have significantly changed the degree of class-linked discrimination in the system. Data from earlier periods are scarce, and they are not directly comparable to the 1986 figures either because different occupational categories are used or because of the changes in the structure of the system itself. A careful assessment of all the available data suggests that there has been little apparent change in the social class selectivity in Chilean postsecondary education since 1973.

In sum, the net effect of the structural and funding reforms of Chilean higher education had been to significantly reduce the level of public expenditure on this educational sector (in constant currency) without either reducing enrollment or changing its social class distribution. This shifting of part of the cost burden to students or their families, particularly during a period of severe economic recession, must mean that many poor and middle-class families are making great financial sacrifices to provide some form of post-secondary education for their children.

The Counter-Academy

The political-ideological "purification" campaign of the military government had, as one of its results, the removal from the universities of thousands of academics who were, for whatever reason, politically suspect. Many left the country, either voluntarily or under duress. However, several hundred remained in the nation and many of them formed, under the aegis and protection of the Catholic church and various international agencies, an extensive network of nongovernmental academic institutes. Using funds obtained primarily from aid agencies outside of Chile, these institutions are carrying on the tradition of critical academic research and cultural action that has been eliminated from the universities. Most of these institutions also provide noncredit university-level courses and seminars which are heavily attended by students enrolled in the uni-

Table 3

Postsecondary Enrollment (1986) by Type of Institution and Occupation of Household Head of Student's Family

Type of Institution	Occupation of Household Head						Total
	Big business & high exec.		Professionals, Technicians, office workers & small business		Workers & Artisans		
	N	%	N	%	N	%	
University with public support	2,931	36.6	93,793	57.0	25,402	59.2	1,221
University without public support	1,517	18.9	4,677	2.8	101	0.2	6,295
Total University	4,448	55.5	98,470	59.8	25,503	59.4	128,422
Professional institute with public support	251	3.1	5,483	3.3	4,710	11.0	10,443
Professional institute without public support	1,460	18.2	15,797	9.6	1,460	3.8	18,717
Total Professional Institutes	1,711	21.3	21,280	12.9	6,710	14.4	29,160
Technical institute*	1,851	23.1	44,777	27.2	11,223	26.0	57,852
Total postsecondary	8,010	100.0	164,527	100.0	42,896	100.0	215,433
Institutions with public support	3,482	39.7	99,276	60.3	30,112	70.2	
Institutions without public support	4,828	60.3	65,251	39.7	12,784	29.8	

* Data available only for technical institutes approved by the Ministry of Education.

Source: Ministry of Education Statistics.

versities and professional institutes, as well as educational programs for the general public, in which material that cannot be covered in the formal educational system is discussed.

A recent survey catalogued thirty-two of these nongovernmental academic institutions. Some are quite small, employing fewer than ten researchers. Others, however, are quite large, involving more than sixty researchers and large cadres of support staff.

The government has tried in various ways to harass these institutions. Staff members are occasionally arrested and held for a time. Government officials, such as tax inspectors, come to carefully check the records for "irregularities" that would allow the government to close down an institution. In one recent case, an institution was raided by security forces, all of its equipment, furnishings, records, and documents were removed, and several staff members arrested. (In this case, other institutions in the network immediately started to contribute funds to allow it to reopen.) But the system has continued to operate, indeed to thrive. Collectively, the counter-academy has constituted one of the most vigorous and lively centers of intellectual activity in all of Latin America. In spite of its evident desire to do so, the military government has not been able to seriously affect this network.

What one has, then, is a parallel postsecondary system, which has carried on all of the traditional functions of the university (research, teaching, community action), in which dissident opinions thrive, and which has operated outside the effective arena of control of a powerful authoritarian government. In a comparative context this is a unique phenomenon. Careful investigation is warranted to attempt to explain its existence. Here, only some preliminary thoughts are offered.

The existence and survival of these institutions have been partly due simply to the dedication, persistence, and courage of a large number of Chilean academics. The political protection provided by the association with the Catholic church, which has been the main source of effective institutional opposition within the society, is very important. Many of these institutes have been members of the Academy of Christian Humanism, an umbrella foundation established by the Church precisely to provide legal status and protection to such agencies. The fact that much of their activity is funded by external aid agencies (governmental, intergovernmental, and private) may be important. Part of the explanation must lie deep within the political and intellectual history of Chile. Their continued existence may also be seen as a part of, or a reflection of, the gradual but steady reemergence over the past decade of traditional pluralist and democratic values in Chile. This reemergence has increasingly limited the effective sphere of government power in restraining or eliminating dissidence.

Toward the Future

As noted at the beginning of this chapter, as these words are being written Chile is in the midst of a profound political transformation. During the past few years there has been a slow, but steadily increasing, diminution of "political" control of the postsecondary system. Although officially proscribed, elections within universities for department heads, and, more recently deans have been tolerated. Researchers associated with the counter-academy have increasingly been permitted, and in some cases invited, to participate in "official" academic meetings, and have had access to government research funds. Very recently, the Academy of Christian Humanism, and many of its associated institutions, has converted itself into the University of Christian Humanism, with Ministry of Education approval, and will offer its first courses leading to degrees in 1989. An educational research institute

Table 4

Proportion of Total Enrollment Derived From Three Occupational Groups (1986) by Type of Institution

Type of Institution	Occupation of Household Head					Total
	Big business & high exec.		Professionals, Technicians, office workers & small business		Workers & Artisans	
University with public support	2.4%	(.83)*	76.8%	(2.4)	20.8%	(.32)	100%
University without public support	24.1%	(8.3)	74.3%	(2.3)	1.6%	(.02)	100%
Total University	3.9%	(1.4)	76.9%	(2.4)	19.2%	(.29)	100%
Professional institute with public support	2.4%	(.83)	52.5%	(1.7)	45.1%	(.69)	100%
Professional institute without public support	7.8%	(2.7)	84.4%	(2.7)	7.8%	(.12)	100%
Total Professional Institutes	6.3%	(2.2)	76.3%	(2.4)	17.4%	(.27)	100%
Technical institute	3.2%	(1.1)	77.4%	(2.4)	19.4%	(.30)	100%
Total Postsecondary	3.7%	(1.3)	76.4%	(2.4)	19.9%	(.30)	100%
Total Labor Force	2.9%		31.7%		65.4%		

* Figures in parentheses are selectivity indexes. Enrollment %/total labor force %.

Source: Ministry of Education Statistics.

associated with that new university is currently sponsoring systematic discussion among representatives of a wide array of political parties and groups, seeking agreement on a core of needed educational changes that could form the basis for an educational reform to be introduced by whatever group wins the coming election. Although postsecondary education is part of those discussions, it is now not clear what direction proposed changes will take. But there is a considerable probability that, by the time these words are printed and read, Chilean higher education will be very different from what it has been during the past fifteen years. Time will tell.

Notes

1.   K. Fischer, "Political Ideology and Educational Reform in Chile," (Ph.D. diss., University of Southern California, 1977), 233.

2.   Ivan Nunez, *Evolucion de la politica educacional del regimen militar* (Santiago, Chile: Programa Interdisciplinario de Investigaciones en Educacion, 1982), 13–14.

3.   Jose Juaquin Brunner, *Informe sobre la educacion superior en Chile* (Santiago, Chile: FLACSO, 1981), 44.

4.   Juan de Dios Vial Correa, "El verdadero dasafio universitario," *Realidad Ano* 3, no. 35 (1982): 21.

5.   Nunez, *Evolucion*, 55.

6.   Ibid., 56.

7.   Guillermo Briones, *Las universidades Chilenas en el modelo de economia neo-liberal: 1973–1981* (Santiago, Chile: Programa Interdisciplinario

de Investigaciones en Educacion, 1981), 17.

8. Ibid., 15.

9. Christian Cox, "Autoritarismo, mercados y conocimiento: Evolucion de las politicas de educacion superior en Chile en los '80"(Paper presented at the seminar La Universidad en America Latina: Participacion y Gestion,

Brasilia, Brazil, October 1988), 9.

10. Ibid., 7–8.

11. Ibid., 17–18.

12. Ernesto Schiefelbein and Joseph P. Farrell, *Eight Years of Their Lives: Through Schooling to the Labour Market in Chile* (Ottawa, Canada: IDRC, 1982).

Colombia

Rosa C. Briceño

◆

The Colombian University in Historical Perspective

Origins

As in most Latin American countries, universities in Colombia were started by religious orders during the colonial period (1500–1810). Among the first founded were the Universidad de Santo Tomás (1580), the Academia Javeriana (1622), and the Colegio del Rosario (1653)—all still functioning today. Patterned after the Spanish universities of Salamanca and Alcala, colonial universities concentrated on the teaching of philosophy, art, and jurisprudence, and were primarily oriented to the training of the clerics and functionaries required by the vice-royalty. They contributed as well to the education of a small colonial aristocracy of Spanish descent and increasingly differentiated from the majority mestizo and Indian population.[1]

Shaping of the Traditional University

With independence from Spain in 1819 came the first struggles for control of higher education. Under the leadership of Bolivar and other independence leaders, there emerged a parallel system of higher education of a Napoleonic character that emphasized professionalization, secularity, and state control. From this period date the universities of Antioquia (1822), Cartagena (1827), and Cauca (1827).[2]

Throughout the nineteenth and first half of the twentieth century, the history of higher education in Colombia was strongly shaped by the struggles between conservatives and liberals—the two traditional groups that have governed the country since its independence. Essentially, the conservatives advocated a scholastic, religious, and privately controlled educational system, while the liberals pushed for a secular and public system. Under the influence of the latter, the Universidad Nacional de Colombia (UNC) was founded in 1867, as a national institution of higher education granted by law relative autonomy and full state funding. A liberal curriculum was established and new schools were created in arts and crafts, natural sciences, and engineering.[3]

The period of radical liberalism to which the UNC owes its founding came to an end with the establishment of what is known as the Conservative Republic, a long phase of conservative hegemony that lasted until 1930. During this period a new constitution (1886) and a concordat with the Vatican (1887)—still valid today—were established, reinforcing the power of the Catholic church and its conservative allies in Colombian society. Religious education was made compulsory and the church was given the power to veto any state measure on education.[4]

First Attempts at Modernization

The 1930s can be considered one of the most significant periods for shaping the profile of modern Colombian society. Under the impetus of industrialization—a process that gained momentum after the 1929 world capitalist crisis—the country underwent a redefinition of its productive base, an intense process of social diversification, and a reformulation of the role of the state in social development.[5] In 1934 the liberal presidency of Lopez Pumarejo launched a major program geared toward the modernization and capitalist development of the country. This was a period of considerable state support for the development of the public university, and in particular, of the UNC, which acquired a normative and pilot status within the higher education system. Between 1934 and 1946 funding for the UNC grew eleven and a half times in current *pesos*. Its enrollment tripled, from 1,159 to 3,673 students, half of the university population in 1946. New programs were created in areas such as agriculture, chemistry, architecture, economics, and business administration.[6]

With the fall of the liberal regime in 1945, and the assassination of the popular leader Jorge Eliecer Gaitán in 1948, Colombia entered one of the most bloody periods in its history, known as *La Violencia*. Interestingly, the years most characterized by violence and political instability, from the mid-1940s to the mid-1950s, were also marked by a notable economic and industrial growth. By then, capitalism had entered a new, transitional phase, with the United States as the center of the system. Multinational corporations spread their production worldwide, becoming a dominant force in the modernization and industrialization processes of Latin American societies.[7] United States investments in Colombia, in the form of international bank loans and industrial investments, doubled from 1943 to 1956, and foreign capital came to occupy a hegemonic position in the most dynamic sectors of the country's economy.[8]

These developments within the productive system together with other processes—such as the fast pace of urbanization (from 29.1 percent of the population in 1938 to 53.3 percent in 1964), an accelerated demographic growth, the emergence of new urban middle classes, and the growth of a university-age population for whom education appeared as the main channel for upward mobility—created increasing pressures for the expansion and modernization of higher education. Accordingly, in the mid-1940s higher education began a process of unprecedented growth, both in enrollments and creation of institutions. New "enclave" institutions patterned after the North American university were established with the support of transnationalized sectors. Among them were the Universidad del Valle (1947) and the Universidad de los Andes (1948). The state, for its part, designed its first policies to regulate higher education and promote the training of technical personnel abroad. For these purposes, it created the Colombian Institute for Educational Credit and Studies Abroad (ICETEX) in 1950, and the National University Fund (FUN) in 1954.

Launching a Modernizing University Project

To understand the dynamics of higher education in the more recent decades, it is necessary to take into account the new international forces impinging upon the university.[9] At a macrolevel, a series of political events in the Latin American region during the late 1950s—the Cuban Revolution in 1958, together with the fall of a number of dictators including Perez Jimenez in Venezuela, Odria in Peru, and Rojas Pinilla in Colombia—reflected the crisis of the old order in Latin America. Meanwhile the alternatives appeared clear. Either these societies would undergo revolutions as in Cuba, or full support would be given to the relatively new and dynamic social forces behind industrial modernization.

It was this context that new modernization theories emerged at the center of the world capitalist system to explain underdevelopment in peripheral countries. Under President John F. Kennedy's administration, the Alliance for Progress (1961) translated this ideology of modernization into a package of reforms in the economic, political, and sociocultural arenas.[10] In education, indigenous universities were considered key agencies for institution- and competency-building in underdeveloped nations, and became the targets of international aid for these purposes.[11]

Colombia entered the 1960s with high social expectations for participation and development. After the crude years of La Violencia (1946–53) and a military dictatorship (1953–57), the country returned to a democratic—albeit limited—civilian rule with the establishment of the National Front in 1958. The Colombian elites agreed that for a period of sixteen years (1958–74) the presidency would alternate every four years between conservatives and liberals, who would share other government powers equally. The country lived under this parity formula until 1978. The National Front was a political restructuring that consolidated the position of the dominant classes at a political as well as at an economic level. With the ascent of the industrial bourgeoisie to a leading position within the ruling elites, the state became an increasingly important agent for modernization and development. Adopting a "developmentalist" perspective, the elite hoped to spur economic growth, with the assumption that it would have a spillover effect that eventually would improve the economic lot of the poor majority.[12]

In higher education the state undertook a concerted effort to reform the university in order to eliminate its most traditional features and reorient it according to developmentalist goals and needs.[13] For this task it followed the guidelines set at the Alliance for Progress, of which Colombia became a showcase. It drew from modernization proposals elaborated by United States advisors for the reform of Latin American universities, in particular the Atcon Report,[14] and it relied increasingly on an international network of aid and knowledge diffusion that provided the expertise

and financial assistance for the design and implementation of its programs. From 1960 to 1967 foreign aid directed to education amounted to forty-eight million dollars. Just for the expansion and reform of higher education the country received more than twenty-five million dollars.[15]

The Rectorship of Jose Felix Patiño (1964–66) represents the most ambitious attempt at implementing a full-scale modernization project in the National University. The reform, entitled "Towards the Development University" and inspired by the North American university model, included among others the following objectives: changing the system of twenty-seven semiautonomous faculties into nine integrated schools; diversifying the professions and creating new graduate programs; fortifying the department as the basic university unit; emphasizing the notion of general studies; reorganizing and rationalizing the administrative system; standardizing admission and crediting procedures; creating a body of full-time professors and providing possibilities for their specialization and international exchange; intensifying research activities; and promoting the links with other knowledge-producing institutions at home and abroad, as well as with the international aid network.[16]

University Conflict

The implementation of these reforms was anything but smooth. A university movement gained force in Colombia during the 1960s that constituted one of the main forces of opposition to the National Front regime.[17] University conflict reached its peak during the so-called Crisis of 1971, which led to an almost total paralysis of higher education activities in the country. By then, the climate of crisis extended beyond the university, to include mobilizations by secondary students and primary school teachers, the peasantry, and some segments of labor.[18]

Accounts of the Colombian university movement also show the process of ideological differentiation and internal fragmentation that this movement experienced as a result of its involvement in the social struggles of the 1960s and 1970s. Three distinct tendencies emerged and clashed around the reform of the university during this period. The first was a modernizing tendency, under the lead of dominant national and transnational groups that sought to adjust the university to the needs and requirements of dependent capitalist development in the country. These groups strived for reforms that focused on issues of internal and external efficiency, and emphasized the notion of technocracy, rationalization, and depoliticization of the university. The second was a democratizing tendency, which expressed the demands of the growing middle-class sectors and the university public for greater justice and equality. These groups worked for reforms designed to increase participation, focusing on such issues as university autonomy, democratic governance, and the strengthening and growth of the public university.

The foreign influence in the university was an all-pervading theme. The third was a radical tendency, which differed from both the modernizing and democratizing tendencies in that it primarily challenged the inherent inequalities of the society. These groups considered the struggle for university reforms as tactical movements, part of a broader revolutionary process for structural change in Colombia.[19]

All these contradictory forces—acting simultaneously upon the Colombian university—led this institution into a deep state of crisis and to the configuration of a postsecondary education system that assumed the characteristics and trends discussed in the next section.

Trends and Currents in Postsecondary Education

The modernization process that Colombia experienced during the last decades has been accompanied by an un-

Table 1

Enrollment in Colombian Higher Education by Gender and Institutional Origin (1935–1984)

Year	Total Enrollment	Gender			Institutional Origin		
		Men	Women	%Women	Public	Private	% Private
1935	4,137	4,079	58	1.4	2,948	1,189	28.7
1945	6,512	6,275	237	3.6	4,730	1,782	27.4
1955	13,284	11,079	2,205	15.2	8,252	5,032	37.9
1960	23,013	18,779	4,234	18.4	13,639	9,374	40.7
1964	36,617	28,785	7,832	21.4	21,377	15,240	41.6
1970	85,560	62,624	22,930	26.8	46,618	38,942	45.5
1974	148,021	95,982	52,059	35.1	72,243	75,778	51.2
1980	271,630	150,515	121,115	44.6	100,783	170,847	62.9
1984	378,586	197,677	180,909	47.8	147,970	230,616	60.9

Source: ICFES, *Estadísticas de la Educación Superior 1975* (Bogotá: n.d.), p. 257. ICFES, *Estadísticas de la Educación Superior 1980* (Bogotá: Mayo 1982), p. 17. ICFES, *Estadísticas de la Educación Superior 1984* (Bogotá: Abril 1986), p. 23.

precedented expansion of its educational system. According to data by DANE, the National Department of Statistics, from 1958 to 1980 the population in primary education increased from 1,493,100 to 4,102,200 students, in secondary education from 175,500 to 1,733,200, and in higher education from 19,200 to 303,100.[20] This expansion has been the most impressive at the tertiary level. During this period enrollments grew at an annual rate of 4.7 percent in primary, 11 percent in secondary, and 13.4 percent in higher education.

In spite of the efforts to expand education at all levels, enormous educational disparities exist today between departments (states), between rural and urban areas, between socioeconomic groups, and between the sexes. Access to education remains relatively low compared to other countries in the region: 74.9 percent for primary, 42.7 percent for secondary, and 7.5 percent for higher education in 1980.[21] A 1974 report by the Ministry of Education estimates that for every 1,000 seven-year-olds in the country, only 770 enter primary school. Of these, 216 complete primary school, thirty-seven finish high school, and only seven receive a university degree.[22]

The Expansion of Higher Education

Table 1 presents the evolution of university enrollment in Colombia from 1935 to 1984, showing its distribution by gender and sector. Together with an enormous expansion—from 4,137 students in 1935 to 378,586 in 1984—there was a massive entrance of women to higher education. While in 1945 women constituted a mere fraction (only 3.6 percent) of university enrollments, in 1984 they represented almost half (47.8 percent) of the student population. Access to higher education, however, is but one dimension of educational equality that must be considered in conjunction with other factors in order to assess how knowledge and educational opportunities are being distributed among the sexes. More empirical research is needed to determine the patterns and outcomes of women's participation in Colombian higher education.[23] As will be shown below, women tend to be concentrated in traditional female fields, and their proportion decreases in the higher levels of postsecondary education. Also, female participation is larger in the private than in the public universities.

While today almost all of Colombia's twenty-four departments (states) have a university, higher education remains concentrated in a few regions, with the highest levels of urbanization and industrial development in the country. Five regions accounted for 79 percent of the 434,623 students enrolled in postsecondary institutions in 1987. The capital alone—Special District of Bogota—absorbed 42 percent of the students, followed by Antioquia (14 percent), Valle (10 percent), Atlantico (9 percent), and Santander (4 percent).[24]

Privatization of Higher Education

Higher education expansion in Colombia has also been characterized by an increasing privatization, both in terms of enrollments and institutions. As shown in Table 1, private education increased its share in enrollments from 28.7 percent in 1935 to 60.9 percent in 1984.

The public university not only grew at a slower pace than the private, but its leading institution—the National University—experienced a sharp decline in its participation within the system. While in 1950 the UNC had almost half of all the university students and a larger population than all the private institutions combined, by 1976 it accounted for only 14 percent of the total enrollments.[25]

The type of expansion that the Colombian University has experienced constitutes a case of what Daniel Levy has called a "third wave" of private-sector growth. Essentially, this is a form of adaptation to the rapid expansion of social demand for higher education in which public institutions are either unable or unwilling to accommodate the spiraling demand, which overflows into private institutions—either established universities or more modest institutions created largely to satisfy this demand.[26]

Colombia entered its explosive growth phase with a private sector that more or less paralleled its public institutions, having both Catholic and secular universities of recognized quality. Its third wave occurred in the 1970s with the proliferation of secular, nonelite institutions representing the "low end" of higher education. A majority of these new institutions were under private control.[27]

Proliferation of Institutions

Higher education expansion in Colombia has taken place via the proliferation of institutions rather than the enlargement of existing ones. As shown in Table 2, in 1966 there were forty-three universities in the country—thirty-one of which were created after 1940. By 1976 the number grew to 111 institutions, 59 percent of them private; in addition to the eighty-five universities there were twenty-six technological institutes offering postsecondary degrees. Decree 80 of 1980 differentiated the system by three types of institutions: intermediate professional schools (relabeled as technical-professional in 1987), technological schools, and universities. More recently, a distinction was made between universities and university institutions, the former concentrating on

Table 2

Higher Education Institutions in Colombia by Origin and Academic Character

Origin & Academic Character	1966	1976	1980	1987
Universities	43	85	102	72
Public	23	32	40	30
Private	20	53	62	42
University Institution	—	—	—	61
Public	—	—	—	18
Private	—	—	—	43
Technological Institution	—	26	21	37
Public	—	13	9	13
Private	—	13	12	24
Technological-Professional Inst.	—	—	60	62
Public	—	—	2	10
Private	—	—	58	52
Total Institutions	43	111	183	232
Public	23	45	51	71
Private	20	66	132	161

Source: ICFES, *Estadísticas de la Educación Superior 1976* (Bogotá: Noviembre 1977). ICFES, *Estadísticas de la Educación Superior 1980* (Bogotá: Mayo 1982). ICFES, *Estadísticas de la Educación Superior 1987* (Bogotá: Abril 1988).

graduate-level programs. Table 2 shows that in 1987 there were 232 postsecondary institutions operating in Colombia. Of these, 31 percent were universities, 26.4 percent were university institutions, 15.9 percent were technological institutes, and 26.7 percent were technical-professional institutes. While the proliferation of institutions has occurred for the system as a whole, more private ones have been created in all categories; the private sector accounted for 69.4 percent of all postsecondary institutions in the country.

Stratification of Higher Education

This expansion via the proliferation of institutions has resulted in a stratification of the higher education system, according to the academic level and social prestige of the institutions and to the socioeconomic background of the students. At the top end of the system are what Rama denotes as "Type A" institutions, a handful of top private (Andes, Javeriana, Rosario, Bolivariana) and public universities (Nacional, Valle, Antioquia, Santander) with comparable high standards and selective admissions. Analysis of the socioeconomic characteristics of students in these types of institutions leads Rama to conclude that the university is the inverted image of the society: the largest socio-occupational categories in the society have an insignificant representation in university enrollments and vice versa.

Covering the rest of the social spectrum are other private and public institutions, where the students tend to have poorer academic preparation, come from lower social backgrounds, and attend part time. The private sector, in particular, is highly hierarchical. Its growth has been achieved through a progressive differentiation of the units that compose it. Hence, in contrast to other Latin American countries, the private university system in Colombia is more heterogeneous than the public one,

with the highest and lowest levels of social stratification found in the private sector.[28] This and other analyses suggest that in spite of its quantitative expansion, the Colombian university has not been democratized, but has served more to maintain a certain class position for upper and middle groups in the society.[29]

The Changing Professoriate

The tremendous expansion of higher education has been accompanied by a corresponding growth of university faculty. The number of professors, adjusted to full-time equivalency, increased from 1,661 to 1960 to 13,973 in 1977.[30] In 1987 teaching positions in the university surpassed the 40,000 mark; it is estimated that by the year 2000 more than 100,000 university professors will be needed in the country. Their education, recruitment, and upgrading are among the main challenges facing higher education today.

Table 3 shows the distribution of professors by academic area, sex, and level of education in 1987. The largest number of professors was in the area of economics, administration, and accounting (24.5 percent), followed by engineering, architecture, and related fields (19.9 percent) and by education sciences (16.6 percent). The percentage of women faculty was 23.3 percent, and their participation was larger in traditional female fields such as humanities (40.2 percent) and education (33 percent). The large proportion of women in health sciences (34.8 percent) reflects their predominance in the nursing profession.

The need for more faculty training has long been recognized. Hundreds of Colombians have received scholarships and loans for advanced training abroad, both from Colombian institutions such as ICETEX and from international organizations, especially North American foundations and the Agency for International Development.[31] However, the education level of the professoriate remains very low. The typical preparation for a professorship is still professional training. Half of the professors in 1987 had professional degrees. Only 12.6 percent had specialized first degrees, 13.2 percent had master's degrees, and no more than 3.2 percent had Ph.D.'s (see Table 3).

During the 1960s there was a conscious effort to increase the proportion of full-time university faculty. As shown in Table 4, the percentage of full-time professors in the Colombian university almost doubled from 20.4 percent in 1960 to 37.8 percent in 1975—one of the highest proportions in all Latin America. The gains were particularly impressive in the public sector, where the proportion of full-time personnel grew from 29.1 to 61.7 percent during that period.

This effort was part of a broader reform program that considered the institutionalization of the full-time faculty crucial for modernizing the university. The rapid expansion of teaching ranks and of the full-time professoriate initiated a transformation of the academic role in Colombian universities.[32] In contrast to their predecessors, the new academics tended to be young, to come from middle-class backgrounds, and to see academia as a full-time career rather than a part-time activity. Moreover, the efforts to create a full-time academic staff paid off in better performances by professors. Pelczar's study of the faculty in six Colombian universities found that full-time professors were not only better teachers than their part-time colleagues and predecessors but they also performed better on measures of scholarly

Table 3

University Faculty in Colombia by Academic Area, Sex, and Education (1987)

Academic Areas*	Total**		% of Women	Level of Education (%)***			
	No.	%		Bachelor	Special.	Master	Ph.D.
Argon., Vet. & Related	1,300	2.9	15.0	56.0	5.7	23.4	3.8
Fine Arts	1,739	3.9	27.4	22.1	7.6	4.0	4.0
Education Sciences	7,353	16.6	33.0	21.1	3.4	19.9	2.3
Health Sciences	7,023	15.9	34.8	35.9	35.8	12.3	4.3
Soc. Sci., Law & Pol. Science	4,956	11.2	23.4	55.2	17.3	9.1	7.0
Econ., Adm., Acc. & Rel.	10,819	24.5	16.7	62.8	9.5	9.7	1.4
Humanities and Theo.	691	1.6	40.2	23.7	5.6	23.6	11.6
Eng., Arch., Urban St.	8,819	19.9	13.5	65.2	6.8	12.3	1.5
Math. & Nat. Sciences	1,569	3.5	21.4	44.1	4.5	25.8	10.3
Total	44,269	100.0	23.3	49.3	12.6	13.2	3.2

*   Decree 80 of 1980 established this new classification by nine academic areas.
**   In the last decade, the statistics compiled for faculty refer to "plazas docentes," meaning the number of teaching positions filled. Therefore, the numbers provided do not correspond to the number of faculty, since one person may teach in various institutions.
*** Data for technological and other degrees below the bachelor's level are not included in the table.

Source: ICFES, *Estadísticas de la Educación Superior 1987, Avance Informativo* (Bogotá: Abril 1986), p. 65.

Table 4

University Faculty in Colombia by Type of Institution
(1960, 1975, & 1987)

Affiliat.	Public Univ. (%)			Private Univ. (%)			Total Univ. (%)		
	1960	1975	1987	1960	1975	1987	1960	1975	1987
Full Time	29.1	61.7	49.5	4.7	12.8	12.1	20.4	37.8	27.8
Part Time	17.3	11.6	9.8	19.7	12.3	11.2	18.2	12.0	10.6
Hourly Basis	53.5	26.7	40.7	75.5	74.9	76.7	61.4	50.2	61.6
Total No.	2,523	10,150	18,595	1,418	9,671	25,674	3,941	19,821	44,269

Source: ICFES, *Estadísticas de la Educación Superior 1975* (Bogotá: n.d.). ICFES, *Estadísticas de la Educación Superior 1987, Avance Informativo* (Bogotá: Abril 1988).

productivity, disciplinary participation, intrauniversity involvement, and extension activities.[33]

However, by the mid-1970s the proportion of full-time staff in the Colombian university began to decline, while the practice of hiring personnel on an hourly basis regained force. By 1987 the proportion of full-time academics dropped to 27 percent and the hourly-basis category climbed again to 61 percent (see Table 4). Factors to explain this decline of full-time faculty include a combination of economic and political reasons. Professors' salaries already take the bulk of strained university budgets and full-time professors usually raise the cost per student. But low salaries, few fringe benefits, and other unsupportive conditions in the university have made academia a less attractive career option for highly trained individuals. In the political arena, many conservatives viewed full-time faculty as a threat. The early 1970s made clear that full-time professors were leading faculty movements that rose to question the path that the Colombian university was following, and to demand greater participation in the definition and direction of its activities—an example being the "Claustros" movement at the UNC. Moreover, full-time personnel were behind the unionization movement that led to the creation of ASPU in 1968, a national unionized association of univer-

sity professors established to win better salaries and work conditions for faculty.[34]

Curricular Developments

In the last decades higher education has experienced a "curricular modernization" characterized by the growth and predominance of those areas of knowledge more directly related to the administration and rationalization of the state apparatus and private firms, with the social demand for formal education, and with industrial development. As shown in Table 5, the largest program areas in 1980 were administration and economics, education, and engineering, which together accounted for 62 percent of the student population. Administration and economics experienced the fastest annual rate of growth (22.2 percent), followed by education (20.7 percent) and the social sciences (17 percent). In terms of the private/public distinction, a majority of the students in the areas of sciences, agronomy, and education were enrolled in the public sector. Private universities had a majority of enrollments in all other areas of knowledge.[35]

Despite the efforts to diversify the university curriculum, a look at the distribution of students by academic programs shows an alarming rigidity in the higher education system. Of the 381 academic programs offered in 1981, just eight enrolled 42.4 percent of higher education students. These were the programs of law (9.3 percent), accounting (7.5 percent), business administration (6.4 percent), economics (5.5 percent), medicine (4.2 percent), civil engineering (3.6 percent), architecture (3.1 percent), and industrial engineering (2.8 percent). The stability of this trend poses serious questions regarding the university's role in development. As noted by ICFES, areas that at first glance would seem more appropriate for the country's development have a very low participation in the overall system. Examples are agronomy (1.3 percent), food engineering (0.3 percent), fishing engineering (0.18 percent), petroleum engineering (0.16 percent), and geology, (0.18 percent).[36]

University and Employment

The explosive expansion of higher education, without a corresponding emergence of the conditions required for the utilization and remuneration of these new professionals, resulted in a brain drain of highly trained personnel, increasing un-

employment and subemployment of university graduates, and what is now being called the devaluation of higher education.

During the 1960s Colombia became one of the Latin American countries with the highest emigration of professionals in relation to the number of graduates that its university produced. This brain drain to industrialized nations was especially large among health professionals and engineers.[37] The Colombian government has established incentive programs (Decree 1397 of 1972; Decree 1318 of 1982) to promote the return of these professionals, with partial success.[38] As some authors argue, the solution to this problem rests primarily in creating the educational climate, competitive salaries, economic conditions that would make this brain drain unnecessary.[39]

While the brain drain of professionals slowed down in the 1970s, the internal unemployment and subemployment of professionals became more visible. Data collected in 1976 for the four largest cities shows a rate of university unemployment ranging between 6 and 9 percent, which is lower than the average for the country as a

---

Table 5

University Enrollment by Academic Areas in Colombia (1960 & 1980)

Academic Areas	Enrollments				Annual Growth Rate
	1960	%	1980	%	
Administration and Economics	1,609	7.0	88,192	32.5	22.2
Agronomy & Related Fields	1,507	6.5	10,363	3.8	10.1
Architecture & Fine Arts	2,577	11.2	17,805	6.5	10.2
Natural & Exact Sciences	747	3.2	5,830	2.1	10.8
Health Sciences	4,802	20.9	25,934	9.5	8.8
Social Sciences	607	2.6	14,069	5.2	17.0
Law	4,123	17.9	25,646	9.4	9.6
Education	1,031	4.5	44,379	16.3	20.7
Humanities	595	2.6	2,755	1.0	8.0
Engineering & Related Fields	5,416	23.5	36,357	13.5	10.0
Total	23,014	99.9	271,630	99.8	13.1

Source: ICFES, *Estadísticas de la Educación Superior 1975* (Bogotá: n.d.). ICFES, *Estadísticas de la Educación Superior 1980* (Bogotá: Mayo 1982), p. 37.

whole (between 9 and 13 percent). While unemployment is affecting professionals in all fields, it is higher among people with technical training than among university professionals (16.5 percent), a phenomena that might be due to a subemployment of the latter.[40]

The fate of university graduates also seems to be related to the stratified higher education system discussed earlier. A case study concludes that the massification and differentiation of the universities have led to an occupational stratification in which graduates from top institutions secure the best positions in the areas of employment of greater prestige, while graduates of mass universities compete for the lower professional positions in institutions of lower prestige. Hence, there has been a differential devaluation of higher education in which the loss of value of this education is greater for the graduates of mass universities. Moreover, the study considers that the devaluation of education affects the graduates of technical schools more than those with university degrees because the technical and instrumental areas of the economy have a fluctuating employment structure.[41]

Recent Developments

The Reform of 1980

Recognizing the disorderly and incoherent growth of higher education—described by a prominent Colombian educator as "laissez faire in all its glory"[42]—its deteriorating quality, its internal disarticulation and lack of integration with the productive sector, the state launched a major reform (Decrees 80 to 84) in 1980, reorganizing the system of postsecondary education. While there were no great innovations in the Reform of 1980, its main virtue lies in providing a legal framework that attempts to integrate and regulate the higher education system. Among other things, Decree 80 establishes the principles and objectives of higher education, its organization by academic modalities and institutions, and the norms regulating the activity of private and public universities. Decree 81 refers specifically to ICFES, and Decree 82 to the National University. No secondary evidence exists at this point to access the impact of this reform on the rationalization and integration of higher education activities in the country. Two aspects are commented on here: the academic differentiation of higher education, and the relationship between the universities and the state.

Differentiation by Academic Modalities

The main innovation of the reform of 1980 is the subdivision of postsecondary education into four modalities, differentiated by their practical/instrumental versus scientific/theoretic content. The first is *intermediate-professional education* (more recently labeled technical-professional), defined by Decree 80 as "a predominantly practical education for the exercise of auxiliary or instrumental activities." The second is *technological education*, offering technological training with a practical emphasis. The third is *university education*, characterized in the law by its social and humanistic content, its scientific grounding, and its orientation toward academic disciplines and liberal professions. And the fourth is *advanced or graduate education*, offering specialization and graduate degrees.

In this way the state has sought to make higher education responsive to the subjective and objective demands for higher education by offering possibilities for students to acquire different types of academic training and to exit school into the labor market at various levels in the system. Despite these efforts, professional education continues to be the preferred alternative: 75 percent of the 200,694 applications to postsecondary institutions in 1987 were to university education programs. As Table 6 indicates, in that year university education had the largest proportion both of students (78 percent) and academic programs (51 percent). Students in technological education absorbed another 13 percent, technical-professional 7.2 percent, and advanced education 2.1 percent. In terms of private/public participation, the data shows that 60 percent of graduate programs were offered by public universities, but enrollments at this level were larger in the private sector. The latter also accounted for 59 percent of the students in university education, 36 percent of the students in technological education, and 90 percent of those enrolled in technical-professional programs.

Official data for 1984 disaggregates this information by gender, providing some idea of women's status within the various modalities. According to these figures, there are more women in the private sector (51 percent) than in the public (43 percent), and their participation is larger in the lower levels of postsecondary education: 61 percent in technical-professional education, 53 percent in technological education, 46 percent in university education, and 37 percent in advanced education.[43]

State Control Over the Universities

Historically, the relationship between the state and universities has been very tense and difficult. On the one hand, public universities have reacted very strongly against state policies and measures that they have seen as threats to their autonomy and the university principles established since the famous Cordoba Manifesto of 1918. The National University, in particular, seeing itself as a leading institution, has tried to maintain this role in determining future directions for Colombian higher education. Voices in defense of the public university were quieted with the repression and decline of the university movement in the mid-1970s. Decree 80 of 1980 estab-lished the regime for the creation and functioning of public universities, and defined their governing structure as follows: the highest university authority, the Superior Council, is composed of the rector—who has a voice but no vote—and an equal number of representatives from the government and the university community.

Private universities, on the other hand, tend to view many activities of the government and its specialized agency ICFES as threats to their power, especially when it comes to issues of monitoring and inspection. Accredited private universities are associated in ASCUN (Asociación Colombiana de Universidades) and constitute a politically powerful interest group in Colombian higher education.[44] The Reform Law of 1980 defined higher education as "a public service, offered by the State and private individuals authorized by the former to provide this service." Private legitimacy within the system is thus recognized, while the state legislates on conditions for the creation and functioning of private university programs.

By law, the Colombian Institute for the Promotion of Higher Education (ICFES) is the public agency in charge of the inspection and monitoring of higher education. The fact that there are currently in Colombia more than two hundred institutions offering more than two thousand academic programs gives an idea of the magnitude of the task that ICFES faces in order to fulfill its constitutional functions.

The Open University Strategy

In the last decade, ICFES has been also in charge of providing existing private and public universities with the technical and logistical support to offer open university programs. The Universidad Abierta y a Distancia (Open and Distance University) has been considered the best strategy for expanding higher education while at the same time providing more equal opportunities and improving the efficiency of the

Table 6

Academic Programs and Enrollments in Colombian Postsecondary Education by Type of Institution and Academic Modality (1987)

Institutions by Origin & Acad. Mode	Academic Programs				Students Enrolled			
	Technic.	Technol.	Univ.	Post.	Technic.	Technol.	Univ.	Post.
Universities	1	70	856	401	98	19,617	275,441	7,938
Public (%)	100.0	72.8	54.2	60.3	100.0	78.8	45.9	42.0
Private (%)	—	27.2	45.8	39.7	—	21.2	54.1	58.0
University Inst.	—	59	216	31	—	15,617	61,501	1,294
Public (%)	—	47.5	24.5	25.8	—	69.3	19.6	30.9
Private (%)	—	52.5	75.5	74.2	—	30.7	80.4	69.1
Technol. Inst.	19	145	2	—	1,486	19,827	420	—
Public (%)	5.3	35.1	—	—	—	46.1	—	—
Private (%)	94.7	64.9	100.0	—	100.0	53.9	100.0	—
Techn. Prof. Inst.	294	—	—	—	31,384	—	—	—
Public (%)	12.9	—	—	—	10.4	—	—	—
Private (%)	87.1	—	—	—	89.6	—	—	—
Grand Total	314	274	1,074	432	32,968	55,061	337,362	9,232
Public (%)	12.7	47.4	48.1	57.9	10.2	64.3	41.0	40.5
Private (%)	87.3	52.6	51.9	42.1	89.8	35.7	59.0	59.5

Source: ICFES, *Estadísticas de la Educación Superior 1987, Avance Informativo* (Bogotá: Abril 1988), pp. 25 & 27.

system. According to the development plan "Change with Equity," this strategy would allow an additional enrollment of 200,000 students between 1983 and 1986, a better use of available resources, a more equal distribution of educational opportunities by regions, and a diversification of programs more harmonious with regional and local needs.[45]

Its accomplishments, however, have been far more modest. Of the sixty-seven programs in operation in 1984, half were in the traditional university education modality, and concentrated in the most oversubscribed academic areas: forty-five were in education, eight in economics and related fields, and six in engineering.[46] In 1987, there were 53,614 open university students, representing 12 percent of the total population.[47] It is still an open question as to what position the open university occupies within the highly stratified postsecondary system, and what the value of its degrees are within the labor market.

Conclusions

Despite the enormous transformations that the Colombian university has experienced in recent decades, it is still far from fulfilling the principles in the Law of 1980 that define it as a democratic, scientific, and critical institution. As this overview shows, the expansion of higher education has not resulted in its democraticization, nor in greater educational opportunities for lower-income groups in society. First, the inequity and selectivity of the educational system, which begins at the primary education level, considerably limits the democratization of access at the tertiary level. Second, the privatization and stratification trends characterizing the expansion of higher education have reinforced the university's role in reproducing and perpetuating the inequalities that exist in Colombian society. The 1980s diversification and open university strategies do not seem to have accomplished much to improve this situation.

Moreover, the economic crisis that has affected the whole region since the early 1980s has created a profound crisis for Latin American governments and for higher education. The primary cause of the Colombian fiscal deficit in 1983 was the educational sector. The deficit of the public university alone amounted in that year to 8,000 million pesos.[48] This situation has paved the way for proposals to counter university dependency on government funding by tapping into private resources. Among the measures proposed are shifting costs to a greater degree to the beneficiaries of higher education, establishing loans from national banks to universities, and generating income through university investments.[49] Thus, while private-sector growth seems to have stabilized—hovering near 60 percent of enrollments since 1980—a new privatization trend is emerging as a result of the government's fiscal crisis and the financial deficits in higher education: finding nongovernmental resources for higher education.

Finally, the development of scientific and technological research in the university continues to be a major challenge today. Despite numerous efforts to promote university research, defined in the Law of 1980 as a fundamental higher education activity, it is one of the least developed functions in the university as a whole. Research is concentrated in a few top public and private universities, and its diffusion and utilization remains very limited. Studies that have analyzed this situation point to some of the obstacles for the development of university research.[50] Among them are the lack of funding and institutional support for research activities, insufficient faculty incentives and numbers of trained research personnel, inadequate laborato-

ries, libraries, and other facilities, limited means for publication and diffusion of results, and the lack of interest on the part of the private and public sectors for the research produced in the universities.

The productive sector—heavily dependent on foreign capital and technology—has relied mainly on imported technologies that do not demand university research in the country. A strengthening of the scientific research capabilities of the university and indigenous research in areas that seem the most promising for national development would therefore require a major commitment and involvement of the state. But the prospects for the future are not encouraging. Colombia's social institutions have been severely shaken by the terror and violence that has gripped the country in recent years, adding yet another obstacle to achieving a truly democratic, scientific, and critical university system.

Notes

1. Jaime Jaramillo Uribe, *Ensayos sobre la Historia Social Colombiana* (Bogotá: Universidad Nacional, 1969).

2. Gerardo Molina, "Universidad Estatal y Universidad Privada," in *Universidad Oficial o Universidad Privada?*, ed. Gerardo Molina et al. (Bogotá: Tercer Mundo, 1978), 67–109.

3. William Lee Magnusson, "Reform at the National University of Colombia: Administrative Strategy in Institution Building" (Ph.D. diss., University of California, Berkeley, 1970), 28.

4. Yvon Lebot, *Educación e Ideología en Colombia* (Bogotá: La Carreta, 1979).

5. See collection of essays in Mario Arrubla et al., *Colombia: Hoy* (Bogotá: Siglo XXI, 1978).

6. Fernán Torres León, *Trayectoria Histórica de la Universidad Colombiana*, 2d ed. (Bogotá: ICOLPE, 1975).

7. Osvaldo Sunkel and Edmundo Fuenzalida, "Transnationalization and Its National Consequences," *Transnational Capitalism and National Development: New Perspective on Dependence*, ed. Jose Villamil (Atlanta Highlands, N.J.: Humanities Press, 1979), 67–93.

8. Jesus A. Bejarano, *El Capital Monopolista y la Inversión Norteamericana en Colombia* (Bogotá: La Carreta, 1978).

9. Robert Arnove, "Comparative Education and World Systems Analysis," *Comparative Educa-*

tion Review 24 (February 1980): pp. 42–62.

10. Oswaldo Sunkel, "The Development of Thinking," in *Transnational Capitalism and National Development: New Perspective on Dependence*, ed. Jose Villamil (Atlanta Highlands, N.J.: Humanities Press, 1979), 19–30.

11. Robert Arnove, *Philanthropy and Cultural Imperialism* (Bloomington: Indiana University Press, 1982).

12. See collection of essays in, Albert Berry et al., eds. *Politics of Compromise* (New Brunswick, New Jersey: Transaction, 1980).

13. Rosa Cecilia Briceño, "University Reform, Social Conflict, and the Intellectuals: The Case of the National University of Colombia" (Ph.D diss., Stanford University, 1988), 96–109.

14. Rudolph Acton, *La Universidad Latinoamericana: Propuesta para un Enfoque Integral del Desarrollo Social, Económico y Educacional en America Latina* (Bogotá: Editores ECO, 1966).

15. Robert Arnove, "Education Policies of the National Front," in *Politics of Compromise*, ed. Albert Berry et al. (New Jersey: Transaction, 1980), 381.

16. Jose Felix Patiño, *La Reforma de la Universidad Nacional de Colombia, Informe del Rector*, 3 vols. (Bogotá: Universidad Nacional de Colombia, 1966).

17. See Francisco Leal Buitrago, "La Frustración Política de una Generación. La Universidad Colombiana y la Formación de un Movimiento Estudiantil 1958–1967," *Desarrollo y Sociedad* 6 (Bogotá: Universidad de los Andes, 1981): 299–325.

18. Yvon Lebot, "El Movimiento Estudiantil durante el Frente Nacional," *Ideología y Sociedad* 19 (Bogotá: October–December 1976), 65.

19. Rosa Cecilia Briceño, "The University as a Microcosm of Social Conflict" (Paper presented at the Annual Conference of the American Education Research Association, San Francisco, 30 March 1989).

20. DANE, *50 años de Estadísticas Universitarias* (Bogotá: DANE, Mayo 1985), 116.

21. Ibid., 113.

22. Ministerio de Educación, *Memoria presentada al Congreso en 1974*, cited by Augusto Franco and Carlos Tunnermann in *La Educación Superior en Colombia* (Bogotá: Tercer Mundo, 1978), 221.

23. See Elssy Bonilla de Ramos, "La Mujer y el Sistema Educativo en Colombia," *Revista Colombiana de Educación* 2 (Bogotá: II Semestre, 1978): 37–47.

24. ICFES, *Estadísticas de la Educación Superior, Avance Informativo 1987* (Bogotá: ICFES, April 1988), 4.

25. DANE, "Universidad Nacional: Estadísticas Basicas," *Boletin Mensual de Estadística* 230 (Bogotá: DANE, 1970): 51–70, cited in Franco

and Tunnermann, "La Educación Superior," 232.

26. Daniel Levy, *Higher Education and the State in Latin America* (Chicago: University of Chicago Press, 1986).

27. Roger Geiger, "Privatization of Higher Education: International Trends and Issue" (Princeton, N. J.: International Council for Educational Development, 1988), 27.

28. German Rama, *El Sistema Universitario en Colombia* (Bogotá: Universidad Nacional de Colombia, 1970).

29. Jaime Rodriguez Forero, "Universidad y Estructura Socio-Económica: El Caso de Colombia," in *La Universidad Latinoamericana. Enfoques Tipologicos* (Chile: Corporación de Promoción Universitaria, 1973), 208–274. See also Rodrigo Parra Sandoval, *Analisis de un Mito. La Educación como factor de la Movilidad Social en Colombia* (Bogotá: Universidad de los Andes, 1975).

30. ICFES, *Historia Estadística de la Educación Superior Colombiana* (Bogota: ICFES, 1977), 107.

31. Richard Pelczar, "University Reform in Latin America: The Case of Colombia," *Comparative Education Review* 16 (June 1972): 230–250.

32. Ibid.

33. Richard Pelczar, "The University Professor in Colombia" (Ph.D. diss., University of Chicago, 1971).

34. Briceño, "University Reform."

35. ICFES, *Estadísticas de la Educación Superior 1980* (Bogota: ICFES, Mayo 1982), 37.

36. ICFES, *Estadísticas de la Educación Superior 1981* (Bogota: ICFES, Junio 1983), 283.

37. Rama, *El Sistema Universitario*, 165.

38. Ramiro Cardona and Sara Rubiano de Velasquez, *El Exodo de Colombianos: Un Estudio de la Corriente Migratoria a Estados Unidos y un Intento de Propiciar el Retorno* (Bogotá: Tercer Mundo, 1980).

39. Franco and Tunnermann, *La Educación Superior*, 403.

40. Cecilia Lopez de Rodriguez and Gina Bayera, "Anotaciones Generales sobre el Mercado Universitario en Colombia," in ANIF, *Indicadores Socio-Económicos*, (Bogota: ANIF, Diciembre 1977), 2873–81.

41. Rodrigo Parra Sandoval and Maria Elvira Carvajal, "La Universidad Colombiana: De la Filosofía a la Tecnocracia Estratificada," *Revista Colombiana de Educación* 4 (Bogotá: II Semestre, 1979).

42. Alfonso Ocampo Londoño, "Financiamiento de la Educación Superior," Reunion Nacional de Universidades, La Ceja, 23–25 January 1969 (Medelleín: Universidad de Antioquia, 1969), 22.

43. ICFES, *Estadísticas de la Educación Superior* 1984 (Bogotá: ICFES, Abril 1986), p. 23.

44. Lebot, *Educación e Ideología*, 52.

45. Departamento Nacional de Planeación, *Cambio con Equidad* (Bogotá: Antares, 1983).

46. Jaime Luis Gutierrez Giraldo, "Los Programs de Educación a Distancia en Colombia Hoy," *Educación Superior y Desarrollo* 3 (Bogotá: ICFES, Octubre–Diciembre 1984): 40–43.

47. ICFES, *Estadísticas de la Educación Superior, Avance Informativo* 1987, 29.

48. Luis Carlos Galan, "Evolución y Perspectivas de la Educación Superior," *Educación Superior y Desarrollo* 2 (Bogotá: Abril–Junio 1983): 49–62.

49. ICFES, "Algunas Alternativas para el Financiamiento de las Universidades Publicas," *Educación Superior y Desarrollo* 3 (Bogotá: Enero-Marzo, 1984): 5–47.

50. Milciades Chaves, "Obstáculos para la Investigación en la Universidad," *Ciencia, Tecnología y Desarrollo* 2 (Bogotá: Abril-Junio 1978): 171–97. See also Franco and Tunnermann, *La Educacíon Superior*, 323–31.

♦

Cuba

Rolland G. Paulston

✦

In January 1989, when the Cuban Revolution celebrated its thirtieth anniversary, Cuban higher education could look back on three decades of unprecedented change in size, historical role, and contributions to national development. If one compares Cuban efforts in this regard with other developing countries, few if any can match or even come close to Cuban achievements. Rather, using participation and expenditure indicators, as presented in Figure 1 and Figure 2, Cuban higher education has advanced to levels more characteristic of developed societies. How and why this expansion and reorientation has taken place, along with an assessment of continuing problems and emerging trends, will be the theme of this chapter.

Ideological Orientation

In Chapter 4 of the Cuban Constitution, "Education and Culture," Cuban revolutionaries have clearly spelled out the bedrock principles upon which all educational policy is formulated. Higher education is a monopoly of the state. All policy is centrally developed, implemented, and evaluated within a Marxist-Leninist "scientific" worldview. The rationale for all higher studies is to provide communist education

in which study, work, sports, and military training are combined to serve the interests of the state. Education is largely free of charge. It seeks to promote the integral development of all citizens. It is accessible to all who support the revolution. It stresses a Marxist scientific approach to solving problems of society and human well-being.[1] Thus higher education in Cuba has a

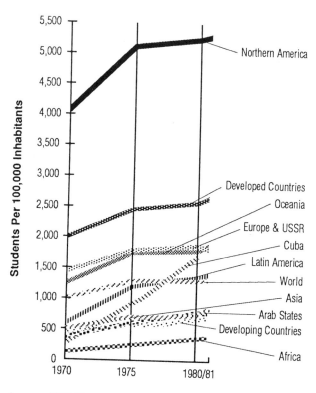

Figure 1

Higher Education Students per 100,000 Population

Northern America
Developed Countries
Oceania
Europe & USSR
Cuba
Latin America
World
Asia
Arab States
Developing Countries
Africa

Source: UNESCO, 1974–1983.

broad and ambitious mandate, especially for a small Caribbean nation of some eleven million people with a long history of colonial exploitation and dependence on a sugar economy. In sum, it seeks the utopian aims of creating a new socialist person in a socialist culture.[2]

As the chief architect of this bold vision, Fidel Castro has clearly given the charge to higher education: "the new man must be by basic nature communistic. Not because he has arrived there by reason, or conviction, or class consciousness: but because all his manner of being, of thinking is part of a communist culture. We must develop with great precision the pedagogy required to make this communist man. For without it we will have neither the correct ideological structure in our youth, nor the possibility to create the first truly communist society."[3]

Before examining how higher education has struggled with utopian goals and difficult conditions in the period of revolutionary reconstruction, we should first turn to the earlier political struggles carried out in Cuban universities before 1959.

Historical Trends

Cuban higher education, until recently only carried out at the University of Havana, played a central political role in Cuba's historical efforts to gain independence from Spain, to replace the dictators Machado and Batista with honest democratic rule, and to establish revolutionary socialist reconstruction after 1959.[4]

Founded in 1728 and secularized in 1842, the University of Havana had become a stronghold of *criollo*, or nationalist, forces by 1870.[5] On November 27, 1871, Spanish authorities tried and executed eight medical students and imprisoned thirty-four others for anti-Spanish subversive activities. This punitive act increased

Figure 2

Educational Expenditures (Estimated) as a Percentage of GNP

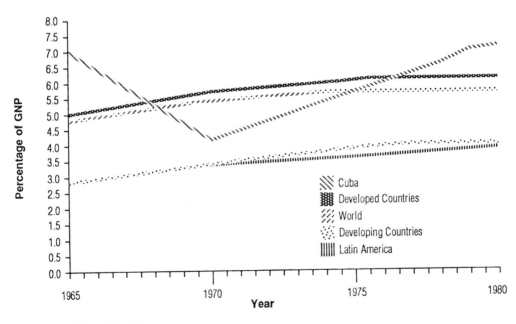

Source: UNESCO, 1974, 1983.

Table 1

Main Indicators for the Development of Higher Education, 1959–1982

	1959/60	1960/61	1961/62	1962/63	1963/64	1964/65
Higher Education Centers	6	6	3	3	3	3
Students	25,295	19,454	17,888	17,257	20,393	26,271
1st year students	—	—	—	—	—	—
Professors	1,046	1,845	992	1,482	1,987	2,600
Graduates	1,331	2,430	1,693	1,372	1,363	86

	1965/66	1966/67	1967/68	1968/69	1969/70	1970/71
Higher Education Centers	3	3	3	3	4	4
Students	26,162	28,243	29,238	32,327	34,520	35,137
1st year students	—	—	6,917	7,433	6,225	9,408
Professors	3,032	4,220	4,499	4,641	4,545	4,415
Graduates	1,830	2,834	2,758	2,769	3,832	3,624

	1971/72	1972/73	1973/74	1974/75	1975/76	1976/77
Higher Education Centers	4	4	4	4	4	27
Students	36,877	48,735	55,435	68,051	83,957	110,148*
1st year students	9,161	16,398	17,459	21,466	26,985	29,897
Professors	4,484	4,697	5,022	5,847	6,326	8,539+
Graduates	4,253	4,472	4,443	6,106	5,894	9,256

	1977/78	1978/79	1979/80	1980/81	1981/82
Higher Education Centers	27	28	30	32	32
Students	128,524*	139,991*	188,898~	176,735~	185,536~
1st year students	34,020	34,366	81,517-	61,886-	65,217-
Professors	10,235+	13,785+	14,836+	14,760+	17,420+
Graduates	11,461	15,343	20,615	25,848	21,009

* Includes the preparatory faculties attached to universities and students abroad.
~ Includes "Directed Teaching" ("Free Teaching"), the preparatory faculties, and students abroad.
- Includes "Directed Teaching" ("Free Teaching"), and the preparatory faculties.
+ Includes students and technocrats who assist the faculty.
** At the beginning of the school year. (Does not include data on the centers for higher military education and the Communist party higher education school, "Ñico López.")

Source: Nikolai Kolesnikov, *Cuba: Education Popular y Preparation de los Cuadros Nacionales, 1959–1982)* (Moscow: Editorial Progreso, 1983), pp. 41–44.

---

anti-Spanish sentiment and placed the university at the forefront of the independence movement led by the young student José Martí.[6]

With independence from Spain in 1898, two periods of United States military occupation (1899–1902 and 1906–09), and continued American economic domination, the University of Havana became increasingly divorced from the social and economic needs of the country.[7] The disciplines of law and medicine reigned supreme: the first as a road to a political career, the second as a means to high social status. With the university reform movement of 1923, the students once again took up political activism, this time addressed to the need for a modern university directed toward social and political development. Influenced by the Córdoba reform movement and the Mexican and Russian revolutions, this movement also opposed United States supervision of Cuban affairs and instead proposed nationalism and democratic reforms.[8] With the able leadership of Julio Mella, a student, a more radical part of the reform movement created the Cuban Communist party and sought for the first time to transcend the university's walls and make the cause of university reform "another battle of the class struggle."[9]

From 1927 to 1933 university students used urban violence to oppose President Gerardo Machado's repressive rule and the continuation of the humiliating Platt Amendment which permitted direct United States intervention in Cuban affairs. Machado closed the university from 1930 to 1933 while students fought for termination of the Platt Amendment and Cuba's financial dependence on the United States, for land reform and the eventual nationalization of the sugar and mining industries, and for the creation of an autonomous university removed from political interference. With Machado's overthrow, Ramón Grau, a professor and ex-student leader, eventually became president in 1933 to lead a government that was for labor and against exploitive foreign investment. Although Grau granted autonomy to the University of Havana, the students soon withdrew their support from him as military participation in his government increased. On January 14, 1934, army chief Fulgencio Batista forced President Grau to resign and within five days received United States government recognition. Previously the United States had refused to recognize Grau's constitutionally elected government.[10]

From 1934 to Fidel Castro's triumph in 1959, with a hiatus during World War II, the Cuban student movement became increasingly radicalized and politicized. The powerful Federation of University Students (the *Federación de estudiantes universitarios* or FEU) called for social justice and attacked widespread corruption in government and immorality in public life, especially during the violent and materialistic years after World War II. At the same time, *bonches* (gangs of armed students) and others used the university's autonomy to carry out political warfare, assassination, and gangsterism. The university council rejected police entrance into the campus, while acknowledging its own total inability to repress the *bonches*.[11]

During this turbulent period in the late 1940s and early 1950s Fidel Castro studied law at the University of Havana and became actively involved in student politics. Castro generally shared the goals of the student movement: economic independence, political liberty, social justice, and an end to corruption. In the absence of national leaders, the university students assumed leadership of the anti-Batista struggle. The University of Havana was closed from 1956 to 1959. In 1956 the leaders of the FEU unsuccessfully attempted to assassinate Batista at the presidential palace, while Castro began rural guerrilla warfare in the mountains of Oriente province.[12]

Although the University of Havana retained its dominant position during the period of quasi-independence, from 1898 to 1959, a number of lesser universities came into being during the 1940s and 1950s. Most important among these was Villanova University, founded by Catholic Augustinian monks in 1940. Wealthier families who could afford the tuition favored this stable and disciplined institution over the highly politicized public universities. The University of Havana opened branch campuses at Santiago de Cuba (1947), Las Villas (1959), Camagüey (1953), and Pinar del Río (1954). A number of small private universities, commercial ventures seeking to capitalize on the closing of the University of Havana, flourished briefly during the late 1950s.

Upon taking power in 1959, Castro proclaimed the state and the university to be identical. The university reopened in 1959, and the students, with government support, formed the University Reform Commission to purge pro-Batista students, professors, and staff and to plan a revolutionary new curriculum and university structure. On December 31, 1960, university autonomy ended with the government's creation of the Higher Council of Universities—headed by the minister of education and composed of government representatives, faculty members, and students—to run the state universities operating at Havana, Las Villas, and Oriente.[13] In January 1962, Juan Marinello, president of the Cuban Communist party, became rector of the university and dedicated its efforts "to the complete service of the revolution."[14] Also in 1962 the Union of Young Communists (*Unión de jovenes comunistas* or UJC) organized the University Bureau, with responsibility for political indoctrination. And in the same year, on the anniversary of Mella's death, the Higher Council of Universities presented a comprehensive university reform plan, which continues to serve as the foundation for Cuban higher education.

Following two years of conflict between the revolutionary government and the still powerful democratic elements in the universities, the reform of 1962 had profound effects on Cuban higher education. The reform eventually eliminated university autonomy, terminated or nationalized all private universities, and concentrated instruction in the national universities at Havana, Las Villas, and Oriente. In 1975 the University of Havana's regional center at Camagüey became Cuba's fourth university. Renamed Ignacio Agramonte University, the institution enrolls over 3,200 students in twelve undergraduate career programs, mainly in rural development.

In 1964 the Higher Council of Universities was replaced by a National Council of Universities, responsible to the minister of education. Similarly, the university council, composed of the representatives of the faculties at each university, was replaced by a new university advisory board, including deans, representatives from the Union of Young Communists and the Federation of Students Board, and other members. University faculties became departmentalized, and the departments were organized in a manner similar to the advisory board. Faculty tenure was abolished, and the rectors were made government appointees subject to dismissal by the minister of education.

In addition to basic structural changes, the reform clearly spelled out the government's expectation that the university would contribute to the creation of a socialist society. The university, a citadel of revolt during the colonial and republican periods, would now be integrated into the revolution. This strategy, called *universalización*, attempted to break down the high walls isolating the universities from society. Large numbers of workers and farmers would attend special programs on university campuses, while professional work teams of students and faculty, or *equipos*, would carry their special skills out to fields and factories.[15]

The reform also called for emphasis on ideological instruction in Marxism-Leninism and a shift in priority from theoretical to practical studies, with heavy emphasis on work-study programs. In contrast to prerevolutionary university studies—which, for the most part, gave middle- and upper-class students a broad liberal education in the humanities and professions—university programs would henceforth prepare Marxist specialists of high quality in technical fields.[16]

The Present System

Following the First Congress of the Cuban Communist Party in 1975, a major policy initiative reform known as *perfeccionamiento* sought to implement additional administrative and curricular reforms. Control of higher education moved out of the Ministry of Education into a new Ministry of Higher Education responsible for all research and teaching in universities and affiliated institutions. Higher education would be expanded to include more workers and address social and economic development needs. Other goals were to improve the quality of research and teaching, and to increase the effectiveness of ideological studies.[17]

By 1986 over forty-five university-level facilities enrolled some 268,000 students. The University of Havana alone enrolled 60,000, with an additional 11,000 nondegree students in the Worker-Farmer Faculty, or "open university."[18] With strong commitment to the policy of universalization, an ever larger segment of the total population aged twenty to twenty-four participated in higher education. In 1982 the percentage enrolled reached 19 percent, according to the World Bank, a percentage higher than in Italy or the United Kingdom. In 1985/86 Castro claimed that higher education enrolled thirty-five of every thousand Cubans aged eighteen or over.[19] Table 1 summarizes main indicators for the entire educational system from 1959 to 1982 and clearly indicates a pattern of sustained growth.

While rapidly expanding enrollment—especially among workers, blacks, and women—may be seen as a response to Castro's commitment to provide all Cuban citizens with a "university" education, it also serves more practical purposes. It is a benefit granted those who actively support revolutionary policies. It helps the government deal with the potentially explosive surplus of labor. And with *masification*, the state reduces the university's elitist tendencies and makes higher education more akin to the other mass popular organizations under strict Communist party control.[20]

Vastly expanded enrollment also means that studies must be more closely linked with central planning and development priorities.[21] Shifts here are made clearly apparent in Figure 3. In general, enrollments in law, humanities, and social sciences have declined, while those in education, engineering, and agricultural sciences have increased sharply.[22]

University admission requirements include a mix of academic records, interviews to assess each applicant's attitudes toward the revolution, and support from one of the mass organizations where the applicant is well known. For those students seeking entrance to natural sciences or technological studies, more objective criteria are used. Those seeking admission to social or behavioral sciences, philosophy, or the diplomatic corps, in contrast, are assessed using more ideological criteria. While students may express a preference for a field of study, placement is made on the basis of guidelines, quotas, and plan requirements. Many applicants are placed in fields for which they have little interest, as in agronomy, and poor motivation and dropout remain continuing problems.[23]

Academic Staff

As indicated in Table 1, the number of academic staff, both professors and adjunct faculty, experienced a large increase following the 1975/76 reforms. Interests of the state, as with students, are determined by the Communist party, and university authorities dictate all aspects of professional work. Marxism-Leninism guides all curriculum and research problems, especially in the less technical areas, and all faculty publications are subject to rigorous review for "ideological correctness." The state has a total monopoly on publishing. Academic publications tend to be studies of prerevolutionary history, or papers in

Figure 4

Higher Education Enrollments by Selected Fields of Study

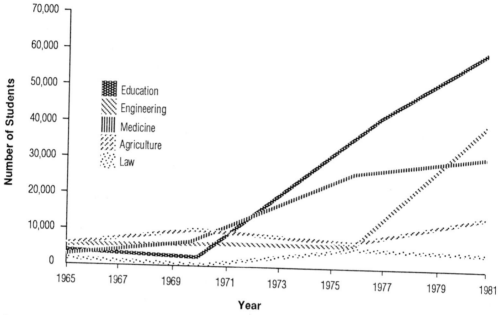

Source: UNESCO, 1974, 1983.

the natural sciences. No mention is made of faculty rights to free intellectual inquiry or academic freedom in Cuban university documents. Today, as a large sign on the gates of the University of Havana proclaims, "The University is only for revolutionaries."

Although faculty are still marked by the titles of *profesores, profesores auxiliares,* and *instructores,* status differences between professors, students, and staff in higher education have been vastly reduced since the prerevolutionary period. Professors and UJC-FEU student representatives jointly plan curriculum, evaluate each other's goals and accomplishments, consult on promotions, and jointly collaborate in the administrative policy and practice of *cogobierno,* or cogovernance. During weekend and summer periods of voluntary productive labor, an obligation for all who are "integrated into the revolution," senior ad-

ministrators, faculty, and students, along with staff and plant-maintenance people, for example, eat and sleep in the men's and women's barracks and work from 7:00 A.M. to 5:00 P.M. in the university farm fields without distinctions or special privileges.[24]

Since the reform of 1962 eliminated faculty tenure, professors are hired on the basis of annual contracts, which can be terminated at any time. Professors are expected to teach in strict conformity with revolutionary ideology; that is, they must demonstrate their subject's contribution to revolutionary goals for socioeconomic development and the creation of a new, socialist man. Those unable to meet these expectations are dropped from the university. The remaining professors receive great social prestige and many of the special rewards reserved for the ruling group, such as access to an automobile, access to foreign currency stores, and other material rewards.

To meet requirements for contract renewal, faculty members are required to take periodic courses in Marxism-Leninism, in teaching methods, and in subject knowledge. In-service training courses are offered during the summer months at all universities and related institutions. Faculty members receive full salaries while attending these courses, which also qualify them for promotion and salary increases.[25]

Faculty members are relatively well paid. All salaries (professional and staff salaries) in higher education are determined by the Ministry of Higher Education according to a fixed salary schedule. All who work in higher education are employees of the ministry and, from the rectors and deans down, are responsible to the minister and subject to his direction as the government's representative. Thus, the concept of academic freedom as it is espoused in many Western countries does not exist. In fact, the concept is officially rejected as a middle-class sham and incompatible with the revolutionary role of Cuban universities today.

Higher Education and Employment

With higher education tightly integrated into Cuba's Marxist economy, university graduates move easily into technical and professional employment in state ministries, agencies, and mass organizations. Relations between higher education and industry are increasingly close. *Equipos* contribute to the planning and construction of industrial facilities and to the increased efficiency of industrial processes and worker training; and university graduates frequently devote their years of public service to work in industry, especially the sugar industry. Since all Cuban industry is in the public sector, the flow of university personnel and skills into the productive process is relatively uncomplicated. In addition, managers and technicians from industry often teach courses in higher education.[26]

In the worker-farmer program workers from industry and agriculture study on campus and participate in student affairs and university governance. Also, university faculty in the program teach classes at the factories and in rural settings as well. Through these joint programs and exchanges universities have become closely linked with industrial development and manpower training. Here the Soviet model, although adapted to Cuban needs, has been put into operation.[27]

During the past decade many Cuban graduates have joined technical assistance projects in Angloa, Ethiopia, and other allied African countries. Although little data is available on this form of employment, it would seem that international service placement possibilities are now declining due to détente. The domestic Cuban economy will be under increased pressure to provide employment for both returning technicians and the growing number of graduates at home.

Continuing Problems

Cuban universities have traditionally shared the Latin American university's emphasis on preparing professionals.[28] There was, accordingly, a scant tradition of research when the 1975 reorientation took place. And just as the United States attempted to develop research capabilities in Latin American universities through Alliance for Progress programs and foundation assistance, so too the Soviet Union, with support from the German Democratic Republic and other socialist countries, has sought with some success to develop research capabilities in Cuban higher education institutions and in the Cuban National Academy of Sciences.[29] Most research studies are the responsibility of the National Center of Scientific Research and the National Academy of Sciences. All research in Cuba is thus directed and funded by the government as a state monopoly. Most research studies address practical problems in the areas of technological development, tropical agriculture, and tropical medicine. Some basic research is also carried out, usually in collaboration with Soviet academics and scientific institutions.[30]

With the press toward pragmatism and specialization in the universities, as indicated in Figure 3, graduates who have been taught research skills are expected to apply them to the task of rural development and production. The Ministry of Education claims that the universities do not produce researchers; instead, they produce knowledgeable, practical people who can run factories and provide basic health services.[31] University professors, for example, are promoted by student-faculty committees on the basis of their teaching ability and revolutionary commitment rather than their research contributions.

Perhaps the major problem in Cuban higher education is the attempted creation of a revolutionary socialist consciousness in all students. This effort to form the so-called new man takes place in educational programs at all levels. Achieving success in this effort is most difficult with older students, who typically manifest greater independence of thought and action.[32] In 1971 the discrepancy between goals for ideological formation in education and actual student behavior had become so great that the government convened the First National Congress of Education and Culture to address the problem. As a result, discipline and regimentation were increased, individual choice in the selection of a field of training was diminished, and time spent outside the university in work teams and rural extension facilities was considerably increased.[33]

This unremitting effort to orient and discipline a new generation of Cuban youth who know the revolutionary struggle of the 1950s only as history and mythology has, in turn, contributed to the chronic problem of low academic achievement and inadequate skills development. Combining study with productive labor may or may not help to form the new man. What is certain, however, is that such efforts seriously reduce the time and energy available for learning the special skills and behaviors needed to become a competent engineer or a physician or a chemist.[34]

Recent Reforms

Major reforms attempted in higher education during the past decade or so have been part of larger national campaigns to achieve greater economic efficiency and ideological orthodoxy. The *perfeccionamiento* reforms, begun in 1975, followed from the creation of a national five-year plan to replace the largely futile and haphazard annual plans. As noted, consequences for Cuban universities included the creation of a new Ministry of Higher Education and the establishment of *Centros de Educación Superior*, postsecondary institutions to prepare technical specialists for local industry and agriculture.

Curriculum was revised and upgraded, with special attention given to practical aspects and ideological correctness.[35] All faculty were required to take additional courses in Marxist-Leninist history, philosophy, and political economy. Students were required to take four courses, or some 10 percent of their load, on the same subjects plus principles of dialectical materialism.

Volunteer productive labor requirements of at least twenty hours a week, usually in study-related areas, plus compulsory one-day-a-week service in the national militia were increased. The law continued to guarantee all higher education students free tuition and support, but with a new requirement that graduates must serve national development needs for three years wherever they are most needed.

The UJC was given authority to coordinate voluntary labor and enforce the regime's political line among university students. Methods used by the UJC to deal with uncooperative or uncommitted students include disciplinary courts, suspension, and expulsion. The F.E.U., a student association with a long history of revolutionary activity before the revolution, has been changed into a mass service organization involved in cultural and athletic activities along with the everyday concerns of university life.

The shock of the *Mariel* exodus in April 1980, and declining Soviet support, a consequence of superpower détente, caused Castro to launch a national "rectification" campaign in April 1986, the twenty-fifth anniversary of the Bay of Pigs invasion. In education, Castro attacked low promotion rates in secondary schools and blamed *finalismo* or overemphasis on final exams; *promocionalismo*, or automatic promotion; overemphasis on memorization; poor preparation of teachers in specialized subject matter; lack of parental involvement; and, inter alia, excessive specialization within the university system. The campaign once again called for closer links between the university curriculum and national economic needs. Castro also denounced the "generalized passivity" seen to be prevalent in universities and the educational bureaucracy, and in the tightly controlled faculty and the students. This serious situation, he cautioned, would require redoubled efforts by the educational organs of the state to secure committed communist orthodoxy.[36]

Conclusions

With the emergence of new technical elites in the USSR under the leadership of Gorbachev who want to move the Soviet Union toward greater openness and economic efficiency, it is problematic how long

Castro will be able to pursue a counter-policy of ideological rigidification. Given Soviet economic influence in Cuba (the USSR contributes over one-quarter of the national GNP), plus the problems of an aging leadership, it would seem likely that the next major reform in Cuban universities will be in the direction of greater productivity and efficiency at the expense of ideological purity, a trend already present in the USSR and in several other Marxist-Leninist states.

Castro has been able to place the ideological returns of higher education over the economic returns in large measure because of massive Soviet economic contributions to the Cuban economy. Future priorities for higher education must, however, take into account Cuba's changing relations with the dominant world powers.[37] As a small, underdeveloped country, Cuba is attempting to create a more egalitarian society and to implant the requisite values of social conscience to support such a vast undertaking. Supporters of this utopian effort argue that the revolution has created a new university system that now serves the Cuban masses and has helped Cuba replace a dependent capitalist system of production with more equitable structures.[38] Critics argue that any equity gains have been overwhelmed by losses of personal liberty, and by bureaucratic inefficiency.[39] While the evaluation of the Cuban people has been generally positive, the extent to which university students will continue to endure intense programing and ideological indoctrination, and especially if the economy weakens, remains to be seen.

Notes

1. Iliana Rojas Requena, "La concepcíon marxista del hombre en la historia de la pedagogía," *Revista Cubana de Educación Superior* 5 (1985): 3–11.

2. Eduardo Ramos, *La Universidad de Oriente y la industria azucarera* (Santiago: Universidad de Oriente, 1951). See also Rolland G. Paulston,

"Cultural Revitalization and Educational Change in Cuba," *Comparative Education Review* 16 (October 1972): 474–85; and Rolland G. Paulston, "Education," in *Revolutionary Change in Cuba*, ed. C. Mesa-Lago (Pittsburgh: University of Pittsburgh Press, 1971), 375–98.

3. Primer congreso nacional de educacíon y cultura, *The Principle of the Combination of Study and Work in Cuban Higher Education*. Report of Cuban Delegation to the Ninth Conference of Higher Education in Socialist Countries (Havana: Ministry of Education, 1974), 3.

4. Jaime Suchlicki, *University Students and Revolution in Cuba* (Coral Gables, Fla.: University of Miami Press, 1969), 15–68.

5. R. L. Packland, *Education in Cuba, Puerto Rico, and the Philippines: Report of the Commissioner of Education, 1897–98* (Washington, D. C.: U.S. Government Printing Office, 1899), 43–46.

6. Enrique Varona y Pera, *Las reformas en la ensenanza superior* (Havana: El Figaro, 1900), 39–44.

7. Olga Caberera and Carmen Almodobar, *Las Luchas Estudiantiles Universitarias, 1923–1934* (Havana: Editorial de Ciencias Sociales, 1975), 22–30.

8. Eduardo Aiguesvives, "University Reform in Cordova and Cuba," *Granma Weekly Review*, 30 January 1989, p. 2.

9. Olga Caberera, *Julio Antonio Mella, Reforma Estudiantil, y Antimperealismo* (Havana: Editorial de Ciencias Sociales, 1977), 46.

10. Juan Marinello, *Revolucion y Universidad* (Havana: Gobierno provincial revolucionario de la Habana, 1960), 41–42.

11. Moirla Perez Rojas, *El Movemiento Estudiantil Universitario de 1934–1940* (Havana: Editorial de Ciencias Sociales, 1975), 65.

12. Juan M. Lafitade, *Brigada Universitaria Jose A. Echeverria y Bon 154* (Havana: Editora Politica, 1983), 33–35.

13. Carlos Rafael Rodriguez, "La reforma universitaria," *Cuba Socialista* 2 (February 1962): 22–44.

14. Juan Marinello, "Universidad y Cultura," *Universidad de La Habana* 159 (January–February 1963): 122–46.

15. See Fidel Castro, "The Large-Scale Application of Study and Work in All Three of Our Universities Is Undoubtedly a Historic Step," *Granma Weekly Review*, 17 December 1972, pp. 9–10; and Nelson P. Valdes and Roland E. Bonachea, eds., *The Selected Works of Fidel Castro* (Cambridge: MIT Press, 1972), passim.

16. Fidel Castro, "The Mission of the Universities Is Not Just to Train Technicians, but Revolutionary Technicians," *Granma Weekly Review*, 18 December 1966, 6.

17. Fernando Alegret Vecino, *Algunas tendencias en el desarrollo de la educacíon superior en Cuba* (Havana: Editorial Pueblo y Educacíon, 1986), 63–65; and Beltran José Gómez, "Tendencias que se presentan en los systemas de control que se aplican en la Educacíon Superior en los paises socialistas," *Revista Cubana de Educacíon Superior* 8 (1987): 39–49.

18. Alfred Padula and Lois M. Smith, "The Revolutionary Transformation of Cuban Education, 1959–1987," in *Making the Future: Politics and Educational Reform in the United States, England, the Soviet Union, China, and Cuba*, ed. Edgar B. Gumbert (Atlanta: Georgia State University, 1988), 126–31.

19. See Eusebio Mujal-Leon, *The Cuban University Under the Revolution* (Washington, D. C.: Cuban American National Foundation, 1988), 25–27; and Cuba, Comite-Estatal de Estadisticas, *Anuario Estadistico de Cuba* (Havana: Comite-Estatal de Estadistics, 1985), 53–55.

20. Carlos M. Alvarez Zayas, "Cuenta del ministro de Educacion Superior a la asemblea nacional de poder popular," *Revista Cubana de Educacíon Superior* 3 (1985): 87–89.

21. Jesús Pérez Othón and Victor I. Mijaliov, "Analisis functional y de objectivos del sistema de direccíon de la educacíon superior en Cuba," *La Educacíon Superior Contemporanea* 3 (1982): 31–45; and Rolland G. Paulston, "Impacto de la reforma eductiva en Cuba," *Revista Latinoamericana de Estudios Educativos* 10 (1980): 99–124.

22. UNESCO, *Statistical Yearbook* (Paris: UNESCO, 1974–88). See also Rolland G. Paulston, *The Educational System of Cuba* (Washington, D. C.: U.S. Government Printing Office, 1975).

23. Theodore MacDonald, *Making a New People: Education in Revolutionary Cuba* (Vancouver, British Columbia: New Star Books, 1985), 169.

24. Miguel Hernández Torres, "La elaboracíon de planes de estudio y programas y su perfeccionamiento en la República de Cuba," *Revista international de Países Socialistas* 2 (1983): 45–53.

25. See Cuba, Ministerio de Educacion Superior, *La Educacion Superior en Cuba* (Havana: Ministerio de Educacion Superior, 1984); and Orlando Mirabal Gonzalez, "El Financiamienlo de la Educacíon Superior cubana en venticinco anos de edificacion socialista," *Revista Cubana de Educacíon Superior* 7 (1987): 67–73.

26. Ministry of Education, *Informe de la delegacion de la Republica de Cuba a la VII Conferencia de Ministros de Educacion Superior y Media especializada en los paises socialistas, Praga, Junio 1972* (Havana: Instituto de Libro, 1972), 12–14.

27. Daniel Novigrod, "La equivalencia de los grados cientificos en Cuba," *Revista Cubana de Educacíon Superior* 6 (1986): 97–109.

28. Joseph Maier and Richard W. Weatherhead, eds., *The Latin American University* (Albuquerque: University of New Mexico Press, 1979). See also Rolland G. Paulston, "Educational Development in Latin America and the Caribbean," *Handbook of Latin American Studies* 51 (Washington, D. C.: Library of Congress, 1990).

29. Nikolai Kolesnikov, *Cuba: Educacion Popular y Preparacion de los Cuadros Nacionales, 1959–1982* (Moscow: Editorial Progreso, 1983), 41–44.

30. Juan Albarz Tehume and V. A. Bogomolov, "Experiencia en normacíon del trabajo de los profesores los CES de la USSR y de la República de Cuba," *Revista internacional de Países Socialistas,* 2 (1983): 103–20.

31. Tirso W. Sáenz and Emilio Gracía Capote, *Cuestiones de la ciencia y la tecnología en Cuba* (Havana: Editorial Academia, 1981), 61–63.

32. Alberto Martínez, "El proceso de motivacíon en las classes de la Educacíon Superior," *Revista Cubana de Educacíon Superior* 7 (1987): 49–58.

33. Greta Crespo Gómez et al., "Los Gastos del proceso de formacion de especialistas de nivel superior. Probelmas para su determinacion," *Revista Cubana de Educacíon Superior* 7 (1987): 73–88.

34. Gary W. Wynia, *The Politics of Latin American Development* (New York: Cambridge University Press, 1987), 288–89.

35. Nora Arrechavaleta, "Algunas consideraciones téoricas para el analisis de la eficiencia de la educacíon superior en Cuba," *Revista internacional de Países Socialistas* 3 (1983): 41–42. See also Rolland G. Paulston, "Problems of Educational Reform and Rural Development in Latin America: Some Lessons from Cuba," in *Rural Change and Public Policy,* ed. William P. Avery et al. (New York: Pergamon Press, 1980), 168–71.

36. Isabel Cabrera Villarrubia, "La conferencia del Marxismo-Leninismo como medio para la preparacion teórica-metodologica y politico-ideologica de los estudientes," *Revista Cubana de Educacíon Superior* 6 (1986): 53–61.

37. Purcell Kaufman, "Is Cuba Changing?," *National Interest* 14 (Winter 1988/89): 7–8.

38. See, for example, Samuel Bowles, "Education and Socialist Man in Cuba," in *Schooling in a Corporate Society,* ed. Martin Carnoy (New York: McKay, 1979); Martin Carnoy and J. Werthein, *Cuba: Cambio Economica y Reforma Educativa* (Mexico, D.F.: Nueva Imagen, 1980); and J. Werthein, "Cuba," in *The Encyclopedia of Comparative Education and National Systems of Education,* ed. T. Neville Postlethwaite (Oxford: Pergamon Press, 1987), 212–17.

39. See, for example, Mujal-Leon, *The Cuban University;* Padula and Smith, "Revolutionary Transformation of Cuban Education," 136–37; and Kaufman, "Is Cuba Changing?," 8.

Mexico

Carlos Ornelas and Daniel C. Levy

◆

Background

Overview

A central challenge to major systems is to adapt to their environment's changing needs while maintaining their own stability. Historically, Mexican higher education has also faced a corollary challenge: to find constructive roles within significantly changing political contexts. Since the 1930s, however, the Mexican political system has finally achieved a notable stability, accommodating itself, whether for good or bad, to changing economic and social conditions. In turn, higher education has been challenged to adapt.

Most observers argue that higher education has failed that challenge in spite of, or, for some, partly because of the system's spectacular enrollment and institutional growth in recent years. In addition to providing some basic information, this chapter attempts to sketch the system's main historical adaptations and the more contemporary problems of reform.

Perhaps the most striking higher education trend of recent decades has been growth. "Massification" has provided access and some social mobility for students from the middle and even lower-middle classes. But it has also provoked strong criticisms from key business and government groups and has stimulated privatizing alternatives to those of public growth.[1] Enrollments jumped from less than 100,000 in 1960 to 1,206,000 in 1988. The relevant cohort percentages grew from 4.5 percent to 12 percent during that same period. To a large extent such growth parallels that of Latin American higher education as a whole, but

steady, continued growth in the 1970s, averaging 13 percent per year, contrasted with reversals in some South American nations under military rule. Mexico's enrollment thus overtook Argentina's to become second only to Brazil in terms of size. Then, in the 1980s, the growth rate finally fell to under 7 percent per year, quite below official estimations at the decade's outset.[2] Strong decline began in 1983 as a direct consequence of the nation's severe economic crisis.

Table 1 shows the female/male student proportions. Note that the female enrollment rate has risen from 28 to 40 percent in the last ten years. But most women are still enrolled in such traditionally female fields as education, nursing, social work, psychology, and social and administrative studies.

Mexico's higher education students are taught by over 100,000 professors and other instructional personnel, in nearly five hundred institutions. Table 2 shows the number of teachers according to the time they devote to the institutions of higher education. (Until 1984 the normal schools or teaching colleges, both private and public, were not considered part of the higher education system.)

The Two Sectors

Spectacular growth, along with a search for adaptation, has produced a higher education system composed of a complex set of institutions that serve diverse groups, pursue different goals, and display distinctive features. This system consists of two sectors, the public and the private, each of which in turn is subdivided.

The public sector is divided mainly into universities and technical institutes. There are also some specialized institutions such as the National School of Anthropology, the National Institute of Fine Arts, military and diplomatic schools, and so forth. The sector's formal aims are to prepare professionals who contribute to national development, to preserve and expand culture, and to develop new knowledge.[3] The public institutions are also expected to promote social mobility.

The private sector, which currently enrolls 17 percent of Mexico's tertiary students, is also complex. It divides into universities, technical institutes, and other independent schools. This sector reflects individual and group initiatives to mold

or adapt higher education to their desires. That is, middle-class, business, and religious interests came to see public institutions as not fulfilling their chief higher education goals: the provision of high status; skilled manpower; academic quality; conservative or apolitical-technocrat orientations. Other private institutions have arisen principally as profit-making institutions to absorb the demand for higher education not satisfied by the public sector. All these factors typify privatizing adaptive trends in much of Latin America.[4]

By quantitative indicators—student enrollments, numbers of teaching personnel, financial resources, facilities—the public universities comprise easily the most important subsector. This subsector

Table 1

Mexican Higher Education

Enrollments Licenciatura*	1978–1979				1987–1988			
	Male	Female	%	Sum	Male	Female	%	Sum
Public								
Universities	341,032	148,695	30	489,727	433,346	279,066	39	712,412
Technical Institutes	94,496	19,557	17	114,053	108,734	42,550	28	151,284
Other	4,544	1,235	21	5,779	4,783	2,755	37	7,538
Sum of Public	440,072	169,487	28	609,559	546,863	324,371	37	871,234
Private	59,421	29,159	33	88,580	90,901	71,072	44	161,973
Sum of Licenciatura	499,493	198,646	28	698,139	637,764	395,443	38	1,033,207
Normal Education								
Public	—	—	—	—	37,487	55,844	60	93,331
Private	—	—	—	—	17,519	22,617	56	40,136
Sum	—	—	—	—	55,066	78,461	59	133,467
Graduate Public and Private								
M.A.	11,696	3,985	25	15,681 Pub.	21,414	9,800	31	31,214
Doctorate	429	276	40	705 Pri.	5,513	2,778	33	8,291
Sum Graduate	12,125	4,261	26	16,386	26,927	12,578	32	39,505
Total National	511,618	202,907	28	714,525	719,697	486,482	40	1,206,179

Graduate	Public	Private	Sum
Specialization**	12,369	1,157	13,526
M.A.	17,773	6,903	24,676
Doctorate	1,072	231	1,303
Total	31,214	8,291	39,505

* First-level university degree.
** Most of them in medicine.

Source: Our own calculations from Asociacion Nacional de Universidades e Institutos de Enseñanza Superior, *Anuario Estadístico* 1979 and 1988.

Table 2

Mexican Higher Education

Teaching Staff	Full-time	Part-time	Catedráticos	Sum
1978–1979*	10.572	5.840	42.059	58.291
1987–1988	28.018	10.587	84.426	123.031
Licenciatura	22.957	8.233	69.775	100.965
Graduate Level	2.715	646.000	6.491	9.852
Normal	2.346	1.708	8.160	12.214

* Licenciatura and graduate.

Source: Our own calculations from Asociacion Nacional de Universidades e Institutos de Enseñanza Superior, *Anuario Estadístico* 1979 and 1988.

includes thirty-three state universities (only three of which are not formally autonomous, and depend heavily on their state governments for top appointments); some state colleges and schools; the National Autonomous University of Mexico (UNAM); the Metropolitan Autonomous University; the National Pedagogical University; and the University of the Army and the Air Force.[5] Except for a few institutions such as the last one, Mexico's public universities are not administered directly by the government, even though they are directly financed almost fully by it. They are characterized by their enormous size, not only because they enroll thousands at the higher education level, but because many also include a preparatory level (the last three years of secondary education). This feature makes the UNAM the largest university in the world with over 350,000 students; three state universities (Guadalajara, Puebla, and Nuevo Leon) have over 100,000 students each, while ten others have over 50,000 each.

The technical subsector was designed to meet distinct economic needs not sufficiently met by traditional public universities, and specifically to provide manpower for industrial and agricultural development. This subsector includes the National Polytechnic Institute (IPN); fifty-two technical institutes in the states; thirty agricultural institutes; three institutes of marine technology; and one technical institute of forestry. More than the public universities, the institutes depend financially and administratively on the federal government. Also within the technical subsector, but dependent on the Ministry of Agriculture, not the Ministry of Education, and with autonomy in governance, are three agricultural universities: Chapingo, Antonio Narro, and Hermanos Escobar. Most of the institutes in the technical subsector are rather small and specialized, though together they offer programs for a variety of engineering and administrative professions.

Within the private sector, which in contrast to the public sector depends fully on nongovernment funds (mostly tuition), there exists a marked hierarchy, topped by such elite institutions as the Technological Institute of Monterrey, the Iberoamerican University, the Autonomous Technological Institute of Mexico, the Anáhuac University, the Autonomous University of Guadalajara, and the University of the Americas (formerly Mexico City College). But the sector overall is composed of nearly 250 institutions, and only a handful are prestigious. Most are small universities or institutes that function like businesses, are poorly equipped, and attract students who cannot gain entrance to better places. Many offer evening courses and fast programs (mostly in accounting and administrative fields), and charge relatively low fees. Likewise, the private teachers colleges are sharply divided between such inferior institutions and older, more prestigious normal schools in the capital and other important cities.

Historical Trends

Before the Revolution

Although the origins of the Mexican higher education system are commonly traced to the sixteenth century, in reality contemporary institutions are much more the children of Mexico's relatively recent experiences with "positivism" and revolution. The colonial Royal and Pontifical University of Mexico, representative of the scholastic, Catholic, and Spanish universities of Europe, was first closed by the liberals in 1833; although repeatedly reopened by conservative governments, it was also repeatedly closed by their liberal successors, who were provoked by the university's conservative ties. Lacking solid institutional life, it was definitively closed during the French intervention (under Maximilian) in the 1860s, by which time it was almost a phantom with but three faculty members and fewer than twenty students, all studying theology and living in a borrowed house.[6]

In 1867 the reform government of Benito Juárez welcomed Gabino Barreda, a former student of positivist philosopher Auguste Comte, and his plan to create the National Preparatory School, oriented toward science and progress. In the following decades several national professional schools (medicine, law, etc.) emerged from this school. All were based on the French system of higher education, especially the *grandes écoles*. Higher education in such schools served the professions. But for other needs some Mexican leaders advocated a major institutional change: creation of a modern university.[7]

A key figure in the university movement was Justo Sierra, who rose to ministerial prominence during Porfirio Diaz's positivist-oriented dictatorship (subsequent to the Reform's demise). In 1910, just two months before the beginning of the Mexican Revolution, the National University of Mexico was inaugurated. The universities of Paris, Salamanca, and Berkeley helped guide the university. In truth, however, the new university merely put under one administration the set of independent national schools, with the National Preparatory School as its base, and the recently created National School of Advanced Studies (later the Faculty of Philosophy and Letters). So from its outset the Mexican university, like most Latin American universities, was marked by a sharp separation of professions, which were taught in semiautonomous schools.[8]

The teachers were not full time but *catedráticos*, professionals who devoted only a few hours a week to teaching and received little salary, but who taught for social and professional prestige, or to recruit promising youth, and/or to offer public service.

Adaptation in the Revolutionary Period

The Mexican Revolution, which took the lives of one citizen in ten and exiled another one in ten, naturally made for a precarious life for the National University. With the ascension to the rectorate (1920) of José Vasconcelos, a leading revolutionary intellectual, the university began a slow expansion, and other public universities were created. An ongoing problem, however, was the university's criticism of the revolutionary governments and the latter's disenchantment with an institution out of step with the revolution. In punitive frustration, the government conferred first partial and then full autonomy (1929, 1933) that deprived the university of its national nomenclature and its annual subsidy.[9] The government intended instead to mold higher education to its needs through alternative institutions.

From 1933 to 1945 Mexico's main university was characterized by continual struggles over power and academic orientation. Some faculty and students wanted to reembrace the government, to promote socialist education, and to direct attention to the lower classes, but others wanted to forge an elite academic institution with high academic status. The latter group dominated.

Meanwhile, the government sought alternatives. Most important was the inauguration of the technical subsector with the creation of the IPN. The institute had a twofold aim: to offer higher education, and thus social mobility, to the working and peasant classes, and to prepare cadres with a strong socialist and nationalist ideology to promote national development. The National University had resisted government efforts to establish programs in technical fields.[10] Similarly, other public universities were created or reformed along these lines (in the states of Nuevo León, Jalisco, and Sinaloa).

In the private sector other actors sought to create institutions oriented to their social, economic, and political views. Government remained too much in alien hands for these groups to find satisfaction in the public sector, but the revolution had moderated enough to allow private options. Still, the revolution's antireligious tendencies remained sufficiently strong to preclude formation of the typical Latin American Catholic universities, though some religious flavor could be found at Iberoamericana, La Salle, and, arguably, the Autonomous University of Guadalajara. The clearest manifestation of the secular, socioeconomic thrust of Mexico's early privatization was the Monterrey Technological Institute. This institution typified the effort to prepare highly qualified engineers and administrators to run business enterprises. It was founded in 1943 by leaders of Monterrey, Mexico's northern industrial city, on the model of the Massachusetts Institute of Technology. (It now has campuses throughout the republic.) In sharp contrast to Mexico's public universities, it was organized in departments and divisions (rather than faculties), and hired many full-time professors.[11] Notably, all such early, elite, private institutions survive to this day, strengthened and intensified by the perceived decline of public universities since the 1960s—and all are basically successful in terms of their own political-economic goals.

The Postrevolutionary Search for Consolidation

Conservative higher education adaptations would not be limited to the private sector, however. As the revolutionary regime retreated from its policies of socialist education, popular mobilization, and revolutionary nationalism, its higher education policy shifted again. Leading public universities entered a period of consolidation, with close ties to the state. For roughly a quarter century, this consolidation was fueled by the nation's economic growth and unprecedented political stability, and by the rise of civilian control (i.e., the replacement of revolutionary military men in top spheres of public life). The public universities, especially the UNAM, became the principal sites of recruitment of new cadres for the state.[12]

Thus from the 1940s to 1968 the universities and the state lived in comparative harmony. "Socialist" universities were renamed "public" or "autonomous" and shifted again to embrace liberalism. Reflecting the smoother university-government relations was the creation of a governing body of key people to oversee UNAM's affairs. This board has since played a major role in selecting rectors, avoiding the pitfalls of participatory elections by faculty, students, and workers, on the one hand, and direct government appointment, on the other hand.

Other public universities were created, always following the UNAM model in most respects. In other words, times were regarded as good and the accent was on reproducing the dominant forms, not on seeking alternatives. This is not to say, however, that institutional adaptation or proliferation stopped. Rather, it was more a time of replication and modification than of rejection and experimentation. In the public technical subsector, the federal government began (1948) the creation of regional institutes on the curriculum model of the IPN. Little was left of the earlier purpose to attract the lower classes or to offer social mobility. Instead, these institutes echoed the IPN's developmental ideology and attempted to prepare people to serve industry, manage technology, and generally support the reigning economic model. Still, this wave of institutional creation implied some criticisms of the autonomous universities' liberal education, which still avoided technical fields. In any case, the technical emphasis has never gained the social prestige associated with the universities (a worldwide problem); the technical institutes usually remain a second option for preparatory school graduates. One might argue, therefore, that higher education adaptations in the public technical subsector have been less successful than in the private sector in terms of fulfilling their own original goals.

Recent Years: Growth but Disenchantment

The era of government-university harmony came to a cataclysmic end. For years Mexico's authoritarian system had repressed political dissent and placed peasants and workers under corporatist control within its official party. But it had allowed leftist intellectuals refuge in the public universities. Inherent tensions intensified in the 1960s as the Cuban revolu-

tion and other international events exerted a tremendous influence on students. A wave of activism spread over Mexico. In this Mexico was not very different from many other Latin American nations. But in 1968 the government of Díaz Ordaz sent the army and police against protesting students, killing a still indeterminate number (but in the hundreds) and jailing all of the student and professional leadership.

Nonetheless, blatant repression did not become the rule for government-university relations. Instead, the government of Luis Echeverría (1970–76) wanted to recover the universities for the state. It therefore attempted to reform from above. Indeed, his government reflected a widespread perception that the decades of the "Mexican miracle"—economically, politically, and socially—were over and in any case had been overestimated. Many realized that Mexico had failed to fulfill even the more realistic aspects of its revolutionary promise. Higher education should accordingly be remolded to lead an expansive national reform.

However, surpassing reformist zeal was basic acquiescence to growth along existing and even less educationally demanding lines. Subsidies from the federal government to public universities grew at a tremendous rate. Many student demands, such as open-door admissions and cogovernment with parity on all academic councils, were readily granted in the public sector. New universities and technical and agricultural institutes were created. Massification resulted, bringing with it new problems. New faculty without experience in teaching or even in the professions they would be teaching were hired. The administrative apparatus grew bewilderingly and uncontrollably. Soon unionism rose to the point where university workers became major actors in the struggle to shape the public sector.[13] In short, growth meant not an orderly plan of relating higher education to societal needs but a complex, largely ad hoc, and conflictual process that left the orientations of higher education unresolved, or even unfathomable, and meanwhile the quality of higher education deteriorated.

To be sure, the government hoped to implement some reforms with its financial largess. It proposed changes in organization (e.g., departmentalization), curriculum (e.g., creation of new fields), and pedagogy (e.g., the incorporation of educational technology). But the government has been just one actor in the struggle to shape contemporary Mexican higher education. It is not nearly the all-powerful actor long postulated in much literature on Mexican politics.[14]

Thus, the future remains uncertain and the tension between two models of reform, which we will call "modernist" and "democratic," remains evident. As we will see, although this tension has some relevance to the private sector, it is more characteristic of the public sector. The private elite institutions are much more tied to the modernist vision, which has had a rough time in the great majority of public institutions. In contrast, the democratic model is the source of conflict in the public sector but is nearly ignored in the private sector.

Current Trends: Conflicting Models of Reform

One way to see current trends in Mexican higher education is to focus on five key "modernizing" versus "democratizing" orientations for change. Critics of the former current complain that its proponents take a limited, technocratic view of modernization; critics of the latter current complain that its adherents confuse democracy with irresponsible egalitarianism. We dichotomize here for clarity but in real life the models are not usually so explicitly or coherently laid out, and in specific institutions elements of both models overlap so that what results are mixes that confuse even the actors themselves.[15] Finally, many features of this Mexican struggle to reform higher education are central to struggles in other Latin American nations as well.

The Modernist Model

The modernist model aims at transforming higher education institutions to make them more rational and efficient so that they will better fit the requirements of the dominant economic interests. The model includes changes in structure, content, and even pedagogy. Accordingly, the universities and related institutions would become the sites to produce human resources to advance technology, an ideology favorable to modern society, and the personal traits necessary to comprehend the industrial order which, according to advocates of this model of reform, is the basis of modern societies. The pedagogical theory behind this model draws heavily on behaviorism.

The modernist model was supported by substantial financial resources until the economic crisis of the 1980s. Funds on the private side have come in part from business, but mostly from families who pay tuition. The government has coupled its financial effort with the propagandist means at hand, including agencies such as the National Association of Universities and Institutions of Higher Education. At the programmatic level the model is promoted by various plans, including the National Plan of Higher Education (1979), the National Program of Higher Education (1984), and the Integral National Program of Higher Education (1986) with a functional planning structure. Predictably, a measure of harsher persuasion is also used to further the modernist model but the government is unwilling to incur the enormous potential costs of imposing its model through large-scale repression.

The modernist model is defined by the following central elements. First, regarding curriculum, emphasis is placed on new fields, especially in science and technology, and also on business administration and enterprise economics. Moreover, one controlling idea is to reorient humanities toward "relevant" fields such as industrial psychology and labor sociology. State resources should be channeled effectively to fields strongly linked to the economy—for example, engineering, chemistry, computer science—which generally have a high cost per student and depend greatly on imported technology (even though others point out that graduates in many of these fields lack easy access to employment).

Second, enrollment policies should be quite selective and meritocratic. Many proponents of the modernist model want to use IQ and other standardized tests to select students. They assume that such tests would be neutral indicators of students' capabilities without social class biases. They also want to collect tuition and other enrollment fees, even in public universities, though they do intend to set up loan plans to help overcome socioeconomic barriers. In practice, such enrollment policies have not been implemented in the public sector mostly because of strong resistance from students and even professors and administrators. In 1986/87, for example, there was a massive student movement opposing the modernizing enrollment proposals made by UNAM rector Jorge Carpizo.[16]

Third, and perhaps most critical to the entire modernist vision, is the idea of implanting a governance form capable of carrying out the package. The modernists desire a hierarchical and centralized form of decision making in which all members of the tertiary educational community have specific functions: pupils to study, faculty to teach, and central bureaucratic staff to make decisions about institutional policy. All this implies a "depoliticization"

in which rational and legal rules attempt to create a corporate enterprise with pure administrative decisions.

Fourth, regarding research, many modernists would encourage practical and applied investigation. They would concentrate on fields related to labor productivity and the dominant sectors of the economy. Indeed, they propose to link university research centers with the most dynamic economic sectors. In all fairness, however, we must mention that other modernists believe in the benefits of open, objective research without immediate application.

In reality, however, research is not heavily supported. Little money is channeled to projects, pay is low, and a brain drain exists from the universities to government and business jobs. In addition, the modern economy relies on imported technology so that national research is not often tied to economic development. Much of the more relevant research that is carried on according to international standards of methods and quality is performed in structures protected from the democratized mainstream of Mexican higher education—less in the faculties of the large public universities than in those universities' institutes isolated from the student masses as well as in free-standing institutes outside the universities altogether. At the pinnacle of such free-standing institutes in the social sciences and the humanities is El Colegio de México, with a strong international reputation. While such academic units make desired homes for many of the nation's academic elite, often after their return from foreign graduate studies, they have contributed little to a necessary restructuring of the higher education system overall.

The modernists believe that cultural diffusion and university extension should be organized and conceived as entertainment for students and other university personnel. As with sports, these pursuits are perceived to be the proper complements—unlike participation in governance—to the basic academic tasks. The modernist approach is paternalistic to worker and peasant communities. Extension beyond the university walls emphasizes the production or sale of services.

The Democratizing Model

The second reform model emphasizes participation. In some respects it harks back to the socialist initiatives of the 1930s in both the public universities and the technical subsectors. At the same time, it defies the basic United States model in which democratic society rests on plural institutions, not all of which (e.g., universities) need be internally ruled by majorities. In contrast, the Mexican (and Latin American) democratic reform model calls for substantial political rule by the student and worker masses. It sees reform as a political, not a technocratic matter. Indeed, its advocates claim to be the heirs of the historically significant Latin American student-based reform movement launched in Córdoba, Argentina, in 1918 and to be harbingers of socialism. And, increasingly, these reformers see themselves as leaders of a broader national democratization that has gripped Mexico in recent years. Freedoms that have long existed to some degree, such as freedom of speech, have been greatly expanded. Freedoms with much less precedent, such as the freedom to organize and participate in truly independent leftist parties, have likewise expanded. In 1988 Mexico held its most competitive, democratic election since the Revolution: the leftist coalition received enthusiastic support from many who promote the democratizing university model.

University democratizers are concerned with power. They want radical change in the university structure and decision-making process. Academic affairs play only a secondary role in programmatic aspects of this model. Instead, it is expected that democratic institutions of higher education will help to produce political leaders to oppose the state's dominant ideology. The democratic forces do not systematically present a strong pedagogical theory, though they do draw on some Marxist ideas to combine education with productive labor as a means of creating less alienated and oppressed citizenry.

The democratic model is defined by the following major elements. First, regarding curriculum, emphasis is put on the social sciences, though without explicitly rejecting scientific and technological fields. The aim is to create new teaching programs that somehow relate curriculum to the needs and aspirations of the working and popular classes. Democratizers believe that subsidies from the state should be channeled to increase the influence of fields in which Marxism has preeminence in Mexico (political economy, sociology, history, philosophy, and others that usually do not carry a high cost per student and therefore allow for expanded enrollments). Second, concerning enrollment policies, the democratic model posits zero fees and zero tuition as a means to permit children of the deprived classes to enroll. It also proposes to arrange academic schedules to facilitate part-time study. Crucially, the democratizers oppose admissions exams and other policies designed to select out, which tend to favor privileged groups.

Third, in governance, the model favors participatory decision making in which university members elect their own authorities and select faculty. The model finds its most radical expression in cogovernment demands in which collective bodies composed equally of faculty, students, and workers set university policies. Power in the hands of these groups would presumably promote a democratizing reform package.

Fourth, concerning research, democratizers regard as irrelevant or worse the replication of orientations dominant in developed nations. Instead they seek research results to solve the problems of the masses or to raise their historical and social consciousness. This implies the support of of multitudinous small projects directed at the concrete problems of a region or of the nation as a whole, without squandering grand sums on pure research or on applied research helpful to privileged groups. In the social sciences the principal objective is to struggle against the dominant ideology by promoting a progressive world outlook among faculty and students.

Fifth, the democratizers conceive university extension and cultural diffusion programs as crucial bridges between the university community and the popular classes. Their aim is to integrate the university in day-to-day working-class experience and to promote art and culture among the people. How much time and effort partisans of such theories are truly prepared to devote to even the programs that now exist along these lines is another matter.

Reformist Models in Practice

What, then, is the relative strength of the two reformist models? Where are their main features most visible? In general, we might argue that neither model has achieved or is likely to achieve the dominance needed to implement its major notions. Instead, each vision is constrained by the other. Compromises are made within many institutions. In a few universities one view is dominant, but these institutions hardly influence the bulk of Mexican higher education. More commonly, even where one vision is dominant, reform is constrained by traditional structures and practices, a striking lack of resources (though the democratizers see that as a political more than an economic constraint), flaws in the models themselves, and a lesser commitment to the sacrifices reform requires than to the rhetoric of reform.

Because the modernist model mirrors many features of United States higher education, it receives its more enthusiastic support in many private universities that look positively upon their neighbor, praise

its educational and other achievements, and denounce a Mexican xenophobia that tries to block foreign influence. In terms of the five key orientations of the modernist model, several elite private universities emphasize curriculum relevant to business and to the ascendent technocratic tendencies of the state (e.g., in fields such as computer science) and have moved further than public universities with structural changes such as departmentalization as channels for such curriculum. They carefully limit enrollment—avoiding massification—through stringent admissions exams, relatively demanding study requirements, and tuition. Governance is hierarchical, with at most limited student or even faculty participation. The leading private universities also carry out research and extension helpful to leading economic interests, but one must emphasize that such activities are in fact still sparse. Moreover, most private institutions have gone much less far in these areas or even in curriculum reform, though even they implement the modernist principles of tuition and especially hierarchy.

In the public sector, technical institutes adopted modernist features by ministerial decree, but there is little evidence that they are actually changing old teaching patterns. While they have come closer than the public universities to other modernist concepts such as hierarchical governance and relevant research for industrial development, they still fall far short of original aspirations in these respects. In the public university subsector, partial exceptions to the modernist weakness are found in certain young universities, such as the state university in Aguascalientes and the Autonomous Metropolitan University. But, for example, the latter is also highly constrained by democratic participation and has largely failed in its research thrusts. Meanwhile, at many public universities, there are top administrators who favor modernization but who are blocked by the political strength of their opponents. Similarly, most government officials are unwilling to risk the political costs involved in forcefully promoting the model. The massive and so far successful student protest versus the reform proposed by UNAM's rector in 1986 serves for many as another reminder of the difficulty of implementing such reform.[17] But neither are the democratizers able to impose their model.

The democratic model is supported by the more radical elements of the middle class, especially intellectuals and students. It is strongest and has been partly implemented in states where there is a convergence of diverse Marxist groups (e.g., Puebla, Sinaloa, and Guerrero). However, the political machinery of these groups is still weak and highly fragmented into ideological sects. A related problem is a continual struggle between faculty and labor unions committed to variants of the model. But a more fundamental weakness of the democratizing model is that it lacks support in the broader political arena. Thus, where university majorities incline toward democratic reform, they often find themselves in open conflict with government authorities. This leaves them in grave danger since, for example, the institutions depend financially almost totally on the government. In other words, it leaves such universities in a position like that of the National University in the 1930s when it was granted autonomy but at the same time denied government funding.

Even allowing for problems of external opposition, one might conclude that democratizers have accomplished little when given a chance. After changing the patterns of electing authorities, universities conquered by leftist militants have done little to enforce other elements of their model. State universities such as the ones in Puebla, Sinaloa, and Guerrero, which are directly governed by left-wing professors and students, have not effected structural or curriculum changes, nor introduced new methods of faculty recruit-

ment. Scientific research is weak, or, as in Puebla, it is mainly done in institutes independent of democratized faculties. University extension practically does not exist and cultural diffusion is mostly entertainment addressed chiefly to the students themselves. In sum, while leadership of these universities opposes many academic innovations as modernist, capitalist, or United States-oriented, it has done little to create alternatives. Thus, in essence such leadership sustains the existing order.

And, ideology aside, the strongest protectors of the traditional university, unreformed, are the authorities, professors, and students of most of the public universities who oppose almost any type of change because of inertia, apathy, vested interests, and fear of changes that would make them compete in a modernized world. After all, unhappily, many in higher education are heavily committed not to any model of reform but to other ends ranging from personal power and advancement to social peace and nonconfrontation. Most public and private higher education institutions strongly pursue neither modernist nor democratizing reforms but traditionalism and academic mediocrity.

The Failure of Reform: Problems of Employment and Autonomy

The failure of any viable reformist model to take hold of the bulk of the system produces sad consequences of many kinds. Employment offers one example. Higher education does not routinely lead to good jobs. The picture is especially bleak for the many who do not finish their studies, instead dropping out. Violating the modernist vision, most students are not considered desirable by employers in the productive sphere. Public university students are sometimes told not to bother to apply. Violating the democratizing vision, few students develop their potential to change society.

Even though we lack recent empirical studies on unemployment among university graduates, newspapers and magazine reports confirm popular perceptions that problems are severe for health science professionals, architects, agricultural engineers, economists, sociologists, and professionals in the hard sciences such as physics and biology. Partly, this problem is the result of higher education continuing to satisfy student demands for admission to fields saturated on the job market: the overproduction of doctors, lawyers, and other liberal professionals is notorious. But partly it is a problem of the type of training provided, insufficiently modernist given the realities of employment needs in Mexico. The few higher education institutions that defy this generalization, mostly the private elite universities, have further marginalized the bulk of higher education graduates by successfully capturing an increased share of the top positions.

Nor has higher education developed a large reliable market of its own for graduates. In fact, the academic profession has been relatively weak and poorly compensated in Mexico by international standards and also by comparison to Mexico's other professions. The great majority of teachers are part-timers who rarely conduct research. Though institutes have been founded since the 1940s to carry on research, they have typically existed separate from the teaching faculties. So the emerging academic profession has been divided between researchers, usually full time, and teachers, usually part time (though full-timers dedicated only partly to research have also emerged in the faculties). In short, while massification led to a multiplication of employment within higher education, only in isolated pockets has it led to a viable job market there.[17]

The nature of autonomy also illustrates the problems of unimplemented reform. Granted, partisans of modernizing reform have been gratified by the performance of elite private universities, which are highly autonomous of the government. These universities are also largely unconstrained by the interests and beliefs of most groups inside and outside the university that do not share their conceptions. But one might question how autonomous they are with regard to the business interests that contribute financially to them and hire their graduates. And one might question how much freedom exists for alternative visions to get an effective hearing. Then, too, partisans of modernizing reform face the reality that for the bulk of Mexican higher education institutions, relative (though variable) autonomy from government and business interests has provided license to continue inefficient policies that fail to meet the needs of an increasingly technocratic government and competitive economy; in fact, autonomy often provides a sanctuary for those most opposed by the modernizers.

On the other hand, for adherents of the democratizing model, relative autonomy has often left the university too cut off from the political and economic power needed for fundamental reform. Moreover, autonomy may provide a legitimizing cover for the state, which often allows significant academic freedom and a place for dissidents to blow off steam but not to achieve major socioeconomic change.

Conclusions

Mexican higher education has a long and proud but checkered history. In recent decades expansion has been remarkable and has made important contributions, but overall higher education has not kept up with society in qualitative terms. Nor do major reform models appear to offer sufficient basis for optimism. Institutional diversification has helped, and many institutions, parts of institutions, and indeed industrious and inspired individuals have contributed mightily. Still, such contributions must be weighed against a mass of unreformed growth.

Notes

1. Guillermo Villaseñor, *Estado y Universidad: 1976–1982* (Mexico City: Universidad Autónoma Metropolitana–Xochimilco and Centro de Estudios Educativos, 1988), 76–78.
2. Figures from Carlos Ornelas and Noel McGinn, *Perspectivas de la Universidad en México* (Mexico City: Fundación Javier Barros Sierra, 1980), 42; and Plan Nacional de Educación Superior, *Lineamientos 1981–1991* (Mexico City: Secretaría de Educación Publica–Asociación Nacional de Universidades e Institutos de Enseñanza Superior [ANUIES], 1981), 127.
3. ANUIES, *Plan Nacional de Educación Superior* (Mexico City: ANUIES, 1979).
4. Daniel C. Levy, *Higher Education and the State in Latin America: Private Challenges to Public Dominance* (Chicago: University of Chicago Press, 1986). All subsequent references to the private sector can be pursued in this work, unless otherwise noted.
5. ANUIES, *Anuario Estadístico 1988* (Mexico City: ANUIES, 1989).
6. Ernesto Meneses, *Tendencias Educativas Oficiales en México: 1821–1911* (Mexico City: Porrua, 1983), 50–52, 102; Isidro Castillo, *México: Sus Revoluciones Sociales y la Educación* (Morelia: Gobierno del Estado de Michoacán, 1976), 2: 160–67.
7. Leopoldo Zea, *El positivismo en México: Nacimiento, Apogeo y Decadencia* (Mexico City: Fondo de Cultura Económica, 1944).
8. Alfonso de Maria y Campos, *Estudio Histórico-Jurídico de la Universidad Nacional* (Mexico City: UNAM, 1975), chap. 2.
9. Jesús Silva Herzog, *Una Historia de la Universidad de México y sus Problemas* (Mexico City: Siglo Veintiuno, 1974).
10. Carlos Ornelas, "La Educación Técnica y la Ideología de la Revolución Mexicana," in *La Ideología Educativa de la Revolucion Mexicana*, ed. Graciela Lechuga (Mexico City: Universidad Autónoma Metropolitana–Xochimilco, 1984), 33–63.
11. Francisco Javier Azcúnaga, "Cultural Dependency of Curricula: A Case Study in Mexican Higher Education" (Ph.D. diss., University of California at Berkeley, 1985).
12. Roderic A. Camp, *The Making of a Government: Political Leaders in Modern Mexico* (Tucson: University of Arizona, 1984).
13. See Gilberto Guevara, *La Democracia en la Calle: Crónica del Movimiento Estudiantil Mexicano* (Mexico City: Instituto de Investigaciones Sociales de la UNAM and Siglo Veintiuno, 1988); and Eliezer Morales, *El SPAUNAM ante los Problemas de la Universidad* (Mexico City: Sindicato del Personal Académico de la UNAM, 1976).
14. Daniel C. Levy, *University and Government in Mexico: Autonomy in an Authoritarian System* (New York: Praeger, 1980).
15. Carlos Ornelas, "El Estado y las Fuerzas Democráticas: La Lucha por la Reforma Universitaria," *Foro Universitario* 43 (June 1984): 23–34.
16. Daniel C. Levy, "Student Politics in Mexico," in *Student Political Activism: An International Reference Handbook*, ed. Philip G. Altbach (Westport, Ct.: Greenwood, 1989), pp. 383–394.
17. Carlos Ornelas, "La Profesión Académica y la Autoridad," *Cuadernos de Legislación Universitaria* 3, no. 6 (May–August 1988): 103–16.

Nicaragua

Robert F. Arnove

◆

After briefly reviewing the historical development of higher education in Nicaragua, this chapter focuses on the social and educational changes that have occurred since the 1979 Sandinista revolution. The achievements as well as the problems that beset higher education are examined in the light of a revolutionary society that is at war.

Pre-1979 Educational Development

Higher education in Nicaragua can be traced back to the founding of the Seminario Conciliar de San Ramón, in the city of León, in December 1670. The seminary was granted university status as the University of León by decree of the Court of Cádiz in January 1812.[1] It was to be the last university created by Spain in the Americas during the colonial period. As former minister of education (1979–84) Carlos Tünnermann Bernheim noted, "After Guatemala, it was in the Province of Nicaragua where the most important experiments in higher education occurred during the colonial period."[2] Although the university was to play an important role in the formation of many leading educators of Central America, it also suffered a number of setbacks and closings throughout the nineteenth century: its fortunes waxed and waned in accordance with the state of the economy and the political system.

From as early as 1822, students and faculty have played a role in championing progressive social and political causes and vigorously resisting attempts at foreign interference in the internal affairs of the country.[3] During the period of rule by the Somoza family (from the mid-1930s to 1979), student and faculty political militancy led to repressive action by governmental authorities—but also to university reform. In March 1947 the University of León achieved the status of National University and was designated as such. That same year a branch campus of the National University was established in Managua. In 1958 the National University was granted partial autonomy; and in 1966, in accordance with article 105 of the Constitution of the Republic, it officially became the Universidad Nacional Autónoma de Nicaragua (UNAN, National Autonomy University of Nicaragua).[4]

Until 1960 UNAN was the only university in Nicaragua. The National School of Agriculture and Animal Husbandry (ENAG) and the National School of Nursing (ENE) comprised the other institutions of higher education.

In 1960 the Universidad Centroamericana (UCA, Central American University) was founded in Managua. UCA was, and is, administered by the Society of Jesus and governed by a board of directors, the majority of whom were, and continue to be, members of the Jesuit order. Originally viewed as a nonpoliticized alternative to the National University, and as a university turning out the high-level human resources that would contribute to the economic development of the country, UCA, by the mid-1970s, also had become a seedbed of Liberation Theology and opposition to the Somoza regime.[5]

The 1960s and early 1970s were a period of rapid economic growth fueled by

Nicaragua's participation in the newly formed Central American Common Market and substantial foreign aid, mostly from the United States. This period also witnessed the rapid expansion of higher education enrollments and the founding of third-level institutions, both of a religious and a secular nature. At the outset of the 1960s approximately 1,500 students were enrolled in postsecondary institutions. By 1978 enrollment had reached 23,791 in the UNAN (León and Managua campuses), UCA, and ENE. Other higher education institutions included the Polytechnical University (UPOLI), established and administered by the Baptist church; the Private University of Higher Studies (UPACES); the School of Commercial Studies (CCC); the School of Public Accountants of Managua (ECPN); the National Center of Education and Sciences (CENEC); the Nicaraguan Technological Institute of Higher Studies (ITESNIC); and the Central American Institute of Business Administration (INCAE), which served as a regional school for Central America.

Despite this impressive expansion, the higher education system manifested serious problems. It was poorly planned and tenuously related to national development. Major problems included duplication of efforts, a proliferation of programs in fields like business administration, which were frequently profit-making enterprises, and a surfeit of students in economics, social sciences, humanities, and law—in 1978–79 these four fields claimed 60 percent of enrollments. At the same time, there were insufficient enrollments and institutional offerings in key areas such as agricultural sciences, medical sciences, technology, and education. Moreover, with the downturn in the Nicaraguan economy that occurred in the late 1970s, per capita allocations to higher education fell steadily. Finally, a substantial portion of the higher education physical plant was either destroyed or damaged by a 1972 earthquake and subsequently by the struggle to topple the Somoza regime during the period 1978–79. By 1979 higher education enrollments had declined to under 21,000.

Post-1979 Educational Development

Since the triumph (*triunfo*) of the Frente Sandinista de Liberación Nacional (FSLN, Sandinista National Liberation Front), in July 1979, higher education has undergone dramatic changes. In the words of Vladimir Cordero (director of higher education planning): "The university, higher education, is obligated to give . . . to the revolution . . . the professionals the country demands, and now more than ever form them with an eye to transforming the country, even in the limiting conditions of poverty."[6]

While facing serious constraints, political and educational policymakers have initiated significant steps to democratize, improve, and transform the higher education system in line with the new political agenda of the revolution. The general education goals of the revolution involve shaping a "new person," a more critically conscious and participatory citizen who is motivated by collective ends; and imparting the skills and necessary knowledge to overcome decades of underdevelopment and set the nation on the path of self-sustaining growth. As the above quote by Cordero underscores, higher education has a critical role to play in turning out the high-level human resources that will contribute to economic growth and more socially conscious leaders in various fields of endeavor.

The following sections will discuss achievements of the Nicaraguan higher education system over the past ten years in relation to challenges, constraints, and contradictions—to problems created by the reform process itself.

Democratization

The Sandinista government equates the expansion of education and provision of opportunities for previously excluded groups to attend higher education, free of cost, with the democratization of the system. By 1984 higher education enrollment had expanded to over 39,000 in four universities, one extension campus (in education, in Estelí), and twelve technical training centers. Two national research centers and six hospitals were serving as training institutions for doctors, dentists, and nurses. The two campuses of UNAN (in León and Managua) each had become a separate, autonomous, degree-granting university. UCA continued as a private institution with substantial private subsidization. A new National Engineering Institute (UNI, Universidad Nacional de Ingeniería) was opened in 1983. Among the institutions closed by the new government were CCC, ECPN, ENE, CENEC, and UPACES. Reasons for terminating the centers included poor quality, duplication of scarce resources, and irrelevance to national development plans.

Along with the expansion of student enrollments and facilities there was a substantial increase in faculty. At the time of the revolution, there were 450 faculty members; five years later there were 1,750 faculty members.

Government financing of higher education increased dramatically so that by the mid-1980s it accounted for approximately 95 percent of all expenditures at this level of the school system. With less than 4 percent of total school enrollment, higher education has received almost one-fifth of all state allocations to education. In this sense, students who attend higher education institutions are indeed privileged.

Higher education students universally represent a privileged minority, both with regard to benefits and opportunities. But it is also the case in post-1979 Nicaragua that steps have been taken to broaden the social class composition of the student body. Access has been considerably democratized by charging no tuition, other than a minimal matriculation fee to cover the costs of a student identification card and a contribution to student government; by instituting a quota system to guarantee enrollments from all regions of the country, especially those most underrepresented; and by establishing a Preparatory Faculty (FP, Facultad Preparatoria) to provide an accelerated high school program for over 1,600 students who otherwise would not be able to attend a university.

Despite these democratizing efforts, a plurality of students today are still from middle-class and upper-class backgrounds. This is especially the case in fields like medicine and architecture. Precise data are not available on the social class origins of entering students. But given the past advantages of middle-class students with regard to the quality of their primary and secondary schooling, and the greater likelihood of their passing entrance examinations (required in mathematics, Spanish, and social studies), in addition to their ability to forego work in order to study, it will be some time before working-class students constitute a majority.

The government has made a major effort to provide fellowships to low-income students. In 1984 the number of fellowships for study within and outside the country was 5,600. By 1988 7,200 fellowships were available for study within Nicaragua, with another 3,000 available for overseas study (mainly in socialist countries). The demand for financial assistance, however, exceeds available resources; and the amount of the stipends is inadequate to defray major expenses of studying—especially in the face of an inflation rate running in the thousands since 1988.

With regard to female participation rates, there have been remarkable changes. Five years after the revolution women comprised 44 percent of enrollments, as compared with 35 percent in 1977. In 1984, because of the intensifying war situation in the country and the draft, females were, for the first time, a majority of higher education students. In 1988 they represented 80 percent of students in UCA and 55 percent in UNAN. Although they are mostly concentrated in the fields of education, medicine, and humanities, they also represent a significant proportion of students in agricultural fields and are increasing their numbers in various engineering specializations.

Because many students work in order to sustain themselves, night classes provide one way to make higher education more accessible to the general population. Night students, since 1979, have represented over 40 percent of enrollments. In certain fields, such as education, where many in-service teachers study at night and on Saturdays to obtain certification, only the UNAN/Managua has day students, who represent about one-fourth of teacher education enrollments. Night students study six years for their degrees as against the five-year course established for day students; they study four nights a week (twelve to sixteen hours total) with one day set aside for consultation with faculty.

The expansion of education has also brought problems. Perhaps the most serious is that of high drop-out rates. Between one-fourth and one-fifth of students dropped out during the first semester of 1988. Fifty percent or less of any student cohort fails to graduate. Reasons for high attrition include the poor preparation of students at lower levels of education and the economic difficulties of many students, resulting from and compounded by the external aggression of counterrevolutionaries and the economic boycott of the country by the United States. Many students have volunteered for military service, been drafted, or have been mobilized as members of reserve battalions. Educational authorities also candidly admit that the shortage of educational materials, unstimulating curricula, and uninspiring pedagogy further contribute to attrition.

Improvements

Higher education policymakers have attempted to confront, as best as possible under the circumstances, the backlog of problems they inherited from the previous educational system, as well as recent challenges. It should be noted that the Sandinista government equates improvements with the enhancement of the capacity of the education system to contribute to economic development. Toward this end, major reforms involve the creation of new specializations as well as the upgrading and realignment of curricular offerings with national development plans, and the hiring and systematic upgrading of full-time faculty.

The National Higher Education Council (CNES, Conejo Nacional de Educacion Superior) was established in 1980 to coordinate higher educational policy with national development priorities. Between 1980 and 1988 the number of higher education career offerings increased from eighty-three to 116. These offerings now include sixteen medical specializations and four master's degree programs (including one in environmental sciences). Prior to 1979, there were only 120 students enrolled in medicine and fifty in agronomy and agricultural engineering; in 1988 these fields enrolled 550 and 660 students, respectively. The fields of agricultural sciences, medical sciences, education sciences, and technology comprised less than half (42 percent) of enrollments in 1980 but represented 70 percent of enrollments five years later. Since 1979 an average of 2,200 high-level professionals have graduated each year.

Among the significant curricular changes introduced by CNES was the formulation of study plans for each field of specialization. The plans set forth in detail the sequence of courses students are able to take, the objectives and content of each course, and the amount of time to be allocated to lecture, recitation, laboratory, and practical experiences. These study plans correspond to occupational profiles prepared by national commissions of leading experts in the field of study. The profiles specify the types of knowledge and skills necessary for competence in particular careers. Faculty are expected to follow the plans closely with regard to content, activities, and allocation of time for defined topics.

Besides the close linkage to economic decision making, the plans are deemed necessary to compensate for deficiencies in the professoriate. It is claimed that a young and inexperienced faculty will benefit from a well-designed curriculum planned by specialists. Higher education planners maintain that given pre-1979 abuses by faculty, the still considerable number of part-time faculty, and the constant disruptions in academic life generated by the revolutionary environment, certain curriculum requirements must be mandated. Also, the study plans indicate areas where outside expertise must be sought and national competence developed if the higher education system is to prepare qualified professionals.

Students also do not have the freedom to design their own programs. The pre-1979 credit system, according to CNES officials, allowed students to proceed through a curriculum at their own pace, with many falling behind or taking far too long to complete their studies. Under the present system, once students come on track, their schedule of courses is determined for the duration of their studies. Moreover, if students fail two courses in any year they must repeat that year. This may be done two times before they are required to leave the university.

In line with academic reorganization, standards and demands also have risen. The current semester system of sixteen weeks (compared with fourteen previously) has increased the number of classroom contact hours per week for day students from a range of twenty-one to twenty-five to a range of twenty-five to thirty-two.

The overall demands per student for classroom hourly attendance and time set aside for final examinations and practical experiences has increased the student load by one-fourth to one-third.

Despite efforts to guarantee the quality of instruction and to ensure through a highly structured curriculum that basic areas of knowledge are covered, the results of top-down planning are mixed. Besides the difficulty of rigorously following a national curriculum, staff in the higher education planning office admit that curricular expectations may be set unrealistically high. Outside consultants have indicated to the Ministry of Education that in certain fields, such as mathematics and physics, the level of expectations would correspond to that of graduate schools in North America.

Many faculty view the national curriculum plans as severely limiting their professional judgment. Even students who recognize some of the positive outcomes of the study plans express concerns over teaching that is reduced to simplistic and mechanistic delivery of prescribed materials. At the highest level of the Ministry of Education and other governmental entities involved with education, there is outspoken criticism of the plans as being antithetical to the nature and mission of a university. It is widely agreed among higher education planners that there is a great need for universities to contribute to the creation of knowledge, and to the expansion of intellectual horizons as well as to the raising of critical consciousness. It is questionable that policies aimed at standardizing instruction in accordance with a technocratic and bureaucratic model of education will accomplish these goals.

Fortunately, these bureaucratizing forces do not have a stranglehold on creativity. There are many encouraging signs of teacher inventiveness in redesigning and adapting curricula to fit changing times. Furthermore, greater numbers of faculty are engaging in research. Various departments and higher education institutions are on the cutting edge of knowledge generation and application in Nicaragua in such fields as fisheries and aquaculture, forest ecology, nutritional sciences, and biochemistry.[7]

Realistically, however, it must be recognized that Nicaragua suffers from serious resource constraints. Even with expanded investments in higher education, capital expenditures constitute only 20 percent of a limited budget. Working conditions do not afford what is considered bare essentials in certain specializations. The conditions in Nicaragua are not unlike those in other underdeveloped countries: electricity frequently shuts down, telephone lines may not be working for months, heavy rains may cause mudslides and block entrances to campuses, photocopying machines—even typewriters—are luxuries. Essential books, scholarly journals, and laboratory equipment are not available because of lack of foreign exchange.

In the other key areas of improvement—the recruitment and retention of full-time, qualified faculty and in-service upgrading of instructional staff—there have been noticeable reforms compared with the pre-1979 period. Achievements here too, however, have been counterbalanced by setbacks. In the initial year of the revolution (1979–80), over two hundred faculty, including some of the most experienced and talented academics, left the university to accept appointments in key government posts. These and other departures have created a situation in which over three-fourths of higher education faculty now working have been employed only since 1979. Five years after the revolution, the average age of faculty was twenty-eight, and today remains under thirty. Be-

yond the youth and inexperience of the faculty, there were only a handful of Nicaraguans with doctorates teaching in higher education. In many scientific fields there were no faculty with advanced graduate training.

Improvements have been made in increasing the number of full-time faculty who can devote their energies and talents solely to teaching, research, and community service. In 1980/81, 44 percent of a total 1,474 faculty members worked full time. By 1984 70 percent of more than 1,750 faculty were working on a full-time basis, but that percentage had fallen to 62 percent by 1988.

Although efforts have been initiated to establish a salary schedule and to provide adequate compensation, education cannot compete with the private sector—or even public-sector employment outside the field of education. A dean with a doctorate, in 1988, could earn 16,900 cordobas, a professor 6,000; but employment in a management position in a publicly owned enterprise would pay two to three times more. A professor of medicine could earn 11,000 cordobas as a teacher, but 20,000 as an official of the Ministry of Health (MINSA). This economic situation has contributed to the loss of talented faculty.

Against the exodus, Nicaraguan higher educational officials, borrowing from the Cuban case, turned to its students to meet instructional needs. Alumnos Ayudantes (Student Assistants) provide a basic source of recruits to supplement and replenish the teaching force. Chosen at the end of the first year of studies, these students serve as teacher aides the next two years and as instructors with significant classroom and laboratory responsibilities the last two years of their academic careers. They comprise between one-third and one-fourth of instructors in the universities (438 out of 1,512 faculty in 1988). Frequently they are sent abroad for graduate study and return as full-fledged faculty members. Many of them are highly regarded as teachers, and some have gone on to become deans and vice-rectors.

Visiting international faculty help supplement the Nicaraguan faculty. In 1986 there were 236 "internationalists" from thirty-six countries, comprising over 15 percent of higher education faculty. Their presence further enabled Nicaraguan faculty to study abroad. For example, the UCA, which has a significant number of foreign faculty, had forty-five of its professors studying in thirteen countries in 1988.

Ongoing in-service activities are also an integral part of national, university, and departmental plans. In the universities, faculty are expected to invest four to eight hours a week in the improvement of their teaching and research activities. In addition to upgrading scientific knowledge, attention is given to diversifying teaching methodologies and enhancing the ideological commitment of faculty to the principles of the Sandinista revolution. Emphasis is placed on moving faculty in the direction of a more "formative," inquiry-oriented pedagogy; other priorities involve multidisciplinary and team approaches to basic and applied research. At the same time, all faculty have to take courses in the History of the (Sandinista) Revolution, and Philosophy (i.e., Scientific Materialism), and a foreign language. Despite the emphasis on political commitment, it would be a mistake to believe that political fervor without technical competence is condoned by university authorities.

Establishing guidelines for teaching loads comprise another effort aimed at improving the quality of faculty and making careers in higher education more attractive. The teaching load for full-time faculty has been set at a maximum of two separate courses per semester with approximately fifteen contact hours per week. In addition, faculty are to be available ten hours a week for student consultation.

Faculty are expected to enter into a close mentoring role with students. This notion of faculty and students working together to analyze societal problems and contribute to their resolution accords with attempts to transform higher education.

Transformations in Higher Education

Transformations in the education system of Nicaragua are viewed as contributions to a "new model of capital accumulation," that is, a mixed economy with both a public sector (in charge of planning the key areas of finance, foreign trade, and industrial development) and a substantial cooperatively owned and managed sector. Discussion of transformations frequently hinges on changing the social relations of learning to accord with a different set of social relations of production that are more cooperative and democratic in nature.

Since 1979 the degree of verticality or hierarchy in teacher-student interactions has changed. The shift has been in the direction of closer faculty-student relations. Such a situation is possible because, as noted above, a greater percentage of faculty teach full time and an important component of academic work loads consists of supervising work-study and practical experiences. Also greater emphasis is placed on the application of scientific theory and course knowledge to concrete social situations. Science fairs involving over six hundred students and as many as 116 faculty are a good example of joint research undertakings. Past entries in the national fairs have concerned raising productivity of various economic enterprises, improving social services, and resolving a variety of everyday problems such as improving sanitary conditions in the dairy industry, or using solar energy to drive machines or to dehydrate foods.

Curricular reforms, similarly, aim at overcoming the distance between theory and practice, intellectual and manual work. To this end, five weeks per semester are devoted to field work and practical experience. During the first two years of higher education students engage in orientation and "familiarization" visits to work sites; during the third and fourth years they specialize in a particular field of work as apprentices or aides; in the final and fifth year of study students write their theses. Examples of socially valuable and professionally relevant training include social science students conducting housing surveys and recording nutritional deficiencies,[8] law students helping establish and run legal aid clinics for low-income people, and engineering students working in sugar mills.

The most systematic inclusion of community-related services as part of professional formation is found in the medical school. Although there are a limited number of professionals to supervise the students, and the student-faculty ratio is much higher than in a North American medical school, the Nicaraguan students are entrusted with considerably more responsibility than their North American counterparts. The Nicaraguan students' mark-ups, for example, become part of the patients' medical records, which is not the case in countries like the United States.

Not all practical experience is as relevant and professionally worthwhile as that in medicine. Agreements remain to be worked out between relevant ministries and a number of academic programs to provide meaningful work opportunities. In priority areas like agronomy or agricultural engineering, where there should be an abundance of opportunities for hands-on experience, work-study activities are frequently criticized as having little practical value.

Opportunities, however, abound for students as well as faculty to learn firsthand the national reality by participating in various national mobilizations related to defense and production activities. The mobilizations are integrally linked to the formal curriculum. Special make-up sessions and examinations have been provided to accommodate participating students,

who, in the case of UNAN/Managua, have numbered over five thousand for different harvests. Significantly, the national university calendar was changed in 1982 to coincide with the harvest period of major export crops such as coffee. Two months (mid-January to mid-March) were added to the traditional Christmas break to extend the period available for participation in production activities.

These activities, beyond whatever ideological commitment and party allegiances may be shared in common, contribute to closer student-faculty relations. However, students who do not share the same loyalty to the Sandinista revolution also may be estranged by what they consider to be favoritism shown to progovernment followers.

Political Culture on Campus

Since 1979 the constant mobilizations of youth around defense and production, as well as the intense politicization of many youths, have left their mark on higher education, and to a certain extent have transformed the university milieu. In many respects, there is a greater sense of purpose, a more profound seriousness, and, during the first five years of the revolution, even joy, in being a university student—which was not the case in the pre-1979 period. During the final years of the Somoza regime it was considered a crime to be a youth, many students were arbitrarily and brutally victimized by the National Guard, and many youths turned to drugs as a means of escape.[9]

The seriousness comes from being entrusted with significant responsibilities in the construction of a new social order. Current student leaders claim that, unlike previous generations of student militants whose task was to oppose and destroy, their role is to construct and to promote. This assessment has merit. Moreover, student representatives are accorded key roles in departmental and universitywide decision making; and at the national level, through the National Union of Nicaraguan Students (UNEN) and the "19th of July" Sandinista Youth organization (JS-19J), they have input into the highest consultative and policy councils shaping higher education.

By 1988 the high spirits and high jinx (such as heaving students into the air or forming human pyramids) that accompanied many mobilizations and festivities on campus had given way to a more somber atmosphere, almost one of lassitude. This atmosphere reflected the consequences of five years and more of "low-intensity" warfare waged against the government and people of Nicaragua by counterrevolutionaries backed by the United States government.

Consequences of War

MED officials estimate that approximately one hundred university faculty and students have been killed or seriously wounded in combat with the counterrevolutionaries. Such a situation creates conflicting responses. Sadness and resignation is matched by resolve to fight on. While intensifying commitment to the revolution on the part of what is still a substantial number of students and faculty, the protracted struggle has resulted in many fleeing the country. These are people so involved in the struggle for mere existence that they are drained of the enthusiasm and energy they once had to contribute to social transformations.

Since 1979 the national mobilizing theme of the Sandinista government has changed from that of "National Reconstruction" to that of "National Survival." Survival is not only a question of military defense but of rescuing an economy that has declined steadily since the initial years of the revolution.[10] At the beginning of 1988 inflation was running in the thou-

sands; by the end of 1988 in the tens of thousands. The consequences of this situation were cutbacks in all social services. In the first half of 1988, all governmental ministries underwent a *compactación* (a "compacting" or streamlining of services). The Ministry of Culture and the National Higher Education Council were "compacted" into the Ministry of Education, with the result that dozens of functionaries lost their jobs. CNES, which had functioned for some eight years as almost a separate ministry, was restructured and renamed the General Office of Higher Education, within MED. With this reorganization might come a shift of greater authority to university administrators and the national council of rectors. Thus, opportunities for the exercise of greater autonomy, as well as responsibility, on the part of university officials have been opened by the economic crisis.

The upheavals and setbacks have contributed to a decline in student enrollments in higher education. By 1988 enrollments were down to 25,000 students. Erosion of gains in the number of full-time faculty and the difficulty of maintaining talented instructors in academia also have been noted.

At the beginning of 1989 a second *compactación* took place. Funds for higher education were cut even further with a concomitant reduction of faculty and high-level university administrators. Trial balloons also were floated concerning the prospect of limiting enrollments only to priority fields directly related to economic production and the provision of basic social services.

Conclusions

The expansion, improvement, and transformation of higher education in Nicaragua since 1979 has taken place within the context of a revolutionary society under siege. While there have been marked changes in the direction of a national system of higher education more closely tied to national development plans and to the creation of a new political culture—that is, to the construction of a more just social order—the national as well as international contexts have placed severe limitations on what could be accomplished over the period 1979 to 1989. Problems, tensions, and contradictions, furthermore, have been generated by the very processes of social transformation—of attempting to do so much in so short a period. While constraining, the historical legacy and the international context are not determinative. What is more certain is that the form Nicaraguan higher education takes will be decided by Nicaraguans themselves in accordance with the realities of their situation.

Notes

1. Juan B. Arríen, "Nicaragua, Republic of," in *The International Encyclopedia of Higher Education*, ed. Asa S. Knowles (San Francisco: Jossey-Bass, 1977), 7:3016.
2. Carlos Tünnermann Bernheim, "Bases para una Reforma Universitaria," in his collection of essays *Estudios Sobre Teoría de la Educación* (San José, Costa Rica: Editorial Universitaria Centroamericana, 1983), 483.
3. Ibid.
4. Arríen, "Nicaragua," 3016.
5. For further discussion of the different stages of institutional development of the Central American University, see Daniel Levy, *Higher Education and the State in Latin America: Private Challenges to Public Dominance* (Chicago: University of Chicago Press, 1986), 56–58.
6. Vladimir Cordero, "Educación Superior y Política en Nicaragua" (Ministry of Education: CNES, 1987), 7.
7. See, for example, Rolland G. Paulston and Fay Henderson Franklin, "U.S. Professors in Nicaraguan Universities: The LASPAU/AID Managua Project" (November 1983, Mimeographed).
8. Ibid., 28.
9. According to many observers of the university scene in the pre-1979 period, the National Guard was the main distributor of drugs on university campuses. Drugs were a source of income for corrupt guardsmen and one means of diverting students from politics.
10. For a discussion of economic growth in Nicaragua, prior to intensification of the external aggression against the country, see Michael E. Conroy, "Differing Perspectives on the Economic Strategies of Post-Revolutionary Nicaragua," *Third World Quarterly* 6 (October 1984): 993–1032.

Venezuela

Orlando Albornoz

♦

In Venezuela, as elsewhere, the educational system is very much tied to the political organization of society and to the power structure. Whatever the characteristics of an educational system, it necessarily reflects the balance of political power of the different interest groups in its society. The main tendencies affecting the educational system in Venezuela are the consequences of structural tendencies clearly visible in the Venezuelan social organization.

On February 2, 1988, a new government took over in Venezuela. This means that the Social Democrat party will stay in power for another five years. It also means political continuity. And for education it signals more of the same, since no dramatic changes are expected to take place in the next five years. The main tendencies of the educational system will prevail in all levels of the system, but more so in higher education.

Privatization

One of the main tendencies of higher education in Latin America as a whole is the privatization process. In the Venezuelan case, one of the main purposes of the new government is to advance a social process through which the state will give up a number of its responsibilities to the private sector. Private universities are a recent institutional innovation in Venezuela. Table 1 shows how important the private sector has become in Venezuelan higher education.

Between the academic years 1971/72 and 1986/87 the percentage of university graduates coming from the private sector rose from 7.35 to 19.92 percent. The percentage of university students enrolled in private institutions increased from 8.47 percent in 1971/72 to 15 percent in 1986/87. The faculty in the private sector has increased from 7.34 percent in 1971/72 to 13.48 percent in 1986/87.

Almost all new institutions of higher learning planned for the near future will be private. For instance, in the first session of the University National Council after the election of the new government, two new private universities were created, as well as two new institutions belonging to nonuniversity higher education.

Politicization

The second main characteristic of the Venezuelan higher educational system is politicization. The institutions of higher learning in Venezuela are linked to the political system. This structure makes the institutions dependent on whatever party holds power. There are only five autonomous universities in the country; these five are considered to be the most powerful and important institutions of higher education. But after the reform of 1970 the government created a nonautonomous sector of the higher educational system, controlled by the Ministry of Education and through the ministry by the political party in power. Even the private sector is highly susceptible to political pressure.

The Role of the "Gremios"

The third characteristic of the Venezuelan higher education system is *gremialization*, the process through which members of the faculty of Venezuelan universities happen to become members of their *gremio*, which has a very important role in defining the duties of the Venezuelan teaching staff in higher education. The Venezuelan teacher or researcher does not exist by himself, but as part of his or her *gremio*. Individual competition as known in American universities, for instance, does not exist in Venezuelan universities. The dictum "publish or perish" is not a part of Venezuelan academic life. People will often go through an entire career at the university without ever publishing or conducting any academic research of any kind. Being a member of the faculty in Venezuelan higher education means being a teacher, since the institutions of higher learning in Venezuela are almost strictly teaching institutions.

Venezuelan higher education has created a large educational bureaucracy, but it has not created a true academic establishment, since the production and dissemination of knowledge is not the main objective of the system. Venezuelan universities are not intellectual institutions devoted to learning but rather professional training bodies. In fact, one might say that for the Venezuelan higher educational community the institutional reference is not university life as such but the lecture hall or the laboratory; not the research library or the book, but the teacher and the oral tradition of the classroom.

The educational system in Venezuela did not even begin to modernize until 1958, when after a long period of rule by *caudillos* and strongmen Venezuela finally developed a very stable political system that is now one of the most democratic political systems in Latin America. Only in the past two decades has the private sector in education become active and consolidated a challenge to the state, which even now still controls almost 90 percent of the higher educational system.

After 1959 a massive educational expansion took place in Venezuela, supported by public investment in this area as well as by public desire to spread educational opportunities to more members of the population. In the years between 1958 and the present educational budgets have approached 20 percent of the total national budget; and from this almost a third of the total education budget was devoted to higher education. This pattern of budget allocation has created a distortion through which higher education, and especially the university, has grown beyond national economic needs. As we can see in Table 1, with a population of about twenty million people, Venezuela has almost one hundred institutions of higher learning. Academic quality among them is necessarily

---

Table 1

Total of Institutions of Higher Education in Venezuela 1984–1985

Universities	26
Public	16
Private	10
University Institutes	39
Public	18
Private	21
University Colleges	13
Public	8
Private	5
Pedagogical Institutes	7
Public	6
Private	1
Polytechnic Institutes	4
Public	4
Private	0
Total	89
Public	52
Private	37

very uneven. The critical expansion of the higher educational system began after 1958; and most Venezuelan institutions of higher learning are so new that they are still searching for an academic identity.

So we can distinguish two very distinct periods in the history of Venezuelan higher education, before 1958 and after 1958, when the last of the military dictatorships was overthrown. Democracy brought with it increasing social expenditures, including expenditures for education. Another critical year was 1982, when, forced by new economic circumstances, Venezuela devalued its currency and entered into the vicious circle of external debt accumulation. The year 1982 marked the beginning of a period of institutional contraction that has meant academic stagnation for the universities, particularly those in the public sector.

Since 1982 research facilities have lacked the resources to import scientific equipment and to subscribe to scientific journals and books. They have not been able to afford to send their scientists abroad for scholarly conferences or advanced training. Devaluation has made life harder for scientists in universities and government-financed research institutes. Many researchers are looking for jobs in private companies. A brain-drain trend is growing, particularly among younger members of the Venezuelan academic community. Teachers with doctoral degrees obtained in American or European universities find that they can earn much more outside of academia, where salaries and fringe benefits are distributed in such a way as to discourage individual competition—a subject I will return to below.

Higher Education in Venezuela

Colonial universities were created under the Spaniards, but university life did not flourish in the long period between 1830, when independence was secured, and 1945, which marked the beginning of the country's first democratic period. During the ten years following 1948 Venezuela was again under a very tight dictatorship and academic life was restricted because of political repression. It was at this time that the country's first private universities were opened. It was only after 1958 that democratic governments became stable and the enormous educational expansion mentioned above began. In 1982 a period of contraction began, which is still going on. The 1980s have been a period of institutional adjustment that has proved painful and difficult, since it is, of course, easier to expand than to contract.

The educational system allows both the public and private sectors to organize parallel educational subsystems. Because Venezuela is a highly centralized society in terms of both population and resources, the capital area of Caracas concentrates most of the academic resources, including not only institutions, but the whole cultural context that grows along with academic life, such as publishers, cultural events, and intellectual life per se. Of the ninety-two institutions of higher education in Venezuela, forty-five are in Caracas, while forty-seven are spread elsewhere throughout the country. Some of them have very poor physical and academic facilities.

The state finances all public institutions and partially finances private institutions. There are no reliable data on finance to private institutions, but one way or the other all private institutions receive some financial assistance from the state. Public institutions are completely financed by the state; they charge no fee at all and offer a number of free or low-cost services to both students and members of the faculty.

Until 1970 the university system in Venezuela consisted of the traditional autonomous universities created in the nineteenth century plus two private universities opened before 1958. But in 1970 the government decided on a policy of educational diversification. New types of institutions, all under the direct control of the government, were created: colleges, teacher training institutions, technological institutions, and some others under the ambiguous category of *institutos universitarios* (three-year colleges devoted entirely to training in technical areas). The monopoly of the universities over higher learning that had lasted so long came to an end. Today only one out of four higher education institutions is a university.

Even today, however, universities are the only type of institution that provide graduate studies and research. All other tertiary institutions are training schools devoted to preparing people for the job market. These nonuniversity institutions offer a formal representation of the segmentation format of the educational system beyond the secondary level, both in regional and occupational terms. That is to say that almost every middle-sized town in the country would like to have its own higher education institution or at least a *núcleo* (branch) of a higher educational institution located elsewhere.

In terms of curriculum design, the only research-oriented tertiary institutions are the autonomous universities. Unlike other Latin American universities, Venezuelan institutions do not have a multicampus scheme, with the exception of the Universidad de Oriente, created under the influence of the American university model in 1958. The Open University is also multicampus. The main characteristic of Venezuelan universities, both public and private, is their nonresidential nature.

The private university sector is the consequence of many social pressures. The first two private universities were created during the last military dictatorship. The Catholic church took advantage of the close relationship between the church and the army at the time to obtain authorization from the government to open the Catholic University. Secular interests, too,

also managed to open a private university as an alternative to the governmentally controlled public institutions. Both new universities opened in October 1953. A third private university opened in 1965. Many others have been created since 1970.

In the public sector there are two types of universities. The traditional autonomous universities are run by the academic community itself, consisting of members of the faculty, students, and employees. They are fully subsidized by the state, charging no fee to their students. Governmental universities are run directly by the government through the Ministry of Education; the academic community has little if any kind of participation in making the policies of the institution. Governmental universities are tuition-free.

The private sector in Venezuela has three types of universities. First, there are what we could call the elite institutions that care for the educational needs of the children of the upper classes. These institutions are oriented toward modern careers and offer the homogeneous social environment that is a requirement of any upper-class social group. In the case of Venezuelan society, this means that no students from the social minorities can enroll at these universities. No students from African or Indian stock would be found in any of these universities.

We might call the second type of university in the private sector the popular university. This is a large institution, where the social environment is totally different from that at the elite schools. Popular universities enroll mostly evening students from the working-class sector of society. They desire careers in the traditional professions and their level of quality and academic demands are not very strong.

For the academic year 1984/85 the available information shows that 3,615 students were enrolled in the elite Universidad Metropolitana, while 22,845 students were enrolled in popular universities. The two student groups belong to two different social worlds. Those at the elite institution would qualify as upper class: they do not have to work to make a living, they own cars, and they move around in a very homogeneous society, in the "white" Venezuelan world. At the second type of private university we find working class students, working class both in terms of their social origins and because they usually work full time while attending the university.

A third type of institution in the private sector is what could be called the informal type of universities. These are institutions that operate outside the legal procedures set up by the *Ley de Universidades*. At the *Universidad Popular Oropeza Castillo*, for example, they train community leaders and social activists. It charges a fee, publishes ads in the papers, and has a building where it conducts its activities. Another example is the *Universidad de la Tercera Edad*, which serves those over fifty. It charges a fee, publishes ads in the papers, and owns a building. Neither of these universities has been officially approved. Neither can be found in any official statistics. But both do exist and both do attract students. Since it cannot legally offer professional degrees, the *Universidad de la Tercera Edad* offers its degrees through an accredited Panamanian university. Other "informal" universities exist outside the institutional structures established by the government and succeed, to varying degrees, in offering alternate forms of education to a wide variety of constituencies.

The Faculty

Members of the faculty have more power than any other group within or outside the public Venezuelan university. In fact, they run these universities. The faculty organizations tell the university administrators how many hours they will work every week, and under what conditions, how many days they will have for holidays, what benefit plans and other fringe benefits they deserve, when and how faculty members will retire, and when and how they will accept any kind of administrative control or technical supervision. The faculty establish their own salary scale, and they tell the government when they want raises and how much they should be. If the government does not comply, the faculty simply closes down the public universities.

To understand the present power of the faculty, we must go back to 1958, immediately after the overthrow of the military dictatorship. Autonomy was restored to the public universities. One of the first independent steps they took was to make teaching an independent profession, not just a part-time job, and to promote the whole notion that research was an important part of the activities of a member of the faculty.

Two main points were established in 1958. First, university professors at public autonomous universities were to be taken into institutional consideration as a group, as a *gremio*. Rights and privileges were to be assigned to all of them; no individual negotiation was possible, nor would individual competition be tolerated. Second, the members of the faculty obtained full job security, meaning that no member of the faculty was ever at risk of being fired, without due legal process, to be taken only by the university. In this way, professors tried to protect themselves from governmental intervention and control. By doing so, in terms of the professionalization of the academic role, they created the category of *dedicación exclusiva*, meaning that the university was to provide members of the faculty adequate salary and social security so as to allow them to devote themselves exclusively to the university.

Between 1958 and 1982 members of the faculty felt very secure at Venezuelan public universities. So many benefits were granted to them and so minimal were their working obligations that to become a member of the faculty was actually to obtain one of the best jobs any Venezuelan could get. It offered lifetime employment, retirement after twenty-five years with full salary, including any subsequent raises or fringe benefits granted to the active members of the faculty. Faculty received medical insurance, loans to buy cars or homes, a month's payment for holidays, and a month's bonus at the end of the year. Bonuses were also given for children and for home expenses. And if a member of the faculty was appointed to a given position in the public administration, he would be kept on the university payroll without salary but still accumulating work years toward retirement.

This obviously expensive scheme was possible while the country enjoyed almost unlimited public funds. But the system entered a crisis with the 1982 economic situation. At that time the faculty *gremios* obtained a guarantee from the government that salaries were to be increased every two years according to the equivalent increase in the cost of living. In 1988, when the government could not pay an increase of 46 percent, the faculties went on strike. The government offered a 5 percent increase in salaries. Finally the strike was settled at an agreed 15 percent increase.

The teaching load of university professors is a maximum twelve hours a week; the majority of faculty members do much less. Faculty members are not obliged to do research or to perform any other duty beside teaching. They are free from any institutional control or supervision because their responsibility is not primarily to the institution but to the *gremio*. People are rewarded not for their intellectual or academic production, but because they belong to that *gremio*, which operates under the principle that duties and rights are not an individual concept but come under the concept of *escalafón*, meaning a closed labor market. Their remuneration has no relationship whatsoever to the market value of the activity they perform,

but only to the rules defined by this closed labor market. All members of the faculty at Venezuelan public institutions of higher education in the academic year 1984/85—29,196 of them—were under the control of the *gremio*. While any strike takes place, salaries are paid to all members of the faculty, including those already retired from active academic life.

In the academic year 1984/85 6,336 persons were teaching at private universities. Unlike those working in public institutions, they have no *gremios* and no working guarantee of any sort. They are hired as part-time teachers and have no job security. In fact, they are hired or fired at will and are paid according to their market value. Though no information is available on this subject, apparently the majority of those teaching at private universities are members of the faculty at public universities. No empirical research on university *profesores* (every person teaching at any level in Venezuela is called "profesor") has ever been conducted in Venezuela; that would be difficult to do, because the *gremios* would probably see any such research as a way to control their academic, professional, and even personal activities.

Members of the faculty come into the public universities by means of *concursos*, which are competitive public exams. Actually they are often organized in such a way that access to the faculty is controlled by political pressure groups and thus quite closed in their procedures. Once faculty members are in, they will not be out until retirement, because there is no turnover whatsoever in Venezuelan universities.

People do not change universities during their academic careers. Professors begin at an average age of twenty-five; after twenty-five years of employment faculty members are entitled to retirement. Retirement is quite attractive: retired faculty continue to receive their full salaries and fringe benefits, and retired people pay no taxes to the government. Thus faculty often live better after retirement than before.

The *escalafón* hierarchy allows members of the faculty to rise to the highest rank in fifteen years. They have to present proof of academic work in order to be able to rise to the next level, of which there are five: instructor, *asistente*, *agregado*, *asociado*, and *titular*. Not all members of the faculty achieve the highest level. In fact, most retire either at the third or fourth rank because they do not present the obligatory academic work required of them. Academic control is nonexistent. Members of the public faculty are quite self-sufficient, with no responsibility to anyone but to themselves.

Faculty in Venezuela constitute a closed and powerful academic bureaucracy. To change this closed bureaucracy into an open meritocracy a number of radical institutional changes would be required, but at this moment they seem only a distant possibility.

Members of the faculty are paid according to the principle of no individual competition. They are paid a minimum and a maximum and salary increases are paid to all or to none. If a member of the faculty does some extraordinary work, he receives no special compensation. There is no way to pay a faculty member less for poor work, or to fire a member of the faculty, or even to impose any administrative sanction. The faculty is a closed system in which all can be rewarded but none can be punished.

The whole process through which members of the faculty enter and retire from the universities is suspected of being full of administrative corruption. The present faculty situation may explain the acceptance of a teaching model of the university instead of a research model. Faculty have nothing to gain, and much to lose, if the present system changes.

The Students

Of the 383,537 students in Venezuelan higher education, 285,785 are enrolled at universities, with some 242,960 in public institutions, and 42,285 in the private sector. This 15 percent of the university student population seems to be the maximum size of the private sector able to pay their way into the professions. They might increase their participation in the future up to some 20 percent, but the role of the state will still be crucial in order to explain the distribution of Venezuelan university students.

This university population does not mirror the Venezuelan social structure. On the contrary, it provides an excellent way to look at the discriminatory pattern typical of that society. Discrimination and inequality are the main characteristics of the Venezuelan social structure. Natives and blacks are grossly underrepresented in the university population. Racism and social discrimination are key concepts for understanding the social mechanism of this South American society. Social democracy is still to be achieved in Venezuelan society, where the more income a family has the greater are its chances of sending its children to higher levels of schooling. In a very general but true sense, it could be said that the richest members of Venezuelan society (the top 15 to 20 percent of the population) have all the opportunities to send their children to higher education; the bottom 40 percent have almost no chances at all to do that; and the middle 40 percent have some opportunities open to them but also many obstacles in their way.

The only chance of the poor social classes to get into any type of higher education is through the public sector, though once they have entered the labor market they can pay their way at mass private universities. There has been little or no quantitative or empirical research on Venezuelan students, so their attitudes and characteristics cannot be categorized or analyzed. A high proportion of those students entering public universities (40 percent) do so as evening students. Of those attending private institutions, only about 15 percent are day students. With the exception of the students at elite private universities and elite institutions in the public sector, most Venezuelan university students are either day students with part-time jobs or night students with full-time jobs.

Venezuelan university students are nonresidential. They live with their families whenever possible, in keeping with tradition. Some of them still live with their families long after they have finished their university careers. This is particularly true for girls, who remain part of the family until they get married. When they have to continue their studies away from home, students usually live with relatives or in family *pensiones* where family life is reproduced. The nonresidential nature of the university creates an academic environment with its own characteristics. The whole academic community commutes from home to the university. Contacts among the members of the community follow this type of relationship. Students and their teachers attend their *aulas*, laboratories or workshops, but the academic life occurs mostly away from the university.

Access to the public university is through a national system of enrollment. Private universities each have their own mechanisms of selection. Places at public universities are given according to the results of the national scholastic test and the academic index, completed by every student before finishing secondary school. Social selection is more important than academic capacities. And performance is closely related to the social origin of the student as well as to the type of secondary school they attend: public or private. The great ambition in Venezuelan society is the obtaining of any kind of degree at the postsecondary level. The tradition in Venezuela in these terms is to be a "doctor,"

more than a technician. Most students aspire to traditional careers instead of the new technical possibilities.

A crucial point that must be mentioned, again without any empirical evidence to substantiate the argument, is that unemployment among professionals has grown quite considerably since the crisis of 1982. Before that, almost any student who graduated in the professions found a job, either in the private sector or in the huge and apparently insatiable public administration. But even before the crisis began jobs became difficult to find. The private sector can now be more selective in choosing employees; private-sector employment is beginning to be affected by such factors as study program, quality of the institution, and so forth. But the main factor to finding a place in the labor market continues to be the social connection of the person. Those further up in the social scale stand a better chance than the rest. Unemployment seems to be highest among graduates in the traditional careers, but there are no data on this topic. Nonsystematic information indicates that all graduates from the elite universities will find jobs immediately after their graduation, while those graduating from mass universities in the traditional careers will find a very narrow labor market.

The Venezuelan student is not expected to go on to graduate studies. After his professional degree he will try to find a job. His main goal in life is to raise a family, to be well-off financially, and live a "normal" middle-class or better life. Interestingly enough, he will have no desire to become an intellectual or a member of the local intelligentisia. Nor will he have the desire to participate in political life, beyond the necessary political affiliation common to almost every Venezuelan.

Conclusions

Venezuelan universities are not research-oriented. Graduate studies are still embryonic. The main university in the country still manages to graduate only some ten doctoral students every year. The private sector does almost no research and offers no graduate programs. Graduate-level expansion has been quite slow in Venezuela. The recent economic crisis will slow this process down even more. Venezuelan universities cannot keep themselves abreast of international academic trends. Fewer members of the faculty can now travel abroad, either to do graduate studies or to attend academic meetings. Foreign books are difficult to obtain.

In the future a kind of academic stagnation will characterize Venezuelan higher education. Even so, demands for places in universities are higher than ever and institutions will have problems accomodating all the students who want to get in.

Venezuelan higher education will not change its institutional pattern in the immediate future. The new government does not have any innovative plan to change the structural tendencies of the higher educational level or the rest of the educational system, for that matter. They will be in the future what they are now, teaching institutions devoted to training people for the professions and for the technical needs of the society.

Most institutions in the Venezuelan educational system are new. With the exception of the private sector, no growth is expected in the higher educational system in Venezuela. And, as I have said, a deep process of deterioration and academic stagnation is setting in, which stands in contrast to the expansion that took place between 1958 and 1982.

MIDDLE EAST

The Arab World

Byron G. Massialas

◆

The Arab World, which includes twenty-one sovereign states plus Palestine, extends over an area of 5.4 million square miles at the crossroads of Africa, Asia, and Europe. The region's total population is estimated to be about two hundred million. Over the years, the region experienced several invasions and occupations by such groups as the Romans, Persians, European Crusaders, Ottomans, Italians, French, and British. These occupiers left their imprint on the Arab countries they occupied in such areas as law and public administration, architecture, religion, and education, as well as political process. Table 1 provides a summary view of the population, population growth patterns, and area for each Arab country.

Arab society, as it has evolved through the years, presents elements that, on the one hand, tend to unify it, and on the other hand, fragment it. The unifying elements include the common cultural past, especially as manifested in customs, language, and religion. The fragmenting elements include the multitude of loyalties characterizing present-day society, loyalties that are based on different ethnic, tribal, religious, or kinship relations. Substantive differences among the countries in the region in the operation of their political, economic, and social institutions and processes contribute to Arab fragmentation. In the past quarter of a century, there have also been significant changes in Arab society, primarily as a result of successful oil exploitation in some of the Arab states. As one analyst of the contemporary Arab scene said, "Oil and movement of manpower and money across country lines is one of the Arab World's silent revolutions. Its impact is the birth of a new Arab social order. A major feature of that order is a new stratification system among the Arab states and within each state."[1] The New Arab Social Order includes such individual types as the "mechanized Bedouin," the "Saudi entrepreneur," the "lumpen capitalist," the "Egyptian peasant" (the person who made good after spending time providing his services to an oil-rich country), the "veiled medical student," and the "angry Muslim militant."[2] Oil wealth has significantly transformed the age-old social arrangements in the Arab world. The key questions now are: What type of society will manifest itself in the postoil era? Will education play a role in advancing the cause of a unified Arab society?

The Present State of Arab Higher Education

There were only eight Arab universities in the 1940s, increasing steadily to twenty-three in the 1960s and to seventy-two in 1986. Twelve of these universities are private and the rest are state-controlled.[3] Sixty-five of these universities, for which figures are available, enrolled a total of 1.3 million students during the period 1983–85. The country with the largest number of universities was Egypt, with thirteen and an enrollment of 716,800 students. Countries with only one university include Tunisia, Kuwait, United Arab Emirates, Qatar, Yemen Arab Republic, and Oman. The latter country has only recently created a university, with an initial enrollment of 540 students. Of the total enrollments available for the sixty-five Arab universities, 43,500 or 3.3 percent were in private institutions. These institutions were located in Lebanon (several institutions), in Jordan's West Bank (four institutions), and in Egypt (one institution).[4] If we were to add to the number of universities all the institutions in the Arab world that offer some form of postsecondary education, the total would be between four and five hundred.[5]

Student enrollments at the third-level or postsecondary Arab institutions have grown dramatically during the recent past. Table 2 indicates that enrollments at this level of education in the Arab world grew from 444,000 students in 1970 to 1,972,000

in 1985. This phenomenal growth (more than a fourfold increase) outpaced comparative enrollment increases in the world as a whole, including developed as well as developing countries. As Table 2 indicates, the decade of the 1970s recorded a 12.5 percent increase in third-level enrollments in the Arab world as compared to a 9.4 percent and a 3.5 percent increase for developing and developed countries respectively. During the first five years of the 1980s, percentage growth slowed down (to 6.5 percent) but still outpaced that of the world (3.3 percent).

Gross enrollment ratios for the region, as shown in Table 2, point to the same

Table 1

General Statistics on Arab Countries

Country	Population Mid-1986 in thousands	Area in Sq. Miles	Per Capita in 1987	Life Expectancy	% of Urban Pop.	Children under 1 yr. per 1000 newborn/1985	No of People per Dr. 1985
Algeria	22.4	919,951	$2,828	62	44	81	2,521
Bahrain	0.435	255	7,241	70	82	35	991*
Djibouti	0.373	8,996	2,197*	49	75	200	6,324
Egypt	49.7	386,872	1,324	61	47	93	670
Iraq	16.5	172,000	2,804	63	72	73	2,213
Jordan	3.6	37,297	1,640	65	66	49	1,046
Kuwait	1.8	7,780	14,254	73	95	22	671
Lebanon	2.7	4,015	29*	65*	81*	44.4	260*
Libya	3.9	679,536	6,285	61	67	90	732
Mauritania	1.8	419,229	449	47	38	132	19,737
Morocco	22.5	171,953	775	60	46	90	7,259*
Oman	1.3	82,500	5,341	54	10	109	3,299
Qatar	0.369	4,247	11,980	69	89	36	622
Saudi Arabia	12	873,000	6,284	63	74	61	1,500
Somalia	5.5	246,155	277	47	35	152	27,660
Sudan	22.6	967,491	326	49	21	112	8,182
Syria	10.8	71,498	914	64	51	54	1,686
Tunisia	7.3	63,379	1,297	63	58	78	3,871
UAE	1.4	32,278	13,241	69	76	35	553
YAR	8.2	75,290	548	46	22	154	4,287
YPDR	2.2	111,000	543	50	41	145	6,050
Total or Av.	197.377	5,364,222	1,991	59	48	91	4,011

Density: 36.81 p.s.q.mi.

* Estimated from earlier years.

Source: The Statistical File, *Al Mustaqbal al Arabi,* The Arab Future, Center for Arab Unity Studies, Vol. 119, No. 1, 1989, pp. 193–94; based on World Development Report, 1988 (World Bank, the Unified Arab Economic Report, Arab League; and the UN Statistical Yearbook (In Arabic).)

trend in growth patterns at the third level of education. From a gross enrollment ratio of 4.3 percent in 1970, it reached 9.8 percent in 1985. This enrollment ratio for the Arab states comes close to the world ratio (11.8 percent) and substantially surpasses the ratio for developing countries (6.4 percent). Needless to say, while the general growth rate has been dramatic, the actual figures still lag significantly behind those of developed countries (33.1 percent). Particularly interesting has been a substantial increase in gross enrollment ratios for female students from 2.0 percent in 1970 to 6.9 percent in 1985. The corresponding male enrollment figures for the period were 6.5 percent for 1970 and 19.5 percent for 1985. Female enrollment growth patterns in both developing and developed countries are considerably slower than those for the Arab countries. The general trend toward democratization of education in the Arab world has apparently affected favorably the opportunities of young females to pursue studies in postsecondary education.

In passing, it should be noted that UNESCO enrollment figures for the third level of education include those for postsecondary institutions in addition to those of universities. As pointed out earlier, institutions of this type may number more than four-hundred. In Morocco, for example, while five state universities enrolled the bulk of the students, in the school year 1982/83 about twenty-four institutes also admitted graduates of secondary schools. These institutes included the National School for Public Administration, with an enrollment of 974 students; the Hassan II School of Civil Engineering, with 1,081 students; and the Hassan II Institute of Agronomy and Veterinary Studies, with 1,868 students.[6] Similar establishments are common throughout the Arab world. It is estimated that out of 1,972,000 third-level students in the Arab countries, approximately 662,000, or about one-third of the total, are enrolled in postsecondary, nonuniversity institutions.

Historical Antecedents

The history of Arab higher education dates back to the seventh century and the rise of Islam. In the beginning, mosques formed the centers of study, including advanced studies. Students would congregate around a teacher who would normally provide instruction in three forms: lectures to fairly large groups; instruction in a smaller "circle," where verbal exchanges with students were encouraged; and "discipleship," where one student would serve as an apprentice "to acquire most of his master's learning."[7] Naturally the stress of instruction in the beginning was on the Koran and the Arabic language, but teaching gradually extended to include other subjects. Characteristic of medieval Arab education was the fact that education was not institutionalized; it was marked by a close, rather intimate relationship between the teacher and the taught, with an emphasis on memorizing the notes of lectures and presentations of the teacher.[8]

Beginning in the eleventh century and side by side with this informal type of instruction in the mosques, a new type of institution appeared, known as *al-madrasah*, or college. The best known among these early colleges, and the one that provided a model for others to follow, was Al-Madrasa Al-Nizammiya, founded in Baghdad in 1067. In this type of institution, lectures by well-known professors constituted the heart of instruction. While no regular schedule of activities was followed, the professor-scholar normally "started his course by giving an outline of the material to be studied, followed by a general explanation of the subject and the ways in which the authorities differed about it."[9] In this setting, the student was encouraged by the professor "to learn logic and rhetoric, so as to know how to avoid ambiguity of language and thought."[10] It is interesting to note that, while the professors were considered to be "true scholars," they had a major shortcoming: a "tendency to imitate rather than to create."[11] It appears that over the years this tendency survived, for it characterizes much of contemporary Arab professorial performance.

The medieval curriculum consisted of two parts, with emphasis given to the first part: the "Revealed Sciences and Sciences of the Arabic Religion and Language" and the "Rational Sciences." The first part consisted of the Arabic language, grammar, rhetoric, literature, Koranic readings and exegesis (commentary), prophetic traditions (*al-hadith*), law, and theology. The second part was devoted to mathematics and logic.[12] The primary purpose of the curriculum was to enable the students "to accept the truths revealed to the prophet and interpreted by the forefathers."[13] The medieval curriculum is very important because it has had a profound impact on the curriculum of the modern Arab university. As I shall indicate later, the present

stress on humanistic-religious studies, indicated by the number of curricular offerings and student enrollments, can be traced back to the medieval period.

By the end of the fourteenth century colleges had been established in the major centers in the Arab World. The largest number of these colleges were located in Cairo and in Damascus, which, respectively, had an estimated seventy-four and seventy-three such institutions.[14] Other colleges were located in such cities as Jerusalem, Baghdad, Aleppo, and Tripoli. The most important medieval institution of higher learning, one that survives today, was Al-Azhar, founded in 970 at Cairo. This institution, claimed to be the oldest university in the world, was initially established on a strictly religious basis but has evolved into an all-purpose, modern Arab university.

The resurgence of Arab higher education occurred during the second half of the nineteenth century when Western-style institutions were introduced, primarily

Table 2

Estimated Total Enrollment at Third Level of Education (in thousands)

Year	World Enrollment	World Teaching Staff	Developed Countries Enrollment	Developed Countries Teaching Staff	Developing Countries Enrollment	Developing Countries Teaching Staff	Arab World Enrollment	Arab World Teaching Staff
1970	28,097	2,129	20,779	1,516	7,318	613	444	25
1975	39,556	2,877	26,714	1,924	12,842	953	896	44
1980	47,285	3,611	29,238	2,309	18,047	1,302	1,440	72
1984	53,952	3,835	30,777	2,243	23,175	1,596	1,860	101
1985	55,669	3,944	30,963	2,255	24,706	1,689	1,972	107
% increase								
70–80	5.3	5.4	3.5	4.3	9.4	7.8	12.5	11.2
80–85	3.3	1.8	1.2	-0.5	6.5	5.3	6.5	8.2

Gross Enrollment Ratios at Third Level of Education by Sex

Year	MF	M	F	MF	M	F	MF	M	F	MF	M	F
1970	8.8	10.8	6.7	23.2	27.2	19.1	3.1	4.3	1.8	4.3	6.5	2.0
1975	10.3	12.2	8.5	28.1	31.0	25.2	4.3	5.7	2.8	6.9	9.6	4.0
1980	11.2	12.6	9.7	29.9	30.7	29.0	5.4	7.1	3.7	8.4	11.2	5.4
1985	11.8	13.4	10.2	33.1	33.9	32.2	6.4	8.1	4.6	9.8	12.5	6.9

Source: UNESCO Statistical Yearbook, 1987.

based on the French, British, and American models. A preparatory school for medicine and pharmacy was founded in Algeria as early as 1859, and was followed in 1879 by schools of higher learning in medicine, law, and arts and sciences. Through the work of missionaries, a Syrian Protestant College (now the American University of Beirut) was established in Lebanon in 1866. This was followed by a French, Jesuit-supported institution in 1881, now known as Saint Joseph University in Beirut, Lebanon. With the advent of the twentieth century, Arab institutions of higher education began to proliferate. Many of these institutions provided the foundation for the subsequent development of a modern university. Most important among them were the institutions established in Khartoum in 1902; Baghdad in 1908; and Rabat and Umdurman (Sudan) in 1912. During this time, there were other private universities established, primarily in Egypt. They were the Egyptian University (1908) and the American University of Cairo (1919). The former would eventually become a state institution, Cairo University. Other notable institutions that had their beginning as Islamic centers are Qaraouiyine University, which traces its origins to a mosque established in 859 in Fez, Morocco, and the University of Tunis, which traces its past to Al-Zaytounah Islamic Institute in Tunis, established during the medieval period.

Although there were indigenous historical antecedents to present-day higher education institutions in Arab lands, most modern universities are basically replicas of Western institutions, developed on the French, British, or American models. The cultural heritage of Arab Islamic civilization has not, on the whole, contributed much to the identities of modern universities in the Arab world. We cannot refer to an Arab-style university as we do to British-, French-, or American-style universities. The discontinuities in the history of higher education in the region probably played a significant role in the loss of the early Arab-Islamic educational character and traditions. Certainly, the Ottoman period brought about a decline in the pace of educational development. As one author puts it, "The Ottoman rule and its neglect of education in the Arab and the Islamic world shattered the momentum of this cultural stride and brought it to a complete standstill. For the five hundred years of this rule, the light of learning was flickering, the research for truth was suppressed, and the advance of literature and science was hindered on all fronts."[15]

Trends in Arab Higher Education and Persistent Issues and Concerns

The contemporary Arab university, primarily a product of the twentieth century, shares most of the characteristics, conditions, and problems of growth of universities throughout the world, especially universities in the developing world. For example, the trend toward democratization of higher education evidenced in Arab countries is a worldwide phenomenon. Many of the problems resulting from this phenomenon are as common to the Arab as to the world community of universities.

Democratization has been accompanied by a trend toward Arabization of education. Both of these major developments are a consequence of national independence—the achievement of state sovereignty from Ottoman, French, British, or Italian colonial rule. Under foreign rule, most of the educational institutions in the region aimed at training a small group of the native population in the culture of the colonial rule, thereby using education as a means of perpetuating and expanding the political and cultural hegemony of the colonizer. This was particularly true of the countries in the Maghreb region. Given this situation, it was only natural that, upon liberation, Arab countries would use education as an instrument of the resocialization of youth into the knowledge and values of the Arab nation. One of the first acts of the independent Arab governments was usually to make education free at all levels, thereby extending opportunity to all Arab children and youth. With this reform came a series of related acts that sought to decolonize, as rapidly as possible, the schools. This was to be achieved primarily through the use of Arabic, rather than the language of the colonizer, as the medium of instruction; through the use of textbooks developed locally; and through a major reduction in the number of foreign teachers employed in Arab schools.

As I pointed out earlier, democratization of education as exemplified through enrollment expansion at all levels of education has been and continues to be a major trend.[16] In comparison to other countries, the Arab countries have a higher percentage of individuals in the respective age group who participate in programs of studies at the postsecondary education level. Despite unceasing attempts to open enrollments, however, problems still persist. First, there is the problem of male-dominated student enrollment at the universities. Although there have been significant improvements, Arab third-level institutions enroll almost twice as many men as women. Table 2 indicates that gross enrollment ratios for men at Arab postsecondary institutions in 1985 were 12.5 percent but for women only 6.9 percent.

Another major issue is whether individuals from the lower socioeconomic classes and/or from rural backgrounds have a chance of getting into university. The few studies available suggest that opportunity for schooling is, to a large degree, a function of the socioeconomic background of the individual, including family income, family size, parents' education, occupation of the head of the family,

and location of residence. The lower the socioeconomic background of the individual, the poorer his or her chances are for getting an education. Moreover, rural-urban disparities in the distribution of educational opportunity definitely exist. This general phenomenon is prevalent in most of the countries in the Arab world, even among those that officially espouse a socialist ideology.

Studies of the determinants of university attendance in the Arab world are scarce. One of the very few studies in the field found that, at the university level, offspring of professionals and owners of farms constituted the bulk of enrollment. At Cairo University in 1968 33.2 percent and 29.3 percent of the students, respectively, had fathers who were professionals or owners of farms. Only 5.6 percent and 5.8 percent of the students, respectively, had fathers who were workers or peasant farmers.[17] In Somalia, nomadic or seminomadic populations were likewise restricted in their opportunity to pursue basic as well as advanced studies.[18]

Arabization of education by means of the language of instruction and the national origin of the teaching staff remains an issue in several countries. While, as a rule, Arabic is the official medium of instruction in most faculties, there are exceptions. In Lebanon, Kuwait, Egypt, Algeria, and Tunisia faculties of sciences, engineering, and medicine continue to use French or English as the language of instruction. Private universities, such as the American University of Beirut, Saint Joseph University in Beirut, and Bier Zeit University in the West Bank, use English or French almost exclusively in all of their faculties. According to one calculation, Arabic constitutes the only language of instruction in fifteen out of sixty-four universities in the region.[19] Twenty-seven universities use both Arabic and English and ten universities use both Arabic and French.

The two reasons usually given for continuing use of a foreign language as the language of instruction (primarily in fields connected with science and technology) are the dearth of qualified national faculty, and the dearth of appropriate texts and reference books of a technical nature available in Arabic. At Yarmouk University in Jordan (an institution established in 1976), English is used in the faculties of natural sciences, engineering, economics, and administrative sciences, because about 20 percent of the faculty cannot speak Arabic.[20] In Libya, English is utilized in the faculties of medicine, science, and pharmacy since the majority of the teaching staff on these faculties are non-Libyans. In the early 1980s, for example, Gar Yunis University had 301 non-Libyans out of a total of 788 faculty members. Libyans occupied only the lower professorial ranks.[21]

One of the major problems resulting from the fact that English or French is used in many faculties is that many Arab students are not well trained in the use of the language of instruction before entering the university. Thus students at the University of Kuwait whose English language proficiency is relatively low have serious problems in following instruction. At that university, English is used in four out of nine colleges, affecting about 43 percent of the total student body.[22]

Given the language problem, Arab governments have taken measures, individually and collectively, to remedy the situation. New textbooks have been written in order to alleviate the problem of dependence on foreign instructional materials. Efforts to train native talent to assume key instructional positions in universities have been accelerated. ALECSO (Arab League Educational, Scientific, and Cultural Organization) established an office in Tunis to coordinate the Arabization efforts among Arab states.

Higher Education and Employment

One of the perennial questions asked is whether education contributes directly or indirectly to employment. Studies in the West found that, as a general rule, there is a correlation between education and labor force participation.[23] But there are very few studies on this subject in the Arab world, especially concerning the tertiary level.[24]

Any discussion of higher education and employment necessitates an analysis of the goals of higher education in the region. As mentioned earlier, medieval Arabic educational institutions were established primarily for Islamic learning and perpetuation of the faith. The twentieth-century Arab universities, however, much like their counterparts in the West, became all-purpose universities, emphasizing education, professional training, research, and public service. While universities in the most traditional Arab countries (e.g., Saudi Arabia) maintain as a major goal "the preservation and promotion of Islamic faith and Arabic language," in actuality all universities seek to prepare students for gainful employment.[25] In addition to the propagation of the faith and preparation for employment, Saudi universities seek to contribute to the general welfare and development of the individual and the society and to advance the state of knowledge.[26]

The most comprehensive study of higher education and employment in the Arab world was conducted in Egypt in the late 1970s. The study confirmed the proposition that there is a mismatch between education and employment.[27] This phenomenon, certainly not peculiar to Egypt, is attributed to several factors. First, dramatic enrollment expansion at the tertiary level was not accompanied by a corresponding expansion in the labor market. Second, students persist in majoring in theoretical rather than practical fields, resulting in graduates with very few, if any, marketable skills (labor demands in land reclamation and other areas of agriculture and in the rapidly expanding service sector of the economy went unfulfilled for lack of qualified personnel). Third, female graduates are not effectively utilized (only 9 percent of the women in Egypt were participating in the labor force in 1976 as compared to 52 percent of the men). Fourth, governments that guarantee employment upon graduation (in some cases, graduates, in spite of these guarantees, had to wait several years before being placed in a job) stifle graduate incentive to seek work and disrupt the labor market. Fifth, universities themselves do not provide adequate services, such as career counseling and job placement mechanisms for their graduates. The study's main implication is that universities, insofar as they prepare students to enter the labor movement, have not done an adequate job. "Universities tend to go on with their traditional courses, which are highly academic without consideration of their relevance to the field of work."[28] Egyptian employers interviewed in the study thought that university "graduates lack required training" (60.7 percent shared this view). Some 44.4 percent of the employers also felt that "good academic performance does not mean good job performance," while 38.2 percent indicated that there are "no links between university studies and employment prerequisites."[29] Significantly, university students, more so than alumni or employers, felt that work experience is a prerequisite in the world of work. In fact, the study concluded that experience more than any other factor, including education, determined the size of annual earnings.

The phenomenon of mismatch between university education and employment is prevalent throughout the Arab world. Two recent studies in Libya concluded that higher education in that country did not meet national development requirements. To meet these requirements, universities need to attend to more powerful mechanisms in order to recruit more women in higher education and provide career education as part of the curriculum.[30] A major higher education curriculum revision is, in fact, recommended in all fields to meet national development objectives.[31]

There have been attempts in most of the Arab countries to provide some coordination between education and work. This has been accomplished primarily through government agencies administering various development plans. In Saudi Arabia, for example, where the government is administering its fourth Five-Year Plan (1985–1990), a Manpower Council was established and held responsible for training and development of the labor force. This council coordinates the programs of all government agencies and makes sure that all education and training programs "are in compliance with the requirements of the development of manpower and its capability to develop the skills needed in the kingdom in the future."[32] It would certainly be a worthwhile endeavor to study the effects of these development plans in the Arab world to determine whether the apparent mismatch between higher education and employment has subsided as a result.

In many Arab countries the education and employment of women presents a major problem. In the Gulf countries, for example, women are not supposed to mix with men in school or in the workplace. Consequently, segregated facilities that separate the two sexes are the rule. The occupational choice of women is highly restricted. A Kuwaiti woman, for example, is limited in her occupational choice by the wishes of her family, the wishes of her husband (if married), and the conditions of work. As a result of the traditional belief system about the role of women prevailing in the Gulf states, women enter only traditional occupations, such as teaching, nursing, and social work, where segregation of the sexes is still possible. While the situation is slowly changing, women constitute only a very small portion of the labor force. In Kuwait, for example, only 24,803, or 3.7 percent, of the labor force in 1985 were women.[33] It is of interest to note, however, that education in Kuwait "bears a direct linear relationship to support for women's economic participation, but only among less religious respondents."[34] It appears that education, for both men and women, has a liberalizing influence on attitudes toward the social roles of members of the two sexes. In other Arab countries, Tunisia and Egypt, for example, women have been able to enter virtually all sections of the economy and public service. In fact, it is no coincidence that in these countries legal restrictions affecting women have been removed. When such restrictions are removed, there is more likelihood that female literacy, overall employment, and participation in nonagricultural economic activity will increase.[35] In Egypt, as early as 1980, there were 154,000 women holders of a university degree or its equivalent who were engaged in such occupations as medicine, engineering, aeronautics, agriculture, and animal husbandry.[36] It should be noted that traditionally all of these employment fields were exclusively for men. While tradition still holds back many women in Arab lands, forces of change are enabling more women to move forward in education and employment outside the home.

Higher Education and the Political System

As I observed earlier, the overwhelming majority of the Arab universities—sixty out of seventy-two—are public universities. As such, they are controlled and financed by the state. The mechanism of control is usually exercised through the Ministry of Education or the Ministry of Higher Education. It is the minister's responsibility to ensure that the operation of the university system, including matters related to student admission and what is to be taught, by whom, and for how long, is consistent with overall government policy. Specific policies on university matters are developed in most cases in a Council for Higher Education. This council is comprised of high-level members of the government, such as cabinet ministers, university rectors or presidents, and representatives from various other segments of society including business and industry. The rector or the university president is the government's agent in the university, making sure that day-to-day university operation is in line with government policies. The rector is assisted by a university council. In some countries, Egypt and Kuwait, for example, the minister of education is the titular head of the university. In other countries, the rector is normally nominated by the university council and approved by the cabinet. In some Arab countries, rectors are appointed by the government without consultation with a university council or similar body, the position being thought of as being part of the civil service network.

The scope and power of the higher education councils in the Arab world are broad. The National Council for Higher Education in Sudan, for example, created by legislative act in 1975, performs the following main functions:

○ The planning and policy-making function: The council is responsible for determining the role of each institution of higher education, the annual student intake, and distribution of students among different branches and disciplines.

○ The financial function: The council is authorized to recommend to the president of the republic the funds to be allocated to each institution after examining the annual budgets of the institutions within the system.

○ The regulatory function: The council is charged with regulating general requirements and terms for academic appointments, and for evaluating the functioning of institutions of higher education and reporting it to the president of the republic.[37]

It is obvious from the above that the council's power over the university reaches out to all of its major functions. Thus the autonomy of the university is highly restricted. In fact, this restrictive situation holds for most of the universities in the region.

Without a measure of autonomy, universities cannot nurture true academic freedom. There have been cases in which faculty and administrators were dismissed from the university simply because a new group assumed political power. As one recent report states, there have also been cases where members of the university community "were imprisoned or pressured/forced to leave the country."[38]

State universities throughout the world are in some measure subject to state control, especially since the bulk of the finances for recurrent as well as development costs are provided by the state. This control is all the greater in most of the Arab countries' universities because they are integrated into the state enterprise system. Long-term development planning and manpower planning by the government tends to strip universities of much of their power to determine their own affairs.

On the other hand, private universities in the Arab world are governed by boards of trustees and usually are quite removed from the national government and its various control mechanisms. This type of university is represented by the American University, one in Beirut, one in Cairo; Haigazian College in Beirut; and the Beirut University College.

The political nature of the universities is manifested, according to one author, in the names that these universities bear. The names change in accordance with the dominant national or political trend.[39] For example, present-day Cairo University was originally known as Egyptian University

(1925) and later as Fuad I University (1936). When the Egyptian-Syrian union was declared, the Syrian University was renamed Damascus University because "it was felt appropriate to de-emphasize country names."[40] Examples such as these abound.

In addition to power relations between higher education and the state, there are other mechanisms through which one entity relates to the other. Universities, for example, relate to the political system through the recruitment, training, and placement of political elites. There are presently no systematic studies of Arab elites such as the one, for example, conducted by Frey in Turkey, on patterns of elite recruitment and the role of education.[41] In Egypt university education is a prerequisite to a position in the civil service, but a degree or university certificate, in itself, will not automatically ensure one of membership in the bureaucratic elites.[42] In fact, the relations between the intellectual community and government leaders seem to be somewhat asymmetrical, the reasons being that "(1) the politico-military elite is culturally non-ideologically inclined and anti-intellectual (2) intellectuals themselves have a low political standing . . . ; (3) intellectuals in Egypt are not concerned with development and modernization, but often with a formalized, humanistically conceived body of knowledge."[43]

In postindependence Tunisia education both as an institution and as a process was used as a primary means to accelerate and strengthen the process of political change. In this sense education served "as a major element in creating a new elite" and served as "the most important single factor in broadening the social and geographical base of political participation in Tunisia."[44] Tunisia, through education, reportedly secured the necessary cadres to run the government. Thus, during this early period of national sovereignty, there was "a conscious and deliberate effort . . . to use education as the vanguard of the proposed social revolution."[45] As the need for political and social solidarity in Tunisia subsided, the government exercised more and more political control over the university. As one author put it, "the social gains of the past decade have shown Bourguiba to be a master of public relations and propaganda. His paternalism reflects a culture in which father has unlimited authority."[46] The pattern of the relation between education and the polity described above was replicated in many of the Arab countries as they strived to establish their national identity and power after independence.

There have been some studies on the role of education in the political socialization of youth.[47] They generally indicate that educational establishments, including universities, socialize students into accepting regime norms and developing attachment to the country and its leaders. In general, it appears that pan-Arab nationalism is subordinate to nationalism identified with the individual's own state; family, tribal, and religious affiliations are also strong, especially among Arabs in the Gulf states.

With the exception of Egypt and, most recently, Palestine, university students in the Arab world have not engaged in student political activism. In Egypt university students have been involved in antigovernment protests since 1919. Later, students either joined existing political parties or formed their own organizations to bring about political and social change. In the mid-1940s students were involved in the movement for national liberation. Their activities culminated in strikes and demonstrations which, in some measure, led to the withdrawal of the British troops from the Cairo and Delta regions in 1946.[48] Students also influenced the process of the Free Officers movement in bringing about the revolution in 1952. Additional incidents of major student protests took place after the humiliating defeat of 1967 under Nasser. The students demanded the punishment of those responsible for the defeat, more freedom of expression and of the press, and a reduction of police surveillance and assaults on university students.[49] Throughout this period the student demand was for wider participation in the decision-making process. In all, it is claimed that the student movement in Egypt contributed "to major changes in the political system—changes which took place gradually in the years following the June war of 1967 and, more rapidly, in the aftermath of the October war of 1973."[50]

Internal Matters in Higher Education

Internally, the university is governed by the rector and a university council or senate. The council, which includes high-level university officials as well as other members from the public and private sectors, is generally responsible for overall university policies, and for the curriculum, faculty appointments, student admission guidelines, and budgeting. The specific responsibilities of each university council vary from country to country. Universities are normally comprised of a number of faculties or colleges, each headed by a dean. The deans, in turn, conduct the business of the college through a college council, a body consisting of department heads, faculty members, and Ministry of Education representatives, as well as distinguished representatives from the community. Faculty members (usually one from each department) are either elected or appointed to council membership. The college council normally attends to matters concerning the college. On most issues, however, approval by the higher authorities, the university council and the rector, is needed. With the exception of some of the private universities, Arab universities are controlled internally by the administrators and their associates. Faculty members, unlike their colleagues in United States institutions, are virtually powerless in the university decision-making apparatus.

The academic structure of each university varies, depending on the model used in creating the university. Universities established on the Egyptian model which, in turn, stems from French and British university traditions, were characterized, initially, by an emphasis on the arts and the humanities. In this system universities are comprised of a number of faculties. The academic program is based on a year-long course of study. Students are obligated to take an examination at the end of each year. Successful performance on the examination allows students to advance to the next term year. Students may take the end-of-year examinations without ever attending classes.

Universities based on the American model are run on a semester basis; programs of study are figured on a credit unit system. Evaluation of student performance is normally ongoing. This system allows more free choice in the form of electives. In addition to the private universities such as AUB, BUC, AUC, and Bier Zeit on the West Bank, public institutions such as Jordan University, Kuwait University, and the University of Petroleum and Research in Saudi Arabia, among others, follow the semester term system. Certain faculties in Syrian universities have also gradually accepted the semester system. As a rule, universities established after 1975 follow the semester plan.

The most significant difference between the two systems (the Egyptian, based on the French and English, and the American) is the matter of specialization. In the former system, specialization begins upon entering the university; in the latter, specialization begins after a period (one or two years) of general studies in the liberal arts. There are advantages and disadvantages in each system. Early specialization permits students to concentrate on the field of study of their interest, but at the expense of a broad education. Liberal arts studies can prolong the term of study in one's own field, thus creating a potential hardship in job placement and in professional attainment. In recent years, there have been cases of extreme specialization, with certain institutions offering specialized training in a narrow field of study. Mu'tah University in Jordan, for example, offers just two programs, one in military/police studies and one in civilian studies; the University of Technology in Baghdad and the University of Science and Technology, with campuses in Algiers and Oran, also offer extremely specialized study programs.[51]

Some of the inflexibility characteristic of the Arab universities may be traced to the fact that many universities were created from a number of faculties or colleges that were originally independent. Even after these colleges become part of a new university system, many of them maintain their separate traditions (e.g., the year-long term program or the semester program). It is reported, for example, that the University of Baghdad has colleges based on the French, British, American, or mixed models, all operating within the same university system.[52] The separate identities of these faculties are still maintained in the sense that rarely are students from one faculty permitted to take courses in another. Thus, core courses in math, sciences, and social sciences are duplicated in all faculties, resulting in a waste of scarce human resources and facilities. Coordination efforts are underway, but the forces of tradition and vested interests still prevail.

The European style of university atmosphere has generally persisted in those establishments that adopted the Egyptian model. Students generally attend large lecture halls where a professor communicates to them by means of a lecture or a lecture-type presentation. With five hundred students in the hall, there is rarely any student-teacher exchange and there is no room for questions. Professorial lectures are also available in bound form for the students to purchase. To pass the year-end exam, students must memorize the lectures or the lecture notes and any assigned textbooks. Memorization rather than critical inquiry becomes the standard mode of operation for the students. In institutions following the American pattern, classes are generally smaller and students are given the opportunity to interact with their instructors, in and out of class.

One of the major problems facing Arab universities, regardless of the type of academic model they follow, is the matter of dramatic student enrollment increases without commensurate increases in faculty, staff, and facilities. The dearth of qualified faculty has sustained and reinforced the pattern of large lecture halls and methods of instruction that lead to memorization rather than critical thinking. For example, the average faculty-student ratio in humanities colleges at Mansoura University in Egypt is reported to be 1:85. In fact, the overall average at Mansoura, the highest in Egypt, is 1:452.[53] As a rule, science and technology faculties have a better teacher-student ratio. Relatively high admission criteria usually operate as a deterrent to large enrollments in these faculties.

High enrollments have also affected the ability to provide adequate facilities for instruction in the form of classroom space, laboratories, and libraries. With the exception of the oil-rich countries, where universities enjoy the most modern facilities and equipment, Arab universities have very little in the way of science laboratories and libraries. The King Saud University library and the Cairo University library are reported to have 1.1 million and 1 million volumes, respectively, but Ain Shams University (with the highest student enrollment in the region) is reported to have only 92,000 volumes in its library.[54] Science laboratories are also scarce. Where scientific equipment is available, it is too often poorly maintained. A visitor to some of the laboratories in the region is often amazed to discover up-to-date equipment that is in a totally unoperative state, this being the result of improper installation, inexperienced staff, or inability to replace damaged parts. The overall poor state of science laboratories in the Arab world accounts, in good measure, for the apparent emphasis on theory rather than on practice through "hands-on" experience. Thus, while students may observe their instructors conducting an experiment on stage, they rarely have the opportunity to conduct one themselves.

The Quest for Reform

An Arab observer of the higher education system in the region noted that there have been six major positive developments in the system in recent years.[55] First, the democratization process of higher education now taking place in the region enables more students to achieve advanced education. Second, the establishment of new kinds of postsecondary institutions (e.g., junior colleges in Jordan and Kuwait, technical institutes in Egypt and Sudan) allows students to pursue studies and commensurate careers outside the traditional university. This trend has created a diversified system of education beyond the secondary school and has encouraged students to explore and cultivate their special interests and needs. Third, the creation of technological or polytechnic universities in the Arab region has promoted a more modern orientation in line with worldwide developments in science and technology. Most of these institutions have been established since the 1970s; they include the University of King Faisal in Saudi Arabia (with campuses in Dammam and Al-Ihsa'), Halwan University in Cairo, Egypt, the University of Science and Technology of Oran, Algeria, the University of Technology in Baghdad, Iraq, al-Ba'th University in Syria, and Mersi Barka University in Libya. Fourth, Islamic scholarship has revived. This revival of concentrated Islamic learning and study has manifested itself in a number of Islamic universities, such as Al-Madina and Al-Imam Mohammad Bin Saud in Saudi Arabia and the Islamic University of

Um-Durman in Sudan. Islamic-Arab studies are also available through the traditional universities (now all-purpose universities), such as the University of Tunis (formerly Al-Zeitouniyya University) and Al-Azhar University in Cairo, both of which have well-established faculties of theology and Islamic jurisprudence. Fifth, the creation of regional universities has stimulated a sense of Arab identity. This type of university seeks to involve a number of Arab states on a cooperative basis and to draw students from the entire region. The Gulf Arab University created in 1980 is such a university, operating under the Gulf Cooperation Council and drawing students from its member states: Bahrain, Iraq, Saudi Arabia, Qatar, U.A.E., and Iraq. The regional university seeks to provide fields of study in areas not covered by the offerings of the individual national universities. Sixth, the establishment of ALECSO (Arab League Educational, Cultural, and Scientific Organization) has been a positive development in bringing about inter-Arab collaboration and coordination. This organization has provided statistical information on the state of education and culture in the member states, conducted research, and organized regional meetings to plan for the future.

In addition to attempts at constructive change described above, there have been other efforts to introduce reforms in higher education. I have already mentioned the effort to Arabize instruction in terms of teaching staffs and language of instruction. The bureau established under ALECSO has sought to provide a comprehensive Arabization plan to be in full operation by the year 2000. In North Africa, where the problem of foreign, non-Arab teachers providing instruction at all levels of education has gradually been minimized, qualified Arab-speaking staff are steadily recruited into educational institutions to replace foreign staff. There are also concurrent efforts to replace foreign textbooks with textbooks written in Arabic.

Another very important movement, also referred to earlier, has been the quest to provide women with the opportunity to study at the university level. I have already noted that in recent years the rate of increase of female students at the tertiary level has outpaced that of male students. Also, with the exception of the Gulf States, most Arab universities are coeducational. The universities in the Gulf (with the exception of the University of Bahrain and Kuwait University) continue to be sex-segregated, both in class and in the residential facilities. In these universities, students are normally taught by instructors of the same gender. In Saudi Arabia, closed-circuit TV is utilized to provide cross-gender instruction.

The quest for democratization has led many Arab governments to eliminate tuition fees for students in postsecondary educational institutions. In Morocco, for example, in addition to not paying tuition, the overwhelming majority of the students receive one type of scholarship. Housing at university residence halls as well as meals are provided at nominal costs. In Jordan, students are charged only nominal fees, but even these are waived when students cannot afford them. Private universities, on the other hand, charge relatively high tuition fees, thus generally restricting enrollment to the well-to-do.

Current Conditions Affecting Students and Academic Staff

One of the most important factors affecting both students and faculty is university admissions policies. In many Arab countries (e.g., Algeria, Morocco, Iraq, and Tunisia), students are admitted into the university after passing the national General Secondary Certificate of Education Examination or what is known as the Baccalaureate Examination. The courses of study or tracks pursued at the upper secondary school and the degree of success on the GSCE are generally taken into account when students are selected to enroll in the various faculties. As a rule, faculties of science, technology, medicine, and dentistry have more stringent admission requirements, given the limited space and personnel available for instruction. Faculties of letters, law, and commerce are more easily accessible to the students who pass the GSCE. The excessive number of students enrolled in these three faculties and the relatively low quality of education offered to them prompted one author to refer to these faculties, in the case of Egypt, as university "dumping grounds."[56] Naturally, the open admissions policy prevalent in the majority of the Arab universities leads to a relatively high failure rate, especially during the first years of study. In Algeria, Morocco, and Tunisia, student failure rate at the faculties of letters, law, and science was between 70 and 80 percent in the first two years of attendance.[57] Other countries in the region in which university mass education is encouraged exhibit similar failure rates. It appears that as long as tertiary education expansion is considered a politically advantageous policy, Arab governments will not seek to employ a more rational plan for selection of university students.

In addition to a lower quality of instruction as the result of uncontrolled enrollments, there is the problem of the qualifications of university faculty. While a doctoral degree or its equivalent is sought as a minimum qualification for entering the professorial ranks, very few universities in the region have been able to attain this goal. In a study conducted in 1977–78 of higher education faculty members in seven Arab countries (Bahrain, Jordan, Kuwait, Libya, Saudi Arabia, Tunisia, and UAE), it was found that only 18.2 percent of the faculty had doctoral degrees or their equivalent.[58] In fact, only 25.8 percent of the faculty had any graduate degree. Also, in these countries the faculty consisted

of 53.1 percent nationals; 28.8 percent Arabs; and 18.1 percent non-Arabs. Over the years, minimum faculty qualifications have improved somewhat, mainly as a result of the availability of funds for graduate study abroad. The newer universities, primarily in the Gulf area, are continuing to experience the problem of recruitment and retention of native faculty. In Kuwait, for example, non-Kuwaiti members of the faculty constituted 70 percent of the total in the mid-1980s.[59] The pressure for instruction in these faculties generally leaves very little time for faculty research. Non-native instructors are usually constrained in their research efforts, too, because they are appointed on a short-term basis and have limited access to needed resources.[60]

The pressure for undergraduate instruction, while maintaining a university open admissions policy, had a number of adverse effects in addition to the ones listed previously. Many faculty members, especially in the oil-poor countries, left jobs in their native land and accepted appointments at faculties of universities in oil-rich countries. This is particularly true for university faculties in Egypt and Sudan, where relatively low faculty salaries prompt the best professors to seek employment in the more affluent countries, thus contributing to the brain drain. In Sudan, for example, 110 faculty members emigrated between 1975 and 1979.[61]

Although there are some reports of continued increase in postgraduate enrollments, this level of study is not a major focus of higher education programs in the Arab world. During the period 1982–84 in nine countries for which data are available, there were only 86,225 students in graduate programs of study.[62] Of these students, 71 percent were attending Egyptian universities. It is obvious that the overall graduate enrollments constitute a very small fraction of total university enrollments. Research output is also on the rise, as calculated by the number of articles authored by Arabs in scientific and technological research publications.[63] However, scientific research is still in its infancy. What is available is generally of poor quality. The relatively low percentage of GNP invested in research in the Arab world—0.27 percent versus 1.78 percent for the world—which is the lowest for all continents, may have something to do, in addition to other factors, with the relatively low research performance level of Arab scientists.[64]

The main obstacles that prevent or limit the development of research in the Arab world have been summarized as follows: "weak graduate study and/or its absence, scientific literature not easily available, limited financial resources, lack of properly trained support staff, translation problems, inadequate facilities, heavy teaching loads, the transient nature of a large proportion of faculty in many Gulf universities, and resort to external employment by faculty members in universities of poor countries."[65]

Conclusions

Higher education in the Arab world has a long and distinguished history. Its roots can be traced back to the rise of Islam and the mosque-related educational practices. Al-Azhar in Cairo dates back to the tenth century; other famous institutions in the region are almost as old. These institutions survived several colonial occupations. In modern times, Arab universities, influenced by the French, English, or American models, evolved into all-purpose universities, much like their counterparts in the West. There are presently about seventy-five universities in operation in the Arab world.

Given the problems inherited from years of colonial rule, Arab universities have in many respects fared well in meeting the development needs of their respective countries. Those responsible for making higher education decisions have succeeded in opening opportunities for higher education to significant numbers of students. Female enrollment has been increased and

inequalities based on socioeconomic background, place of residence, and religious beliefs, etc., have been reduced. In many Arab countries the Arabization process has been successful. Instruction has been Arabized by recruiting more native instructors into the university facilities and by legitimizing the use of Arabic as the main instrument of communication. The decision makers have also sought to coordinate university coursework with manpower needs in the respective country and in the region.

While the higher education goals above have been sought, and, in many instances, achieved, there are other problems yet to be resolved. These include:

The problems of university governance. Too much authority is concentrated in the hands of the education minister and the rector, and too little in the hands of the faculty and students. Major decisions about such matters as admissions, curriculum, examinations, textbooks, and attendance requirements are not made by those who are being most affected by them. The patriarchal social orientation based on the authoritarian structure inherited from the past seems to extend to all major decisions on educational matters.[66]

The problem of coordination among colleges within a university. Since each college is relatively autonomous, especially under the Egyptian, French, and British patterns, there is little coordination in terms of offerings, core courses, and resources. This results in duplication of effort, and wastage of course credit should a student decide to transfer from one college to another.

The problem of outdated textbooks and other instructional materials. Very little effort is expended on faculty research and publication. At best, faculty members publish their lectures in note form, which in turn are used by students in studying for the year-end examinations. Textbooks imported from abroad unduly tax the student who, as a rule, is not proficient in the language of the text.

The problem of planning to match university programs of study and employment. As indicated, Arab countries experience a general mismatch between university offerings and knowledge/skills needed to become gainfully employed. As a result, many university graduates are unemployed, underemployed, or are employed in occupations that do not require university training.

The problem of insufficient university contributions to knowledge. Given all the factors mentioned earlier that mitigate against scientific research, faculty at Arab universities have not, as a rule, made major contributions to knowledge. One of the traditional functions of the university, research, is presently not being performed. Moreover, the Arab world has a scarcity of significant programs of graduate study.

The problem of unequal distribution of opportunity for higher education. Notwithstanding government and ALECSO efforts to the contrary, factors such as gender, socioeconomic status, and place of residence still adversely affect adversely the opportunity to attend a postsecondary institution. Male, middle-class, urban dwellers are still favored in higher education enrollments. While the respective agencies acknowledge the importance of democratization of all levels of education, in actual practice the removal of the aforementioned obstacles is taking place at an extremely low pace.

There is no doubt that Arab higher education is in a period of transition. The question is how to maintain the valuable elements of the Arab-Islamic civilization while at the same time attending to national and regional development needs. Issues that need to be carefully attended to include:

○ The striking difference in knowledge and skill among graduates of universities in the region.
○ The lack of uniformity (standardization) in courses of study, curricula, and evaluation methods, which make interuniversity or interfaculty cooperation virtually impossible.
○ The lack of systematic guidance and career counseling services, a situation that compounds the problem of graduate job placement.
○ The preoccupation of faculty, especially new faculty, with bureaucratic trivia that precludes investment of time and effort in research and development activities.
○ The lack of general coordination between agencies controlling national development and universities, resulting in unemployment or underemployment of university graduates.
○ The inability to offer on a large scale alternate routes to postsecondary education (e.g., through the establishment and the expanded use of polytechnic institutes and community colleges).
○ The lack of realistic measures for writing new textbooks and instructional materials or providing translations of extant materials.
○ The apparent noninvolvement of community and business leaders in the affairs of higher education.

Other issues also confront Arab universities today. While these issues sometimes appear to be overwhelming, positive changes are possible through careful planning. Most important, however, is the willingness of Arab top administrators to learn from the experience of others and to look to the future with optimism and a determination to succeed. As a former president of the University of Jordan said, "We are now more on the receiving end than on the donating end. . . . We look to the world with an open mind and we hope to make our modest contribution to human knowledge and international understanding."[67]

Notes

1. Saad Eddin Ibrahim, *The New Arab Social Order: A Study of the Social Impact of Oil Wealth* (Boulder, Colo.: Westview, 1982), 3.
2. Ibid., 5–25.
3. George I. Za'rour, *Universities in Arab Countries* (Washington, D.C: International Bank for Reconstruction and Development/World Bank, 1988), 3.
4. Ibid.
5. Munir Bashshur, *Similarities and Contrasts in Patterns of Higher Education in the Arab World* (Paper delivered at the Nordic Conference on Higher Education in the Arab World and the Middle East at Lund University, Sweden, 28 March 1985), 1.
6. Byron G. Massialas, "Morocco," in *World Education Encyclopedia*, ed. G. T. Kurian (New York: Facts on File, 1988), 883.
7. Bayard Dodge, *Muslim Education in Medieval Times* (Washington, D.C.: Middle East Institute, 1962), 8–9.
8. Ibid., 10
9. Ibid., 21.
10. Ibid.
11. Ibid.
12. Ibid., 29.
13. Ibid.
14. Ibid., 23.
15. A. S. Majali, *The Development of Higher Education in the Arab World* (London: Longmans for the University of Essex, 1971), 6.
16. Byron Massialas and Samir A. Jarrar, *Arab Education in Transition* (New York: Garland, forthcoming).
17. A. Shaban, "Social Justice and Efficiency in Egyptian Education" (Ph.D. diss., University of Pittsburgh, 1981), 198.
18. Improving the Efficiency of Educational Systems (IEES), *Somalia: Education and Human Resources Sector Assessment* (Tallahassee, Fla.: Learning Systems Institute, Florida State University, 1984).
19. Za'rour, *Universities in Arab Countries*, 18.
20. Ibid., 19.
21. Byron G. Massialas, "Libya," in *World Education Encyclopedia*, ed. G. T. Kurian (New York: Facts on File, 1988), 815.
22. Za'rour, *Universities in Arab Countries*, 19.
23. Rati Ram, "Sex Differences in the Labor Market Outcomes of Education," *Comparative Education Review* 24 (June 1980): 553–77.
24. Byron G. Massialas and Jamileh F. Mikati, "Trends in Women's Education and Employment in the Arab World," in *Women and Economic Development in the Arab World*, ed., J. A. Nasr and I. Lorfing (Beirut, Lebanon: Institute for Women's Studies in the Arab World, Beirut University College, 1988), 231–52.
25. Abdul-Rahman Ahmed Saeh, "Higher Education and Modernization in Saudi Arabia: An Inquiry into the Societal Values of Saudi Colleges and Universities and Their Roles in the Economic and Non-Economic Development of the Kingdom" (Ph.D. diss., Claremont Graduate School, 1983), 179.
26. Ibid., 179–85.
27. Bikas C. Sanyal et al., *University Education and the Labour Market in the Arab Republic of Egypt* (Oxford: Pergamon Press, 1982).
28. Ibid., 63.
29. Ibid., 163.
30. Mohamed Masud Mogassbi, "Perceptions of the Higher Education System and Manpower Development in Libya" (Ed.D. diss., George Washington University, 1983).
31. Hamid Ali Muftah, "Analysis of the Development of a Higher-Education System in Libya and Its Impact on the Libyan Students" (Ph.D. diss., University of Kansas, 1982).
32. Joy Winkie Viola, *Human Resources Development in Saudi Arabia* (Boston, Mass: International Human Resources Development Corporation, 1986), 159.
33. Jamil A. Sanad and Mark A. Tessler, "The Economic Orientations of Kuwaiti Women: Their Nature, Determinants, and Consequences," *International Journal of Middle East Studies* 20 (November 1988): 443–60.
34. Ibid., 461.
35. Elizabeth H. White, "Legal Reform as an Indicator of Women's Status in Muslim Nations," in *Women in the Muslim World*, ed. Lois Beck and Nikki Keddie (Cambridge: Harvard University Press, 1978), 63–67.
36. Byron J. Massialas and Samir A. Jarrar, *Education in the Arab World* (New York: Praeger, 1983), 260.
37. Ibid., 195.
38. Za'rour, *Universities in Arab Countries*, 5.
39. Ibid., 6.
40. Ibid.
41. Frederick W. Frey, *The Turkish Political Elite* (Cambridge: MIT Press, 1965).
42. Malcolm H. Kerr, "Egypt," in *Education and Political Development*, ed. James S. Coleman (Princeton: Princeton University Press, 1965), 169–94.
43. Leonard Binder, "Egypt: The Integrative Revolution," *Political Culture and Political Development*, ed. Lucian W. Pye and Sidney Verba (Princeton: Princeton University Press, 1965), 445–46.
44. Leon Carl Brown, "Tunisia," in *Education and Political Development*, ed. James S. Coleman

(Princeton: Princeton University Press, 1965), 168.

45. Ibid.
46. Catherine Tompkins Sizer, "The Development of Education in Tunisia," (M.A. thesis, The American University, 1971).
47. Tawfic E. Farah, ed., *Political Behavior in the Arab States* (Boulder, Colo.: Westview Press, 1983).
48. Ahmed Abdalla, *The Student Movement and National Politics in Egypt, 1923–1973* (London: Al Saqi Books, Distributed by Zed Books, 1985).
49. Ibid.
50. Ibid., 218-19.
51. Za'rour, *Universities in Arab Countries,* 8.
52. Ibid.
53. Ibid., 13.
54. Ibid., 15
55. Bashshur, *Patterns of Higher Education in the Arab World,* 32–39.

56. Za'rour, *Universities in Arab Countries,* 11.
57. Massialas and Jarrar, *Education in the Arab World,* 204.
58. Ibid., 200.
59. Qayum Safi, "Kuwait University and Its Evaluation Program," *Higher Education* 15 (1986): 421–47.
60. Ibid., 431.
61. Bashshur, *Patterns of Higher Education in the Arab World,* 23.
62. Za'rour, *Universities in Arab Countries,* 17.
63. Ibid.
64. Ibid.
65. Ibid., 18.
66. Hisham Sharabi, *Neopatriarchy: A Theory of Distorted Change in Arab Society* (New York: Oxford, 1988).
67. Majali, *Development of Higher Education in the Arab World,* 14.

Egypt

Samir A. Jarrar

◆

Egypt lies at the crossroads of Africa and Asia in the center of the Arab world. Its area covers 386,000 square miles (1,001,710 square kilometers). Egypt has the longest recorded history of any modern nation, dating back to 3200 B.C. Since early times Egypt has experienced periods of strength, during which it dominated neighboring countries. In periods of relative weakness Egypt has been controlled by Greeks, Romans, Persians, Ottomans, French, and British forces.

Culturally, geographically, and economically Egypt is in the center of the Arab world. Egypt was a founding member of the League of Arab States and the United Nations—both established in 1945. The Egyptian population was estimated to be about 50.5 million in late 1988, with an annual growth rate of 2.75 percent for the last decade.[1] The high rate of population growth has placed tremendous pressures on the Egyptian economy and is affecting the development of the educational system in the country.

Educational System Background

The evolution of the educational system in Egypt dates back to the pharaohs' times, when special schools were established to educate royalty and other members of the court. Formal education peaked during the Islamic era, starting around A.D. 640. The *Kuttab*, or Koranic schools, taught children the Koran and the three Rs. The *Madrassa* started as adult learning centers, then developed to provide advanced specialization equivalent to higher education.

Al-Azhar Mosque, founded in A.D. 970, is the oldest university in the world.[2] Traditional Islamic studies continued to be the basis for all formal education in Egypt until the end of the eighteenth century.

Modern secular education in Egypt can be traced to the early nineteenth century. The invasion of the country by the French in 1798 triggered an outcry for reform and modernization led by the sheikh of Al-Azhar. He believed that education was the key to change and that new subjects needed to be added to the traditional curriculum.

Mohammad Ali emerged as the strong man of Egypt (1805–49), beginning a dynasty that ruled the country until the revolution of 1952. Mohammad Ali wanted independence from the Ottoman empire. To achieve his goal, he needed a modern, well-trained army. And a modern army, like Napoleon's, required an educated officer corps. With the purpose of creating skilled professionals for his army and the state bureaucracy, he embarked on a grand scheme to establish institutes of higher education, as well as technical and professional schools. He invited instructors and trainers from France and, by 1809, sent the first of a series of student missions abroad to be trained.

Mohammad Ali faced a major obstacle in trying to establish institutes of higher education. Egypt's educational system taught religious studies and the humanities. The pool of available applicants for his new schools lacked the basic skills in math and science needed for modern professional and technical training. Therefore, after establishing military academies and a school of engineering in 1816, Mohammad Ali established preparatory schools in 1825 and elementary schools by 1832. He founded Qasr Al-Aini medical in 1827. By 1835, higher institutes established by Mohammad Ali included schools for agriculture, administration, accounting, music, pharmacy, veterinary medicine, languages, and an industrial school run by the government's Department of War.

The system founded by Mohammad Ali had a European orientation with syllabi and curricula emulating the French model. Instruction was in French with a few courses in Arabic. In the beginning, instructors were recruited from Europe; once Egyptians sent to study abroad returned, they were drafted to teach. By 1880 a central teacher-training institute was opened to prepare the teachers needed to expand the modern system.

Mohammad Ali's attempts to provide an educational system to service his army led to the creation of a system parallel to the religious schools. The Western orientation that characterized the new institutions was not totally welcomed by the people. Conservatives attacked the new system as an affront to Egypt's traditions, values, and culture. But modern education gradually ousted the traditional system.[3]

The arrival of the British colonial forces in Egypt by 1882 changed the educational scene. The British wanted to rule Egypt without allowing it to develop. The educational system suffered from lack of funds. Access to higher education became more limited and higher education became a privilege for the elite.

Trends in Higher Education

The aspirations for nationhood that led to the Orabi revolt succeeded in mobilizing Egyptian leaders to push for the establishment of a privately funded national university in 1908. This university was supposed to enhance the knowledge base and character of the students rather than to train them to become bureaucrats and officers. By 1917 the government of Egypt had decided to unite all the different higher schools into one university. In 1925 Cairo University (originally known as Fuad 1st University), consisting of four colleges, humanities, sciences, medicine, and law, was established. In 1935 the Institute of Agriculture, the higher Commerce Institute, and the Veterinary Medicine Institute were upgraded to colleges and joined to Cairo University. Alexandria University (originally known as Farouk 1st University) was established in 1942. Ain-Shams University (originally known as Ibraheem Pasha University), formed from existing higher institutes of vocational and technical education, was established in Cairo in 1950. In the same year, the Supreme Council of Universities was established to coordinate the activities of higher education. The council was composed of presidents of universities, academic vice-presidents, and ministry officials.

The expansion of the higher education system was quantitative. Qualitatively, little changed; aims and objectives were not changed, nor were the delivery systems. The 1952 revolution, which abolished the monarchy, brought with it a new philosophy of education. The new theme was democratization of education, providing equal educational opportunities based on aptitude and ability to all Egyptians. Educational reforms were introduced, and open access to higher education became available. More universities were established, especially in the rural areas of the country. New vocational, technical, and industrial schools were also created, as were new teacher-training institutes. Assiut University (formerly known as Mohammad Ali University) was conceived of in 1951 but not established until 1957.[4]

Up to the early 1970s institutes of higher education were concentrated in Cairo, the capital city, and two other major urban areas, Alexandria and Assiut, with only a few branch campuses outside these metropolitan areas. The Ministry of Higher Education (MOHE) decided to open new universities to serve other regions of the country. MOHE wanted to make higher education more accessible to people living in rural areas and to involve the universities in the economic development of these rural areas. As a result, Tanta University and Al-Mansoura University were established in 1972, Zagazig University in 1974, and Helwan University in 1975. In 1976, three new universities were established in Al-Minya, Al-Manoufia, and Suez Canal (see Table 1).

The revolution of 1952 was instrumental in expanding technical education at the tertiary level. Higher institutes of technology were established in Egypt to graduate technicians. By 1952 there were nine institutes enrolling 1,500 students.[5] Most of these institutes concentrated on training business graduates. Higher institutes of agriculture and commerce were established in the mid-1950s under the auspices of the Ministry of Higher Education.

After the establishment of the Ministry of Higher Education in 1961, special attention was given to technical institutes. Major reforms were introduced to the curricula to improve their quality. By 1962, there were thirty-nine institutes of higher education. By 1970, a new law was promulgated to increase the number of technical schools, improve their quality, and revise the curriculum. In the early 1980s the government decided to channel more secondary school graduates to technical institutes to meet the changing demands of Egyptian society, and to relieve some of the pressure caused by students seeking to enter universities.

Governance of Higher Education

Tertiary education in Egypt is publicly funded and highly centralized. The Supreme Council of Universities (established in 1950) and the Ministry of Higher Education (es-

tablished in 1961) provide policy guidelines and coordination among universities. The council and the ministry play different roles in fostering higher education. Currently, the council develops general policies, approves new colleges and universities, and oversees the establishment of new specialties and departments to keep pace with the latest developments in different fields of knowledge. It also regulates and sets equitable admissions standards. MOHE handles international cooperation and exchange and monitors Egyptians studying abroad.[6]

The Supreme Council of (technical) Institutes was established to set policies for higher and intermediate institutes; higher institutes offer study programs that take four or five years and intermediate institutes offer programs that take two years. The Supreme Council has been instrumental in planning for the establishment of higher institutes of technology and for the creation of quality teacher-training colleges. It has also planned the revision of the curriculum in all institutes and teacher-training colleges.

The concept of private education is not widely accepted in Egypt, in part because of the orthodox interpretation of the Egyptian constitution, which states that "education is a right for every citizen and should be offered free-of-charge." The constitution, however, did not specify to what level and type of school such free education should extend. Public Law 52 does stipulate that the government has the right to establish a private, tuition-charging higher education institution under its supervision. Currently, the government is studying the question of establishment of a private fee-based university.

At present there is only one private university in Egypt, the American University in Cairo. There are also a few private technical colleges run by private associations, individuals, or religious sects. In 1988 a private four-year higher institute of technology was established. All these schools

Table 1

Overview of Egyptian Universities

University	Year Established	Number of Branches	Number of Colleges	Languages[†]
Ain-Shams	1950	—	13	A
Al-Azhar	970	8	36	A
Alexandria	1942	1	18	A,E
Assiut	1957	3	20	A,E
Cairo	1908	2	30	A,E,F
Helwan	1975	1	18	A,E
Mansoura	1972	1	12	A
Menoufia	1976	—	8	A,E
Minya	1976	—	9	A,E
Suez Canal	1976	3	10	A,E
Tanta	1972	1	13	A,E
Zagazig	1974	1	21	A,E,F
American University in Cairo	1919	—	N.A.	A,E

[†] A = Arabic; E = English; F = French

[††] These data for the number of students and for the number of faculty members are for 1984–1985.

Sources: The Arabic Republic of Egypt, Ministry of Higher Education Statistical Data, 1989 (Mimeograph). Ahmad Fathi Srour, *The Strategy for Developing Education in Egypt,* 1987, pp. 216–224. George I. Za'rour. *Universities in Arab Countries.* The World Bank, 1988, pp. 36–39.

have to follow the policies and guidelines promulgated by MOHE and the two Supreme Councils.

Article 18 of the Egyptian Constitution of 1971 guarantees the independence of higher education institutions and centers of research, provided that these institutions and centers aim to serve the community and to increase its productivity. The independence of higher education is, therefore, tied to its achievement of social goals.[7] The concept of independence as applied to Egyptian institutes of higher education means autonomy in the management of academic affairs; it does not imply total autonomy, since all universities rely on public financing. This concept of semi-independence is shared by most institutions of higher education in the Arab world. Problems arise between higher education and the government because the limits and degrees of academic freedom allowed are nowhere specified. Authorities can interpret this freedom according to their

Table 1 (continued)

Overview of Egyptian Universities

Students 1987–88	Faculty 1987–88	Library Holdings	Academic Calendar	Major Faculties* and Degrees**
108,860	4,835	92,000	Year	A,Ag,Ar,E, Ed,L,M,S
115,294	4,806	80,000	Year	Ag,D,Ed,L, Ln,P,R,S
78,783	4,365	210,000	Semester	A,D,E,Ed,L, M,P,S,Vm
47,139	2,413	N.A.	Semester	Ag,E,Ed,L, M,P,S,Vm
114,396	6,814	1,000,000	Year	Ag,Ar,D,E,L, M,S,Vm
33,091	2,475	920,000	Year	A,E,Ed,S,
46,174	1,998	N.A.	Year	A,Ag,D,E, Ed,L,M,P,S,
17,223	1,014	N.A.	Year	Ag,E,Ed,S,
14,885	1,199	88,500	Semester	A,Ag,E,Ed, M,S
12,176	908	N.A.	—	Ag,E,Ed,M,S,
45,164	1,861	190,000	Year	A,Ed,D,L,M, P,S
75,900	4,008	N.A.	Semester	A,Ag,E,Ed,L, M,P,S,T,Vm
2,587††	149††	185,000	Semester	A,Cs,E,S

* A=Arts
  Ag=Agriculture
  Ar=Architecture
  Cs=Computer Science
  D=Dentistry

E=Engineering
Ed=Education
L=Law
M=Medicine
P=Pharmacy

R=Religious Studies
S=Technician
T=Technology
Vm=Veterinary Medicine

** All award B.A., M.A., and Ph.D., except American University in Cairo, which awards only B.A. and M.A. degrees.

---

needs and, thus, can deny academic freedom when it contradicts their agenda.

Presidents and vice-presidents of Egyptian universities are appointed by the president of the republic, based on nominations by the minister of higher education. The minister of higher education has the power to decide policy measures; he must inform the Supreme Council of Universities, but is not required to gain their approval.

Enrollments

The Egyptian university system consists of thirteen universities with twenty-one branches and two hundred and eight colleges (see Table 1). Latest figures indicate a total enrollment of about 826,100 students, of which 732,921 were undergraduate students. Between 1971/72 and 1980/81 females constituted between 29 percent and 33 percent of the student population (see Table 2). Female enroll-

Table 2

Distribution of Students in Higher Education in the Arab Republic of Egypt by Field of Study
1960–1985

Year	Humanities, Education, and Fine Arts			Law and Social Sciences		
	Number	% Female	% of Total	Number	% Female	% of Total
1960	25,630	23.0	23.9	38,587	13.0	36.1
1965	36,119	31.0	20.6	59,393	22.0	33.9
1970	49,488	35.0	22.7	65,924	31.0	30.2
1974	100,467	37.0	26.4	134,076	31.0	35.2
1980	144,529	43.4	27.3	193,805	28.2	36.7
1985	170,131	N.A.	31.4	225,520	N.A.	41.7

Note: Totals do not always add up to 100% since a small number of students, whose fields of study were not identified, is not included.

ments in certain colleges, such as education, liberal arts, and mass communication, exceed male enrollments.

Distribution of students by field of study shows that, in 1985/86, 31.4 percent were enrolled in the humanities, education, or fine arts, 44.7 percent were enrolled in law or social sciences, and 26.9 percent were enrolled in natural sciences, medical sciences, engineering, or agriculture. Egypt enrolls a smaller percentage of science students than most other Arab countries; average enrollment in science, medical, and technical fields for the Arab world for the same period was about 37 percent. The increase in enrollments in the humanities and social sciences over the last twenty-five years may be attributed to the expansion of the system and the pressures to admit more students to higher education, for it is easier, and much less expensive, to increase student numbers in these areas. Some of the decrease in enrollments in the sciences, along with the drop in the absolute number of enrollees, can be attributed to the efforts of MOHE to improve quality by lowering student-teacher ratios.

Table 3 shows that business colleges attracted the highest number of enrollees. This situation may be attributed to the new economic orientation of the country, for Egypt is now moving from a socialist to an open-market economy (*Infitah*). Law and arts colleges attracted the second and third largest number of enrollees, followed by education, engineering, agriculture, medicine, and veterinary medicine colleges, which witnessed a slight but gradual decrease in enrollees, prompted by an effort to improve the quality of instruction.

Student-teacher ratios have been increasing to meet the increased demand for higher education: in law colleges the ratio is 105:1; in business colleges 61:1; and in education colleges 27:1.[8] A review of Table 4 and Table 5 shows that, between 1981/82 and 1984/85, enrollments increased by 8.9 percent, 5.6 percent, and 3.4 percent, while number of faculty in the same period increased by 4.4 percent, 3.2 percent, and 4.6 percent, respectively. These figures show that faculty development and recruitment are not matching the ever-increasing number of students enrolled,

Table 2 (continued)

Distribution fo Students in Higher Education in the Arab Republic of Egypt by Field of Study 1960–1985

Natural and Medical Sciences, Engineering, and Agriculture			Total		
Number	% Female	% of Total	Number	% Female	% of Total
41,169	9.0	38.5	106,830	17.0	98.5
79,733	15.0	45.0	175,245	21.0	99.5
102,966	17.0	47.1	218,278	27.0	100.0
146,474	22.0	38.4	381,017	29.0	100.0
185,621	26.8	35.1	528,751	31.8	99.1
145,238	N.A.	26.9	540,889	N.A.	100.0

Sources: UNESCO Statistical Yearbooks for relevant years; Ahmad Fathi Srour, *The Strategy for Developing Education in Egypt,* 1987, p. 219.

thus affecting the quality of teaching. Facilities are not keeping up with the ever-increasing demands on the higher education system. The high density of students in some colleges is affecting the proper utilization of laboratories and workshops. The Business College of Ain-Shams University, for example, has over 34,000 enrollees, and the Medical College at Cairo University has about 6,300 students.

Enrollments in tertiary education in Egypt outside the university system have been improving.[9] In an effort to diversify higher education and produce highly qualified technicians and professionals, MOHE has been trying to increase enrollment in higher institutes and intermediate colleges. The share of enrollees in these technically oriented institutes and colleges has been increasing from 14.2 percent of total enrollments in 1982/83 to 20.6 percent in 1986/87. The gradual growth in technical institutes coincides with a general decline in annual growth at the tertiary level. Between 1981/82 and 1985/86, annual growth in tertiary education dropped from 8.2 percent to 1.8 percent (see Table 6).

Issues and Trends in Higher Education

Higher education in Egypt has passed through many phases in which its aims, objectives, and orientation changed. In the beginning, higher education aimed at serving the faith by producing religious leaders at Al-Azhar. Next came the aim of serving the state by training officers, professionals, and bureaucrats in Mohammad Ali's colleges and higher institutes. The founders of the National University (1908) aimed at serving the individual by attempting to cater to his intellectual, aesthetic, and cultural well-being, but could only reach a few students—mainly, from the social elite. The revolution of 1952 aimed at democratizing higher education: making it tuition-free, equitable, and available to the masses. Then came the planning decades of the 1960s and 1970s, when higher education was supposed to meet the developmental goals of the society. To encourage entry to higher education and to serve communities, new colleges and universities were established in different provinces of the country. Graduates were guaranteed government jobs. During this period special attention was given to the establishment of intermediate colleges and higher institutes to serve the development needs of the country.

Egyptian universities used to be the flagship institutions of higher education in the Arab world, but rapidly rising enrollments combined with shrinking financial resources and the stagnation in the economy to severely damage the higher education system. Overexpansion of the Egyptian university system, growing num-

bers of students, the outdated libraries and poorly equipped laboratories, a brain drain, and scarce resources have undoubtedly affected the quality of tertiary education by lowering productivity. It became necessary in the last few years to introduce qualitative measures to remedy the situation. Such measures include a long-range linkage program with American universities financed by the the United States Agency for International Development, bilateral collaborative research efforts with major European and Asian institutions, and the establishment of a National Center for the Development of Higher Education

Table 3

Number of Students by Field of Study*

College	1981–82	1982–83	1983–84	1984–85	1985–86
Agriculture	35,176	34,569	33,250	32,131	31,717
Arabic Studies	8,428	7,712	9,372	10,065	9,843
Archaeology	1,083	991	972	934	930
Art Education	5,549	5,512	5,687	5,873	5,797
Arts	61,211	67,997	70,337	66,819	66,169
Business	125,025	134,052	142,956	145,297	143,821
Communications	1,047	1,190	1,286	1,423	1,422
Dentistry	3,858	3,793	3,638	3,421	3,281
Economics & Political Science	1,234	1,186	1,186	1,168	1,094
Education	63,399	68,392	74,233	75,927	74,918
Engineering	49,457	49,583	49,140	48,689	48,123
Home Economics	1,143	491	1,231	1,324	1,312
Law	66,793	72,104	76,495	79,025	78,090
Linguistics	1,630	1,653	1,695	1,802	1,750
Medicine	33,074	30,688	27,531	26,819	26,249
Music Education	496	534	594	675	553
Natural Therapy	419	382	342	308	328
Nursing	892	1,000	1,253	1,436	1,422
Pharmacy	8,172	7,705	7,393	6,888	6,776
Physical Education	4,816	5,339	5,765	6,419	6,562
Sciences	20,850	21,206	21,371	21,366	21,327
Social Science	2,556	2,224	2,376	2,529	2,515
Tourism and Hotel Management	532	603	740	887	875
Veterinary Medicine	6,703	6,584	6,437	6,094	6,015
Women's Colleges	5,445	5,477	5,952	6,020	5,960
Total	508,438	531,667	551,333	553,313	546,849

* Al-Azhar University and the American University in Cairo are not included.

Source: Ahmad Fathi Srour, *The Strategy for Developing Education in Egypt,* 1987, p. 214.

Table 4

Graduate Studies Enrollment by Level and Number of Graduates

Year	Enrollments				Graduates			
	Diploma	M.A.	Ph.D.	Total	Diploma	M.A.	Ph.D.	Total
1975–76	16,854	10,915	4,546	32,315	3,214	1,434	561	5,119
1981–82	25,034	26,331	7,325	58,690	2,890	3,540	1,148	7,578
1982–83	23,456	24,911	8,973	57,340	3,418	3,799	1,359	8,576
1983–84	27,594	25,354	8,386	61,334	3,739	3,997	1,254	8,990
1984–85	35,513	30,665	8,804	74,982	4,161	4,225	1,301	9,687
1985–86	41,542	33,542	9,023	84,097	—	—	—	—

Source: Ahmad Fathi Srour, *The Strategy for Developing Education in Egypt*, 1987, pp. 220–221.

(NCDHE). In an attempt to improve both quality and productivity in higher education and to increase its relevance to the economic and social development of Egypt, this center—established by the Ministry of Higher Education—is entrusted with four tasks: upgrading policy and planning, enhancing curriculum methods and materials, upgrading academic management, and increasing management information capabilities and data bases.

Admission to tertiary education is centralized through three offices: one under the auspices of the Supreme Council of Universities, another under the Supreme Council of Institutes, and a third that handles Al-Azhar. More restrictive admission policies are supposed to curb enrollments in universities and direct a larger number of high school graduates to higher technical institutes. The aim of these policies is to reorient university admissions to meet local and regional needs and to avoid unemployment problems.

Applicants are assigned to universities, colleges, and institutes using grades obtained at the secondary schools' completion exam (a nationally administered examination, based on the last year of studies). Students' aptitudes, abilities, and other factors are considered only for certain colleges, such as education, physical education, fine arts, applied arts, and music.

Faculty recruitment has not kept up with the increasing pool of students. Institutional financial constraints prevent the hiring of necessary numbers of faculty members and low salaries cause many of the best-qualified people to seek employment elsewhere. It is not uncommon to find hundreds of students enrolled in one class, especially in the nonprofessional schools and colleges. Faculty members often teach in more than one university in order to improve their income. In many instances, faculty members spend most of their time commuting and/or working in more than one job. All this leads to poor performance. Financial pressures often force full professors to teach introductory courses in which enrollments are high, thus providing a good source of income through the sale of their books and/ or notes to students. Shortages in faculty lead to increased teaching loads and poor supervision of graduate students.

The proliferation of higher education in other parts of the Arab world has had a negative effect on higher education in Egypt. Arab universities, especially in the oil-rich countries, attract many of the better, more qualified Egyptian faculty members. MOHE has been trying to regulate the flow of its faculty members abroad by imposing a four-year maximum period of work outside the country. However, many faculty members opt to resign from their university posts in order to serve as visiting professors in other countries. The main reason for this brain drain is financial reward; other reasons include greater availability of research facilities and funds, and smaller classes.

Faculty promotion is another area of discontent in Egyptian universities. Rules and regulations that govern promotions vary from one institution to another. Well-established institutions, especially those in metropolitan areas, normally are more prestigious and are highly sought after. In order to encourage faculty members to join colleges and faculties in newly established institutions, a fewer number of years of service is required as part of the promotion process. Faculty members who cannot get a promotion in their own institutions often try to gain a second appointment in a less-known university in order to get promoted.

Faculty promotion regulations follow the traditional, rigid British system. Seniority, rank, number of publications, and service to the community are prerequisites for promotion. It takes at least ten to twelve years for an assistant professor to become a full professor. To qualify for a senior position in the management and administration of a university, a professor usually must serve a minimum of five years as a full professor. Such prerequisites for senior management positions lead many university managers to retire before serving their full term in office.

Egyptian universities are autonomous institutions, headed by a president, who is assisted by three vice-presidents (one for graduate studies and research, one for student affairs, and one for community development), and a secretary general, who handles fiscal and administrative affairs, and the institution is governed by a university council. This council, chaired by the president, is composed of the vice-presidents, the secretary general, college deans, and five public figures. There are two auxiliary councils: one for student affairs, headed by the vice-president and composed of the vice-deans for student affairs, an assistant secretary general, and five public figures, and the other for graduate studies and research, headed by the vice-president and composed of the vice-deans for graduate studies and research, an assistant secretary general, and five public figures. Individual colleges have structures similar to the universities: dean, vice-deans, college registrar, and the college council. The college council is composed of a dean, vice-deans, registrar, chairs of departments, senior professors, and the most senior associate and assistant professors in the college. College councils may have external members from related ministries and the private sector.

Table 5

Number of Faculty by Rank

Year	Professor	Associate Professor	Assistant Professor	Sub-Total	Instructor	Assistant	Sub-Total	Total
1975–76	1,542	1,534	2,528	5,604	3,523	5,931	9,454	15,058
1980–81	2,587	2,507	4,577	9,751	6,301	7,831	14,132	23,883
1981–82	2,725	2,786	5,033	10,544	6,886	8,073	14,959	25,503
1982–83	2,919	2,844	5,324	11,087	7,361	8,183	15,544	26,631
1983–84	3,189	2,911	5,621	11,721	7,643	8,121	15,764	27,485
1984–85	3,570	3,209	5,888	12,667	8,109	7,978	16,087	28,754
1987–88	5,119	4,821	8,077	18,017	10,437	8,252	18,689	36,706

Source: Ahmad Fathi Srour, *The Strategy for Developing Education in Egypt*, 1987, pp. 222–223.

Table 6

Number of Students in Tertiary Education in Egypt by Level and Type of Institution

Year	Total Enrollment	Universities	Higher Institutes (4-Year)	Intermediate Colleges (2-Year)	Annual Growth	Population	Percent of Enrollment in Tertiary Education
81–82	698,692	589,562	55,782	53,348	8.2%	43,465,000	1.61
82–83	746,896	632,360	59,423	55,113	6.9%	44,673,000	1.67
83–84	790,895	667,987	65,256	57,652	5.9%	45,913,000	1.72
84–85	814,620	690,726	85,630	58,264	30%	46,958,000	1.73
85–86	829,100	668,849	101,394	58,857	1.8%	48,189,000	1.72
86–87	793,101	629,723	102,793	60,585	4.3%	49,012,000	1.61
87–88	na	824,080	na	na	na	50,776,180	—

Sources: Ahmad Fathi Srour, *The Strategy for Developing Education in Egypt*, 1987, p. 215. The Arabic Republic of Egypt, Ministry of Higher Education Statistical Data, 1989 (Mimeograph).

Universities enjoy considerable autonomy in running their own programs within budgetary limitations. This tradition, good as it is, led to variations among universities that had negative effects on the system of higher education. One example that illustrates this issue is the different models that regulate academic years and requirements. Egyptian universities follow different models, including a full-year program, a semester-based program, and a credit-system program. The variations may be attributed to institutional tradition and philosophy. However, most of these philosophies and aims have not been revised to reflect changes in the needs and/or orientations of Egyptian higher education as a whole. The result is a mix of systems that makes transfer of students from one college to another, even within the same institution, next to impossible without the loss of credit. The Supreme Council of Universities is trying to coordinate program matters to facilitate, among other things, student transfers.

Methods of instruction and the reference materials available are another problem area. Most Egyptian students depend mainly on textbooks and on notes dictated by teachers. Lecturing and rote memorization are still the main mode of education.

Textbooks are, on the whole, outdated. To ensure equity and facilitate student access to textbooks, universities subsidize the production of textbooks. An Egyptian paperback textbook of four to five hundred pages is sold to students at a cost of $3.00 or less. Some university textbooks are produced by MOHE and are distributed free of charge or at a nominal cost. Because of serious shortages in library holdings, students face the problem of having to depend on textbooks and lecture notes as their main source of information.

Pressured by time and the large number of students, many faculty members depend on lecturing as the main mode of delivery. Faculty-student interaction rarely takes place. End-of-course exams are the main method of evaluation. Exams normally are geared toward testing students' memories rather than their analytical skills or problem-solving abilities. A student's creativity is hardly challenged.

Such approaches rarely encourage students to stretch their capabilities or explore their potential. As long as these practices continue Egypt will never realize one of the central goals of its educational reform, which is the preparation of "a generation of inventors and creative thinkers."

Table 7

Enrollment Distribution by Level, Type of Program, and University 1987–1988

| University | Undergraduate Studies | | | Graduate Studies Enrolled | | | |
	Admitted	Enrolled	Graduated	Diploma	M.A.	Ph.D.	Total
Ain-Shams	9,543	88,259	15,483	13,195	5,890	1,516	20,601
Al-Azhar	12,261	106,689	14,340	4,715	2,780	1,110	8,605
Alexandria	9,038	65,964	12,990	4,959	6,156	1,704	12,819
Assiut	9,139	41,386	7,646	3,729	1,340	684	5,753
Cairo	16,201	97,765	16,439	8,023	6,270	2,338	16,631
Helwan	4,543	30,246	6,595	1,022	1,302	521	2,845
Mansoura	5,716	36,319	7,360	3,027	1,307	521	4,855
Menoufia	3,375	15,755	272	640	608	256	1,468
Minya	5,291	13,633	2,963	226	809	217	1,252
Suez Canal	2,210	9,720	2,007	1,758	512	186	2,456
Tanta	6,953	41,930	8,973	1,694	1,100	435	3,229
Zagazig	10,688	65,255	12,712	4,462	4,753	1,430	10,645
Total	94,958	732,921	108,780	47,450	32,827	10,918	91,159

Source: Arab Republic of Egypt, Ministry of Higher Education Statistical Data, 1989 (Mimeograph).

Graduate education and research are the main vehicles through which a university can contribute to the development of society. While undergraduate studies aim at training students and equipping them with skills, graduate education serves the community through monitoring developments in the field of knowledge, adding to them, and adapting what is best to serve the communal needs. If properly monitored and trained, graduate students are supposed to develop their analytical and creative skills, research capabilities, and independence. In Egyptian universities, graduate studies are taking a second place to undergraduate studies across the board. A high percentage of graduate students are enrolled on a part-time basis. In 1987/88, 11.1 percent of all students enrolled in universities were pursuing graduate studies. Aim-Shams University had the highest percentage of students enrolled in graduate studies (23.3 percent), while Al-Azhar University had the lowest percentage of students enrolled in graduate studies (7.5 percent). Only two institutions had more than 20 percent of their students enrolled in graduate studies; five institutions had less than 10 percent of their students enrolled in graduate studies (see Table 7).

Graduate studies and research in Egyptian universities suffer from lack of attention by faculty members, who are more involved in undergraduate teaching. Faculty who try to put an effort into promoting graduate studies and research are inundated by requests to serve on committees or to advise students. Most research in graduate schools is theoretical in nature and rarely up-to-date, since resources and references are not always available to graduate students. Data bases, computer time, and mastery of foreign languages are scarce in Egyptian graduate schools.[10] Egypt desperately needs a specialized graduate university with sufficient resources to attract the most qualified faculty and graduate students on a full-time basis. The

Table 7 (continued)

Enrollment Distribution by Level, Type of Program, and University 1987–1988

| Diploma | Graduate Studies Graduated | | | % of Graduate Students | Total Enrollment |
	M.A.	Ph.D.	Total		
1,353	682	293	2,328	23.5	108,860
468	451	239	1,158	7.5	115,294
1,042	722	204	1,968	16.3	78,783
387	208	94	689	12.2	47,139
1,280	1,237	446	2,963	14.5	114,396
321	186	95	602	8.6	33,091
431	206	83	720	10.5	46,174
81	45	21	147	8.5	17,223
84	73	34	191	8.4	14,885
238	73	19	330	20.2	12,176
454	239	78	771	7.1	45,164
378	675	178	1,231	16.3	75,900
6,517	4,797	1,784	13,098	11.1	824,080

presence of such an institution could entice some of the faculty members who emigrated from Egypt to return. By reversing the brain drain, Egypt might be able to regain its position as the hub of tertiary education in the region. A graduate studies and research policy should be adopted by all universities. External funding from the private sector should be solicited. Programs should be geared to solving problems and to serving the community.

Higher Education and Employment

In a study of tertiary graduates and job opportunities, Abdel-Maksoud observes that the rapid expansion in higher education in the last three decades, the higher demand for university graduates to meet the goals of development plans, and the external demands exerted on the Egyptian labor force by the wealthy Arab states led to an increasing demand on higher education. This caused the expansion of higher education to get out of hand, leading to large universities with over 100,000 students (see Table 1). Quantity increased at the expense of quality. The higher education system output suffered, and graduates found that they could not get jobs because of their low skill levels. The decline in migration possibilities due to the economic stagnation after the drop in oil prices, coupled with the slow movement of development plans in the country, led to a high rate of unemployment.[11]

University enrollments in aggregate numbers were increasing between 1981/82 and 1983/84. During the following two years enrollments decreased, due to new policies by the government of Egypt to reduce admissions to universities and to increase admissions to the technical institutes and colleges (see Table 6). In 1987/88 enrollments in universities increased by 30.9 percent over the previous year. Some contributing factors were poor flow, repeaters (thanks to a free system!), transfers from other Arab universities (when parents of students had to leave oil-rich countries after their economies slowed down), and backdoor entry via foreign universities. The total aggregate number includes an increasing percentage of foreign students coming from Arab and African countries who seek inexpensive higher education.

Graduates from Egyptian universities gradually increased in number from a low of 86,841 in 1981/82 to a high of 119,216 in 1985/86, then dropped to 115,056 in 1986/87. If we add all the graduates from higher institutes, intermediate colleges, teacher-training institutes, and technical secondary schools to these figures, about 450,000 new graduates enter the labor force annually.[12]

Conclusions

Higher education in Egypt grew rapidly during the period from 1960 to 1989. This was mainly due to the availability of free higher education at an increasing number of institutions spread throughout the nation. The rapid growth in enrollments led to an increase in the number of graduates. This process had two major negative effects: on the one hand, standards dropped because resources were strained; and on the other hand, the government did not have the capacity to employ all the new graduates.

Tertiary education institutions are faced with the task of preparing the manpower required for national development. The balance between the number of degree holders and the capacity of the country to employ these graduates has to be monitored closely. Recent attempts to direct and reduce enrollments have not been very successful, since the streaming of enrollees into fields with current or projected manpower shortages has not been systematically addressed. More secondary school graduates need to be steered into technical programs and career specialties that are needed by society.

Other needs that are plaguing tertiary education in Egypt include low productivity, the lack of relevance of research to the needs of the country, and the absence of sufficient facilities and resources.

Egypt has made strong efforts to improve tertiary education. The system is still not responding properly to the developmental needs of the country. Substantial manpower surpluses are being graduated. Admission objectives must be designed to meet parallel manpower needs. Students should be discouraged from entering certain fields. Selected fields of study need to be strengthened. Streaming enrollments should be geared to meet deficiencies in the labor force structure.

The Ministry of Higher Education has initiated a comprehensive reform of the tertiary system, in which the needs of the many sectors are being reconsidered and recognized. Reform measures include:

○ Pedagogy training of university faculty members before entering the teaching cadre
○ Establishment of curriculum development committees
○ Introduction of advanced college-bound curriculum for secondary schools
○ Increasing linkages between universities and productive sectors
○ Establishment of accreditation systems to assure quality standards in programs
○ Introducing limits to university expansion
○ Encouraging privatization, especially in highly needed fields, such as biotechnology, food and nutrition technology, and agricultural and electronic technologies
○ Considering additional admission criterion measures, such as college admission examinations, and contingency admission (on probation)

Egypt hopes to achieve, through the implementation of such measures, the re-alignment of its higher education system, making it demand-driven and development-oriented.

Notes

1. Ahmad Fathi Srour, *Tatweer Al-Taleem fi Misr: Siyasatoho wa Istratiegiatoho wa Khuttat Tanfeethiya, Al-Taleem Kabl Al-Jamea* (Educational development in Egypt: Policies, strategies, and action plans, pre-college education), 2d ed. (Cairo: ALAHRAM Press, 1989), 12.
2. Byron G. Massialas and Samir A. Jarrar, "Egypt," in *World Education Encyclopedia,* ed. George Kurian (New York: Facts on File Publications, 1988), 353.
3. Ahmad Fathi Srour, *Istratiegiat Tatweer Al-Taleem fi Misr* (The strategy for developing education in Egypt) (Cairo: Central Agency for University School Books, 1987), 12.
4. Amir Bokhtar, *The Development and Expansion of Education in the United Arab Republic* (Cairo: American University in Cairo Press, 1963), 27-28.
5. Ahmad Fathi Srour, *Istratiegiat Tatweer Al-Taleem fi Misr,* 18.
6. Ibid., 49.
7. Ibid., 21.
8. Ibid., 51.
9. Ibid., 16.
10. Ibid., 54–56.
11. Sayed Abdel-Maksoud, *Towards a Policy for Developing Job Opportunities and the Employment of Tertiary Graduates in Egypt* (Mimeograph, 1989), 4-6.
12. Ibid., 8.

Iraq

A. A. Al-Rubaiy

The increase in oil revenues in past years gave Iraq the opportunity to accelerate the process of educational development. These revenues affected educational policies and practices, which in turn affected manpower resources for economic development. Since achieving its independence from Turkish rule after the post-World War I disintegration of the Ottoman empire, Iraq has maintained a system of centralized state control in the educational, political, and economic fields. Iraqi governments have devoted increasing attention to providing not only general, but also higher and specialized education. Although radical changes occurred in government forms and political attitudes following the Iraqi Revolution of July 14, 1958 (when the political system changed from a monarchy to a republic), the concept of centralized government control of the nation's affairs continued to prevail as a necessity for the state to protect the public interest and individual rights and to achieve national unity.

The Educational System and Its Development

Today, the basis of educational policy is clear: "Education must focus comprehensively on the building of an educational system in harmony with the principles and aims of the 17th July Revolution [1968] . . . a system that rears generations infused with the ideals of national and socialist democracy and capable of realizing the ambition of the leading party [BASP]. . . . Time will not be on the

side of the Revolution if we maintain the pace in education of the last ten years.[1]

General education takes place in three stages: primary, intermediate, and secondary. Primary education begins at age six and continues for six years in both single-sex and mixed schools. The former are more prevalent in rural areas, while the latter are becoming the rule in urban localities. Students who complete the sixth grade in primary school proceed to the intermediate level for a further stage lasting three years. Intermediate education follows a broad syllabus, and ends with a public examination. At age fifteen students begin secondary education, which becomes increasingly specialized as the students proceed. Most enter into a general secondary scheme that covers a wide range of subjects during the first year.

Vocational and technical programs in secondary education are available at industrial or agricultural schools; graduates of these schools are awarded a secondary vocational certificate. Alternatively, students can choose to enter commercial schools for a three-year course of study that leads to a secondary commercial certificate. Female secondary students also have the option of studying home economics.

Higher education begins normally at age eighteen years for both male and female students who have earned the secondary certificate and attained a stipulated average grade; this average varies from year to year, but generally exceeds 60 percent for science-based and 70 percent for art-based subjects. Again, a wide range of options exist. Those having a general secondary certificate may find a place in a university or college. Higher education in a broad range of subjects is available at the universities of Baghdad, Basrah, Mosul, Salahiddin (Sulimaniya), Almustansiria, the University of Technology, and the Foundation of Technical Institutes (FTI). FTI offers degree and nondegree courses taught at junior colleges for teachers, science and mathematics centers, and postsecondary technical and vocational institutes.

Enrollment

If progress can be measured by expansion of student enrollment, then the education and training sectors in Iraq have developed substantially from 1968 to 1984. The number of preprimary/kindergarten school children increased from 15,553 in 1967/68 to 76,663 in 1983/84, an annual increase of 25 percent. The number of primary school pupils increased from 990,718 in 1967/68 to 2,698,542 in 1983/84, and reached about three million in 1984/85, an annual increase of 14 percent. The number of students in the technical/vocational schools increased from slightly over 10,000 to well over 77,000; this rate of growth represents a total increase of 65 percent or a 36 percent annual increase.[2] The number of students enrolled in higher education increased from about 11,000 in 1968/69 to over 31,000 in 1979/80, an annual growth rate of 16 percent.

This kind of quantitative expansion in all sectors of education has frequently resulted in a limited utilization of capacity.[3] Despite Iraq's desperate need for increased manpower with technical skills, the use of facilities designed for technical and vocational training has often fallen below 50 percent of the student capacity available.

The number of graduates from universities, colleges, and technical institutes has increased from 6,323 in 1968/69 to 21,404 in 1979/80. The total number of graduates (B.S./B.A. or diploma) during that period was 115,204, distributed among disciplines as follows:

7,712	Medical Sciences: Medicine, Dentistry, Pharmacy
17,270	Engineering and Technology
14,350	Basic Sciences
9,123	Agricultural and Veterinary Studies
20,085	Administration and Economics
34,661	Humanities and Social Sciences
8,309	Education
2,070	Physical Education/Sport Sciences
1,624	Fine Arts[4]

Between 1975 and 1980 the number of male students studying to become teachers declined, while female enrollments in this sector more than doubled. The total number of enrollees increased from slightly over 15,000 to well over 36,000, an average increase of 9 percent per year. This increase was particularly significant for females, whose number increased by an annual rate of 16.5 percent.[5] There are several possible explanations for the reduction in male students attending teacher training schools, not the least of which is the low remuneration paid to teachers and their relative low prestige. Another significant trend is the increased female enrollment in vocational-technical education. The enrollment in 1983/84 was 1,626 in agricultural, 2,498 in industrial, and 18,625 in commercial institutes. Such increases are explained in part by changes in social attitudes toward nonacademic education for women and in part by the low standards required for admission to technical schools.

Parameters of the Higher Education System

From a modest beginning with a single institution in 1908, a comprehensive system of higher education institutions had emerged by the 1980s. Beginning of with a single four-year college of law, the monarchical period experienced a slow expansion of higher education. By 1956 twelve institutions, of varying degrees of sophistication and quality, were in place. These institutions served about one thousand students by 1940, and over five thousand by 1958.[6]

During the Republican period, since 1958, an uneven but demonstrable expansion in higher educational development was clearly in evidence. The present era has witnessed a period of measurable growth both in terms of quantity and quality of higher education development. Six major institutions of higher education have existed since 1987–88, three of which are located in the capital, Baghdad. In addition, five new universities are planned. Expansion has been driven by large increases in the number of high school graduates, the desire to produce a professional class to lead Iraq's development, and the need to serve tertiary demand in Iraq's outlying areas.

The Ministry of Higher Education and Scientific Research, now in charge of university education, planned to admit about 100,000 students by 1985. Students were enrolled as follows: 20,455 in the academic years 1981/82; 21,705 in 1982/83; 22,725 in 1983/84; and 23,230 in 1984/85. The ministry set a target of 91,406 male and female graduates to be distributed in the following manner: 17,159 in 1981/82; 20,447 in 1982/83; 19,768 in 1983/84; and 19,589 in 1984/85.[7]

Primary education is now free and compulsory. The government hoped to enroll all six-year-old boys and girls in primary schools by 1984. This goal has almost been achieved, although not all children who live in the rural areas attend school full time. Rural families are less likely to send girls to school; those who do attend are less likely to go full time or to receive as many years of schooling as boys.

Coping with a massive expansion of students has put pressure on the educational sector and its staff. Student-teacher ratios have climbed. Some schools have had to introduce double sessions (16 per-

cent) and a few have even gone to triple sessions (5 percent). Of 9,477 primary schools in 1979/80, 25 percent were unsuitable.[8]

Lack of Iraqi teachers forced recruitment of non-Iraqi teachers, especially in higher education. But by 1980 over two-thirds of the teaching staff in universities were Iraqis; the rest were Arab expatriates (mainly Egyptians) and foreign personnel. The ratio of Iraqi to non-Iraqi faculty varies from one university to another; for example, in Baghdad University (a leading institution), the indigenous teaching staff in 1980 constituted 92 percent of the total, while in Salahiddin (then Sulimaniya) Iraqis constituted only 59 percent of the staff. The teacher-student ratio also varied. In Baghdad University it was 1 to 18; in Mosul 1 to 16; in Basrah 1 to 20; in Salahiddin 1 to 13; in Al-Mustansiriya 1 to 29; and in the University of Technology 1 to 41 during the 1979/80 academic year. The ratio also varied according to specialization. It was 1 to 12 in medical subjects; 1 to 29 in engineering and technology; 1 to 9 in veterinary medicine and agriculture; 1 to 11 in basic sciences; 1 to 43 in administration and economics; and 1 to 20 for humanities and social sciences.[9]

Undergraduate Education

Universities offer the bachelor's degree in a number of professional fields, most of which require four years of study. Engineering, dental surgery, pharmacy, and veterinary medicine require five years, while medicine and surgery require six years plus an additional year of internship.

During the 1980s English was deleted from the list of required courses in most bachelor's degree programs. Arab National Social Studies, sometimes called Cultural Education, is now a required course in all bachelor's degree programs, requiring sixty hours of instruction per year for four years. Beginning with the 1986/87 academic year, two hours of compulsory study in computer science were added to the first year, with two additional hours planned in 1987/88 for each bachelor's degree program.

Graduate Studies

The most common degree is the master of science, offered in most areas including education. It requires two years of study, one year of course work and one year of thesis research.

Doctor of philosophy degree programs require three years of study beyond a master's degree, with one year devoted to course work and two years to dissertation research. Admission is highly selective: most departments have only one or two doctoral candidates at any one time. Usually, the doctoral thesis panel includes a foreign professor.

For all practical purposes undergraduate studies tend to transmit information rather than produce knowledge. Furthermore, these studies tend to provide the students with limited opportunity for indepth learning and research. Thus, it is a great challenge for the graduate programs to provide opportunities for conducting research and developing knowledge needed in the process of change and development. The government recognizes that any country that does not create the facilities and foster the intellectual atmosphere for such studies risks remaining at the mercy of the advanced countries.

Since 1960 graduate education has expanded significantly. The number of students admitted to graduate-level programs increased from fourteen in 1960/61 to over 1,047 in 1975.[10] The master's program now provides a wider range of subjects. The University of Baghdad (UB) is no longer the only university to offer graduate programs. In 1970 the University of Baghdad initiated Ph.D. programs in three fields: history, geography, and chemistry. Enrollment in the graduate programs is more balanced than in the undergraduate programs. The official policy has tended to encourage enrollment in the fields of

medicine and science since their graduates can be absorbed easily into the expanding economy. The quality of these graduates tends to be equal to or perhaps better than those of other Arab universities. The theses produced tend to be of good quality and show extensive research and thoroughness. Most theses tend to deal with Iraq; by focusing on Iraq the researcher often solves problems related to his or her country's needs. Students pursuing graduate work who are not working or receiving support from any agency receive support from the government.

Graduate programs in general face a number of challenges: a shortage of qualified staff, a shortage of library and laboratory facilities, and duplication of programs. For example, each new university rushes to establish its own graduate programs, despite countrywide, critical shortages in staffs and facilities. This rush is motivated by the desire for prestige and the urge to compete with the University of Baghdad. Most students take much more than the two years required for a master's program; this failure to proceed through the program in the expected time is caused by the shortage of faculty and facilities. The drop-out rate for graduate students and the limited female enrollment in undergraduate programs. The basic reason for this low percentage is graduate programs are also serious concerns. In the 1970s females represented 24 percent of the graduate program enrollment, significantly less than their percentage of enrollment in undergraduate programs. The basic reason for this low percentage is that many women choose marriage after obtaining an undergraduate degree, and consequently are discouraged from pursuing advanced degrees.

Technical Institutes

The objective of the technical institutes is to train middle-level technicians in fields such as agriculture, business administration, forestry, industrial training, laboratory technology, and technology. While most institutes offer a variety of academic programs, some specialize in one area, such as agriculture.

The first technical institutes were established in the early 1950s to meet the growing need for highly trained technicians. By 1969 there were five technical institutes, all located in Baghdad: administration, applied arts, technology, agriculture, and medicine. By 1972 the institutes admitted 940 students.

In 1976 the Foundation of Technical Institutes was established as a division of the Ministry of Higher Education and Scientific Research, and all of the technical institutes became independent institutions under its jurisdiction. Since then the number of technical institutes and their enrollments have increased dramatically. In 1975/76 there were eight institutes with 285 faculty members and 5,766 students. In 1978/79 there were seventeen institutes with 9,328 students; in 1984/85 there were twenty-one institutes with an estimated 24,000 students; and in 1986/87 there were twenty institutes with an estimated 50,000 students. The technical institutes currently enroll about 25 percent of postsecondary students and are expected to eventually enroll more than 50 percent of all postsecondary students.[11]

Private Institutions

Private institutions at the postsecondary level, including private universities, are now being developed. In 1988 four new private universities were established, partly by a reorganization of existing private colleges and technical institutes and partly by the establishment of new colleges. In 1987 the government approved the reintroduction of private institutions at the higher education level, each to be governed by its own board of trustees. A pattern of allowing and forbidding private institutions has recurred over the years in Iraq. When private universities are disallowed, they are usually reorganized into colleges and attached to one of the universities. Private institutions are required to follow government policies governing the public institutions. The government seems to be reintroducing private institutions as part of its general plan to encourage the private sector of the economy.

Admission Procedures

A preparatory school baccalaureate is required for admission to any university program, while a preparatory school baccalaureate or a vocational school baccalaureate is required for admission to any technical institute. The type of institution and academic program to which a student can be admitted depends upon the type of baccalaureate received (literary, scientific, agricultural, commercial, industrial, or veterinary), and upon the scores received on the baccalaureate examinations.

Admission to all university programs is selective. For university admission, a preparatory baccalaureate score of 504 (an average of 84 percent in each of six subjects) is considered average. A score below 390 (an average of 67 percent) is considered weak.[12] Some scientific programs, such as engineering and medicine, have minimum grade requirements (usually 70) for specified individual subjects, including biology, chemistry, mathematics, or physics. Programs in art require a portfolio, in music require an audition, and in physical education require evidence of physical fitness.

In 1986 the minimum baccalaureate total scores of students admitted to the University of Baghdad ranged from a high of 569 for the College of Medicine (an average of 94.8 percent in each subject on the preparatory baccalaureate, scientific section) to a low of 438 for the Department of Geography in the College of Arts (an average of 73 percent in each subject on the preparatory baccalaureate, literacy section).

University programs in medicine, architectural engineering, civil engineering, and other engineering fields are the most popular and the most highly selective. They are followed in selectivity by university programs in other science fields, programs in nonscience fields (administration and economics, agriculture, arts, education, humanities, social studies), programs offered by the technical institutes, programs offered by postpreparatory teacher training institutes, and programs offered by the specialized institutions administered by other ministries (such as midwifery, military, police science, nursing, and social welfare).

Students apply for admission to a specific department, not to a college, university, technical institute, or specialized institution. A student can list several department and university choices in order of preference, such as electrical engineering at the University of Baghdad, electrical engineering at the University of Mosul, physics at the University of Baghdad, physics at the University of Mosul, and electrical engineering at a technical institute.

Each department of each institution has an enrollment quota, determined in relation to Iraq's Development Plan. The number of students to be admitted is set annually via a joint consultation between the department, the college, the university, the Ministry of Higher Education and Scientific Research, and the Ministry of Planning. In popular fields, such as electrical engineering, most students do not gain admittance to their first- and second-choice program or department. In an unpopular field, such as geography, students who list a geography program or department as their third or fourth choice might well be admitted because so few students apply that the quota is not filled by first- and second-choice applicants.

For the 1985/86 academic year, an applicant whose father or husband was killed in the Iran-Iraq war was admitted to any science program if the baccalaureate score was 420 or higher, and to any college of arts if the baccalaureate score was 300 or higher, no matter what the competitive requirements for regular applicants might have been. Beginning with the 1986/87 academic year, these applicants received a five-point bonus in each subject (30 points total) when their baccalaureate grades were considered for admission to bachelor's degree programs.

In 1986 the technical institutes and universities were instructed to accept all eligible preparatory school graduates. Thus, everyone who achieves a preparatory examination score of 300 or higher is guaranteed admission to some type of tertiary-level program. (Preliminary discussion is underway to reverse this policy.)

In a typical year, 45 percent to 55 percent of the preparatory school graduates do not make the cutoff for admission to a university program. If they wish, they can be placed at a technical institute, a postpreparatory teacher training institute, or a specialized postpreparatory institute supervised by one of the other ministries. Much of the increase in enrollment in postsecondary institutions during the past ten years has occurred at these institutions, particularly at the technical institutes.

Recent Significant Developments

There have been a number of fundamental developments in Iraqi education with relevance to higher education in the last twenty years. From age six every child is entitled to free education. This task was accomplished through the Compulsory Primary Education Act of 1974, which was implemented in 1978 and achieved its goal of total enrollment in 1983/84, when 2.7 million Iraqi children were in primary school. The National Campaign against

Illiteracy begun in 1980 has since enrolled 2.25 million males and females, aged fifteen to forty-five, in literacy classes. Educational opportunities for females have been greatly expanded although segregation of the sexes is still maintained at the secondary level. These trends were aimed at overcoming personnel shortages associated with economic development.

The government recognizes that education can be used to raise the productivity of the Iraqi labor force and to equip the country with indigenous skilled labor. Unfortunately, the development of the educational system in line with the requirements of industry and the economy has been hindered by rural traditionalism. Even so, considerable progress has been made at all levels of education.

Literacy Campaigns

The Revolution of 1968 marked a new era in the campaign against illiteracy and has been characterized by a serious mobilization of government support and resources. The party believes that literacy is the foundation for social change and development, and a prerequisite for the elimination of backwardness and exploitation. The report of the party's 1974 Eighth Regional Congress states: "The illiteracy of vast sections of the population, especially in rural areas, is one of the most formidable obstacles to the political, economic, and social progress of the country. As long as illiteracy rates remain high, it will be impossible to raise the standards of the people or to build a progressive society capable of tackling the complex problems of our era."[13]

The BASP recognized that gains in literacy had been inadequate due to the noncompulsory aspect of primary education. The government therefore concluded that primary schooling should be compulsory in Iraq. In 1974 a Free Education Law was enacted under which the government undertook to underwrite all

education costs from kindergarten through university level.

As a result of determined government effort, the number of primary schools increased during ten years after 1968 by 71 percent; secondary schools by 83 percent; and universities by 19 percent. The number of students enrolled in primary schools increased by 107 percent; those in secondary schools by 83 percent; and those at the universities by 110 percent.

The Literacy Law of 1971 provided for the formation of a Supreme Literacy Board to carry out the literacy campaign. As of 1973 it was estimated that 40 percent of the males and 76 percent of the females in the fifteen to forty-five age group were illiterate. In order to lend full government support to the effort, literacy was made a condition for employment in government positions.[14]

Enabling legislation was passed in 1976 to implement Article 27 of the 1970 Interim Constitution calling for free, universal, and compulsory primary schooling. Becoming effective in 1978, Public Law 118 mandated free compulsory education for all six- to fifteen-year-olds. The law established a six-year primary level and a three-year intermediate level of schooling. In May 1978 the National Comprehensive Campaign for Literacy was launched by the BASP, "making the eradication of illiteracy a national issue to which all the country's energies on both official and popular levels would be oriented," with the president of the republic as the supreme chairman of the campaign.[15]

By September 1980 Iraq claimed to have entered a new era, as illiteracy was well on its way to extinction; over one and a half million citizens had been freed from the burden of illiteracy. This figure represents 76.4 percent of the 2.3 million involved.[16] Considering the size and complexity of the task, not to mention the burdens imposed on Iraq society by an extended war, an important step forward has been taken.

Role of Women

Women had a limited role in the pre-1968 period. Recent economic realities have compelled women to abandon their traditional role and join the country's social and economic expansion. One result of this development has been the doubling of the number of nursery schools throughout Iraq.

All universities in today's Iraq are co-educational, and many more Iraqi women proceed to higher education. Today, women in universities represent an estimated 33 percent of the total enrollment.

The overall general low enrollment of women in the past was partially due to fewer women graduates from high school. Even in the mid-1970s women enrolled in high schools represented less than 30 percent of the total high school population. Iraqi society still tends to discourage women from pursuing a college education. During the last two decades, however, Iraqis have experienced radical change in many traditional beliefs, including the education of women. Women's high school enrollment has expanded faster than men's, which will eventually increase the enrollment of women in the universities.

Until recently, the overwhelming majority of women entered women's colleges or specialized in the humanities. These choices reflected their specialization in high school, when women tended to concentrate in the liberal arts fields, and Iraqi society's attitude that the liberal arts were an appropriate field of study for women. Since 1980 the percentage of women in science and the related fields has been increasing to an estimated 50 percent.[17] Changes in women's opportunities for obtaining education reflect changes in Iraqi society. More and more women are seeking jobs outside the home that require training only made available at the higher levels of education.

This increasing enrollment in science and related fields, however, has been uneven. There is a tendency for women to choose pure science and medicine more frequently than such fields as engineering and agriculture. Most of the women enrolled in colleges continue to come from such large cities as Baghdad, Basra, and Mosul.[18] These cities have their own universities, of course, so that women do not have to go away from home and stay in dormitories, and high school education for women in these cities is more available than elsewhere.

Higher Education and the Political System

The paramount aim of Iraqi education today is to realize the ambitions of the Arab nation and the Arab Baath Socialist Party's principles of unity, liberty, and socialism. The responses of the state to the problem of education can be seen from the party literature. The party first came to power in 1963 and has held power continuously since 1968. The 1974 political report of the Eighth Congress of the Arab Baath Socialist Party of Iraq stated the central goals in the field of education: to eradicate illiteracy; to make education, and in particular primary education, a right available to all; to ensure free education to all; and to coordinate and link education to national development needs.[19]

Shared Administration

A unique system of administrative management exists in Iraqi higher education at the present. While such institutions of postsecondary education as teacher training, vocational, commercial, home economic, and agriculture programs are under the supervision of the Ministry of Education, all other higher education institutions are under the supervision of the Ministry of Higher Education and Scientific Research. (Administration of first-level education and literacy programs are under the Ministry of the Interior, while the Ministry of Education has direct control over secondary-level education.) The Ministry of Higher Education and Scientific Research supervises the two major groups of institutions, the universities and the technical institutes. It makes most decisions concerning university curricula, admissions requirements, facilities, financing, and assignment of faculty members. This ministry supervises the existing ten universities and twenty technical institutes. Universities have some responsibility for designing their own curricula, but within ministry guidelines, while those for the technical institutes are set by the Foundation of Technical Institutes.

Educational policy is formulated at the national level by the Revolutionary Command Council, which represents the public interest. Policy adoption, however, is the domain of the Ministry of Education. Educational policy is implemented through the local administrations, inspectors, and teachers.

While the universities are administered by the Ministry of Higher Education and Scientific Research, they are autonomous in most professional and technical matters. The ministry finances both the universities and postsecondary technical education.

Faculty

The qualifications of the faculty in higher education are respectable, and much improved from previous eras. University and technical institute professors are assigned to their positions by the Ministry of Higher Education and Scientific Research, after consultation with university or technical institute administrators. Most professors have completed graduate work at foreign universities. Some professors, especially in highly specialized areas, are foreigners. Approximately three hundred foreign scholars come to Iraq each year to serve as short-term visiting professors for periods ranging from three weeks to three months or longer.

Two valuable or innovative research papers are required for promotion from assistant lecturer to lecturer, three for promotion from lecturer to assistant professor, four for promotion to associate professor, and another four for promotion to professor. The typical full-time teaching load of a faculty member is twenty to twenty-five hours per week of lecture and laboratory instruction. Only associate professors and professors are allowed to supervise the research of doctoral students.

To meet the need for new faculty members caused by a dramatic increase both in the number of programs and in the enrollment of students in 1986/87 and 1987/88, employees of government agencies who have master's or doctoral degrees have been added to the faculties as part-time professors. They are required to devote six hours per week in addition to their regular employment responsibilities. Those with master's degrees serve as part-time professors at the technical institutes and in the bachelor's degree programs at the universities, while those with doctoral degrees serve as part-time professors in master's and doctoral programs or as thesis advisors.

Most colleges at each university are self-contained—the college's faculty members teach all required and elective courses that a student may take in the college's degree program. As a result, each university (with few exceptions) is likely to have four or more departments of mathematics, physics, and other commonly required subjects.

Faculty members are eligible for a one-year sabbatical after four years of service at the rank of assistant professor or higher. A research project approved by the department, the college, the university, and the Ministry of Higher Education and Scientific Research is required before a sabbatical is granted. Although promotion of faculty is based upon research, salaries are based upon seniority. The retirement age is sixty-three, but it can be extended to sixty-five, and retirees can give lectures after retirement for extra income.

Education and Ideology

Nationalism and education have had a long history of interaction in Iraq. Nationalism has exerted particular kinds of influence on educational practices. It is considered essential to the modern state since it can promote unity and social cohesiveness.

Modern Arab nationalism is essentially an educational movement. While Iraqi education has sustained nationalism, it has in turn been influenced by it. Manifestations of nationalism and their influence on the Iraqi educational system evolved in three areas: degree of reliance on foreign expertise and the utilization of foreign personnel, the distribution of enrollments, and the education of minority groups.[20]

Nationalism manifested itself at an early age as a hostile attitude toward foreign elements. However, since the mandate period (1921–32), foreign expertise and skills have been introduced for educational development. Throughout successive periods, nationalism can be seen in the desire to reduce or eliminate reliance on foreign expertise. In spite of the Western orientation of the ruling elite during the monarchical period, foreign personnel employed by the Ministry of Education gradually decreased. During the republican era, despite the intensity of nationalistic feelings that accompanied it, a wide range of new foreign contacts with socialist countries was sought. These new contacts not only encouraged the utilization of foreign expertise, but they provided new opportunities for students to study and train abroad. However, the sending of graduate student missions to socialist countries did not totally eliminate the practice of sending students to educational institutions in the Western nations. Iraqi nationalism

has gradually begun to abandon its previous negative attitude toward foreign elements. Today's Iraq is a more tolerant nation.

Iraqi society is a mosaic of elements based on differing religious, linguistic, and cultural traditions. Among all the institutions and practices that can make a significant contribution to the stability and social integration of Iraqi society, education looms large. Cultural and linguistic harmony and national feelings can be fostered through education. The educational system remains the most effective means of creating an ideal of national unity. Since the coming of the Republican era, the general trend is unmistakably toward secularization of education.

Problems and Prospects

The common feature of all forms of education in Iraq is a tremendous growth in educational facilities and opportunities. Problems include an imbalance favoring academic education at the expense of badly needed vocational/technical education, the relative reluctance on the part of students (especially male students) to take full advantage of vocational training, and quantitative growth that often has not been accompanied by qualitative improvement in staffing and course offerings.

In secondary education students manifest a preference for humanities tracks as opposed to scientific tracks. Women in particular avoid scientific and technical studies. This preference continues into higher education, where scientific and technical remain undersubscribed.

While the figures show an increased proportion of total enrollments, they disguise a large proportion (nearly 50 percent) of students taking degree courses that lead to white-collar jobs (administration/economics/social sciences). The growth of general secondary education enrollments has placed increased burdens upon university placement in literary-based, nonvocational courses.

Notes

1. Baath Arab Socialist Party (BASP), *Proceedings of the 8th and 9th Political Reports* (Baghdad, Iraq: Dar Al-Huria Press, 1974, 1982), 167–68.
2. Ministry of Education, *Trends and Parameters of the Educational Sectors in Iraq* (Baghdad, Iraq: Ministry of Education, 1981).
3. Ministry of Planning, *Annual Abstracts of Statistics, 1980* (Baghdad: Republic of Iraq, 1980).
4. Ayad Al-Qazzaz, "Higher Education in Iraq" (A paper presented at the Annual Meeting of the Comparative and International Education Society, New Orleans, 17 February 1977.
5. *Alef-Ba Weekly*, no. 836 (1984), p. 27.
6. Abid Al-Maryati, *A Diplomatic History of Iraq* (New York: Robert Speller & Sons, 1961), 170.
7. Ibid.
8. Ministry of Planning, *Annual Abstracts*, 1980.
9. Ministry of Education, "A Blueprint for Education and Higher Education Sector in Iraq," submitted for the *Educational Debate*, July 1981.
10. Ministry of Planning, *Statistical Abstracts, 1975* (Baghdad: Republic of Iraq: Ministry of Planning, 1975), 408.
11. James S. Frey, *Iraq*. *World Education Series* (Washington, D.C.: American Association of Collegiate Registrars and Admissions Officers, 1988), 39.
12. Ibid., 40.
13. Baath Arab Socialist Party, *Proceedings*, 167–68.
14. Alya Sousa, "The Eradication of Illiteracy in Iraq," in *Iraq: The Contemporary State*, ed. Tim Niblock (New York: St. Martin's Press, 1982), 103.
15. Ministry of Education, *Education in Iraq* (Baghdad, Iraq: General Directorate of Education Planning, 1977).
16. N. Y. Syala, "Strategic Stand for the Question of Literacy and Adult Education in Iraq," *Al-Thawra Newspaper*, 11 February 1983, 3.
17. Abdul Jalil Al-Zawbai and Muhamad Al-Kanam, *Higher Education in Iraq* (Baghdad, Iraq: Al-Hakima Press, 1968), 30.
18. Ministry of Planning, *Statistical Abstracts*, 1971–72 (Baghdad: Republic of Iraq: Ministry of Planning, 1971–72), 275.
19. Baath Arab Socialist Party, *Proceedings*, 1974, 1982.
20. Abdul A. Al-Rubaiy, "Nationalism and Education: A Study of the Nationalistic Tendencies in Iraqi Education" (Ph.D. diss., Kent State University, 1972), 178–80.

Israel

Yaacov Iram

◆

Tertiary education in Israel can be divided into three major subsystems. The main division differentiates statutorily between postsecondary education and higher education. Within the higher education system a distinction is made between university and nonuniversity institutions of higher education.

The term "postsecondary education" refers to vocational or professional training after secondary school that does not necessarily require completion of the state leaving examination (Bagrut), a prerequisite for entry to higher education. The postsecondary subsystem includes a variety of small institutions for the training of technical, nursing, paramedical, clerical, and business professionals as well as most of the primary-level teacher training colleges. Some of these sectors opt for academization, official recognition of higher education status. In 1987 some 34,000 students attended postsecondary institutions, with some 13,700 enrolled in practical engineering and technicians' schools and 12,000 students enrolled in thirty teacher training colleges.[1]

"Higher education," as defined by "The Council for Higher Education Law, 5718–1958," "includes teaching, science, and research" that are conducted in universities and other academic degree-granting institutions.[2] The higher education system in Israel as of 1989 is divided into four distinctive groups. The first group consists of seven universities and the Open University, which is authorized to award only the bachelor's degree. The Planning and Grants Committee (PGC) of the Council for Higher Education (CHE) is responsible for their budgets, as will be discussed later. The second group consists of seven specialized institutions of higher education that are not universities or teacher training colleges. These institutions are authorized to award only the bachelor's degree. They, too, fall under the control of the PGC. The third group consists of six teacher training institutions in the process of acquiring academic status. They have received permission from the Council for Higher Education to award the bachelor of education degree either for the entire institution or for certain programs of study. These institutions are financed by the Ministry of Education and Culture. The Council for Higher Education set up a special permanent subcommittee to oversee their accreditation process. The fourth group includes eight regional colleges, which, in addition to serving as centers of adult education, provide certain academic courses under the academic responsibility of one of the universities, which appoint their teachers and award their degrees. Though these are not independent institutions of higher education, they must be taken into account in any overall review of the system.[3] The regional colleges are financed by the Ministry of Education and Culture and by various local and regional authorities that are supported by the Ministry of the Interior. The Council for Higher Education has appointed a subcommittee to deal with academic courses at regional colleges "in order to make higher education more accessible to broader segments of the population"[4] and as of 1985 made direct allocations to their academic programs. Only the seven universities are authorized to award degrees beyond the bachelor's degree in a variety of fields of study and advanced professional training. The eight "other institutions of higher education" are authorized to award the bachelor's degree only in specified fields of study or training, as shown in Table 1, and the six teacher training colleges award the B.Ed. to teachers for primary and junior high schools (K–9).

Israel does not have liberal arts colleges that specialize in teaching undergraduates. This function is performed by universities that also pursue research and engage in the the training of professionals in law, medicine, engineering, business, and other fields. The typical bachelor's program in the humanities and social sciences is designed for three years of study. The student specializes in two disciplinary fields (departments) provided he or she meets the admission criteria of the two concerned departments. The two fields/departments/disciplines system has no stated rationale; it presumably exists to provide the potential schoolteacher with two school subjects so that he or she will be able to obtain a full-time job in one school. The natural sciences and social sciences departments in many universities are moving gradually toward single-discipline majors. Professional education in law, medicine, engineering, and other fields commences in the first year of studies at the undergraduate level and continues for three and a half to five years. Three years are generally required for the completion of the master's degree. The Ph.D. degree has minimal formal requirements; it is designed individually according to the candidate's research project.

The number of students at the seven university-level institutions reached 67,900 in 1988, an increase of more than 25 percent over the last ten years. Some 60 percent of the students are studying humanities, social sciences, and law, 23.3 percent natural sciences, agriculture, and medicine, and 16.7 percent engineering. Some 72 percent are studying for the first degree (bachelor's), 21 percent for the second degree (master's), 5 percent for the doctorate, and 2 percent for academic diplomas, mainly secondary school teaching diplomas. The thirteen nonuniversity institutions of higher education enrolled some

Table 1

Fields of Study in the Institution of Higher Education

	Humanities	Social Sci.	Law	Arts	Social Work	Teacher Train.	Math., Nat. Sci.	Eng., Tech.	Agriculture	Medicine	Dentistry	Para-Med. Profs
Hebrew University	●	●	●	●	●	●	●		●	●	●	●
Technion-IIT		●					●	●	●			
Tel Aviv University	●	●	●	●	●	●	●	●		●	●	●
Bar-Ilan University	●	●	●	●	●	●	●					
University of Haifa	●	●		●	●	●	●					
Ben-Gurion University	●	●			●	●	●	●		●		●
Weizmann Inst. Science							●					
Everyman's (Open) Univ.	●	●					●					
Bezalel Academy Arts				●								
Jerusalem Acad. Music				●		●						
Jerusalem Coll. Technol.							●	●				
Shenkar—Text. & Fash.				●				●				
Ruppin Institute		●										
Coll. of Administration		●										
Teacher Training Colleges						●						

Source: Council for Higher Education, Report No. 14, 1988, p. 60.

5,800 students. About 13,500 students were enrolled in academic courses at the Open University; this number is approximately equivalent to 2,300 students in full-time study programs at a regular university.[5]

It is difficult to compare the rate of study in Israel with the rate in Western countries because of variations in the division between university and postsecondary education in different countries. Also, the principal age group attending universities in Israel, ages twenty to twenty-nine, differs from that in other countries due to three years required military service for men and two years for women. In Israel about 20 percent of the twenty to twenty-nine age cohort received university education and about 30 percent some form of higher education. This rate is higher than in most developed nations, similar to Japan, but lower than the rate in the United States and Canada. In 1983 the student-to-teacher ratio was about 15:1 in the humanities and social sciences and about 8:1 in the natural sciences, medicine, agriculture, and engineering. The overall average ratio was about 11.5:1; this compares well with the desired ratio of 10:1 accepted in England. Tuition fees are set by the government and ranged from about 10 percent of the ordinary budget in the mid-1970s to a low of 4 percent in 1982 and to a high of 17.5 percent in 1987.[6]

The academic staff of the universities consists of assistants, instructors, senior instructors, lecturers, senior lecturers, associate professors, and full professors. Those at the senior instructor and above levels are required to hold a Ph.D. degree. Only senior lecturers and above are granted tenure. The academic staff in 1986 numbered the equivalent of some 7,818 full-time positions, and 9,679 technical and administrative staff.

Wages and salaries are negotiated jointly by all institutions of higher education with the PGC and coordinated with the Ministry of Finance.

The principal sources of income for the higher education system are: (1) allocations from the government, determined and paid by the PGC; (2) income from current donations; (3) revenue from endowment funds; (4) tuition fees; (5) income from research contracts and research grants from government and private sources, at home and abroad; (6) sale of services (including teaching services). The share of each source is shown in Table 2.

Government participation in the ordinary budget of higher education remained unchanged in real terms over the past decade in relation to the Consumer Price Index; however, it did not compensate the universities for a 25 percent growth in student population and for the significant increase in wages and salaries of all employees in Israel, including those in higher education.

Historical Developments and Current Characteristics

Higher education in Israel shares most of the goals of tertiary systems elsewhere: training manpower, furthering economic development, promoting scientific research, enriching the culture, and transmitting and advancing knowledge in general.[7] In addition to these general goals, Israel's higher education institutions are expected to strengthen Jewish scholarship, transmit Jewish culture, and forge cultural links with the Jewish people in the Diaspora. Indeed, the sociohistorical roots of higher education in Israel are connected with the Zionist idea of cultural and national revival.[8] Thus the two institutions that were founded before the establishment of the State of Israel, the Technion (Israel Institute of Technology) in 1924, and the Hebrew University in 1925, were meant to help generate the Jewish cultural revival and the realization of the Zionist program by providing the pragmatic technological and technical needs of the Yishuv, the Jewish community in Palestine.[9]

The establishment of the Jewish state produced a growing demand for higher education. Indeed four new universities were established between 1955 and 1964 (Bar-Ilan, Tel-Aviv, Haifa, and Ben Gurion universities). The Weizmann Institute of Science was established in 1949 as a research institute, and in 1958 it opened a graduate school to award M.Sc. and Ph.D. degrees. The Open University opened in 1976, was accredited in 1980, and was authorized to award the bachelor's degree in 1980.[10] Rapid growth in the number of students became the most conspicuous feature of the expansion of the higher educational system (see Table 2) though not the most important feature.

Three of the five new universities founded since 1955—Tel Aviv, Haifa, and Ben Gurion—Beer Sheva universities—owe their establishment to local initiative; one—Bar-Ilan University—to that of the Zionist religious organization; and one—the Open University—to governmental initiative and philanthropic support (from the Rothschild Foundation). However, in spite of the disparate origins of the new universities established in the 1950s and 1960s, they tended to imitate the two veteran higher education institutions, the Hebrew University and the Haifa Technion, by stressing research as a measure of strength and success. Indeed, the long-standing Jewish tradition of the unity of research and teaching is responsible for the growth of research in Israeli universities, their single most important feature.[11] Trow's assertion that "competition accounts for the 'drift' . . . of new institutions and sectors toward the academic forms and styles, the curriculum and standards of elite institutions"[12] applies also to the Is-

Table 2

Ordinary Budget of the Higher Education System by Sources of Income and Academic Years

Academic Year[1]	Donations Various[4]	Tuition from Abroad	Allocations Fees	Earmarked Matching and various[3]	Direct Allocations[2]	Ordinary Allocations	Total	Budget
			N.I.S. Thousands, at Current Prices					
1979/80	159	126	64	52	50	867	969	(5)1,318
1980/81	450	260	133	108	225	2,228	2,561	(5)3,404
1984/82	1,132	505	272	150	400	4,138	4,688	(5)6,597
1982/83	3,754	1,205	1,405	569	600	13,326	14,495	(5)20,859
1983/84	25,763	5,944	3,290	3,702	1,363	36,623	41,688	(6)76,685
1984/85	43,387	42,199	29,603	24,079	8,820	153,075	185,974	(7)301,163
1985/86	43,500	57,741	99,256	38,629	38,254	253,037	329,920	(7)530,420
1986/87	89,179	80,087	124,085	49,540	43,904	324,625	418,069	(7)711,420
			Percentages					
1979/80	12.1	9.6	4.8	5.9	3.8	65.8	73.5	100.0
1980/81	13.2	7.6	3.9	3.2	6.6	65.5	75.3	100.0
1981/82	17.2	7.6	4.1	2.3	6.1	62.7	71.1	100.0
1982/83	18.0	5.8	6.7	2.7	2.9	63.9	69.5	100.0
1983/84	33.6	7.7	4.3	4.8	1.8	47.8	54.4	100.0
1984/85	14.4	14.0	9.8	8.0	3.0	50.8	61.8	100.0
1985/86	8.2	10.9	18.7	7.3	7.2	47.7	62.2	100.0
1986/87	12.5	11.3	17.4	7.0	6.2	45.6	58.8	100.0

(1) From October up to September 30. (2) To endowment funds at the institutions. (3) Included allocations for research and for special subjects (earmarked allocations, inter-university activities, aid to students, budgetary transfers, and miscellaneous subjects). (4) Included deficits. (5) According to the balance sheets of the institutions. (6) According to financial reports received from the institutions. (7) Final budget at updated prices.

Source: Council for Higher Education, Higher Education in Israel-Statistical Abstracts, 1986/87, p. 56.

Table 3

Students in Universities, by Academic Years

Year	Growth Indexes		Annual Percentage of Growth	Total*
	1969/70=100.0	1964/65=100.0		
1948/49	—	—	—	1,635
1949/50	—	—	—	2,450
1959/60	—	—	14.8**	10,202
1964/65	—	100.0	12.5**	18,368
1969/70	100.0	197.3	14.6**	36,239
1970/71	110.6	218.2	10.6	40,087
1971/72	125.2	247.0	13.2	45,365
1972/73	135.1	266.5	7.9	48,942
1973/74	132.8	262.1	-1.6	48,140
1974/75	143.7	283.6	8.2	52,088
1975/76	144.9	285.9	0.8	52,510
1976/77	146.2	288.4	0.9	52,980
1977/78	149.2	294.3	2.0	54,060
1978/79	154.0	303.7	3.2	55,790
1979/80	158.7	313.0	3.1	57,500
1980/81	162.7	321.0	2.6	58,970
1981/82	167.6	330.7	3.0	60,735
1982/83	172.1	339.5	2.7	62,365
1983/84	178.3	351.7	3.6	64,605
1984/85	179.5	354.1	0.7	65,050
1985/86	182.6	360.2	1.7	66,160
1986/87	185.3	365.6	1.5	67,160
1987/88	187.4	369.7	1.1	67,900

* Including foreign students and students in special programs.
** On the assumption of linear growth within the years.

Source: Council for Higher Education, Planning and Grants Committee. *Higher Education in Israel—Statistical Abstracts* 1983/84; 1986/87. *Statistical Abstracts of Israel, No. 39, 1988.*

raeli case. The similarity of Israel's higher education institutions may also be explained by the direct supervision exercised by the Hebrew University and the Technion on the new universities in the initial years of their development and the indirect supervision exercised by the Council of Higher Education (established in 1958 and headed by senior faculty members of the two older institutions and the Weizmann Institute of Science). In the 1950s two discernible groups exerted decisive influence on the development of higher education in Israel. One group consisted of prominent scientists and scholars who immigrated to Israel during the 1920s and particularly during the 1930s following the rise of nazism. This group had received its academic training mainly in the authoritarian academic atmosphere of central European universities. These scholars and scientists became the basis for academic development in the country. In the late 1940s a second group of scientists and scholars emerged from among the outstanding graduates of the local institutions and from England and the United States. The political circumstances at that time (British rule) and the rigid academic norms of the Hebrew University and the Technion combined to limit their academic influence.[13] But in the 1950s this group emerged to play a decisive role in the establishment and consolidation of the Weizmann Institute, brought about a reform in teaching and the adoption of the three-level degree structure at the Hebrew University and the Technion, and were instrumental in the establishment of Bar-Ilan and Tel-Aviv universities[14] in the 1950s and Haifa[15] and Ben Gurion[16] universities in the 1960s.

These developments enabled Israel's universities to conform in curricula, degree structure, and offerings to those of the United States and Britain. It resulted also in the increased democratization of research organization and in academic government. As a result Israel's higher education became an up-to-date scientific enterprise and some of its institutions achieved international status. Indeed, the universities' affirmation of research as their supreme goal continues to guide the higher education system even in times of financial constraints. This truth was emphasized by the chairman of the Planning and Grants Committee of the Council for Higher Education in his 1986/87 annual report: "The universities are engaged both in teaching and research . . . teaching not accompanied by research cannot ensure proper academic level for any length of time."[17] It is estimated that about 30 percent of all research and development in Israel, including military research, and about 45 percent of the civilian research and development in the natural sciences, medicine, agriculture, and engineering is carried out in the universities. Most of the research in the humanities and social sciences and virtually all the basic research in the country is done in the universities,[18] with implications that will be discussed below.

Higher Education and Employment

One of the basic issues of higher education is its relevancy to the labor market. Educational policies are affected by social concepts and policies as much as by academic considerations. In Israel, as is the case in many other democratic societies, education is free and universal and its consumption is determined largely by the individual's interests and ability. In principle, education is not subordinated to the functional needs of society, the state, or the labor market. This might well result in a gap between the output of the universities and the needs of the labor market. Such a gap might well increase as a result of technological and applied research innovations that outpace policy and curricula changes in higher education institutions. Israel's higher education institutions have tried with various degrees of success to adapt to social, economic, and technological changes, the needs of the labor market, and the prospects for employment of their graduates. The profile of the student body in Israel's higher education reflects their attitude toward studies in general, their interest in matching graduates to employment, and their approach to occupational training.

The socioeconomic and geopolitical realities of Israel are responsible for some of the distinct characteristics of its students.[19] The majority of students are two or three years older than those in other countries because of compulsory military service. About half are married at the time of their studies. Although tuition fees are relatively low, they are a burden for the majority of students and particularly for those who are married. The majority of students work either full time or part time. Thus, three variables distinguish the Israeli students from their counterparts in academic institutions elsewhere: they are older, often married, and usually are working.[20]

One of the most important links between higher education and society at large is manifested in the use of university studies as a means for social mobility. In response to the increased demand in the newly established state of Israel for professional and administrative personnel, the higher education system in Israel has expanded since the 1950s with one of the highest rates of growth in the world, as shown in Table 3.[21] The expectations of university students to fill professional and administrative jobs in the expanding economy and administration were met by universities quite successfully during the 1950s, 1960s, and 1970s both through expansion and through the transformation of structure, content, and aims. Changes to meet the needs of the labor market and student expectations started with the introduction of the three-year bachelor's degree in 1950.[22] This was followed by the establishment and growth of professional schools in education, social work, and business administration, as well as by changes in individual science, humanities, and social science departments. After two or three years of army service, students were in a hurry to learn something that would make them proficient in a given field; the changes mentioned above were intended to fulfill this student desire.[23]

A comprehensive study on higher education and employment in Israel from 1971 to 1976,[24] focusing on humanities and social sciences students, found that "64 percent of the graduates had been working when they started their studies. In the course of studies, the percentage rose to 90 percent after graduation. Practically all graduates who wanted to work found employment . . . this is the peak participation rate of any group in Israel."[25] A considerable portion of the graduates, approximately one-third, remained in the same job where they had been employed during their studies. A possible explanation for the high occupational rate is the older age and marital status of the students. Most of the graduates felt that their work was closely associated with their academic training.[26]

These findings were generally supported by a background document submitted by the PGC to the CHE in 1987 which stated: "Graduates are absorbed into the labor market with no major difficulty. One reason for this smooth absorption in the labor market is the gradual process of transition from studies to employment, which begins for many of them while they are still students, working to support themselves during their studies."[27] Based on economic and manpower planning the PGC forecasts "a balance between the general demand for and supply of academically qualified manpower in the economy."[28]

Government-University Relations

When the State of Israel was established in 1948, there were two small higher education institutions, The Hebrew University of Jerusalem and the Haifa Technion. The Humboldtian German university provided the academic model for both institutions. They emphasized research and scholarship in a few selected areas, technological training, and applied research. They provided opportunities for higher education to very few students; high fees and a small demand for the courses and skills taught combined to limit enrollment. Indeed, the number of students in the two institutions in 1948 was 1,635.

Although the Hebrew University and the Technion were intended to play a key role both in "the realization of Jewish culture and the Zionist program of building up the country physically,"[29] they were private institutions, mainly supported by foreign donors, and run like a corporation, in the manner of American private universities. Their relative isolation from political controversies and factional feuds safeguarded their autonomy from the Zionist organization that first created and supported them, and later, in the 1950s, from the emerging governmental bureaucracy. The universities continued to have full institutional autonomy and their academic staffs enjoyed almost unrestricted academic freedom for teaching and conducting research, in the manner of British elitist institutions. The academic staff played a decisive role in administrative matters of the university.[30]

The postindependence years witnessed the growth of the Israeli university system in size and in the quality and scope of its research and training activities. Between 1955 and 1964 four new universities were founded; the number of students rose from 3,022 in 1950/51 to 18,368 in 1964/65; and faculty numbers rose from 135 professors and lecturers in 1950/51 to 2,814 in 1968/69. New departments in the social sciences and humanities and professional schools in law and medicine were established in both the old and the new universities.[31]

The expansion of the higher education system and its increased demand for public and governmental funds have brought to light three interrelated issues: accreditation of new universities; criteria and means for channeling public funds to the individual institutions; and governmental control over the system. Indeed, since World War II Israeli governments have tended to intervene in higher education in order to democratize access and governance, to make studies more relevant to student careers and/or the economy, and to augment their influence over the magnitude, the cost, and the future direction of the higher education enterprise.[32] This trend became apparent in Israel in 1958 when the government established the Council for Higher Education (CHE) as a statutory body, to serve as "the State Institution for matters of higher education in the State."[33] The CHE has the sole authority to recommend to the government whether a permit to open a new institution of higher education should be granted; CHE itself grants academic recognition or accreditation and the right to confer academic degrees.

The continuous quantitative expansion of the higher education system was accompanied by a massive increase in public expenditure, which rose steadily to 45.5 percent in 1959/60 and to almost 80 percent of the ordinary budget in 1974/75. Increased government spending on higher education naturally intensified the basic issue of how to reconcile the inherent conflict between academic freedom and accountability to the public. From 1948 to 1971 the presidents of the universities maintained direct contact with political figures and submitted their budgetary requests independently to senior officials in the Finance Ministry, who were not always familiar with the issues in higher education. Thus, doubts began to grow concerning the competency of the government to cope with the rapid expansion of higher education.[34]

The autonomous governing body of each university decided on its own development policy without coordination with other universities, the CHE, or the government. As a result almost all universities incurred increasing deficits and the government was continually being asked for additional resources. There was an obvious need to find a mechanism that would make the universities more accountable to the public and particularly to work out an equitable system for financing higher education. A committee appointed in 1972 by the minister of education and culture to examine alternative models of university finance recommended establishing a "Planning and Grants Committee" on the lines of the British University Grants Committee (UGC).[35] In 1974 the Council for Higher Education was put in charge of planning and appointed the first Planning and Grants Committee (PGC). To safeguard against government intervention at least four of PGC's six members, including the chairman, were to be full professors; the other two members were to come from business and industry. "The four professors represent 'the two cultures': two from the humanities, social sciences, law, or education; two from the natural sciences, engineering, medicine, or agriculture."[36]

The duties of the Planning and Grants Committee, as set forth in Government Decision No. 666 of June 5, 1977, are as follows: "(1) To be an independent body coming between the Government and the national institutions, on the one hand, and the institutions of higher education, on the other, in all matters relating to allocations for higher education. . . . (2) To submit the ordinary and development budget proposals for higher education. . . . (3) To allocate to the institutions of higher education the global approved ordinary and development budgets. (4) To submit to the Government and to the Council for Higher Education plans for the development of higher education, including their financing. (5) To encourage efficiency in the institutions of higher education and coordination between them. . . . (6) To ensure that budgets are balanced. . . . (7) To express its opinion to the Council for Higher Education before the Council reaches a decision on the opening of a new institution or a new unit in an existing institution having financial implications."[37]

The PGC submits annual reports to the council at the end of each academic year. Its composition, terms of reference, and modes of operation were meant, in theory, to guarantee against the erosion of academic freedom within the higher education system as a whole while providing for greater accountability by the universities, who now negotiate their budgets only with the PGC. In practice, however, the freedom of the individual institution both in academic and fiscal matters has shrunk considerably in recent years, as I will discuss below.

Trends in Higher Education

The higher education system during the past four decades went though several phases, both quantitative and qualitative in nature, some of which have been de-scribed and analyzed above. The 1950s and 1960s were marked by a dramatic quantitative expansion in terms of new universities, new programs of study, growing numbers of students, a major structural reform, and the introduction of undergraduate studies. The 1970s witnessed further expansion and diversification of higher education opportunities within the existing universities and also in the nonuniversity sector, where regional colleges began offering academic studies in association with established universities. Another expression of this diversification was the academization of other nonuniversity institutions, particularly those for the paramedical professions and primary school teaching. The early and mid-1980s were marked by severe cuts in government expenditure on social services including education due to economic slowdown and inflation.[38] These harsh fiscal measures have resulted in a major crisis in higher education with long-term implications. While the number of students increased by some 30 percent between 1974 and 1983, academic staff decreased and administrative staff was reduced. A definite trend of substantial disinvestment in higher education was reflected by the share of higher education in the national budget, excluding defense expenditure and debt payment, which fell by some 44 percent (see Table 4). These reductions have heightened tension between the government and the institutions of higher education, and between higher education and the Planning and Grants Committee of the Council for Higher Education. PGC's chairman admitted that "during some of this time [1979–85] the Ministry of Finance's attitude toward the higher education system bordered on open hostility."[39]

Another and related trend during the 1980s was an increase in the indirect power of the government through the Planning and Grants Committee. The PGC has become a centralized power in matters of funding, planning, policy initiatives, and evaluation. It ceased to be a more or less passive participant in budgeting for universities and became an active initiator of development in higher education. At a time when governmental allocations were cut time and again and research funds, national and international, became scarce (see Table 2) "PGC's authority in the allocation of the higher education budget to the higher education system is, essentially, unlimited."[40]

The PGC operates through five budgetary channels: direct global allocation, matching allocations, allocations for research, earmarked allocations, and allocations for development. Through each of these channels, and by determining their relative share in the general budget, the PGC exerts influence on higher education. The increased control of the PGC is reflected in its policy in regard to the largest item of the budget, namely, the direct allocations to the institutions of higher education. This item made up about 85 percent of the total PGC budget in 1979/80 but decreased to 73.3 percent in 1985/86, and decreased again to about 71 percent in 1986/87 (excluding allocations for computers) because "the PGC preferred to preserve, and even increase, the real value of its special allocations"[41] (see Table 5). This

trend is evident even more in PGC's direct allocations to the ordinary budget of the universities, which decreased from 65.8 percent in 1979/80 to 45.6 percent in 1986/87 while the share of tuition fees increased in the same period from 4.8 percent to 17.4 percent (see Table 2). In this way the PGC has used the budget to support activities in accordance with its own determined priorities. Thus, it increased its funding earmarked for basic research and special projects, two areas that suffered severely in the early 1970s.

Another example of the PGC's increased influence on higher education relates to its method of and criteria for apportioning the direct allocation between higher education institutions. Since 1981, in addition to determined indices for budgetary allocations to each university, the PGC also uses "productivity" data that reflect the "output" of graduates and the scope and quality of research of the individual institutions. However, there is no single formula upon which calculations of an institution's "productivity" are based, since "the PGC believes that no such unequivocal formula is possible." The PGC's rationale for refraining from formulating a binding formula for funding is that "a single, pre-determined formula gives the

Table 4

Trends in the University System, 1974–1983

	1974	1983	Percentage Change
No. of students	48,140	62,500	+30%
Academic staff (positions)	6,630	6,451	-3%
Administrative and technical staff (positions)	9,120	8,094	-11%
Non-salary expenditure	3,754	2,791	-26%
Share of higher education in state ordinary budget, excluding expenditure on defense or interest on debts (percentage)	7.9	4.4	-44%

Source: The Higher Education System in Israel, 1984.

Table 5

Apportionment of PGC Allocations (In NIS and as Percentage of Total Allocations)

Total (NIS Thousands)	1985/86		1986/87	
	331,121.4	100%	439,381.4	100%
Direct allocation to the institutions of higher education	242,912.0	76.4%	311,905.0	73.9%
Allocations for electronics and computers	10,125.0		12,855.0	
Matching allocations to endowment funds	38,253.7	11.5%	43,904.4	10.0%
Earmarked allocations for research and special subjects*	20,398.5	6.2%	28,172.1	6.4%
Other allocations**	18,230.7	5.5%	41,144.9	9.4%
PGC's administrative budget	1,201.5	0.4%	1,430.0	0.3%

* Includes allocations for research, earmarked allocations, and inter-university activities.
** Includes aid to students, miscellaneous subjects, and budgetary transfers.

Source: Council of Higher Education, *PGC Annual Report No. 13*, 1985/86, No. 14, 1986/87.

omnipotent computer the power of decision rather than the collective balanced judgment of the committee members."[42] Not surprisingly, the universities have questioned the validity of the allocation methods employed by the PGC and particularly the lack of an established definite formula for "productivity" of an institution, which leaves to the PGC the authority to "assess" the "quality" of the universities' performance.

The PGC's controlling power is reflected in its requirement that the universities inform it of their plans to open new units, of any organizational change in an existing unit, or of any development project "regardless of how marginal or unimportant it may seem" even when no request is made for government funding. The PGC also has at its disposal "Competitive Funds" and "Scientific Equipment Funds" which amounted to 6.2 percent in 1985/86 and 6.4 percent in 1986/87 of the total govern-

mental budget to higher education; these funds are allocated by selection committees who evaluate the quality of research programs. The apportionment of the budget is detailed in Table 5.

Additional means for evaluating the quality of teaching and research consists of periodic inspection of departments and research units by "review committees" from outside the institution. Although "the PGC's policy is not to take part in these checks but to recommend that the university administration appoint from time to time external review committees which would present their reports to the administration,"[43] it encouraged individual institutions to act on these lines. PGC periodically reviews fields of study within the higher education system as a whole by means of "survey committees." In 1987, for example, the PGC appointed an "international visiting committee" to review "the place and role of the universities' schools of education in the framework of the educational system in Israel and within their institutional framework." The committee submitted its report, which included far-reaching recommendations, on December 1988.[44] If its recommendations are accepted, the report will have a decisive restructuring effect on schools of education in content, structure, teacher training, and research.

The PGC also initiated a comprehensive study of undergraduate programs which was submitted in 1987 to the Council for Higher Education.[45] If adopted by the council the duration, structure, and content of undergraduate studies in the social sciences and humanities will change dramatically. The study also recommends the creation of colleges specializing in general undergraduate teaching. Such institutions might be established by private initiative outside of the existing public system, be wholly financed by tuition fees rather than funded by the government, and operate under different academic terms. Such a development would result in differentiation and diversification of the largely unitary higher education system.

All these policy initiatives and administrative measures of the PGC weakened the integrity of universities in Israel and limited their institutional autonomy. A similar trend has been observed in many national systems from the 1960s through the 1980s.[46]

Conclusions

The degree of expansion of higher education in Israel between the 1950s and 1970s was among the highest in the world. Increasing access to higher education was not an important political issue, since both the universities and the government were in favor of providing higher education to all qualified applicants. The proportion of Israelis of an age cohort attending higher education is very high, matched only by Japan and Sweden and surpassed only by the United States and Canada. As a result, the proportions of college-educated persons in Israel's labor force, whether defined by years of schooling or by occupational classification—scientific, professional, technical, or managerial—is among the world's highest.[47] However, a significant difference in the rate of participation appears according to socioeconomic and ethnic background. Thus, in 1985, the participation rate among Israeli-born students whose fathers were born in Europe, America, or Israel was 3.8 times higher than those whose fathers were born in Africa or Asia. As a result of various measures, in the last decade (1976–85) the rate of participation of students of oriental origin has increased from 19 percent to 30 percent among undergraduate students while their percentage in the twenty to twenty-nine age cohort has changed only slightly, from 43 percent to 45 percent.[48] However, more effective steps have to be taken to reduce this gap, which is inconsistent with Israel's stated social philosophy. In a related development, rising tuition fees and declining employment opportunities have combined to produce stagnation in the attendance rate since 1984. Thus between 1984 and 1986 it remained unchanged in spite of an almost 10 percent increase in the number of recipients of high school matriculation certificates.

The government provided the lion's share in funding the expansion of the system in the 1950s and 1960s regardless of real economic demand. The universities demonstrated flexibility in adjusting their programs to accommodate the changing expectations of the students and the economy by introducing undergraduate and professional bachelor's degrees. However, the basic commitment of the system to research as a hallmark of excellence continued to characterize both the old and the new institutions; higher education continued to avoid a utilitarian approach.[49] It is reasonable to conclude that worsening economic conditions by the mid-1970s, resulting in reductions in public expenditures including annual allocations to the universities, created a new policy climate. This policy climate might continue to affect the delicate balance of control and autonomy between direct governmental intervention and the statutory roles of the CHE and the PGC on the one hand and the universities on the other. This, for example, nationally negotiated wage agreements with faculty and staff as well as student tuition fees were imposed on the universities without consulting with individual universities and without commensurate provisions for funding.

Another development of far-reaching consequences was the drastic change in the composition of funding higher education, with a sharp decline in government's share and a rise in both tuition fees and private funding. The substitution of private for government funding resulted in shortages in general-purpose expenditure on basic research infrastructure such as libraries, laboratories, and computers. This trend, if continued, will adversely affect the quality of education and research in the country's higher education system. To restore the equilibrium of the research infrastructure, additional public funds will be required.[50] This demand was echoed in the 1985/86 PGC chairman's annual report: "to repeat previous warnings and stress that if higher education does not very soon advance in the national order of priorities, it will no longer be possible to repair the damage that higher education has suffered in recent years."[51] In 1988 PGC's chairman in his annual review chose to discuss "the central and vital question: is the higher education system in danger of losing its independence?"[52] as a result of financial dependence on the government allocation, built-in deficits, and divestment of universities' assets. To halt the risk of further deterioration of the system both in academic standards and in its function of manpower training, the PGC has submit-

ted to the government a plan "for increasing the basic higher education budget by 25 percent in four years" (1987–90).[53]

On the other hand, demands for accountability were expressed by proposing that expanding and even existing needs for higher education could be met only by a more efficient and vocationally oriented system. These demands were followed by growing pressure for higher productivity, more efficient and/or joint utilization of facilities and equipment, and interuniversity cooperation in research. University faculties and administrators tended to see some of these demands as a disguised desire for more direct state control at the expense of institutional autonomy.

It seems at this point that Israel's higher education system reached a crossroad. In order to overcome the present crisis, both the universities and the government will have to explore new ways that will allow effective planning, financing, and policy-making at the university and national levels, while taking into account both the legitimate public and national interests, academic freedom, and institutional autonomy.

Notes

1. Central Bureau of Statistics, *Statistical Abstracts of Israel 1988*, No. 39 (Jerusalem: Central Bureau of Statistics, 1988), Table XXII/32, p. 636.
2. Ruth Stanner, *The Legal Basis of Education in Israel* (Jerusalem: Ministry of Education and Culture, 1963), 244.
3. Council for Higher Education, Planning and Grants Committee, *Annual Report No. 14, Academic Year 1986–1987* (Jerusalem: Planning and Grants Committee, 1988), 18–20. The most comprehensive and up-to-date information on Israel's higher education system is published by the Council for Higher Education (CHE), and the Planning and Grants Committee (PGC) in their annual reports published in Hebrew and English, and in their occasional publication *Higher Education in Israel—Statistical Abstracts*, which presents cumulative data on various quantitative aspects of the system. Further references to the annual reports will be as follows: "PGC, *Annual Report No.*"
4. PGC, *Annual Report No. 14*, 78.

5. *Statistical Abstracts of Israel* 1988, Table XXII/32, p. 636; Table XXII/34, pp. 638–39.

6. Council for Higher Education, Planning and Grants Committee, *The Higher Education System in Israel: Guidelines on the Development of the System and Its Planning for 1988 with a First Glance at 1995* (Jerusalem: Planning and Grants Committee, 1984), 19, 22; see also State of Israel, Ministry of Education and Culture, *Facts and Figures on the Education and Culture System in Israel* (Jerusalem: Publications Department, Ministry of Education and Culture, 1988); 55–56. The comparison is based on UNESCO's *Statistical Yearbook* 1987 and *Statistical Digest* 1987, quoted in the ministry's publication.

7. Burton R. Clark, *The Higher Education System: Academic Organization in Cross-National Perspectives* (Berkeley and Los Angeles: University of California Press, 1983); Clark Kerr, "A Critical Age in the University World: Accumulated Heritage Versus Modern Imperatives," *European Journal of Education* 22, no. 2 (1987): 185.

8. The sociohistorical background and developments are discussed by Joseph Ben-David, "Universities in Israel: Dilemmas of Growth, Diversification, and Administration," *Studies in Higher Education* 11, no. 2 (1986): 105–30; Yaacov Iram, "Higher Education in Transition—The Case of Israel: A Comparative Study," *Higher Education* 9 (1980): 81–95; Yaacov Iram, "Vision and Fulfillment: The Evolution of the Hebrew University, 1901–1950," *History of Higher Education Annual* 3 (1983): 123–43.

9. On the establishment of the Technion and the Hebrew University, see Technion, Israel Institute of Technology, *History of the Technion in the Beginning: 1908–1925* (Haifa, Israel: Public Relations Department of the Technion, 1953) (in Hebrew); *The Hebrew University, History and Development: Year Book* (Jerusalem: 1928); *The Hebrew University of Jerusalem: 1925–1950* (Jerusalem: 1950).

10. Samuel Halperin, *Any Home a Campus: Everyman's University of Israel* (Washington, D.C.: Institute for Educational Leadership, 1984).

11. Ben David, "Universities in Israel," 113. For the high status of research and the training of researchers, as well as various indices of Israeli scientists' high research productivity, see Ben David, 114–17.

12. Martin A. Trow, "The Analysis of Status," in *Perspectives on Higher Education*, ed. Burton R. Clark (Berkeley and Los Angeles: University of California Press, 1984), 143.

13. On the influences of German, British, and American higher education traditions on the development of higher education in Israel, see Yaacov Iram, "Higher Education Traditions of Germany, England, the U.S.A., and Israel," *Paedagogica Historica* 22 (1982): 93–118. Of particular interest are the conflicting attitudes expressed by senior faculty members of different academic origin toward academic issues.

14. On the development of these two institutions, see Israel Efrat, "The Beginning: On the History of Tel Aviv University," *Moznayim* (1971): 33–36 (in Hebrew); Arye Ben Yosef, *Bar Ilan Annual* 4–5 (1967): 12–29 (in Hebrew); "Bar-Ilan University 30th Anniversary: 1955–1985, *Jerusalem Post Supplement*, 24 May 1985.

15. Schewach Weiss,""Haifa University: Aims and Their Realization," *Beminhal Hachinuch* (Educational administration), 1972 (in Hebrew).

16. Zeev Hadari, "The Ben Gurion University—The Beginning of a Period in the Negev," in *Erez Hanegev, Adam Umidbar* (The land of the Negev, man and desert), no. 2 (Tel Aviv, Israel: Ministry of Defense, 1979) (in Hebrew).

17. PGC, *Annual Report No. 14*, 62.

18. Israel Academy of Sciences and Humanities, *Scientific Research Activity in Israel: A Blueprint for Basic Research* (Jerusalem: 1986) (in Hebrew); PGC, Annual Report No. 14, 62–67.

19. For a general study on the Israeli students, see Rina Shapira and Hava Etzioni-Halevi, *Who is the Israeli Student?* (Tel Aviv, Israel: Am Oved, 1973) (in Hebrew).

20. A profile of students in humanities and the social sciences is sketched in Arye Globerson, *Higher Education and Employment: A Case Study of Israel* (New York: Praeger, 1978), 1–18. For a comprehensive survey on undergraduate students, see Ruth Silberg, *Undergraduate Studies in the Higher Education System* (Jerusalem: Planning and Grants Committee, 1987) (in Hebrew).

21. For a comparative perspective, see Trow, in *The Higher Education System*, 139–44.

22. On the structural reform that led to the introduction of undergraduate studies at the Hebrew University, see Iram, "Vision and Fulfillment," 132–35.

23. Ben David, "Universities in Israel," 121.

24. Globerson, *Higher Education and Employment*.

25. Globerson, *Higher Education and Employment*, 14. Various statistical sources indicate that the percentage of American and European students who work through studies ranges from 20 to 30 percent (Globerson, *Higher Education and Employment*, 18, fn. 23).

26. Globerson, *Higher Education and Employment*, 148–49.

27. Silberberg, *Undergraduate Studies*, 49–53.

28. PGC, *Annual Report No. 14*, 37.

29. Ben David, "Universities in Israel," 105. For

historical background, see also Iram, "Vision and Fulfillment," and Chaim Schatzker, "Tradition and Reform at the Universities in Israel," in *Tradition and Reform of the University under an International Perspective—An Interdisciplinary Approach*, ed. Hermann Rohrs (Frankfurt am Main: Verlag Peter Lang, 1987), 185–202.

30. The power of the professoriate at the Hebrew University and the Technion is close to Clark's "discipline-rooted authority" classification (Clark, *The Higher Education System*, 110–16).

31. On the growth of the higher education system, see Aharon F. Kleinberger, *Society Schools and Progress in Israel* (Oxford: Pergamon Press, 1969), 245–74.

32. Trow, in *Perspectives on Higher Education*, 142; and Clark, *The Higher Education System*, 119–23.

33. Council for Higher Education Law, 5718–1958, in Stanner, *Legal Basis of Education*, 244–49, section 3.

34. Meir Zadok, "The Israeli Planning and Grants Committee at the Crossroads: From Shock Absorber to Steering Wheel," *Higher Education* 13 (1984): 535–44. For possible options of governmental involvement in higher education before the decision to establish the PGC, see Lydia Aranne, *Government Policy toward Higher Education in Israel* (Jerusalem: Center for Policy Studies, 1970).

35. "The Chairman's Summary of the Planning and Grants Committee's Activities 1979–1985," in PGC *Annual Report No. 12*, 95. The British model is described by Frederick Dainton, "University Grants Committees," in *International Encyclopedia of Higher Education*, ed. Asa S. Knowles (San Francisco: Jossey Bass, 1977), 1724–29. For recent developments in the status of the British UGC, see John H. Farrant, "Central Control of the University Sector," in *British Higher Education*, ed. Tony Becher (London: Allen & Unwin, 1987), 29–52.

36. PGC, *Annual Report No. 12*, 95. This report includes the chairman's summary of PGC's activities for 1979–85, 95–128.

37. Quoted in Council for Higher Education, Planning and Grants Committee *Annual Report No. 13, Academic Year 1985/86* (Jerusalem: Planning and Grants Committee, 1987), 12–13.

38. Yaakov Kop, "Social Services in the Eighties—A Turning Point?", in *Israel's Outlay for Human Services 1984*, ed. Yaakov Kop (Jerusalem: Center for Social Policy Studies in Israel, 1985), 7–18. See also Ofer Gur, Yaakov Kop, and Joel Blanket, "Government Outlays on Social Services," *Israel's Outlay for Human Services 1984*, 20–59.

39. PGC, *Annual Report No. 12*, 124.

40. Ibid, 96.

41. Ibid, 101.

42. Ibid, 102; and PGC, *Annual Report No. 14*, 6. For a detailed analysis on budgetary deliberation procedures, see Yaacov Iram, "Quality and Control in Higher Education in Israel," *European Journal of Education* 22, no. 2 (1987): 155–57.

43. PGC, *The Higher Education System in Israel*, 1984, 67.

44. In addition to three Israeli members, including the chair, there were three foreign members: Dean Patricia Albjerg Graham of the Harvard Graduate School of Education, James Coleman of the University of Chicago, and Lee Shulman of Stanford University. The committee was appointed on April 9, 1987, and its thirty-page report was submitted to the PGC on December 7, 1988.

45. Silberberg, *Undergraduate Studies*.

46. *The Future of Higher Education in Israel*, Discussion Paper No. 5-88 (Tel Aviv University, The Pinhas Sapir Center for Development, March 1988) (in Hebrew). For similar trends and developments in other countries, see *Higher Education Policy* 1, no. 3 (1988), a special issue on "the response of higher education to new priorities." See also James Perkins and Barbara Baird Israel, eds., *Higher Education: From Autonomy to Systems* (New York: International Council for Educational Development, 1972); and Trow, in *Perspectives on Higher Education*, 144–47.

47. Ruth Klinov, *Allocation of Public Resources to Education*, Israel's Educational System: Issues and Options, Discussion Paper No. 1 (Jerusalem: Center for Policy Studies in Israel, June 1988), 9.

48. PGC, *Annual Report No. 14*, 36; Silberberg, *Undergraduate Studies*, 31–35.

49. Ben David, "Universities in Israel," 113.

50. Israel Academy of Sciences and Humanities, *Scientific Research Activity*, 49–56. The academy has recommended the establishment of a National Committee for Research with an annual budget of twenty million dollars for basic research.

51. PGC, *Annual Report No. 13*, 5.

52. PGC, *Annual Report No. 14*, 5–7.

53. Ibid, 6.

Kuwait

H. A. Al-Ebraheem

◆

Kuwait, located on the northwestern shore of the Arabian Gulf, has little, if any, recorded history. While some scattered information and a few archaeological studies exist,[1] the country's modern history spans little more than two and a quarter centuries. Prior to the discovery of oil in 1936 Kuwait was extremely poor. Its small population survived mostly on fishing, trade, and pearl-diving. Lacking even supplies of fresh water, Kuwait had never attained an important place in the region. Such education as existed before 1912 was based on Koranic instruction. The teaching of religion, the study of the Koran, reading, and bookkeeping were the main activities of the *kutaba* (Koranic schools).

In 1912, with private donations, the Al-Mubarakiyya School was opened with a broader curriculum. However, the world depression in the early 1930s had a devastating impact upon the pearl-diving industry, and this school was closed because of lack of financial support. It was not until 1936, with the establishment of a Department of Education, that modern education truly began. A board of education was then authorized to levy an education tax that enabled the government to open four primary schools, including one for girls. A Palestinian Mission composed of four teachers was seconded from the Supreme Muslim Council in Jerusalem to assist this development. Following World War II and the advent of oil revenues, Kuwait's education system witnessed a vast expansion that has continued to the present.[2] Unfortunately, despite lavish expenditure, educational development has favored quantity at the expense of quality.[3]

Historical Background

Kuwait's higher education system is composed of one university and a number of two-year and four-year institutions. The entire system is run by the Public Authority for Applied Education and Training (PAAET). Although higher education dates back to October 1966, when Kuwait University was opened, the government's scholarship program was initiated earlier, in 1957. This program enabled any student who passed the final examination in high school to pursue study abroad in the field of his choice. But this unplanned and haphazard approach to higher education subsequently emerged as a major problem for Kuwait University as it attempted to avoid unwarranted expansion.

In 1960 the Department of Education issued an invitation to three distinguished scholars, Sir Ivor Jennings (Cambridge, U.K.), Dr. Suleiman Huzain (Egypt), and Dr. Constantine Zureig (American University of Beirut) to make recommendations concerning the establishment of Kuwait University. The commission's report stressed five major points. First, the major justification for the establishment of a university should be to produce skilled people in various fields and to produce an institution that would assume a leadership role in society as a whole. Second, the university should be competent to play a significant role in culture and science both regionally and in the Arab world as a whole. Third, the university should be relevant to the environment and should therefore cater to such local needs as greater understanding of marine biology, oil-related subjects, and the desert. Fourth, the university should be able to guarantee quality of staff, quality of teaching, and adequate research. If high standards were not established from the beginning, the commission noted, the university could not serve its function and might even hinder the development of the country. Fifth, the commission warned against the danger of simply copying any existing Arab university.[4]

This well-reasoned report continued to be discussed by various committees until 1965 when a political decision was finally reached to establish a university. This decision was based less on thorough planning than upon a desire to assert Kuwait's identity in the face of strong pressures that would deny the country's very existence. Kuwait University opened its doors in 1966 with two colleges, the College of Arts and Science and the Women's College. The first class was comprised of 418 students, of whom 175 were women.

Kuwait University's first class was indicative of two trends. First, despite the smaller number of female students in the high schools, women constituted about 42 percent of the class. Second, most members of the first class enrolled in arts and education. Subsequent efforts by the university to tighten admissions in 1985 only accelerated the first trend to the point that today females constitute the majority of new entrants. The second trend, a preference for arts rather than science, reflects a problem common to the entire Arab world, where it has been estimated that three-fourths of the student population enroll in the humanities.

In 1967/68 two more colleges were established in Kuwait University, the College of Law and Shari'a and the College of Commerce, Economics, and Political Science, both based on Egyptian models. In 1971 the College of Science was separated from the College of Arts. In 1981 the College of Shari'a and Islamic Studies was separated from the College of Law.

The period from 1975 to 1982 also witnessed the emergence of other colleges. The College of Engineering and Petroleum was established in 1975, and the College of Medicine in 1976. A College of Graduate Studies was founded in 1977. The College of Education was separated from the College of Arts in 1981. In 1982 the College of Allied Health Science and Nursing was separated from the College of Medicine. Thus, over a twenty-three-year period Kuwait University expanded from two to ten colleges and saw an increase in student enrollment from 418 in 1966/67 to 13,993 for the academic year 1987/88.[5] Notwithstanding various positive aspects of this expansion, which has undoubtedly shaped higher education as a whole in the country, the lack of planning that has characterized much of the process has contributed to a number of crises in management.

Organization and Management

In 1966, contrary to the advice of the commission's report, Law Number 29, regulating higher education, borrowed heavily from the existing Arab, and especially the Egyptian, university model. A Higher Education Advisor, brought from Egypt was made responsible for carrying out the law, and a Secretary of Kuwaiti nationality was given administrative and financial responsibility under the "supervision" of the advisor. The law indicated that a Higher Education Council was to be formed by the minister of education and that deans were to be nominated from among professors. The higher education law revealed the absence of a consolidated plan for university organization and development. Restrictions on the new university were clearly manifested in the areas of budgeting and personnel. The current rector has clearly stated his intention to correct this situation in his report for 1988:

What we are asking for is a flexible budget to allow us to do the following:

Generate income through consultancy and contract research and also campaign for project donations or chairs.

Create a better compensation system especially for Kuwaitis to encourage Kuwaitization of quality calibre and reduce dependence.

Develop flexibility in our construction budget so that we are not tied down to line items (an impossible task) in making estimates.

What is saved from the current year should go to the next to encourage savings.[6]

What the university received was not a charter that would enable it to develop and implement an educational philosophy, but rigid prescriptions that tied it to Kuwait's general civil service regulations. Matters elsewhere usually assumed to fall within the province of a university council or senate became the ongoing concern of the cabinet, and, sometimes, parliament. Although steps were taken in 1975 to advance a new university law, it has made little progress beyond becoming the subject of numerous parliamentary committees and council of ministers' sessions. In 1988 a Ministry of Higher Education was finally created. Some critics hope this ministry will solve all the administrative and organizational problems arising from Law Number 29. Other critics believe that the new ministry will just complicate matters by placing a more restrictive and rigid bureaucracy on top of the one that already exists.

In summary, the organization and administrative structure of Kuwait University followed the common practice of universities in the Arab world. By means of appointments of top leadership in the university the state reserves for itself ultimate control over all aspects of university affairs. In 1985 Kuwait University attempted to implement a freer and more rational practice regarding the appointment of the university rector, deans, and chairpersons of academic departments through the introduction of search committees. This effort had a precedent: in 1975 the first Kuwaiti rector insisted that the University Council should be consulted about his nomination. Since that time, in accordance with Law 29, the rector, secretary-general, and assistant secretary-general have been appointed by government decree after approval by the council of ministers. There has been no requirement that the University Council be consulted. Only the vice-rectors, a recent innovation, are appointed by the University Council. The University Council is composed of the rector, the secretary-general, the vice-rectors, the deans of colleges, the dean of student affairs, and the dean of admissions and registration. In addition to the minister of higher education, who presides as chancellor, the other members of the government and people from the private sector also sit on the council. Aside from a newly formed consultative university senate, there is no statutory basis for faculty participation in decision making.

In its formal structure—spelled out by law or developed through bureaucratic traditions—Kuwait University, like other Gulf and Arabian Peninsula universities, was essentially conditioned by the Egyptian university traditions, academically and administratively. The first university rector, appointed in 1965, was Egyptian and brought with him not only the bulk of the teaching staff but an Egyptian bureaucratic organization. Duplication of Egyptian university forms and procedures extended even to stationery and applications. But the Egyptian model was not confined to the university; it exerted a strong influence throughout the entire state bureaucracy. Recent efforts in Kuwait to rationalize managerial and administrative structures have essentially reflected a desire to overcome the negative consequences of the Egyptian legacy.

Problems of Enrollment and Admissions

From its inception Kuwait University followed an open-door admissions policy that made it possible for all high school graduates to apply. But whereas the 1960 commission report had recommended an annual intake of three hundred male and seventy-five female students so as to maintain a total undergraduate body of between 1,200 and 1,500 students, the first intake far exceeded the initial projection. This trend continued into the 1970s, as Table 1 and Table 2 indicate.

Table 2 demonstrates that the growth rate of the 1980s surpassed that of the previous decade. Table 2 also shows the impact of the adoption of a more restrictive admissions policy in 1985; under this new policy the number of students admitted dropped by a little under half from the high of 1984/85. This is reflected by a decrease in total enrollment of 4,193 from a high of 18,187 in 1985/86 to 13,994 in 1987/88.

Ever-increasing political and social pressures led in some years to a doubling or tripling of enrollment. These massive leaps in enrollment were characterized by a total lack of planning and a consequent significant drop in student quality. When the new admissions policy was adopted in 1985, and cut the student intake in half, strenuous objections were raised in parliament. Such objections were natural in a social context that associates university degrees with government jobs and in which salary scales are stratified according to degrees earned rather than job performance.

The increase in student numbers at Kuwait University has been coupled with the university's inability to control the quality of the students admitted. The only criterion for admission into the university is the final score a student attains on a test given in the last year of high school. Lack of admissions standards results in a tremendous gap between high school curricula and that of the university. The influence exercised over American high schools by the College Entrance Examination Board or over Lebanese high schools by the American University of Beirut Entrance Examination is completely absent in Kuwait. What students study in secondary school often leaves them totally unprepared to study at the university.

Kuwait University's student body is somewhat unique in its composition since it is characterized by a large percentage of nonnationals and more females than males. Although the first-year intake in 1966 totaled 418 students, of

Table 1

Enrollment Growth

Year	New Students	% of increase	Total
1966/67	418	—	418
1967/68	516	24	874
1968/69	557	10	1,337
1969/70	564	1	1,713
1970/71	654	16	1,988
1971/72	1,018	56	2,453
1972/73	1,271	25	2,286
1973/74	1,245	2	3,836
1974/75	1,552	24.7	4,445
1975/76	1,658	6.8	5,832
1976/77	1,630	4	5,968
1977/78	2,800	19.2	7,500

Source: Report on Admission Policy of Kuwait University March 1978 (in Arabic).

whom 358 or 86 percent were Kuwaiti, by 1977 the Kuwaiti percentage in the university as a whole had dropped to 59 percent. Recently, as the result of raising the admission requirements for non-Kuwaitis, the percentage of Kuwaiti students has increased to 71 percent. Similarly, although females (149) accounted for 42 percent of the Kuwaiti intake in 1966, by 1977 females accounted for 56 percent of the Kuwaiti intake and 58 percent of all Kuwaiti students in the university. By 1988 females represented 67 percent of the total student population.

There are many reasons for the increasing percentage of females at the university. The most significant reason is that females have limited alternatives other than a university education. Male students can study abroad at their own expense or on government scholarship, but young women do not have this freedom. The conservatism of the Kuwaiti middle- and lower-middle-class families also helps to explain high female enrollment. Women are encouraged to enroll in education and nursing courses so that they can have professional-level jobs and yet work in a totally female environment.

Faculty Recruitment and Development

One of the major problems that has confronted Kuwait University from the beginning is the recruitment and development of a highly qualified and dedicated faculty. This was one of the major goals set forth by the 1960 commission report: "It is generally acknowledged that of the main elements which comprise a university, the faculty is the principal constituency. Indeed, it is axiomatic that the stature of a university is primarily determined by the quality,

Table 2

University Enrollment

Year	New Admission	Total Enrollment
1980/81	2,717	9,640
1981/82	3,122	10,335
1982/83	4,123	11,708
1983/84	4,884	14,394
1984/85	5,084	17,141
1985/86	2,946	18,187
1986/87	3,115	17,419
1987/88	3,039	13,994

Source: University Admission 1988/89 Kuwait University.

intellectual vigour and renown of its faculty members. That is, of course, as is to be expected, or should be, for they are the ones that set the tone of academic life within the scholarly community, and they are the ones on whom society primarily depends for the discharge of two of the university's most fundamental missions: the expansion of the frontiers of knowledge, and the training and certification of academic competence of students entrusted to its care."[7]

The major reasons for continued and ever-increasing difficulties in recruiting qualified faculty are the absence of a retirement plan for non-Kuwaitis, the lack of research facilities, the absence of qualified support staff, a fragmented faculty with no sustained academic life, and the absence of a democratic structure wherein faculty can effectively participate in decision making. The current rector of Kuwait University has addressed the non-Kuwaiti faculty problem:

As for non-Kuwaiti, the reappointment process has given rise to much concern, and the feeling of insecurity, sometimes caused by pressure groups. Even until recently, some prominent Arab scientists, who are helping with the present restructuring of Kuwait University, had been threatened with future dismissal, when a new administration takes over. Such occurrences illustrate the importance of adopting new personnel policies which should remove the element of threat from any source, whether internal or external. The new appointment, reappointment, termination and tenure policies are at the final stage of study and should be ready for final discussion and approval. Briefly, it stresses the right of the University to maintain quality and provide security on the one hand and the rights of the individual to a just and equitable decision making process on the other.[8]

The development and retention of a qualified Kuwaiti staff is another problem confronting the university. The university began a scholarship program in 1967 to secure future Kuwaiti faculty by sending selected nominees abroad on scholarship for advanced degrees. Upon their return, however, many of these students are enticed away by the lure of higher salaries in the private sector. And the automatic tenure enjoyed by those returning with their Ph.D.'s tends to have severe negative effects for the university: "The present personnel policies leave much to be desired. The policy of appointment of Kuwaitis to the teaching staff at Kuwait University is not practiced anywhere in the world where there are high-quality universities. A fresh university graduate, once awarded a Ph.D., has tenure from day one. Such a policy can only breed mediocrity, for it is well known that not all holders of a Ph.D. are successful academics."[9] The negative impact of this policy is abundantly clear and obviously affects interfaculty relations. The university is currently evaluating this serious problem and proposes to make certain recommendations for improvement.

Higher Education and Employment

The initiation of the scholarship program in 1957 meant the adoption in higher education of the concept of entitlement. Students were sent abroad after finishing high school with little attention given to their field of study or performance. When the university opened in 1966, its admissions policy reflected the same philosophy. The only requirement for admission during the university's first twelve years was the achievement of a 55 percent grade in the high school final examination. In 1978 a new admissions policy was adopted that linked the annual university intake to its overall capacity; thereafter a minimum 60 percent score on the final exam was required for admission. But a lax period of four years witnessed another large increase in student enrollment. In the early 1980s the university again tightened its requirements for intake, cutting the rate of enrollment almost in half by 1985.

With the adoption of an unconditional entitlement approach to higher education, Kuwait was left with no mechanism for producing leadership in the public or private sectors. The majority of higher education graduates seek government employment, usually characterized by bureaucratic criteria. Promotion, remuneration, and esteem are not tied to job performance. Because of an increasing number of graduates, the government was forced to enlarge its own work force. But since there were limits to such an enlargement, the problem of unemployment began to surface. Meanwhile, other sectors of society that require high-level management skills are being run by non-Kuwaitis.

These policies have left Kuwait in a most peculiar condition. While possessing some characteristics that place it in the advanced, developed world, other characteristics place Kuwait among the less developed countries. As a rentier state Kuwait has the following characteristics:

1. Of a total population of approximately 1.9 million, less than 30 percent are Kuwaitis.
2. Of a total labor force of approximately 798,249, less than 15 percent are Kuwaitis. Of all Kuwaitis employed, 40.5 percent are in the government sector. The government has used employment as a means of distributing oil wealth. Government employment is looked at as an entitlement by the Kuwaiti. The net result is continued reliance on expatriate labor, which leaves Kuwait with few options for economic development and diversification. Kuwait's investment in human capital, which compares favorably with that of some advanced countries, will produce few returns unless the government takes bold political steps to address the situation, for example, by changing the civil service salary scale to link hard work and productivity with pay incentives.
3. The composition of the Kuwait University student body, as previously noted, is unique. It is characterized by a large percentage of nonnationals and more females than males. In 1987/88 females accounted for about 67 percent of the total student enrollment. The success rate of non-Kuwaiti students was considerably higher than that of Kuwaiti students.
4. Many high-income Kuwaiti families have provided their children with such comfortable lives that they have no economic incentive to work. The relationship between normal wages or salaries in return for hard work has become blurred. This problem helps to explain why so many Kuwaitis enroll in humanities and ignore scientific and technological studies.

Reforming the Academic Structure

In the advisory commission report of 1960 it was properly noted that the structure of a new university is affected by the conditions under which it is established. In some Arab countries universities were preceded by colleges and other institutions of higher learning. While in some cases these preexisting institutions made the establishment of universities easier, artificial unification by government fiat often led to technical and administrative difficulties of a permanent nature. The experts hoped that the proposed University of Kuwait, unhampered by any preexisting institutions or traditions, would be unrestricted in planning its structure and administration.

The report referred to a pattern whereby several competing departments were established for the same science in the same university. For example, the college of science, the college of engineering, and the college of pharmacy each might have a chemistry department. Or the college of arts and the faculty of commerce might each have a geography department. Such duplication, plus a lack of coordination, an absence of channels of communication, extreme decentralization, etc. often characterizes the university created by amalgamating former independent institutions. Each college maintains its own separate teaching staff, courses, laboratories, and scientific associations, and its students are prevented from cross-registering for courses in any other college.

Arab universities suffer from many shared flaws that can be traced back to their origins. Egypt created a National University in 1908 that became the model for most other Arab universities in the Near East. But the Egyptian university itself was modeled on nineteenth-century British and French universities, with heavy emphasis on arts and humanities. Although lack of concern with science, technology, and research was not unusual for the time, a subsequent failure to readjust priorities in keeping with the demands of industrialization left the Arab universities far behind their western counterparts. Moreover, the French and British who ruled most of the Near East until after World War II geared the entire educational structure toward the servicing of colonial needs, in particular the production of bureaucrats. Despite the end of colonial rule, traditions established by the colonial powers persist. Thus the university systems in most Arab nations continue, directly and indirectly, to pursue the mission of producing civil servants. In the absence of financial incentives to study subjects that would have practical or developmental consequences, Arab students continue to aspire to become professional bureaucrats. As mentioned above, the development of separate professional schools and colleges in the Arab world preceded the creation of universities. In Egypt, for example, the professional schools of medicine, engineering, pharmacy, law, and agriculture were founded in the nineteenth century. The first university in Egypt, as elsewhere throughout the Near East, was created by joining together these separate institutions. This type of organization presented obstacles. The independent traditions of various departments and colleges prevented the universities formed in this way from becoming unified, cohesive bodies—a problem that persists today.

In a major change of course, breaking with the Egyptian model, Kuwait University in 1975/76 adopted a new educational philosophy embodied in the course unit system of the American model. Having first proved its value and success on a provisional basis in the College of Commerce, Economics, and Political Science, the course unit system became the norm throughout the university. It was adopted to provide greater flexibility and adaptability in accordance with student interest and national needs. It was also intended to rationalize teacher-student work loads, reduce reliance upon year-end examinations, and promote student responsibility in shouldering academic decisions affecting their own lives.

Although adoption of the course unit system brought numerous benefits to the university, many of the teaching staff charged with its implementation had no prior experience with it and failed to grasp its philosophy. In the absence of such experience, students have frequently been poorly advised, grades have not been scientifically assessed, and the full potential of the system has yet to be realized.

Table 3

Population and Work Force

Population According to Nationalities December 1988

Nationality	Number	%
Kuwaiti	534,827	28
Non-Kuwaiti	1,380,599	72
Total	1,915,426	100

Total Work Force December 1988

Nationality	Number	%
Kuwaiti	112,689	14
Non-Kuwaiti	685,560	86
Total	798,249	100

Work Force According to Sectors December 1988

Sector	Number	%
Government	249,847	32
Private	539,337	68
Total	789,184	100

Work Force According to Nationality and Sector December 1988

Nationality	Government	Private	Total
Kuwaiti	101,261 (40.5%)	8,595 (1.6%)	109,856
Non-Kuwaiti	148,586 (59.5%)	530,742 (98.4%)	789,184

Table 4

Kuwait University Faculty—Student Statistics

Faculty	Number of the Academic Staff 1988–1989			Number of Enrolled Students 2nd Semester 1988–1989			Ratio of Staff to Students
	Kuwaiti	Non-Kuwaiti	Sum Total	Kuwaiti	Non-Kuwaiti	Sum Total	
Science	63	135	198	1,442	939	2,381	1:12
Arts	71	109	180	1,739	630	2,369	1:13.2
Law	16	23	39	746	159	905	1:23.2
Commerce, Economics, and Pol. Science	41	73	114	1,411	463	1,874	1:16.4
Engineering and Petroleum	48	52	100	941	546	1,487	1:14.9
Medicine	23	143	166	406	121	527	1:3.2
Education	40	28	68	1,837	293	2,130	1:31.3
Shari'a	3	36	39	317	150	467	1:12
Allied Health Sciences and Nursing	—	14	14	262	213	475	1:33.9
Sum Total	305	613	918	9,101	3,514	12,614	1:13.7

The Public Authority for Applied Education and Training

Postsecondary technical and vocational education began in Kuwait in the 1970s with the establishment of the postsecondary Commercial Institute. This institute was supposed to offer technical training in accounting and the use of business equipment and to tailor various study programs according to market needs. In 1969 a postsecondary Teachers Training Institute for men and another one for women were established; both offered a two-year course to train primary school teachers. In 1986 the two-year program was extended to a four-year program and the name of the institute was changed to the College of Basic Education. In the mid-1970s an Institute of Health was set up to offer nursing training to secondary school graduates. To provide a more systematic approach to these specialized studies in 1981 the parliament established the Pub-

lic Authority for Technical Education and Training with the purpose of developing Kuwait's manpower to compensate for the shortage in national technical manpower and meet the requirements for the country's development.

The Public Authority is composed of the following applied institutes, corresponding to the professional, commercial, and technological activities of the country: the College of Technological Studies, the College of Basic Education, the College of Business Studies, and the College of Health Sciences. The training component of the Public Authority is composed of the following training centers: the Telecommunication and Air Navigation Training Center, the Water and Electricity Training Center, and the Industrial Training Center.

The establishment of the Public Authority for Applied Education and Training (PAAET) in 1982 marked the government's awareness of the country's need for blue-collar workers to offset continuing reliance upon non-Kuwaitis. Although the objectives listed in the charter of the Public Authority seem to be appropriate to the country's needs for skilled workers, few, if any, of these aims have been accomplished. Although the reasons for the contradiction between the aims and the accomplishments of PAAET are many, some of the major reasons include the lack of well-defined strategies, a growing reliance upon theoretical studies, the government salary structure, staffing problems reflected in heavy emphasis on academic qualifications at the expense of practical experience, and, lack of adequate buildings and equipment. All of these problems are interlinked with prevailing Kuwaiti social values that denigrate manual work. As one expert noted, "A major public relations campaign is needed to get across the importance of the more difficult work. It may be that salary scales, etc., are wrong, and that government effort is needed to put them right, but a country which does not give proper esteem to those activities on which it places fundamental dependence is heading for trouble."[10]

Conclusions

Kuwait's higher education system is now twenty-four years old. It has been estimated that the country has spent more than four billion dollars on the system. Now it is imperative that Kuwait should re-evaluate and rethink its higher education system to determine whether its objectives have been accomplished.

Of crucial importance is the introduction of the concept of planning in higher education in order to redefine its role in the development of the country. The output of the system must be linked with the manpower needs of the country or at least related in broad outline to the future needs of the country in various specialties. A reconsideration of the mass approach to higher education is long overdue. The system would profit from the introduction of entrance examinations designed to weed out the weaker students. The government should consider a program of elite education for the purpose of training leaders.

Kuwait University has been under severe pressure to accept ever-increasing numbers of students. The rigidity of government salary structures, which admit no avenue for promotion except through university degrees, is a major cause of this public pressure. Efforts in the early 1980s to restrict enrollment in Kuwait University led to an outcry against the minister of education.

As long as Kuwait University represents the only avenue to higher education, problems will become worse. The solution is to rethink the whole educational system, starting with the primary level, with the purpose of creating more educational avenues. This drastic reform should be coupled with a reform of the government

Table 5

Enrollment in the Public Authority Institutes 1981–1982 to 1988–1989

Year	Male	Female	Total
1980–81	1,743	2,269	4,012
1981–82	2,294	2,549	4,843
1982–83	2,793	2,948	5,741
1983–84	2,780	2,901	5,681
1984–85	2,570	2,840	5,410
1985–86	2,894	3,310	6,204
1986–87	3,575	4,150	7,725
1987–88	3,581	4,570	8,151
1988–89	3,518	5,222	—

Source: Public Authority for Applied Education and Training, Dean of Students and Trainees Affairs, April 1989 (in Arabic).

bureaucracy, beginning with its salary structure.

Higher education in Kuwait, as in the rest of the Arab world, has not succeeded in meeting the development needs of the country.[11] Kuwait, because of its small population and its scarcity of human resources, is in dire need of development. It requires a university that will be a center of excellence and a leader of development. The Public Authority needs to be reformed so that it will not be a dumping place for those who are rejected by the university. The development of Kuwait, like all modern nations, depends upon the development of people and the intelligent organization of human activity, which should be the mission of the Kuwait higher education system.

Table 6

Public Authority Academic Staff April 1989

Nationality	Ph.D.	Non-Ph.D.	Total
Kuwaiti	23	203	226
Non-Kuwaiti	184	91	275
Total	207	294	501

Public Authority Training Staff April 1989

Kuwaiti	89
Non-Kuwaiti	50
	139

Notes

1. *Kuwait Official Gazette*, March 1989. See also Kuwait Ministry of Education, *Archeological Investigations in the Island of Failaka, 1958–1964* (Kuwait: 1964) (in Arabic).
2. See A. L. Tibawi, *Islamic Education* (London: Luzak & Co., 1979); H. A. Al-Ebraheem, *Kuwait and the Future: Education and Development* (Kuwait: 1989) (in Arabic).
3. For details, see Kuwait Ministry of Education, *Report on the Evaluation of the Kuwait Educational System* (1987) (in Arabic).
4. Kuwait Department of Education, *Report of the University Advisors Commission* (1960).
5. *Report of the Kuwait University Admissions and Registration Office*, May 1988 (in Arabic).
6. *Rector's Report*, Kuwait University, September 1988.
7. Kuwait Department of Education, *Report of the University Advisors Commission* (1960). For details on faculty recruitment at Kuwait University, see H. A. Al-Ebraheem and S. N. Anabtawi, "Patterns of Faculty Recruitment in Development Setting: Some Preliminary Findings at Kuwait University," in *The Arab Brain Drain*, ed. A. B. Zahlan (Ithaca Press, 1981), 59–68.
8. *Rector's Report*, Kuwait University, 12 September 1987.
9. Ibid.
10. Sir Alex Smith, *Report on a Visit to Kuwait*, 31 March–13 April 1984, 16.
11. G. A. Sinclair, *Education in Kuwait, Bahrain, and Qatar: An Economic Assessment* (Ph.D. diss., Durham University, United Kingdom, 1977), 314.

Lebanon

Samir A. Jarrar

◆

Lebanon lies on the eastern shores of the Mediterranean Sea, at the crossroads of the Middle East. Lebanon has witnessed many waves of invaders and settlers since the dawn of civilization. Cultures and convictions mixed on its shores, sometimes merging and occasionally colliding. In its recent history, Lebanon was part of the Ottoman Empire that dominated the region for four centuries (1516–1918). After World War I, the region was placed under French and British mandate by the League of Nations. The state of "Greater Lebanon" was established by the French Mandatory Authority on August 31, 1920. The Republic of Lebanon was declared on May 23, 1926, and a constitution was drafted. Lebanon became an independent state on November 22, 1943.

Culturally, geographically, and economically, Lebanon is part of the Arab World. It was a founding member of the League of Arab States and the United Nations, both established in 1945. The Lebanese population, estimated at three million in 1989, comprises a mosaic of religious and ethnic groups. The country is small, with an area of 4,160 square miles.

Educational System Background

Lebanon's educational system can only be understood in relation to its particular social structure. Lebanon is the only Arab country with a large number of minorities, some religious, others ethnic. Under Ottoman rule, minorities were allowed to regulate their personal and community affairs under the "Millah" system. This system, established in the early days of the Muslim expansion, allowed minorities to handle their religious, personal, and educational needs in accordance with their cultural traditions and heritage. The Franco-Ottoman Concordat, signed in 1535, gave French subjects living in the Ottoman Empire the right to conduct their own religious and community affairs, including education. These rights, known as the "capitulations," were extended in time to include all Catholics and eventually other Christians who lived in territories ruled by the empire.[1] By the late nineteenth century, non-Islamic religious groups in the region looked to various Western powers to guarantee their rights. As a result, the Catholics and Maronites allied themselves with the Holy See in Rome, and France; the Shiites allied themselves with Iraq and Iran; the Greek Orthodox believers allied themselves with czarist Russia; and the Druses and Protestants allied themselves with Britain.

The capitulations became a fixture in the Lebanese political structure. They have affected the educational system to a great extent, enabling private education to dominate. The establishment of "Greater Lebanon" as a state under the mandate system did not change the educational scene. In fact, Article 8 of the mandate agreement stipulated the following: "The right of each community to maintain its own schools for the instruction and education of its own members in its own language while conforming to such educational requirements of a general nature as the administration may impose, shall not be denied or impaired."[2] The article opened the doors for all groups to run their own education systems. This trend was further strengthened when the Lebanese Constitution was adopted in 1926. Article 10 of the constitution reads as follows: "There shall be no interference with public instruction as long as the latter is not contrary to public order and morals and does not impinge upon the free exercise of the various creeds. The religious communities shall be entitled to maintain their own schools, provided they conform to the general requirements relating to public instruction set forth by the state."[3] As a result, private education became the rule in Lebanon. By the time Lebanon achieved independence in 1943, public schools accounted for only 16.5 percent of student enrollment at the elementary and intermediate levels, and 2.7 percent of the enrollment at the secondary and normal (teaching training) levels.[4] Higher education was totally private.

Under Ottoman rule, education in the empire served one main purpose, to train servants of the state, bureaucrats, and military personnel. Other educational needs were ignored. As a result, private education flourished in what became Lebanon. Private education in Lebanon dates back to 1770, when Jesuit missionaries established two schools. In 1782 the first national private school for elementary and secondary education was established in Ain-Waraqa.

Protestant missionaries started a school system after their arrival in 1820. By the end of the nineteenth century they had 123 schools, including the first school for girls. In 1866 the Evangelical Mission to Syria established the Syrian Protestant College, later known as the American University of Beirut (AUB). Its founder, Dr. Bliss, is claimed to have said that he was going to establish two universities. When asked to explain, he said, "Once an American university is established the French will open one." He was proven right when, in 1875, the Jesuits founded Saint Joseph University. Thus, the foundations of the present higher education system in Lebanon were laid in the second half of the nineteenth century.

Trends in Higher Education

Higher education in Lebanon predates the creation of the state. The birthplace of the alphabet, Lebanon was exposed to higher education as early as the fifteenth century B.C. when the "Beirut School of Law" was established. The school scholars produced and codified the laws of many ancient countries, including the Roman Law codes of Justinian. The school had a major library, and was a center for publishing and keeping records of the laws until it was destroyed by an earthquake in A.D. 555.[5]

Modern higher education started with the establishment of the Syrian Protestant College in 1866 and Saint Joseph University in 1875. Other than the West Bank and Ghaza, Lebanon is the only Arab country where higher education is mainly private. In 1989 there were nineteen institutions of higher education of which only one, the Lebanese University, was public. As noted in Table 1, in 1979/80 a majority of the students, 51 percent, were in private institutions. By 1981/82 the public university enrollment had dropped to 41.3 percent of the total student population.

Up until the mid–1970s most tertiary institutions were concentrated in the metropolitan Beirut area. The civil war and the fragmentation of the country have had one positive result, namely, the creation of new campuses in other parts of the country. By 1988 the Lebanese University had thirty-one campuses scattered in all the five governates of the Lebanese republic. These satellite campuses were established between 1976 and 1982.[6] AUB has established an off-campus program, while Beirut University college has an affiliation with the Notre Dame de Louaize order, and another with the Makassed philanthropic

Table 1

Enrollments in Lebanese Universities by Nationality and Sex

Univ.	Year Begun	1979/80			1981/82		
		No. of Students	% of non-Lebanese	% of Females	No. of Students	% of non-Lebanese	% of Females
Al-Hikema Law Inst.	1961	245	0.4	46.1	151	0.0	54.3
Amer. Univ. of Beirut	1866	4,530	24.7	38.5	4,709	23.9	40.3
Beirut Arab Univ.	1960	28,698	87.4	19.5	24,856	88.9	20.6
Beirut Univ. College*	1924	1,420	25.0	56.1	1,813	24.5	55.0
Haigazian College	1955	225	23.6	40.9	275	18.9	45.5
Holy Spirit Univ. (Kaslik)	1962	2,116	2.4	44.5	2,244	3.4	43.2
Imam Al-Ouzai Islamic Faculty	——	——	——	——	147	41.5	14.3
Islamic College (Tripoli)	——	——	——	——	——	——	——
Lebanese Acad. of Fine Arts	1937	460	4.1	51.7	589	4.4	56.4
Lebanese Univ.	1952	41,684	7.0	44.5	29,048	6.9	47.7
Louvin Univ. (Baabda)	——	165	0.6	27.9	338	0.0	25.7
Makassed Center for Higher Ed. (Saida)	1979	——	——	——	65	12.3	58.5
Middle East College	1946	69	23.2	39.1	149	20.8	43.6
Near East School of Theology	1932	10	70.0	10.0	25	68.0	20.0
Saddam Hussein Faculty of Medicine	——	——	——	——	24	8.3	54.2
St. John of ** Damascus Inst.		33	42.4	18.2	53	37.7	18.9
St. Joseph Univ.	1875	5,265	3.8	46.5	5,381	5.9	47.0
St. Mary U. (Louizeh)	1978	140	7.9	30.7	394	8.6	33.0
St. Paul Inst. (Harissa)	——	27	51.9	3.7	53	41.5	3.8
Totals		85,087	35.1	36.0	70,314	37.5	37.4

* Earlier known as Beirut College for Women. In 1970 males were admitted and name was changed to Beirut University College.

** Changed name to Balamand University in 1987.

Source: Computed from preliminary statistics for the years 1979–80 and 1981–82. Ministry for Education, Center for Educational Development and Research, Beirut.

association in Saidon, South Lebanon. Saint Joseph University has established branches in Tripoli, Sidon, and Zahle. Decentralization of higher education was needed before the war to serve people in different regions of the country who could not afford to live in Beirut. Decentralization could have helped the economy by linking university research to the regions. However, forced decentralization due to the war has led to the establishment of campuses that have few resources (i.e., buildings, libraries, and laboratories). As a result, the newly established campuses are mainly social sciences and humanities colleges that do not satisfy the economic needs of the regions. It is estimated that 70 percent of the students of the Lebanese University are enrolled in such colleges. This situation will only increase the problem of unemployment that plagues Lebanon.

Table 2 provides a breakdown of enrollments by field of study. Though the figures available are dated, they do indicate that between 1959 and 1983 student enrollment in the sciences and applied studies has dropped from 27.4 percent to 19.3 percent, while enrollments in the humanities and social sciences increased from 72.6 percent to 80.7 percent. The one positive factor is the increase in the percentage of women enrolled, from 23 percent in 1959 to 37.3 percent in 1983.

Governance of Higher Education

By the time Lebanon got its independence in 1943, all institutions of higher education were private. The American University of Beirut and the Beirut University College (known at the time as Beirut College for Women) were chartered by the Board of Regents of the State of New York, and pursued an American liberal arts tradition. Saint Joseph University was affiliated with the University of Lyons in

Table 2

Distribution of Lebanese Students in Tertiary Education by Field of Study and Percentage of Females, 1959–83

Field of Study:	Humanities, Education, and Fine Arts			Law and Social Sciences			Natural Sciences, Medical Sciences, Engineering, and Agriculture			TOTAL		
	T	%F	%	T	%F	%	T	%F	%	T	%F	%
1959	2,710	24.0	39.8	2,228	28.0	32.7	1,862	16.0	27.4	6,800	23.0	100.0
1965	8,115	27.0	39.9	9,273	10.0	45.6	2,957	22.0	14.5	20,345	19.0	100.0
1969	19,467	30.0	50.5	14,108	13.0	36.6	4,482	20.0	11.6	38,519	23.0	98.8*
1980	14,823	57.0	18.7	47,498	31.0	60.0	16,321	31.0	20.6	79,073	36.0	99.5*
1983				58,974		80.7	14,078	36.9	19.3	73,052	37.3	100.0

*Some fields of study were not identifiable

Sources: UNESCO Statistical Year Books, 1960–86; M. Bashshur, *Similarities and Contrasts in Patterns of Higher Education in the Arab World* (Sweden: Lund University, 1985). (Mimeograph).

Table 3

Lebanese Universities: Language of Instruction, Library Holdings, Academic Calendar, Major Faculties, and Degrees Awarded

University	Language of Instruction	Academic Staff 1984/85	Library Holdings	Academic Year	Major Faculties/ Degrees
Al-Hikma Law Institute	F	n/a	n/a	Year	L/Lic., Dip.
Amer. Univ. of Beirut	E	367 F.T.	435,000	Sem.	M, E, Ar, Ag, Ed, Cs/BA, MA, Ph.d, MD
Beirut Arab University	A, E	67 F.T. 194 P.T.	200,500	Year	A, L, E, A, S/Lic BA, MA
Beirut Univ. College	E, A	60 F.T. 130 P.T.	40,000	Sem.	S, A, Ln, Ed, Cs, E, BA
Haigazian College	E	20 F.T. 30 P.T.	38,000	Sem.	Bus., BA S, A, Armenian, Ed
Holy Spirit Univ.	A, F	67 F.T. 298 P.T.	140,000	Sem.	R, A, L, Ed, Bus. Lic, Dip., Ph.D.
Imam Al-Ouzai Islamic Faculty	A	n/a	n/a	Year	BA
Islamic College	A	n/a	n/a	Year	BA
Lebanese Acad. of Fine Arts	F	n/a	n/a	Year	A, Ar, Music, Int. Des., Dip
Lebanese Univ.	A, E, F	530	n/a	Sem.	S, L, Ed, A, Lic, Dip., Ph.d.
Louvin Univ.	F	n/a	n/a	Sem.	M, D, E Lic., Dip.
Makassed Center for Higher Ed.	——	——	——	Sem.	Ed., Bus, BA
Middle East College	E	n/a	n/a	Sem.	S, BA R, T, Ed., Bus.
Near East School of Theology	E	——	——	Sem.	MA, Dip. T, Divinity, BA
Saddam Hussein Faculty of Medicine	A, E	n/a	n/a	Year	Medical Sciences BA, M, MD
St. John-Balamand Coll.	E	n/a	n/a	Sem.	T, Hum., BA
St. Joseph University	F, E	230 F.T. 681 P.T.	n/a	Sem.	R, M, P, D, E, L, A Lic, Dip, Ph.d, MD
St. Mary University	E	n/a	n/a	Sem.	Bus, Cs, E, Sec. Se. R.A.
St. Paul Institute	E	n/a	n/a	Sem.	T/BA

Ag=Agriculture; Ar=Architecture; A=Arts; Cs=Computer Sc; D=Dentistry; Ed=Education; E=Engineering; Ft=Food Techn; Ln=Languages; L=Law; M=Medicine; P=Pharmacy; R=Religious Studies; S=Sciences; T=Technology; Vm=Veterinary Med.

Source: Adapted from George I. Za'rour, *Universities in Arab Countries* (Washington, D.C.: World Bank, 1988); Leslie Schmida, ed., *Education in the Middle East* (Washington, D.C.: AMIDEAST, 1983).

France and governed by a board of trustees. It followed a traditional French program of study, with courses in French culture and professional training.

The Lebanese University, established in 1952, is the only university in Lebanon that is now under the direct control of the Ministry of Education.

With the exception of the Beirut Arab University, established in 1960, which is sponsored and controlled by Alexandria University in Egypt, all institutions follow either the American or French models. All universities in Lebanon are governed by a president or a rector, aided by a university council or its equivalent. The Ministry of Education, in principle, supervises all institutions of higher education. However, once an institution meets the requirements set by the government for establishing an institute of higher education and is accredited, very little supervision follows. Universities have a high degree of freedom in running their programs, setting their requirements, and carrying out instruction.

Admission requirements vary among institutions. While most faculties at the Lebanese University and the Beirut Arab University do not require entrance exams, most private universities do require entrance exams. Students who choose subject areas taught in either English or French must take their entrance exams in that language. The American University of Beirut developed a battery of exams that are used by most institutions. Foreign nationals applying at tertiary institutions in Lebanon must have a high school diploma or certificate that is recognized by the Ministry of Education. They must sit for entrance exams, and are usually admitted to the freshman class, or its equivalent.

After the beginning of the civil war in 1975, the educational system was faced with interruptions and cancellations of government baccalaureate exams. High school diplomas and full entrance exams have since become the norm for admission. The influx of foreign students dropped, except at Beirut Arab University (BAU), where class attendance is not a requirement. End-of-year exams for BAU are held in neighboring countries like Egypt and Jordan.

The Lebanese civil war has had a major negative effect on the educational system. Political, religious, and cultural differences already present in Lebanon have been exacerbated to the great harm of intellectual life. Beirut, home to most of Lebanon's colleges and universities, has become a dangerous and unliveable city. As a result, universities and colleges had to establish branches in the regions.

The Lebanese University (LU) was the first to branch out. On August 24, 1976, a decree promulgated by the Council of Ministers allowed the establishment of branches of LU in different regions since the main campus was no longer accessible to all students. Though some considered this move as a partitioning gesture, most critics later accepted it as a measure of decentralization. A series of decrees issued by the Council of Ministers in 1977 and 1978 established units of LU in Tripoli, to serve North Lebanon; in Nabatiyah, to serve South Lebanon; and in Ksara, to serve the Biqa' region. The directors of these new branches were given broad administrative, financial, and academic responsibilities.

Private institutions dealt with the issue of branching out differently. AUB started an "off-campus program" as a temporary measure to serve students in parts of the country whose population was isolated from the main campus. Saint Joseph University, which already had some branch campuses, added more as the need arose. Beirut University College established two off-campus branches affiliated with other organizations as part of their diversification plan. Haigazian College and the Lebanese Academy for Fine Arts also added regional campuses.

Aside from starting satellite campuses and temporary branches, the civil war had other effects on tertiary education. The movement of students and faculty from one part of the country to another became hazardous. The interruption of the academic year led to the shortening of content hours and the abolition of final exams. Security and economic problems forced many established faculty members to seek employment outside the country, leading to major shortages in qualified and experienced faculty. Universities had to depend on adjunct faculty, and in many instances had to lower their standards in recruiting new instructors.

The civil war in Lebanon also had a marked effect on the quality of new students entering tertiary education. Graduates from secondary schools varied in the degree of their academic preparation due to the interruption of their education. The end of cycle exam, used to screen graduates, was often suspended because security problems interfered with the proper running of exams or the safe movement of students and instructors. High school diplomas became the main criteria for admission. Some institutions introduced entrance exams, while others expanded their exams to cover more subjects. Most institutions introduced remedial courses to assist students.

Some institutions reported that the pool of able students actually increased. The economic crisis prevented many students from studying abroad. These students helped some of the private universities to maintain their standards.

Higher Education and the Political System

Until the beginning of the civil war in 1975, Lebanon was one of the few democracies in the region. The constitution and tradition allowed for greater degrees of freedom in cultural and intellectual discourse than was usual in the Arab world.

Since the turn of the century universities in Lebanon have been centers of student activism. Many leaders of national movements and many members of the intellectual elite were trained in Lebanese universities. In the late 1960s and early

Table 4

Lebanese Students in Tertiary Education Studying Abroad in Fifty Selected Countries

Country	1974	1980	1983
Algeria	35*	180*	——
Belgium	309	699	640
Canada	237	229*	299
Egypt	n/a	349	——
France	2,499	4,408	4,066
Greece	37	117	——
Italy	165	421	682
Kuwait	59	86*	——
Morocco	12	60	——
Pakistan	11	n.a.	——
Saudi Arabia	n/a	197	——
Spain	210	150	——
Syria	268	——	——
W. Germany	199	284	313
U. K.	143	234	——
U. S. A.	1,580	6,800	5,903
Yugoslavia	44	93	——
Other	794	793	——
Total	7,250	15,117	14,225

n/a—not available
*—1979 date

Source: UNESCO Statistical Yearbook, 1976, 1983, 1986.

1970s the student movement in Lebanon became more militant. Students became more involved in shaping their future by insisting on, and getting, more active student councils and representation on university committees. Their militancy was expressed in strikes and forced closure of universities during the struggle for greater representation in higher education governance (1969–71).

The presence of foreign institutions such as the American University of Beirut and Saint Joseph University, with their Western educational philosophies, opened the door for the introduction of Western values, many of which were alien to the Arab region. Scholarly research and publication by faculty members in Lebanese universities is among the most active in the region. The level of freedom in the country prior to the civil war allowed faculty members to undertake studies and to publish articles and books that could not be published in most countries of the region. But the Western tradition of academic freedom was not always maintained due to social pressures exerted by political and religious leaders in the country. In the late 1960s a philosophy professor's contract was not renewed at the American University of Beirut because he had published a controversial book deemed heretical by religious leaders. A sociologist was denied tenure and promotion at the same university because the administration was angered by his involvement in student strikes. Although students and faculty rallied for the retention of the sociologist, his contract was terminated.

The advent of the civil war, the disintegration of the Lebanese government, and the absence of security has definitely affected academic freedoms. Many faculty members have been threatened and some have been kidnapped.

Higher Education and Employment

Higher education in Lebanon follows a liberal policy vis-à-vis employment, with very little involvement from the government. Lebanon has no manpower planning agency or other government body to regulate higher education enrollment by subject area or to set goals for the production of various kinds of professionals. Lebanon is one of the few Arab countries that has not adopted five-year plans that try to link human resource development to the needs of the country. As a result, institutions of higher education in Lebanon respond to the labor market but do not attempt to anticipate its needs. Some universities have closed facilities when they determined that enrollments in a particular faculty were dropping, or when there was an obvious surplus of graduates. AUB closed its schools of dentistry and pharmacy, and other institutions have closed their law facilities.

As we saw earlier, the majority of students are enrolled in the humanities and the social sciences. This pattern had led to serious graduate unemployment. As a result, many Lebanese graduates have immigrated to other Arab countries where employment was available. The regional picture has changed with the proliferation of institutions of higher education. This will definitely lead to new approaches in higher education planning because private institutions will have to adjust to market demands. Some of the universities have started to review their offerings and to introduce new disciplines in technology, computer sciences, and allied medical fields.

Another major force that played a role in reorienting tertiary education in Lebanon was the establishment of the Hariri Foundation in 1983. The foundation is a private, nonprofit, nonsectarian educational organization. It aims at helping to build the human resources of Lebanon through education and training, with emphasis on technology and the sciences. Through its research and development arm, the foundation undertook a general survey of basic needs in the villages, towns, and city centers of Lebanon. These research activities led to the identification of human resources needed for the country. The foundation, through its education and training program, has already served over 15,000 Lebanese students at the tertiary level. The foundation is also providing funds for universities to establish faculty development programs and to start new centers and research institutions. These efforts will be instrumental in redirecting the education and training of Lebanese toward employable skills. It is estimated that over 15 percent of Lebanese students enrolled in higher education institutions in Lebanon or abroad are sponsored by the Hariri Foundation. The foundation is also instrumental in helping its graduates find employment in Lebanon and other Arab countries.

Conclusions

The tertiary education system in Lebanon is one of the oldest in the region. The predominance of private institutions founded on varying models stimulated a higher education tradition characterized by a degree of freedom that was unique in the region. Some of Lebanon's institutions,

like the American University of Beirut and the Saint Joseph University, used to be considered among the best institutions in the region. They were able to attract exceptional faculty and students from the region and the world.

The effect of the civil war on higher education has been terrible. Physical facilities have been destroyed, faculty members have immigrated, and overall academic standards have suffered tremendously. Chaos has led the government to clamp down on academic freedom.

It is hoped that once the civil war comes to an end, and the government re-establishes its power, tertiary education can be revived to play a major role in the development of the country.

Notes

1. Munir Bashshur, "The Role of Education in the Fragmentation of the Lebanese Society," (Unpublished paper, 1984), 2.
2. Muhammad Khalil, *The Arab States and the Arab Leagues: A Documentary Record.* Vol. 1: *Constitutional Developments* (Beirut: Khayats, 1962), 96.
3. Antoine E. El-Gemayel, *The Lebanese Legal System*, Washington, D.C.: International Law Institute, 1985, 1:24.
4. R. D. Matthews and M. Akahwi, *Education in Arab Countries in the Near East* (Washington, D.C.: American Council on Education, 1949), 423.
5. El-Gemayal, *Lebanese Legal System*, 14–15.
6. Munir Bashshur, "The Demise of the Lebanese Educational System," *Al Mustaqbal Al-Arabi* 3 (May 1988): 48.

NORTH AMERICA

Canada

Michael L. Skolnik

---◆---

Broad Parameters

Canada is a bilingual, federal state with a population of 26 million unevenly dispersed over an immense geographical area. Constitutionally, education has been regarded as falling primarily within provincial jurisdiction, although the federal government influences higher education in important ways, particularly through revenue-sharing arrangements with the provinces, direct support of university research, provision of student loans and graduate scholarships, and exercise of its responsibility for ensuring adequacy of skilled manpower for the economy. Owing to the differences in historical development and perceptions of societal needs among the provinces, there are major differences among the systems of higher education of the ten provinces and two territories, making it difficult to produce valid generalizations about higher education at a national level.

Nevertheless, there are four noteworthy structural characteristics that the provincial systems share to a considerable degree. First, all provinces have binary systems with clear demarcations between the degree and nondegree sectors. In seven provinces universities concentrate on degree-level instruction and community colleges and technical institutes (which will be referred to in this chapter simply as "colleges") on nondegree instruction. In British Columbia and Alberta, community and junior colleges offer lower-level university courses for which the universities grant credit. The highest level of articulation between the two sectors is in Quebec, where the *collèges d'enseignement général et*

professionnel (CEGEPs) provide both a two-year preuniversity stream, which all Quebec students must enter in order to qualify for university, and three-year terminal vocational programs. The other seven provinces have no systemic linkages between universities and nondegree institutions, although there are several joint programs and bilateral agreements under which a university recognizes certain courses in a college for entry qualification or credit toward a degree.

A second characteristic is that all institutions that award secular degrees, as opposed to those that only train clergy for religious denominations, are public institutions in the sense that their legal status derives from an act of a provincial legislature and they receive the vast bulk of their operating revenue from a provincial government (the only exception being two small religious-affiliated institutions that offer secular degrees).

A third characteristic is the prevalence of affiliation and federation arrangements among institutions that are legally, and often financially, autonomous, but which through formal agreement operate in concert in certain, but not necessarily all, respects. Several institutions hold their own degree-granting power in abeyance, and their students earn the degrees of the larger institutions with which they are affiliated.

Fourth, public policy has encouraged the development of a network of comprehensive postsecondary institutions of approximately comparable standards rather than specialized institutions or stratified systems. One writer has observed that the Canadian university system is more egalitarian than that of the United States in terms of equal standards; but less egalitarian insofar as these standards preclude the admission of some students who might find a place in the more stratified United States system—though if not admissible to a Canadian university, students would be admissible to a college, most of which have an open-door policy.[1]

The basic statistical information, summarized in Table 1, shows that there are sixty-eight universities and 197 community colleges and technical institutes, with little change in the number of institutions since the mid-1970s. Total full-time enrollment is just under 800,000, almost 60 percent of which is in the university sector. While almost all community college enrollment was in career programs in 1966/67, by 1986/87 about one-third of the enrollment in that sector was in university transfer programs, reflecting the development of the CEGEPs in the second largest province, Quebec, in the late 1960s. Part-time enrollment in universities increased by almost three and a half times between 1966/67 and 1986/87, while full-time enrollment more than doubled. Total expenditures of colleges and universities in 1986/87 exceeded ten billion dollars.

Full-time postsecondary enrollment as a proportion of the relevant age population was 25.5 in 1986/87, an increase from the 1966/67 figure of 14.2. The greatest increase in participation rate occurred in the community college sector, from 5.8 to 19.1, compared to the increase from 10.6 to 15.2 for the university sector. Pineo and Goyder report that about 70 percent of those who complete secondary school go on to some form of postsecondary education.[2] Postsecondary participation rates differ substantially among the provinces (see Table 2), with Quebec having by far the highest rate in the community college sector.

Nova Scotia, with a population under 900,000 and eleven-degree granting institutions, but no comprehensive community college, has the highest university participation rate and the lowest community college rate. Overall postsecondary participation rates among the provinces range from 17 or 18 percent in the Atlantic and western provinces to 34.5 percent in Quebec. It should be noted, however, that postsecondary education in Quebec commences one year earlier than in the other provinces.

Table 1

Basic Parameters of Canadian Higher Education, 1966–67, 1976–77, and 1986–87

	1966–67	1976–77	1986–87[1]
Universities	57[2]	66	68
Community Colleges	125[2]	189	197
University Teachers	16,675	31,353	35,570
Com. College Teachers	n.a.	19,674	23,550
Full-time Enrollment	310,540	603,537	796,399
Univ, Undergraduate	210,618	335,866	418,267
Univ, Graduate	19,719	40,640	57,147
Com, College.Career	77,527	150,361	219,945
Com, College.Transfer	2,676	76,670	101,040
Part-time Univ. Enrol.	85,814	190,957	287,500
Degrees & Diplomas:			
Bachelor's & 1st Prof.	42,716	83,276	101,668[3]
Master's	5,256	11,555	15,948[3]
Doctor's	780	1,693	2,218[3]
Com. College Dipl./Cert.	9,182	55,414	82,144[3]
Expenditures: ($Millions)			
University	991.6[4]	2,976.7	7,353.4
Com. College	61.05[4]	1,084.5	2,812.4

[1] Preliminary figures.
[2] Figures are for 1969.
[3] Figures are for 1985–86.
[4] Figures are for calendar year 1966.

Source: Education in Canada (Statistics Canada Catalogue No. 81,229, Annual, various years).

Table 2

Full-Time Post-Secondary Education Participation Rates, Community College and University, Canada, and the Provinces and Territories, 1986–87

	Community College Enrollment Relative to Population aged 18–21	University Undergraduate Enrollment Relative to Population aged 18–21	Total Relative to Population aged 18–21	Total Relative to Population aged 18–24[1]
Newfoundland	6.3	21.6	27.9	17.3
Prince Edward Island	12.0	21.6	33.6	17.9
Nova Scotia	3.8	35.2	39.0	22.8
New Brunswick	4.6	27.9	32.5	18.6
Quebec	37.8	22.8	60.6	34.5
Ontario	15.7	27.6	43.3	25.2
Manitoba	5.5	24.7	30.2	18.1
Saskatchewan	4.5	28.8	33.3	18.9
Alberta	15.1	24.0	39.1	22.3
British Columbia	13.2	17.7	30.9	18.2
Yukon	3.7	—	3.7	2.2
Northwest Territories	2.9	—	2.9	1.7
Canada	19.1	24.9	44.0	25.5

[1]Includes university graduate enrollment.

Source: *Education in Canada 1987* (Ottawa: Statistics Canada, Catalogue No. 81-229).

Historical Forces

The earliest influences on the structure of Canadian higher education were the desires of the many religious denominations to have their own institutions and the geographic dispersal of the population. As a result of these forces, Canada, at the time of confederation (1867), with a population of about 3.5 million, had eighteen degree-granting institutions. At the same time, England and Wales, with a population of 22 million, had four universities; Scotland, with a population of 3.3 million, had four; and Australia, with a population of 1.7 million, had two.[3] All Canadian universities then were denominational institutions (Roman Catholic, Church of England, Baptist, Methodist, or Presbyterian) except Dalhousie, McGill, and Toronto. Ultimately, however, all of the denominational universities became public in order to qualify for full provincial financial support, even though some federated or affiliated colleges within the secular universities retain denominational affiliation.

Concern over dispersal of resources has been a major issue for universities since earliest times, and attempts to consolidate universities date back at least to an unsuccessful attempt in 1876 to create an umbrella University of Halifax, and the more successful reduction of six Ontario universities that existed in 1867 to three by 1910. Largely in reaction to the proliferation of degree-granting institutions in Ontario and the maritime provinces, the western provinces, which were settled later than the eastern provinces, adopted a policy of restricting university operations to one provincial institution, nondenominational and publicly funded, much along the lines of the contemporary land grant universities that were being established in the United States. This policy did not give way fully until the 1970s, by which time, commensurate with the growth of other population centers, additional institutions were established in these provinces. In the 1980s the historic concern over dispersion of resources is still manifested in stringent provincial control over the proliferation of graduate and professional programs, periodic recommendations—seldom acted upon—for amalgamation of institutions, especially in Ontario and Nova Scotia, and the stringent control over the extension of degree-granting rights and the prohibition against private universities in all provinces.[4]

To the early influence of the British liberal model and the prerevolutionary French Jesuit college model was added in the late nineteenth century a strong concern for practical studies, the vehicle for which was government intervention in the affairs of universities. For example, in 1872 the Ontario Government established a School of Practical Science which was subsequently absorbed into the University of Toronto as its Faculty of Applied Science and Engineering, and it created the Ontario Agricultural College at Guelph in 1874 which became the foundation for the University of Guelph. Between 1873 and 1910 Quebec gave direct provincial support to the establishment of schools of engineering, commerce, forestry, agriculture, dentistry, and pharmacy, all of which subsequently became affiliated with Université Laval. In the 1960s and 1970s the traditions of government influence over professional education resulted in moves by provincial governments to transfer autonomous teacher training institutes and hospital nursing programs into universities and/or colleges, and in government direction over the location, facilities, and sometimes enrollment quotas for medical, veterinary, and, at times,

other professional schools within the universities. As an extension of its assumption of responsibility for guiding the development of university activities that are perceived to have direct utilitarian outcomes, governments have had a major influence on the development of university research through provision of facilities and support of direct costs, augmented recently by the designation of centers of excellence which, again, illustrate attempts through public policy to correct the dispersion of resources that would result from natural forces.

Arguably, the most dramatic influence on the development of Canadian higher education subsequent to the push for professional education and research in the early twentieth century was the broad commitment to social equity that motivated and fueled the rather spectacular expansion of postsecondary education that commenced in the 1960s. Slightly preceding, but exemplified and galvanized by then Prime Minister Trudeau's vision of a "Just Society," social policy became increasingly focused upon redressing social and economic inequities and reducing barriers that had prevented many groups from fully partaking in Canada's affluence and cultural development (i.e., women, francophones, visible minorities, native peoples, and the rural and northern population). Postsecondary education was an important area of such social policies, as it was deemed an intrinsically valuable element of a good life and a key vehicle for social and economic mobility. If sometimes the achievements did not seem to match the exuberant social aspirations, and a few critics maintained that the primary motive for the expansion of higher education was not to promote social equity but rather to provide the literate and appropriately skilled workers for an expanding economy in the context of a knowledge explosion and technological revolution,[5] the sheer rate of expansion of postsecondary education in the 1960s and 1970s was nevertheless impressive. The means through which the expansion was achieved reflected in part the commitment to achieving greater equity. Existing programs in the existing universities were expanded; new universities were created in areas that did not have one, particularly in the northern regions; new institutional forms were introduced, most notably the community colleges and the University of Quebec, a network of constituent campuses across the province that helped Quebec achieve the largest percentage increase in university participation of any province; world-renowned distance education programs were established, especially in Quebec, Alberta, and British Columbia; the Saskatchewan Indian Federated College, the only autonomous degree-granting institution in North America that is controlled by indigenous peoples, was created; and a host of programs in special subject areas were instituted.

Flashpoints of Controversy

Fulfilling the commitment to social equity with respect to providing accessibility to postsecondary education that was made in the 1960s has been the central focus of recent controversies in postsecondary education. On the one hand, there has been heated debate as to whether significant progress has been made toward greater equality of opportunity for postsecondary education and whether enough is being done to make mass higher education genuinely accessible. On the other hand, concerns have been expressed as to whether sufficient funds are being allocated by governments, and governments in all provinces have been roundly criticized for not matching their rhetoric about accessibility with the levels of funding necessary to realize those noble objectives. Further, many university and college faculty, administrators, and students have argued that by expanding enrollment with

static or declining levels of real funding, universities and colleges face an alarming decline in the quality of their activities. The major flashpoints of controversy at the end of the 1980s—easy to identify and difficult to resolve—are captured by three words: accessibility, funding, and quality.

Accessibility has been the most extensively researched subject in Canadian higher education. Yet owing to differences in theoretical models, definitions, and data sources among different studies, there is an absence of consensus as to the nature and extent of persisting inequities.[6] One area where it appears that substantial changes have occurred is with respect to gender imbalance, as females comprise about half the student body in universities today compared to about one-third in the mid-1960s. The increase has been particularly notable in professional programs, from 15 percent in 1969 to 49 percent in 1983, led by jumps from 7 to 44 percent in law, 7 to 40 percent in commerce, 5 to 25 percent in dentistry, 26 to 42 percent in medicine, and 46 to 77 percent in pharmacy. However, a few fields remain segregated (engineering is 92 percent male and nursing is 98 percent female); and females are still underrepresented in postgraduate programs (about 40 percent of enrollment). The gender imbalance is greater among professors than students, with the percentage of women faculty members increasing only from 13 to 17 percent between 1971 and 1985. Moreover, the average salary of female professors is only about 83 percent of the salary of male professors, and there are only a few female university presidents across the country.

While there has been considerable reduction of gender imbalance, there appears to have been only modest reduction over the past two decades in the extent of inequality in university participation with respect to socioeconomic status as measured by family income or parents' education. However, for postsecondary education as a whole, there has been a substantial increase in participation from lower socioeconomic groups through their penetration of the community college sector. Indeed, as the postsecondary participation of women, minorities, and other disadvantaged groups has increased, attention has begun to focus more on type than extent of participation (e.g., college or university, full time or part time, and types of program).

An indication of the breadth and intensity of concern about accessibility is that it was the major issue identified by participants at the National Forum on Postsecondary Education, a unique national conference on postsecondary education held in 1987 that brought together federal and provincial politicians, civil servants, educators, employers, unions, and a wide range of groups concerned with postsecondary education.[7] A strong consensus emerged that vigourous action is needed to make postsecondary education "available to the sons and daughters of people who have not themselves had the opportunity," with certain groups being identified as having not had equal opportunity: native peoples, some visible minorities, francophones outside Quebec, the disabled, and women in certain fields. It is recognized that many of the factors that inhibit postsecondary participation by these groups are beyond the scope of the postsecondary system to alter, particularly the formative influences of the home and early schooling on subsequent education and career aspirations. What has been the subject of intense controversy is the extent to which reduction of inequalities is dependent upon the amount of money which colleges and universities have to spend.

Canadian universities get over 80 percent of their operating income from government grants (the other sources being tuition fees—16 percent, gifts—0.7 percent, and investment income—1.2 percent); community colleges receive 90 percent of their operating revenue and most of their capital funding from governments. For

several years since the late 1970s increases in provincial government grants to universities and colleges in various provinces were less than the rate of inflation, and more often than not were insufficient to compensate for the combined effects of inflation and enrollment increase. While the national statistics agency, Statistics Canada, publishes extensive data on higher education finance and enrollment, it does not regularly publish estimates of constant dollar funding per full-time equivalent student. However, numerous provincial and national education organizations and researchers have made such estimates. While these estimates differ somewhat, the general picture they reveal is one of declining real revenue per student. One report shows that the combined total of real provincial operating grants and tuition fees, the latter controlled by provincial governments, per full-time equivalent student declined continuously from a peak of $7,692 in 1977/78 to $6,051 in 1985/86 ($1,981).[8] Another study identified 1983/84 as a watershed year when the current dollar value of provincial operating grants per student declined for the first time.[9] Indicative of concerns about funding, there have been public demonstrations over funding (and rarely, if at all, over anything else) in almost all provinces; money has been at the center of nearly all of the strikes that have occurred in universities and colleges in the past decade; and strident criticism of government funding practices by representatives of the higher education community has become commonplace. Most of this criticism has been directed at provincial governments, as they are the direct providers of operating grants to universities and colleges.

The provinces receive funding from the federal government for postsecondary education through a complex formula involving unconditional transfer of taxation rights and cash grants—under the Federal-Provincial Fiscal Arrangements and Established Programs Financing Act of 1977. It is not possible to authoritatively calculate the amount of federal transfers that are targeted to postsecondary education. However, by making certain assumptions that relate to the structure of federal funding for postsecondary education and health that existed under the cost-sharing arrangements that preceded the present act, estimates have been made. These estimates show that the provinces have been increasingly diverting federal funds for postsecondary education to other expenditure areas, notably health, and that half the provinces are now spending less on postsecondary education than they receive for it from the federal government.[10] Needless to say, provincial politicians have refuted these calculations and have tended to blame the federal government for the declines in postsecondary funding. Universities and colleges, not caring which level of government supports them, have urged greater cooperation between the federal and provincial governments and a more effective national strategy for funding. One of the hopes for the National Forum, which was sponsored jointly by the federal government and the Council of (Provincial) Ministers of Education, Canada, was that it might usher in a new era of federal-provincial coordination in higher education policymaking, but these hopes have not yet been realized. In short, funding has become the focal point of discussion of higher education policy and the center of heated confrontation, pitting provincial against federal government; universities and colleges against government; increasingly, one university against another over the distribution of funds within each province; but surprisingly infrequently, faculty against administration, except in community colleges in some provinces.

Within the university community, there has been increasing tension between those who feel that the universities should continue to increase enrollment even with existing funding limitations, and those who feel that continuing to expand enrollment

jeopardizes both the viability of research and the quality of education. This tension has produced a few stirring polemical indictments of the quality of Canadian higher education[11] and an outpouring of studies by higher education agencies that attempt to convince provincial governments of the adverse effects of their funding policies on the quality of education. Neither category of writing has yet produced convincing evidence on the alleged deterioration in the quality of higher education or has appreciably influenced government funding policies. In part, this may be because of the inherent difficulties in measuring quality,[12] and in part because one might easily mistake the inevitable changes in the form and appearance of higher education that are coincident with the transition from elite to mass higher education for changes in quality.[13] Be that as it may, a widespread feeling exists in the higher education community that quality has deteriorated as a result of trying to increase accessibility in the face of severe funding limitations—or, at least, that a major deterioration is just around the corner.

This section would be incomplete without acknowledging, at least briefly, a minority view that the most fundamental problems in Canadian higher education are not funding, accessibility, and quality, but crises of confidence and purpose. According to this view, underfunding is a symptom of the public's lack of confidence in the capacity of higher education, as it is now oriented, to make a significant contribution to the quality of life, standard of living, or to the host of societal problems that threaten our planet, and that what is needed is a fundamental transformation of the epistemological and institutional basis of higher education. The university, it is alleged, has been taken over by an alliance of scholastic guilds that are preoccupied with narrow disciplinary specialization, the members of which value method over substance and relevance, communicate only with one another, and use concern for quality as a defense against change. Canadian criticisms of higher education along these lines are a part of a worldwide movement that challenges positivist epistemology and post-Academic Revolution professional norms that provide the underpinning of the contemporary university. This debate about the nature and purpose of the university is less animated in Canada than in some other Western countries, possibly owing to conformist traditions and the weakness of competitive forces in Canadian higher education.[14]

Higher Education and Employment

Canadian universities have explicitly rejected the idea of determining how many students to admit to each program on the basis of forecasts of the numbers of workers required in the corresponding occupations at some future date, except to a limited extent in certain professional programs.[15] The universities, and the colleges as well in their two- and three-year occupational programs (as opposed to their short-term programs for which training seats are purchased directly through the national employment service), tend to follow the "social demand" approach: student preference that is the predominant determinant of the numbers of students enrolled in most programs. Student demand for program entry, in turn, seems to be strongly influenced by students' perceptions of subsequent employment opportunities, which was evidenced, for example, by the substantial shift in applications from liberal subjects to commerce and computer science in the past decade. Surveys have revealed that improvement of career prospects is the most important reason for students' postsecondary enrollment decisions, ahead of general interest, personal development, or acquisition of communications, social, and reasoning skills.[16]

While Canada has had relatively high levels of unemployment in recent years, the rates for the highly educated have tended to be no more than half the overall rate, and there is an inverse relationship between level of education and unemployment rate. Surveys also show a positive correlation between level of education and job satisfaction, continuation of education, and utilization of knowledge and skills attained through education. Among college graduates, unemployment rates have been highest for humanities and arts graduates, lowest for health and business graduates; among university graduates, unemployment has been highest for humanities and social science graduates, lowest for graduates in business, education, and natural and applied sciences. Similarly, the highest proportions of graduates working in jobs not related to their education have been in the social sciences and humanities, particularly history, geography, political science, sociology, and English.

There is an apparent contradiction between, on the one hand, the higher incidence of unemployment and underemployment among humanities and arts graduates, and on the other, the widespread reports that employers are dissatisfied with the communications, reasoning, problem-solving, and other generic skills and knowledge of graduates. Employers recently have been urging colleges and universities to strengthen their liberal arts and general education offerings, and many employers have instituted their own literacy and basic skills training programs in the workplace. At the same time, however, graduates of career-specific programs continue to enjoy a competitive advantage in the job market. The chief executive of one large corporation acknowledged at a recent conference that while he travels the country giving speeches on the importance of liberal education, his personnel manager continues to give preference to graduates of career-specific programs over arts graduates. Probably, the answer to this paradox is that employers want colleges and universities to provide career-specific training, but they want it to rest on a solid foundation of liberal arts and general education.

Higher Education and the Political System

As recently as the late nineteenth century the Ontario Legislature appointed professors to chairs in the University of Toronto, and well into the twentieth century a university president might well comply if a provincial government wanted him to fire a professor whose views were unpalatable to the government. However, at least until recently, overt attempts by governments to influence the behavior of universities have been unnecessary because there was general agreement between government and the universities with respect to the objectives of the universities and how best to achieve them.[17]

With the emergence of the funding problems outlined earlier, the shift of control of the university from the president to the faculty, and growth of faculty unionization, there is increasing divergence between the interests of government and those of the universities. Increasingly over the past decade and a half governments have sought to influence the behavior of postsecondary institutions through the use of earmarked funding (which the universities denounce and accept, and the colleges, as agents of government policy, are only too happy to receive); external program review schemes that are intended to reduce program proliferation, but have rarely done so; and periodic royal commissions that have recommended various strategies for rationalization of programs and institutions, but which governments have generally been too timid to implement, even in regard to modest recommendations for amalgamation of facilities. However, the pressures for rationalization

are likely to increase, and the universities show increasing signs of a willingness to break ranks, with those institutions or faculties that expect to benefit from rationalization showing more inclination to support a proposed government intervention. The combination of increased government determination and division among the universities may foreshadow a significant move toward government direction over the universities in the 1990s. And such provincial influence, to the extent that it does occur, likely will be wielded directly by the government, for intermediary bodies between government and the universities exist in only half the provinces and generally have quite limited influence. As units of a protected public monopoly, almost totally dependent upon government funding, and lacking in strong political allies, the universities are quite vulnerable to the designs of elected officials, and they can only hope that politicians will act with restraint and enlightenment. Having said that, however, it should be noted that Canadian universities still enjoy an extraordinary degree of autonomy for public institutions; essentially, government gives them money, and except for some professional fields, confines its attempts at influence to exhortation.

Nor do the imminent threats to institutional autonomy bode ill for academic freedom. Though of relatively recent origin, traditions of professorial freedom from government are robust and well guarded by the Canadian Association of University Teachers and its provincial affiliates. Although the practice of earmarking funds for research in areas that are deemed to be of national or provincial importance sometimes evokes cries of infringement on academic freedom by professors in nontargeted areas, Canadian professors enjoy a degree of freedom with respect to their teaching, research, and external activities that is the envy of their counterparts in many areas of the world. An attempt by the government in British Columbia a few years ago to introduce legislation that would give the universities the authority to dismiss faculty without cause was met by such an outcry that the government had to retreat, leaving the responsibility for staff termination policies to negotiation between the universities and their employees.[18]

Not protected by traditions of independence, and having been established as explicit vehicles of provincial, and to a degree federal, social, and economic policy, the community colleges are in a quite different situation than the universities with respect to their relations with government. In most provinces the colleges have local boards with ambiguous and varying authority. In only one province did colleges ever receive some of their funding from a municipal levy (no longer the case), but in several provinces local boards once enjoyed a considerable degree of autonomy. Over the past decade the pendulum has everywhere swung in the direction of centralized provincial authority over the colleges—even though they are still popularly called community colleges—and the colleges tend to function almost as departments of the provincial governments, which indeed they are by statute in two provinces. There have been calls in some provinces to have the pendulum swing back toward decentralization, but this seems unlikely given the provinces' interests in controlling costs, rationalizing programs and facilities, and using the colleges even more instrumentally to serve provincial economic, technological, social, and cultural objectives. So far as academic freedom for community college teachers is concerned—who in most provinces have no recognized research function—expectations are far from clear. It is generally assumed, but rarely if ever codified, that community college teachers should have at least as much, and perhaps slightly more, academic freedom as secondary school teachers, but clearly not the same as university professors.

Internal Trends in Higher Education Institutions

Since early in the twentieth century Canadian universities have employed a bicameral form of governance, with a board of governors responsible for financial management and an academic senate responsible for academic matters. Beginning in the 1960s most universities, in response to demands for greater faculty and student participation in institutional governance, reorganized their governance structures while retaining the basic bicameral form. Most boards, composed predominantly of lay appointees, now include faculty and student representation, and most senates, consisting mainly of faculty, include external members and student representation. The University of Toronto's creation of a unicameral structure in 1971 catalyzed interest in the idea of a single governing council composed of both internal and external members, but the Toronto structure has been an object of almost continual review and readjustment, and interest elsewhere in the unicameral model has waned.

During the 1970s Canadian universities were swept by a wave of unionization, motivated primarily by concern over conditions of employment and a felt need to ensure greater faculty influence in institutional policymaking. By 1980 the majority of universities had faculty unions, but there has been little formation of faculty unions in the other universities since then. During the early years of faculty unionization there was concern about the possible erosion of the role of academic senates, but these fears proved largely groundless as a stable accommodation was reached between the exercise of faculty influence through the collective bargaining process and through the senate. College faculty, by contrast, are almost all unionized, but historically have had little influence in their institutions outside the collective bargaining arena. In recent years there has been widespread pressure for increased faculty and student participation in institutional governance, but colleges still tend to be run more along the lines of a top-down, bureaucratic model than the more collegial model that characterizes the universities.

With regard to programs and curricula, recent years have seen the establishment of a multitude of specialized, semiautonomous centers and institutes within the universities. Important stimuli for this development have been the research funding policies of governments which have encouraged the creation of centers of excellence; the desire to attract more private funding and develop corporate-university partnerships in research and technology transfer; the development of interdisciplinary studies, of which women's studies has perhaps been the most rapidly growing area; and the increased scale of activities with a specialized international focus, especially centers focused on the Pacific Rim. Almost all universities and colleges have become substantially more internationally oriented and have increased the volume of their research and service contracts that involve activities in or with other countries.

Reflecting Canada's national commitment to bilingualism in general, and the identified needs of francophone students outside Quebec—as well as those of native English-speaking graduates of the French immersion streams in the secondary schools—governments have been providing special grants to universities and colleges for the purpose of facilitating bilingual programs. However, leaders of francophone communities have expressed concern about the limited progress that has been made in providing opportunities for French-language university education outside Quebec.[19] Indicative, perhaps, of concerns about the effectiveness of bilingual institutions in serving the minority language group, Ontario—which already has several bilingual community colleges—and the federal government recently announced the joint establishment of a new French-language community college in Ottawa.

There has also been increased attention to the special instructional needs of the disabled, including the establishment in one university of a college for the hearing impaired. Concerned about high levels of attrition, many community colleges have started to implement more systematic procedures for entry-level testing and placement, early warning for students in academic difficulty, peer counseling, and remediation. Colleges have also made considerable headway in the development of modularized curricula, computer-assisted and computer-managed learning, and self-paced study, the latter often through independent learning centers.

Programming for part-time students and liberal/general education are two areas where there have been widespread calls for change, but thus far only modest responses to those calls. Many postsecondary programs, especially in the professions, are available only to full-time students; evening students are often denied full access to academic support services; and part-time students are usually taught by part-time instructors, who are thought to be less qualified than full-time instructors. These problems are likely to get more attention in the 1990s, as part-time enrollment continues to expand faster than full-time enrollment.

In response to concerns about the lack of curricular coherence in undergraduate arts and science, several universities have moved to strengthen requirements for core courses and/or to provide newly designed liberal arts curricula. Over the past decade there has been a significant decline in the general education component in two- and three-year career programs in the community colleges, owing mainly to budget constraints and pressures to increase the amount of time devoted to career-specific courses. However, in response to widespread employer concerns about the communications and other basic skills of graduates, a reexamination of the appropriate balance between general and career-specific components in college curricula is being conducted.

Reforms in Higher Education

The major reforms in Canadian higher education occurred in the 1960s, when community college systems were established across the country, new universities were created, the entire educational system in Quebec was overhauled, and colleges and universities were given a broad mandate to serve as engines for achieving social equity and economic and technological advancement. In contrast, the 1980s have been a period of little reform. This decade has been characterized by continued expansion within existing structures, efforts to improve efficiency, and the selective filling in of gaps in the higher education mosaic. Reforms in Canadian higher education have usually involved considerable expenditure of funds, and the funds necessary for major reforms were not available in the past decade.

During the 1980s commissions and task forces in most provinces have been charged with articulating visions of Canadian higher education for the twenty-first century. While it is too early to tell if the types of reforms currently under discussion will be implemented, mention of them may give some idea of possible future directions and emphases in Canadian higher education. These include: systematic redesign of the relationships among the various levels of the education system, particularly the linkages between the community colleges and the universities; the development of polytechnic education, bridging the gap between the colleges

and the universities; greater differentiation of institutions by function and areas of specialization; extension of opportunity for university education in regions not presently served by a university, especially in British Columbia; and increased rationalization of programs and facilities through interinstitution cooperation and amalgamation. In order to plan and guide such initiatives, it may also be necessary to introduce reforms in the forms of relationships among institutions, their publics, and governments.

Factors Affecting Students and Academic Staff

Judged by the comments of the organizations that represent them, the major factor affecting both students and faculty for the past decade has been the chronic insufficiency of funds for higher education. Student federations have complained about excessively large classes, obsolete or insufficient facilities and equipment, inadequate levels of financial assistance, and shortages of places in certain programs for which there is high student demand. Real faculty salaries in universities have declined by less than most other items of expenditure—between only 5 and 10 percent since 1971—and faculty members' major complaints have been similar to those of their students. Teaching loads of faculty are substantially higher in the community colleges than in the universities, and with the increase in student-contact hours in the early 1980s workload became a major source of dissatisfaction among college faculty in most provinces—and the major issue in two provincewide strikes of college faculty.

In addition to factors that are financial in origin, students have been affected also by the growth in size and complexity of institutions and by changes in the relationship between higher education and employment. Students often complain of feeling lost on large impersonal campuses and demoralized by routines which they liken metaphorically to factory assembly line processes. With increased complexity and apparent instability in the labor market opportunities associated with different fields of study, students feel bewildered in the face of the various postsecondary education choices available to them. The softness of the labor market for arts and humanities graduates has been a particular source of distress, and it is now not uncommon for university graduates in these fields to subsequently enroll in a community college or private vocational school to obtain a more marketable skill.

The more than 25,000 foreign students in Canadian universities complain about loneliness and their difficulties making friends with local people. They also criticize the high foreign student fee differentials that most provinces have imposed in recent years.[20]

Some of the most significant issues pertaining to faculty have to do with aging. The largest cadre of faculty were hired between the mid-1960s and early 1970s, and accordingly the predominant age group in the universities is now in the late forties to late fifties range. With relatively little new hiring in the past decade, the universities now have a quite top-heavy age structure, and there are widespread concerns about the loss of continuity that will occur with the large numbers of retirements expected in the late 1990s. As retirements presently provide one of the main sources of funds for hiring new scholars, the compulsory retirement policies that most universities have—usually at age 65—have become a focus of heated controversy and litigation, pitting the interests of the older against those of the younger faculty. Another factor affecting faculty is the increased use of formal program review by agencies external to the university. While supporting the concern for quality assurance that underlies these reviews, many faculty are discomforted by the resultant heavy demands for administrative work, the increased pressure to publish, and the possibly adverse steering effects that these reviews often have on their professional activities, and in a way, on their academic freedom.[21]

Conclusions

Entering the last decade of the twentieth century, Canada has an exclusively public system of higher education that emphasizes both providing a wide range of opportunities to its diverse and geographically dispersed population and serving as an intellectual and research base for the technological and professional knowledge and skill requirements of its growing economy. In its breadth and quality Canadian higher education is well poised to meet the challenges of an increasingly multicultural society that is committed to further redressing social inequity, and of an increasingly interdependent competitive world economy.

However, the rapid expansion of the past two decades and the financial austerity of the past decade have imposed strains that will demand attention during the remainder of this century. Among the weak spots that may be in need of attention are: the continued underrepresentation of native peoples, francophones outside Quebec, the disabled, women in some fields, and certain other minorities in higher education; the inferior opportunities afforded to part-time students and the fact that lifelong learning has yet to become a reality; the historic tendencies toward dispersal of resources for research and advanced study; weaknesses in liberal and general education; the absence, except in Quebec, of effective coordination and linkages between colleges and universities; and the lack of mechanisms for coordination between federal and provincial policies and funding for higher education. Yet, working from the base of achievements of the past twenty-five years, and drawing upon the high-quality intellectual and related organizational infrastructure that presently exists, there are good grounds for optimism that the challenges of the next century can be addressed effectively.

Notes

The author wishes to thank Glen A. Jones, a doctoral candidate in the Higher Education Group, for assistance in preparing this chapter.

1. Peter Leslie, *Canadian Universities 1980 and Beyond: Enrolment, Structural Change, and Finance* (Ottawa: Association of Universities and Colleges of Canada, 1980), 61.
2. Peter C. Pineo and John Goyder, "The Growth of the Canadian Education System: An Analysis of Transition Probabilities," *Canadian Journal of Higher Education* 18, no. 2 (1988): 42–43.
3. R. S. Harris, "The Universities of Canada," in *Commonwealth Universities Yearbook* 1980, vol. 2 (London: The Association of Commonwealth Universities, 1980), 811.
4. Michael L. Skolnik, "State Control of Degree Granting: The Establishment of a Public Monopoly in Canada," in *Governments and Higher Education: The Legitimacy of Intervention*, ed. Cicely Watson (Toronto: Ontario Institute for Studies in Education, 1987), 67–78.
5. The theme of Paul Axelrod, in his *Scholars and Dollars: Politics, Economics, and the Universities of Ontario, 1945–1980* (Toronto: University of Toronto Press, 1982).
6. Paul Anisef with Marie-Andree Bertrand, Ulrike Hortian, and Carl James, *Accessibility to Postsecondary Education in Canada: A Review of the Literature* (Ottawa: Canada Secretary of State, 1985), 97–103. Other sources for the comments here on accessibility are: Neil Guppy, "Accessibility to Higher Education—New Trend Data," CAUT *Bulletin* (June 1988), 15–16; and Neil Guppy, Doug Balson, and Susan Vellutini, "Women and Higher Education in Canadian Society," in *Women and Education: A Canadian Perspective*, ed. Jane Gaskell and Arlene McLaren (Calgary: Detselig, 1987), 173–87.
7. *Report to the Secretary of State, Canada, and the Council of Ministers of Education, Canada, on the National Forum on Postsecondary Education, Saskatoon, Saskatchewan, October, 1987*, submitted by Brian Segal, Forum Chairperson (Ottawa: Institute for Research on Public Policy, 10 December 1987).
8. Canadian Association of University Teachers, *The Academic Staff and the University* (Ottawa: Canadian Association of University Teachers, 1987), 14.
9. Sheila Slaughter and Michael L. Skolnik, "Continued Efforts to Cope with Declining Resources: Selected Postsecondary Education Systems in the United States and Canada, an Introductory Essay," *Higher Education* 16 (1987): 131.
10. A. W. Johnson, *Giving Greater Point and Purpose to the Federal Financing of Postsecondary Education and Research in Canada* (Ottawa: Canada Secretary of State, 1985), 10-12.
11. David J. Bercuson, Robert Bothwell, and J. L. Granatstein, *The Great Brain Robbery: Canada's Universities on the Road to Ruin* (Toronto: McClelland and Stewart, 1984).
12. Michael L. Skolnik, "If the Cut Is So Deep, Where Is the Blood? Problems in Research on the Effects of Financial Restraint," *Review of Higher Education* 9, no. 4 (1986): 435–55.
13. Martin Trow, *Problems in the Transition from Elite to Mass Higher Education* (Berkeley: Carnegie Commission on Higher Education, 1973), 35–38.
14. See Gilles Paquet, "An Academic's Perspective: The Social Sciences and Humanities in Modern Society, or Two Tramps in Mud Time," in *The Human Sciences*, ed. B. Abu-Laban and B. G. Rule (Edmonton: University of Alberta Press, 1988).
15. Michael L. Skolnik, "The University and Manpower Planning: A Re-examination of the Issues in the Light of Changing Economic Conditions and New Developments in Labour Market Information," *Canadian Journal of Higher Education* 13, no. 3 (1983): 84–86.
16. Warren Clark, Margaret Laing, and Edith Rechnitzer, *The Class of 82: Summary Report on the Findings of the 1984 National Survey of the Graduates of 1982* (Ottawa: Canada Secretary of State and Statistics Canada, 1986), 81–85.
17. H. Blair Neatby, "The Historical Perspective," in *Governments and Higher Education: The Legitimacy of Intervention*, 35.
18. John Dennison, "Universities Under Financial Crises: The Case of British Columbia," *Higher Education* 16 (1987): 137–38.
19. Paul Ruest, "The Future of Francophone University Centres in a Minority Environment," *Canadian Journal of Higher Education* 18, no. 3 (1988): 7.
20. Edward Holdaway, Wendy M. Bryan, and Wilfred Allan, "International University Students in Canada," *Canadian Journal of Higher Education* 18, no. 3 (1989): 20.
21. A. E. Malloch, "Academic Freedom and Its Limits," CAUT *Bulletin* (April 1988), 1, 7.

The United States

Marian L. Gade

◆

What are the distinctive characteristics of higher education in the United States? Colleges and universities everywhere have similar goals and functions: to generate new knowledge through scholarship and research; to preserve and transmit a body of culture and knowledge to succeeding generations; to meet the needs of society and the labor market for educated, skilled, and productive citizens and workers. But nations differ in the emphasis they put on these and other goals; they differ in the ways they structure, govern, organize, and finance colleges and universities; and they differ in their expectations of which and how many people should participate in the educational enterprise.

Perhaps most obvious to an outside observer is the diversity and decentralization of postsecondary education in the United States. T. R. McConnell said over thirty years ago—and it is still true—that, "There is no *system* of American higher education. It is safe to say there never will be. Diversity of support, control, organization, aims, programs, and students will continue to be the most evident characteristics of post high-school education in this country."[1]

A second distinctive feature of the American system is its heavy reliance upon market forces rather than planning. Competition is intense among institutions—for students, high-quality faculty, and research support. Planning has come late, is carried out at the level of individual institutions and states rather than nationally, and is concerned principally with public institutions, although some states include the private sector in their planning mechanisms.

Another characteristic feature is differentiation within institutions. Several elements have been combined to produce the distinctive American university—the British undergraduate liberal arts college, the German research and graduate faculty, and professional schools—so that there exists a diversity of curriculum, standards, and degrees within as well as among institutions.

A fourth characteristic consists of a cluster of aspects relating to curriculum and teaching, including a general education component at the undergraduate level, patterns of electives and distribution requirements, and a system of academic credits that, taken together, link the whole system of institutions together. The unit or credit is the academic currency that allows students flexibility and mobility among programs and institutions.

A fifth defining characteristic is the system of governance of higher education, based on strong leadership by presidents (or chancellors) at the campus level and on boards of lay (i.e., nonacademic) trustees who are the legal owners (in the case of private institutions) and policymakers for institutions and systems. Governance by boards of trustees stands in contrast to governance directly by a government agency or ministry, or by guilds of faculty members. The almost 2,500 governing boards with their 55,000 trustees provide both a buffer for institutions from short-term vicissitudes in society, and at the same time act as a bridge between the institutions and the larger society, ensuring institutional responsiveness, on the one hand, and some measure of autonomy for the institutions, on the other.[2]

These characteristics are direct outgrowths of the historical forces that have shaped postsecondary education in the United States. Higher education began in the British Massachusetts Bay Colony where Harvard College (now Harvard University) was chartered in 1636. The model for the curriculum was the college at Oxford or Cambridge, and undergraduate education in the United States still exists largely as an outgrowth of the British college model. Eight more colleges were established in the thirteen American colonies prior to the American Revolution, all of them jointly sponsored and financed by public and private groups, usually the colonial government and one or more Protestant denominations.[3] It was not until after the U.S. Supreme Court decided the famous Dartmouth College case in the early nineteenth century that the modern distinction between "public" and "private" institutions became important.[4]

It was also in the nineteenth century that another model of education was imported into the United States, that of the German research university. Rather than developing separate institutions for research and advanced instruction, these functions were grafted onto existing institutions, turning many colleges into universities and creating another distinctive American form, the comprehensive institution, containing undergraduate education on the British model, and research and graduate work on the German model, as well as a variety of professional programs.

Structure of American Higher Education

Education at all levels in the United States is principally a state and local responsibility, and mainly falls upon the individual fifty states, their public colleges and universities, and the private institutions they charter.

The federal, or national, government sponsors service schools (e.g., United States Military Academy) and provides major funding for two institutions in the District of Columbia. As a general rule, however, the historical pattern has been for federal funding to support specific public purposes rather than institutions as such. Thus, the Morrill Land-Grant Act of 1862 provided states with funds to build colleges that would, as a major purpose, improve agricultural practices. The GI Bill (Servicemen's Readjustment Act) after World War II provided funds for former members of the armed forces to attend college. A variety of programs to support scientific research in colleges and universities have been established, principally in the past half-century. Based on a belief that the nation requires a highly educated citizenry and work force, and an ideology that educational opportunities should not be limited by ability to pay, federal student aid programs were inaugurated in the early 1970s.

Historical reliance on the states and private initiatives rather than upon a national plan for higher education underlies the diversity of institutions in the United States. State and regional history and political culture are embodied in public colleges, while many private colleges reflect the values and missions of the religious denominations that founded and often still support them. For example, the location of many colleges in rural areas, removed from centers of population, reflects a historical mistrust of urban life and a belief that young people would be corrupted by it.

In 1987 the Carnegie Foundation for the Advancement of Teaching, using data gathered by the United States National Center for Education Statistics, classified the 3,389 degree-granting higher education institutions into categories based on the level of degree offered and the comprehensiveness of their missions. There are roughly 1,800 private and 1,500 public institutions altogether; about 2,000 offer programs lasting four years or more, while 1,300 (900 of them public community colleges) offer two-year programs. (The basic categories and the numbers of institutions in each are shown in Table 1.)

Research universities (e.g., the University of California, Harvard University, or the University of Michigan) are included in the category of Doctorate-Granting Institutions; there are seventy "Research University I" institutions, forty-five public and twenty-five private, which each receive at least $33.5 million in federal support each year and which each award at least fifty Ph.D. degrees each year. Almost all offer degree programs at the bachelor's and master's level, as well as the Ph.D. and a variety of professional degrees. They constitute a major portion of the basic research enterprise in the United States.

The Comprehensive Colleges and Universities offer four- or five-year programs leading to a bachelor's, master's, or terminal professional degree below the level of the doctorate. Many are former teachers' colleges and they still educate the bulk of the teachers for the nation's public schools.

Liberal Arts Colleges I are relatively small, highly selective of their students, and concentrate on undergraduate education in the arts and sciences. Liberal Arts II colleges are both less selective and more professionally oriented than Liberal Arts I institutions. Many are affiliated with religious denominations or were founded to provide education for blacks. Twenty percent of them (eighty-six) have fewer than five hundred students each.

The largest segment is made up of the 985 community colleges (public two-year institutions). These provide education leading to an associate degree; recipients may continue their education toward a bachelor's degree at a four-year institution. They also serve large adult populations in a variety of ways: job and skills training, personal development, and remedial education, for example. Over one-third of all students are enrolled in a public community college.

Table 1

Numbers of Institutions by Type

Type of Institution	Number of Institutions Public	Private
Doctorate-Granting Institutions	134	79
Comprehensive Universities and Colleges	331	264
Liberal Arts Colleges		
Liberal Arts I (Selective)	2	140
Liberal Arts II (Less Selective)	30	400
Two-year Institutions	985	382
Specialized Institutions	66	576
Total	1,548	1,841

Source: Adapted from *A Classification of Institutions of Higher Education, 1987 Edition* (Princeton, NJ: The Carnegie Foundation for the Advancement of Teaching, 1987), Table 4.

The Students

Over half of all high school graduates enter postsecondary education at some point. On a full-time equivalency basis, 37 percent of the nineteen- to twenty-four-year-old age cohort is enrolled in higher education, the highest rate in the world. But students are no longer confined, as they once were, to the immediate postsecondary age group. Almost half (45 percent) of all students are now over age twenty-five, adult students. Women outnumber men slightly in the student population, 53 percent to 47 percent. Only about two million of the approximately 12.5 million persons enrolled are traditional students, full-time students aged eighteen to twenty-five. Part-time students now number over five million, 43 percent of all students.

Members of racial and ethnic minority groups now constitute a significant number of students—18 percent of all enrollments—but they make up a smaller proportion of higher education enrollment than they do of the total population. Blacks and Hispanics constitute less than 14 percent of enrollments but are 21 percent of the eighteen to twenty-one-year-old population.

Table 2 gives headcount enrollment by type of institution. Table 3 gives headcount enrollment by selected characteristics.

The Faculty

There are approximately 700,000 faculty members in American colleges and universities, two-thirds of them full-time and one-third part-time. About one-third of them are members of collective bargaining units (faculty unions), mostly in the public two-year sector. A high proportion of the full-time faculty, perhaps as many as 75 percent, have job security in the form of tenure.[5]

Women hold about one-third of the faculty positions, mostly concentrated in the lower academic ranks (only 10 percent are full professors) and in institutions of lesser academic quality. The number of Ph.D.'s awarded to women has increased sharply in recent years so that female representation in the academic labor force may also increase in coming years. Minorities constitute about 10 percent of total faculty members.

Financing Higher Education

Expenditures by all kinds of colleges and universities were estimated to be slightly over $100 billion in the mid-1980s, about 2.5 percent of gross national product (GNP). One of the salient characteristics of American higher education is the diversity of sources from which colleges and universities derive their support. Government at all levels (federal, state, and local) provides almost half the total, with states alone accounting for one-third. These figures exclude student aid going directly to students, which shows up in college accounts as tuition, fees, or payments for board and room.

While public institutions derive about 60 percent of their revenue from government sources (almost half from state governments), and less than one-fourth from tuition and fees from students, private institutions have a very different pattern. They receive less than one-fifth of their support from governmental sources (only 2.5 percent from state and local entities), but almost half from students in the form of tuition and fees. In both public and private institutions, gifts and grants, investment income, and sales and services (e.g., dormitories, bookstores, hospitals) account for the remaining income.

Table 2

Enrollment by Type of Institution

Type of Institution	Enrollment (000)	
	Public	**Private**
Doctorate-Granting Institutions	2,655	774
Comprehensive Universities and Colleges	2,377	926
Liberal Arts I Colleges	5	209
Liberal Arts II Colleges	39	331
Two-Year Institutions	4,250	268
Specialized Institutions	131	336
Total	9,457	2,844

Source: Adapted from *A Classification of Institutions of Higher Education, 1987 Edition* (Princeton, NJ: The Carnegie Foundation for the Advancement of Teaching, 1987), Table 4.

The federal government is a major funder of research in colleges and universities. In fiscal year 1986 over two-thirds of the university research and development (R&D) budget came from the federal government. Colleges and universities spent only 12 percent of all R&D funds in the nation, but over half of the basic research funds, mainly federal funds.

Special Issues

The overall structure of American higher education is relatively stable. But there have been some changes and trends in recent years, and others that are anticipated in the near future, that may have significant impacts upon the system or parts of it. For example, as noted above, student numbers and the composition of the student body have changed and will continue to change, with consequent impacts upon faculty, the curriculum, and subsequent labor market participation. Issues of governance arise as education becomes more central to the economic and social vitality of the nation. A few of these current and emerging issues will be considered here.

Access and Enrollments

Predicting enrollments, in the United States as elsewhere, has proven to be akin to looking into a very cloudy crystal ball. Predictions have been almost invariably wrong. The much-vaunted drop in the number of people in the traditional college-going age cohort that began in the late 1980s did not bring the expected declines in enrollment levels which, in fact, increased.[6] This unanticipated development stemmed principally from increased

Table 3

Enrollment by Selected Characteristics—1986

Attendance Status	Enrollment	%
Full-time	7,113,000	56.9
Part-time	5,388,000	43.1
Sex		
Women	6,613,000	52.9
Men	5,888,000	47.1
Minority	2,238,000	17.9
Asian and Pacific Island	448,000	3.6
Black	1,081,000	8.6
Hispanic	624,000	5.0
Native American	90,000	0.7
Foreign Students	344,000	2.7

Source: *The Chronicle of Higher Education Almanac,* September 1, 1988.

participation rates by older persons, by part-time students, and by women and minorities.

The number of high school graduates is expected to continue to decline—by 11 percent between 1989 and 1994—after which they will rise sharply at least until 2005 as the grandchildren of the post-World War II baby-boomers move into the college-going age group.

Institutional policymakers are concerned about overall demographic trends as well as with changes in the educational participation rates of different population groups, for changes in either may produce increases or decreases in enrollments with consequences for financing, staffing, and programs. For the nation at large and for public policymakers, a critical issue continues to be the ability of students from all socioeconomic, racial, and ethnic groups to attend college in order to fulfill dreams and promises of social justice and to ensure a productive and well-trained labor force. One-third of the nation will be comprised of non-white minority groups by the end of the century; these groups have traditionally been outside the mainstream of educational and occupational opportunities.[7]

In addition to a shift in racial and ethnic composition, the age distribution of the population in the nation is changing: by 1992 half of all college students will be over twenty-five and one-fifth over thirty-five years of age.[8] The growing number of older persons also means that there will be a larger number of retired persons compared to those in the active labor force. Estimates indicate that by the year 2035 there will be fewer than three workers to support each retiree, compared to five in 1988. At the same time, the average age of persons in the growing minority groups is considerably younger than in the population as a whole and in the white majority (in 1980, the average white American was thirty-one, the average black was twenty-five, and the average Hispanic was twenty-two years old).

Thus, we face the prospect of large numbers of young people from minority racial and ethnic groups that have not in the past participated in higher education at the levels of the majority. They will leave the educational system to enter a highly technological economy that requires an ever more highly educated labor force to operate. They will be expected not only to compete in the international marketplace but to reach levels of productivity that will support growing numbers of persons outside the labor force, the very young and the aged. The challenge to higher education is enormous: to provide access and opportunities for all; to develop modes of teaching and learning appropriate for large numbers of older and other nontraditional students; and to deliver high levels of education and skills for a competitive and education-dependent labor force. These are not only matters of social justice, important as those are, but also of national vitality and viability. Equality of access to the higher education system depends to a large extent upon the ability of students to meet the costs of attendance. There is a widespread perception that college attendance, particularly at high-cost private institutions, has been priced out of the reach of many individuals and families. In 1988 tuition and fees averaged $1,414 at four-year public institutions and $6,658 at four-year private colleges and universities. Total costs (tuition, fees, room and board, books, personal items) can run over $20,000 a year at some private institutions.

One reason for the concern with rapidly increasing costs is the switch from grants to loans as a basic component of federal student aid packages: between 1975 and 1985 grants dropped from 75 percent to 29 percent of federal student aid while loans increased from 21 percent to 66 percent.[9] Many students, especially those from minority groups with cultural biases against incurring debt, simply do not attend college rather than apply for student loans. In order to counteract the effects of the federal shift from grants, many institutions have greatly increased the amount of aid they award from their own resources. Between 1980 and 1987 institutionally awarded aid increased by 65.7 percent in constant dollars, a substantial portion of it coming from higher tuition paid by those students whose families could afford the full amount. Institutions thus play a "Robin Hood" role in shifting resources from the more affluent to the less wealthy. Many believe this is a function better performed through public tax policy and need-based student aid in the form of grants.

Serving these changing student populations, ensuring that participation rates reflect the demographics of the population, and providing opportunities for students from all segments of the population to enter into and benefit from higher education is probably the greatest challenge facing American higher education institutions and policymakers in the coming decades.

Quality and Content

Concern about equality of educational opportunity is linked with growing concern with the quality of education at all levels, including higher education. It is widely agreed that at the highest levels—doctoral education, research, and professional training—American institutions are among the best in the world. But in some other areas, particularly secondary education and undergraduate collegiate education, the record is uneven, with precollegiate education being eroded, according to one report, "by a rising tide of mediocrity."[10] A further series of reports in the early 1980s examining undergraduate education decried lack of rigor, low standards of achievement, and a fragmented curriculum.[11] Some of these reports were excessive in their negativism, but concern about quality has led to widespread reexamination of the undergraduate curriculum and, perhaps more important from a public-policy perspective, to concern with accountability (Do institutions do what they promise? Do they produce results commensurate with money spent?) and assessment (How do we know? How can we do better?).

By the end of 1988 about fifteen states had some sort of initiatives in place to require or encourage institutions to assess the quality of undergraduate teaching and learning by evaluating the outcomes of those processes. In general, state action has constituted a call to assessment of undergraduate teaching and learning rather than a mandated blueprint for how to do it. The actual assessment techniques and instruments have generally been left up to the individual institutions as an academic decision, contrary to the expectations of many on campuses who believe that legislators "really" want standardized testing. Because some of the first mandates (as in Florida) did involve statewide testing, in other states where testing forms a part of the assessment process, it has often received excessive attention.

Assessment of the outcomes of education is coming to be used as a tool for internal improvement as well as for accountability to outside forces. Many state leaders believe that improvement and accountability can go hand-in-hand, and are couching their legislation accordingly. Faculty support the development and use of assessment on campuses to improve undergraduate education (almost 70 percent did so in one 1988 survey),[13] but at the same time almost 80 percent fear misuse of the results by state authorities. Especially where state resources for higher education have been scarce in the past, and where cutbacks have taken place, educators view assessment as a way of justifying further reductions in support.[13]

Growing numbers of institutions are taking assessment of educational outcomes seriously. Faculty across a variety of types of institutions have reported that, once underway, assessment efforts have brought unanticipated program improvements. It may be that once again, as sometimes in the past, it has taken external pressure for reform to be undertaken by those inside higher education institutions. Benjamin Jowett, master of Balliol, once commented, "We cannot reform ourselves."[14]

The problem is to devise models and methods that will perform the dual tasks of improving teaching and learning on the campuses while, at the same time, serving to satisfy state officials and external publics that the large amounts of money expended on education are serving intended purposes.

Not only has there been concern about how well teaching and learning is being done, but also about the content of what is taught and learned: the curriculum. In 1971 bachelor's degrees awarded were divided almost equally between arts and sciences and job-related subjects (business, education, etc.) By 1983 the arts and sciences share had dropped to about 36 percent of degrees awarded while job-related degrees constituted 64 percent of the total. As early as 1977, several years before the spate of reform reports of the 1980s, general education (that component of the curriculum that once provided a common experience of liberal education for all students) was labeled "a disaster area."[15]

Many recent observers of higher education, including authors of some of the reform reports noted above, believe that the flight from liberal education, especially the humanities, constitutes a danger to a free society that depends heavily upon a common culture to hold it together, a society always threatening to come apart under the centrifugal forces of pluralism and diversity. Rather than constituting a debate between the arts and sciences, on the one hand, and the job-related or professional schools on the other—that battle has apparently already been won by the professional schools—it now more frequently takes the form of discussions about what minimum of common curriculum for all students will provide the essential societal glue. One group urges required courses in Western civilization, believing that only a common background of subject matter, stressing the historical sources of present-day values and political structures, can create the necessary cohesion. Another group, instead, urges required courses that will move beyond the traditional "Western civ" orientation to include the history and culture of newer immigrant populations, women, and racial and ethnic minorities, arguing that an understanding and mutual respect for the variety of American cultures represented in the population will provide a better underpinning for a multiracial, multicultural society. The prescriptions differ, but the problem is the same: how to accommodate and nurture different cultural heritages and practices while creating sufficient common bonds and experiences to make a democratic society possible.

Faculty for the Twenty-First Century

As always and everywhere, the real business of higher education—teaching, research, and service—lies in the hands of the faculty, individually and collectively. Structures and incentives can only create the climate in which faculty and students work together. Yet by the mid-1980s surveys and studies showed a high degree of dissatisfaction among faculty of American colleges and universities.[16] After rising steadily throughout the 1960s, their salaries leveled off and purchasing power decreased steadily from 1972/73 into the early 1980s. In addition, faculty compensation lagged behind that in jobs in other parts of the economy requiring comparable qualifications. Steady increases in compensation that exceeded the rise in the cost of living each year from 1982 to 1989 were viewed by some as too little, too late.

Continued predictions of falling enrollments during the late 1970s and throughout the 1980s, even when in error, created an aura of instability and lack of job security. A deterioration of working conditions due to erosion of public support, lack of mobility following upon stable enrollments, and deep fragmentation of the faculty as a result of specialization and subspecialization, among other causes, led to falling morale among faculty members at all kinds of institutions. Over half the faculty surveyed in 1985 said they would seriously consider a position in another institution, and almost half were willing to leave academe entirely. One-fifth said if they had to start all over again, they would choose a different profession.[17]

As noted above, 65 percent of full-time faculty have job tenure, and at some institutions the number is more than 80 percent. Low morale within the profession, along with a scarcity of job openings, have discouraged many young people from planning an academic career. They see Ph.D.'s from the 1970s unable to secure permanent positions in colleges and universities, and although the academic unemployment rate is, in actuality, quite low, by 1985 some 43 percent of all Ph.D. holders were working outside the academic milieu.[18] Many fewer college students expressed aspirations to a career as a college teacher or researcher in the 1980s than had done so in the 1960s.

In addition to noting the discouragement and low morale of those now in the profession, many who graduate with a bachelor's degree in fields such as engineering, mathematics, the sciences, or economics find that they can immediately command salaries outside academe approaching those of their faculty, who have spent long years earning advanced degrees. They have no incentive to continue graduate studies and work toward an academic career.

These problems and conditions are expected to continue until about the middle of the 1990s when a quite different scenario unfolds. As noted above, enrollments will begin to rise again about 1995 as the grandchildren of the baby-boomers enter higher education. In addition, the bulk of the faculty who were hired in the expansionist years of the 1960s will reach retirement age. Overall, it is expected that a number of new faculty—probably equal to two-thirds of those working in 1985—will need to be recruited between that date and 2010—some 500,000 people. There are some troubling factors:[19]

○ There is a potential lowering of the overall quality of the faculty as many of the brightest college graduates turn to other fields. The quality of teachers and researchers for the period extending well into the twenty-first century will depend upon whether students of the highest intellectual quality can be persuaded into the pipeline leading to academic careers.
○ Those disciplines that must compete with higher salaries outside the university may find themselves without enough full-time faculty, necessitating hiring more part-time or adjunct faculty.
○ Few minority students are attending graduate school and preparing for academic careers, so that institutional affirmative action goals and hopes for faculty to serve as models for students may be unfilled.
○ Colleges and universities will need to pay attention to a variety of issues affecting the quality of faculty life in order to recruit high-quality people under conditions of competition. Those that can offer affordable housing, assistance in finding jobs for spouses, child care, and other quality of life perquisites, will have an advantage.

Some institutions are already stockpiling young faculty, hiring against anticipated retirements. But with no sure way to predict future enrollments, institutions with marginal financial resources cannot afford to hire faculty who may not actually be needed.

Governance and Control

Whose responsibility ought it to be to provide access, support students and institutions, and worry about staffing colleges with high-quality faculty? Higher education in the United States, as noted above, has historically been a joint effort between governmental entities, mainly the states, and private initiatives—by individuals, churches, and others. Even though the majority of institutions are privately controlled, enrollments are overwhelmingly (over three-fourths) in the public sector. The extent to which the states that establish and support higher education institutions ought to direct and control them has been a subject of discussion and sometimes bitter political debate around the country for many years, and continues.

One of the proud traditions of American public higher education is that it has provided the same kind of academic freedom and institutional autonomy as the private sector. Academic freedom appears to be thriving (with some reservations as noted below), but institutional autonomy in the public sector is widely considered to be under stress.

As higher education has become more central to society—in generating new knowledge and technology for economic competitiveness and quality of life, in training and upgrading the labor force, aiding in state and regional economic development, undergirding interstate and international economic competition, producing an educated citizenry with a common intellectual culture, etc.—state officials, governors and legislators, have taken a greater interest in their higher education institutions. This has come about as a consequence of the centrality of higher education to the economic and cultural life of the states, but also because higher education constitutes a major item in the budget of every state. I have already noted that gubernatorial and legislative attention has recently focused on the quality of education and institutional accountability for results, and commented upon public pressure for higher education to take the lead in generating economic competitiveness. Much of that interest has been both entirely appropriate and beneficial to colleges and universities.

At the same time, such interest brings with it some threats to the independence and autonomy of public higher education. State authorities wish that the complexity of higher education could be reduced; that there might be just one telephone number that the governor could call to get answers about the whole system; that the rules for purchasing, hiring architects, salary schedules, faculty workloads, etc., were the same for all institutions so that they could be readily grasped and administered; that there were a hierarchy of command through

which things could easily be mandated for campus performance, as in other executive departments, rather than the messy, time-consuming, bottom-up set of arrangements for consultation and consensus that pervade campus governance, especially where faculty have a part in "shared governance."

The result of deliberations about the relationship between a state's government and its colleges and universities has been a wide diversity of arrangements for support and direction. The overall trend since the great expansion of public institutions in the 1960s has been toward greater centralization and control of those institutions by the states. As noted above, the principal pattern of governance in the United States has been through a board of trustees. In half the states a single board (along with an implementing agency) either governs all public higher education institutions in the state (fourteen states), or governs all senior institutions with separate arrangements for two-year institutions (eleven states). All but four of the remaining twenty-five states have coordinating boards with varying powers.[20]

A number of states have reviewed their governance structures in recent years, and most that have done so have ended by strengthening but not completely centralizing the powers of the coordinating board. Only one of the fifteen states that considered moving to a centralized governing board in the past ten years actually did so (Massachusetts), although one other (Maryland) established a system covering all but two of the senior institutions. The trend has been toward centralization, but with provision for institutional autonomy to varying degrees.

The problem was succinctly stated by T. R. McConnell over thirty years ago: statewide coordination must be judged in terms of "its effectiveness in stimulating both unity and diversity among institutions, encouraging appropriate differentiation of functions, and avoiding unnecessary or undesirable duplication of educational facilities."[21] But centralization tends toward unity rather than diversity, toward homogenization of institutions, processes, and functions. Differentiation means making conscious judgments about institutions and programs that require different and unequal levels of support. In a nation with an ideology of equality, it is politically difficult to justify unequal treatment—different salary schedules and work loads for research universities, for example. And state governments, as outlined above, prefer simplicity and hierarchy to complexity and diffused patterns of authority. Thus, the intrinsic needs of higher education do not always correspond to the needs and desires of the supporting state, although both are legitimate. There will always be a tension between them, and it will emerge in discussions of how to govern and manage the higher education enterprise. Frank Newman has commented, "The real need is not simply for more autonomy [for universities] but for a relationship between the university and the state that is constructive for both, built up over a long period of time by careful attention on the part of all parties."[22]

Preserving the Private Sector

A major shift took place in the United States over the past forty years as both financing and enrollments in higher education moved from the private sector to the public sector. In 1950 students were evenly divided between public and private institutions, but by 1975, a quarter-century later, the private share of enrollment had dropped to about 21 percent of total enrollments, where it has remained.

This shift resulted from rapid expansion of the public sector, not only in numbers of institutions but also in size of individual campuses, rather than from any absolute decline in the private sector. In fact, private enrollments increased absolutely, even while falling as a share of the total, and as private institutions continue to outnumber public.

Private colleges enroll 21 percent of the students, but figure disproportionately in the overall contributions that higher education makes to society. These institutions award 33 percent of baccalaureate degrees, 40 percent of master's degrees, 36 percent of doctoral degrees, and 60 percent of first professional degrees in law, medicine, engineering, and other fields. The sector contains a range of institutions with a diversity of missions and affiliations that provide a wide choice of educational environments for students, including a number affiliated with religious denominations.

The cost of education is estimated to be comparable in similar types of institutions in the public and private sectors, but the price to the consumer—the student—is quite different because of the built-in subsidy to students attending publicly supported institutions. Even in private institutions students pay nowhere near the total cost of education (about two-fifths of the revenue of these colleges came from tuition and fees in 1985/86), and gifts, grants, and other sources of private income bring the total revenue from private sources up to 80 percent of all revenues. Less than 20 percent of revenue comes from governmental sources. It is estimated that if public institutions had to assume the responsibility for educating these 2.6 million students, the additional cost to the taxpayers would exceed twelve billion dollars annually.

The rationale for maintaining a diverse and healthy private sector is widely accepted, but questions arise about just how to do that. Private institutions are principally concerned about the "tuition gap," the difference in what it costs a student to attend a private versus a public institution caused by the subsidy to students in public institutions. The National Association of Independent Colleges and Universities estimates the average state appropriation for a student attending a public college in 1987 at $4,900, compared with an average state appropriation of $590 to a student in a private college (mainly financial assistance for needy students).

States are increasingly aware of the value of the private sector and have themselves increased their support of it; student aid from state programs increased almost 44 percent from 1980 to 1985. But the question remains, how much more can the private sector shrink (on a comparative basis) and still maintain its health and its position as innovator and principal source of diversity to the whole higher education enterprise. Also remaining is the question of what appropriate public policies can be adopted to support the sector without unduly eroding its autonomy and independence.

Enduring Issues

In addition to these topics that are of special concern as we reach the final decade of the twentieth century, there are at least two other issues that permeate higher education discussions at all times: academic freedom for those laboring in universities and colleges, and the ways in which those institutions serve the needs of the labor market.

Academic Freedom

As mentioned earlier, academic freedom has been accepted as essential to the conduct of colleges and universities, and external threats, such as those from boards of trustees or public officials concerned with the economic or political views of individual professors, have subsided. One survey showed that more than 80 percent of faculty leaders believe their board of trustees performs at a "good" or "excellent" level in providing "freedom of teaching and research for faculty."[23]

There are two areas, however, where future developments may not justify so sanguine a view. First, threats to academic freedom appear to come more from inside the academy than from outside in recent years. Professors and students alike have occasionally prevented a full range of viewpoints from being expressed on campuses, usually on politically sensitive issues and often outside the classroom. Martin Trow has said that there are "two major forces restricting the kinds and range of views it is possible to invite to our campuses: one is sheer physical intimidation and disruption; the other is a prior restraint on the invitation of 'controversial' speakers, exercised by academics and academic committees, administrators and student groups which have the authority to invite speakers from outside the academic community."[24] The ability of the university to serve as a place where all ideas can be examined and disputed, while the institution itself maintains a position of neutrality, has become open to question.

A second threat to academic freedom arises from the relationships between the university and businesses or corporations as they cooperate to develop and market the products of research and technology. One report, prepared by the National Governor's Association and the Conference Board, concluded, "Education was viewed by all three groups in business, academia, and government—as the key to the nation's competitiveness."[25] Around the nation, governors, legislators, businesspersons, and civic leaders are urging increased attention to education, and to higher education, to train workers for a technological era, to speed up transfer of technology from the laboratory to the marketplace, to cooperate with business and industry in creating new products and new markets. In the process they may be placing pressures on the educational system that it cannot withstand and continue to serve other functions. For example, one article reported that "campus patent officials fear that many have not developed adequate measures to guard against potential ethical, legal, and financial problems involved in bringing technology to the marketplace."[26]

Especially problematical are situations in which "a scholar or an institution assumes substantial authority, responsibility, and/or interest in two or more entities with divergent missions," as, for instance, where faculty members become stockholders or heavily involved as consultants in firms (e.g., computers or pharmaceuticals) developing products based on their university research. Potential conflicts of interest arise, with consequences for academic freedom: publication of research results may be delayed or suppressed in the interests of favoring one commercial developer; choice of research topics may be dictated by the needs of the marketplace rather than by the potential contributions to knowledge and the state of the discipline; the public may be deprived of an important source of neutral judgment on the impact of science and technology upon political and social processes.[27] Harvard president Derek Bok has also warned of the dangers inherent in too close relations between the academy and industry in fulfilling the bright promises of "technology transfer," as the field is coming to be called. He said, "the newfound concern with technology transfer is disturbing not only because it could alter the practice of science in the university but also because it threatens the central values and ideals of academic research."[28]

Both of these concerns deal as much with the values and behavior of those inside the institution as outside. Academic freedom, like governance, can no longer be considered a sacrosanct area in which any outside pressures are automatically considered as unwarranted intrusion, and anything that academics decide to do is, by definition, correct. Academic freedom and institutional autonomy carry obligations as well as rights for faculty, students, and administrators. Careful thought will be needed to establish productive rela-tionships that link the university with its political, economic, and social environment while preserving essential freedom and autonomy for those working within the special academic milieu.[29]

Higher Education and the Economy

At all times and in all places a major function of higher education has been service to the labor market. The medieval universities educated lawyers and accountants, priests and doctors, at Bologna and Paris and elsewhere. In colonial America, the first college had the function of educating leaders for the state and church, as Harvard was founded "to advance Learning and perpetuate it to Posterity; dreading to leave an illiterate Ministry to the Churches, when our present Ministers shall lie in the Dust."[30] Today, higher education still is the avenue to the professions, and, in addition, trains persons for a myriad of semiprofessions and vocations. Some believe it overeducates, producing more educated persons than the economy can productively absorb.[31] How many college-educated workers are there, and is the market producing about the right number?

In the mid-1980s slightly more than one-quarter of the employed labor force (ages twenty-five to sixty-four) had completed four or more years of college, while 45 percent had attended for one year or more.[32] At the same time, the *Workforce* 2000 report estimated that 42 percent of jobs required one or more years of college, and Daniel Bell recently wrote that "more than half the labor force is in white-collar, middle-class, and education-requiring categories."[33] The U.S. Department of Labor estimates put the proportion of the labor force in managerial, scientific, and technical occupations at 25 percent.

These estimates produce a slight overproduction of college-trained employees, but there are advantages to an educated populace other than ability to fill particular slots in the labor force. More educated employees tend to restructure jobs to make use of their knowledge and skills, often improving productivity in the process. More highly educated persons in the population tend to participate more as citizens, to enjoy better health, and to manage personal finances better, among many other effects that benefit both the individual and the society.[34]

It is probable, however, that higher education makes its greatest direct contributions to the American economy through advances in knowledge rather than through education for the labor market. Based on work by Edward Denison, it has been estimated that, for the 1929–82 period, about 20 percent of the growth rate in national income (on the basis of per person employed) came from increasing education per worker; 40 percent of the growth was attributable to advances in knowledge, a large portion of which occur within universities or by those trained in them. Recognizing that a large part of the educational contribution comes from secondary education and from on-the-job training, the portion of the educational component that higher education can claim is probably nearer 5 percent.[35]

Conclusions

Higher education appears to have performed well in serving the needs of the labor market and economy, although challenges lie ahead, as outlined earlier with respect to demographic changes and also with respect to heightened expectations for service to the economy, with its possible implications for academic freedom and autonomy.

It is less clear that American higher education has served equally well the needs of all its citizens. A major challenge is to provide access to high-quality education for members of educationally disadvantaged racial and ethnic groups. Major responsibility for providing access, as well

as for ensuring excellence in the educational process itself, lies with the fifty states and with individual institutions. It is likely that the federal government will continue its role in financing research and some level of access (through student aid), in line with its tradition of undertaking missions that are both limited in scope and national in their impacts.

Notes

1. T. R. McConnell, "The Diversification of American Higher Education: A Research Program," *Educational Record* 38 (October 1957): 315. This list of defining characteristics also draws on Martin Trow, "American Higher Education: Past, Present, and Future," in *State and Welfare: USA/USSR*, ed. Gail W. Lapidus and Guy E. Swanson (Berkeley and Los Angeles: University of California Press, Institute of International Studies, 1988).

2. For a history of governing boards in higher education, see William H. Cowley, *Presidents, Professors, and Trustees* (San Francisco: Jossey-Bass, 1980), chap. 2. For current analysis of boards and trustees, their tasks, and an assessment of their performance, see Clark Kerr and Marian L. Gade, *The Guardians: Boards of Trustees in American Colleges and Universities* (Washington, D.C.: Association of Governing Boards of Universities and Colleges, 1989). The "bridge" and "buffer" analogy is found in James A. Perkins, "Conflicting Responsibilities of Governing Boards," *The University as an Organization*, ed. James A. Perkins (New York: McGraw-Hill, 1973), chap. 11.

3. Jurgen Herbst, *From Crisis to Crisis: American College Government, 1636–1819* (Cambridge: Harvard University Press, 1982).

4. For a history of the genesis of the public-private distinction, see Herbst, *Crisis to Crisis*. For a different interpretation, see John Whitehead, *The Separation of College and State* (New Haven: Yale University Press, 1973). Both deal with the "Dartmouth College Case" in detail.

5. Howard R. Bowen and Jack H. Schuster, *American Professors: A National Resource Imperiled* (New York: Oxford University Press, 1986), 45.

6. For one such prediction, and a criticism of others, see *Three Thousand Futures: The Next Twenty Years for Higher Education*, Final Report of the Carnegie Council on Policy Studies in Higher Education (San Francisco: Jossey-Bass,

1980).

7. Harold L. Hodgkinson, *All One System: Demographics of Education—Kindergarten through Graduate School* (Washington, D.C.: Institute for Educational Leadership, 1986), 7.

8. Hodgkinson, *All One System*, 3.

9. Carol Frances,"1986: Major Trends Shaping the Outlook for Higher Education," *AAHE Bulletin* 38 (December 1985): 5.

10. National Commission on Excellence in Education, *A Nation at Risk* (Washington, D.C.: 1983), 5.

11. The most important reports included: *Integrity in the Academic Curriculum: A Report to the Academic Community* (Washington, D.C.: Association of American Colleges, February 1985); William J. Bennett, *To Reclaim a Legacy: A Report on the Humanities in Higher Education* (Washington, D.C.: National Endowment for the Humanities, November 1984); Ernest L. Boyer, *College: The Undergraduate Experience in America* (New York: Harper & Row, 1987); *Time for Results: The Governors 1991 Report on Education* (Washington, D.C.: National Governors' Association, 1986); *Involvement in Learning: Realizing the Potential of American Higher Education* (Washington, D.C.: Study Group on the Conditions of Excellence in American Higher Education, National Institute of Education/ U.S. Department of Education, October 1984); Frank Newman, *Higher Education and the American Resurgence* (Princeton: Princeton University Press, 1985); *Transforming the State Role in Undergraduate Education* (Denver, Colo.: Education Commission of the States, July 1986); *Access to Quality Undergraduate Education* (Atlanta: Southern Regional Education Board, July 1986).

12. Elaine El-Khawas, *Campus Trends, 1988* (Washington, D.C.: American Council on Education, 1988).

13 Peter T. Ewell and Carol M. Boyer, "Acting Out State-Mandated Assessment: Evidence From Five States," *Change* 20 (July–August 1988): 40–47.

14. Letter from Jowett to Roundell Palmer, Esq., Member of Parliament, November 15, 1847, *Life and Letters of Benjamin Jowett*, ed. Evelyn Abbott and Lewis Campbell (London: John Murray, 1897), 1:189.

15. *Missions of the College Curriculum: A Contemporary Review with Suggestions*, A commentary of The Carnegie Foundation for the Advancement of Teaching (San Francisco: Jossey-Bass, 1977), 11.

16. See, for example, "Change Trendlines. The Faculty: Deeply Troubled," *Change* 17 (September–October 1985): 31–34.

17. "The Faculty: Deeply Troubled," 32.

18. Bowen and Schuster, *American Professors*, 177.

19. Carolyn J. Mooney, "Uncertainty Is Rampant as Colleges Begin to Brace for Faculty Shortage Expected to Begin in 1990s," *Chronicle of Higher Education* 35 (25 January 1989): A14–A17.

20. For a classification and evaluation of state governing and coordinating boards, see Kerr and Gade, *The Guardians*, chap. 10.

21. McConnell, "Diversification of American Higher Education," 302.

22. Frank Newman, *Choosing Quality: Reducing Conflict Between the State and the University* (Denver, Colo.: Education Commission of the States, 1987), xiii.

23. Kerr and Gade, *The Guardians*, chap. 8.

24. Martin Trow, "On a Board's Stance toward Social and Political Issues: Trustees and the Open Campus" (Paper prepared for the National Conference of the Association of Governing Boards of Universities and Colleges, 15 March 1988), 6. The paper was a commentary on Alan Pifer's *The Board's Role in Dealing with Social and Political Issues* (Washington, D.C.: Association of Governing Boards of Universities and Colleges, 1988).

25. *The Role of Science and Technology in Economic Competitiveness*, Report Prepared for the National Science Foundation by the National Governors' Association and the Conference Board (Washington, D.C.: September 1987), 1.

26. Gilbert Fuchsberg, "Universities Said to Go Too Fast in Quest of Profit from Research," *Chronicle of Higher Education* 35 (12 April 1989): A28.

27. Elisabeth A. Zinser, "The Development and Transfer of Technology: On a Handout or a Handshake?" *Proceedings of the Annual Meeting of the North Carolina Association of Colleges and Universities, 3–4 November 1988*, 17–36.

28. Derek Bok, *Beyond the Ivory Tower: Social Responsibilities of the Modern University* (Cambridge: Harvard University Press, 1982), 142.

29. For discussion of the obligations of those inside the university, see Clark Kerr, "The Academic Ethic and University Teachers: A 'Disintegrating Profession?'" *Minerva* (forthcoming, 1989).

30. "New England's First Fruits, 1643," in *American Higher Education: A Documentary History*, ed. Richard Hofstadter and Wilson Smith (Chicago: University of Chicago Press, 1961), 1:6.

31. See, for example, Richard B. Freeman, *The Overeducated American* (New York: Academic Press, 1976).

32. U.S. Bureau of the Census, Current Population Reports, *Population Characteristics*, Series P-20, No. 4115, "Educational Attainment in the

U.S.: March 1982 to 1985" (Washington, D.C.: November 1987), Table 6.

33. William B. Johnston, *Workforce* 2000 (Indianapolis, Ind.: Hudson Institute, 1987), 98; Daniel Bell, "The World and the United States in 2013," *Daedalus* 116 (Summer 1987): 27.

34. Howard R. Bowen, *Investment in Learning: The Individual and Social Value of American Higher Education* (San Francisco: Jossey-Bass, 1977).

35. Edward F. Denison, *Trends in Economic Growth, 1929–1982* (Washington, D.C.: Brookings Institute, 1985). Also see the discussion of Denison and related data in Clark Kerr, *Higher Education and Service to the Labor Market: Contributions and Distortions* (Paper delivered at the Higher Education Research Program, sponsored by the Pew Charitable Trusts, Philadelphia, 25 February 1988).

◆

BIBLIOGRAPHY

Bibliography

◆

(These short bibliographies relate to the chapters in this volume and were prepared by the authors of each chapter. An effort has been made to provide a highly selective listing of key items concerning each country, region, and topic.)

Topics
Academic Freedom

Hook, Sidney, ed. *Academic Freedom and Academic Anarchy*. New York: Cowles, 1970.

Joughin, Louis, ed. *Academic Freedom and Tenure*. Madison, Wis.: University of Wisconsin Press, 1969.

Lewis, Lionel S. *Cold War on Campus*. New Brunswick, N.J.: Transaction, 1988.

Metzger, Walter, S. Kadish, A. DeBardeleben and E.J. Bloustein. *Dimensions of Academic Freedom*. Urbana: University of Illinois Press, 1969.

Pincoffs, Edmund L., ed. *The Concept of Academic Freedom*. Austin: University of Texas Press, 1975.

Schrecker, Ellen W. *No Ivory Tower: McCarthyism and the Universities*. New York: Oxford University Press, 1986.

Slaughter, Sheila. "Academic Freedom in the Modern University." In *Higher Education in American Society*, edited by Philip G. Altbach and Robert Berdahl, 77–106. Buffalo, N.Y.: Prometheus, 1987.

Academic Profession

Altbach, Philip G., ed. *Comparative Perspectives on the Academic Profession*. New York: Praeger, 1977.

Bourdieu, Pierre. *Homo Academicus*. Stanford: Stanford University Press, 1988.

Bowen, Howard, and Jack H. Schuster. *American Professors: A National Resource Imperiled*. New York: Oxford University Press, 1986.

Bowen, William G., and Julie Ann Sosa. *Prospects for Faculty in the Arts and Sciences*. Princeton: Princeton University Press, 1989.

Burke, Dolores L. *A New Academic Marketplace*. Westport, Conn.: Greenwood, 1988.

Chitnis, Suma, and Philip G. Altbach, eds. *The Indian Academic Profession*. New Delhi: Macmillan, 1979.

Clark, Burton. *The Academic Life: Small Worlds, Different Worlds*. Princeton, N.J.: Carnegie Foundation for the Advancement of Teaching, 1987.

———, ed. *The Academic Profession: National ,Disciplinary, and Institutional Settings*. Berkeley and Los Angeles: University of California Press, 1987.

Finkelstein, Martin J. *The American Academic Profession*. Columbus: Ohio State University Press, 1984.

————, ed. ASHE *Reader on Faculty and Faculty Issues in Colleges and Universities.* Lexington, Mass.: Ginn, 1985.

Halsey, A. H., and M. A. Trow. *The British Academics.* Cambridge: Harvard University Press, 1971.

Kerr, Clark. "The Academic Ethic and University Teachers: A 'Disintegrating Profession'?" *Minerva* 27 (Summer–Autumn 1989): 139–56.

Lewis, Lionel S. *Scaling the Ivory Tower: Merit and Its Limits in Academic Careers.* Baltimore: Johns Hopkins University Press, 1975.

Regional Institute for Higher Education and Development. *Staff and Faculty Development in Southeast Asian Universities.* Singapore: Regional Institute for Higher Education and Development, 1981.

Ringer, Fritz K. *The Decline of the German Mandarins: The German Academic Community, 1890–1933.* Cambridge: Harvard University Press, 1969.

Shils, Edward. *The Academic Ethic.* Chicago: University of Chicago Press, 1983.

Startup, Richard. *The University Teacher and His World.* Westmead, England: Saxon House, 1979.

Sutherland, Margaret. *Women Who Teach in Universities.* Trentham, England: Trentham Books, 1985.

Trow, Martin, ed. *Teachers and Students.* New York: McGraw-Hill, 1975.

Van den Berghe, Pierre L. *Power and Privilege at an African University.* London: Routledge and Kegan Paul, 1973.

Accountability

Billing, David, ed. *Indicators of Performance.* Guildford, Surrey, England: Society for Research into Higher Education, 1980.

Bligh, Donald, ed. *Accountability or Freedom for Teachers?* Guildford, Surrey, England: Society for Research into Higher Education, 1982.

Bourke, Paul. *Quality Measures in Universities.* Canberra, Australia: Commonwealth Tertiary Education Commission, 1986.

Bowen, Howard R. *Investment in Learning.* San Francisco: Jossey-Bass, 1977.

Cave, Martin, et al. *The Use of Performance Indicators in Higher Education: A Critical Analysis of Developing Practice.* London: Jessica Kingsley, 1988.

Commonwealth Tertiary Education Commission. *Review of Efficiency and Effectiveness in Higher Education.* Canberra, Australia: Australian Government Publishing Service, 1986.

Goodlad, Sinclair, ed. *Economies of Scale in Higher Education.* Guildford, Surrey, England: Society for Research into Higher Education, 1983.

Hufner, Klaus, Thomas R. Hummel, and Einhard Rau. *Efficiency in Higher Education: An Annotated Bibliography.* Frankfurt am Main, Federal Republic of Germany: Peter Lang, 1987.

Lumsden, Keith G., ed. *Efficiency in Universities: The La Paz Papers.* Amsterdam: Elsevier, 1974.

Organization for Economic Cooperation and Development. *Universities under Scrutiny.* Paris: OECD, 1987.

Sheldrake, Peter, and Russell Linke, eds. *Accountability in Higher Education*. Sydney, Australia: Allen and Unwin, 1979.

Verry, Donald, and Bleddyn Davies. *University Costs and Outputs*. Amsterdam: Elsevier, 1976.

Expansion of Higher Education

Altbach, Philip G. *Higher Education in the Third World: Themes and Variations*. New York: Advent, 1987.

Ben-David, Joseph. *Centers of Learning: Britain, France, Germany, and the United States*. New York: McGraw-Hill, 1977.

Ben-David, Joseph, and Abraham Zloczower. "Universities and Academic Systems in Modern Societies." *European Journal of Sociology* 3 (1962): 45–84.

Clark, Burton R. "The 'Cooling-out' Function in Higher Education." *American Journal of Sociology* 65 (1960): 569–76.

————, ed. *Perspectives on Higher Education: Eight Disciplinary and Comparative Views*. Berkeley and Los Angeles: University of California Press, 1984.

Collins, Randall. *The Credential Society*. New York: Academic Press, 1979.

Cummings, William K., Edward R. Beauchamp, Shogo Ichikawa, Victor N. Kobayashi, and Morikazu Ushiogi, eds. *Educational Policies in Crisis*. New York: Praeger, 1986.

Geiger, Roger L. *Private Sectors in Higher Education: Structure, Function, and Change in Eight Countries*. Ann Arbor: University of Michigan Press, 1986.

Hetland, Atle, ed. *Universities and National Development*. Stockholm: Almquist & Wiksell International, 1984.

Hinchliffe, Keith. *Higher Education in Sub-Saharan Africa*. London: Croom Helm, 1987.

Kerr, Clark. "A Critical Age in the University World: Accumulated Heritage Versus Modern Imperatives." *European Journal of Education* 22 (1987): 183–93.

Levy, Daniel C. *Higher Education and the State in Latin America: Private Challenges to Public Dominance*. Chicago: University of Chicago Press, 1986.

Meyer, John W. "The Effects of Education as an Institution." *American Journal of Sociology* 83 (1977): 55–77.

Neave, Guy. "On the Edge of the Abyss: An Overview of Recent Developments in European Higher Education." *European Journal of Education* 17 (1982): 123–44.

Psacharopoulos, George. "The Economics of Higher Education in Developing Countries." *Comparative Education Review* 26 (June 1982): 139–59.

Sirowy, Larry, and Aaron Benavot. "Higher Education in an Era of Equality: A Cross-National Study of Institutional Differentiation on the Tertiary Level." *Research in Sociology of Education and Socialization* 6 (1986): 1–44.

Financing of Higher Education

Bowen, Howard R. *The Costs of Higher Education*. San Francisco: Jossey-Bass, 1980.

Coombs, Philip H., and Jacques Hallack. *Cost Analysis in Education*. Baltimore: Johns Hopkins University Press, 1987.

Gaines, Adam, and Nigel Turner. *Student Loans: The Costs and the Consequences. A Review of Student Financial Support in North America and Scandinavia.* London: National Union of Students, 1985.

Glenny, Lyman A. *Funding Higher Education: A Six-Nation Analysis.* New York: Praeger, 1979.

Johansson, Olof, and Lars Ricknell. *Study Assistance in Ten European Countries—Overview and Conceptual Framework.* Umea, Sweden: Department of Political Science, University of Umea, 1986.

Johnstone, D. Bruce. "International Perspectives on Student Financial Aid." *Journal of Student Financial Aid* 17 (Spring 1987): 30–44.

———. *Sharing the Costs of Higher Education: Student Financial Assistance in the United Kingdom, the Federal Republic of Germany, France, Sweden, and the United States.* New York: College Board, 1986.

Mingat, Alain, and Jee-Peng Tan. "Financing Higher Education in Developing Countries." *Higher Education* 15 (1986): 283–97.

Psacharopoulos, George, and Maureen Woodhall. *Education for Development.* New York: Oxford University Press, 1985.

Tsang, Mun C. "Cost Analysis for Educational Policymaking: A Review of Cost Studies in Education in Developing Countries." *Review of Educational Research* 58 (Summer 1988): 181–230.

Vorbeck, Michael. "Financial Aid to Students in Europe: A Summary Analysis." *International Journal of Institutional Management in Higher Education* 7 (November 1983): 289–305.

Woodhall, Maureen. "Designing a Student Loan Program for a Developing Country: The Relevance of International Experience." *Economics of Education Review* 7 (1988): 153–61.

———. *Review of Student Support Schemes in Selected OECD Countries.* Paris: Organization for Economic Cooperation and Development, 1978.

Foreign Students

Altbach, Philip G., David H. Kelly, and Y. G. M. Lulat. *Research on Foreign Students and International Study: An Overview and Bibliography.* New York: Praeger, 1985.

Altbach, Philip G., and Jing Wang. *Foreign Students and International Study: Bibliography and Analysis, 1984–1988.* Washington, D.C.: University Press of America, 1989.

Barber, Elinor, Philip G. Altbach, and Robert G. Myers, eds. *Bridges to Knowledge: Foreign Students in Comparative Perspectives.* Chicago: University of Chicago Press, 1984.

Chandler, Alice. *Obligation or Opportunity: Foreign Student Policy in Six Major Receiving Countries.* New York: Institute of International Education, 1989.

Cummings, William K. "Trends Seen in the Flow of Asian Students to the United States." *NAFSA Newsletter* 40, no. 5 (March 1989): 1, 10–19; continued in no. 6 (April–May 1989): 13–15, 26.

———. "Going Overseas for Higher Education: The Asian Experience." *Comparative Education Review* 28 (May 1984): 241–5.

Cummings, William K., and Wing-Cheung So. "The Preference of Asian Overseas Students for the United States: An Examination of the Context." *Higher Education* 14 (1985): 403–23.

Goodwin, C. D., and M. Nacht. *Absence of Decision*. New York: Institute of International Education, 1983.

Jenkins, Hugh, ed. *Educating Students from Other Nations*. San Francisco: Jossey-Bass, 1983.

Sirowy, Larry, and Alex Inkeles. "University-Level Student Exchanges: The U.S. Role in Global Perspective." In *Foreign Student Flows*, edited by Elinor Barber, 29–85. New York: Institute of International Education, 1985.

Zikopoulos, Marianthi, ed. *Open Doors: 1987/88*. New York: Institute of International Education, forthcoming.

Graduate Education

Ben-David, Joseph. *Centers of Learning: Britain, France, Germany, and the United States*. New York: McGraw-Hill, 1977.

Berelson, Bernard. *Graduate Education in the United States*. New York: McGraw-Hill, 1960.

Blume, Stuart. *Post-Graduate Education: Structures and Policies*. Paris: Organization for Economic Cooperation and Development, 1972.

Blume, Stuart, and Olga Amsterdamska. *Post-Graduate Education in the 1980s*. Paris: Organization for Economic Cooperation and Development, 1987.

Clark, Burton R. *The Higher Education System: Academic Organization in Cross-National Perspective*. Berkeley and Los Angeles: University of California Press, 1983.

Clark, Terry. *Prophets and Patrons: The French University and the Emergence of the Social Sciences*. Cambridge: Harvard University Press, 1973.

Dahllof, Urban. *The Ecology and Merit-Value of Postgraduate Studies*. Stockholm: National Swedish Board of Universities and Colleges, 1986.

Glazer, Judith. *The Master's Degree: Tradition, Diversity, Innovation*, Washington, D.C.: Association for the Study of Higher Education, 1986. (ASHE-ERIC Higher Education Report No. 6.)

Hirsch, Wendy. "Postgraduate Training of Researchers." In *The Future of Research*, edited by Geoffrey Oldham. Guildford, Surrey, England: Society for Research into Higher Education, 1982.

Malaney, Gary. "Graduate Education as an Area of Research in the Field of Higher Education." In *Higher Education: Handbook of Theory and Research, Vol. 4*, edited by John C. Smart. New York: Agathon Press, 1988, pp. 397–454.

Rudd, Ernest. *A New Look at Postgraduate Failure*. Guildford, Surrey, England: Society for Research into Higher Education, 1985.

————. *Higher Education: A Study of Graduate Education in Britain*. London: Routledge and Kegan Paul, 1975.

Simpson, Renate. *How the Ph.D. Came to Britain: A Century of Struggle for Postgraduate Education*. Guildford, Surrey, England: Society for Research into Higher Education, 1983.

Smith, Bruce L. R., ed. *The State of Graduate Education*. Washington, D.C.: Brookings Institute, 1985.

Smith, Bruce L. R., and Joseph Karlesky, eds. *The State of Academic Science: The Universities in the Nation's Research Effort*. New York: Change Magazine Press, 1977.

Smith, Bruce L. R., and Joseph Karlesky, eds. *The State of Academic Science: Background Papers*.

New York: Change Magazine Press, 1978.

Special issue of *European Journal of Education* 21, no. 3 (1986) on graduate education.

Special issue of *Higher Education in Europe* 6, no. 4 (1981) on graduate education.

Higher Education and the Labor Market

Blaug, M. *Education and the Employment Problem in Developing Countries.* Geneva, Switzerland: ILO, 1973.

Carnoy, M. "High Technology and International Labour Markets." *International Labour Review* 24, no. 6 (1987): 643–69.

Carnoy, M., and H. M. Levin. *Schooling and Work in the Democratic State.* Stanford: Stanford University Press, 1985.

Freeman, R. B. "Evaluating the European View That the United States Has No Unemployed Problem." *American Economic Review* 78 (May 1988): 294–99.

————. *The Over-Educated American.* New York: Academic Press, 1976.

Hallak, J., and F. Caillods. *Education, Work, and Employment.* Vol. 1. Paris: UNESCO, 1980.

Hinchliffe, K. "Employment and Education." In *The International Encyclopaedia of Education*, 1661–67. Oxford: Pergamon Books, 1985.

International Labour Organization. *Paper Qualification Syndrome and Unemployment of School Leavers.* Geneva, Switzerland: ILO, 1982.

Jallade, J. P., ed. *Employment and Unemployment in Europe.* Staffordshire, England: Trentham Books, 1981.

Oxenham, J., ed. *Education Versus Qualifications.* London: Allen and Unwin, 1984.

Reich, M., D. M. Gordon, and R. C. Edwards. "Dual Labor Markets: A Theory of Labor Market Segmentation." *American Economic Review* 63 (1973): 359–66.

Rumberger, R. W., and H. M. Levin. "Forecasting the Impact of New Technologies on the Future Job Market." *Technological Forecasting and Social Change* 27 (1985): 399–417.

Sanyal, B. C. *Higher Education and Employment: An International Comparative Analysis.* London: Falmer Press, 1987.

Sanyal, B., et al. *University Education and the Labour Market in the Arab Republic of Egypt.* Oxford: Pergamon Press, 1982.

Spence, M. "Job Market Signalling." *Quarterly Journal of Economics* 87 (1973): 355–75.

Task Force on Education and Employment. *Education for Employment: Knowledge for Action.* Washington, D.C.: Acropolis Books, 1979.

Teichler, U., and B. Sanyal. *Higher Education and the Labour Market in the Federal Republic of Germany.* Paris: UNESCO, 1982.

History

Altbach, Philip G. *Comparative Higher Education: Research Trends and Bibliography.* London: Mansell, 1979.

Armytage, W. H. G. *Civic Universities.* London: Benn, 1955.

Ashby, Eric. *Any Person, Any Study: An Essay on Higher Education in the United States.* New York:

McGraw-Hill, 1971.

————. *Universities: British, Indian, African.* Cambridge: Harvard University Press, 1966.

Brooke, Christopher, et al. *Oxford and Cambridge.* Cambridge: Cambridge University Press, 1988.

Clark, Burton R., ed. *The Academic Profession.* Berkeley and Los Angeles: University of California Press, 1987.

————. *Perspectives on Higher Education.* Berkeley and Los Angeles: University of California Press, 1984.

Cobban, A. B. *The Medieval Universities.* London: Methuen, 1975.

Cummings, W. K., I. Amano, and K. Kitamura. *Changes in the Japanese University.* New York: Praeger, 1979.

Edwards, E. G. *Education for Everyone.* Nottingham, England: Spokesman, 1982.

Flexner, Abraham. *Universities: American, English, German.* London: Oxford University Press, 1930.

Haskins, C. H. *The Rise of the Medieval Universities.* Ithaca, N.Y.: Cornell University Press, 1957.

Hofstadter, Richard, and Wilson Smith, eds. *American Higher Education: A Documentary History.* 2 vols. Chicago: University of Chicago Press, 1961.

Jarausch, K. H., ed., *The Transformation of Higher Learning: 1860–1930.* Chicago: University of Chicago Press, 1982.

Jilek, Lubor, ed. *Historical Compendium of European Universities.* Geneva, Switzerland: Standing Conference of Rectors, Presidents, and Vice-Chancellors of European Universities, 1984.

Kearney, Hugh. *Science and Change, 1500–1700.* New York: McGraw-Hill, 1971.

Kittelson, J. M., and Pamela J. Johnson, eds. *Rebirth, Reform, and Resilience: Universities in Transition, 1300–1700.* Columbus: Ohio State University Press, 1984.

Lipset, S. M., and P. G. Altbach, eds. *Students in Revolt.* Boston: Houghton-Mifflin, 1969.

Makdisi, George. *The Rise of Colleges: Institutions of Learning in Islam and the West.* Edinburgh, Scotland: Edinburgh University Press, 1981.

McClelland, Charles E. *State, Society, and University in Germany, 1700–1914.* Cambridge: Cambridge University Press, 1980.

McClelland, James C. *Advocates and Academics: Education, Culture, and Society in Tsarist Russia.* Chicago: University of Chicago Press, 1979.

Nagai, Michio. *Higher Education in Japan.* Tokyo: Tokyo University Press, 1971.

Perkin, Harold. *Key Profession: The History of the Association of University Teachers.* London: Routledge and Kegan Paul, 1969.

————. *The Rise of Professional Society: England Since 1880.* London: Routledge and Kegan Paul, 1989.

Piltz, Anders. *The World of Medieval Learning.* Oxford: Blackwell, 1981.

Rashdall, Hastings. *The Universities of Europe in the Middle Ages.* 3 vols. Oxford: Clarendon Press, 1936, 1987.

Ringer, Fritz. *Education and Society in Modern Europe.* Bloomington: Indiana University Press, 1979.

Rudy, Willis. *The Universities of Europe, 1100–1914.* London: Associated University Presses, 1984.

Rothblatt, Sheldon. *The Revolution of the Dons.* Cambridge: Cambridge University Press, 1981.

Sanderson, Michael. *The Universities and British Industry, 1850–1970.* London: Routledge and Kegan Paul, 1972.

Scott, D. F. *Wilhelm von Humboldt and the Idea of a University.* Durham, England: University of Durham Press, 1960.

Touraine, Alain. *The Academic System in American Society.* New York: McGraw-Hill, 1974.

Veysey, L. R. *The Emergence of the American University.* Chicago: University of Chicago Press, 1965.

New Universities

Acherman, J. D., and R. Brons. *Changing Financial Relations between Government and Higher Education.* Enschede, Netherlands: Uitgeverij Lemma, 1989.

Barblan, A., ed. *From Infancy to Maturity: Creating a University.* Geneva, Switzerland: European Rectors' Conference, 1986.

Becher, Tony, and Maurice Kogan. *Process and Structure in Higher Education.* London: Heinemann, 1980.

Berger, Guy, et al. "Higher Education and Regional Development: Five Case Studies in Europe." *Paedogogica Europaea* 11 (1976).

Bosworth, Stuart, et al. "Management of Staffing Reductions: Series of Articles and Cases on Personnel Policies and Institutional Survival." *International Journal of Institutional Management in Higher Education* 8 (March 1984).

Bullock, Matthew. *Academic Enterprise: Industrial Innovation and the Development of High-Technology Financing in the United States.* London: Brand Brothers, 1983.

Clark, Burton R. *The Academic Life.* Princeton, N.J.: Carnegie Foundation for the Advancement of Teaching, 1987.

————, ed. *The Academic Profession.* Berkeley and Los Angeles: University of California Press, 1987.

Davies, John. *The Entrepreneurial and Adaptive University.* Paris: OECD, 1987.

Keller, George. *Academic Strategy.* Baltimore: Johns Hopkins University Press, 1983.

Lockwood, Geoffrey, and John Davies. *Universities: The Management Challenge.* Windsor, England: NFER-Nelson, 1985.

Mayhew, Lewis B., and Ronald Bennett. *Surviving the Eighties.* New York: McGraw-Hill, 1979.

Neave, Guy. "Education and Regional Development: An Overview of a Growing Controversy." *European Journal of Education* 14, no. 3 (1979).

Private Higher Education

Breneman, David W., and Chester E. Finn, Jr., eds. *Public Policy and Private Higher Education.* Washington, D.C.: Brookings Institute, 1978.

Carnegie Commission. *The States and Private Higher Education.* San Francisco: Jossey-Bass, 1977.

Geiger, Roger L. "Creating Private Alternatives in Higher Education," *European Journal of Education* 20 (1985): 385-98.

————. *Private Sectors in Higher Education: Structure, Function, and Change in Eight Countries.* Ann Arbor: University of Michigan Press, 1986.

————. *Privatization of Higher Education: International Trends and Issues.* Princeton, N.J.: International Council for Educational Development, 1988.

————. "Public and Private Sectors in Higher Education: A Comparison of International Patterns." *Higher Education* 17 (1988): 699–711.

Grant, Gerald, and David Riesman. *The Perpetual Dream: Reform and Experiment in American Education.* Chicago: University of Chicago Press, 1978.

Jones, David, and John Anwyl, eds. *Privatizing Australian Higher Education: A New Australian Issue.* Melbourne, Australia: Centre for the Study of Higher Education, University of Melbourne, 1987.

Levy, Daniel. "Private Versus Public Financing of Higher Education: U.S. Policy in Comparative Perspective." *Higher Education* 11 (1982): 607–28.

————. "Latin America's Private Universities: How Successful Are They?" *Comparative Education Review* 29 (1985): 440–59.

————. *Higher Education and the State in Latin America: Private Challenges to Public Dominance.* Chicago: University of Chicago Press, 1986.

————, ed. *Private Education: Studies in Choice and Public Policy.* New York: Oxford University Press, 1986.

Powell, Walter W., ed. *The Nonprofit Sector: A Research Handbook.* New Haven: Yale University Press, 1987.

Research Institute for Higher Education. *Public and Private Sectors in Asian Higher Education.* Hiroshima, Japan: Research Institute for Higher Education, 1987.

Shils, Edward. "The American Private University," *Minerva* 11 (1973): 6–29.

Research and the Development of Scientific Activity

Altbach, P. G., et al. *Scientific Development and Higher Education in Newly Industrialized Countries.* New York: Praeger, 1989.

Davis, C. H. "Institutional Sectors of Mainstream Science Production in Subsaharan Africa, 1970–1979." *Scientometrics* 5 (1983): 163–75.

————. "L'Unesco et la promotion des politiques scientifiques nationales en Afrique subsaharienne, 1960–1979." *Etudes internationales* 14 (1983): 621–38.

Dedijer, S. "Underdeveloped Science in Underdeveloped Countries." *Minerva* 2 (1964): 61–81.

Eisemon, T. O. *The Science Profession in the Third World: Studies from India and Kenya.* New York: Praeger, 1982.

————. "The Implantation of Science in Nigeria and Kenya." *Minerva* 27 (1979): 504–26.

Garfield, E. "Mapping Science in the Third World." *Science and Public Policy* 10 (1983): 112–27.

Henry, Reg. "Science, Technology, and Development in Asia: New Trends and Old Models." *Prometheus* 6 (1988): 305–26.

Hinchliffe, K. *Higher Education in Sub-Saharan Africa.* London: Croom Helm, 1987.

Irele, A. "Education and Access to Modern Knowledge." *Daedalus* 118 (1989): 125–37.

Kolm, E. Jan. "Regional and National Consequences of Globalizing Industries of the Pacific Rim." *Technological Forecasting and Social Change* 35 (1989): 63–91.

McMahon, W. W. "The Relation of Education and R & D to Productivity Growth in the Developing Countries of Africa." *Economics of Education Review* 6 (1987): 183–94.

Standke, Klaus-Heinrich. "International Cooperation in Science and Technology: Classical Options and New Opportunities for Africa." *International Journal of Technology Management* 3 (1988): 439–60.

Ukaegbu, C. C. "Are Nigerian Scientists and Engineers Effectively Utilized? Issues on the Deployment of Scientific and Technological Labor for National Development." *World Development* 13 (1985): 499–512.

Yuthavong, Y. "Bibliometric Indicators of Scientific Activity in Thailand." *Scientometrics* 9 (1986): 139–43.

Student Political Activism

Altbach, Philip G. *Student Politics in America.* New York: McGraw-Hill, 1974.

Altbach, Philip G., ed. *Student Political Activism: An International Reference Handbook.* Westport, Conn.: Greenwood Press, 1989.

Altbach, Philip G., ed. *Student Politics: Perspectives for the Eighties.* Metuchen, N.J.: Scarecrow, 1981.

Altbach, Philip G., ed. *Turmoil and Transition: Higher Education and Student Politics in India.* New York: Basic Books, 1968.

Astin, Alexander, H. S. Astin, A. E. Bayer, and A. S. Bisconti. *The Power of Protest.* San Francisco: Jossey-Bass, 1975.

Barkan, Joel. *An African Dilemma: University Students, Development, and Politics in Ghana, Tanzania, and Uganda.* Nairobi, Kenya: Oxford University Press, 1975.

Douglas, S. A. *Political Socialization and Student Activism in Indonesia.* Urbana: University of Illinois Press, 1970.

Emmerson, Donald K., ed. *Students and Politics in Developing Nations.* New York: Praeger, 1968.

Feuer, Lewis. *The Conflict of Generations.* New York: Basic Books, 1969.

Fraser, Ronald, ed. *1968: A Student Generation in Revolt.* New York: Pantheon, 1988.

Gitlin, Todd. *The Sixties: Years of Hope, Days of Rage.* New York: Bantam, 1987.

Horowitz, H. L. *Campus Life: Undergraduate Cultures from the End of the 18th Century to the Present.* Chicago: University of Chicago Press, 1988.

Jarausch, Konrad H. *Students, Society, and Politics in Imperial Germany.* Princeton: Princeton University Press, 1982.

Klineberg, Otto, et al. *Students, Values, and Politics: A Cross-Cultural Comparison.* New York: Free Press, 1979.

Levitt, Cyril. *Children of Privilege: Student Revolt in the Sixties.* Toronto: University of Toronto Press, 1984.

Liebman, Arthur, et al. *Latin American University Students: A Six-Nation Study.* Cambridge: Harvard University Press, 1972.

Lipset, S. M., *Rebellion in the University.* Chicago: University of Chicago Press, 1976.

Lipset, S. M., and P. G. Altbach, eds. *Students in Revolt.* Boston: Beacon Press, 1969.

Miller, James. *Democracy Is In the Streets: From Port Huron to the Siege of Chicago*. New York: Simon and Schuster, 1987.

Sale, Kirkpatrick. SDS. New York: Random House, 1973.

Steinberg, M. S. *Sabers and Brown Shirts: The German Students' Path to National Socialism, 1918–1935*. Chicago: University of Chicago Press, 1979.

University Reform

Altbach, Philip G. *University Reform: An International Perspective*. Washington, D.C.: American Association for Higher Education, 1980.

Altbach, Philip G., ed. *University Reform: Comparative Perspectives for the Seventies*. Cambridge, Mass.: Schenkman, 1974.

Bergandal, G. "U68: A Reform Proposal for Swedish Higher Education." *Higher Education* 3 (August 1974): 353–64.

Cerych, L., and P. Sabatier. *Great Expectations and Mixed Performance: The Implementation of Higher Education Reforms in Europe*. Trentham, England: Trentham Books, 1986.

Clark, Burton. *The Higher Education System*. Berkeley and Los Angeles: University of California Press, 1983.

Cohen, Habiba. *Elusive Reform: The French Universities, 1968–1978*. Boulder, Colo.: Westview Press, 1978.

Hefferlin, J. B. Lon. *Dynamics of Academic Reform*. San Francisco: Jossey-Bass, 1969.

Levine, Arthur. *Why Innovation Fails: The Institutionalization and Termination of Innovation in Higher Education*. Albany, N.Y.: SUNY Press, 1980.

Levine, Arthur, and John Weingart. *Reform of Undergraduate Education*. San Francisco: Jossey-Bass, 1973.

Levy, Daniel C. *Higher Education and the State in Latin America*. Chicago: University of Chicago Press, 1986.

Mayhew, Lewis B., and Patrick J. Ford. *Reform in Graduate and Professional Education*. San Francisco: Jossey-Bass, 1974.

Nitsch, Wolfgang, et al. *Hochschule in Der Demokratie*. Berlin: Luchterhand, 1965.

Perry, Walter. *The Open University*. San Francisco: Jossey-Bass, 1977.

Riesman, David, and Verne A. Stadtman, eds. *Academic Transformation: Seventeen Institutions Under Pressure*. New York: McGraw-Hill, 1973.

Teichler, Ulrich. *Changing Patterns of the Higher Education System*. London: Jessica Kingsley, 1989.

Women in Higher Education

Abramson, J. *The Invisible Woman: Discrimination in the Academic Profession*. San Francisco: Jossey-Bass, 1975.

Acker, Sandra. "Women: The Other Academics." *British Journal of Sociology of Education* 1 (1980): 81–91.

Baba, Y., and E. Monk-Turner. "Gender and College Opportunities: Changes Over Time in the United States and Japan." *Sociological Inquiry* 57 (Summer 1987): 292–303.

Balbo, Laura, and Ergas Yasmine. *Women's Studies in Italy.* Old Westbury, Conn.: The Feminist Press, 1982.

Battel, Roisin, et al., eds. "So Far, So Good—So What: Women's Studies in the UK." (Special Issue.) *Women's Studies: International Forum* 6 (1983).

Blackstone, Tessa, and Oliver Fulton. "Sex Discrimination Among University Teachers: A British-American Comparison." *British Journal of Sociology* 26 (1975): 261–75.

Bramley, Gwenda M., and Marion Ward. *The Role of Women in the Australian National University.* Canberra: Australian National University, 1976.

Bridges, J. S. "College Females' Perception of Adult Roles and Occupational Fields for Women." *Sex Roles* 16 (June 1984): 591–604.

Chang, Sei-wha, ed. *Challenges for Women: Women's Studies in Korea.* Seoul: Ewha Women's University Press, 1986.

Craney, J., and C. O'Donnell. "Women in Advanced Education: Advancement for Whom?" *Higher Education Research and Development* 2 (1983): 129–46.

Dach, Z. "Women's Participation in Higher Education in Poland, 1970–1984," *Higher Education* 17, no. 1 (1988): 27–39.

DuBois, Ellen Carol, G. P. Kelly, C. Kursmeyer, and L. Robinson, *Feminist Scholarship: Kindling in the Groves of Academe.* Champaign: University of Illinois Press, 1985.

Eaton, J. S., ed. "Women in Community Colleges." (Symposium.) *New Directions for Community Colleges*, no. 34 (1981): 1–90.

Fujimura-Fanselow, K. "Women's Participation in Higher Education in Japan." *Comparative Education Review* 29 (November 1985): 471–89.

Gannik, D., and K. Sjrup, eds. "Special Issue on Women's Studies." *Acta Sociologica* 30, no. 2 (1987): 133–232.

Horning, L. S. "Untenured and Tenuous: The Status of Women Faculty." *American Academy of Political and Social Science Annals* 448 (March 1980): 115–25.

Kashif-Badri, Hagga. "The History, Development, Organization, and Position of Women's Studies in the Sudan." In *Social Science Research and Women in the Arab World*, edited by UNESCO. Dover, N.H.: Frances Pinter, 1984.

Krishnaraj, Maithreyi. "Employment Pattern of University-Educated Women and Its Implications." *Journal of Higher Education* 2 (Spring 1977): 317–27.

Lindsay, Beverly. "Pursuing the Baccalaureate Degree in the United States: The Case of African-American Women." In *World Yearbook of Education 1984: Women and Education*, edited by Sandra Acker et al. London: Kogan Page, 1984.

Luukkonen-Gronow, T. "University Career Opportunities for Women in Finland in the 1980s," *Acta Sociologica* 30, no. 2 (1987): 193–206.

Moore, Kathryn. "Women's Access and Opportunity in Higher Education: Toward the Twenty-First Century." *Comparative Education* 23, no. 1 (1987): 23–34.

Palmier, L. "Degree and Gender Distinctions Among Indonesian Graduate Officials." *Higher Education* 15, no. 5 (1986): 459–73.

Randour, Mary Lou, Georgia L. Strasburg, and Jean Lipman-Blumen. "Women in Higher Education: Trends in Enrollment and Degrees Earned." *Harvard Educational Review* 52, no. 2 (1982): 189–202.

Reilly, Shalini. "Gender Divisions in the Academic Workplace." *Compare* 15 (1985): 41–52.

"Sex Stereotyping and Higher Education of Women." (Symposium.) *Western European Education* 14 (Spring–Summer 1982): 4–183.

Simeone, Angela. *Academic Women: Working Toward Equality.* South Hadley, Mass.: Bergin and Garvey, 1987.

Solomon, Barbara Miller. *In the Company of Educated Women: A History of Women and Higher Education in America.* New Haven: Yale University Press, 1985.

Sutherland, M. B. "The Situation of Women Who Teach in Universities: Contrasts and Common Ground." *Comparative Education* 21, no. 1 (1985): 21–28.

Tinsley, A., et al., eds. "Women in Higher Education Administration." (Symposium.) *New Directions for Higher Education* no. 45 (1984): 1–91.

Regions and Countries

Africa

Sub-Saharan Africa

Ashby, Eric. *African Universities and Western Tradition.* London: Oxford University Press, 1964.

Ashby, Eric. *Universities, British, Indian and African.* Cambridge: Harvard University Press, 1966.

Coleman, James S. "The Academic Freedom and Responsibilities of Foreign Scholars in African Universities." *Issue* 7 (1977): 14-33.

Coombe, Carol. *International Development Programmes in Higher Education.* London: Commonwealth Secretariat, 1989.

Court, David. "The Development Ideal in Higher Education: The Experience of Kenya and Tanzania." *Higher Education,* 7 (1980): 657-680.

Hetland, Atle. *Universities and National Development.* Stockholm: Almquist & Wiksell, 1984.

Hinchliffe, Keith. *Higher Education in Sub Saharan Africa.* London: Croom Helm, 1987.

Malyiamkono, ed., T. L. *University Capacity in Eastern and Southern African Countries.* London: James Currey Ltd, 1987.

Mazrui, Ali. *Political Values and the Educated Class in Africa.* London: Heinmann, 1978.

Thompson, Kenneth, Barbara Fogel and H. E. Danner. *Higher Education and Social Change.* New York: Praeger, 1976.

Van Den Berghe, Pierre L. *Power and Privilege at an African University.* London: Routledge and Kegan Paul, 1873.

Wandira, Asavia. *The African University in Development.* Johannesburg: Raven Press, 1978.

World Bank. *Education in Sub Saharan Africa.* Washington, D.C.: World Bank, 1988.

Yesufu, J. M. *Creating the African University.* Ibadan: Oxford University Press, 1973.

Francophone West Africa

Belloncle, Guy. *La Question educative en Afrique Noire*. Paris: Karthala, 1984.

Bureau International du Travail, Programme des Emplois et des Competence Technique pour l'Afrique. *Le Syndrome du diplome et le chomage des diplomes*. Addis Ababa, Ethiopia: 1982.

Hinchliffe, Keith. *Higher Education in Sub-Saharan Africa*. London: Croom Helm, 1987.

Ki-Zerbo, Joseph. *Histoire de l'Afrique Noire*. Paris: Hatier, 1972.

Manning, Patrick. *Francophone Sub-Saharan Africa*. Cambridge: Cambridge University Press, 1986.

Moumouni, Abdou. *Education in Africa*. New York: Praeger, 1968.

Ransom, Angela. *Financing Higher Education in Francophone West Africa: Report on a Series of Meetings Held in Dakar, Senegal, March 1985, in Yamoussoukro, Côte d'Ivoire, March 1986, and Victoria Falls, Zimbabwe, January 1987*. EDI Policy Seminar Report, No. 12. Washington, D.C.: World Bank, 1988.

Salifou, Andre. *Perspectives du developpement de l'enseignement superieur en Afrique dans les prochaines decennies*. Paris: UNESCO, 1983.

World Bank. *Education in Sub-Saharan Africa: Policies for Adjustment, Revitalization, and Expansion*. Washington, D.C.: World Bank, 1988.

Kenya

Barkan, J. "African University Students: Presumptive Elite or Upper-Middle Class?" In *Education and Political Values*, edited by Kenneth Prewitt. Nairobi, Kenya: East African Publishing House, 1971.

Court, D. "The Development Ideal in Higher Education: The Experience of Kenya and Tanzania." *Higher Education* 9 (1980), 657–680.

———. "Educational Research Environments In Kenya." In *Educational Research Environments in the Third World*, edited by S. Shaeffer and J. Nkinyangi. Ottawa: International Development Research Centre, 1983.

———. "The Education System as a Response to Inequality." In *Politics and Public Policy in Kenya and Tanzania*, edited by J. Barkan. Nairobi, Kenya: Heinemann, 1984.

Eshiwani, G. S. "Women's Access to Higher Education in Kenya: A Study of Opportunities and Attainment in Science and Mathematics Education." In *Women and Development in Africa*, edited by G. S. Were. Nairobi, Kenya: Gideon S. Were Press, 1985.

Hughes, R. "Revisiting the Fortunate Few: University Graduates in the Kenyan Labor Market." *Comparative Education Review* 31 (November 1987): 583–601.

Hughes, R., and K. Mwiria, "Kenyan Women, Higher Education, and the Labour Market." *Comparative Education*, forthcoming.

———. "An Essay on the Implications of University Expansion in Kenya." *Higher Education*, forthcoming.

Kinyanjui, K., S. Migot-Adholla, and P. Amanyi. "Notes on the Evolution of Overseas Training Policy in Kenya." In *Policy Development in Overseas Training*, edited by T. L. Maliyamkono. Dar es Salaam, Tanzania: Eastern African Universities Research Project and Black Star Agencies, 1980.

Migot-Adholla, S. E. "The Evolution of Higher Education—Kenya." In *The Development of Higher Education in Eastern and Southern Africa*, edited by L. Tembo, M. Dilogassa, P. Makhurance, and P. L. Pitso. Nairobi, Kenya: Hedaya Educational Books, 1985.

Njenga, A. W. "Career Patterns and Prospects Among Women and Men Agriculturists, Veterinary Doctors, and Engineers." Kenya Educational Research Award (KERA) Series 3.2. Nairobi, Kenya: Kenyatta University, Bureau of Educational Research, 1986.

Van den Berghe, P. "An African Elite Revisited." *Mawazo* 1 (1986): 57–71.

Nigeria

Adesina, Segun. *Planning and Educational Development in Nigeria*. Lagos, Nigeria: Educational Industries, 1977.

Ahimie, F. A. "The Roots of Educated Youth Unemployment in Nigeria." *Economics* 23, no. 97 (Spring 1987): 195–96.

Akpan, P. A. "The Spatial Aspects of Higher Education in Nigeria." *Higher Education* 16 (1987): 545–55.

Beckett, Paul, and James O'Connell. *Education and Power in Nigeria*. New York: Africana Publishing Company, 1977.

Biraimah, Karen L. "Class, Gender, and Life Chances: A Nigerian University Case Study." *Comparative Education Review* 31 (November 1987): 570–82.

Chuta, E. J. "Free Education in Nigeria: Socioeconomic Implications and Emerging Issues." *Comparative Education Review* 30 (November 1986): 523–31.

Enaohwa, J. O. "Education and the National Economy of Nigeria." *International Social Science Journal* 37, no. 2 (1985): 237–46.

———. "Emerging Issues in Nigerian Universities—The Case of the Level and Scope of Growth of Nigerian Universities." *Higher Education* 14 (1985): 307–19.

Fafunwa, A. Babs. *History of Education in Nigeria*. London: Allen and Unwin, 1974.

Kolinsky, Martin. "Universities and the British Aid Programme: The Case of Nigeria During the 1970s." *Higher Education* 16 (1987): 199–219.

Obasi, Emma. "Manpower Planning and Occupational Choice in Nigeria." *Higher Education Review* 20, no. 1 (1987): 27–34.

Oduleye, S. O. "Decline in Nigerian Universities." *Higher Education* 14 (February 1985): 17–40.

Okafor, Nduka. *The Development of Universities in Nigeria*. London: Longman, 1971.

Osunde, Egerton O. "General Education in Nigerian Universities: An Analysis of Recent Curricular Reforms." *Journal of General Education* 37, no. 1 (1985): 47–62.

Rathgeber, Eva M. "A Tenuous Relationship: The African University and Development Policymaking in the 1980s." *Higher Education* 17 (1988): 397–410.

Taiwo, C. O. *The Nigerian Education System: Past, Present, and Future*. Lagos, Nigeria: Thomas Nelson, 1980.

Yesufu, T. M., ed. *Creating the African University*. Ibadan, Nigeria: Oxford University Press, 1973.

South Africa

Behr, A. H. "South African Universities Today: Perceptions for a Changing Society." *South Africa Journal of Higher Education* 1, no. 1 (1987): 3–9.

———. *Education in South Africa: Origins, Issues, and Trends.* Pretoria: Academica, 1988.

File, Jon. "The Politics of Excellence: University Education in the South African Context." *Social Dynamics* 12 (1986): 26–42.

Gwala, Nkosinathi. "State Control, Student Politics, and the Crisis in Black Universities." In *Popular Struggles in South Africa*, edited by William Cobbett and Robin Cohen, 163–82. London: James Curry, 1988.

Hofmeyr, Jane, and Rod Spence. "Bridge to the Future." *Optima* 37 (1989): 37–48.

Kallaway, Peter. *Apartheid and Education.* Johannesburg: Raven Press, 1984.

Keenan, J. H. "Open Minds and Closed Systems: Comments on the Functions and Future of the 'Urban', 'English-Speaking University' in South Africa." *Social Dynamics* 6 (1980): 36–47.

Mitchell, Graham, and Peter Fridjohn. "Matriculation Examinations and University Performance." *South African Journal of Science* 83 (1987): 555–59.

Moulder, James. "'Africanizing' Our Universities: Some Ideas for a Debate." *Theoria* 72 (1988): 1–16.

Mphahlele, Es'kia. "Black Educators and White Institutions." In *Education, Race, and Social Change in South Africa*, compiled by John A. Marcum, 136–40. Berkeley and Los Angeles: University of California Press, 1982.

Nkomo, Mokubung. "Foreign Policy and Scholarship Programs for Black South Africans: A Preliminary Critical Assessment." *Perspectives in Education*, forthcoming.

Nkondo, G. M., ed. *Turfloop Testimony: The Dilemma of a Black University in South Africa.* Johannesburg: Raven Press, 1976.

Orkin, F. M., L. O. Nicolaysen, and M. Price. "The Future of the Urban University in South Africa: Some Practical Considerations." *Social Dynamics* 5 (1979): 26–37.

Taylor, Rupert. "University of the Witwatersrand Ltd.: Big Business Connections and Influence on the University Council." *Perspectives in Education* 10 (1988–89): 71–76.

Trotter, George J. "An Alternative for University Financing in South Africa." *South African Journal of Higher Education* 2 (1988): 94–102.

Webster, Eddie. "The State, Crisis, and the University: The Social Scientist's Dilemma." *Perspectives in Education* 6 (1982): 1–14.

Zimbabwe

Murphree, M. W., and E. A. Ngara. *Inter-University Cooperation in Eastern and Southern Africa: Report of the Vice-Chancellors' Workshop on Regional Cooperation Among Universities.* Harare, Zimbabwe: AESAU, 1984.

Chideya, N. T., ed. *The Vice-Chancellor Speaks: A Collection of Some Major Speeches by Professor Walter J. Kamba (1980–88).* Harare, Zimbabwe: University of Zimbabwe Information Office, 1988.

Chideya, N. T., et al., eds. *The Role of the University and Its Future in Zimbabwe.* Harare, Zimbabwe: Harare Publishing House, 1982.

Asia
China

Bastid, Marianne. "Chinese Educational Policies in the 1980s and Economic Development." *China Quarterly* 98 (June 1984): 189–219.

Bernstein, Thomas. *Up to the Mountains and Down to the Villages: The Transfer of Youth from Urban to Rural China.* New Haven: Yale University Press, 1977.

Chen Hsi-en, Theodore. *Chinese Education Since 1949: Academic and Revolutionary Models.* New York: Pergamon Press, 1981.

Goldman, Merle. *China's Intellectuals: Advise and Dissent.* Cambridge: Harvard University Press, 1981.

Grieder, Jerome. *Intellectuals and the State in Modern China.* New York: Free Press, 1981.

Gu, Mingyuan. "The Development and Reform of Higher Education in China." *Comparative Education* 20, no. 1 (1984): 141–49.

Hawkins, John N. "Higher Education Alternatives in China: The Transition from Revolutionary to Postrevolutionary Forms." *Comparative Education Review* 29 (November 1985): 425–39.

Hayhoe, Ruth. *China's Universities and the Open Door.* Armonk, N.Y.: M. E. Sharpe, 1989.

Hayhoe, Ruth, and Marianne Bastid, eds. *China's Education and the Industrialized World: Studies in Cultural Transfer.* Armonk, N.Y.: M. E. Sharpe, 1987.

Henze, Jurgen. "Higher Education: The Tension between Quality and Equality." In *Contemporary Education in Chinese Education,* edited by Ruth Hayhoe, 241–56. London: Croom Helm, 1984.

Huang, Shiqi. "China's Educational Relations with Foreign Countries." *Canadian and International Education* 16 (1987): 33–39.

Hunter, Carmen St. John, and Martha McKee Keehn, eds. *Adult Education in China.* London: Croom Helm, 1985.

Liu, Wenxiu. "The Significance of Recent Reforms for Higher Education." *Canadian and International Education* 16 (1987): 33–39.

Pepper, Suzanne. "Chinese Education After Mao: Two Steps Forward, Two Steps Back and Begin Again?" *China Quarterly* 8 No. 1 (March 1989): 1–63.

Rosen, Stanley. "Education and the Political Socialization of Chinese Youths." In *Education and Social Change in the People's Republic of China,* edited by John N. Hawkins. New York: Praeger, 1983.

———. "Recentralization, Decentralization, and Rationalization: Deng Xiaoping's Bifurcate Educational Policy." *Modern China* 11 (July 1985): 301–46.

———. *Red Guard Factionalism and the Cultural Revolution in Guangzhou.* Boulder, Colo.: Westview Press, 1982.

Shirk, Susan. *Competitive Comrades: Career Incentives and Student Strategies in China.* Berkeley and Los Angeles: University of California Press, 1982.

Unger, Jonathan. *Education Under Mao: Class and Competition in Canton Schools, 1960–1980.* New York: Columbia University Press, 1982.

White, Gordon. *Party and Professionals: The Political Role of Teachers in Contemporary China.* New York: M. E. Sharpe, 1981.

World Bank. *China: Management and Finance of Higher Education*. Washington, D.C.: World Bank, 1986.

Zhang, Xing. "Research Into Higher Education in China." *Canadian and International Education* 16 (1987): 33–39.

India

Altbach, Philip, ed. *Turmoil and Transition*. New York: Basic Books, 1968.

Bose, P. K., S. P. Mukerjee, and B. C. Sanyal. *Graduate Employment and Higher Education in West Bengal*. New Delhi: Wiley Eastern, 1983.

Chitnis, Suma, and Philip G. Altbach, eds. *The Indian Academic Profession*. New Delhi: Macmillan, 1979.

Gaudino, Robert. *The Indian University*. Bombay: Popular Prakashan, 1965.

Government of India, Ministry of Education. *Education and National Development—Report of the Education Commission 1964–66*. New Delhi: Ministry of Education, 1966.

Kamat, A. R. *Education and Social Change*. Bombay: Somaiya, 1985.

Kaul, J. N., ed. *Higher Education, National Development, and Social Chance*. Simla: Indian Institute of Advanced Study, 1975.

Malik, S. C., ed. *Management and Governance of India Universities*. Simla: Indian Institute of Advanced Study, 1971.

Panchmukhi, P. R., ed. *Educational Reforms in India*. Delhi: Himalaya, 1988.

Singh, Amrik, and G. D. Sharma, eds. *Higher Education in India*. Delhi: Konrak, 1988.

Singh, Amrik, and Philip Altbach, eds. *The Higher Learning in India*. Delhi: Vikas, 1973.

Veeraraghaven, J., ed. *Higher Education in the Eighties*. Delhi: Lancers, 1985.

Indonesia

Atmakusuma, Achjani. "Problems of University Growth in Indonesia." In *The Growth of Southeast Asian Universities: Expansion Versus Consolidation*, edited by Amnuay Tapingkae, 1–10. Singapore: Regional Institute for Higher Education and Development, 1974.

Bachtiar, Harsja. "The University and Society in Indonesia: A Country Report." In *Higher Education and Commitment*, edited by S. Nasution and Banphot Virasai, 42–49. Singapore: Regional Institute for Higher Education and Development, 1978.

Cummings, William K. "Notes on Higher Education and Indonesian Society." *Prisma* 21 (June 1981): 16–39.

Cummings, William K., and Salman Kasenda. "The Origin of Modern Indonesian Higher Education." In *From Dependence to Autonomy*, edited by P. G. Altbach and V. Selvaratnam. Dordrecht, The Netherlands: Kluwer Academic Publishers, 1989.

Pearse, R. "The Role of Selection Based on Academic Criteria in the Recruitment Process at an Indonesian Government University." *Higher Education* 7 (1978): 157–76.

Smith, Theodore M., and Harold F. Carpenter. "Indonesian University Students and Their Career Aspirations." *Asian Survey* 14, no. 9 (1974): 807–26.

Soemardjan, Selo. "General Problems and Issues of Higher Education Development in Indonesia." In *Development of Higher Education in Southeast Asia: Problems and Issues*, edited by Yip Yat Hoong, 41–56. Singapore: Regional Institute for Higher Education and Development, 1973.

Thomas, R. Murray. *A Chronicle of Indonesian Higher Education: The First Half-Century—1920 to 1970.* Singapore: Chopmen Enterprises, 1973.

Japan

Abe, Y., ed. *Non-University Sector Higher Education in Japan.* Hiroshima: Research Institute for Higher Education, Hiroshima University, 1989.

Beauchamp, E. R., and R. Rubinger. *Education in Japan—A Source Book.* New York: Garland, 1989.

Cummings, W. K., et al., eds. *Educational Policies in Crisis.* New York: Praeger, 1984.

———. *Changes in the Japanese University.* New York: Praeger, 1979.

Japan Association of Private Colleges and Universities. *Japan's Private Colleges and Universities.* Tokyo: Japan Association of Private Colleges and Universities, 1987.

Kaneko, M. *Enrollment Expansion in Postwar Japan.* Hiroshima: Research Institute for Higher Education, Hiroshima University, 1987.

———. *Financing Higher Education in Japan.* Hiroshima: Research Institute for Higher Education, Hiroshima University, 1989.

Monbusho (Ministry of Education, Science, and Culture, Japan). *Basic Guidelines for the Reform of Education Report of the Central Council for Education.* Tokyo: Ministry of Education, 1972.

———. *Outline of Education in Japan 1989.* Tokyo: Ministry of Education, 1989.

Nagai, M. *Higher Education in Japan: Its Take-Off and Crash.* Tokyo: University of Tokyo Press, 1971.

O.E.C.D. *Reviews of National Policies for Education: Japan.* Paris: OECD, 1981.

Teichler, U. *Geschichte und Struktur des japanischen Hoschschulwesens.* Stuttgart, West Germany: Ernest Klettverlag, 1975.

U.S. Department of Education. *Japanese Education Today.* Washington, D.C.: U.S. Government Printing Office, 1987.

Korea, Republic of

Kim, Chul-Hwan, and Wha-Kuk Lee, eds. *Higher Education and the Asia-Pacific Century.* Seoul: Ajou University and KCUE, 1988.

Kim, Ransoo. *Korean Education in Research Perspectives.* Seoul: Jong-Gak, 1984.

Kim, Sang-Hyup. "The Direction for the Reform of University Education in Korea." In *Innovation in Higher Education,* edited by T. S. Park. Seoul: Yonsei University Press, 1972.

Korean Council for University Education. *Inter-Institutional Cooperation in Higher Education: Proceedings of the 1st AASCU-KCUE Seminar.* Seoul: Korean Council for University Education, 1984.

———. *Korean Higher Education: Its Development, Aspects, and Prospect.* Seoul: Korean Council for University Education, 1988.

Korean Educational Development Institute. *Korean Education 2000.* Seoul: Korean Educational Development Institute, 1985.

Lee, Sungho. "The Emergence of the Modern University in Korea," *Higher Education* 18 (1989): 87–116.

McGinn, N. F., et al. *Education and Development in Korea.* Cambridge: Harvard University Press, 1980.

Ministry of Education. *Education in Korea* 1988. Seoul: Ministry of Education, Republic of Korea, 1988.

Presidential Commission for Educational Reform. *Korean Education Reform Toward the 21st Century.* Seoul: Presidential Commission for Education Reform, Republic of Korea, 1987.

Malaysia

Ahmat, Sharom. "Nation-Building and the University in Developing Countries: The Case of Malaysia." *Higher Education* 9 (1980): 721–41.

Aziz, U. A., Chew Sing Baun, Lee Kiong Hock, and Bikas C. Sanyal, eds. *University Education and Employment in Malaysia.* Paris: International Institute for Educational Planning, 1987.

Hoong, Yip Yat, ed. *Development Planning in Southeast Asia: Role of the University.* Singapore: Regional Institute for Higher Education and Development, 1973.

Hui, Lim Mah. "Affirmative Action, Ethnicity, and Integration: The Case of Malaysia." *Ethnic and Racial Studies* 8 (April 1985): 251–76.

Inglis, C. "Educational Policy and Occupational Structures in Peninsular Malaysia." In *Issues in Malaysian Development,* edited by J. C. Jackson and M. Rudner. Kuala Lumpur, Malaysia: Heinemann, 1979.

Mahathir, B. Mohammed. *The Malay Dilemma.* Kuala Lumpur, Malaysia: Federal Publications, 1981.

Marimuthu, T. *Student Development in Malaysian Universities.* Singapore: RIHED Occasional Paper No. 19, 1984.

Mehmet, Ozay, and Yip Yat Hoong. "An Empirical Evaluation of Government Scholarship Policy in Malaysia." *Higher Education* 14 (1985): 197–210.

———. *Human Capital Formation in Malaysian Universities: A Socio-Economic Profile of the 1983 Graduates.* Kuala Lumpur, Malaysia: Institute of Advanced Studies, University of Malaya, 1986.

Mukherjee, Hena, and Jasbir Sarjit Singh. "Education and Social Policy: The Malaysian Case." *Prospects* 15, no. 2 (1985): 189–300.

———. "Scientific Personnel, Research Environment, and Higher Education in Malaysia." In *Scientific Development and Higher Education in Newly Industrialized Nations,* edited by P. G. Altbach, et al. New York: Praeger, 1989.

Selvaratnam, V. "Dependency, Change, and Continuity in a Western University Model: The Malaysian Case." *Southeast Asian Journal of Social Science* 14 (1986): 29–51.

———. "The Higher Education System in Malaysia: Metropolitan, Cross-National, Peripheral, or National." *Higher Education* 14 (1985), 477-96.

_____. "Ethnicity, Inequality, and Higher Education in Malaysia." *Comparative Education Review* 32 (May 1988): 173–96.

Silcock, T. H. *Southeast Asian University: A Comparative Account of Some Development Problems.* Durham, N.C.: Duke University Press, 1964.

Singh Sarjit Jasbir. "Higher Education and Social Mobility: The Role of the University of Malaya." *Southeast Asian Journal of Social Science* (1981): 55–63.

Thomas, R. Murray. "Malaysia: Cooperation versus Competition—Or National Unity Versus Favored Access to Education." In *Politics and Education: Cases from Eleven Nations,* edited by R. Murray Thomas. Oxford: Pergamon Press, 1983.

Woon, Toh Kim. "Education as a Vehicle for Reducing Economic Inequality." In *Ethnicity, Class, and Development: Malaysia,* edited by S. Husain Ali. Kuala Lumpur, Malaysia: Social Science Association, Malaysia, 1984.

Pakistan

Guisinger, Stephen E., James Henderson, and Gerald Scully. "Earnings, Rate of Return to Education, and the Earnings Distribution in Pakistan." *Economics of Education Review* 3 (1984): 257–67.

Hussain, Tahir, et al. *Higher Education and Employment Opportunities in Pakistan.* Paris: IIEP (UNESCO) Research Report No. 60, 1987.

Khan, Shakrukh R., and M. Irfan. "Rates of Returns to Education and Determinants of Earnings in Pakistan." *Pakistan Development Review* 24 (Autumn–Winter 1985).

Khan, Shakrukh R., and Syed Z. Ali. "Some Findings on Higher Educated Unemployment in Pakistan." *Canadian Journal of Development Studies* 11 (Summer 1988): 261–78.

Qureshi, I. H. *Education in Pakistan.* Karachi, Pakistan: MA'AREF, 1975.

Rado, E. R. *Unemployment Among the Educated in Pakistan.* Geneva, Switzerland: International Labour Organization, 1976.

Philippines

Association of Catholic Universities of the Phillipines Secretariat. *The Filipino Teacher in the 80's: An Empirical Study.* Manila: Association of Catholic Universities of the Philippines, 1985.

Arcelo, Adrian A., and Bikas C. Sanyal. *Employment and Higher Education in the Philippines* (HELMS II Report). Manila: Ministry of Education, Culture, and Sports, Fund for Assistance to Private Education, International Institute of Educational Planning, 1983.

Bazaco, Evergisto, O. P. *History of Education in the Philippines.* Manila: University of Santo Tomas Press, 1953.

Fund for Assistance to Private Education. *FAPE Atlas.* Manila: FAPE, 1975.

Gonzalez, Andrew F. S. C., and Anicia del Corro. *Doctoral Programs in the Philippines.* Manila: Research Council, De La Salle University/United Publishing Company, 1978.

Taiwan

Altbach, Philip G. "Academic Freedom in Asia: Learning the Limitations." *Far Eastern Economic Review* (June 1988): 24–25.

Chang, Clement Chien-pang. A *Study of Bureaucratic, Collegial, and Political Models of Governance in Six Universities in Taiwan.* Taipei, Taiwan: Ching Sheng Book Co., 1981.

Kao, Charles H. C. "Taiwan's Brain Drain." In *Contemporary Republic of China: Taiwan Experience 1950–1980,* edited by James Hsiung, et al. New York: American Association for Chinese Studies, 1981.

Ministry of Education. *Education in the Republic of China.* Taipei, Taiwan: Ministry of Education, 1988.

———. *Educational Statistics of the Republic of China.* Taipei, Taiwan: Ministry of Education, 1988.

Wu, Wen-hsing, Shun-fen Chen, and Chen-tsou Wu. "The Development of Higher Education in Taiwan." *Higher Education* 18 (1989): 117–36.

Yang, Shun-jane. *The Role of the Ministry of Education in the Governance of Higher Education in Taiwan, The Republic of China.* Ed.D. diss., University of Kansas, 1987.

Thailand

Amnuay, Taping Kae, and Louis Setti, eds. *Education in Thailand: Some Thai Perspectives.* Washington, D.C.: U.S. Department of Health, Education, and Welfare, 1973.

Danskin, Edith. *Increasing Opportunities for Higher Education: Implications of the Thai Solution.* EDC Occasional Paper No. 4. London: University of London Institute of Education, 1983.

Darling, F. C. "Student Protest and Political Change in Thailand." *Pacific Affairs* 47 (1974).

Ketudet, S. "Higher Education in Thailand." *Bulletin of the* UNESCO *Regional Office for Education in Asia,* No. 7. Bangkok, Thailand: UNESCO, 1972.

Ketudet, Sipponandha, et al. *Systems of Higher Education: Thailand.* New York: International Council for Educational Development, 1978.

Nakata, T. *Problems of Democracy in Thailand: A Study of Political Culture and Socialization of College Students.* Bangkok, Thailand: Praepittya, 1975.

Sailhoo, P., S. Chantavanich, and U. Thongutai. *Research Environmental Study: Thailand.* Bangkok, Thailand: National Education Commission, 1981.

Silcock, T. H., ed. *Thailand: Social and Economic Development.* Canberra: Australian National Press, 1971.

Sukontarangsi, Surat. *The Development of Thai Educational Bureaucracy.* Bangkok, Thailand: National Institute of Development Administration, 1967.

Watson, K. *Educational Development in Thailand.* Hong Kong: Heinemann Asia, 1980.

Watson, Keith. "The Higher Education Dilemma in Developing Countries: Thailand's Two Decades of Reform." *Higher Education* 10 (1981): 297–314.

———. "Looking West and East: Thailand's Academic Development." In *From Dependence to Autonomy,* edited by P. G. Altbach and V. Selvaratnam. Dordrecht, The Netherlands: Kluwer Academic Publishers, 1989.

Turkey

Dogramaci, Ihsan. *The Higher Education Reform in Turkey: Results After Three Years.* Ankara, Turkey: January, 1985.

Hirsch, Ernst. *Dunya Universiteleri ve Turkiye'de Universitelerin Gelismesi* (World Universities and the Development of Universities in Turkey). Istanbul, Turkey: A. U. Yayinlari, 1950.

Kocer, H. Ali. "Turkiye'de Universiteler (1453–1960)," 1968 *Yili Ogrenci Hareketleri* [Universities in Turkey (1453–1960)]. Ankara, Turkey: A. U. Egitim Fak/Yayinlari, 1969.

Miller, Barnette. *The Palace School of Muhammad the Conqueror*. New York: Harvard University Press, 1973.

Reed, Howard A. "Hacettepe and Middle East Technical Universities in Turkey." *Minerva* 13, no. 2 (1975): 200–235.

Umunc, Himmet. "In Search of Improvement: The Reorganization of Higher Education in Turkey." *Minerva* 24, no. 4 (1986): 433–55.

Australia

Anderson, D. S., and A. E. Vervoorn. *Access to Privilege: Patterns of Participation in Australian Post-Secondary Education*. Canberra: Australian National University Press, 1983.

Beswick, D. G., M. Hayden, and H. Schofield. *Evaluation of the Tertiary Education Assistance Scheme: An Investigation and Review of Policy on Student Financial Assistance in Australia*. Canberra: Australian Government Publishing Service, 1983.

Bourke, P. *Quality Measures in Universities*. Canberra: Commonwealth Tertiary Education Commission, 1986.

Davies, Susan. *The Martin Committee and the Binary Policy of Higher Education in Australia*. Surrey Hills, Australia: Ashwood House, 1989.

Dow, Hume, ed. *Memories of the University of Melbourne: Undergraduate Life in the Years Since 1917*. Melbourne, Australia: Hutchinson, 1983.

Gallagher, A. P. *Co-ordinating Australian University Development: A Study of the Australian Universities Commission, 1959–70*. St. Lucia, Australia: University of Queensland Press, 1982.

Grimshaw, Patricia, and Lynne Strahan, eds. *The Half Open Door: Sixteen Modern Australian Women Look at Professional Life and Achievement*. Sydney, Australia: Hale and Iremonger, 1982.

Harman, G. S., and V. L. Meek, eds. *Australian Higher Education Reconstructed? Analysis of the Proposals and Assumptions of the Dawkins Green Paper*. Armidale, Australia: Department of Administrative and Higher Education Studies, University of New England, 1988.

Harman, Grant, and Don Smart, eds. *Federal Intervention in Australian Education*. Melbourne, Australia: Georgian House, 1983.

Jones, David R., and John Anwyl, eds. *Privatizing Higher Education: A New Australian Issue*. Parkville, Australia: Centre for the Study of Higher Education, University of Melbourne, 1987.

Moses, Ingrid. *Academic Staff Evaluation and Development: A University Case Study*. St. Lucia, Australia: University of Queensland Press, 1988.

Partridge, P. H. *Society, Schools, and Progress in Australia*. Oxford: Pergamon Press, 1988.

Powles, M. *Women's Participation in Tertiary Education: A Review of Recent Research*. Canberra, Australia: Commonwealth Tertiary Education Commission, 1986.

Smith, Christopher Selby. *The Costs of Post-Secondary Education: An Australian Study*. Melbourne, Australia: Macmillan, 1975.

Toombs, William, and Grant Harman, eds. *Higher Education and Social Goals in Australia and New Zealand*. University Park: Australian and New Zealand Studies Center, Pennsylvania

State University, 1988.

West, Leo, et al. *The Impact of Higher Education on Mature Age Students.* Canberra, Australia: Commonwealth Tertiary Education Commission, 1986.

Williams, Bruce. *Systems of Higher Education: Australia.* New York: International Council of Educational Development, 1978.

Europe
Western Europe

Altbach, Philip G., and David H. Kelly. *Higher Education in International Perspective: A Survey and Bibliography.* London: Mansell, 1985.

Becher, Tony, ed. *British Higher Education.* London: Allen and Unwin, 1987.

————. *Academic Tribes and Territories: Intellectual Enquiry and the Cultures of Disciplines.* Milton Keynes, England: SPHE & Open University Press, 1989.

Becher, Tony, and Maurice Kogan. *Process and Structure in Higher Education.* London: Heinemann, 1980.

Boys, Chris J., et al. *Higher Education and the Preparation for Work.* London: Kingsley, 1988.

Cave, Martin, et al. *The Use of Performance Indicators in Higher Education.* London: Kingsley, 1988.

Cerych, Ladislav, and Paul Sabatier. *Great Expectations and Mixed Performance: The Implementation of Higher Education Reforms in Europe.* Stoke-on-Trent, England: Trentham, 1986.

Clark, Burton R., ed. *The School and the University: An International Perspective.* Berkeley and Los Angeles: University of California Press, 1985.

De Moor, R. A., ed. *Changing Tertiary Education in Modern European Society.* Strasbourg, France: Council of Europe, 1978.

Friedberg, Erhard, and Christine Musselin. *En quete d'universites: Etude comparee des universitees en France et en RFA.* Paris: l'Harmattan, 1989.

Fulton, Oliver, Alan Gordon, and Gareth Williams. *Higher Education and Manpower Planning.* Geneva: International Labour Office, 1982.

Goedegebuure, L. C. J., and V. L. Meek, eds. *Changes in Higher Education: The Non-University Sector.* Culemborg, Netherlands: Lemma, 1988.

Kogan, Maurice, ed. *Evaluating Higher Education.* London: Kingsley, 1988.

Nicolae, Valentin, Rene H. M. Smulders, and Mihai Korka, eds. *Statistics on Higher Education.* Bucharest, Romania: CEPES, 1989.

OECD. *Policies for Higher Education in the 1980s.* Paris: OECD, 1987.

————. *Universities Under Scrutiny.* Paris: OECD, 1987.

Teichler, Ulrich. *Changing Patterns of the Higher Education System.* London: Kingsley, 1988.

————. *Convergence or Growing Variety: The Changing Organization of Studies.* Strasbourg, France: Council of Europe, 1988.

————. *Europaische Hochschulsysteme.* Frankfurt am Main, West Germany: Campus, 1990.

Van de Graff, John H., et al. *Academic Power: Patterns of Authority in Seven National Systems.* New York: Praeger, 1978.

Van Vught, Frans A., ed. *Governmental Strategies and Innovation in Higher Education.* London: Kingsley, 1989.

Wittrock, Bjorn, and Aant Elzinga, eds. *The University Research System.* Stockholm: Almquist & Wiksell International, 1985.

Wolter, Werner, et al. *Planning in Higher Education.* Bucharest, Romania: CEPES, 1986.

Czechoslovakia

Juva, Vladimir. *Vysoka skola a vychova* (University and education process). Brno: Univerzita J. E. Purkyne, 1981.

Kopp, Botho von. *Hochschulen in der CSSR* (Higher education institutions in the CSSR). Weinheim-Basel: Beltz Verlag, 1981.

Koucky, Jan, et al. *Prognozy vysokych skol* (Prognosis of higher education institutions). Prague: Ustav rozvoje vysokych skol CSR, 1988.

Mokosin, Vladislav, et al. *Koncepce rozvoje vysokeho skolstvi v CSSR v devacesatych letech* (The policy of the development of Czechoslovak higher education in the 1990s). Prague: Ustav rozvoje vysokych skol CSR, 1988.

France

Aron, R. *La revolution introuvable.* Paris: Fayard, 1968.

Bienayme, A. *L'enseignement superieur et l'idee d'universite.* Paris: Economica, 1986.

Bienayme, A., F. Bourricaud, et al. *Systems of Higher Education: France.* New York: ICED, 1978.

Bourdieu, P. *La noblesse d'etat: Grandes ecoles et esprit de corps.* Paris: Editions de Minuit, 1989.

Bourricaud, F. *La reforme universitaire et ses deboires.* Amsterdam: European Cultural Foundations, 1977.

Campus, P. *Reconstruire l'universite.* Paris: Albatros, 1986.

Carpentier, A. *Le mal universitaire: Diagnostic et traitement.* Paris: R. Lafont, 1988.

Cerych, L., and P. Sabatier. *Great Expectations and Mixed Performances.* Stoke-on-Trent, England: Trentham Books, 1986.

De Romilly, J. *L'enseignement en detresse.* Paris: Fayard, 1984.

Faure, E. *Philosophie d'une reforme.* Paris: Plon, 1969.

Gusdorf, G. *L'Universite en question.* Paris: Payot, 1964.

Lesourne, J. *Education et societe: Les defis de l'an 2000.* Paris: La Decouverte, 1988.

Milner, J. C. *De l'ecole.* Paris: Le Seuil, 1984.

Schwartz, L. *Sauver l'Universite.* Paris: Seuil, 1983.

Vuillemin, J. *Rebatir l'Universite.* Paris: Fayard, 1983.

German Democratic Republic

Akademie der Padagogischen Wissenschaften der DDR. *Das Bildungswesen der Deutschen Demokratischen Republik.* 2d ed. Berlin (East): Volk und Wissen Volkseigener Verlag, 1983.

Baylis, Thomas A. *The Technical Intelligentsia and the East German Elite.* Berkeley and Los Angeles: University of California Press, 1974.

Childs, David, Thomas A. Baylis, and Erwin L. Collier, eds. *East Germany: Politics and Society.* Beckenham, England: Croom Helm, 1988.

Federal Ministry for Intra-German Affairs. "Universitaten und Hochschulen." In *DDR Handbuch*, 3d ed., 1382–94. Cologne, West Germany: Verlag Wissenschaft und Politik, 1985.

Giles, Geoffrey J. "The Structure of Higher Education in the German Democratic Republic." *Higher Education* 7 (May 1978): 131–56.

Honecker, Margot. *Zur Bildungspolitik und Padagogik in der Deutschen Demokratischen Republik.* Berlin (East): Volk und Wissen Volkseigener Verlag, 1986.

Husner, Gabriele. *Studenten und Studium in der DDR.* Cologne, West Germany: Verlag Wissenschaft und Politik, 1985.

Irmer, H., and B. Wilms. "New Forms of Cooperation for Research in the German Democratic Republic between Higher Education and Industry." *Higher Education in Europe* 9 (October–December 1984): 35–40.

Korn, K., G. Feierabend, G. Hersing, et al. *Education, Employment, and Development in the German Democratic Republic.* Paris: UNESCO International Institute for Educational Planning, 1984.

Page, John. "Education Under the Honeckers." In *Honecker's Germany*, edited by David Childs, 50–65. London: Allen and Unwin, 1985.

Panorama DDR. *Education in the GDR: Objectives, Contents, and Results.* Dresden, East Germany: Verlag Zeit im Bild, 1987.

Richter, Hans-Joachim. "Present Trends in Research in Higher Education in the German Democratic Republic." *Higher Education in Europe* 12 (January–March 1987): 95–100.

Sontheimer, Kurt, and Wilhelm Bleek. "The Educational System." In *The Government and Politics of East Germany*, 126–42. London: Hutchinson, 1975.

Waterkamp, Dieter. *Hanbuch zum Bildungswesen der DDR.* Berlin (West): Verlag Arno Spitz, 1987.

German Federal Republic

Cerych, Ladislav, and Paul Sabatier, *Great Expectations and Mixed Performance. The Implementation of Higher Education Reform in Europe.* Trentham, Stoke-on-Trent, England: Trentham Books, 1986.

Conze, Werner, and Jurgen Kocka, eds. *Bildungsburgertum im 19. Jahrhundert. Teil I: Bildungssystem und Professionalisierung in internationalen Vergleichen.* Stuttgart, West Germany: Klett-Cotta, 1985.

Fallon, Daniel. *The German University: A Heroic Ideal in Conflict with the Modern World.* Boulder, Colo.: Colorado Associated University Press, 1980.

Gellert, Claudius. "Politics and Higher Education in the Federal Republic of Germany." *European Journal of Education* 19 (1984): 217–32.

Goldschmidt, Dietrich. "Transatlantic Influences: History of Mutual Interactions between American and German Education." *Between Elite and Mass Education: Education in the Federal Republic of Germany.* Albany, N.Y.: SUNY Press, 1983.

Goldschmidt, Dietrich, Ulrich Teichler, and Wolff-Dietrich Webler, eds. *Forschungsgegenstand Hochschule. Uberblick und Trendbericht.* Frankfurt am Main: Campus, 1984.

Huber, Ludwig, and Eckart Liebau. "Die Kulturen der Facher." *Neue Sammlung* 25 (1985): 314–39.

Jarausch, Konrad H. *Students, Society, and Politics in Imperial Germany: The Rise of Academic Illiberalism.* Princeton: Princeton University Press, 1982.

Over, Albert. *Die deutschsprachige Forschung uber Hochschulen in der Bundesrepublik Deutschland, Eine kommentierte Bibliographie 1965-1985.* Munich, West Germany: K. G. Saur, 1988.

Peisert, Hansgert, Tino Bargel, and Gerhild Framhein. *Studiensituation und studentische Orientierungen an Universitaten und Fachhochschulen.* Bad Honnef: Boch, 1988.

Ringer, Fritz K. *The Decline of the German Mandarins. The German Academic Community 1890–1933.* Cambridge: Harvard University Press, 1969.

Rudolph, Hedwig, and Rudolf Husemann. *Hochschulpolitik zwischen Expansion und Restriktion. Ein Verglecih der Entwicklungen in der Bundesrepublik Deutschland und der Eutschen Demokratischen Republik.* Frankfurt am Main, West Germany: Campus, 1984.

Schelsky, Helmut. *Einsamkeit und Freiheit. Idee und Gestalt der deutschen Universitat und ihrer Reformen.* Hamburg, West Germany: Rowohlt, 1963.

Teichler, Ulrich. *Higher Education in the Federal Republic of Germany.* New York: Center for European Studies, Graduate School and University Center of the City University of New York, 1986.

Von Friedeburg, Ludwig. *Bildungsreform in deutschland. Geschichte und gesellschafflicher Widerspruch.* Frankfurt, West Germany: Suhrkamp, 1989.

Hungary

Halasz, Gabor. "A New Educational Act." *New Hungarian Quarterly* 28 (Summer 1987).

Klement, Tamas. *Higher Education in Hungary.* Budapest: Tankonyvkiado, 1973.

Kozma, Tamas. "Teacher Education in Hungary: System, Process, and Perspectives." *European Journal of Teacher Education* 7, no. 3 (1984): 225–66.

Ladanyi, Andor, ed. *A felsooktatas tavlati fejlesztesenek kerdesei* (The questions of the development of higher education). Budapest: Oktataskutato Intezet (Hungarian Institute for Educational Research), 1985.

———. *Felsooktatasi politika 1949–1958* (Higher education policy 1949–1958). Budapest: Kossuth, 1986.

Palovecz, Janos, ed. *A magyar felsooktatas helyzete* (The state of Hungarian higher education). Budapest: Oktataskutato Intezet (Hungarian Institute for Educational Research), 1983.

———. "Current Problems of Higher Education Following the Passage of the New Hungarian Education Law." *Higher Education in Europe* 12, no. 3 (1987).

Pokol, Bela. *Az egyetemi-tudomanyos szfera* (The academic sphere). Budapest: Kutatasok a felsooktatas korebol, No. 3, 1988.

Polinszky, Karoly, and Eva Szechy, eds. *Higher Education in Hungary.* Budapest: UNESCO-CEPES, 1985.

Voros, Laszlo. *Vitairat a felsooktatasrol* (Treatise on higher education). Budapest: Oktataskutato Intezet (Hungarian Institute for Educational Research), 1988.

Italy

Barbagli, Marzio. *Educating for Unemployment: Politics, Labor Markets, and the School System—Italy, 1959–1973.* New York: Columbia University Press, 1982.

Bruno, Sergio, Ute Lindner, and Marina Capparucci. *Universita e istruzione superiore come risorse strategiche.* Milan: Angeli, 1989.

Clark, Burton R. *Academic Power in Italy: Bureaucracy and Oligarchy in a National University System.* Chicago: Chicago University Press, 1977.

Giglioli, Pier Paolo. *Baroni e burocrati: Il ceto accademico italiano.* Bologna: Il Mulino, 1979.

Luzzatto, Giunio. "The Debate on the University and the Reforms Proposals in Italy." *European Journal of Education* 23 (June 1988): 216–56.

Manghi, Sergio. *Il barone e l'apprendista: Ricerche sulla condizione accademica nell'universita di massa.* Milan: Angeli, 1987.

Merritt, Robert L., and Robert L. Leonardi. "The Politics of Upper Secondary School Reform in Italy: Immobilism or Accommodation?" *Comparative Education Review* 25 (July 1981): 369–83.

Moscati, Roberto. "Higher Education in Southern Europe: Different Speeds or Different Paths Toward Modernization?" *European Journal of Education* 23 (June 1988): 189–94.

———, ed. *I cicli brevi nell'istruzione superiore.* Milan: Angeli, 1986.

———, ed. *La sociologia dell'educazione in Italia.* Bologna: Zanichelli, 1989.

———. "Reflections on Higher Education and the Polity in Italy." *European Journal of Education* 20 (June 1985): 127–39.

———. *Universita: Fine o transformazione del mito?* Bologna: Il Mulino, 1983.

The Netherlands

Acherman, H. A. "Termination of Degree and Research Programmes: An Exercise in University Cooperation." *International Journal of Institutional Management in Higher Education* 8, no. 1 (1984): 67–69.

Bormans, M. J., R. Brouwer, R. J. In't Veld, and F. Mertens. "The Role of Performance Indicators in Improving the Dialogue between Government and Universities." *International Journal of Institutional Management in Higher Education* 11, no. 2 (1987): 181–95.

Brons, R. "Changing the National Funding System for Higher Education in the Netherlands: A Challenge for Institutional Management." In *Changing Financial Relations between Government and Higher Education,* edited by J. A. Acherman and R. Brons. Culemborg, Netherlands: Lemma, 1989.

Daalder, H. "The Netherlands: Universities between the 'New Democracy' and the 'New Management'." In *Universities, Politicians, and Bureaucrats,* edited by H. Daalder and E. Shils. Cambridge: Cambridge University Press, 1982.

Gevers, J. K. "Co-operative Planning: Some First and Second Thoughts." *International Journal of Institutional Management in Higher Education* 7, no. 1 (1983): 63–71.

Goedegebuure, L. C. J., and H. J. Vos. "Blown on the Steel Breeze: Institutional Mergers in Dutch Higher Vocational Education." In *Change in Higher Education: The Non-University Sector,* edited by L. C. J. Goedegebuure and V. L. Meek. Culemborg, Netherlands: Lemma, 1988.

Ligthart, W. J. N., O. C. McDaneil, F. J. H. Mertens, H. de Groot, J. Ritzen, T. Steenkamp, P. B. Boorsma, J. B. J. Koelman, and M. J. C. M. de Kok. "Policies of Retrenchment in the Dutch University System." *International Journal of Institutional Management in Higher Education* 10, no. 1 (1986): 62–75.

Luttikhold, H. "Universities in the Netherlands: In Search of a New Understanding." *European Journal of Education* 21, no. 1 (1986): 57–66.

Maassen, P. A. M. "Quality Control in Dutch Higher Education: Internal Versus External Evaluation." *European Journal of Education* 22, no. 2 (1987): 161–71.

Maassen, P. A. M., and F. A. van Vught. "An Intriguing Janus-Head: The Two Faces of the New Governmental Strategy for Higher Education in the Netherlands." *European Journal of Education* 23, nos. 1 & 2 (1988): 65–76.

Ministry of Education and Science. *Dutch Higher Education and Research: Major Issues, Facts, and Figures.* The Hague: Soetermeer, 1988.

Rosenberg, H. "Recent Developments in 'Buffer' Agencies in Higher Education in the Netherlands." *International Journal of Institutional Management in Higher Education* 7, no. 2 (1983): 191–201.

Spee, A. J. J., and R. P. van Brouwershaven. "The Relationship between Government Planning and Financing and Institutional Management of Higher Vocational Education in the Netherlands." In *Change in Higher Education: The Non-University Sector,* edited by L. C. J. Goedegebuure and V. L. Meek. Culemborg, Netherlands: Lemma, 1988.

Van Vught, F. A. "Negative Incentive Steering in a Policy Network: The Case of the Policy Development Process Concerning the Retrenchment Operation in the Dutch University System in 1982 and 1983." *Higher Education* 14 (1985): 593–616.

———. "A New Autonomy in European Higher Education?" In *Self-Regulation, Self-Study, and Program Review in Higher Education,* edited by H. R. Kells and F. A. van Vught. Culemborg, Netherlands: Lemma, 1988.

———. *Governmental Strategies and Innovation in Higher Education.* London: Jessica Kingsley, 1989.

———. "A New Autonomy in European Higher Education?" *International Journal of Institutional Management in Higher Education* 12, no. 1 (1988): 16–26.

Poland

Adamski, Wladyslaw. *Educational Opportunities in Poland: State Policy v. Structural Determinants.* Paris: European Institute of Education and Social Policy, 1983.

Borzymowski, Jan. "Higher Education Network in Poland." *Zycie Szkoly Wyzszej* (English Edition 1986): 271–86.

Cerych, L., and P. Sabatier. "Reform in a Socialist Country: The Polish Preferential System." In *Great Expectations and Mixed Performance—The Implementation of Higher Education Reforms in Europe.* Paris: European Institute of Education and Social Policy/Trentham Books, 1986.

Glikman, Pawel. "Polskie szkolnictwo wyzsze wobec syzwan strukturalnych gospodarki." *Zycie Szkoly Wyzszej* 36 (November 1988): 145–58.

Gmytrasiewicz, Michal. "Economic Aspects of Training at Institutions of Higher Education in People's Poland." *Zycie Szkoly Wyzszej* (English edition 1986): 235–53.

Gorski, Janusz. "Open University in Poland—Assumptions and Prospects." *Zycie Szkoly Wyzszej* (English edition 1986): 211–22.

Jablonska-Skinder, Hanna. "Higher Education in Poland in Comparison with Other Countries of the World." *Zycie Szkoly Wyzszej* (English edition 1986): 255–70.

———. "Participation of Women in Polish Higher Education." *Higher Education in Europe* 9 (July 1982): 13–18.

Jozefowicz, A., J. Kluczynski, and T. Obrebski. "Manpower and Education Planning and Policy Experience in Poland 1960–1980." In *Forecasting Skilled Manpower Needs: The Experience of Eleven Countries*, edited by R. V. Youdi and K. Hinchliffe. Paris: UNESCO-IIEP, 1985.

Jozefowicz, Adam, and Jan Kluczynski. *Determinants and Options in the Development of Higher Education in Poland.* Paris: UNESCO, 1980.

Kluczynski, Jan. *Higher Education in Poland.* Bucharest, Romania: UNESCO-CEPES, 1987.

———, ed. *Perspektywy ksztalcenia w szkolnictwie syzszym.* Warsaw: PWN, 1985.

———. "Polish Higher Education Quantitative Growth and Policy Dilemmas." CRE-*Action* 1 (January 1988): 362–82.

Mucha, Janusz. "University Legislation and the Decline of Academic Autonomy in Poland." *Minerva* 23 (Autumn 1985): 362–82.

Pastwa, Marta. *Ksztaltowanie struktury organizacyjnej szkoly wyzszej.* Warsaw: PWN, 1987.

Struzek, Marian. "Perspektywy rozwoju wyzszego szkolnictwa ekonomicznego do roku 2000." *Zycie Szkoly Wyzszej* 36 (November 1988): 105–25.

Szczepanski, Jan. "Institutions of Higher Education and Economic and Social Crisis." *Zycie Szkoly Wyzszej* (English edition 1986): 65–76.

Romania

Bala, Constantin. "University Industry Relations: Romanian Case Study." *Higher Education in Europe* 8 (October 1983): 17–25.

Belis, Mariana. "Rumanian Women in Technology." *European Journal of Engineering Education* 5 (January 1980): 32–37.

Burloiu, Petre. *Planification de l'education en Roumanie.* Paris: UNESCO-IIEP, 1975.

———. "Methodology of Educational Planning." *Higher Education in Europe* 5 (January 1980): 32–37.

Dimitriu, Emilian, et al. *A Concise History of Education in Romania.* Bucharest, Romania: Academy of Social Sciences/Editura stiintifica si enciclopedica, 1981.

Ghimpu, Sanda. "Characteristic Traits of the Status of Higher Education Personnel in the Socialist Republic of Romania." *Higher Education in Europe* 10 (April 1985): 28–36.

Ionescu, Bucur. "Aspects of Scientific Research on Higher Education in the Socialist Republic of Romania." *Higher Education in Europe* 8 (January 1983): 23–26.

Pestisanu, C., D. F. Lazaroiu, and P. Burloiu. *L'Enseignement superieur et la main-d'oeuvre dans la Republic Socialist de Roumanie.* Geneva/Bucharest: ILO/UNESCO-CEPES, 1977.

"Romania—Universities and Technical Universities." In *International Handbook of Universities*, 10th ed., edited by D. J. Aitken. Paris: International Association of Universities, 1986.

Stefanescu, Stefan. "Romania." In *Historical Compendium of European Universities*, edited by L. Jilek. Geneva: Standing Conference of Rectors, Presidents, and Vice-Chancellors of the European Universities, 1984.

Soviet Union

Ailes, Catherine P., and Francis W. Rushing. *The Science Race: Training and Utilization of Scientists and Engineers, US and USSR*. New York: Crane Russak, 1982.

Avakov, R., B. C. Sanyal, M. Buttgereit, and U. Teichler, eds. *Higher Education and Employment in the USSR and in the Federal Republic of Germany*. Paris: UNESCO, International Institute for Educational Planning, 1984.

Avis, George. "Access to Higher Education in the Soviet Union." In *Soviet Education in the 1980s*, edited by J. J. Tomiak, 199–239. London: Croom Helm, 1983.

———. "Soviet Students: Lifestyle and Attitudes." In *Soviet Education Under Scrutiny*, edited by John Dunstan, 88–120. Glasgow, Scotland: Jordanhill College Publications, 1987.

———, ed. *Soviet Higher and Vocational Education: From Khrushchev to Gorbachev*. Bradford Occasional Papers No. 8, Special Issue on Soviet Education. Bradford, England: Modern Languages Centre, University of Bradford, 1987.

Buttgereit, Michael, and Ulrich Teichler, eds. *Probleme der Hochschulplanung in der Sowjetunion*. Kassel, West Germany: Wissenschaftliches Zentrum fur Berufs- und Hochschulforschung an der Gesamthochschule Kassel, 1984.

Chuprunov, D., R. Avakov, and E. Jiltsov. *Enseignement superieur, emploi et progres technique en URSS*. Paris: UNESCO, Institut International de planification de l'education, 1982.

Dobson, Richard, ed. "The Restructuring of Soviet Higher and Secondary Specialized Education: Phase I." *Soviet Education* 29 (Nos. 9–10).

Dobson, Richard B. "Social Status and Inequality of Access to Higher Education in the USSR." In *Power and Ideology in Education*, edited by Jerome Karabel and A. H. Halsey, 254–74. New York: Oxford University Press, 1977.

Glowka, Detlef. "Problems of Access to Higher Education in the USSR." In *Western Perspectives on Soviet Education in the 1980s*, edited by J. J. Tomiak, 123–37. London: Macmillan, 1986.

Gruson, Pascale, and Janina Markiewicz-Lagneau. *L'enseignement superieur et son efficacite: France, Etats-Unis, URSS, Pologne*. Paris: La Documentation française, 1983.

Karklins, Rasma. "Ethnic Politics and Access to Higher Education: The Soviet Case." *Comparative Politics* 16 (April 1984): 277–94.

Kerr, Stephen T. "The Soviet Reform of Higher Education." *Review of Higher Education* 11, no. 3 (1988): 215–46.

Matthews, Mervyn. *Education in the Soviet Union: Policies and Institutions Since Stalin*. London: Allen and Unwin, 1982.

Mitter, Wolfgang, and Leonid Novikov. "Tendenzen der Hochschulpolitik in der Sowjetunion." In *Bildungssysteme in Osteuropa: Reform oder Krise?*, edited by Oskar Anweiler and Friedrich Kuebart, 261–76. Berlin, West Germany: Berlin Verlag, 1984.

Novikov, Leonid. *Hochschulen in der Sowjetunion: Studien und Dokumentationen zur vergleichenden Bildungsforschung*. Cologne, West Germany: Bohlau Verlag, 1981.

Yelyutin, V. P. "Higher Education in a Country of Developed Socialism." *Soviet Education* 26 (nos. 9–10); (nos. 1–2); (nos. 8–12) (1984–85).

Spain

Alvarez de Morales, A. *Genesis de la Universidad espanola contemporanea.* Madrid: Instituto de Estudios Administrativos, 1972.

Consejo de Universidades. *Anuario de estadistica universitaria 1988.* Madrid: Ministerio de Educacion y Ciencia, 1989.

————. *Guia de la Universidad.* Madrid: Ministerio de Educacion y Ciencia, 1988.

————. *Legislacion universitaria 1: Normative general y autonomica.* 2d. ed. Madrid: Tecnos, 1986.

————. *La reforma de las ensenazas universitarias.* Madrid: Ministerio de Educacion y Ciencia, 1987.

Garcia Garrido, J. L. "Universidades durante el franquismo." In *Historia de la Educacion en Espana y America.* Madrid: Fundacion Santamaria, 1990.

International Council for Educational Development. "La reforma universitaria espanola: Evaluacion e informe." In *La educacion postsecundaira.* Madrid: Santillana, 1988.

Jimenez Frau, A. *Historia de la Universidad espanola.* Madrid: Alianza, 1971.

Lain Entralgo, P. *El problema de la Universidad.* Madrid: Edicusa, 1968.

Martin Mareno, J., and A. de Miguel. *Universidad, fabrica de parados.* Barcelona: Vicens Vives, 1979.

McNair, J. M. *Education for a Changing Spain.* Manchester, England: Manchester University Press, 1983.

Ortega y Gasset, J. *Mision de la Universidad.* Madrid: Revista de Occidente, 1960.

Vilar, S. *La Universidad, entre el fraude y la irractionalidad.* Barcelona: Plaza y Janes, 1987.

Sweden

Lane, Jan-Erik. *Institutional Reform.* Aldershot, England: Dartmouth, 1989.

Lindensjo, Bo. *Hogskolereformen.* Stockholm: Stockholm University Press, 1981.

Premfors, Rune. *Svensk forskningspolitik.* Lund, Sweden: Studentlitteratur, 1986.

Premfors, Rune, and Bertil Ostergren. *Sweden: Systems of Higher Education.* New York: International Council for Educational Development, 1978.

Statskontoret. *Hogskolans administration.* Stockholm: Statskontoret, 1986.

Teichler, Ulrich. *Changing Patterns of the Higher Education System.* London: Jessica Kingsley, 1988.

United Kingdom

Barnett, R. A. "The Maintenance of Quality in the Public Sector of UK Higher Education." *Higher Education* 16 (1987): 279–301.

Berdahl, R. O., and M. L. Shattock. "The British University Grants Committee, 1919–83: Changing Relationships with Government and the Universities." *Higher Education* 12 (1983): 331–47.

Cantor, L. M., and I. F. Roberts. *Further Education Today: A Critical Review.* 3d ed. London: Routledge and Kegan Paul, 1986.

Carswell, John. *Government and the Universities in Britain: Programme and Performance, 1960–1980.* Cambridge: Cambridge University Press, 1985.

Eggins, Heather, ed. *Restructuring Higher Education.* Milton Keynes, England: SRHE and Open University Press, 1988.

Eustace, Rowland. "The Criteria of Staff Selection: Do They Exist?" *Studies in Higher Education* 13, no. 1 (1988): 69–88.

Fulton, Oliver, ed. *Access to Higher Education.* Guildford, England: SRHE, 1981.

Halsey, A. H., and Martin Trow. *The British Academics.* London: Faber, 1971.

Jones, David R. *The Origins of Civic Universities: Manchester, Leeds, and Liverpool.* London: Routledge, 1988.

Moodie, Graeme C. "Le Roi est Mort; Vive le quoi? Croham and the Death of the UGC," *Higher Education Quarterly* 41, no. 4 (1987): 329–43.

Moodie, Graeme C., ed. *Standards and Criteria in Higher Education.* Guildford, England: SRHE and NFER/Nelson, 1986.

Moodie, Graeme C., and Rowland Eustace. *Power and Authority in British Universities.* London: Allen and Unwin, 1974.

Rudd, E. "The Educational Qualifications and Social Class of Parents of Undergraduates Entering British Universities in 1984." *Journal of the Royal Statistical Society, Series A* 150, no. 4 (1987): 346–72.

Scott, Peter. *The Crisis of the University.* London: Croom Helm, 1984.

Sharp, Paul R. *The Creation of the Local Authority Sector of Higher Education.* Lewes, England: Falmer Press, 1987.

Shinn, Christine Helen. *Paying the Piper: The Development of the University Grants Committee 1919–1946.* Lewes, England: Falmer Press, 1986.

Trow, Martin. "Academic Standards and Mass Higher Education." *Higher Education Quarterly* 41, no. 3 (1987): 268–92.

———. "The Robbins Trap: British Attitudes and the Limits of Expansion." *Higher Education Quarterly* 43, no. 1 (1989): 55–75.

Williams, Gareth, and Tessa Blackstone. *Response to Adversity: Higher Education in a Harsh Climate.* Guildford, England: SRHE, 1983.

Latin America

Argentina

Ferrer, Aldo. *La Economia Argentina.* Buenos Aires: Fondo de Cultura Economica, 1963.

Gillespie, Richard. *Montoneros. Soldados de Peron.* Buenos Aires: Grijalbo, 1987.

Mignone, Emilio Fermin. "Argentina Republic." In *The International Encyclopedia of Higher Education,* edited by Asa S. Knowles, 465–72. San Francisco: Jossey-Bass, 1977.

Perez Lindo, Augusto. *Universidad, Politica y Sociedad.* Buenos Aires: EUDEBA, 1985.

Puryear, Jeffrey M. *Higher Education, Development Assistance, and Repressive Regimes.* New York: Ford Foundation, 1983.

Tedesco, Juan Carlos. *Educacion y Sociedad en la Argentina* (1880–1900). Buenos Aires: Pannedille, 1982.

Brazil

Azevedo, Fernando de. *Brazilian Culture.* New York: Macmillan, 1950.

Canuto, Vera Regina Albuquerque. *Politicos e educadores: A organizacao de ensino superior no Brasil.* Petropolis, Brazil: 1987.

Castro, Claudio de Moura. "The Impact of European and American Influences on Brazilian Higher Education." *European Journal of Education* 18, no. 2 (1983): 367–81.

Coelho, Eduardo Campos. A *Sinecura academica: A etica universitaria em questao.* São Paulo, Brazil: Vertice, Ed. Revista de Tribunais, 1988.

Cunha, Luis Antonio. A *Universidade critica.* Rio de Janeiro: Francisco Alves, 1983.

———. A *Universidade reformanda.* Rio de Janeiro: Francisco Alves, 1988.

———. A *Universidade tempora.* Rio de Janeiro: Civilizacao Brasileira, 1980.

Fagundes, Jose. *Universidade e compromisso social: Extensao, limites e perspectivas.* Campinas, Brazil: UNICAMP, 1986.

Fernandes, Florestan. *Universidade brasileira: Reforma ou revolucao?* São Paulo, Brazil: Alfa-Omega, 1975.

Graciani, Maria Stela Santos. O *Ensino superior no Brasil: A estrutura de poder na universidade em questao.* Petropolis, Brazil: Vozes, 1982.

Haar, Jerry. *The Politics of Higher Education in Brazil.* New York: Praeger, 1977.

Haussman, Fay, and Jerry Haar. *Education in Brazil.* Hamden, Conn.: Archon, 1978.

Levy, Daniel. *Higher Education and the State in Latin America: Private Challenges to Public Dominance.* Chicago: University of Chicago Press, 1986.

Mendes, Candido, and Claudio de Moura Castro, eds. *Qualidade, expansao e financiamento de ension superior privado.* Brasilia, Brazil: Educam ABM, 1984.

Schwartzman, Simon. *Formacao da comunidade cientifica no Brasil.* Rio de Janeiro: FINEP, 1979.

Schwartzman, Simon, and Claudio de Moura Castro. *Pesquisa universitaria em questao.* Campinas, Brazil: Editora de UNICAMP; São Paulo, Brazil: Icone, 1986.

Chile

Apablaza, Viterbo, and Hugo Lavados, eds. *La educacion superior privada en Chile.* Santiago, Chile: Corporacion de Promocion Universitario, 1988.

Briones, G., et al., eds. *Desigualdad educative en Chile.* Santiago, Chile: Programa Interdisciplinario de Investigaciones en Educacion, 1985.

———. *Las universidades Chilenas en el modelo de economia neo-liberal.* Santiago, Chile: Programa Interdisciplinario de Investigaciones en Educacion, 1981.

Brunner, Jose Juaquin. *Informe sobre la educacion superior en Chile.* Santiago, Chile: FLACSO, 1981.

Farrell, Joseph P. *The National Unified School in Allende's Chile: The Role of Education in the Destruction of a Revolution.* Vancouver, British Columbia: University of British Columbia Press, 1986.

Fischer, Kathleen. "Political Ideology and Educational Reform in Chile." Ph.D. diss., University of Southern California, 1977.

Grossi, Maria Clara, and Ernesto Schiefelbein. *Bibliografia de la educacion Chilena 1973/1980.* Santiago, Chile: Corporation de Promocion Universitaria, 1980.

Lavado, Hugo, et al., eds. *Educacion Chilena.* Santiago, Chile: Corporacion de Promocion Universitario, 1986.

Nunez, Ivan. *Evolucion de la politica educacional del regimen militar.* Santiago, Chile: Programa Interdisciplinario de Investigaciones en Educacion, 1982.

Schiefelbein, Ernesto. *Antecedentes para el analisis de la politica educacional Chilena en 1982.* Santiago, Chile: Corporacion de Promocion Universitaria, 1982.

Schiefelbein, Ernesto, and Joseph P. Farrell. *Eight Years of Their Lives: Through Schooling to the Labour Market in Chile.* Ottawa, Canada: IDRC, 1982.

Colombia

Berry, Albert, et al., eds. *Politics of Compromise.* New Brunswick, New Jersey: Transaction, 1980.

Briceno, Rosa Cecilia. "University Reform, Social Conflict, and the Intellectuals: The Case of the National University of Colombia." Ph.D. diss., Stanford University, 1988.

Franco, Augusto, and Carlos Tunnermann. *La Educacion Superior en Colombia.* Bogota, Colombia: Tercer Mundo, 1978.

Garcia, Antonio. *La Crisis de la Universidad.* Bogota, Colombia: Plaza & Janes, 1985.

Instituto Colombiano para el Fomento de la Educacion Superior. *Diagnostico de la Educacion Superior 1973–1983: Analisis Cuantitativo de Variables.* 2d ed. Bogota, Colombia: ICFES, 1985.

Leal Buitrago, Francisco. "La Frustracion Politica de una Generacion. La Universidad Colombiana y la Formacion de un Movimiento Estudiantil 1958–1967." *Desarrollo y Sociedad* 6 (1981): 299–325.

Lebot, Yvon. "El Movimiento Estudiantil durante el Frente Nacional." *Ideologia y Sociedad* 19 (October–December 1976): 49–70.

———. *Educacion e Ideologia en Colombia.* Bogota, Colombia: La Carreta, 1979.

Levy, Daniel. *Higher Education and the State in Latin America.* Chicago: University of Chicago Press, 1986.

Maier, Joseph, and Richard Weatherhead. *The Latin American University.* Albuquerque: University of New Mexico Press, 1979.

Molina, Gerardo, et al. *Universidad Oficial o Universidad Privada?* Bogota, Colombia: Tercer Mundo, 1978.

Parada Caicedo, Jorge Humberto. *Bibliografía Comentada sobre Educacion Superior en Colombia 1970–1979.* Serie Bibliografica, Vol. 6, no. 1. Bogota, Colombia: ICFES, 1981.

Parra Sandoval, Rodrigo. *La Educacion Superior en Colombia.* Caracas, Venezuela: CRESALC-UNESCO, 1985.

Parra Sandoval, Rodrigo, and Maria Elvira Carvajal. "La Universidad Colombiana: De la Filosofia a la Tecnocracia Estratificada," *Revista Colombiana de Educacion* 4, no. 2 (1979): 131–41.

Pelczar, Richard. "The University Professor in Colombia." Ph.D. diss., University of Chicago, 1971.

Pelczar, Richard. "University Reform in Latin America: The Case of Colombia." *Comparative Education Review* 16 (June 1972): 230–50.

Rama, German. *El Sistema Universitario en Colombia*. Bogota, Colombia: Universidad Nacional de Colombia, 1970.

Torres-Leon, Fernan. *Trayectoria Historica de la Universidad Colombiana*. Bogota, Colombia: ICOLPE, 1975.

Cuba

Carnoy, Martin, and J. Werthein. *Cuba: Cambio Economica y Reforma Educativa*. Mexico, D.F.: Nueva Imagen, 1980.

Galvez, Luis Felipe. *La Universidad de La Habana: Sintesis historica*. Havana: Imprenta de la Universidad, 1960.

MacDonald, Theodore. *Making a New People: Education in Revolutionary Cuba*. Vancouver, British Columbia: New Star Books, 1985.

Maier, Joseph, and Richard W. Weatherhead, eds. *The Latin American University*. Albuquerque: University of New Mexico Press, 1979.

Marinello, Juan. "Universidad y Cultura." *Universidad de La Habana* 159 (January–February 1963): 122–46.

Ministerio de Educacion Superior. *La Educacion Superior en Cuba*. Havana: Ministerio de Educacion Superior, 1984.

Mujal-Leon, Eusebio. *The Cuban University Under the Revolution*. Washington, D.C.: Cuban American National Foundation, 1988.

Padula, Alfred, and Lois M. Smith. "The Revolutionary Transformation of Cuban Education, 1959–1987." In *Making the Future: Politics and Educational Reform in the United States, England, the Soviet Union, China, and Cuba*, edited by Edgar B. Gumbert. Atlanta: Georgia State University, 1988.

Paulston, Rolland G. *The Educational System of Cuba*. Washington, D.C.: U.S. Government Printing Office, 1975.

———. "Impacto de la reforma eductiva en Cuba." *Revista Latinoamericana de Estudios Educativos* 10, no. 1 (1980): 99–124.

———. "Educational Development in Latin America and the Caribbean." In *Handbook of Latin American Studies*, 51. Washington, D.C.: Library of Congress, 1990.

Suchlicki, Jaime. *University Students and Revolution in Cuba*. Coral Gables, Fla.: University of Miami Press, 1969.

Vecino Alegret, Fernando. *Algunas tendencias en el desarrollo de la educacion superior en Cuba*. Havana: Editorial Pueblo y Educacion, 1986.

Mexico

Arce, Francisco, et al. *Historia de las Professiones en Mexico*. Mexico City: El Colegio de Mexico, 1982.

Barquin, Manuel, and Carlos Ornelas, eds. *Superacion Academica y Reforma Universitaria.* Mexico City: UNAM, 1989.

Camp, Roderic A. *The Making of a Government: Political Leaders in Modern Mexico.* Tucson: University of Arizona Press, 1984.

Castrejon, Jaime, and Marizol Perez, eds. *Historia de las Universidades Estatales.* Mexico City: SEP, 1976.

Cleaves, Robert. *Professions and the State: The Mexican Case.* Tucson: University of Arizona Press, 1987.

King, Richard, et al. *The Provincial Universities of Mexico.* New York: Praeger, 1971.

Leon, Enrique G. *El Instituto Politecnico Nacional: Origen y Evolucion Historica.* Mexico City: SEP, 1975.

Levy, Daniel C. *University and Government in Mexico: Autonomy in an Authoritarian System.* New York: Praeger, 1980.

———. *Higher Education and the State in Latin America: Private Challenges to Public Dominance.* Chicago: University of Chicago Press, 1986.

Lomnitz, Larissa. "Conflict and Mediation in a Latin American University." *Journal of Interamerican Studies and World Affairs* 19, no. 3 (1977): 321–29.

Mabry, Donald J. *The Mexican University and the State: Student Conflicts, 1910–1971.* College Station: Texas A&M University Press, 1982.

Mohar, Oscar B., ed. *Crisis y Contradicciones de la Educacion Tecnica en Mexico.* Mexico City: Gaceta, 1984.

Orozco, Jose de Jesus. *Regimen de las Relaciones Colectivas de Trabajo en las Universidades Publicas Mexicanas.* Mexico City: UNAM, 1984.

Osborn, Thomas Noel. *Higher Education in Mexico.* El Paso, Tex.: Western Press, 1976.

Rangel, Alfonso. *Systems of Higher Education: Mexico.* New York: International Council for International Development, 1978.

Teran, Liberato. *Nueva Universidad.* Culiacan, Sin., Mexico: Universidad Autonoma de Sinaloa, 1984.

Villasenor, Guillermo. *Estado y Universidad: 1976–1982.* Mexico City: Universidad Autonoma Metropolitana-Xochimilco and Centro de Estudios Educativos, 1988.

Venezuela

Albornoz, Orlando. "Higher Education and the Politics of Development in Venezuela." *Journal of Interamerican Studies and World Affairs* (August 1977): 291–314.

———. *La Educacion Superior en Venezuela.* Caracas, Venezuela: Fundarte, 1977.

———. *Teoria y Praxis de la Educacion Superior Venezolana.* Caracas, Venezuela: Universidad Central de Venezuela, 1979.

Arnove, Robert F. *Student Alienation: A Venezuelan Study.* New York: Praeger, 1971.

Bracho Sierra, Jose. *El Problema del Financiamiento de la Educacion Universitaria.* Caracas, Venezuela: Universidad Central de Venezuela, 1980.

La Educacion Superior. Caracas, Venezuela: Congreso Nacional de Educacion, 1989.

La Educacion Superior en Venezuela. Caracas, Venezuela: Consejo Nacional de Universidades, 1985.

Leal, Ildefonso. *Historia de la Universidad Central de Venezuela*. Caracas, Venezuela: Universidad Central de Venezuela, 1981.

Marta Sosa, Joaquin. *El Estado y la Educacion Superior en Venezuela*. Caracas, Venezuela: Universidad Simon Bolivar, 1984.

Mayz Vallenilla, Ernesto. *El Ocaso de las Universidades*. Caracas, Venezuela: Monte Avila Editores, 1984.

Middle East
The Arab World

Al-Ebraheem, H. A., and R. P. Stevens. "Organization, Management, and Academic Problems in the Arab University: The Kuwait University Experience." *Higher Education* 9 (1980): 203–18.

Al-Misnad, Sheikha. *The Development of Modern Education in the Gulf*. London: Ithaca Press, 1985.

Beck, Lois, and Nikki Keddie, eds. *Women in the Muslim World*. Cambridge: Harvard University Press, 1978.

Farah, Tawfic E., and Yasumasa Kuroda, eds. *Political Socialization in the Arab States*. Boulder, Colo.: Lynne Rienner Publishers, 1987.

Hussain, Freda, ed. *Muslim Women*. London: Croom Helm, 1984.

Ibrahim, Saad Eddin. *The New Arab Social Order: A Study of the Social Impact of Oil Wealth*. Boulder, Colo.: Westview Press, 1982.

Jones, H. T. "Allocation of Students in North African Universities." *Higher Education* 10 (1981): 315–34.

Massialas, Byron G., and Samir A. Jarrar. *Arab Education in Transition*. New York: Garland, 1990.

―――. *Education in the Arab World*. New York: Praeger, 1983.

―――. "Conflicts in Education in the Arab World: The Present Challenge." *Arab Studies Quarterly* 21 (1987): 34–52.

Nasr, J. A., and I. Lorfing, eds. *Women and Economic Development in the Arab World*. Beirut, Lebanon: Institute for Women's Studies in the Arab World, Beirut University College, 1988.

Qubain, Fahim. *Education and Science in the Arab World*. Baltimore: Johns Hopkins University Press, 1965.

Sharabi, Hisham. *Neopatriarchy: A Theory of Distorted Change in Arab Society*. New York: Oxford University Press, 1988.

Szyliowicz, Joseph S. *Education and Modernization in the Middle East*. Ithaca, N.Y.: Cornell University Press, 1973.

Zahlan, A. R., ed. *The Arab Brain Drain*. London: Ithaca Press, 1981.

Egypt

Hyde, Georgie. *Education in Modern Egypt*. New York: Praeger, 1983.

Kerr, Malcolm. "Egypt." In *Education and Political Development*, edited by James Coleman. Princeton: Princeton University Press, 1965.

Massialas, Byron G., and Samir A. Jarrar. *Education in the Arab World*. New York: Praeger, 1983.

———. "Egypt." In *World Education Encyclopedia*, edited by George Kurian, 352–72. New York: Facts on File, 1988.

———. *Arab Education in Transition*. New York: Garland, 1990.

Saleh, Saneya Abdel Wahab. *The Brain Drain in Egypt*. Cairo Papers in Social Sciences, Volume 2, Monograph 5. 2d ed. Cairo: AUC, 1983.

Sanyal, Bikas C., et al. *University Education and the Labor Market in the Arab Republic of Egypt*. Oxford: Pergamon Press, 1982.

Schmida, Leslie C., ed. *Education in the Middle East*. Washington, D.C.: AMIDEAST, 1983.

Szyliowicz, Joseph S. *Education and Modernization in the Middle East*. Ithaca, N.Y.: Cornell University Press, 1973.

Iraq

Al-Kanam, Muhamad, and Abdul Jalil Al-Zawbai. *Higher Education in Iraq*. Baghdad, Iraq: Al-Hakima Press, 1968.

Frey, James S. *Iraq*. World Education Series, American Association of Collegiate Registrars and Admissions Officers. Washington, D.C.: 1988.

Penrose, Edith, and E. F. Penrose. *Iraq: International Relations and National Development*. Boulder, Colo.: Westview Press, 1978.

Qubain, Fahim I. *Education and Science in the Arab World*. Baltimore: Johns Hopkins University Press, 1966.

Israel

Alpert, Carl. *Technion: The Story of Israel's Institute of Technology*. New York: American Technion Society, Israel Institute of Technology, 1982.

Ben-David, Joseph. "Research on Higher Education in Israel." *Higher Education in Europe* 8 (1983): 76–79.

———. "Universities in Israel: Dilemmas of Growth, Diversification, and Administration." *Studies in Higher Education* 11 (1986): 105–30.

Bendor, Shmuel. "University Education in the State of Israel." In *International Encyclopedia of Higher Education*, edited by Asa S. Knowles, 2331–41 San Francisco: Jossey-Bass, 1977.

Beytan, Max, Serge Cuenin, and Jean-Claude Elcher. *L'evolution de l'enseignement superieur en France et en Israel (1972–1983)*. Dijon, France: Institute de Recherche sur l'economie de l'education, Universite de Dijon, no date.

Council for Higher Education, Planning and Grants Committee. *The Higher Education System in Israel—Guidelines on the Development of the System and Its Planning for 1988 with a First Glance at 1995*. Jerusalem: Planning and Grants Committee, 1984.

Council for Higher Education, Planning and Grants Committee. *Higher Education in Israel* 1983/84; 1986/87. Jerusalem: Planning and Grants Committee, 1985; 1988.

Gamson, Zelda, and Tamar Horowitz. "Symbolism and Survival in Developing Organizations: Regional Colleges in Israel." *Higher Education* 12 (1983): 171–90.

Globerson, Arye. *Higher Education and Employment: A Case Study of Israel.* New York: Praeger, 1978.

Halperin, Samuel. *Any Home a Campus: Everyman's University of Israel.* Washington, D.C.: Institute of Educational Leadership, 1984.

Iram, Yaacov. "Higher Education in Transition: The Case of Israel—A Comparative Study." *Higher Education* 9 (1980): 81–95.

———. "Vision and Fulfillment: The Evolution of the Hebrew University, 1901–1950." *History of Higher Education Annual* 3 (1983): 123–43.

———. "Quality and Control in Higher Education in Israel." *European Journal of Education* 22 (1987): 145–59.

Schatzker, Chaim. "Tradition and Reform at the Universities in Israel." In *Tradition and Reform of the University Under an International Perspective—An Interdisciplinary Approach,* edited by Hermann Rohrs, 185–202. Frankfurt am Main, West Germany: Verlag Peter Lang, 1987.

Zadok, Meir. "The Israeli Planning and Grants Committee at the Crossroads: From Shock Absorber to Steering Wheel." *Higher Education* 13 (1984): 535–44.

Lebanon

Bashshur, Munir. *Buniat Al Nizam Al Tarbawi Fi Lubnan* (The structure of the Lebanese educational system). Beirut: Center for Educational Research and Development, 1978.

———. "Tarady Al-Nizam Altarbawi Fi Lubnan" (The demise of the Lebanese educational system)," *Al-Mustaqbal Al-Arabi* 11 (May 1988): 34–55.

Massialas, B. G., and Samir A. Jarrar, eds. *Education in the Arab World.* New York: Praeger, 1983.

———. *Arab Education in Transition.* New York: Garland, 1990.

Schmida, Leslie C., ed. *Education in the Middle East.* Washington, D.C.: AMIDEAST, 1983.

Szyliowicz, Joseph. *Education and Modernization in the Middle East.* Ithaca, N.Y.: Cornell University Press, 1973.

Za'rour, George I. *Universities in Arab Countries.* Washington, D.C.: World Bank, 1988.

North America
Canada

Anisef, Paul, with Marie-Andree Bertrand, Ulrike Hortain, and Carl James. *Accessibility to Postsecondary Education in Canada: A Review of the Literature.* Ottawa: Canada Secretary of State, 1985.

Campbell, Duncan D. *The New Majority: Adult Learners in University.* Edmonton: University of Alberta Press, 1984.

Clark, Warren, Margaret Laing, and Edith Rechnitzer. *The Class of 82: Summary Report on the*

Findings of the 1984 *National Survey of the Graduates of* 1982. Ottawa: Canada Secretary of State and Statistics, 1986.

Dennison, John D., and Paul Gallagher. *Canada's Community Colleges: A Critical Analysis.* Vancouver: University of British Columbia Press, 1986.

Donald, Janet G. "Teaching and Learning in Higher Education in Canada: Changes Over the Last Decade." *Canadian Journal of Higher Education* 16, no. 3 (1986): 77–84.

Harris, R. S. "The Universities of Canada." In *Commonwealth Universities Yearbook* 1980 2: 811–34. London: Association of Commonwealth Universities, 1980.

Konrad, Abram G., and Joanne McNeal. "Goals in Canadian Universities." *Canadian Journal of Higher Education* 14, no. 1 (1984): 31–40.

Leslie, Peter. *Canadian Universities* 1980 *and Beyond: Enrollment, Structure, and Finance.* Ottawa: Association of Universities and Colleges of Canada, 1980.

Sheffield, Edward, Duncan D. Campbell, Jeffrey Holmes, B. B. Kymlicka, and James H. Whitelaw. *Systems of Higher Education: Canada.* 2d ed. New York: International Council for Educational Development, 1982.

Skolnik, Michael L. "Diversity in Higher Education: The Canadian Case." *Higher Education in Europe* 11, no. 2 (1986): 19–32.

Symons, Thomas H. B., and James E. Page. *Some Questions of Balance: Human Resources, Higher Education, and Canadian Studies.* Vol. 2 of *To Know Ourselves: The Report of the Commission on Canadian Studies.* Ottawa: Association of Universities and Colleges of Canada, 1984.

Watson, Cicely, ed. *Government and Higher Education: The Legitimacy of Intervention.* Toronto: Ontario Institute for Studies in Education, 1987.

Winchester, Ian, ed. *The Independence of the University and the Funding of the State: Essays on Academic Freedom in Canada.* Toronto: Ontario Institute for Studies in Education, 1984.

United States

Bok, Derek. *Higher Learning.* Cambridge: Harvard University Press, 1986.

————. *Beyond the Ivory Tower: Social Responsibilities of the Modern University.* Cambridge: Harvard University Press, 1982.

Bowen, Howard R. *Investment in Learning: The Individual and Social Value of American Higher Education.* San Francisco: Jossey-Bass, 1977.

Bowen, Howard R., and Jack H. Schuster. *American Professors: A National Resource Imperiled.* New York: Oxford University Press, 1986.

Boyer, Carol M., and Peter T. Ewell. *State-Based Approaches to Assessment in Undergraduate Education: A Glossary and Selected References.* ECS Working Paper PS-88-2. Denver, Colo.: Education Commission of the States, March 1988.

Boyer, Ernest L. *College: The Undergraduate Experience in America.* New York: Harper & Row, 1987.

Carnegie Council on Policy Studies in Higher Education. *Three Thousand Futures: The Next Twenty Years for Higher Education.* San Francisco: Jossey-Bass, 1980.

Herbst, Jurgen. *From Crisis to Crisis: American College Government,* 1636–1819. Cambridge: Harvard University Press, 1982.

Hofstadter, Richard, and Walter P. Metzger. *The Development of Academic Freedom in the United States.* New York: Columbia University Press, 1955.

Jencks, Christopher, and David Riesman. *The Academic Revolution.* Garden City, N.Y.: Doubleday, 1968.

Kerr, Clark. *The Uses of the University.* 3d rev. ed. Cambridge: Harvard University Press, 1982.

Kerr, Clark, and Marian L. Gade. *The Guardians: Boards of Trustees in American Colleges and Universities.* Washington, D.C.: Association of Governing Boards of Universities and Colleges, 1989.

Newman, Frank. *Choosing Quality: Reducing Conflict Between the State and the University.* Denver, Colo.: Education Commission of the States, 1987.

Study Group on the Conditions of Excellence in American Higher Education. *Involvement in Learning: Realizing the Potential of American Higher Education.* Washington, D.C.: National Institute of Education/ U.S. Department of Education, 1984.

Veysey, Laurence R. *The Emergence of the American University.* Chicago: University of Chicago Press, 1965.

CONTRIBUTORS

Contributors

———————————◆———————————

MILTON N. ADAMS is acting director for policy studies at the Cooperative Institute for International Policies Research and Education at Florida A & M University, Tallahassee.

ORLANDO ALBORNOZ is professor of comparative higher education at the Central University of Venezuela in Caracas. He is the author of many books on higher education in Venezuela and Latin America.

HASSAN ALI AL-EBRAHEEM is president of the Kuwait Society for the Advancement of Arab Children. He is former rector of Kuwait University and former minister of education in Kuwait.

A. A. AL-RUBAIY is professor of international studies at the University of Akron, Ohio.

PHILIP G. ALTBACH is professor and director of the Comparative Education Center, State University of New York at Buffalo. He is the author of *Comparative Higher Education* and is North American editor of *Higher Education*.

ROBERT ARNOVE is professor of education at Indiana University, Bloomington. He is the author of *Education and Revolution in Nicaragua*.

MARK A. ASHWILL is assistant vice provost for internatioal education at the State University of New York at Buffalo.

GEORGE AVIS is senior lecturer in Russian studies and chair of the Russian section at the University of Bradford, England. He has served as editor of the *Journal of Russian Studies*.

IBRAHIMA BAH-LALYA is completing a doctoral program in educational leadership and policy analysis at Florida State University and has been assistant director general of higher education in the Ministry of Education, Republic of Guinea.

ALAIN BIENAYMÉ is professor at the University of Paris-Dauphine.

KAREN BIRAIMAH is associate professor in the Department of Educational Foundations, University of Central Florida, Orlando.

HUBERT O. BROWN is senior lecturer in the Department of Education, University of Hong Kong. He has written extensively on education in China.

ROSA C. BRICEÑO is currently on the faculty of the School of Education, San Jose State University, California, and head of Creating Strong Families, an educational agency in San Mateo County.

SHUN-FEN CHEN is assistant professor of higher education in the Department of Education, National Taiwan Normal University, Taipei, Taiwan, Republic of China.

NGONI CHIDEYA is currently Ambassador of Zimbabwe to the Nordic countries.

DAVID COURT is Rockefeller Foundation representative in Kenya.

WILLIAM K. CUMMINGS is director of international education at the Graduate School of Education, Harvard University, Cambridge, Massachusetts.

JOHN L. DAVIES is professor of higher education management and director of the Center for Education Management, Danbury Park Management Centre, United Kingdom. He is principal consultant in higher education management at the Organization for Economic Cooperation and Development.

CHARLES H. DAVIS is on the staff of the Science Council of Canada, Ottawa, Canada.

THOMAS O. EISEMON is professor and director of the Center for Cognitive and Ethnographic Studies, Faculty of Education, McGill University, Montreal, Canada.

JOSEPH P. FARRELL is a professor in the Department of Adult Education, Ontario Institute for Studies in Education, Toronto, Canada.

MARIAN GADE is research associate in the Office of the President and on the staff of the Center for Studies in Higher Education, University of California, Berkeley.

JOSÉ LUIS GARCIA GARRIDO is professor and vice-rector at the National University of Distance Education, Madrid, Spain. He is the author of *Comparative Education* and other books.

TOKAY GEDIKOGLU teaches in the Faculty of Arts and Sciences, Gaziantep University, Turkey.

ROGER GEIGER is associate professor of higher education at Pennsylvania State University, University Park.

ANDREW GONZALEZ is president of De La Salle University, Manila, Philippines. He has written extensively on higher education and on linguistics.

GÁBOR HALÁSZ is principal research fellow at the Institute for Educational Research, Budapest, Hungary.

GRANT HARMAN is professor of educational administration and head of the Department of Administrative and Higher Education Studies at the University of New England, Armidale, Australia.

KLAUS HÜFNER is professor in the Institute of Political Economy at the Free University of Berlin, Federal Republic of Germany.

REES HUGHES is on the staff of Humboldt State University, Arcata, California.

YAACOV IRAM is professor of education and chair of the Department of Educational Studies at Bar-Ilan University, Ramat Gan, Israel.

SAMIR AHMAD JARRAR is chief executive officer of Educational Development Group International, Washington, D.C. He has served on the staff of the World Bank.

D. BRUCE JOHNSTONE is chancellor of the State University of New York. He is author of *Sharing the Costs of Higher Education*.

GAIL P. KELLY is professor and chair of the Department of Educational Organization, Administration, and Policy, State University of New York at Buffalo.

SHAKRUKH R. KHAN is assistant professor of economics at Vassar College, Poughkeepsie, New York.

RANSOO KIM is president of Kwangju University, Republic of Korea.

KAZUYUKI KITAMURA is professor at the National Institute of Multimedia Education, Tokyo, Japan.

JIRÍ KOTÁSEK is professor of education at the Charles University in Prague, Czechoslovakia, and head of the Department of Higher Education Pedagogy at the Czech Institute for the Development of Higher Education.

BEATE KRAIS is a research assistant at the Max Planck Institute for Human Development and Education, West Berlin, Federal Republic of Germany.

JAN-ERIK LANE is professor of public administration at the University of Lund, Sweden. He is also a researcher for the Swedish Council for Research into the Social Sciences.

DANIEL C. LEVY is professor of Educational Policy and Latin American Studies at the State University of New York at Albany. He is the author of *Higher Education and the State in Latin America* and other books.

T. L. MALIYAMKONO is executive director of the Eastern and Southern African Universities Research Program, Dar es Salaam, Tanzania.

BYRON G. MASSIALAS is professor of education and multicultural studies at Florida State University, Tallahassee, Florida. He is coauthor of *Education in the Arab World* and has also written other books.

GRAEME C. MOODIE is emeritus professor of politics at the University of York, England, where he established the Department of Politics in 1963.

ROBERTO MOSCATI is associate professor of sociology at the University of Milan, Italy.

MWENENE MUKWESO is a doctoral candidate in international/intercultural development education at Florida State University. He has been on the staff of the College of Education at the University of Kisangani, Zaire.

JOHAN MULLER is coordinator of the Educational Policy Unit at the University of the Witwatersrand, Johannesburg, South Africa.

KILEMI MWIRIA is a research fellow at the Bureau of Educational Research, Kenyatta University, Nairobi, Kenya.

JENS NAUMANN is a research assistant at the Max Planck Institute for Human Development Education, West Berlin, Federal Republic of Germany.

CARLOS ORNELAS is professor of education and communications at the Universidad Autonoma Metropolitan-Xochimilco in Mexico City. He is coauthor of *Superacion Academica y reforma Universitaria* and the author of other books.

ROLLAND PAULSTON is professor of education at the University of Pittsburgh, Pennsylvania.

HAROLD PERKIN is professor of history at Northwestern University, Evanston, Illinois.

FRANCISCO O. RAMIREZ is professor in the SIDEC program, School of Education, Stanford University, Stanford, California.

GARY RHOADES is associate professor at the Center for the Study of Higher Education, University of Arizona, Tucson.

PHYLLIS RIDDLE is assistant professor of sociology, Arizona State University, Tempe, Arizona.

RICHARD SACK is an independent consultant working on education and development. He has taught in American, French, and African universities.

JAN SADLAK is research scholar at the Higher Education Group, Ontario Institute for Studies in Education, Toronto, Canada. He has been on the staff of the European Rectors Conference in Switzerland.

BIKAS C. SANYAL is on the staff of the International Institute for Educational Planning in Paris, France. He is the author of many books relating to higher education and employment.

EDWARD SHILS is professor of sociology at the University of Chicago, where he is also a member of the Committee on Social Thought. He is fellow of Peterhouse College, Cambridge University, England, and editor of *Minerva*.

SURESHCHANDRA SHUKLA is professor of education at the Central Institute of Education, University of Delhi, India. He is editor of the *Journal of Higher Education* (India).

JASBIR SARJIT SINGH is on the staff of the Education Department at the Commonwealth Secretariat, London, England. She has been professor of education at the University of Malaya.

MICHAEL L. SKOLNIK is professor of higher education at the Ontario Institute for Studies in Education, Toronto, Canada, and professor in the Graduate Department of Education, University of Toronto. He has written widely on Canadian higher education.

DONALD R. SNODGRASS is an institute fellow at the Harvard Institute for International Development and a lecturer on economics at Harvard University.

NIKSA NIKOLA SOLJAN is professor and dean of the Faculty of Arts at the University of Zagreb, Yugoslavia.

ULRICH TEICHLER is professor and director of the Center for Higher Education and Work at the University of Kassel in the German Federal Republic and Professor of Higher Education at Northwestern University, Evanston, Illinois.

CARLOS ALBERTO TORRES is assistant professor in the Department of Education, University of California at Los Angeles.

FRANS VAN VUGHT is professor of public administration at the University of Twente, The Netherlands, where he is also director of the Center for Higher Education Policy Studies.

ROBERT E. VERHINE is associate professor in the Graduate Program in Education at the Federal University of Bahia in Salvador, Brazil.

KEITH WATSON is professor of comparative education at the University of Reading, England. He is the author of *Educational Development in Thailand*.

INDEX

Topic and Name Index

◆

◆

Country and Region Index

◆